Enigma Books

Also published by Enigma Books

Hitler's Table Talk: 1941–1944
In Stalin's Secret Service
Hitler and Mussolini: The Secret Meetings
The Jews in Fascist Italy: A History
The Man Behind the Rosenbergs
Roosevelt and Hopkins: An Intimate History
Diary 1937–1943 (Galeazzo Ciano)
Secret Affairs: FDR, Cordell Hull, and Sumner Welles
Hitler and His Generals: Military Conferences 1942–1945
Stalin and the Jews: The Red Book
The Secret Front: Nazi Political Espionage
Fighting the Nazis: French Intelligence and Counterintelligence
A Death in Washington: Walter G. Krivitsky and the Stalin Terror
The Battle of the Casbah: Terrorism and Counterterrorism in Algeria
Hitler's Second Book: The Unpublished Sequel to *Mein Kampf*
At Napoleon's Side in Russia: The Classic Eyewitness Account
The Atlantic Wall: Hitler's Defenses for D-Day
Double Lives: Stalin, Willi Münzenberg and the Seduction of the Intellectuals
France and the Nazi Threat: The Collapse of French Diplomacy 1932–1939
Mussolini: The Secrets of His Death
Top Nazi: Karl Wolff—The Man Between Hitler and Himmler
Empire on the Adriatic: Mussolini's Conquest of Yugoslavia
The Origins of the War of 1914 (3-volume set)
Hitler's Foreign Policy: 1933–1939—The Road to World War II
The Origins of Fascist Ideology 1918–1925
Max Corvo: OSS Italy 1942–1945
Hitler's Contract: The Secret History of the Italian Edition of *Mein Kampf*
Secret Intelligence and the Holocaust
Balkan Inferno: Betrayal, War, and Intervention, 1990–2005
Calculated Risk
The Murder of Maxim Gorky
The Kravchenko Case
The Mafia and the Allies
Hitler's Gift to France
The Nazi Party, 1919–1945: A Complete History
Encyclopedia of Cold War Espionage, Spies, and Secret Operations
The Cicero Spy Affair
The Decision to Drop the Atomic Bomb
Target Hitler
The Orlov KGB File
NOC Non-Official Cover: British Secret Operations

Reinhard R. Doerries

Hitler's Intelligence Chief

Walter Schellenberg

Introduction by
Gerhard L. Weinberg

Includes the original
Autobiography
by Walter Schellenberg
and
Annexe
by Franz Göring

Enigma Books

All rights reserved under the
International and Pan-American
Copyright Conventions.
Published by Enigma Books,
New York

Copyright © 2009 by Reinhard R. Doerries

First Edition

No part of this publication may be reproduced, stored in a retrieval system, or transmitted, in any form or by any means, electronic, mechanical, photocopying, recording, or otherwise without the written permission of Enigma Books.

Printed in the United States of America

ISBN 978-1-929631-77-3

Library of Congress Cataloguing in Publication Data

Doerries, Reinhard R.
 Hitler's intelligence chief : Walter Schellenberg / Reinhard R. Doerries ; introduction by Gerhard L. Weinberg. -- 1st ed.

 p. : ill. ; cm.

 Includes the original "Autobiography" by Walter Schellenberg and "Annexe" by Franz Goring.
 Includes bibliographical references and index.
 ISBN: 978-1-929631-77-3

 1. Schellenberg, Walter, 1910-1952. 2. World War, 1939-1945--Secret service--Germany. 3. Military intelligence--Germany--History--20th century. 4. Nazis--Biography. 5. Intelligence officers--Germany--Biography. I. Weinberg, Gerhard L. II. Title.

DD247.S338 D63 2009
940.54/8743/092

Table of Contents

Introduction by Gerhard L. Weinberg		ix
Preface		xiii
I.	Years of Apprenticeship	3
II.	Chief of *Amt* VI Foreign Intelligence	43
III.	Twilight of the Gods	111
IV.	Postlude to Hitler's Germany	219

Appendices

Editor's Comment   293

Appendix I

    Brigadefuehrer Schellenberg. Amtschef VI, Autobiography, Compiled During His Stay in Stockholm   296

Appendix II

    Annexe Written by Hauptsturmfuehrer Göring to Schellenberg's Report on His Transactions with Count Bernadotte and Events in the Last Weeks of the German Reich   350

Appendix III

    Annexe Written by Hauptsturmfuehrer Göring to Schellenberg's Report on His Transactions with Count Bernadotte and Events in the Last Weeks of the German Reich. Part II   357

Abbreviations, Acronyms, Cover Names   363

Glossary. German Intelligence Services   367

Bibliography   374

Index   381

Introduction

by

Gerhard L. Weinberg

The leadership of National Socialist Germany included a large number of individuals who might well be called peculiar. The term applies not only to a lack of moral sense. It also can be applied to someone who does not quite fit in because of considerable intelligence on the one hand and a special personal relationship to one of the most important and highest leaders on the other. Walter Schellenberg certainly fits this characterization.

Decades ago the scholar Robert Koehl called attention to what he called the feudal aspects of National Socialism. Personal allegiances and alignments, rivalries and jurisdictional disputes were so endemic to the system that they effectively displaced what formal structures of state and Party there were. It was in the context of such a personal relationship with the head of the whole German police apparatus, Heinrich Himmler, that Walter Schellenberg rose to prominence. And he was able to do so and retain his position to the end of the regime in spite of having a clearer and earlier perception of the likelihood of German defeat than such allegedly smart men like Albert Speer who did not come to this recognition until the end of January 1945. What tied Himmler and Schellenberg together cannot be explained precisely; but there cannot be any doubt that a special personal tie existed and that Himmler allowed Schellenberg a degree of latitude that was unique in the higher reaches of Nazi Germany.

It is in the context of a man of considerable ability and vast ambition rising to prominence in an evil regime that this study of Schellenberg sheds light on the regime he served. Participating in its horrors, engaging in endless organizational rivalries, inheriting growing responsibilities in the field of intelligence, Schellenberg is seen here as a person who enjoyed a degree of what the Germans call "Narrenfreiheit," the loose reins of the mentally incompetent.

The problem of sources is especially complicated in this case, and Professor Reinhard Doerries has tackled it in a systematic way like no one else. The interrogations by the British after the war—which Doerries has himself carefully edited for publication—the recently declassified records of British and American intelligence agencies, the very confused status of Schellenberg's memoirs, and a host of other materials have all been carefully searched and evaluated. Whether it is Schellenberg's ascent in the hierarchy of the Third Reich, his efforts to sound Allies and neutrals for a way out of Germany's losing war, his hopes of a future for himself by saving Jews destined for death in the final days of fighting—all these and related issues are recounted here in a manner unmatched in the existing literature.

The inclusion in this book of Schellenberg's original autobiography written in Sweden in 1945 and a report by Schellenberg's adjutant, Franz Göring, offers the reader a sense of how these two men saw themselves acting in the last hectic days of Nazi Germany. That as participants in a regime that had engaged in murder on a colossal scale they would emphasize their own efforts at rescuing Jews and others from the death planned for them is hardly surprising. It is, however, not entirely false because it is self-exculpatory. Those saved are unlikely to have been troubled at the time by the prior activities of those who kept them from being slaughtered. This portion of the story is also of interest for understanding the activities of Swedish Count Folke Bernadotte and Jewish organizations trying to rescue victims of the Nazis.

There is in this a further important insight into the extraordinary society that was Nazi Germany. The careers and actions of the regime's leading figures can more easily be seen as to a large extent self-determined. As long as loyalty to Hitler, or to whoever one's immediate superior might be, could safely be assumed, there was a very great degree of latitude. Individual initiative was allowed far greater leeway than one might have expected from a state that prided itself on the "Führerprinzip," the leadership principle. This principle was frequently interpreted to mean unquestioning adherence to whatever was prescribed from above. In practice, however, as long as there was no doubt about personal loyalty, one could voice views and suggest courses of action that at first sight might appear to contradict official policy.

This has important implications for an understanding of the whole system because it sheds important light on those who never thought to take advantage of this opportunity. The point is that whatever the endless jurisdictional disputes, there was far more consensus among those in positions of authority than the postwar memoirs and protestations might lead one to expect. The disputes have left behind masses of records; tacit agreement on policies and objectives did not. It is this combination of a broad consensus with a considerable degree of latitude for any in the system who actually wanted to take advantage of it that contributed to the system's coherence and strength as well as to its ability to maintain itself operating relatively effectively until the bitter end. In this way, the account offered here of one figure of real significance in the political and military system that was Nazi Germany can provide insight into the vanished world of Hitler's government as a whole even as it concentrates on the life and activities of a single individual.

Gerhard L. Weinberg
Efland, North Carolina
April 2009

Preface

It is the original intention of this study to provide a better understanding of the role of intelligence in the decision-making processes at times of international political and military crises. Most publications relating to the field of German intelligence history in both World Wars still tend to be descriptive or sensational. Only few authors have followed in the footsteps of David Kahn and Ladislas Farago who first cleared the path many years ago. More recently studies, such as the highly enlightening history of deception in World War II by Thaddeus Holt, have been the exceptions. While archival research conditions continue to be cumbersome in Germany, to say the least, archival holdings in the United States in most cases have been accessible to scholars. Access to the so-called Captured Records from the National Socialist period even today continues to be easier in Washington than in Germany. In the case of most personnel files of the time and other specific research interests, access continues to be particularly troublesome in all German archives. The more recent availability of the former Communist East German archival holdings may be a first indication of the general improvement of research conditions in Germany.

The absence of thoroughly researched and balanced studies in German intelligence history, however, has not only contributed to what might be described as black holes in general military history, but has also brought about a number of somewhat curious appraisals of major developments in both World Wars. Particularly the history of international relations has suffered from this seemingly almost programmed ignorance, and the consequences are visible. Thus, for instance, we have indications of very personal intelligence lines built by Wilhelm Canaris, the traditional naval officer who was in charge of German military intelligence until 1944, to influential military and political circles in Franco's Spain, but our knowledge of these relationships just below the routine surface of Spanish or for that matter German history is rather spotty and not based on an analytical study of Spanish or German sources.

Regarding Walter Schellenberg, who in World War II for all practical purposes directed an SS intelligence service parallel to Canaris' military intelligence, our knowledge until very recently has been even more incomplete. In marked contrast to the Nazi elite, Walter Schellenberg was not only aware of Germany's standing in the international community, but apparently also had the ability to establish fruitful personal contacts with educated personalities of other cultures. For Schellenberg his committed efforts in that direction not only produced consequential international connections, such as in the case of Prince Hohenlohe, but it can be said without reservation that thanks to his personal and very open contacts, an extraordinarily large number of unfortunate victims held in the infamous German concentration camps were allowed to survive. Few authors have set their sights on Schellenberg, and when he was discussed, it usually resulted in a superficial appraisal. The reason was simple: his multifaceted and in many ways contradictory personality was forced into a somehow precast frame established years ago for the examination of high ranking Nazis who had committed crimes quite beyond comprehension for most of us.

Taking a closer look at the vast amount of documentary material released in recent years, a number of conclusions appear to be unavoidable. In most ways, the Chief of Foreign Intelligence was not what might be described as a typical Nazi officer—I am inclined to argue that there was no such typical person—but Schellenberg's complicated existence somewhere between his official position as a powerful executive within the immoral system and his life outside that almost hermetically sealed world of crime and corruption surely deserves scholarly attention. For that reason this book presents not merely a study of a number of significant aspects of German intelligence during the Nazi period and of the role of German intelligence in the course of World War II, but it is also the first attempt to draw a more realistic portrait of Walter Schellenberg. From the height of his position this man knew of all the indescribable excesses being perpetrated, but earlier than many of his contemporaries he reached an understanding of how all this would have to end. Just over thirty years old, he was in command of a powerful intelligence machine, permitting him to challenge some of the iron controls of the dictatorship and to test its limits. While the early period of this educated lawyer's participation in the organized destruction of any semblance of freedom and democracy—he joined the SS at 23—may be comprehensible to most of us, through an analysis of his youthful years in post-World War I Germany, it is near impossible to penetrate the personality of the mature man. A few years ago Klemens von Klemperer in his study of German resistance against Hitler pointed out that Schellenberg had come up with a way of playing off Heinrich Himmler against Adolf Hitler "to free Germany of the tyrant." Having studied the records, but in the almost complete absence of personal letters and diary notes, one would hesitate to completely subscribe to such a suggestive explanation. Based on the sources, all that can be offered at this stage is an attempt to place this educated young German, a product of his culture and time, in the complicated context of intelligence and, it cannot be forgotten, of the Holocaust. Schellenberg recognized the abyss it represented and lived with that knowledge.

Due to this quasi-biographical approach to the Chief of Foreign Intelligence, the present study is not intended as an informative general overview of Nazi Germany's intelligence activities. For various reasons some areas have had to be excluded. Thus, intelligence operations and covert activities in the Middle East have not been thoroughly examined. The failure to build a functioning network of agents in the United States also has not been investigated. The whole network of relations between the traditional Armed Forces and the National Socialist State, often misunderstood and still misrepresented, could also not be included in this publication.

The rescue operations—freeing a great number of inmates from the camps of human depravity—are, however, of significant historical importance, not just for those whose lives were saved and their descendants.

As with all difficult research projects, this too could not have reached the finishing line without the more than gracious assistance of a great number of friends and colleagues. Gerhard Weinberg over many years has been an irreplaceable friend in the transatlantic community of scholars. Often he has suggested new ways of thinking about the problems of our concern. David Kahn I have also known for a long time, and we have had numerous conversations on the role of intelligence in modern history. I owe much gratitude to both Lord Dacre and Sir Stuart Newton Hampshire and have often regretted that the thoughtful exchanges with Lord Dacre in particular are not to be continued. Much effort went into my search for an explication of Lord Dacre's repeated criticism of Count Folke Bernadotte and Walter Schellenberg, but during our last conversation he was still not quite ready to open up more fully on this point. I owe him gratitude for bearing with me.

Of the archival experts I would like to particularly thank Tim Nenninger who has continually been willing to respond to my very often rather demanding archival wishes. Without his help this book, as other studies before, would not have happened. The many telephone conferences with the Swiss expert Pierre Braunschweig and his readiness to help have been highlights of my research. I thank him for his patience. Ernst Haiger in the course of another project became a valued colleague, and I abused him repeatedly in the course of my search for all kinds of sources in Berlin. He was always available. Reinhard Spitzy was willing to freely exchange views on intelligence, ethics and history. His insights into a different era were of much value. Robert Wolfe, the friend who first, a few decades ago, put the "Final Report" into my hands knows what we historians owe him.

Among the many who assisted and advised in numerous ways, helped locate documents and other sources, translated some texts, showed me the way to lesser known depositories and often just were ready to make significant material available are Richard Aldrich, Doron Arazi, Gideon Botsch, Richard Breitman, Terry Charman, Isabelle Cuvelier-Fiemeyer, Ralph Erskine, Fritz Fellner, Matthias Fifka, Ben Fischer, Michael Foedrowitz, Frank Fox, Detlef Garbe, Paulgerhard Gladen, Daniel Gossel, Ashbel Green, Klaus Harpprecht, Jan Heitmann, Katja Hirmer, Lothar Höbelt, Heinz Höhne, Harald Lönnecker, Heinz Lohfeldt, Henry Mayer, Craig McKay, Dina Porat, Wolfgang Ramsteck, Oliver Rathkolb, Ulrich Schlie, Sara Sherbill, Arnold Sywottek and Michael Wala. May those forgive me whom I did not mention.

I acknowledge with gratitude the permission of the National Archives and Records Administration to publish from their holdings. I also gratefully acknowledge permission from the editors of *After the Battle*, from Ms. Belser of Friedrich Reinhardt AG, from Michael Foedrowitz, from Henry Mayer of the United States Holocaust Memorial Museum Archives, from *Der Spiegel*, Hamburg, and from Pierre Th. Braunschweig to publish photographs identified respectively.

At the National Archives I much benefited from the generous advice of Rich Boylan, Greg Bradsher, Larry McDonald, Ron Swerczek and John Taylor. Efficient research at the Political Archive of the German Foreign Office was possible thanks to the patient assistance from Maria Keipert and Ludwig Biewer. Gunther Fischer of the Staatsarchiv Nuremberg helped me to access the trial records. I appreciate the assistance of the Freedom of Information/Privacy Office, Department of the Army, Fort George G. Meade, MD.

The many thoughtful conversations with Robert Miller, the Enigma Editor, have made the writing of this book more rewarding.

Hitler's Intelligence Chief

Walter Schellenberg

Chapter I

Years of Apprenticeship

While the Danes were out in the streets of Copenhagen happily celebrating the inevitable surrender of the much despised German "Thousand Year Empire," out at Kastrup Airport a most unlikely passenger was boarding a Red Cross plane bound across the Øre Sound for Malmø, Sweden. The special flight on May 5, 1945, had been arranged by Count Folke Bernadotte, a rather reserved member of the Swedish Royal Family and at the time Vice-President of the Swedish Red Cross. The haggard exhausted passenger climbing aboard was Adolf Hitler's last Chief of Foreign Intelligence, the SS-*Brigadeführer* Walter Schellenberg, now traveling as *Gesandter* (Minister) appointed by Count Lutz Schwerin von Krosigk, Foreign Minister of the short-lived post-Hitler Nazi government headed by Grand Admiral Karl Dönitz. The 35-year old SS foreign intelligence boss in the final months of Nazi Germany had played the mysterious role of underling and consultant in one for the infamous Heinrich Himmler. The unclear lines of Schellenberg's short life and career, but also a hesitancy on the part of many historians to include intelligence in their research and analysis may have caused him to be left out of most studies of that German era. Quite to the contrary, fiction writers not surprisingly have discovered the polymorphous SS leader and used him to embellish their admittedly often captivating historical thrillers.[1]

---

1. For instance Glenn Meade, *The Sands of Sakkara* (London: Hodder & Stoughton, 1999). Published in Germany as *Mission Sphinx* (Bergisch Gladbach: Lübbe, 2000). Also Jack Higgins, *The Eagle Has Flown* (London: Penguin, 1998; 1st 1991). A Schellenberg, far removed from reality and described with curious

The colorful and controversial high-ranking Nazi Friedrich Walter Schellenberg was the seventh child born into the middle class family of a piano builder in Saarbrücken on January 16, 1910. His father Guido Franz Bernhard Schellenberg is said to have had a difficult time providing for the needs of the large family. The firm had been founded by Schellenberg's great-grandfather and running it more than fully occupied his father. For this reason, it would appear, Schellenberg saw little of his father, and he later recalled that it was his mother, Katherina Lydia, née Riedel, who raised the children. She exerted a considerable influence on the boy and did her best to give the children "a Christian upbringing." Music was a significant part of family life. Walter's grandfather played the organ and violin, his father played the piano and violin, and Walter took lessons on the cello from the age of eight. Schellenberg's older brothers and sisters do not appear to have been very close to him later. A sister lived in the United States for fourteen years but did not become a citizen and had to leave in 1941. A brother operated a gardening business in Rhode Island but returned after twelve years because he found it difficult to earn a living.[2]

For four years young Walter was sent to an elementary school to prepare him for entry into a *Gymnasium*, to this day the German version of high school offering the *Abitur* or final diploma needed for admission to a university.[3] Some authors have suggested that Schellenberg's recollection that due to poor business conditions after World War I his father had moved to Luxembourg was pure invention. However, personal correspondence between Schellenberg and his father, available in the German Federal Archives, clearly shows that his parents in the 1930s indeed resided in Luxembourg. Moreover, the records of the NSDAP (*Nationalsozialistische Deutsche Arbeiterpartei*, Nazi party) in Luxembourg list Schellenberg's father, the "Music Dealer" Guido Schellenberg, as a party member since December 1937 and residing at Luxembourg/Gare. Schellenberg graduated from the *Gymnasium* in the spring of 1929 and promptly matriculated in the Law School of the University of Marburg. He signed up for standard lectures and seminars in law, but university records clearly indicate that Schellenberg from the beginning seems

---

inaccuracy, plays a major role in Philip Kerr's *Hitler's Peace: A Novel of the Second World War* (New York: G. P. Putnam's Sons/Penguin, 2005).
2. Walter Schellenberg, *The Schellenberg Memoirs* (London: André Deutsch, 1956), 19. Robert Gellately, ed., *The Nuremberg Interviews: An American Psychiatrist's Conversations with the Defendants and Witnesses*. Conducted by Leon Goldensohn (London: Pimlico, 2006; 1st 2004), 423-424. Unpublished text of Leon Goldensohn's conversation with Walter Schellenberg, submitted by Eli Goldensohn to Ashbel Green, 6.
3. At the time that *Gymnasium* was called *Oberrealschule*. Schellenberg also referred to it as *Reformgymnasium*. — Various letters, Bundesarchiv (BA) Berlin, R 58/Anhang 52. "Nazi Party Membership Records Luxembourg," National Archives, College Park, MD (NA), Records of the Army Staff, RG 319, IRR, IS, Box 11.

to have looked for more than a routine legal education. In the course of his five semesters in the colorful university town on the Lahn River, he also enrolled in Church Law (*Kirchenrecht*), Political Science (*Staatslehre*), Finance, Political Economy (*Nationalökonomie*), and indeed a course on socialism and its representatives. Surviving records contain nothing to support the information offered in his memoirs that he began to study Medicine before switching to Law, but even an experienced historian, such as Alan Bullock, in his introduction of 1955 wrote that at the University of Bonn Schellenberg "changed from the study of medicine to that of law" and consequently left university "with few qualifications."[4]

Though seriously strapped for funds, already in his first semester at Marburg, Schellenberg decided to join the *Corps Guestphalia*, a highly reputed traditional student fraternity belonging to the *Kösener Senioren-Convents-Verband* (*KSCV*), Germany's oldest association of student fraternities. Like other German student corps, *Corps Guestphalia* is based on a close brotherhood of the members ("Corpsbrüderlichkeit") meant to last for a lifetime. "Schlägermensuren" or students' fencing was and still is an important ritual required from the student members. As in other German student fraternities of this type, it was and is understood that a high degree of coherence and esprit de corps among members is an important characteristic of the old boys network (*Alte Herren*), and Schellenberg, when interrogated at Nuremberg after World War II, freely admitted that this was a most significant aspect of corps membership.[5] From Marburg in the autumn of 1931 he moved on to the University of Bonn, where he did not participate in the activities of Corps Guestphalia, and on March 18, 1933, passed the junior bar exam (*Referendarexamen*) at the provincial court (*Oberlandesgericht*) in Düsseldorf. His training as a *Referendar* he took at a district court in Sinzig on the Ahr, in the state attorney's office in Bonn, with the secret state police in Düsseldorf, and at the provincial court also in Düsseldorf where on December 18, 1936, he successfully passed the final German legal exam (*grosse juristische Staatsprüfung*).[6]

---

4. Erroneous data in Schellenberg, *The Schellenberg Memoirs*, 20. Matriculation records, Hessisches Staatsarchiv Marburg, show that Schellenberg studied at the University of Marburg from April 24, 1929, to October 16, 1931. Cf. handwritten autobiography, NA, Berlin Document Center (BDC) Microfilm, Roll A3343 SSO-074B. Alan Bullock, "Introduction" to Schellenberg, *The Schellenberg Memoirs*, 9. Other sources suggest that Schellenberg had wanted to study Medicine but in line with the wishes of his father had decided to become a lawyer. Gellately, ed., *The Nuremberg Interviews*, 428. The records also contain nothing about Schellenberg having been a Jesuit. Cf. Edmund L. Blandford, *SS-Intelligence: The Nazi Secret Service* (Shrewsbury: Airlife, 2000), 70.
5. Statement under Oath, January 3, 1947, at Nuremberg before his interrogator Otto Verber, Staatsarchiv Nürnberg (SAN), Rep. 502, VI, S-45c. *Corps Guestphalia* continues to function and now calls itself *Corps Guestphalia et Suevoborussia*.
6. Statement under Oath, Schellenberg, November 14, 1947, SAN, IV E, S-45c. Handwritten brief autobiography by Schellenberg in connection with the usual SS questionnaire at the time of his first marriage.

Possibly caused by his rapid and certainly full-time occupation in the SS hierarchy but nevertheless somewhat unusual for a young man of his ambition is the absence of the Dr. jur., the doctoral degree in Law in his case. Titles had long been an important part of the German class structure, and the Nazis had changed neither the educational system nor the title-ridden administration built on it. Some time during the early phase of his high-pressure career, Schellenberg may have been reminded that he lacked something. Apparently he got in touch with SS-*Standartenführer* Professor Reinhard Höhn of the *Rechts- und Staatswissenschaftliche Fakultät* (School of Law and Political Science) at the University of Berlin.[7] As an academic and a high-ranking SS official, Höhn had often played a decisive role in drafting intelligent young men from the university into the SS, and Schellenberg certainly knew of Höhn's SS functions before talking to him about his plans to obtain a doctoral degree. Surviving personal notes of Schellenberg indicate that the first possible dissertation topic discussed concerned the concept of police in the context of Christian thought. At a further meeting in April 1940 this theme seems to have been discarded and, as Schellenberg noted, Höhn asked him to instead consider the nature of administration as practiced in Yugoslavia. In order to meet formal requirements Schellenberg also in April 1940 enrolled as a law student. Whether he found time to attend any doctoral seminars must remain an open question, but he did realize that he would hardly have the leisure to compose a doctoral dissertation and accordingly corresponded with Professor Fritz Valjavec[8] associated with more than one German institute for Southeastern European studies. From surviving documents it is evident that Valjavec was willing or had to be willing to be of assistance, but for whatever reasons a doctoral dissertation does not appear to have been presented and Schellenberg was not awarded the doctoral degree. Surrounded by men who had obtained this particular German qualification, Schellenberg would have to do without it.[9]

NA, BDC Microfilm, Roll A3343-RS-FO 270. Cf. Official German certificate dated December 17, 1936, giving the date of the exam as December 8, 1936. BA Berlin, R 58-48.
7. Reinhard Heinrich August Höhn (1905-2000), studied Law, Habilitation 1934 University of Heidelberg, Professor in Berlin and Chief of Department II,2 in SD Head Office since 1935, after World War II active as management expert, started academy for management executives in Bad Harzburg 1956. Cf. Lutz Hachmeister, "Die Rolle des SD-Personals in der Nachkriegszeit. Zur nationalsozialistischen Durchdringung der Bundesrepublik," in Michael Wildt, ed., *Nachrichtendienst, politische Elite und Mordeinheit. Der Sicherheitsdienst des Reichsführers SS* (Hamburg: Hamburger Edition, 2003), 347-352.
8. Fritz Valjavec (Vienna 1909-Germany 1960), studied History, NSDAP 1933, Deutsches Auslandswissenschaftliches Institut Berlin under Franz Alfred Six 1940, consultant for SS, member *Einsatzkommando* (special detachment) 1941, Professor University Munich 1958. Conference Report, "Südostforschung im Schatten des Dritten Reiches (1920-1960), Institutionen, Inhalte, Personen," Munich 2002. Valjavec to Schellenberg, August 25, 1941, NA, Records of the Reich Leader of the SS and Chief of the German Police, T 175/239.
9. Various notes and letters by Schellenberg and correspondence with Valjavec, 1940-1941, BA Berlin, R 58/Anhang 52. *Amt* IV to Minister for Education, February 26, 1941, Humboldt Universität zu Berlin/

So much for his otherwise very formal legal education which, with the exception of the training at the secret state police office, would appear to have been rather routine for a young German planning to either open his own or to work in someone else's law office (*Kanzlei*) or to strive for a salaried legal position in a business enterprise or in some governmental institution. The significant political decisions of actually joining the Nazi party (NSDAP) and even the SS (*Schutzstaffel*) had been made three years earlier and the somewhat out of the ordinary training experience with the secret state police may well have been closely related to these political commitments. According to his SS personnel file, Schellenberg joined the Nazi party on April 1, 1933, receiving membership number (*Pg.-Nr.*) 3.504.508, and the SS on the same date with the SS No. 124.817.[10] When questioned after the war he explained that it was dire economic circumstances as a law student that caused him to seek financial assistance from the government and that at the time it was generally assumed that grant recipients were active Nazis. There is no reason to doubt his recollection that some superior had advised him to take the proper step and join the party. Besides, he also recalled, many people at the time saw no other way out of Germany's prolonged economic and political crises than to actively join the Nazi movement and support what to them seemed a common effort.[11] In retrospect, the problem with that postwar explanation is that Walter Schellenberg for much of the rest of his short life did not often act the way most people did. Instead, his joining of the SS in 1933 would appear to suggest a clear decision to enter the still young Nazi structures at an elite level. In the creative imagination of the ambitious 23-year old the SS with its striking uniform, an aura of prestige, and certain social advantages presented a challenge, seemingly far removed, he thought, from the street brawls of "the beer hall rowdies of the SA" storm troopers (*Sturmabteilung*).[12]

While working as a *Referendar* for the secret state police, Schellenberg became acquainted with a man whom his interrogators after the war understood to have been "Prof. Nehlis, a Prof. of philology." This was probably

---

Universitätsarchiv zu Berlin (HUB), R/S No 2111. There also Immatriculation Lists, 1940-1941. — Siegfried Matlok, ed. *Dänemark in Hitler's Hand: Der Bericht des Reichsbevollmächtigten Werner Best* ... (Husum: Husum Verlag, 1988), 169. Reinhard Heydrich also considered earning a doctoral degree in Law, but like Schellenberg did not complete requirements.

10. Himmler's office to *Brigadeführer* Schulz, May 21, 1943, recommending Schellenberg's promotion from SS-*Standartenführer* to SS-*Oberführer*. NA, BDC Microfilm, Roll A3343 SSO-074B. The confusion of some authors regarding the date of his joining the SS may be caused by the fact that he became an "SS-Anwärter" (candidate) on April 1, 1933, but an "SS-Mann" (full-fledged member) on January 10, 1934. Cf. "Dienstlaufbahn" (service career), *Ibid.*

11. "Friedrich Walther Schellenberg," December 29, 1947, NA, Records of the Central Intelligence Agency (CIA), RG 263, Name Files, E A1-86, Box 38. Schellenberg, *The Schellenberg Memoirs*, 20-21. Cf. Walter Schellenberg, *Memoiren* (Köln: Verlag für Politik und Wirtschaft, 1959), 26-27.

12. "Autobiography," June 1945, see edited text below in this publication. Schellenberg, *The Schellenberg Memoirs*, 21.

Heinrich-Josef Nelis, a decorated veteran of World War I who had studied various fields but especially Catholic Theology and then worked as a school teacher of Catholic Religion for seven years. Before 1933 Nelis had been active in the nationalist *Stahlhelm* (Steel Helmet), a kind of veteran organization, and in 1933 he joined the SS and obviously very soon became more than a regular member. Nelis was so impressed by the young lawyer that he brought him to the attention of Wilhelm Albert, an engineer by profession and a former Free Corps (*Freikorps*) member with some standing in the SS. Albert, at the time chief of the administrative section of the SD (*Sicherheitsdienst*) head office in Berlin, was impressed by the impatiently eager youngster and quickly moved him to the capital. Challenging legal work in the area of state reform and more attractive financial arrangements may have played their part to lure Schellenberg to Berlin, but great enticements were not needed to change from what amounted to boring guard duty to assignments requiring some thought and initiative. Schellenberg's personnel file, fully preserved in the Berlin Document Center records, illustrates his rapid rise on the treacherous career ladder of the SS. Recognizing the human weaknesses in his surroundings, he may have been induced to work even harder and avoid all public spectacle. His supervisor in Department II of the *Hauptamt* (head office) was SS-*Oberführer* Dr. Herbert Mehlhorn who apparently found it difficult to keep his critical views to himself. Schellenberg later remembered that his mentor Mehlhorn openly opposed Reinhard Heydrich and in 1936 was dragged before a "Court of Honor" (*Ehrengerichtsverfahren*) and eventually dismissed from the SS head office, being given assignments to travel in different parts of the world and report on political conditions. Mehlhorn, if Schellenberg recalls correctly, thought rather highly of him and apparently was able to talk some sense into the ambitious young man, making him go back to his legal studies in 1936 in order to prepare for the state exam.[13]

There are no reliable data, but it may have been about this time that Schellenberg discarded the idea of having his own law practice and instead, at least for the foreseeable future, decided to pursue a political career in Berlin. It was not a flippant decision for even years later he was to recall the opportunity in Düsseldorf which he had chosen to turn down. Indications are that the prospect of establishing himself as an independent lawyer was quite real.

---

13. "Final Report on the Case of Walter Friedrich Schellenberg" edited by Reinhard R. Doerries, in Doerries, *Hitler's Last Chief of Foreign Intelligence* (London: Frank Cass, 2003), 71. (Hereafter: "Final Report".) Statement under Oath, Dr. Theodor Päffgen, NA, NA Collection of WWII Crimes Records, RG 238, Microfilm M 897, Roll 114, suggesting that it was Mehlhorn who persuaded Schellenberg to complete his law exams in order to join the "political intelligence service." (Transl.) Schellenberg, *Memoiren*, 30-33, where he refers to "Prof. Dr. N.". Personnel File, Heinrich-Josef Nelis, BA Berlin, R 4901/13272. From this file it is not clear whether Nelis had been a priest prior to joining the SS.

Apparently Alfred Bartholomäus, by friends sometimes called Bartolo, a member of *Corps Guestphalia*, and a successful, well-connected lawyer in Düsseldorf, thought very highly of him and planned to have him take over his law office. Schellenberg later recalled: "... I had an especially good connection to a Justizrat Bartholomaeus in Duesseldorf who so to speak, adopted me as his son, not legally but in fact, whose law office I was to take over in Duesseldorf. He was one of the most respected people in the Ruhr area ... From him I have learned a lot."[14] Schellenberg actually spent some time in that Düsseldorf law firm before being lured to Berlin. British intelligence men interrogating him after the war understood him to say that *Justizrat* Bartholomäus was a friend of his father, and this seemed to explain the offer to join that law firm. While the lawyer may have had good connections to Schellenberg's parents, he certainly was also a member of the same student corps and therefore was likely to have thought that he could fully trust the young corps brother. Additionally, it seems rather believable that his interrogators in London understood correctly when they recorded that Schellenberg thought the Nazi system foreshadowed "nationalization" and "that there would be little, if any future," in running a private independent law practice. In the end the corps brother and young Schellenberg agreed that he "should return to Berlin at least for a year," knowing that he was welcome to come back and become a partner in the Düsseldorf *Kanzlei* should he wish to do so.[15]

In Berlin Schellenberg soon acquired a reputation as a workaholic and superiors as well as peers began to regard him as someone likely to be moving up. Wilhelm Höttl, an Austrian trained historian and fellow SS-officer, used by Allied interrogators after the war to double-check Schellenberg's statements, put it this way: "... as far as his personal life is concerned, he was utterly beyond reproach. His manner of life was almost that of an ascetic. He neither drank nor smoked, and worked twenty hours straight for days on end." He was right when he told them that Schellenberg had joined both NSDAP and SS relatively late and therefore could not claim to be an *Alter Kämpfer* (early warrior), the proud label given to the founding generation of Nazis, but Höttl also correctly observed that Schellenberg had "a keen understanding of the potentialities of

---

14. Schellenberg, SAN, Rep. 502, VI, S-45c. Bartholomäus is father-in-law of Kurt Gerstein's brother Alfred and befriended with the Gersteins, talks to them about Schellenberg. Pierre Joffroy, *Der Spion Gottes* (Berlin: Aufbau, 1995; 1st Paris 1992), 150-151.
15. "Final Report," 70. Regarding Schellenberg's connection with Bartholomäus see intelligence report of December 29, 1947, declassified by the CIA in 2001, NA, RG 263, E A1-86, Box 39. Statement under Oath by Dr. Theodor Päffgen, March 12, 1948, SAN, Rep 501, LV, S-3. There also Statement under Oath, Heinz Amthor, who met Schellenberg in the offices of Albert and Mehlhorn. Statement under Oath by SS-*Sturmbannführer* Hans-Hendrik Neumann, of Heydrich's staff, NA, RG 238, Microfilm M 897, Roll 114. Cf. Joffroy, *Der Spion Gottes*, 150-151.

this section" (the administrative office where Schellenberg began his service in Berlin). Schellenberg, as Höttl saw it, "knew how to place himself in the foreground and soon Heydrich's watchful eye had become aware of the young man. The latter [Heydrich] soon accepted Schellenberg into his inner circle, in order to, as he put it, 'train the youngster himself' ... Schellenberg became one of Heydrich's most trusted confidants."[16] This in itself would have been quite an achievement, but the well-educated and quietly reliable performer of a great variety of tasks also succeeded in making himself almost irreplaceable to those in the higher SS echelons in the capital. They in turn rewarded him with more responsibility which he seemed to be craving for.

His employment in legal and administrative tasks may be an indication that his superiors were sufficiently impressed with the young man's abilities. It did not, however, always spare him the less inspiring assignments of guard duty or just standing around to be seen at official functions. While Schellenberg was later to note that he cared little for such calls to duty, there was one such day he would not forget. It was June 29, 1934, and the SS was providing security at the well-known Hotel Dreesen in Bad Godesberg on the Rhine. Standing outside in a gruesome downpour, the 23-year old SS youngster sought cover near the building and found himself looking into the windows of the rooms where Hitler was conferring with a group of Nazi leaders, among them such names as Joseph Goebbels, Hermann Göring and the SS-*Gruppenführer* Sepp Dietrich. Schellenberg had heard that something important was happening, and he understood that he was part of it: "All day strange and disquieting rumors had reached my unit. There were said to be plots, divisions in the Party, and impending disasters."[17] The high-level meeting unraveled only late that evening, and it was past midnight when the Mercedes limousines of Hitler and his entourage were heading off to the nearby airport of Hangelar. It would soon be daybreak of what Heinz Höhne has called "the most murderous day in German pre-war history."[18] It was, as Schellenberg later described it, "the monstrous blood-bath that Hitler's orders let loose among his own followers that night."[19] In retrospect, of course, it is not entirely surprising that Hitler and his cronies not only wiped out SA leaders suspected of taking too seriously the socialist part of so-called national-socialist ideology, but also would not pass up the opportunity of ridding themselves of numerous untrusted and

---

16. Interrogation Report No. 15, July 9, 1945, Secret, NA, RG 319, IRR, PS, Box 617.
17. Schellenberg, *The Schellenberg Memoirs*, 23. Published data in this connection are somewhat confusing. Schellenberg stood guard on June 29 and the conference at the Hotel Dreesen ended after midnight, i.e. on June 30.
18. Heinz Höhne, *Mordsache Röhm: Hitlers Durchbruch zur Alleinherrschaft 1933-1934* (Reinbek: Rowohlt/Spiegel, 1984), 265. (Transl.)
19. Schellenberg, *The Schellenberg Memoirs*, 23.

unappreciated personalities. Among those murdered were General Kurt von Schleicher, high-ranking General Staff officer and *Reich* Chancellor just before Adolf Hitler, and his wife; Gregor Strasser, an early follower of Hitler, a participant in the latter's 1923 putsch attempt and one of the more socialist inclined early Nazi leaders; Edgar Jung, a conservative political writer and close collaborator and supporter of Franz von Papen; and Gustav Ritter von Kahr, important Bavarian leader who had opposed Hitler's political ambitions.

Nothing is known about Schellenberg's private thoughts at the time, but the trained lawyer must have recognized that it was a brutal and immoral system which he was about to join. His SS uniform was still very new when he realized that "June 30 marked the ascendancy within the Nazi structure of the SS, whose black uniform with the death's head insignia I now wore."[20] So, at least, he later wrote. As it were, events witnessed did not shock the ambitious young man enough to consider a still possible withdrawal from the SS career track.

Other jobs assigned to him were in the field of basic observation of individuals and institutions. For several weeks he was dispatched to Paris to spy on the activities of a professor at the Sorbonne. Such assignments as a rule came from the Berlin head office of the *Sicherheitsdienst* (SD) and were handed to him by a surgeon in Bonn. Schellenberg would visit the medical professional in his private home to receive his orders. The meetings in the man's study filled with a library of some substance often turned into reflective conversations on a broad range of topics, particularly intelligence and its development in Britain and the Balkans. Another go-between instructing him on behalf of the SD appears to have been a Jesuit priest who considerably impressed the young SS man. Later Schellenberg was to recall his disappointment about never receiving any reactions to his presumably carefully structured reports in the course of the assignments. Though little is known about these activities, his rapid advance within the SS would suggest that his superiors were more than impressed by his performance in the field. After the war Theodor Päffgen, a Berlin SS colleague, told Allied interrogators: "In the *Amt* Schellenberg was highly regarded for his great diligence, the quality of his written work, and his adroitness in negotiations with superiors."[21]

Upon completion of his final legal exams in December 1936, he was moved back to the head office in Berlin where in January 1937 he became Assistant to the Head of Department in the administrative section I/II of the

---

20. Schellenberg, *The Schellenberg Memoirs*, 24.
21. Statement under Oath, Dr. Theodor Paeffgen, NA, RG 238, Microfilm M 897, Roll 114. (Transl.)

SD. On paper he was taken on by the Ministry of the Interior following the legal exam and the pro-forma appointment to *Gerichtsassessor*, the German legal title signifying that its bearer had completed the highest requirements for the legal profession. In 1937 he became a *Regierungsassessor* with the Ministry of the Interior, the first step to becoming a *Regierungsrat* in 1938. In reality he was loaned out to or worked for the SD. Because much of the documentation available appears unclear and in some cases plainly contradictory, previously published biographical data of Schellenberg are not always reliable.[22] For this particular stage of his career we have the appraisal by his department chief, the SS-*Standartenführer* Wilhelm Albert on March 27, 1937, stating that Schellenberg was back with the Berlin head office "since the middle of December 1936" being occupied with assignments in the area of organization. "This activity brings him together almost only with the influential leaders of the central departments which would urgently suggest his elevation to leadership rank." The result of this recommendation was Schellenberg's promotion to SS-*Untersturmführer*. To all appearances, Schellenberg also must have overcome, at least for the time being, any serious personal doubts he may have had about the ethical qualities of the regime he had decided to serve. If this required adjustments in his personal life, he seems to have been willing to accept that too. His official declaration in the District Court of Berlin on March 31, 1937, that he was leaving the Catholic Church certainly was one of the required adjustments.[23]

Rank, however, did not exempt Schellenberg from risky missions. When Germany decided to absorb Austria in 1938, Schellenberg found himself responsible for the collection of data concerning possible reactions of the Western powers, with particular attention being paid to Italy, Austria's neighbor. How much his paperwork in the *Hauptamt* (head office) contributed to German treachery in an increasingly pro-German Austria is uncertain, but there can be no doubt that Schellenberg was fully informed about what was transpiring,[24] and his memoirs convey the impression that he fully enjoyed the tense atmosphere and probably the challenge of the situation. On March 12, 1938, a day after Hitler had obtained the resignation of Austrian Chancellor Kurt von Schuschnigg and while German military forces were crossing the

---

22. In most cases it would appear recommendable to refer to the personnel files retained in the holdings of the BDC, fully available at the NA. They contain CV sketches written by Schellenberg himself in connection with promotions and other important personal matters.
23. Walter Schellenberg, NA, BDC Microfilm, Roll A 3343 SSO-074B. (Transl.) Amtsgericht Berlin, Abt. 460 Gen. II. 323 ka, April 30, 1937, BA Berlin, R 58/Anhang I/48. — A number of SS officers in the German Foreign Office stayed in the Church.
24. André Brissaud, *The Nazi Secret Service* (New York: W. W. Norton, 1974), 192, without naming his sources, strongly suggests — "I have good reason to believe" — that Schellenberg himself went to Austria in late November or early December 1937. (Brissaud spoke with him shortly before his death. See below.)

border into Austria, Schellenberg received orders to fly to Vienna. From all appearances his mission was to assist in the adjustment of the legal system of what until then had been Austria and would be referred to in Nazi lingua franca henceforth as *Ostmark* (Eastern border region). As it happened, another passenger on his flight was the *Reichsführer* SS Heinrich Himmler whom Schellenberg had not met before personally. He later recalled that Himmler took him to the back of the plane in order to better discuss administrative problems expected in the wake of the German takeover in Austria. Schellenberg: "Himmler was leaning against a door when I noticed that the safety catch was not on. At any moment the door might have opened ... I quickly grasped him by his coat and jerked him away. He glared at me furiously, but when I showed him the door was unlatched he thanked me and said if the opportunity ever arose he would be happy to do as much for me."[25] If the incident is reported correctly, one could be tempted to register that encounter at the door on the flight to Vienna on March 12, 1938, as the possible beginning of the trust or at least as part of the background for the maturation of a feeling of trust that Himmler much later seems to have had at times for Schellenberg.

Once in Vienna the work load must have been considerable and pressure was on the rise largely due to the apparent shortage of ranking German personnel. At least in part, Schellenberg later explained, his responsibility for important tasks in Vienna was caused by the absence of Heinrich Müller, the soon-to-be chief of the *Geheime Staatspolizei* (Secret State Police, Gestapo) who presumably otherwise would have attended to the more pressing matters. One of these undertakings may have been Schellenberg's involvement in the collection, if not to say confiscation of certain Austrian documents wanted in Berlin. Reinhard Heydrich, soon-to-be chief of the *Reichssicherheitshauptamt* (Imperial Security Head Office, RSHA) had personally "told me to secure all the files and documents of the Chief of the Austrian Secret Service, Colonel Ronge."[26] Apparently, no lesser person than Wilhelm Canaris, submarine commander and intelligence operative in World War I and since 1935 head of the *Abwehr* (Military Intelligence) pursued the same target, but, according to Jacques Delarue, Schellenberg, though not yet a formidable competitor in the intelligence business, beat him to it and "carried out his mission which consisted in seizing the statute books and records of the Austrian Secret Service chief." André Brissaud, quite to the contrary, reports that Erwin Edler von Lahousen-Vivremont, formerly of the Austrian Military Intelligence and

---

25. Schellenberg, *The Schellenberg Memoirs*, 51. Cf. same account, but worded slightly differently in Schellenberg, *Memoiren*, 52.
26. Schellenberg, *The Schellenberg Memoirs*, 51.

after the *Anschluss* a ranking member of the German *Abwehr*, told him that Canaris got there first and obtained from Max Ronge the Austrian files created on Canaris, Göring, Heydrich, and Hitler.[27] Not uncommon for Schellenberg, his own description of the operation remains rather sparse: "The papers that I found were not very up-to-date, though there was some interesting material on deciphering codes. Colonel Ronge himself expressed his willingness to work in future for the German Secret Service."[28]

One of the high points of Schellenberg's intelligence activities in Vienna must have been a period of approximately twelve hours during which he was personally responsible for security. The *Führer* (leader, Adolf Hitler) had come to Vienna to bathe in the huge Austrian welcoming crowd and the Gestapo Chief Müller was not on location to take charge. A sudden bomb threat drove tension to a peak and demanded immediate decisive action which Schellenberg apparently was able to provide. Yet even in his satisfaction with having mastered the crisis, he could not have been more pleased "to turn my responsibilities back to Müller."[29]

From Heydrich's perspective events in Vienna apparently had been handled so well that Schellenberg found himself dispatched again, right after his return to Berlin in mid-April, this time to Rome to attend to security preparations for an up-coming visit of Hitler in Italy. Schellenberg's later claim that he infiltrated five hundred Italian speaking agents into Italy dressed up as tourists may be somewhat exaggerated. Their purpose, Schellenberg said after the war, was "to look out for anything which might seem suspicious in connection with Hitler's visit," but also "to note and report on all evidence of popular feeling in Italy and of the attitude of the Italian people towards the Fascist régime." Whatever—as a result of this operation, which incidentally appears to have gone well, Schellenberg was able to gather a great amount of information on the political climate in Italy and, of course, to establish first contacts with Italian secret service personnel, both of which would be useful in the coming years. Among others he encountered Arturo Bocchini, Chief of the

---

27. Brissaud, *The Nazi Secret Service*, 194. André Brissaud, *Canaris* (New York: Grosset & Dunlap, 1974; 1st 1970), 86. Jacques Delarue, *The Gestapo* (New York: Paragon House, 1987; 1st Paris, 1962), 163-164.
28. Schellenberg, *The Schellenberg Memoirs*, 51. Information varies on the nature of the respective documents, but indications are that at least some of them were connected with the murder of the Austrian Chancellor Engelbert Dollfuss on July 25, 1934, by a group of National Socialists, among them Otto Planetta. "Final Report," 71. For details of the murder, committed by Otto Planetta and others, see Gerhard L. Weinberg, *The Foreign Policy of Hitler's Germany* (Chicago: University of Chicago Press, 1970), 101-104. Cf. Schellenberg, *Memoiren*, 53.
29. Details regarding the explosives placed under a bridge on Hitler's route vary somewhat in the different editions of the memoirs.

Italian Police and therefore also in charge of what was often referred to as *Opera per la Vigilanza e la Repressione dell'Antifascismo (OVRA)*.[30]

One would justifiably assume that Schellenberg in the course of these very early assignments must have been under close, if not always visible control of his mentors and superiors in Berlin. It also needs to be recalled that the man whom they chose to thrust into operations of this nature was barely twenty-eight years old. Indications are, at least during this early period, that Schellenberg fully understood the political developments in the locations of his work and indeed much welcomed the challenges and dangers connected with the assignments. The workaholic never took a break. Not surprisingly, the appraisal by his superior, the SS-*Oberführer* Wilhelm Albert, was sufficiently precise to lead to Schellenberg's promotion: "Sch. is an especially able leader, who thoroughly meets his assignments and whose promotion is especially recommended ... The promotion of Sch. to SS-Hauptsturmführer is especially recommended considering especially his extraordinary accomplishments in Austria as well as in Italy. (at the time Schellenberg was not promoted.)"[31]

Besides the intelligence assignments in Austria and Italy and the strenuous security work in connection with Hitler's much publicized triumphal visits to Vienna and Rome, Schellenberg also became involved in destructive covert German activities in Czechoslovakia and the close cooperation with Konrad Henlein and his *Sudetendeutsche Partei* (Sudeten German Party). It would appear that the Germans wished to keep the lid on internal frictions of the Sudeten Germans. If Schellenberg's memoirs can be trusted on this, Konrad Henlein was less interested in the dismemberment of Czechoslovakia than others, such as Karl Hermann Frank, his second-in-command in the party. Henlein, who Schellenberg later recalled had his eyes set on a state of autonomy for the Sudeten Germans, Berlin knew was in contact with "Colonel Christie, a representative of the British Secret Service."[32] Henlein's meetings with the

---

30. When interrogated at Camp 020 by British intelligence in 1945, he spoke of "some 60 or 70 members of the S.D. Hauptamt ... introduced into the country as visiting civilians ... to be posted at strategic points throughout the city." "Final Report," 72. The larger number mentioned could therefore refer to German informers spread across Italy and not directly related to Hitler's visit. — Already in late March 1936 the political police chiefs of Italy and Germany and representatives of the Foreign Offices had convened in Berlin. Bocchini, Himmler, Heydrich and Vicco Karl Alexander von Bülow-Schwante and Emil Johannes Schumburg from the German Foreign Office were among those attending. Hans-Jürgen Döscher, *Das Auswärtige Amt im Dritten Reich: Diplomatie im Schatten der "Endlösung"* (Berlin: Siedler, 1987), 122.

31. Forms signed by SS-*Oberführer* Albert. Dates not clear, but after Schellenberg's marriage. Walter Schellenberg, NA, BDC Microfilm, Roll A 3343 SSO-074B. The text in parenthesis on the document is in Albert's handwriting. (Transl.)

32. Group Captain Malcolm Grahame Christie (1881-1971) studied engineering at Aachen, worked in the Ruhr area until 1914, member of the Royal Flying Corps, from 1922 to 1926 served as Air Attaché in Washington and from 1927 to 1930 in the same position in Berlin. In Washington he came to know Sir Robert Vansittart and in Berlin he is said to have developed a relationship with Hermann Göring. Stephen Dorril, *A Who's Who of the British Secret State* (no publ. data), 19, lists him as "part of the Vansittart 'private

British presumably took place in Switzerland, and in the summer of 1938 Heydrich instructed Schellenberg to have Henlein observed and to uncover the meaning of the mysterious connection. Henlein's message to the British, if Schellenberg reports correctly, could not have come very unexpected: "... to wait any longer would be impossible, both for the Sudeten German Party and for Hitler, and if necessary the problem would have to be solved by force." The events in late 1938 and early 1939 appear to have proven him correct. The destruction of Czechoslovakia took its course after Britain and France acceded to Germany's brash demands at Munich. Schellenberg describes in some detail the surreptitious operations of German intelligence inside Czechoslovakia leading to dismemberment and the consequent "peaceful occupation of Czechoslovakia by German troops" as he calls it. According to the English edition of his memoirs, he was part of Hitler's entourage when the latter, "in order to be the first to arrive at the Hradčany, the ancient and historic castle in Prague ... raced through the night at breakneck speed over icy roads, passing the advancing German columns on the way." If one follows the German memoirs, Schellenberg stayed in Berlin to assure an extensive delay of the return journey of the Czechoslovakian Minister President Emil Hacha, whom the Nazis had pressured into agreeing to the so-called protection of the Czech people by Nazi Germany.[33]

Though one might be tempted to suspect that the date of Schellenberg's marriage to Käthe (Katharina Gertrud) Kortekamp on May 25, 1938, had something to do with the successful completion of his assignments in Austria and Italy, the records clearly show that this was not the case.[34] As an SS-officer Schellenberg was obliged to formally apply for permission to become engaged and to marry. That application form was filled out and presented at the *Sippenamt* SS (SS genealogical office) already on January 27, 1938. Based on the information regarding the presumable racial descent of Schellenberg and his future wife and the health history of the two, considered on January 28 and February 18 respectively, the SS had no objections. Official permission for the marriage was granted on February 22, 1938. As Schellenberg had left the Catholic Church a year earlier, the wedding was a civil ceremony. Käte

---

intelligence agency' close to MI6." F. H. Hinsley and others, *British Intelligence in the Second World War*, vol. I (London: Her Majesty's Stationery Office, 1979), 47-48: "Group Captain M G Christie ... was not as has been claimed, employed by the SIS." Klemens von Klemperer, *German Resistance Against Hitler: the Search for Allies Abroad* (Oxford: Clarendon Press, 1994; 1st 1992), 90-91. Christopher Andrew, *Secret Service: The Making of the British Intelligence Community* (London: Heinemann, 1985), 382-383.
33. Schellenberg, *The Schellenberg Memoirs*, 54-57. Schellenberg, *Memoiren*, 57-58. Cf. Marlis Steinert, *Hitler* (München: C. H. Beck, 1994, 1st ed. Paris, 1991), 384.
34. The date of marriage in Schellenberg's personnel file is given as "25.5.38." During interrogation by British officials, however, the date noted was May 18, 1938. Walter Schellenberg, NA, BDC Microfilm, Roll A 3343 550-074B. "Final Report," 72. Heiratsregister Nr. 440, Berlin, May 25, 1938, BA Berlin, R 58/48.

Kortekamp was born in Bonn in 1907, had attended the *Volksstiftsschule* (elementary school) there, and at age fourteen had begun an apprenticeship as a tailoress for ladies clothes. Since 1925 she had worked as an independent seamstress.[35] Not much is known about this marriage of two people who would appear to have been rather different in most ways. The marriage lasted just over a year, and the divorce proceedings, rather fully documented, turned out to be most trying and unpleasant for both sides. In view of the brevity of the marriage Wilhelm Höttl's later explanation that Schellenberg "divorced his first wife when her age made it appear likely that she would be unable to bear any more children," must be considered erroneous. Schellenberg's unwillingness to accept "a working-class wife … a seamstress," another reason for the divorce according to some authors, also sounds less than plausible.[36] One would be tempted to wonder why Schellenberg had not discovered this problem prior to marriage. As is common in divorce cases, both he and his wife were represented by law firms whose obvious purpose had to be the assemblage of negative information about the other side. This was necessary to impress the Berlin court and reach a decision in favor of one's client. The unpleasant details offered by both sides would appear to suggest that the marriage could not be saved. The records show that Schellenberg and his wife were together or "engaged" for a period of about eight years before their marriage. Why they decided on marriage, must remain an open question, but available sources contain some suggestions that Schellenberg's private affair with Käthe Kortekamp had ceased to be private and that persons in his professional surroundings had put him under pressure to regulate his relationship. The painful and exasperating legal proceedings ending the unhappy marriage finally closed with a decision on December 31, 1939, declaring the marriage ended and Schellenberg's wife as guilty. She had strongly fought for her interests, even going as far as personally visiting Schellenberg's chief, Reinhard Heydrich, and therefore was not much inclined to just give in. Most unfriendly legal correspondence about questions concerning property and payments as a consequence extended to at least the middle of 1942.[37]

What the records do not show is the obvious connection between his personal problems and excessive political and professional pressure at such an

---

35. All documents NA, BDC Microfilm, Roll A 3343-RS-FO 270. Included there is a further formal permission to marry, dated March 3, 1938.
36. "A Character Sketch of Schellenberg" by Wilhelm Höttl, July 12, 1945, NA, RG 319, IRR, PS, Box 195. Leo Kessler, *Betrayal at Venlo: The Secret Story of Appeasement and Treachery, 1939-1945* (London: Leo Cooper, 1991), 67.
37. Letters from Schellenberg's lawyer, Dr. Fritz Jacke, and from her lawyer, Dr. Hans-Heinrich Miller. Also hearings of Schellenberg's witnesses Hans-Hendrik Neumann and Erhard Urbannek. Legal documents relating to the divorce proceedings. All in BA Berlin, R 58/Anhang I/49.

early age. It is more than likely that Schellenberg's marital problems contributed heavily to his "nervous" and general breakdown in May 1939. Unhealthy rumors of a friendship between Reinhard Heydrich's wife Lina and Walter Schellenberg certainly did not help matters and underlined the apparent linkages between his personal and his professional problems. The dinner at which Heydrich threatened to poison Schellenberg if he did not tell him the truth about a walk with Lina along the Plöner See (Lake Plön) may not have happened in quite the manner described in the English-language edition of Schellenberg's memoirs, but there is no reason to doubt the episode and the abysmal context of personal aloofness and all pervasive suspicion in top Nazi echelons.[38]

Circumstances such as these may well have contributed to Schellenberg's desire to seek a change of department. While legal and administrative questions had interested him greatly, his professional curiosity early seems to have turned to the sector of security and its organization. By August 1939 Schellenberg had rather recovered from his psychological and physical bouts with the breakdown, and after conversations with Heydrich he found himself appointed head of the subdivision *Gruppe* (Group) IV E in *Amt* IV of the recently organized *Reichssicherheitshauptamt* (RSHA) in Berlin. No one less than the notorious Heinrich Müller[39] became his boss and chieftain of Department IV that is the *Geheime Staatspolizei* (Gestapo), Heydrich's "strongest and most powerful weapon." Schellenberg's subdivision IV E was working in the area of counterintelligence, inside as well as outside of the country.[40] Consequently, Schellenberg not only increasingly moved from legal questions to intelligence problems, but the confusing disorganization of German intelligence services must have also reinforced his view that only a higher degree of centralization could lead to more effective intelligence work. Forging a single powerful security service appears to have become a major objective for Schellenberg already at this early stage. His 29-page organizational memorandum of February 24, 1939, would seem to leave little to the reader's imagination. The

---

38. Höttl's colorful account during interrogation in 1945 would appear exaggerated but may serve as an indication of the internecine spirit among SS leaders: "The boss also introduced his new protege into the circle of his family, where Schellenberg soon so ingratiated himself, that everybody expected him to marry Heydrich's widow (after the latter's assassination). But by then Schellenberg had become far too clever. A dead Heydrich was no longer of any interest to him." Wilhelm Hoettl, NA, RG 319, IRR, PS, Box 617. Schellenberg, *The Schellenberg Memoirs*, 36-38.
39. Heinrich Müller, born 1909 in Munich, according to the German magazine *Der Spiegel* (vol. 17, no. 42, 1963) was neither a bureaucratic bookkeeper like Adolf Eichmann nor an "intellectual" like Walter Schellenberg, but simply "cunning and brutal." His fate after 1945 remains somewhat uncertain and dubious rumors, such as those referring to his escape to the USSR, continue to have some currency.
40. Allied intelligence in December 1944 reported that Department IV E then had a number of subsections concerned with frontier controls and counterespionage activities in various parts of the world. "Revision Notes No. 2 on 'The German Intelligence Services'," December 25, 1944, Top Secret, NA, RG 319, IRR, IS, Box 5.

SS, he wrote, in line with its "special laws of military discipline and ideological conduct" would absorb the entire governmental sector of the police and create a new state security service (*Staatsschutz-Korps*). This new combined service, Schellenberg cleverly gave it the hazy designation "personnel union" (*Personalunion*), would strive to achieve a political *Ziellinie* (goal line) while also "developing the purely impartial work of a total political intelligence service." Those seeking to detect personal objectives of Schellenberg's in the newly planned mammoth organization were likely to be disappointed. The memorandum with its presumably intended vagueness of expression instead might be seen as a sample of the work of a 29-year old SS-leader and his way of navigating the highly competitive and more often than not unpredictable Nazi elite network. That Schellenberg's paper was to become a center piece of a controversy between Heydrich, who by and large agreed with Schellenberg, and Werner Best, Heydrich's deputy until 1940, may have been somewhat predictable. There is little evidence, however, that Schellenberg intended anything more than to produce a plan of organization for Heydrich and, of course, as much as possible to include his own views in the overall proposal. As the controversy concerned the future role of lawyers in the RSHA and more specifically in the SD, it is necessary to recall that while his supporters Heydrich and Himmler had not studied Law, Schellenberg had completed the study of Law and possessed the qualifications to run his own law firm.[41]

In the complete absence of meaningful political or impressive military opposition from other nations, the Germans could only be expected to continue their drive for aggressive expansion and, looking at the international context and developments in Europe, Poland seems to have been predestined to be the next target. In his memoirs Schellenberg has little to say about German preparations for the attack on Poland, and indications are that he was not much involved in pre-invasion planning. He does, however, recall in some detail a strange meeting with Herbert Mehlhorn, his former mentor in the *Hauptamt*, on August 26, 1939, just days prior to the Gleiwitz operation. If we can believe Schellenberg's report on their conversation during a very private walk, Mehlhorn was in a state of quasi-shock because his enemy Heydrich had personally given him the order to organize the attack on the Gleiwitz station. The impression given in the memoirs that Schellenberg may not have known

---

41. Walter Schellenberg, "Reorganisation des Sicherheitsdienstes des Reichsführers SS im Hinblick auf eine organisatorische und personelle Angleichung mit der Sicherheitspolizei," February 24, 1939, BA Berlin, R 58/826. (Transl.) Regarding this controversy see Michael Wildt, *Generation des Unbedingten: Das Führungskorps des Reichssicherheitshauptamtes* (Hamburg: Hamburger Edition, 2003), 266 ff, referring to a conversation between Felix Kersten and Heinrich Himmler. Ulrich Herbert, *Best: Biographische Studien über Radikalismus, Weltanschauung und Vernunft, 1903-1989* (Bonn: J. H. W. Dietz Nachfolger, 1996; 2nd ed.), 229 ff. Cf. Felix Kersten, *The Kersten Memoirs, 1940-1945* (London: Hutchinson, 1956), 104 ff.

of the respective operational plans seems difficult to believe. His advice to the desperate Mehlhorn to come up with some excuse for just not being able to execute the order with the expected precision, however, may well have been voiced just like that. Mehlhorn then indeed informed Heydrich that he was not sufficiently healthy and strong enough to perform to the usual highest standards. Unbelievable as it may seem, Heydrich apparently accepted Mehlhorn's decision and merely discharged him again from the SD. The Gleiwitz operation on August 31, 1939, was the infamous attack by Germans dressed as Poles on the Gleiwitz radio station, leaving behind some bodies of men they had killed in a concentration camp for that purpose and creating a *casus belli* legitimizing the planned German attack on Poland. It was the beginning of World War II. The operation was largely carried out by Alfred Naujocks who seems to have had no problems performing Heydrich's assignments.[42] Although Schellenberg does not say so in his recollections, it would be reasonable to assume that he was pleased by the circumstance that Russia since the Hitler-Stalin Pact a week earlier was an observing partner of Germany rather than a threatening ally of Britain and France. In any case, his comments on the German unleashing of World War II are paltry to say the least, suggesting that Schellenberg at this point in time still believed that the on-coming war could have positive results for Nazi Germany.

Schellenberg offers more detail on circumstances in Poland following the brutal attack from Nazi Germany and Soviet Russia. Although his assignment to the newly created *Abteilung* IV E would appear to have had no particular connection with the German military campaign in Poland, Schellenberg found himself ordered to travel with Himmler "as the representative of the Reichssicherheitshauptamt." Before his departure Heydrich warned him of SS-*Gruppenführer* Karl Wolff and his adjutants, "a pretty unpleasant lot" surrounding Himmler. In fact, Schellenberg later felt that though officially *Ordonnanzoffizier* (aide-de-camp) he was in fact being tested or screened by Himmler. They were following the quickly advancing German forces when on September 28 Heydrich himself turned up and used Schellenberg to organize security for the up-coming visit of Hitler to vanquished Warsaw. This is what he saw there: " ... ruined and burnt-out houses, starving and grieving people ... smoke hung over the city and everywhere there was the sweetish smell of burnt flesh ... Warsaw was a dead city."[43]

---

42. Schellenberg, *The Schellenberg Memoirs*, 68-70. Schellenberg, *Memoiren*, 69-70. Cf. Heinz Höhne, *The Order of the Death's Head* (New York: Ballantine, 1989; 1st German publ. 1967), 296-299, for a slightly different explanation why Heydrich "jettisoned" Mehlhorn.
43. For the assignment in Poland see Schellenberg, *The Schellenberg Memoirs*, 70-78. The German memoirs do not vary greatly.

Decidedly more important for the recently appointed counter-intelligence officer must have been the information harvest gathered from captured Polish intelligence records. Some 430 Germans according to this material were working for Polish intelligence. As in other cases, the editions of his memoirs differ slightly in detail, but there seems to be little doubt that his quick journey to the Rhine-Ruhr region had one single major purpose, namely to check the controls put in place to prevent precisely what Polish espionage apparently had accomplished so far.[44] Ironically, Schellenberg, of course, had no inkling of the Poles' real intelligence coup just prior to being overrun by the German armies. Polish intelligence had handed over carefully constructed replicas of Germany's Enigma machine. Stunningly timed, just when German submarines were heading for their assigned battle stations in the Atlantic and a massive ground force was closing in on Poland, Colonel Stewart Menzies and his men of MI6 were at Victoria Station, London, to receive the gift of the Poles, the phenomenal importance of which was to become evident in the course of World War II.[45]

With the destruction of Poland well on its way, back in Berlin the ambitious young Schellenberg was about to be drawn into one of the most publicized feats of his relatively short career. Christopher Andrew has labeled the Venlo operation "one of the most embarrassing episodes in the history of the SIS," and the German violation of the Dutch border with the kidnapping of two British agents to this day has remained a controversial matter. Though it seems difficult to determine just what the Germans gained from the exercise, there can be little doubt that British intelligence suffered or rather thought it suffered an unexpected blow, not to mention real or imagined consequences of the episode. Some authors continue to recount events as if the somewhat astonishing contacts between Nazi representatives and British intelligence were part of a general immediate reaction to the onset of World War II, but much of the evidence suggests the existence of such contacts well before September 1939. The British certainly had been aware of a certain restless mood in some quarters of German society, and London was informed about a latent discontent among some military leaders in Germany.

The so-called Z organization run by Claude Edward Marjoribanks Dansey is not unknown. Dansey, the old intelligence hand with MI5 and MI6 experience in World War I more recently had built a network of connections in

---

44. For some detail on Polish operations in the *Ruhrgebiet* see Schellenberg, *Memoiren*, 76-78. "Final Report," 74-75.
45. Anthony Cave Brown, *"C": The Secret Life of Sir Stewart Graham Menzies, Spymaster to Winston Churchill* (New York: Macmillan, 1987), 199-208. For this and much detail on the Polish contribution Wladyslaw Kozaczuk, *Enigma* (Frederick: University Publications of America, 1984; 1st Warsaw, 1979).

Italy that would serve as a starting point for Z. At the time presumably almost no one other than Hugh "Quex" Sinclair, Chief of MI6 from 1923 to 1939, was fully informed about the Z organization and its broad range of activities. While Dansey's operations had their main base in Switzerland, another significant center of Z was in the Netherlands. Early contacts between British and Germans, contrary to published historical studies, were not made by Schellenberg, but appear to have stemmed from Dr. Franz Fischer who is said to have worked for Dansey as an agent, but who also became an SD operative shortly before World War II, keeping in mind his future in case of a German victory. Therefore, depending on one's sources, he was a refugee from Nazi Germany living in France or an agent for one or the other side.[46] Apparently Fischer managed to gain access to a group of German exiles around Dr. Klaus Spieker in Paris. Somehow Fischer was able to get a German officer named Solms to agree to bring members of the supposedly existing military opposition to Holland in order to meet with representatives of Major Richard H. Stevens, an MI6 officer stationed at the British Embassy at The Hague. Major Solms, the man with the mysterious contacts to a German military opposition, was in fact Major Johannes Travaglio of *Abwehr* I/*Luft* (Military Intelligence/Air). Sigismund Payne Best, chief of Z in The Netherlands, was quasi roped into the game by a number of rather curious circumstances. To begin with, Spieker, who was working for Dansey, had informed the latter that Dr. Franz or rather Franz Fischer could be trusted, and Dansey had accepted that recommendation, and, as Andrew has it, "agreed to deal with Fischer through his London headquarters rather than through Best."[47] When war came, it was Dansey who made Best Fischer's case officer and thereby put a finishing touch to the overture of the operatic enterprise called Venlo. Best, being unaware that Fischer was in the service of both British and German intelligence, requested that the trusted agent arrange a meeting with the Germans.

While Schellenberg told British intelligence after the war that he thought contacts with Best and Stevens began some time in August 1939, most accounts record the first real encounter at the beginning of September 1939, at the Hotel Wilhelmina in Venlo on the Dutch-German border. On this occasion Fischer supposedly introduced Captain Best to "Major Solms." For

---

46. On Fischer: Callum A. MacDonald, "The Venlo Affair," *European Studies Review*, vol. 8, no. 4 (1978), 448. Rudolf Ströbinger, *A-54* (München: List, 1965/1966) 140. Brown, *"C": The Secret Life of Sir Stewart Graham Menzies*, 213. Michael Wildt, *Generation des Unbedingten*, 399, suggests that Schellenberg "produced" the "contact." Cf. Schellenberg writing to SS-*Sturmbannführer* Dr. Hellmuth [*sic*] Knochen ("Dear Hellmuth!"), July 9, 1940, that Heydrich had permitted that Fischer become active in Paris and be led by Knochen. Later Fischer, according to Heydrich, could "disappear in some business group in Holland, Belgium or France." (Transl.) BA Berlin, R 58/Anhang 51.
47. Andrew, *Secret Service*, 435.

obvious reasons the accounts of the meeting would differ, but it appears that Fischer afterwards reported to his SD case officer, Dr. Helmut Knochen, and claimed that British intelligence contacts were much interested in discussing chances for an early peace with a ranking German officer. If one is to believe the much later report by *Oberstleutnant* Walter Schulze-Bernett, an *Abwehr* officer stationed in the Netherlands from 1938 to 1941, Fischer telephoned Knochen, unaware of the latter's position in the SD, and passed on Best's desire to contact German circles interested in a quick end to the war.[48]

MacDonald's appraisal that "Schellenberg and Knochen, certainly believed that they were engaged in genuine peace negotiations" fits in well with the apparent political confusion reigning in both Berlin and London. Almost concurrently with the curious developments on the Dutch-German border, Max Egon Prince zu Hohenlohe-Langenburg, an extremely active but somewhat shadowy Nazi emissary, met with British Group Captain Malcolm G. Christie who was well known to German official circles in Berlin from his earlier tour of duty as Air Attaché. The British listened with some interest to intimations suggesting that it might occur to some Germans to replace Hitler with Göring.[49] However one might be inclined to interpret these contacts in Switzerland, it is not at all surprising that some British representatives under the circumstances would consider talking to German military emissaries in Holland with the purpose of examining available contingencies other than war. Curiously, however, British intelligence apparently was not sufficiently informed about these Germans and their schemes.

In the meantime Reinhard Heydrich had selected the young and still relatively inexperienced Walter Schellenberg to conduct the rather risky game of meeting with British intelligence in the still neutral Netherlands. Schellenberg, of course, had no choice but to accept the challenge and indeed may even have welcomed the opportunity to prove his professional acumen. In retrospect, one can't quite escape the impression that much of the Venlo operation was poorly planned, not really thought through, and repeatedly merely reacting to unexpected turns. Dates and locations of the British-German encounters also are less than reliable in the respective sources. This unreliability is of some interest because available memoirs seem to indicate that the first of these meetings already took place on October 20, 1939, at a café in

---

48. "Information obtained from Schellenberg on the Venlo Incident," Top Secret, National Archives Kew (London) (NAK), KV 2/98. Walter Schulze-Bernett, "Der Grenzzwischenfall bei Venlo/Holland," *Die Nachhut*, no. 23/24 (May 1973), 2. *Die Nachhut* was published as a newsletter by and for former members of the *Abwehr*.
49. MacDonald, "The Venlo Affair," 451. For detailed treatment of the Hohenlohe-Cristie contact see Ulrich Schlie, *Kein Friede mit Deutschland: Die geheimen Gespräche im Zweiten Weltkrieg* (München: Langen Müller, 1994), 104 ff.

Zutphen when Captain Copper, in reality the Dutch Lieutenant Dirk Klop, and Dr. Franz Fischer picked up the German visitors at the frontier village of Dinxperlo. Much to the surprise of Stevens and Best, they did not return with the expected German general and his adjutant, but instead brought back with them two young Germans, introducing themselves as Captain von Seidlitz and Lieutenant Grosch. They were, in fact, SS-*Sturmbannführer* Karl von Salisch and SS-*Hauptsturmführer* Bernhard Christensen, respectively.[50] Following the recollections of Best, the atmosphere at the café at Zutphen after some time was felt to be unsafe and even threatening, causing them to drive off to the home of some friends of Best in Arnhem. When Dutch police interfered with the clandestine discussion, a new meeting was agreed for October 25, a date then changed to October 30.[51] While there seems no reason to doubt the recollections of Best concerning this encounter, it should be pointed out that Schellenberg recalls having met Best and Stevens at Arnhem on October 21, after having been picked up at Zutphen by Best himself in his Buick. Callum A. MacDonald, in his brief but sober analysis of the Venlo operation refers to Schellenberg's memory regarding October 21 and states that "Schellenberg is obviously confusing his own activities with those of Salisch and Christensen at this point." This would suggest that what Schellenberg remembers as having been said to him by the British representatives was instead reported to him by his emissaries following their jaunt to The Netherlands: "The British officers assured me that His Majesty's Government were definitely interested in our enterprise and that their Government attached the greatest importance to preventing a further extension of war and to the attainment of peace."[52]

Though beset by all kinds of logistical difficulties, the meeting on October 30 actually took place. Traveling to The Hague were three German officers, named for the occasion Captain Schemmel,[53] Colonel Martini, and Grosch whom the British already knew from the previous encounter. Schemmel was Schellenberg who, like the real Schemmel, an officer attached to the German General Staff, was wearing a monocle for this performance. Colonel Martini, in fact, was Maximinian de Crinis, as of November 1938 successor of Karl Bonhoeffer[54] as Professor of Psychiatry and Neurology at the University of

---

50. Some sources give the cover name as von Seydewitz. Dr. Franz Fischer to Schellenberg, Paris, August 11, 1940, BA Berlin, R 58/Anhang 51.
51. S. Payne Best, *The Venlo Incident* (London: Hutchinson, 1950), 9-11.
52. MacDonald, "The Venlo Affair," 462-463. Schellenberg, *The Schellenberg Memoirs*, 84-86.
53. Also referred to as Schaemmel or Schämmel.
54. Karl Bonhoeffer, a psychiatrist of some reputation and academic success, was the father of Dietrich Bonhoeffer, the theologian closely connected to the *Abwehr* and executed by the Nazis in April 1945. On Karl Bonhoeffer see Edwin Robertson, *The Shame and the Sacrifice: The Life and Teaching of Dietrich Bonhoeffer* (London: Hodder & Stoughton, 1987), 21-26, 45. Cf. positive comments in Robert J. Lifton, *The Nazi Doctors: Medical Killing and the Psychology of Genocide* (New York: Basic Books, 2000; 1st 1986), 81. For critical

Berlin and Director of the Neurological Clinic at the well-known Charité Hospital. Born and educated in Austria, he had been a professor of psychiatry and neurology at the University of Cologne since 1934. The professor was a member of the Nazi Party since 1931 and had joined the SS in 1936. While it is uncertain just when and how de Crinis and Schellenberg first came into contact, by the time of the Venlo operation, according to Schellenberg, de Crinis was his "best friend." In fact, they knew each other well enough for de Crinis to approach Schellenberg to do something for Andreas Morsey who had helped de Crinis back in 1934 when he was arrested for his Nazi activities in Austria. Morsey was now in a German concentration camp. Schellenberg later described the de Crinis home as "a most pleasant and cultivated household, and for years I had been received there like a son." He depicted his much older friend as "elegant, stately, highly intelligent and cultured." Evidently Schellenberg trusted him fully and found him "ideally suited for the role I had in mind."[55]

The adventurous trio drove to Holland and instead of waiting for Captain Copper, or rather Lieutenant Dirk Klop, tried to enter the country without being checked by border controls. As luck would have it, they were picked up and held until Klop arrived. Not surprising, before liberating the Germans, Klop used the unexpected opportunity to closely check their papers and the rest of their belongings. He then proceeded to pilot them to Stevens' office in The Hague. Schellenberg recalls that they discussed ridding Germany of Hitler and arranging peace talks with the Western nations. Austria, Czechoslovakia and Poland would regain independence. Berlin would return to the gold standard. Her colonies, lost in World War I, would be restored. Captain Best's memory of this exchange does not contradict Schellenberg and quotes the latter as saying: "We are Germans and have to think of the interests of our own country first. Before we take any steps against Hitler we want to know whether England and France are ready to grant us a peace which is both just and honourable." Regrettably, Best does not comment on the apparently most agreeable dinner that evening, served to the German guests at his home. The oysters, Schellenberg later remembered, were "marvellous," and Best and de Crinis outdid each other with charming after-dinner speeches. There was even

---

comments regarding the doctor's involvement in Nazi medicine see Thomas Beddies, "Universitätspsychiatrie im Dritten Reich: Die Nervenklinik der Charité unter Karl Bonhoeffer und Maximinian de Crinis," www.charite.de/psychiatrie/ geschichte/Beddies–bonhoeffer pdf–, 7-10.

55. Friedrich Alexander Maximinian de Crinis (1889 Ehrenhausen, Austria–1945 suicide), studied Medicine at Innsbruck and Graz, Habilitation 1920, Professor for Psychiatry Graz 1924, problems and arrest for Nazi activities 1934, Professor at Cologne, Germany 1934, 1938 to Berlin. Officially called himself Max de Crinis. Nachlass de Crinis and Personalakten Professor Dr. M. de Crinis, Humboldt Universität zu Berlin, Universitätsarchiv (HUB). Schellenberg, *The Schellenberg Memoirs*, 86. Cf. Lifton, *The Nazi Doctors*, 120-122.

time to converse on such lighter topics as music and painting, and "it was quite late when we drove back to the villa" where Best had arranged comfortable quarters for them. If Schellenberg has it right, the next morning they were served a sumptuous Dutch breakfast before being picked up for a final work session at Best's office. Either Stevens and Best were much taken up by the German emissaries or they tried to play the game and keep up the good ambience. Whichever, the Germans were even handed a transmitter and the respective instructions for communicating with the British Secret Service in The Hague. The calling number was to be 0–N–4.[56]

Following Best's recollections, the next encounter was arranged by wireless communication for November 7 at Venlo. Stevens and Best apparently were less than pleased with the choice of Venlo. They considered it risky being so close to the German border, but Klop thought it was a perfectly harmless place, and that is where they met. Schemmel and Grosch turned up and there was some follow-up discussion of the questions treated at the previous meeting. The British then were asked to return the next day to meet the "chief" of the resistance group in the German military. When they came back in the afternoon of November 8, Schemmel met them alone and explained that "the general" again had been detained. "The attempt against Hitler" was imminent, Schemmel told them, but the general would want to meet the British representatives and, in fact, deposit certain papers with them for safekeeping in case the plot failed. The date was fixed for the next day, November 9, at 4 p.m.[57]

Schellenberg's memoirs in principle support Best's version of events, except for the added somewhat stunning information that he had not received an official go-ahead for November 7, and his explanation of real—or later invented—plans of what he had in mind to achieve in Holland. The November 8 meeting had to be handled that way, because in the short time available he was unable to produce a fitting opposition general. If Schellenberg tells the truth, it was only on November 8 that he located a businessman whom he thought suitable to take on the role of a leading figure in the anti-Hitler conspiracy.

When all had been put into place for the next day's encounter at Venlo, Schellenberg literally collapsed from exhaustion in his quarters in Düsseldorf where he had stayed, one is led to believe, ever since the critical meeting with the British in The Hague. An unexpected telephone call from Heinrich Himmler shortly thereafter ended his respite. An attempt on Hitler's life had

---

56. Best, *The Venlo Incident*, 11-13. Schellenberg, *The Schellenberg Memoirs*, 87-91, where Klop's cover name is given as Coppens.
57. Best, *The Venlo Incident*, 13-14.

been made the previous evening at the Bürgerbräukeller of Haidhausen in Munich. Himmler was or pretended to be certain that "there is no doubt that the British Secret Service is behind it all." While there remains much uncertainty as to when Hitler or Himmler actually may have decided to turn the ongoing deception game in Holland into a dangerous abduction, there is no particular reason to doubt Schellenberg's report that he had not been informed about a planned kidnapping prior to November 8.

Another curious telephone call Schellenberg claims to have received in Düsseldorf on November 8 after his return from the meeting at the Dutch border would indeed almost suggest that the abduction of the British intelligence men had been planned earlier. Although Schellenberg's memoirs do not divulge the name of the caller, it would appear to have been Alfred Naujocks, the SS-officer commanding the operation into Holland at Venlo the next day. When he spoke to Schellenberg the night before, he informed him that he had been ordered to Düsseldorf with a special unit to cover Schellenberg on the following day and make certain that nothing would happen to him. Whether Schellenberg, according to his memoirs, indeed told the unnamed SS-officer calling that if things developed well the next day, he might actually depart with the British to London, must remain an open question. In retrospect and in view of Naujocks' reckless personality—Callum MacDonald refers to him as "The gunman Naujocks"—such a step by Schellenberg would seem to have been somewhat careless to say the least.[58]

The events of November 9, 1939,[59] are covered in a number of more or less reliable reports. Both Best and Schellenberg have told the story from their perspective and there are no significant differences. Various authors have later interpreted these reports and other documentary texts, but small attention has been given to the curious coincidence that both Best and Schellenberg went to the final encounter at Venlo harboring veritable doubts concerning the operation and its usefulness. Best and Stevens may have been fooled for some time by the Germans playing their part in the game, but it is difficult to overlook that both carried a gun when going to the meeting. Also, they had decided that this would be their final encounter with the Germans in case the latter once again had no real facts to offer. While still considering the

---

58. Schellenberg, *The Schellenberg Memoirs*, 91-94. MacDonald, "The Venlo Affair," 457. Cf. "Notes by Dr.Wilhelm Hoettl on Schellenberg Interrogation Report," NA, Records of the Office of Strategic Services (OSS), RG 226, E 125A, Box 2: "It was generally said that Naujocks was the man who was used by Heydrich for certain secret operations, such as liquidation of persons." Naujocks, calling himself Alfred Donsen, was captured on October 19, 1944, when he attempted to cross American lines. He told his interrogators that the whole "operation was planned and put into execution by Schellenberg." NAK, KV 2/280.
59. Not 1940 as stated by Bob Edwards, M.P. and Kenneth Dunne, *A Study of a Master Spy* (London: Housmans/Chemical Workers Union, 1961), 43.

possibility that they were in touch with a real resistance group, they were also very much aware of the threat of an impending German invasion. Their reaction to the frequent controls by Dutch forces on the road may reflect their less than optimistic composure: They would indeed have much welcomed being told that they could not proceed any farther to the border. Schellenberg, or Schemmel for the British, had reservations of his own. While he had played the game with the British agents and may indeed have had rather unrealistic ideas about going beyond the game, he obviously fully understood the danger of becoming trapped in an international incident of this nature. It is not clear from the sources to what degree Schellenberg was able to present his reservations to Himmler, but it appears certain that not unlike his British contacts he was less than enchanted with what the day might bring. In his memoirs he claims that he went unarmed to Venlo.[60]

On November 9, 1939, Schellenberg also realized that his "great plan of continuing the negotiations in London" had to be scrapped. Instead he found himself at least partially in charge of a dangerous assignment that might include a shoot-out. Schellenberg was indeed worried about losing his life and openly confesses that fear in his memoirs. To be certain the twelve men of the special detachment picked by Alfred Naujocks and Werner Göttsch would not confuse him with Best, as both he and Best were wearing monocles, Schellenberg met with them prior to the operation. Some time between 2:00 p.m. and 3:00 p.m. he and Bernhard Christensen crossed the border and entered the nearby café. They ordered something to drink and registered from the window what to their watchful eyes looked like too many policemen with their dogs. They had no choice but to wait at the Café Backus and speculate what the afternoon might have in store. They knew little about what either the British or the Dutch might have planned, but they were certain that a small detachment of armed SS-men was ready for action just across the border. Around 4:00 p.m. there was a sudden commotion on the road, and when Schellenberg went out on the porch, he lifted his hand, greeting the arriving British intelligence officers—or giving a signal to his SS-men. Only moments later Schellenberg found himself in the middle of a shoot-out. When all was over, Best, Stevens and their driver Jan Frederick Lemmens were kidnapped prisoners of the Germans. Lieutenant Klop was seriously wounded. Best later recalled that their captors marched them across the border. "The black and

---

60. For Best's recollections on the hours before Venlo *The Venlo Incident*, 14–16. For Schellenberg's perspective "Information obtained from Schellenberg on the Venlo Incident," Top Secret, NAK, KV 2/98. "Final Report," 75–76. *The Schellenberg Memoirs*, 94-97. *Trials of War Criminals before the Nuernberg Military Tribunals under Control Council Law No. 10*, vol. 12, (Washington, D.C.: U.S. Government Printing Office, n.d.) (USGPO), 1236–1237.

white barrier closed behind us. We were in Nazi Germany."[61] Schellenberg, lucky not to have been hit in the brief and disorganized exchange of fire, jumped into his car and quickly departed from the scene. Across the border in Düsseldorf at the "evangelical hospital" Dr. Walter Behrends shortly thereafter examined a very seriously wounded man without identity papers but still dressed in a coat with a Dutch label. When the mysterious patient passed away that same evening, German police guarding him had not left his side. Following interrogation, Jan Lemmens was sent back to the Netherlands and eventually became a member of the Dutch resistance.[62]

The appraisal of Venlo as a German intelligence operation and of Schellenberg's role in its rather brazen final act has varied, but in retrospect it would appear justified to assume that Schellenberg might have much preferred to avoid kidnapping his British contacts. His own perspectives instead seem to have included more long-range negotiations with British intelligence in order to carefully examine any, however slim, chances of finding a way out of the war, or as Clinton Gallagher, an American intelligence officer, who in 1945 was able to talk to Schellenberg at the Military Intelligence Interrogation Center at Oberursel, put it: "I am ... prepared to believe his protestations that the abduction ... was contrary to his own ideas regarding long range exploitation of the link to the British service, and that he acquiesced in participating in the kidnapping only with great reluctance."[63] When taking a closer look at the records, one could also be inclined to question the extent to which Schellenberg could have influenced respective decisions from above at this time, not to mention the obvious necessity to avoid being seen as someone striving to the top all too eagerly. His enemies inside the RSHA system might easily have become alerted.

While German motivations behind the kidnapping of Best and Stevens continue to be debated, it seems certain that the capture of the British agents was a rather short-term decision. The actual kidnapping operation was apparently decided in the wake of the Bürgerbräu explosion in Munich and, of course, was used by the German authorities to demonstrate some form of treacherous cooperation between The Netherlands and Britain. In fact, the bombing of the Bürgerbräu beer cellar by Johann Georg Elser and the German attack on The Netherlands do not appear to have been connected at all. After

---

61. Best, *The Venlo Incident*, 17.
62. Statement under Oath, Dr. Walter Behrends, February 6, 1948, SAN, Rep. 502, NG-4671. The doctor was ordered to Berlin in December 1939 and told by Schellenberg to speak to no one about this. — Antony Read and David Fisher, *Colonel Z: The Secret Life of a Master of Spies* (New York: Viking, 1985; Copyright 1984), 220-221, 225.
63. Clinton Gallagher, review of *The Labyrinth-The Memoirs of Hitler's Secret Service Chief* (New York: Harper, 1956), photocopy, *Studies in Intelligence*, Fall 1957, NA, RG 263, E 27, Box 1.

the war Schellenberg himself unmistakably stated: "... the German intention of attacking the West by violating the neutrality of Belgium and the Netherlands, was an accepted fact at the time ... anything which might have established the cooperation of British and Dutch intelligence services could be of no significance for the carrying out of these actions ..."[64] On the personal side, the high-reaching young SS leader had the satisfaction of being awarded, along with Alfred Naujocks, Maximinian de Crinis, and Werner Göttsch, the Iron Cross I. Class for what was presented as a successful undertaking against British treachery. Hitler awarded the honors in person. Incidentally, SS-*Sturmbannführer* Helmut Knochen's role in the operation was not forgotten. He too was awarded "by the Führer personally" the Iron Cross I. Class and II. Class.[65]

While Schellenberg seems to have had little or no part in the quickly developing German military operations against The Netherlands, as head of Group IV E he was instead much involved in the debriefing of Best and Stevens. The interrogations of the two British agents took place at the Concentration Camp Oranienburg just outside of Berlin,[66] and it may be assumed that considerable pressure was exerted on the captured British to extract as much as possible about the organization of British intelligence services, as well as about contingency plans against Germany. The records indicate that Heydrich ordered *Kriminalrat* Dr. Ernst Schambacher to take over the interrogations and that the latter was assisted by *Kriminalrat* Dr. Karl Schaefer and a *Kriminalkommissar* Fehmer. Schellenberg, under interrogation after the war, freely admitted that he himself had questioned the prisoners "on some four or five occasions."[67] The two British agents were interrogated separately and the records indicate that undue methods, such as the application of drugs, were not used. Schellenberg later told his British interrogators that he approached Best with the suggestion to allow himself to be used as a double agent and that Best seemed to be willing to oblige. Schellenberg, however, also

---

64. "Extracts from the Testimony of Defendant Schellenberg," *Trials of War Criminals before the Nuernberg Military Tribunals under Control Council Law No. 10*, vol. 12, 1241.
65. According to Schellenberg's Personnel File, NA, BDC Microfilm, Roll No. A 3343 SSO-074B, the "E.K. I u. II Klasse" was awarded on November 12, 1939. Schellenberg, *The Schellenberg Memoirs*, 101, reports that four men received the Iron Cross I. Class and the rest the Iron Cross II. Class. H. Krausnick, H. C. Deutsch, eds. *Helmuth Groscurth: Tagebücher eines Abwehroffiziers* (Stuttgart: Deutsche Verlags-Anstalt, 1970), 312. Cf. Otto John, *Twice Through the Lines* (London: Futura, 1974), 55. Schulze-Bernett, "Der Grenzzwischenfall bei Venlo/Holland," 8.
66. The history of the Concentration Camp Oranienburg/Sachsenhausen goes back to 1933, first in Oranienburg and from 1936 in Sachsenhausen. The camp was taken over by Russian troops in April 1945.
67. Schellenberg himself later named Dr. Schambacher and Kriminalrat Dr. Wilhelm Clemens as the interrogators. "Information obtained from Schellenberg on the Venlo Incident," Top Secret, NAK, KV 2/98. Schambacher was trusted by Schellenberg, and he was one of the men he took with him from *Amt* IV to *Amt* VI. Statement under Oath, Bruno Grothe, Gestapo officer working under Schambacher, NA, RG 238, Microfilm M 897, Roll 114.

realized that Best's readiness to cooperate might well have been motivated by his desire to return to England. The matter, therefore, was not pursued any further. Evidently Schellenberg's concern was that Hitler would decide to use the captured agents for a sensationalist trial to demonstrate British treachery. In that case, Schellenberg would have lost a valuable means to reconstruct contacts with British intelligence. Following this line of thought, Schellenberg even tried to persuade Himmler to trade the two Englishmen for German POWs. Schellenberg later recalled that he thought Himmler favored such suggestions made in 1943 and 1944 but held back consent for fear that Hitler might suddenly want to have them available for a show trial.[68]

Taking into consideration the miffed reactions of the British concerning the messy end of the intelligence game and the real or uncertain connections between Venlo and the German invasion of The Netherlands, it comes as no surprise that Venlo became part of the legal proceedings against Schellenberg at Nuremberg. Indeed, the SS leader found himself accused of having "participated also in the carrying out of aggressive war [against The Netherlands]." His defense that "in my position ... as a very young Government Councillor—I was 29 at the time—... nobody informed me about the German war plans in the West; nobody gave me the dubious honor of participating in a so-called conspiracy of German leadership," would appear to be a clear understatement of the information level Schellenberg had access to by the autumn of 1939.[69] Looking back, however, indications are that Schellenberg in his position could have had no influential part in the German schemes of aggression, regardless of his successful participation in the intelligence game played by the British and German services and with, it would seem, at least partial knowledge of the Dutch General Staff. Within the larger context of events in late 1939, the game ending at Venlo or rather what German officials may have considered a fruitful debriefing of Best and Stevens, was not of great significance. After the fall of Poland, the real aim of Hitler and his irresponsible advisers had become the defeat of a more substantial enemy. "Und wir fahren gegen Engeland" was soon to become the popular battle cry of Germans in the streets, and Hermann Göring's self-confident air force stood in waiting for the onslaught against Britain.[70]

---

68. "Information obtained from Schellenberg on the Venlo Incident," Top Secret, NAK, KV 2/98. Interrogation Report, August 20, 1945, Secret, NAK, KV 2/97. See, however, comments regarding Schellenberg's "utter vileness" and "refined sadism" in handling the mail of the two prisoners, in Hans Bernd Gisevius, *To the Bitter End* (Boston: Houghton Mifflin, 1947), 40.
69. "Extracts from the Testimony of Defendant Schellenberg," Trials of War Criminals before the Nuernberg Military Tribunals under Control Council Law No. 10, vol. 12, 1240.
70 Cf. Richard Breitman, *The Architect of Genocide: Himmler and the Final Solution* (London: The Bodley Head, 1991), 82. — "And now we go against England" (England spelled in this German song with the extra *e*).

In the aftermath of Venlo Walter Schellenberg, it is true, was decorated by his *Führer* and his standing among the group of up-and-coming Nazi leaders may have taken on a new shine. Reality, however, was somewhat less glamorous. His physical condition had deteriorated under the almost constant pressure of the last weeks, and the young man may have suffered some form of "heart attack." The already mentioned painful and unpleasant extended divorce procedures in 1939 had probably also contributed to the strain.[71] Whether it was indeed his physical malaise that caused him to seek a reprieve from the work in *Amt* IV must remain an open question in the absence of reliable documentary evidence. In the course of the postwar interrogations in London Schellenberg explained that he had been "dissatisfied with the purely executive position" and consequently had felt that a tour of duty in active military service would be desirable, not least to avoid being looked down upon after the war for not having served in action. His request for a leave of absence in order to join the *Wehrmacht* (Armed Forces), Schellenberg recalled, was turned down by Himmler, who instead agreed, as a sort of compensation, "to send him as a liaison officer to the O.K.W. [*Oberkommando der Wehrmacht*/Supreme Command of the Armed Forces] for two months."[72] Otherwise, the winter of 1939/1940 was filled with administrative duties in *Amt* IV and intelligence work assisting in the preparations for *Weserübung*, the code word for the impending German attacks on Norway and Denmark. When German forces launched their offensive in the West, Schellenberg's men produced false radio news broadcasts to the French in order "to create the greatest possible confusion among our enemies." In addition to this, from his perspective very successful operation, a curious air drop over France of grim prophecies made 400 years earlier by Nostradamus "predicted terrifying destruction from 'flying fire-machines'." In retrospect, this undertaking would appear to be one of several peculiar incidents in Schellenberg's professional life that have caused some authors to ridicule the SS leader.[73]

After the Germans had their much desired revenge against France at Compiegne on June 22, 1940, provisions for the forthcoming attack on Britain went into high gear. Following some initial hesitation, Germany was now about to take on the arch enemy. They would bring order to the *Krämervolk* (nation of shopkeepers) and cleanse Aryan British society from its racial impurities. How the Germans would go about that task can be seen from the *Sonderfahndungsliste*

---

71. "Final Report," 76. Cf. Lina Heydrich, *Leben mit einem Kriegsverbrecher* (Pfaffenhofen: W. Ludwig, 1976), 76. David Kahn, *Hitler's Spies: German Military Intelligence in World War II* (New York: Macmillan, 1978), 256-257.
72. "Final Report," 77-78.
73. Schellenberg, *The Schellenberg Memoirs*, 121-122. Schellenberg, *Memoiren*, 105, reports both operations though slightly less positive.

G.B. (Special Wanted List G.B.) said to have been produced by Walter Schellenberg in the summer of 1940. In his memoirs he recalls that "at the end of June 1940 I was ordered to prepare a small handbook for the invading troops and the political and administrative units that would accompany them, describing briefly the most important political, administrative and economic institutions of Great Britain and the leading public figures."[74] The Special Wanted List, apparently part of the assignment, was long and contained persons whom the Germans intended to arrest, imprison or eliminate. Included on the German Special Wanted List, besides such names as Churchill and Eden, were for instance the eighty-year old Polish pianist Ignacy Paderewski, the philosopher Bertrand Russell, the absconded German diplomat Wolfgang Gans Edler Herr zu Putlitz, Klop Ustinov now working for British intelligence, the writer Aldous Huxley, the intelligence officer Claude Edward Marjoribanks Dansey, the politician Harold Nicolson, the German historian Fritz Epstein, the writer Lion Feuchtwanger, the American singer Paul Robeson and the German naval officer and Kaiser's sabotage agent in the U.S. Franz Rintelen. "Sämtliche in der Sonderfahndungsliste G.B. aufgeführten Personen sind festzunehmen" ("All persons listed in the Special Wanted List G.B. are to be arrested") was the unmistakable instruction for the invading army and the accompanying SS. The genocide committed by German forces in Eastern Europe may serve as an indication of what was in store for Britain. Even prior to their planned landing on the shores of England, the German Army command had issued an order to the effect that all "able-bodied" males between seventeen and forty-five were to be deported to Germany for forced labor. The authorship of the brochures, in spite of Schellenberg's recollection, seems less than certain. While it is entirely possible that he busied himself with the outline and structure of the more general handbook entitled *Informationsheft GB (Information Brochure Great Britain)* and its supplement, the *Special Wanted List*, it is certainly evident that a whole team of specialists would have been required to collect and sort the vast amount of personal and institutional data, even faulty as some of them are, and then produce the 20,000 copies Schellenberg claims to have been responsible for. His capability had already been more than strained, and the dubious undertaking of manipulating Edward VIII or rather the Duke of Windsor was about to occupy him so fully that at best he could have performed some kind of supervision of the *Information Brochure* project. Schellenberg's postwar memory that all 20,000 copies were destroyed in the course of an air raid incidentally appears to be as unreliable as his suggested

---

74. Schellenberg, *The Schellenberg Memoirs*, 124. Cf. more detailed version in the unpublished memoirs, Institut für Zeitgeschichte (IFZ), ED 90/6, 10.

authorship.[75] Among other unverifiable reports concerning responsibility for the *Special Wanted List* are suggestions that it was Franz Alfred Six who directed the project. Six had just been designated to become head of security service operations in occupied Britain. His would have been the complex task of turning British society into something sufficiently malleable in order to enable the Germans to impose what they proclaimed to be their superior Germanic structure.[76]

While one might wonder what Schellenberg thought of the Germanization of Britain as outlined in the almost "amusing," often faulty and to this day in its bluntness shocking booklet for the invading forces[77]—he is known to have had considerable respect for Britain and its institutions—his subsequent assignment, also closely related to the planned German invasion of Britain, in retrospect appears to be almost ludicrous. While the origins of the perverse idea are not entirely clear, available information points to Joachim von Ribbentrop, Germany's former Ambassador to the Court of St. James and now Foreign Minister who had come to detest the British.[78] The background of Germany's hackneyed scheme to utilize the Duke of Windsor for its designs against Britain remains confusing and hazy. As recently as 1937 the Duke and his wife had traveled to Germany and paid a visit to Adolf Hitler. Moreover, the Duke had on different occasions voiced opinions that might have been construed as pro-German. All in all, there was an impression in some quarters that the Duke could be brought to assist in the building of political bridges between London and Berlin. Whether the Germans intended to set him up as a kind of pawn in some neutral country, such as Switzerland, to be available as a useful tool in their medium or long range plans for a defeated Britain, or whether, as some sources suggest, he was quite bluntly scheduled to serve as king in a German vassal state, has not been fully clarified.[79]

---

75. *The Black Book (Sonderfahndungsliste G.B.)*, "Introduction" by Terry Charman (London: Imperial War Museum, 1989). The more recent Walter Schellenberg, *Invasion 1940: The Nazi Invasion Plan for Britain*, "Introduction" by John Erikson (London: St. Ermin's Press, 2001) on title page and cover names Schellenberg as author, but the "Introduction" offers no information concerning the authorship. In the "Preface" Nigel West (Rupert Allason) correctly states: "Precisely who wrote the whole of this report remains unclear to this day." Terry Charman, " '... And, if necessary, carry it out': Operation Sealion and the Black Book, fact and fiction," *Imperial War Museum Review*, no. 5 (November 1990).
76. Egbert Kieser, *Hitler on the Doorstep* (London: Arms & Armour, 1997; 1st 1987), 251. Wildt, *Generation des Unbedingten*, 372. Ronald Wheatley, *Operation Sea Lion: German Plans for the Invasion of England 1939-1942* (Oxford: Clarendon Press, 1958), 122-123. Ströbinger, *A-54*, 168, writes that Six "prepared" the Special Wanted List. Comer Clarke, *If the Nazis Had Come* (London: C. Nicholls, 1962), 72-73, reports that Walter zu Christian assisted in putting together the Black Book.
77. Cf. Tom Freeman-Keel, *From Auschwitz to Alderney* (Cravens Arms/Shropshire: Seek, 1995), 92-95.
78. Cf. Michael Bloch, *Ribbentrop* (London: Transworld/Bantam, 1992), 286.
79. Cf. Gerhard L. Weinberg, *A World at Arms: A Global History of World War II* (Cambridge: Cambridge University Press, 1994), 144.

In contrast to this background of somewhat uncertain German planning, the details of Schellenberg's specific assignment in July 1940 are perfectly clear. Schellenberg was authorized to strongly invite the Duke to place himself in some neutral country, preferably Switzerland, and in return for "dissociating himself from the maneuvers of the British Royal Family" accept an offering of some financial security in form of a deposit of 50 million Swiss Francs. If circumstances should turn out to be more difficult than expected, such as in the event of interference from British intelligence, Schellenberg was at liberty to employ more forceful methods in assisting the Duke to arrive at the desired decision. When in the course of his meeting with Ribbentrop it occurred to Schellenberg that the Duke might not be entirely willing to cooperate with the Germans, the Foreign Minister apparently was at a loss for an answer, and instead emphasized Hitler's personal wish to have this operation carried out successfully. Schellenberg was obviously not taken by the idea of interfering with a member of the British Royal Family. When Ribbentrop said "I shall report to the Führer that you have taken on the assignment," Schellenberg thought this to be a good time to take leave. But he had misjudged the situation, for Ribbentrop suddenly picked up the phone and called Hitler, passing the extra receiver to Schellenberg. "Tell him that I shall rely on him" were the final words of Hitler. Ribbentrop rose from his chair, bowed to the telephone and said "Thank you, my Führer ..." After this interlude Schellenberg went to see Heydrich to report on matters. The latter was rather "frosty" and made no secret of his estimation of the Ribbentrop scheme: "... I don't care for the whole plan, but I know that it is impossible to change the Führer's mind when he pursues such ideas ... You will of course realize that you will have front-line contact with an enemy who will not forgive you so easily. I don't want you to go alone. Take two well-trained men with you who speak the language to make certain you are at least bodily protected. For I tell you, if I were the chief of the Secret Service, I would certainly spoil your little enterprise."[80]

We are uncertain whether Schellenberg's men or the *Abwehr* had obtained reliable information about the Duke's upcoming journey from Portugal to the Bahamas where he would reside as Governor. One may assume, however, that German intelligence through direct lines to Britain and more likely through contacts in Spain and Portugal was sufficiently clued in on British policy and

---

80. Unpublished memoirs, IFZ, ED 90/6. Schellenberg, *The Schellenberg Memoirs*, 127-131. Schellenberg, *Memoiren*, 108-111. These sources clearly include Hitler's role, and Schellenberg reports that he informed Heydrich of the assignment. Somewhat surprising, "Final Report" (transcribing what Schellenberg is said to have told his interrogators in Britain), 78: "...without informing Heydrich of his intentions, Schellenberg left Berlin .. .for Madrid." Regarding Ribbentrop's policy in this context cf. Bloch, *Ribbentrop*, 289-291.

Churchill's absolute determination to defend Britain at all costs. German bombers had begun their raids on shipping to Britain and British installations, and it would not be long until England's cities and London itself would be hit. Schellenberg may well have perceived that the plans of Ribbentrop or Hitler, as outlined to him, were not among the options London was considering. He left almost immediately, accompanied by two experienced men for all occasions that might arise. It was common knowledge that Madrid had become a place where agents from many nations had a free run, and the so-called Police-Attaché Paul Winzer, though actually the Gestapo's man in Spain, but now also Schellenberg's subordinate, had some 20 to 30 men in his service. Winzer and the German Ambassador Eberhard von Stohrer were Schellenberg's first contacts.[81]

His memoirs do not contain anything unexpected, except for the astonishing frankness that apparently characterized his conversations with von Stohrer. In this context it needs to be said that candid exchanges of political views, particularly those concerning the Hitler regime or current international developments, were unwise, if not to say outright dangerous, and that this was more so when members of government services, such as the *Sicherheitsdienst* of the SS and the Foreign Office encountered each other. Ambassador von Stohrer, who had replaced the "enthusiastic Nazi" and Major General Wilhelm Faupel in 1937, Schellenberg later recalled, spoke more than openly about the wily Franco's unwillingness to fully commit himself and his nation to a war alliance with Nazi Germany: "...the opinion among well-informed circles was that the war might go on longer than the military and political leaders of Germany wanted to believe. Germany still had not succeeded in destroying Great Britain—which was the prerequisite for final victory." Schellenberg, of course, must have been aware of German plans in the making, including the transport of combat troops through Spain for the purpose of attacking Gibraltar. He knew that for Germany's Mediterranean and Mideastern plans it was certainly essential to remove that British guard post at the entry to the Mediterranean. Schellenberg's view that "Stohrer wanted to use me to warn Berlin against any undue optimism as far as Spain's entry into the war was concerned," in view of Franco's delaying actions, seems to have been fully correct.[82] His encounter shortly thereafter with the German Minister in Lisbon,

---

81. Interrogation Report No. 38, NA, RG 319, IRR, IS, Box 12. Testimony of Walter Schellenberg, January 10, 1946, NA, RG 238, E 7A, Box 18. Liquidation Report No. 7, Secret, NAK, KV 3/114. On von Stohrer (1883-1953) cf. Ulrich Schlie, "Eberhard von Stohrer," *Lebensbilder aus Baden-Württemberg*, vol. 20 (2001), 438-466.
82. Schellenberg, *The Schellenberg Memoirs*, 135. Schellenberg, *Memoiren*, 112-113. On the Spanish context see the still very relevant Charles B. Burdick, *Germany's Military Strategy and Spain in World War II* (Syracuse: Syracuse University Press, 1968). Wilhelm Faupel (1873-1945) had seen military service in China, German-

Oswald Baron von Hoyningen-Huene, apparently also turned out most satisfactorily.[83]

After a few days Schellenberg gained the impression that whatever careless or suggestive political opinions the Duke may have uttered, they ought to be taken with a grain of salt, and when Ribbentrop sent him the unmistakable message "The Führer orders that an abduction is to be organized at once," Schellenberg seems to have arrived at the sensible decision that a kidnapping operation might not be the advisable way to cultivate whatever sympathies for Germany the Duke may have had.[84] His reports on the entire affair are, as would be expected, slightly more positive than the situation in Portugal and Spain would have suggested, but on the whole sober in form and content. All the more one is surprised to register a slip such as this: "An open contact with the Duke which I could have obtained quite routinely seemed less than appropriate, because I saw no prospects of success. He was after all an Englishman."[85] After some rather haphazard moves to develop conditions or feelings on the Duke's part that might contribute to bringing about circumstances in the course of which he could be induced to become a German pawn, Schellenberg simply decided to refrain from direct, not to mention violent interference. When the Duke of Windsor and his American wife boarded the American liner *SS Excalibur* to Bermuda on August 1, 1940, Schellenberg observed the departure of his target with field glasses from the "tower room of the German Embassy [Legation]." Evidently the Duke had been under constant protective scrutiny of the British Secret Service, and Schellenberg certainly had been aware of being shadowed by British agents since the day of his arrival. To all indications, however, neither Schellenberg nor the German Ambassador in Madrid or the German Minister in Lisbon had been much attracted by the prospect of the use of coercive force in the abduction of a member of the British Royal Family. As the vessel slowly made its way down the Rio Tejo to the open sea, Schellenberg was intensely aware that his failure to bring about what Hitler—or was it Ribbentrop's idea?—had planned might expose him to most unpleasant reactions in Berlin.[86] It was not

---

Southwest Africa and in World War I. Franco "resented Faupel's arrogance." Stanley G. Payne, *Fascism in Spain, 1923-1977* (Madison: The University of Wisconsin Press, 1999), 288-289.
83. Oswald Baron von Hoyningen-Huene (1885-1963) was a diplomat of the old school who had entered the Foreign Service in 1920. Biographical data in Maria Keipert, Peter Grupp, eds., *Biographisches Handbuch des deutschen Auswärtigen Dienstes 1871-1945*, vol. 2 (Paderborn: Ferdinand Schöningh, 2005), 380-381.
84. Unpublished memoirs, IFZ, ED 90/6.
85. *Ibid*. These words do not appear in the German *Memoiren*, 115, and only the first sentence is found in Schellenberg, *The Schellenberg Memoirs*, 139.
86. For greater detail on Schellenberg's perspective of Germany's attempt to use the Duke of Windsor see the unpublished memoirs in IFZ, ED 90/6. For the abbreviated published version Schellenberg, *The Schellenberg Memoirs*, 127-142.

a particularly good moment in Berlin to deliver news on what undoubtedly would be seen as another miss in the frustrating efforts to force Great Britain into accepting German hegemony in Western Europe. Preparations for Operation Sea Lion, the German invasion of Britain, were moving ahead, but in retrospect there can be no doubt that Hermann Göring was forced to increasingly accept the fact that his much acclaimed *Luftwaffe* (Air Force) would not be able to defeat the enemy in the air and that the entire grand scheme of occupying Britain was becoming less likely as time went on. Not surprisingly, German leadership kept expectations high and had no hesitations of speaking publicly as if even a minor force would bring Britain to "a complete collapse."[87] Upon arrival in Berlin Schellenberg first went to the Foreign Office to report on the mission. Other than informing Schellenberg that Hitler had read his reports from Madrid and, in spite of his disappointment over the outcome of this entire matter, was fully in agreement with the decisions taken, Ribbentrop had little to say and seemed more interested in Franco's policy toward Germany. Schellenberg later recalled his relief and that he indeed felt a certain respect ("Würdigung") for Hitler's reaction. Schellenberg's personal view of Ribbentrop's lame handshake and his apparent inability or unwillingness to frankly exchange views on the matter was negative and at the time merely confirmed the low opinion he had formed much earlier of the Foreign Minister. "I felt that there was nothing between this man and myself that could have helped to create a really trusting relationship. And this feeling was confirmed until the end [of the Nazi period and World War II]."[88]

The ensuing visit with Heydrich would have been the more dangerous one, but quite different from his feelings about Ribbentrop, Schellenberg had an alert, if at times fearful, respect for Heydrich. Not that it would have been of much use if Ribbentrop had turned Hitler against him, but he was fully aware that both Himmler and Heydrich shared his own deprecatory assessment of the Foreign Minister. Heydrich listened attentively and told Schellenberg: "Don't try to get too close to Ribbentrop. I personally think that you should not even have taken on the assignment. I know you well enough to be certain that you knew from the beginning that this undertaking most likely would end just this way. In spite of it all, carried off rather cleverly." For Schellenberg undoubtedly more important than this welcome approval was Heydrich's passing comment regarding Schellenberg's professional future as he saw it. Once Schellenberg had attended to the organizational work still to be done in counterespionage in *Amt* IV, he could move to *Amt* VI (Foreign Intelligence).

---

87. Peter Fleming, *Operation Sea Lion* (New York: Simon and Schuster, 1957), 130-131.
88. Unpublished memoirs, IFZ 90/6. (Transl.) Cf. slightly more superficial text in Schellenberg, *The Schellenberg Memoirs*, 142-143.

Years of Apprenticeship 39

Heydrich added that he'd like to discuss such matters privately, why not at the upcoming hunt at Parlow.[89]

Though occasionally attending such events at Parlow in the countryside north of Berlin, we don't know whether Schellenberg was able to join that hunting party.[90] He seemed to have been slowed down by grave physical problems ever since his return from Lisbon. While there are hints that he may have been subjected to some kind of poisoning in Portugal, medical records of the Nuremberg hospital, where he was treated after the war, do not give a cause but indicate that he was suffering from Flexner-Ruhr (diarrhoea). Not attending to the problem may have worsened matters.[91] In spite of it all, Schellenberg married again on October 10, 1940. His second wife, Irene Grosse-Schönepauck, was of Polish descent on one side of the family that is her mother was considered to be Polish. Though several authors have suggested that Irene Schönepauck's family was well-to-do or "high in Berlin society," there are no indications of a particularly high financial, political or social standing. Schellenberg was certainly aware that with her Polish background he would be obliged to obtain some form of official consent, and he had approached Heydrich to intercede for him with Himmler. The needed permission was given, but as Schellenberg was to discover shortly thereafter, at a price. His Polish mother-in-law and her family were closely observed by the Gestapo. The Gestapo report landed accidentally on his desk, and Schellenberg later recalled: "There lay a secret report from the State Police in Posen addressed personally to Mueller, the Gestapo Chief ... Among other things it contained a reference to my mother-in-law's sister, who was married to a Jewish mill-owner."[92] In line with his experience inside the SS structures, Schellenberg assumed, probably correctly, that Heydrich had ordered this to conveniently collect some information which could be used against him if the need should arise. Schellenberg also later recalled that Himmler was disturbed by the fact that the photos of the bride clearly showed that she did her

---

89. Unpublished memoirs, IFZ, 90/6. Extremely abbreviated Schellenberg, *The Schellenberg Memoirs*, 143, and Schellenberg, *Memoiren*, 118.
90. Schellenberg was at Parlow once or twice during the fall/winter 1940-1941. Cf. *The Schellenberg Memoirs*, 160-161, where a discussion of Germany's foreign intelligence is covered.
91. "Friedrich Walter Schellenberg," FBM document, December 29, 1947, Secret, NA, RG 263, E A1-86, Box 38. Certificate from Professor D. Jahn, Medical Director of the Municipal Hospital in Nuremberg, May 16, 1949, NA, United States High Commissioner for Germany (HICOG), RG 466, E 53, Box 30. "Final Report," 79.
92. William B. Breuer, *Deceptions of World War II* (Edison: Castle, 2005; 1st 2001), 172. Schellenberg, *The Schellenberg Memoirs*, 39. Paehler's statement in "Espionage, Ideology, and Personal Politics," 257, referring to the same text in the American edition, Schellenberg, *The Labyrinth: Memoirs of Walter Schellenberg* (New York: Harper & Brothers, 1956), 21-22: "Note Schellenberg's insidious attempt in these passages to claim 'Jewish ancestry,' be it only by marriage" is a misrepresentation. There is no passage suggesting that Schellenberg claims to be of Jewish ancestry. Schellenberg, *Memoiren*, 136, offers the same information as the English and the American edition.

eyebrows and used lipstick. Most important at the time, however, the SS-*Standartenführer* Dr. Brustmann, in charge of the physical examination of the bride, found her "racially perfect" and the "dominant racial factor Nordic."[93]

Irene Grosse-Schönepauck was born in 1919, like Schellenberg raised a Roman Catholic, and following elementary school had been sent to an *Oberlyzeum*, a type of high school for girls who at that time in Germany were not admitted, as a rule, to the *Gymnasium* or *Oberschule*. She had wanted to become a dress designer and had therefore enrolled briefly in a fashion college. A short honeymoon journey took the newlyweds to Luxembourg where they stayed with his parents. While some of the dates available from the various records are rather confusing, there seems to be little doubt that Schellenberg's health had deteriorated considerably and that on December 2, 1940, he was shipped off on a cure to Karlsbad for four weeks of professional attendance to his physical condition. His wife apparently was able to adjust somehow. Though not much is known about her, it can be said without reservation that life with the young SS leader more often than not must have been highly uncomfortable and extremely hectic. There was not only the rather constant strain of his work at the *Reichssicherheitshauptamt*, but his activities by necessity required his presence in the *Amt* almost constantly and certain operations were connected with long absences from Berlin.[94]

While still attached to *Amt* IV, in April 1941, almost as if to once more test him before permitting him to move on to *Amt* VI, Schellenberg found himself drawn into another operation of perverse nature. He knew that the matter would be important and unpleasant when Himmler personally ordered him by telephone to report to Hitler in the *Reich* Chancellery that afternoon. There was no further information and Schellenberg, as often, called Heydrich, who knew what it was all about but did not wish to discuss the matter over the telephone. "Also, let's wait and see, how things develop. I am not in agreement with the solution. Anyway, a final decision will only be made this noon." Heydrich invited him to come over and drive with him to the *Reich* Chancellery. At their encounter shortly thereafter Heydrich was, if Schellenberg is to be believed, surprisingly open. Otto Strasser, the surviving brother of Gregor Strasser, had been located in Spain, and German agents had claimed that he planned to assassinate Hitler. The Gestapo representative and Police Attaché at the

---

93. Report on medical check-up at *Rasse- und Siedlungs-Hauptamt-SS* (SS Head Office for Race and Settlement), September 27, 1940; *SS-Ahnentafel* (family tree) of Irene Grosse-Schönepauck; handwritten biographical sketch signed by Irene Grosse-Schönepauck, September 28, 1940; NA, BDC Microfilm, RuSHA, Roll No. A 3343-RS-FO 270. Schellenberg, *Memoiren*, 136.
94. The Carlsbad stay apparently was prescribed for two months but Schellenberg shortened it to four weeks even before he departed. Schellenberg, *Memoiren*, 130. Schellenberg to "Kamerad Keim," November 30, 1940, BA Berlin, R 58/Anhang 51.

German Embassy in Madrid, Paul Winzer, in fact, had been at the Foreign Office in Berlin recently and discussed the search for Strasser with SS-*Obersturmbannführer Legationsrat* Werner Picot. Winzer had then been ordered to go to Lisbon and do all "to get ahold" of Strasser.[95] Heydrich had concluded that Otto Strasser was working hand in hand with British and American agents in Spain. Heydrich even voiced his own suspicion that Strasser was a "double crosser" who as a "national Bolshevik" and in connection with his Black Front (*Schwarze Front*) was actually working for Stalin. Heydrich's operatives had already been dispatched to Portugal to get a better picture of Strasser's exact whereabouts and activities directed against Germany. Heydrich minced no words: "The Führer, however, is pressing with greatest interest for a liquidation of Otto Strasser, and he is unsatisfied with the results of inquiries so far."

When Himmler, Heydrich and Schellenberg finally met with Hitler, the latter came to the point rather quickly: "The order I am giving you now is subject to the strictest secrecy and requires, if need be, risking your life." Hitler then seemed to take a brief respite, appearing to be almost absentminded, only to erupt into a cascade of insults relating to Gregor and Otto Strasser. "The greatest traitor Gregor," Hitler exclaimed, had met his just fate, but his less significant brother due to the support of foreign powers had become a real threat. "I have therefore decided to extinguish Otto Strasser, no matter by what means." When Hitler looked at him directly, Schellenberg found himself responding: "Yes, my Führer." Details of the planned murder were later discussed in Himmler's office. Most of all, Otto Strasser had to be found. That he was or shortly would be in Portugal seemed to be certain, and it became clear to the still somewhat shocked Schellenberg that Himmler and Heydrich had indeed made the preliminary decisions prior to this. Heydrich emphasized that Strasser should not be allowed to leave Portugal alive, and Schellenberg later remembered how he was struck by the hatred in Heydrich's voice. Minutes later a doctor entered the room, identified by Schellenberg only as St. from the University of Munich. The apparently unmoved and very sober medical professional had brought with him two flasks, each containing a bacterial fluid, a drop of which would suffice to put anyone to death. St. may have been SS-*Sturmbannführer* Dr. Horst Strassburger who was an expert in the field of bacteriology and had been brought by Himmler from Munich to Berlin to work on the possibilities of bacteriological warfare.[96]

---

95. Picot to Minister Martin Luther, December 10, 1940, Secret, PA, AA, R 101219.
96. Regarding Dr. Horst Strassburger see Interrogation of Dr. Kurt Blome, July 30, 1945, Secret, NA, Records of the Surgeon General (Army), RG 112, Box 4. Schellenberg's information that the doctor was about 30 years old, rather self-confident, and from the University of Munich is confirmed. He was assistant

When the mysterious medical doctor had departed, Heydrich warned Schellenberg to be "careful with the stuff." Schellenberg, faced with a clear assignment, hurried back to his office and locked the dangerous flasks in a safe. He was thoroughly confused. Why did he need two bottles if a single drop was enough to attend to the matter at hand? Was he being used as a guinea-pig to test some new substance, eventually to be employed in future bacteriological warfare? To prevent the worst, he called one of his technicians and had the bottles encased in steel shells lined with protective rubber coating. If need be, he thought, he might discard them somewhere out on the ocean.

Once in Lisbon, he employed the network he was familiar with—German agents, Japanese contacts, and a number of more or less reliable Portuguese police officials—to search for his target. But Strasser never appeared and after some rather costly and completely fruitless efforts, Schellenberg decided to give up, and with Heydrich's permission returned to Berlin. Otto Strasser, not entirely surprising, must have been on constant guard and certainly not in a mood to face his former friends, now deadly enemies. In contrast to his brother Gregor, who was murdered at the time of the so-called *Röhm-Putsch*, Otto survived the Nazi era only to return to Germany after World War II and indeed try his hands once more in politics. Considering that this was already Schellenberg's second failure in Portugal, it does seem somewhat surprising that he was not only able to return to his position in Berlin but also soon to move on to become Chief of *Amt* VI. One could be tempted to assume that Heydrich and Himmler, for reasons not entirely clear, were protecting the intelligent young SS leader even though he seemed to perform somewhat poorly in their exercises of brutality.[97]

---

to Professor Karl Kisskalt. Cf. Friedrich Hansen, *Biologische Kriegsführung im Dritten Reich* (Frankfurt: Campus, 1993), 144. Erhard Geissler, *Biologische Waffen—nicht in Hitlers Arsenalen* (Münster: LIT, 1999), 330-331.

97. On the confusing political ideas of Strasser cf. Kurt Singer, "Einstein And The German Don Quixote Otto Strasser," *Aufbau*, vol. 65, no. 4 (February 19, 1999), 11-12. The account of the assignment to murder Otto Strasser is based on Schellenberg's unpublished memoirs, IFZ, ED 90/6. Citations are translated. Cf. Schellenberg, *The Schellenberg Memoirs*, 182-189. Geissler, *Biologische Waffen*, 333, without citing respective evidence suggests that Schellenberg could have invented the Strasser story.

Chapter II

Chief of *Amt* VI Foreign Intelligence

There can be no doubt that Schellenberg for some time had looked for an opportunity to move from Heinrich Müller's Gestapo domain of inland security and spying on fellow citizens to the area of foreign intelligence and even diplomacy. When the head office people originally tried to persuade him to come to Berlin rather than joining the law firm of his fraternity brother and paternal friend Alfred Bartholomäus in Düsseldorf, they had indeed promised him that following an initial period of work in Berlin, he would be posted abroad.[98] Therefore, it seems entirely possible that his earlier secret state police work from his perspective was but a way to gain a first foothold in the Nazi structure. To the very young and inexperienced lawyer in training at the courts that type of confidential activity may also have presented new challenges. Certainly a number of SS leaders of some weight, such as Albert, Mehlhorn, Heydrich and Himmler, had taken notice of the extremely ambitious and gifted newcomer, and it may be assumed that his difficult foreign assignments, such as in Austria, Italy, The Netherlands and Portugal, in some way were a consequence of the respect he had been able to gain in parts of the hierarchy. These foreign assignments, of course, also had meant that in fact he had spent very little time on matters of internal security and the unpleasant Gestapo work

---

98. Statement under Oath, *Obersturmbannführer* (*Waffen*-SS) and one of Heydrich's adjutants Hans-Hendrik Neumann, NA, RG 238, Microfilm M897, Roll 114.

of Müller's *Amt* IV. When Robert Kempner asked Schellenberg in 1947 "What was the difference between IV and VI?," he replied: "Amt VI worked only outside of the country. It had nothing to do with police and the interior ... Amt IV was state police." In the strict sense of its official designation, Schellenberg's own subdivision, the Group IV E, however, was not occupied with secret police assignments against German civilians. Instead its explicit purpose actually was counterespionage in the industrial sector, as well as against Western countries in general, particularly Great Britain and the U.S., but also against Poland and the Soviet Union, Southeastern Europe and Turkey.[99]

Looking at the meagre evidence available on so-called counterintelligence cases during the period of Schellenberg's tenure in Group IV E, it is difficult to escape the impression that much of this work was more foreign intelligence than counterintelligence. In addition, it is quite evident that SS counterintelligence (Group IV E) and military intelligence (*Abwehr*) often closely cooperated in Berlin as well as abroad. Typical activities concerned the observation of foreign diplomatic posts in the capital and the respective intelligence lines connected to them. Covering individuals linked to diplomatic posts or foreign businesses constituted another task. In these specific operations those scrutinized could be Germans or foreign citizens. A number of the suspected agents obviously could be put out of action, but others were so well connected to powerful persons in Germany, Schellenberg later remembered, that it was risky if not impossible to touch them. A Swedish Count Roosen, for instance, was suspected of acting as courier for a Chilean singer named Rosita Serrano who in turn was thought to be in the service of another country. As it turned out, Count Roosen was personally acquainted with Hermann Göring and *Amt* IV "did not dare to order his arrest."[100] Also Schellenberg correctly suspected Baron Luigi Parilli, an Italian whose frequent journeys between Munich, Paris and The Hague were closely observed. Actually Parilli had a wide network of contacts. Already prior to World War II he had acted as a representative for certain American business interests in Italy and in the course of the war became closely acquainted with SS officers, as well as with intelligence officials in Switzerland. Eventually he was involved in the

---

99. Interrogation of Schellenberg by Dr. R. M. W. Kempner, November 13, 1947, in presence of Jane Lester, SAN, S-45c. (Transl.) "Translation of Statement by Schellenberg," July 18, 1945, NA, RG 226, E 119A, Box 26. "Situation Report No. 10," Confidential, NA, RG 319, IRR, IS, Box 1.
100. The Germans believed that Swedish intelligence in Germany was headed by a top official of Swedish Aerotransport A.B. Count Roosen was a Swedish pilot of that airline. "Counter-Espionage Cases Dealt with Amt IV (Gruppe IVE) in the Period August 1939-June 1941 on which Schellenberg Had Given Information," dated September 7, 1945, NA, RG 238, E 160, Box 50. — Rosita Serrano (Maria Aldunato del Campo, 1914–1997), a Chilean singer also called the Chilean nightingale, performed in Germany since 1936, supported by Nazi officials such as Goebbels, then suspected of spying, went to Sweden.

negotiations between Allen Dulles and the SS General Karl Wolff leading to Operation Sunrise, that is the very last-minute surrender of German forces in Northern Italy. When Schellenberg cast his eye on this gentleman, Parilli had already been able to create for himself very useful connections to such persons as the SS chief in Paris, Helmut Knochen, and the SS commander in The Hague, Wilhelm Harster, thus in fact making any serious interference from Schellenberg inadvisable.[101] In another possibly significant case, the activities of a large Italian waiters' union in Germany, Group IV E never succeeded in breaking the apparent network which was suspected to have been set up by the Italian Fascist party. Counterintelligence operations first against Poland and later against the Polish underground during German occupation were another notable task for Schellenberg's organization and apparently centered on a Polish agent often identified in the records as Jacubic alias Kuncewicz.[102] This man who is said to have been attached to the Japanese Embassy in Berlin apparently worked together with Salomea Lapinska, a Polish cook in the Manchurian Legation in Berlin. The two, eventually arrested by the Germans in the Berlin Tiergarten, were members of a larger network run at least in part for the benefit of Japan. Schellenberg told Allied interrogators that *Amt* IV prior to his arrival had taken no counterintelligence measures against Japan because it was considered a friendly nation. This courtesy had meant that the Germans were completely overlooking the fact that the Japanese had built a vast network collecting political, economic and military intelligence in Germany. Kuncewicz had been outfitted by the Japanese with a valid Manchurian passport enabling him to painlessly pass German controls on his frequent journeys between Warsaw and Berlin. The touchy point of the whole affair was of course, that Kuncewicz in this context, while working on behalf of the Polish underground, actually was part of the far-flung Japanese intelligence network in Central Europe and therefore directly connected to General Makato Onodera, the Japanese Military Attaché in Sweden. It did not take the Germans very long to discover the line from the Poles in Berlin to Onodera in Stockholm. According to the records, it was most likely a Polish Major by the name of Rybicki or Kybikowski who was actually attached to Onodera's office and in Stockholm moved about as a White Russian called Piotr or Peter Iwanow (Ivanov).

---

101. *Ibid.* Wilhelm Hoettl, *The Secret Front: The Inside Story of Nazi Political Espionage* (London: Phoenix, 2000; Copyright 1953), 295. Allen Dulles, *The Secret Surrender* (New York: Harper & Row, 1966), passim. Peter Grose, *Gentleman Spy: The Life of Allen Dulles* (Amherst: University of Massachusetts Press, 1996; 1st 1994), 226-229, 253.
102. Schellenberg, *The Schellenberg Memoirs*, 144 ff., identifies the agent as "K." In the records he is also called Jacubic or Jerzy Kuncewicz, with the latter being spelled a number of ways. C. G. McKay, *From Information to Intrigue: Studies in Secret Service Based on the Swedish Experience 1939-45* (London: Frank Cass, 1993), 142-143, 145, identifies him as Captain Alfons Jakubaniec (also Jakubianiec) alias Kuncewicz.

Besides the Poles in Germany and Sweden and the Japanese, there was a further, though slightly more unusual recipient of the information, namely the Jesuit General Vladimir Ledochowski in Rome.[103]

While this type of work would have been difficult enough under regular conditions, it was unnecessarily complicated by what would appear to have been a constant moving of functions between departments. To worsen matters there were "difficulties between the Gestapo and the SD regarding competency." Particularly inexpedient friction between *Amt* IV and *Amt* VI turned out to be a real impediment. These interdepartmental problems had certainly not been cleared away when in 1941 Schellenberg moved from a subordinate position under Gestapo Müller in *Amt* IV to the office of Chief of *Amt* VI.[104]

That Schellenberg's apparent lack of success in his previous assignments abroad concerning the Duke of Windsor and the former SA leader Otto Strasser caused no blockage in his hectic pursuit of a more promising position in international work, may be seen as an indication of his rather good standing with some of the more powerful men at the top. His takeover of the SS Foreign Intelligence Service occurred over an extended period of time and eventually also involved a number of difficult changes in personnel. Foreign Intelligence or *Amt* VI had only been organized with the *Reichssicherheitshauptamt* (RSHA) in 1939. Its forerunner had been *Abteilung* III, 3 of *Amt* III in the SD *Hauptamt*. Heinz Jost, like Schellenberg a trained lawyer and an SS functionary,[105] according to some records as far back as 1934 had begun to create a kind of security service which in 1937 became part of *Amt* III. It acted "as an espionage rather than a security service" and, interestingly, demonstrated that if need be "it could extend its interest from Germany itself to territory outside the Reich." It was this particular quality that had led Heydrich to instruct Jost "to prepare the foundations of a proper

---

103. Schellenberg, *The Schellenberg Memoirs*, 147, refers to the diplomatic post in Berlin as "the Manchoukuoan Embassy." In *Memoiren*, 120-121, he calls it both Manchukuoan and Manchurian "Legation." Manchukuo was part of Manchuria and since 1932 under Japanese control. "Counter-Espionage Cases Dealt with by Amt IV (Gruppe IV E)," NA, RG 238, E 160, Box 50. Various documents, NA, RG 263, E ZZ-18, Box 97 (2nd release, CIA Name Files). Memorandum, Strategic Services Unit, October 2, 1946, NA, RG 226, E 212, Box 6. McKay, *From Information to Intrigue*, 142, identifies the Pole as Major Michal Rybikowski alias Piotr Iwanow and (p. 145) refers to the cook as Janina Lapinska.
104. Cf. "Situation Report No. 4 Amt IV of the RSHA," December 7, 1945, Secret, NA, RG 319, IRR, IS, Box 8.
105. Heinz Maria Karl Jost, (1904-1964), worked as a lawyer before becoming a higher police official in Worms and Giessen. Joined NSDAP 1928, changed from SA to SS 1934, Chief of *Einsatzgruppe* A in the U.S.S.R. 1942, drafted into *Waffen*-SS 1944, sentenced to life 1948, later pardoned. On Jost cf. Kahn, *Hitler's Spies*, 251-255. Katrin Paehler, "Ein Spiegel seiner selbst. Der SD-Ausland in Italien," in Wildt, ed. *Nachrichtendienst, politische Elite und Mordeinheit*, 246-247.

Auslandsnachrichtendienst [Foreign Intelligence Service] on the basis of Abteilung III, 3."[106]

Although Schellenberg must have coveted Jost's position in foreign intelligence, the records leave little doubt that Jost's undoing was by and large caused by his own lack of efficiency, if not to say an apparent inability to keep his men and, for that matter, his own name out of troublesome financial irregularities. When interrogated at Nuremberg in 1948, Jost himself spoke of Schellenberg as a very young but extremely successful SS leader. His own enemies, as Jost saw it, were Gestapo Müller and Heydrich who collaborated to destroy him. Whether the respective charges against him were in the end fully justified or not, the overall condition of *Amt* VI certainly seemed to call for drastic change.[107] In the words of an Allied report from London after the war: "... Amt VI activities against Western Europe fall into two well defined parts, as does indeed the history of the Amt as a whole—the periods before and after the appointment of Schellenberg as Amtschef [department chief]. Schellenberg's accession in late 1941 marks a turning point in Amt VI, a change in organisation, in personnel and in policy. The results of Amt VI in the time of Jost were meagre, in the case of Western Europe almost negligible."[108] Schellenberg himself gives June 22, 1941, "the day our armies marched into Russia," as the date of his appointment as Deputy Chief of *Amt* VI. His personnel file contains a letter from Heydrich to Himmler, dating Schellenberg's promotion on July 2, 1941. Wilhelm Höttl, repeatedly interrogated by Allied military and intelligence officers in order to countercheck Schellenberg's statements, told his questioners that Schellenberg "was appointed deputy chief of Amt VI ... and given the specific mission by Heydrich to build up a damaging case against Jost," and added "Schellenberg went about this task with his customary circumspection."[109]

Schellenberg's transfer from Müller's Gestapo to Foreign Intelligence was not only overshadowed by the apparent lack of shining performance in several previous assignments, but the important step-up in his career followed the still not fully explained flight of Rudolf Hess to England on May 10, 1941.[110] While

---

106. "Situation Report No. 10," Confidential, NA, RG 319, IRR, IS, Box 1. For details of the early organizational structure cf. Höhne, *The Order of the Death's Head*, 242-244.
107. Cf. "Final Report," 80-83. Heinz Jost interrogation by Mr. Barr, January 6, 1948, SAN, Rep 502, J 37.
108. SAINT London to SAINT Washington, October 26, 1945, "Liquidation Report No. 7," Secret, NA, RG 226, E 109, Box 45.
109. "Source: SS Sturmbannführer Dr. Wilhelm Hoettl," File XE 00 08 82, NA, RG 319, Box 617.
110. Rudolf Hess (1894 Alexandria, Egypt—1987 Allied prison Berlin-Spandau) served with German Air Force in World War I, early member of NSDAP 1920 (membership number 16), studied geopolitics with Karl Haushofer in Munich, participated in Hitler's unsuccessful putsch 1923, Deputy of the *Führer* 1933,

the records do not suggest any direct links between Schellenberg and Hess, the Hess flight could have easily been used by Schellenberg's enemies to connect his name with men around Hess who suddenly found themselves in deep trouble.[111] Schellenberg certainly knew Kurt Jahnke, the right-hand man of Franz Pfeffer von Salomon, the disgraced former Highest SA Leader (*Oberster SA Führer*/OSAF) who by some miracle had survived the 1934 massacre following the *Röhm Putsch*.[112] The highly regarded and internationally well connected intelligence figure Jahnke had professionally come down to operating a small intelligence service from the offices of Pfeffer von Salomon under Rudolf Hess.[113] Although no reliable evidence has surfaced so far, some authors continue to speculate on Jahnke's role in the preparations for the Hess scheme.[114] Apparently Schellenberg was drawn into the urgent deliberations of Heydrich and Himmler concerning the Hess case. In the course of these lively discussions he registered with some distaste how Martin Bormann was using the situation in order to increase his own influence with Hitler. Schellenberg later recalled that it was Bormann who came up with the splendid idea that Hess was mad, never considering that at home and abroad some might wonder how it was that a mentally deficient Hess could have been Hitler's long-time deputy and close advisor. When Himmler and Schellenberg pondered the stupidity of the explanation of mental illness, they also touched on Martin Bormann's influence on Hitler. If Schellenberg recalls correctly, Himmler took a long look at him, shook his head and said: "It is too late to do something against it." Schellenberg's recollections quite frankly suggest that he tried to keep himself covered in most aspects, but also that he thought he could count on Heydrich's protection, if not open agreement. Schellenberg's opinion, whether based on information obtained from Jahnke we do not know, was quite clear. He felt that Hess had been strongly influenced by Hitler's earlier more positive views of the British. He thought that Hess, not least because of

---

sentenced in Nuremberg to life imprisonment 1946, official cause of death suicide. It has been argued that he was murdered. In neo-Nazi circles Hess continues to be considered a heroic martyr.

111. The British government has not yet declassified all records relating to the Hess flight and the aftermath in England. Much of the literature on Hess and his flight therefore continues to be somewhat speculative.

112. According to Himmler, Pfeffer von Salomon had "educated" the SA "for constant disobediance towards the Führer." (Transl.) Unsigned memory note by Himmler, May 24, 1941, BA Koblenz, NS 19/2817. According to this, Pfeffer von Salomon resigned his SA position only days after the Stennes "mutiny" in 1930.

113. Franz Pfeffer von Salomon (1888-1968), Free Corps leader after World War I, participant in the *Ruhrkampf* (violent campaign against French occupation of Ruhr area 1923), member of NSDAP since 1924, 1926 named by Hitler Highest SA Leader, 1936 as representative for Hermann Göring negotiations with U.S. representatives in connection with Mixed Claims Commission. Cf. Burkhard Jähnicke, *Washington und Berlin zwischen den Kriegen. Die Mixed Claims Commission in den transatlantischen Beziehungen* (Baden-Baden: Nomos, 2003), 283-285.

114. Actually, the Jahnke Büro had already been closed prior to the Hess flight, and Jahnke had something like a working relationship with the SD since 1940. "Final Report," Appendix XV.

his upbringing in Egypt, had been much inclined to see Germany's future in the West, in sharp contrast to the rapprochement with the Russians sought and practiced by considerable sectors of German military leadership following World War I and indeed still very evident in Nazi foreign policy in the late 1930s. Yet, almost as if to leave a kind of directive for later historians, Schellenberg clearly stated: "According to my full knowledge of the records, the course of the investigation by the Abwehr, and the course of the entire Hess affair, it is out of the question that Hitler gave explicit instruction to fly to England in order to present to England a final peace offer."[115]

Schellenberg's position in *Amt* VI officially was acting head or second-in-charge under Heinz Jost. Whether Schellenberg from that desk contributed to the ultimate dismissal of his chief must remain an open question in the absence of more complete documentation. Höttl's later comments in this respect should not be overvalued. Questionable involvement in the affairs of several business enterprises and, most of all, the SD support of Horia Sima and his Iron Guard in their rebellion against Rumania's dictator Marshal Ion Antonescu were quite enough to bring about Jost's demise. Germany evidently had to be interested in preventing any interruption in the shipment of oil from Rumania, and the German Foreign Office under Joachim von Ribbentrop had decided to support the dictator. That the Foreign Office seems to have been less than fully informed about the contacts between Horia Sima and *Amt* VI in Berlin is all the more surprising since Jost's representative in Rumania, SS-*Hauptsturmführer* Otto von Bolschwing, was "maintaining good relations" with Dr. Hermann Neubacher, *Gesandter* (Minister) in Bucharest and Germany's special representative for oil questions in Southeastern Europe. From the records one could conclude that Neubacher had problems with Ribbentrop and his Foreign Office while the Austrian-born Ernst Kaltenbrunner, and therefore the RSHA in Berlin, thought the Austrian-born Neubacher to be "an extremely capable man." Bolschwing was well connected with Horia Sima and assisted him against Antonescu. As it turned out, however, the Iron Guard was put down and Bolschwing had all to do to spirit Horia Sima and some of his confederates out of Bucharest and get them to Berlin where the Germans allowed them to claim to be a government-in-exile. Ribbentrop saw to it that Bolschwing was pulled out from Bucharest and for Jost the uncalled-for SD intervention in foreign policy, as the Foreign Office saw it, turned out to be the

---

115. IFZ, ED 90/6 (Transl.). Cf. Schellenberg, *The Schellenberg Memoirs*, 199-203. Less detailed Schellenberg, *Memoiren*, 159-161.

proverbial straw that broke the camel's back. The whole affair certainly contributed to clearing the road for Schellenberg's takeover of *Amt* VI.[116]

Nevertheless, Schellenberg was not officially appointed *Chef* of the *Amt* until about a year later, though he seems to have assumed full responsibility in the autumn of 1941. It was his first chance to attempt the construction of a workable and reliable foreign intelligence service. The special foreign intelligence branch had been in the making under Jost since 1934, and Schellenberg wasted no time introducing the necessary radical changes, as well as becoming acquainted personally with existing intelligence lines abroad. In order to turn *Amt* VI into a more efficient organization, it was necessary to move people around and place trusted men into key positions. If we can believe the interrogation reports of Martin Karl Sandberger, like Schellenberg a trained lawyer with the respective university degrees, Schellenberg when taking over *Amt* VI "purposely ignored" what Sandberger called "the internal political principles of eligibility of the SS." Even men who were not members of the party (NSDAP) or other Nazi organizations were brought in, "doing away, in practice, with the SS or party character according to which it [*Amt* VI] had been founded." As *Gruppe* IV E had done mostly counterintelligence work, it is also not at all surprising that Schellenberg seems to have taken along several of his former staff members whom he thought capable of handling intelligence assignments. One of these men was *Kriminal-Kommissar* SS-*Obersturmbannführer* Dr. Wilhelm Schmitz who had much wanted to leave *Amt* IV with Schellenberg and now as his personal *Referent* (a type of adjutant) ran the front office in *Amt* VI. He became the liaison officer between Schellenberg and all other sections. Like Schellenberg he was a law school graduate and to all appearances Schellenberg trusted him fully. Another was Franz Göring who later became one of the people Schellenberg trusted and used in his dangerous efforts to rescue large numbers of concentration camp inmates in the final period of the war.[117] His enemies inside the RSHA structure, not least of course those whom he had removed from their positions, loudly criticized Schellenberg, thereby forcing him to act quickly and even to risk possible interruptions of certain operations abroad. Part of the problem was the fact that the SS men stationed abroad, as so-called Police Attachés, remained under

---

116. "Situation Report No. 10," and "Consolidated Interrogation Report No. 3," June 21, 1945, NA, RG 319, IRR, IS, Box 1. Weinberg, *A World at* Arms, 521-522. Wildt, *Generation des Unbedingten*, 398-399. Höhne, *The Order of the Death's Head*, 328-329.
117. "Sandberger Report" (Camp 020), Secret, NA, RG 226, E 119A, Box 33. Statement under Oath, Franz Göring, April 24, 1948, SAN, Rep 501, LV, S9. Statement under Oath, former *Kriminaldirektor* SS-*Sturmbannführer* Kurt Lindow, January 23, 1948, SAN, Rep 502. "Report on Kapitän z. See Freiherr von Bechtolsheim," Secret, July 3, 1945, NAK, KV 3/119. Annex No. IX, Confidential, NA, RG 319, IRR, IS, Box 1.

the control of the Gestapo Chief Müller who was not a friend of Schellenberg's and would have been more than pleased if *Amt* VI had become even more undone. As long as Heydrich was alive, he seemed to hold his hand over Schellenberg, making it difficult for Müller to really damage Schellenberg, but when Heydrich met his violent death in June 1942, Müller must have welcomed the apparent opportunity to finally rid himself of Schellenberg. It was one of the most critical moments in Schellenberg's brief professional career.[118]

Young Schellenberg had lost the man who had the power and apparently the inclination to cover for him. He had been able to rely on that. Heydrich's successor Ernst Kaltenbrunner was a different caliber and Schellenberg correctly expected him to become an undisciplined competitor who would not hesitate to eliminate him if circumstances seemed to demand that.[119] Schellenberg, the records and his memoirs clearly demonstrate this, became permanently aware of the professional, political and indeed personal threat to himself. He sought and slowly gained what turned out to be a kind of continued protection by Heinrich Himmler. How the often questioning and doubting Schellenberg was able to live with his growing and soon nearly complete knowledge of Himmler, must remain an enigma. In fact, there can be no doubt that Schellenberg developed an incredible loyalty to his protector, a loyalty ensuing from his extremely personal relationship and one that would shortly, when the Germans were losing the war and the destruction of their Thousand Year Empire was upon them, lead Schellenberg to earnestly consider Heinrich Himmler as the successor to Adolf Hitler.[120]

From the beginning of his frantic structural changes in *Amt* VI, Schellenberg must have known that his long-term target, the creation of a unified German intelligence service, would clash with the ideas and concepts of the much older head of Germany's military intelligence, the *Abwehr*. He certainly became acquainted with the navy man Wilhelm Canaris at an early stage, and we know from the records that the two men, as different as they may have been, developed what could almost be called a friendship.[121] When Schellenberg was still a very small child, Canaris in 1914 had already served on the German cruiser *Dresden* just off the coast of Mexico when the Germans were assisting the Mexican dictator General Victoriano Huerta against the U.S.

---

118. Cf. Schellenberg, *The Schellenberg Memoirs*, 321-322.
119. Ernst Kaltenbrunner (1903-1946), Austrian born, studied law, SS leader in Austria prior to 1938, successor of Heydrich in the RSHA, sentenced to death by hanging in Nuremberg 1946.
120 Cf. Schellenberg, *The Schellenberg Memoirs*, 336-341.
121. Admiral Wilhelm Canaris (1887-1945), Chief of the *Abwehr*, was arrested after the attempted assassination of Hitler in July 1944, sentenced in a sham court procedure and hanged on April 9, 1945, in the Concentration Camp Flossenbürg.

In World War I Canaris survived the 1915 sinking of the *Dresden* off the shores of Chile by the British cruiser *Glasgow*, escaped from Chilean internment and finally managed to reach Spain. There he became involved in German intelligence operations and, following a bout with malaria in 1918, commanded one of Germany's submarines in the Mediterranean. The war hero, supporter of the far-right *Kapp Putsch*, participant in the *Schwarze Reichswehr* (illegal German armed forces), and since 1935 Admiral and Chief of the *Abwehr*, had apparently taken a liking to the educated, well-mannered and dynamic young SS functionary. While in Berlin Canaris, like some other German men of a certain social class or military status, enjoyed riding out in the large wooded area called Grunewald, and Schellenberg much enjoyed joining him on such occasions. Though both were professional intelligence men and thus clearly not overly talkative on sensitive issues, they apparently got to know each other on a rather personal level, and it would seem more than reasonable to conclude that they knew of each other's serious doubts concerning the future of Nazi Germany.[122] The little that is known about this unusual relationship does not help us reach a full appraisal of the competitive spirit of their intelligence services, and contrary to some previously published views, there is no reliable evidence in the records suggesting that Schellenberg from the start wished to destroy the *Abwehr* and its Chief.[123] Quite to the contrary, there are indications that Schellenberg preferred to deal with representatives of the *Abwehr* rather than with Heinrich Müller's Gestapo men whom he did not trust. Since 1936 there indeed had been a kind of agreement between Canaris' Abwehr and the SD. How much this agreement, known as the Ten Commandments, was linked to the power struggle of the German intelligence organizations and just how effective it was in creating an acceptable working climate are questions beyond the scope of the present study of Walter Schellenberg. When he came to *Amt VI* Foreign Intelligence, diverging interests were still very evident, and in 1942 SD and Abwehr drew up an updated version of the Ten Commandments. Canaris and Heydrich, not Schellenberg, signed the new agreement at a conference of SD and Abwehr officials on May 18, 1942, at the Hradčany Palace in Prague.[124]

---

122. Schellenberg, *The Schellenberg Memoirs*, 115, 207, 399-400. Höhne, *The Order of the Death's Head*, 552. Brissaud, *Canaris*, 235-236.
123. Cf. Ladislas Farago, *The Game of the Foxes: British and German Intelligence Operations and Personalities Which Changed the Course of the Second World War* (London: Hodder & Stoughton, 1972; 1st U.S. ed. 1971), 609. Lauran Paine, *The Abwehr* (London: Robert Hale, 1984), 9, 46, 181. Gert Buchheit, *Die anonyme Macht* (Frankfurt: Akademische Verlagsgesellschaft Athenaion, 1969), 96.
124. Schellenberg's own comments in IFZ, ED 90/3. Cf. Michael Mueller, *Canaris: Hitlers Abwehrchef* (Berlin: Propyläen/Ullstein, 2006), 363, 373-379. Cf. also cooperation with *Fremde Heere Ost* (FHO) in the *Zeppelin* operation. Heinz Höhne, Hermann Zolling, *The General Was a Spy* (New York: Coward, McCann & Geoghegan, 1972), 39-43.

Even before he was able to complete the difficult internal restructuring of *Amt* VI, Schellenberg turned his fierce energy to getting to know the often very covert but also disorganized existing German intelligence networks abroad. With a large part of Europe being occupied by German forces and other parts decidedly being in the Allied camp, places where operatives could move about relatively unhindered and where direct contacts with the enemy were still possible had become few by late 1941. Besides the almost inaccessible Ireland and the more distant Spain and Portugal, there really remained only two neutral nations which could be used for undercover operations and, more importantly, for approaches to Britain, the Soviet Union or the United States. Both Switzerland and Sweden were extremely watchful and carefully guarded their fragile neutrality. Both had no desire to provoke the Germans and risk war and occupation. While such considerations would suggest close supervision of unusual persons and connections, they also may well have contributed to a certain laxness which in both countries in the end allowed for and even tolerated many of the activities of the various Allied and Nazi intelligence networks. Very early, probably already in 1941 at the time of his move to *Amt* VI, Schellenberg had come to the conclusion that Germany might not be able to end this war successfully, and it was therefore a natural reaction that he began to explore ways and means to scrutinize possibilities of first secret contacts to Allied diplomats and intelligence operatives in the two neutral nations. Needless to say, with the German forces being slowed and thrown back in many places and the idea of unconditional surrender also soon being in the air, this was not going to be an easy undertaking. Schellenberg not only had to carefully protect his own standing and safety inside the SS structure, but it was also often difficult to select men who were sufficiently qualified and trustworthy to be sent out on such vague and in every way extremely dangerous missions. Yet, in spite of the perilous nature of such operations, Schellenberg succeeded in setting up valuable contacts in both countries and indeed gaining access to individuals of the highest stature and influence. His education and his seemingly easygoing personality were his most useful assets on the often unpredictable international stage, but evidently he also had a very lucky hand in choosing suitable people from the unassuring twilight zones of the intelligence underground. His apparent hesitancy to employ ruffians and their direct modus operandi may have often given him the edge in the difficult business of creating new international lines.

The foundations of Nazi intelligence work in Switzerland had been laid by Schellenberg's predecessor, Heinz Jost, but early German moves had suffered gravely from a Swiss backlash when some Germans seriously attempted to organize Nazi sympathizers in Switzerland, not only putting together a Fifth

Column, but in fact trying to create a Swiss SS. Although the Germans had reacted to the angry resentment of the Swiss and more or less accepted removal of their compromised representatives, such as Ernst Peter who lasted from March to June 1940, Hans-Ulrich Reiche, Eugen Lang or Willi Gröbl, official relations between Bern and Berlin had become rather vulnerable, and Schellenberg was forced to proceed with utmost care.[125] To all indications Schellenberg not only respected the neutrality of Switzerland, but he created new lines and exposed himself to considerable danger by personally running the Swiss connection. To make certain that Dr. Klaus Hügel, responsible SS leader of both the *Amt* VI branch office and the *Alemannische Arbeitskreis* (AAK, Alemannic Study Group) in Stuttgart, understood what he meant, Schellenberg requested that *Amt* VI relations with Swiss Nazi sympathizers, cultivated by his predecessor Jost, were to stop immediately. Though Schellenberg certainly expressed his own views, it is of some interest to note that Wilhelm Canaris pursued the same policy of respecting Swiss neutrality when he ordered his *Abwehr* representatives to stop espionage activities in Switzerland. Looking back, it is justified to state that the large Soviet spy ring, usually referred to as the Red Orchestra (*Rote Kapelle*) and operating from Switzerland but strongly represented in a number of European nations, was one concern among many for Schellenberg but certainly did not decisively influence his careful steps taken in Switzerland.[126]

Schellenberg's first representative in Switzerland was SS-*Sturmbannführer* Hans-Christian Daufeldt whom he inherited from the Jost period. This supposed expert for Great Britain and the United States had enjoyed a somewhat mixed education, finishing with a degree from a police school in Bad Tölz. In October 1935 he suddenly turned up in England, accompanied by a lady named Hedwig Gut whom he said he intended to marry. He claimed to be a clerk at the Hotel Kaiserhof in Bad Tölz and had come to improve his

---

125. Dr. Ernst Peter (b. 1906), lawyer, sent by Jost, attached to the German Legation in Bern March-June 1940. Peter had a diplomatic passport from the German Foreign Office. SS-*Obersturmführer* Dr. Hans-Ulrich Reiche was attached to the German Consulate in Geneva. *Amt* VI moved him to France already in October 1940. Eugen Lang was attached to the Consulate General in Zurich and against the loud objections of the German Minister Otto Karl Köcher was arrested in late 1942, expelled from Switzerland, and sentenced in absentia to life in prison. SS-*Untersturmführer* Dr. Willi (Wilhelm) Gröbl was attached to the German Consulate General in Zurich and specifically concerned with organizing a Swiss SS. He was expelled in October 1941. Hans Rudolf Fuhrer, *Spionage gegen die Schweiz* (Frauenfeld: Huber, 1982), 74, 124-126. *Bericht des Bundesrates an die Bundesversammlung über die antidemokratische Tätigkeit von Schweizern und Ausländern im Zusammenhang mit dem Kriegsgeschehen 1939-1945*. 1. Teil. Vom 28. Dezember 1945. No publ. data.

126. Pierre Th. Braunschweig, *Secret Channel to Berlin: The Masson-Schellenberg Connection and Swiss Intelligence in World War II* (Philadelphia: Casemate, 2004), 256-257. Fuhrer, *Spionage gegen die Schweiz*, 70. On the Red Orchestra see *The Rote Kapelle: The CIA's History of Soviet Intelligence and Espionage Networks in Western Europe, 1936-1945* (Washington, D.C.: University Publications of America, 1979). Mark A. Tittenhofer, "The Rote Drei: Getting Behind the 'Lucy' Myth," *Studies in Intelligence*, vol. 13, no. 3 (Summer 1969). Differences of opinion on the Red Orchestra, resistance group or Soviet spies, continue to be argued. Also sections of the Red Orchestra plainly continued their work after World War II and the end of the Nazi regime.

English. He must have been called back by his SS bosses, but a year later, in November 1936, he reappeared in London to study, he told officials, at the London School of Economics. However, somewhere along the way, British intelligence had become interested in his travel between Germany and England, and it was decided to bug his telephone which he had listed under a false name. Whatever was said on the telephone, intelligence felt it wise to know more about the mysterious German visitor. No lesser agent than U 35 (Klop Ustinov) was assigned to keep an eye on his activities. Daufeldt's real claim to fame after less than successful tours of duty in Hamburg and Scandinavia was his assignment to escort Karl von Wiegand during his information tour of Nazi Germany. Through Wiegand Daufeldt met other American authors and journalists, and he seems to have enjoyed the restless travel and socializing of the Americans. Wiegand, the Hearst correspondent, knew Germany well and had played a role already in World War I, reporting on the *Kaiser* and his nation. He was obviously also very well connected in Hitler's Third Reich. Following other brief stunts in Berlin, Hof, Hamburg and Scandinavia, Daufeldt's biggest assignment was a report "on the USA and it's preparedness for war," the data for which he gathered from the press and radio programs. Over time Daufeldt had also worked for and with Heydrich, and indications are that it was Heydrich rather than Schellenberg who in the spring of 1942 arranged for the assignment in Switzerland. Most appraisals of Daufeldt's professional abilities and achievements tend to be negative, and Schellenberg's view that "Daufeldt was the biggest failure I know" may not have been unjustified. During interrogation Wilhelm Höttl referred to Daufeldt "as a man that never had his heart in his work and only desired an elegant existence, consequently falling out of favor with Schellenberg."[127] To be certain, Daufeldt must have been able to present himself socially and even leave a favorable impression. There is no other way to explain the very positive reaction to him of Ambassador Ulrich von Hassell, who in his diary noted that Daufeldt had visited him in Berlin. "This young SS man showed himself remarkably well informed on foreign policy, sober in judgment and surprisingly free in his expression. He stayed one and a half hours and talked in directions which I was cautious enough not to pick up."[128]

---

127. Hans-Christian Daufeldt (b. 1908), cover name Dressler, joined NSDAP and SA 1931 and the SS 1933. The police school in Bad Tölz was an SS-leadership school, also referred to as *Junkerschule* or *Führerschule*. His studies in England were sponsored by the SD. Lt. Col. Andrew H. Berding to Chief, CIB, G-2, USFET, July 30, 1945, Secret, NA, RG 226, E 108A, Box 287. NAK, KV 2/141-142, Home Office files and other docs. BA Berlin, R 58/Anhang 51. Fuhrer, *Spionage gegen die Schweiz*, 76. Ray Bearse and Anthony Read, *Conspirator: The Untold Story of Tyler Kent* (New York: Doubleday, 1991), 193.
128. Ulrich von Hassell (1881-executed 1944) was the former German Ambassador to Rome and a member of the resistance in Germany. He is said to have maintained contacts in Switzerland. Friedrich Freiherr Hiller von Gaertringen, ed., *Die Hassel-Tagebücher 1938-1944* (Berlin: Siedler, 1988), 272. (Transl.)

After the war Otto Köcher, the German Minister in Switzerland, told a State Department interrogation team under DeWitt C. Poole that the so-called Vice-Consul Daufeldt received sealed orders from Himmler and Schellenberg and that he reported to Schellenberg. Daufeldt did assure the Minister that he was not operating against Switzerland. Köcher claimed that he saw one of Daufeldt's reports "listing Swiss officers who were Jews or Freemasons." As both were persecuted back home in Germany, Daufeldt's activities in this sector would appear to be routine Gestapo work rather than foreign intelligence. In view of the evidently very close observation of all German activities by the Swiss services and as a consequence of Daufeldt's inability to create a workable Swiss network, Schellenberg was forced to react promptly. Rather than risking another unproductive engagement, he decided to take matters into his own hands, and he invested his reputation in what was nothing less than his own very personal line to Switzerland. His most significant accomplishment was a straight line to Brigadier Colonel (*Oberstbrigadier*) Roger Masson, Chief of the Intelligence Service of the Swiss General Staff, referred to in Schellenberg's messages as "Senner I." That this most unusual contact at the highest level should also produce misunderstandings, all sorts of accusations and even the personal defamation of those involved comes as no surprise.[129]

Although both Swiss and American records are now largely accessible and Swiss specialists have looked into the matter, some of the background of the curious connection between the Swiss Military Intelligence Chief and the head of SS Foreign Intelligence to this day remains rather uncertain. On the German side it was especially Hans Wilhelm Eggen, who paved the way and opened the twisted paths to the highest level in Switzerland. He had been trained as a lawyer but also worked briefly in finance before taking over the management of Warenvertriebs GmbH in Berlin, a family-run internationally active import and export business according to some sources, but also linked to other less visible business interests and personages elsewhere. Purchasing arms and other items for the *Waffen*-SS, he soon made the acquaintance of important people in the German Economic Ministry (*Reichswirtschaftsministerium*) and the SS purchasing agencies, thereby becoming involved in a less public international market and the respective foreign currency transactions, difficult in times of war. It is not surprising that eventually he came into contact with *Amt* VI and

---

129. Roger Masson (1894-1967) became chief of Swiss Military Intelligence in 1936. Originally small and underfinanced, the service in World War II had 120 members. *Büro Ha*, a private intelligence service run by the businessman Hans Hausamann since the 1920s, became attached to Masson's military intelligence in 1939. Hans Rudolf Fuhrer, "Die Schweiz im Nachrichtendienst" in Rudolf L. Bindschedler et al, eds., *Schwedische und schweizerische Neutralität im Zweiten Weltkrieg* (Basel: Helbing & Lichtenhahn, 1985), 405-409. Braunschweig, *Secret Channel to Berlin*, 33-41. Cf. obituary für Masson by Hausamann, *Die Nachhut*, no. 4 (February 15, 1968), 23-24.

its successive chiefs Jost and Schellenberg. If we accept what Eggen told his Allied interrogators after the war, he never officially became part of the structure of *Amt* VI and his connections there were limited to the chief and his staff. Schellenberg confirmed this and added that it allowed for greater freedom of action in the operations in Switzerland.

Because wooden huts (for army camps or concentration camps?) were one of the products Eggen was purchasing in Switzerland for the SS, he came to do business with the Swiss Timber Syndicate (*Holzsyndikat*) and ran into a Dr. Ritzburg who in fact was Captain Meyer or, in actuality, Dr. Paul Meyer-Schwertenbach, a man of diverse interests who also happened to be an officer of Swiss Military Intelligence and in that function an associate and subordinate of Brigadier Colonel Roger Masson. Through the well-connected Meyer-Schwertenbach, referred to in Schellenberg's messages as "Senner II," Eggen was introduced to Paul Holzach, another Swiss intelligence officer working for Masson. Holzach, referred to by Schellenberg as "Senner III," and Eggen apparently then proceeded to set up a cover business in Zurich named *Interkommerz AG* which was engaged in all kinds of international transactions and therefore able to move funds around when needed. Another attractive matter of interest must have been the very handy coincidence that Henry Guisan, Jr., a son of General Henri Guisan, the Swiss Chief of Staff, happened to sit on the board of Extroc S.A., a Swiss company heavily involved among other things in deals with Eggen's Warenvertriebs GmbH. Much of the information concerning this network came to light during Allied interrogations in the postwar years and is now accessible in the vast material on Nazi Germany and the aftermath released by the U.S. Government in recent years. Other data have become known through respective Swiss investigations in the postwar period, and there have been a number of extensive documentary and historical publications, most recently the revealing study by the Swiss expert Pierre Braunschweig.[130]

However one might be inclined to see the Swiss-German contacts during World War II—and some of the appraisals have been highly critical—there can be no doubt that Schellenberg through his network and personal lines not only served his own interests but also those of the Swiss intelligence service. At the same time it must be remembered that the Schellenberg-Masson contact was

---

130. Hans Wilhelm Eggen (b. 1912), son of a legal official, studied Law, brief military service 1939/1940, member of NSDAP, SS, and *Waffen*-SS. He used the aliases Eggi, Mille, Millet, Paul Müller, and Peter Mille-Mueller. "Lebenslauf of Hans Wilhelm Eggen," Secret, CIA Name Files, NA, RG 263, E A1-86, Box 37. Cf. NAK, WO 204/12814. DB5 to SAINT Rome, September 26, 1945, NA, RG 263, E ZZ-16, Box 45. Statement under Oath, Paul E. Meyer, Zurich, May 10, 1948, SAN, Rep 501, LV, S-4. Regarding Holzach cf. "Translation of Statement," Schellenberg, August 13, 1945, NA, RG 226, E 125A, Box 2. Braunschweig, *Secret Channel to Berlin*, 18, 206. Concerning Lieutenant Henry Guisan see *Ibid.*, 135, 138-141.

not at all an extraordinary phenomenon in the arena of international intelligence—and intrigue—in neutral Switzerland. Certainly other powers, among them Great Britain, the U.S., the U.S.S.R. and Japan, maintained their own networks in Switzerland and had no hesitations to recognize and explore even reckless proposals in the uncertain and often dangerous game of covert intelligence. Other than Sweden, Switzerland was the main ball court and results of the games played surely influenced the course of World War II and, it must not be forgotten, created circumstances enabling a great many refugees to escape from Germany and stay alive.

In the absence of reliable information concerning the personal reactions of the young SS leader to the brutal excesses of the Nazi regime at home or to the initial military successes and the subsequent increasing indications that Germany would not be able to gain the much proclaimed *Endsieg* (final victory), the historian is forced to resort to an often difficult comparative and critical examination of the surviving records and the subjective reports and memoirs of Schellenberg's contemporaries. Operation Sea Lion had been put on ice and to informed observers it must have seemed increasingly doubtful that German armed forces would indeed invade and conquer hated *Engeland*. Instead, after divvying up Poland, German armies had attacked their erstwhile ally, the powerful and far-flung Soviet Union, and mass murder committed by SS-*Einsatzgruppen* (special task forces) and regular troops had become the order of the day. While we cannot be certain how Schellenberg digested the daily news on what on the surface still appeared a victorious campaign, it may be assumed that he was rather fully informed on the strength of the Soviet Union and the stamina of its leader Joseph Stalin. We are not aware that Schellenberg at this early stage of the war had already established sufficiently important contacts to Japanese representatives in Berlin, Switzerland, and Stockholm to be realistically informed on Japanese policy and military objectives. Nevertheless, Pearl Harbor and the American declaration of war against Japan, or, probably even more so, Hitler's declaration of war against the United States on December 11, 1941, must have been final indications that the outcome of this war could be catastrophic for Germany unless carefully prepared avenues of mediation and compromise were found almost immediately. Being part of the ruling apparatus and close to men such as Heydrich and Himmler, Schellenberg also must have realized very early that it would not be an easy task to seek contact with the enemy. If he dropped his guard and moved without greatest circumspection, his foes inside the SS structure, he was fully aware, would enjoy nothing more than destroying him. So much for the background of the diverse and complicated initiatives he took in Bern and elsewhere. His grave handicap was a general ignorance of British and American political perceptions, coupled with a total lack of experience in diplomatic manners and procedures. Needless to say, even doubting Germany's grand destination was extremely dangerous in the police state he was part of and which clearly had the support of most Germans. Taking this into consideration, it may not be an error to assume that the Chief of Foreign Intelligence and his emissaries and indeed most of his personal staff in *Amt* VI shared certain views concerning their nation and its government. Far from being part of what later became known as an underground resistance, there nevertheless must have been some such thing as loyalty in Schellenberg's immediate surroundings, and a number of his staff must have shared views on developments in Germany and abroad. If such had not been the case, Schellenberg certainly would have been denounced and destroyed in the manner then prevalent in Germany. The sober if not to say often outright critical appraisals of each other voiced during intensive interrogations after the war suggest that, in the case of Schellenberg and his staff, it was not really friendship but a spirit of reliable loyal cooperation that set the stage for the often very hazardous undertakings. Interestingly this type of working relationship does not appear to have become a risk factor when, during the final hectic months of the Nazi regime, a concern about the aftermath and their individual fate may have become important to most of the men. Instead the records show that Schellenberg was able to function until the very end, because he could rely on those around him regardless of personal character and inclinations. This held true from the earliest approaches to British and American representatives in various countries, to the rescue efforts on behalf of certain individuals over the years and to the last minute transports of large numbers of concentration camp victims to Switzerland and Scandinavia.

While it is more than likely that the difficult task of creating some kind of useful and confidential contact to the British was really his first priority in Switzerland, it was, of course, also necessary to first clear the stage by actively attending to some circumstances considered untenable by the Swiss. One such very visible problem was the so-called *Internationale Presse-Agentur* (IPA) or International Press Agency, a hate propaganda office under the control of a Swiss national of Nazi persuasion by the name of Franz Burri. Disseminating aggressive publications, Burri und his political associates, such as Ernst Leonhardt of the *Schweizer Gesellschaft der Freunde einer autoritären Demokratie* (SGAD, Swiss Association of the Friends of an Authoritarian Democracy) and Otto Alfred Lienhardt, in 1941 in Stuttgart also organized what they called the *Bund der Schweizer in Grossdeutschland* (BSG, Association of the Swiss in Greater Germany). Their immediate purpose seems to have been interference with Swiss neutrality. A long-term target was the eventual union of what they and the Germans considered the Germanic peoples of Europe, and they loudly proclaimed Adolf Hitler as their *Führer*. Some of their published views were outright offensive and directed particularly against the Swiss Chief of Staff, General Henri Guisan. The Swiss, most likely Masson or one of his men, such as Paul Meyer-Schwertenbach, contacted Hans Wilhelm Eggen and expressed their strong desire to tune down or turn off Burri's disturbing German propaganda aimed largely at their Nazi sympathizers in Switzerland. Though specific measures taken in Germany remain rather obscure, Burri apparently was persuaded to move his propaganda organization, and for awhile he operated out of Vienna, Budapest and even Zagreb. Masson himself later credited Schellenberg with having attended to the Burri problem. According to Swiss experts, Eggen's postwar claims that it was he who shut down Burri's IPA operation prior to Schellenberg taking over *Amt* VI are more than dubious. Eggen either confused dates or quite intentionally adjusted to postwar conditions by recalling his own activities on behalf of Switzerland in a more positive light.[131]

Another matter of considerable importance to the Swiss and therefore with some urgency transmitted by Masson to Schellenberg was the Gestapo arrest of Lieutenant Dr. Ernst Mörgeli in March 1942. This man, described by Edgar Bonjour as "a Swiss intelligence officer," had worked in Germany for some time. Officially he functioned as a journalist who for cover was attached as a Secretary to the Swiss Consulate in Stuttgart. His superiors in Bern were sufficiently concerned about Mörgeli's fate in German hands to earnestly consider the arrest of a German consulate official in Switzerland in order to have something to bargain with in a planned prisoner exchange.[132] Mörgeli apparently was held without trial in a prison and then transferred to a concentration camp. Schellenberg later recalled that Mörgeli had been apprehended after he had spied on German Western defenses (*Westwall*) and that he and other such prisoners were to be handed over by Gestapo Chief Müller to the much feared Nazi People's Court (*Volksgerichtshof*).[133] From that so-called German court the death penalty certainly could have followed. Schellenberg managed to extract the Swiss officer from the Gestapo, and it was

---

131. "Attestation" of Masson, May 10, 1948, NA, RG 238, Microfilm 897, Roll 114. "Bericht des Bundesrates," December 28, 1945, *Bundesblatt*, vol. 98, part 1 (January 4, 1946), 88-91, covering organizational details of Swiss-German Nazi groups. Fuhrer, *Spionage gegen die Schweiz*, 81-82, 130. Braunschweig, *Secret Channel to Berlin*, 159-160, 358-359.
132. Major Alfred Ernst (head of the German Bureau and Axis Section of Swiss military intelligence) to Roger Masson, April 19, 1942, Strictly Confidential, approved and sent on by Masson, May 7, 1942. Reproduced in Braunschweig, *Secret Channel to Berlin*, 175. Edgar Bonjour, *Geschichte der schweizerischen Neutralität*, vol. V: *1939-1945* (Basel: Helbig & Lichtenhahn, 1970), 73.
133. Some sources suggest that Mörgeli had been "sentenced to death." Clipping from a Zurich newspaper, October 22, 1945, NAK, WO 204/12814. Cf. "Final Report," 113.

on December 23, 1942, that Mörgeli suddenly found himself released and flown to Switzerland accompanied by Schellenberg's operative Eggen. When he arrived home on Christmas Eve, the overjoyed Mörgeli had no inkling what may have brought about this fortunate turn of events. General Guisan, a few days later on January 11, 1943, in a handwritten note passed on this interesting comment on Schellenberg: "[Schellenberg] has had Mörgeli freed after ten months of detention ...*without asking for anything in exchange*. [He did it] simply out of *prestige* and in order to prove that he keeps his promises [*sic*]."[134] Whatever Schellenberg's motives may have been, he had succeeded in strengthening the contact to neutral Switzerland and by the frank exhibition of what can only be labeled goodwill had considerably improved working conditions.[135]

It is difficult to arrive at some plausible appraisal of the relationship between the SS leader and the somewhat slick and nimble businessman Eggen, other than to surmise that they were able to use each other. Eggen was sufficiently intelligent to realize the profitable aspects of the connection for his own business interests and to comprehend that his work for Schellenberg at the time was also very much an insurance policy for his own personal security. Schellenberg, fully aware of the diverse business interests of Eggen, clearly preferred him to other Nazis or SS functionaries in his difficult confidential undertakings. This preference was a significant factor in such dangerous high-level contacts as those to the Swiss intelligence chief Masson or the Swiss Chief of Staff Guisan, but it was also of primary importance in risky and potentially problematic operations, such as the freeing of the American Brigadier General Arthur Vanaman. That the two men did not really like each other has nothing to do with the fact that in pursuit of their respective interests, they probably served each other very well. [136] As long as that continued to be the case, they relied on each other, knowing well that neither would gain anything by turning on the other. Suggestions that the intelligence services of Nazi Germany and Switzerland may have cooperated and that such cooperation might have been the real purpose behind the maneuvers of Schellenberg must be considered misleading.[137] First of all, there are clear indications that it was Masson who

---

134. Citing from records in the Swiss Federal Archives, Braunschweig, *Secret Channel to Berlin*, 377. For Braunschweig's own critical view *Ibid.*, 184.
135. Regarding the Mörgeli case see Fuhrer, *Spionage gegen die Schweiz*, 81, 130. Bonjour, *Geschichte der schweizerischen Neutralität*, vol. 5: *1939-1945*, 72. Braunschweig, *Secret Channel to Berlin*, 173-176, 183-184. "Attestation" of Roger Masson, May 10, 1948, NA, RG 238, Microfilm 897, Roll 114.
136. The rather critical comments on each other during postwar interrogations may have several reasons, but they do suggest certain fundamental differences. Cf. Interrogation of Hans Eggen by Norbert G. Barr, March 1948, SAN, Rep 502, E 12. DB5 to SAINT Rome, September 26, 1945, Report on Eggen, NA, RG 226, E 210, Box 503.
137. Cf. "Statement by Dr. Wilhelm Hoettl" [during postwar interrogation], NA, RG 226, E 125A, Box 2.

made certain moves to get preparations for such a meeting underway. Secondly, there is no evidence that Schellenberg at any time believed that he could deliver the Swiss service into the Nazi camp, and it would appear that such achievement, while possibly harvesting some short term appreciation from Hitler, would in no way have served the interests of Schellenberg in the long run. Other than certain advantages from an untroubled relationship and the slight chance that either side could benefit from some advance information passed on inadvertently in the course of the contacts, there was no organizational closeness or intimate cooperation between German and Swiss intelligence.[138] Even "a sort of regular interchange of information" between Schellenberg and Masson could not be carried out.[139]

What occurred, however, was a sequence of meetings between Schellenberg, the Chief of SS Foreign Intelligence, and Masson, the Chief of Swiss Military Intelligence, who in May 1942 had received photographs of massacres in Poland and freight cars loaded with corpses. How was this very strange connection possible and what was achieved? The first of these conferences took place in the town of Waldshut, not far from the border town of Laufenburg on September 8, 1942. The very risky and absolutely confidential crossing of the border had been carefully prepared to the last detail by Swiss Captain Paul Meyer-Schwertenbach and Schellenberg's man SS-*Obersturmführer* Hans Wilhelm Eggen. Yet, when Masson and Meyer-Schwertenbach, both in suits and without any identification papers, reached the 40-meter bridge across the Rhine at Laufenburg, some of the preparations obviously had gone astray. The military on both sides, watchful as they were trained to be, did not seem to care much about the secret operation or, more likely, the needed vital information had not filtered down to the men at the border. First Masson and Meyer-Schwertenbach had to overcome difficulties on the Swiss side, and after finally crossing the bridge, they were not exactly welcomed by the German border guards either. To complicate the uncomfortable situation, neither Eggen nor Schellenberg were to be seen anywhere, causing the Swiss emissaries an unplanned and somewhat worrisome wait in the station house of the German border post. Fortunately for Masson, Eggen drove up shortly, explaining that his chief had been involved in a car accident but would arrive soon. Eggen then took Masson and Meyer-Schwertenbach in his car to Waldshut some 10 kilometers down the road where Schellenberg was already expecting them at the inn of the local railroad station. Following introductory courtesies and a brief drink at the inn, the

---

138. Willi Gautschi, *General Henri Guisan* (Zurich: Verlag Neue Zürcher Zeitung, 1989), 528. Wildt, *Generation des Unbedingten*, 718.
139. "Final Report," Appendix XXI, 268. Cf. "Translation of Schellenberg's Report 96a," NAK, KV 2/98.

strange assortment of men took off for a lengthy walk in the nearby woods. We are uncertain what Masson and Schellenberg said to each other because Eggen and Meyer-Schwertenbach were walking some distance behind them. Somewhere in the woods Masson and Schellenberg sat down on a bench to continue their apparently animated conversation, but presumably here too without witnesses because their two companions most likely did not push next to them on the bench. It was about 7:30 p.m. when the four men emerged from the woods, returning to the inn to share a supper of cold cuts and Mosel wine.[140] At about 9:00 p.m. Masson and Meyer-Schwertenbach reentered Switzerland at Laufenburg and most likely considered themselves fortunate to have come out of this hazardous undertaking without personal harm or unpleasant incident.

The German records reveal little about preparations for the meeting or the contents of what must have been a rather tense conversation in the woods of Waldshut. Schellenberg's memoirs are extremely unrevealing on this unusual encounter and his limpid explanation of the background of the intermezzo does not open any vistas on his own plans or objectives. If we accept his later explanation, he had not only come to the personal conclusion that Germany might not be able to win the war, but he had also begun to carefully talk to Himmler about possible ways of contacting the Western Allies. He had actually made some attempts to establish first contacts to British representatives in Switzerland, but those in power in Berlin, particularly Foreign Minister Ribbentrop, had found his initiative totally unacceptable and in fact had gone so far as to threaten him personally. Discussing his steps in neutral Switzerland with Himmler, Schellenberg had found him withdrawing and unwilling to commit himself to support any specific action. When Schellenberg tried to shift the conversation to possibilities of employing neutral channels to pursue similar goals in the future, Himmler responded: "Well, I don't wish to know all those details—that's your responsibility." Picking it up from there, Schellenberg "decided personally to take up certain secret and long-standing service connections with Switzerland for no other purpose than to try to bring peace one step closer. I had a personal conversation with Brigadier Masson ..."[141]

After the war Captain Paul Meyer-Schwertenbach remembered that he had been involved in preparing the Waldshut encounter, that he was active in this on orders from his chief Masson and that he attended the meeting personally.

---

140. This according to Masson cited in Gautschi, *General Henri Guisan*, 528. Braunschweig, *Secret Channel to Berlin*, 180, refers to "some canned food" Eggen had brought along. On the photographs of German crimes in occupied Poland Jonathan Steinberg, *Die Deutsche Bank und ihre Goldtransaktionen während des Zweiten Weltkrieges* (Munich: Beck, 1999), 80.
141. Schellenberg, *The Schellenberg Memoirs*, 372. Schellenberg, *Memoiren*, 295-296.

The walk in the woods and the respite on the bench are not mentioned.[142] Eggen, for his part, later recalled that he had a major role in the preliminaries to the meeting and that the main topic of the two men was a possible German attack on Switzerland. In fact, the meeting had not gotten off to a good start. Possibly Masson was slightly miffed because Schellenberg was not at the border to welcome him. Maybe too, Schellenberg was initially tense because he had not quite collected himself after the car accident on the road down from Berlin. Whatever transpired on the negative side, it did not take long until the charisma of both men brought about a kind of mutual appreciation not always common to such first encounters of a dangerous nature. Masson later recalled: "The meeting with Schellenberg was extremely cordial ... I found myself across from a very fine and cultured man and the conversation therefore was very interesting ... We spoke alone, out in the open, without any witness." Having bridged whatever barriers there had been between them, including Schellenberg's comment that Masson certainly would be aware that he [Masson] was "in the top portion of Germany's list of wanted persons," the Swiss Chief of Military Intelligence quickly got to the point and Schellenberg learned why it was that he had wished to see him. Above all, Masson made it quite clear, he wanted the intelligence officer Mörgeli freed from German prison. Not surprisingly, Schellenberg seemed to have no particular objections. Making the best of the opportunity, Masson quickly added that the Swiss would also much appreciate having the hate campaign of IPA stopped, and being at it he hastened to express his wish to have Heinrich Rothmund given a visa to enter Germany and, last but not least, to finally permit Swiss citizens living in Germany to return to Switzerland for service in the armed forces." Masson had either been well informed about Schellenberg's state of mind or he had indeed captured the moment: "Without his spelling things out, it was my understanding that Schellenberg wanted to find a solution to bring the war to an end..." To make certain his conversation was understood, Masson frankly suggested that he thought Germany would not be able to achieve victory. Her 6th Army under the Supreme Command of Friedrich Paulus would have to surrender to Soviet forces, he added. Schellenberg did not seem taken aback, and in the words of Pierre Braunschweig "the Masson-Schellenberg connection was established."[143]

---

142. "Affidavit by Dr. Paul E. Meyer," May 10, 1948, SAN, Rep 501, LV, S-4.
143. Masson quoted from Gautschi, *General Henri Guisan*, 528. (Transl.) Braunschweig, *Secret Channel to Berlin*, 180-182. Schellenberg later attended to Heinrich Rothmund of Swiss Federal Police and his wish to visit Germany. Indications are that Schellenberg did not much care for the anti-Semitic Rothmund. Cf. Braunschweig, *Secret Channel to Berlin*, 166. Joseph Friedensohn, David Kranzler, *Heroine of Rescue: The Incredible Story of Recha Sternbuch Who Saved Thousands from the Holocaust* (New York: Mesorah, 1984), 30. Winfried Meyer, *Unternehmen Sieben* (Frankfurt: Hain, 1993), 317. Vernehmung Schellenberg, December 13, 1946, SAN, S-45b.

A follow-up encounter took place later that year hosted by Meyer-Schwertenbach and his apparently very sociable wife at Wolfsberg Castle near Ermatingen on the Swiss side of Lake Constance. One of the three days of his visit was shared by Masson. The meetings were extremely cordial and continued along the same line as at Waldshut in September. Schellenberg later recalled—and there is no reason to doubt this—that his real aim in these Swiss visits was to come closer to some sort of contact with representatives of the Western Allies. "... at that time I was already considering preparations towards bringing the war to an end. Masson and his colleague, Dr. Meyer were the contacts with whose help I hoped to bridge the gap either to the British or American Military attaché..." Masson, not surprisingly of course, was in no position to openly promise such contacts and instead somewhat reservedly expressed his willingness to assist Schellenberg in his "political plans." Schellenberg also went out of his way to leave the impression that he would do his part to assist in supporting Swiss neutrality.[144]

Already in March 1943 Schellenberg once again took to the road and the journey turned out to be quite a coup. Although Guisan later remembered that his meeting with the German intelligence chief was almost accidental, the highly risky encounter was, of course, well prepared by Masson, his assistant Meyer-Schwertenbach and Schellenberg's emissary Eggen. If we accept the version of Meyer-Schwertenbach, Eggen told the Swiss that Schellenberg would be willing to meet General Guisan presupposing the agreement of Hitler and Himmler. Through Eggen Schellenberg informed the Swiss that the Germans would much like to have a binding promise of Swiss neutrality. Germany would trust such a promise and in turn abstain from any intentions to occupy Switzerland. Meyer-Schwertenbach, presumably through Masson, was able to obtain a positive reaction from Guisan. Eggen took these tidings to Berlin and evidently Schellenberg obtained the needed go-ahead from Hitler as well as from Himmler. Eggen, Meyer-Schwertenbach and the Swiss police then did their best to minutely plan the journey. This was no time for snags. As a result Schellenberg and Eggen were met by Meyer-Schwertenbach and Zurich police inspector Dr. Albert Wiesendanger at the German-Swiss border town of Kreuzlingen near Constance.[145] Without any delay the Germans were rushed off to Wolfsberg Castle and their German car plates were quickly exchanged for Swiss plates, presumably to minimize public curiosity and to increase

---

144. The second meeting probably took place December 16-18, 1942, but some sources (Gautschi, *General Henri Guisan*, 529) suggest October 16-18. "Translation of Schellenberg's Report–96a," NAK, KV 2/98. Questionnaire for Schellenberg, December 30, 1946, NA, RG 263, E ZZ-16, CIA Name Files, Box 45.
145. Albert Wiesendanger (1893-1970), studied Law in Zurich and Berlin, later high-ranking police official in various functions. More detail in Braunschweig, *Secret Channel to Berlin*, 380-381.

Schellenberg's personal security. After the Venlo incident there had even been some concern that Schellenberg in turn could be kidnapped by British intelligence.

For those interested in the real reasons for the quickly organized meeting at Wolfsberg Castle, the records are not very rewarding. There are some indications that Eggen had become seriously irritated by the extreme close surveillance of his person by Swiss intelligence. He wanted this stopped or rather not constantly be made aware of it. He actually lodged complaints with Meyer-Schwertenbach and police inspector Wiesendanger. In view of the tense situation between Nazi Germany and Switzerland and citizens of each country still living in the other, it can be presumed that Swiss surveillance of Eggen became somewhat less visible. Other than such incidentals, much of the discussion at Wolfsberg Castle on March 2, 1943, must have centered on Swiss declarations of their intent to defend their neutrality against any intruder, as well as on German declarations of full respect for Swiss neutrality.[146]

The next morning saw them drive off to Zurich to meet up with Masson. In the afternoon the group traveled on to Bern where rooms at the Hotel Bellevue had been reserved in advance, naturally without identifying the guests. "Schelli," as Masson and Meyer-Schwertenbach had come to call Schellenberg among themselves, as often did not feel well and suffered from what he explained was a badly upset stomach. However, there was no respite. Dinner with General Guisan was planned at the Hotel Bären in Biglen, a short drive from Bern. At the hotel, well known for its excellent food, dinner for six was served in a separate room. After dessert there was Moët et Chandon, followed by two hours of private, unwitnessed exchange between Guisan and Schellenberg. What exactly was said in that confidential atmosphere behind closed doors remains a matter of conjecture and strewn about small bits of information. We may assume that the two men accepted and trusted each other as much as can be expected in a meeting of high ranking military personnel who were not personally acquainted. Their exchange evidently, among other things, covered the German fear that Switzerland might give in to the Allies and the Swiss fear that Germany might consider a preventive attack. Undoubtedly, the German discovery in 1940 of the so-called Charité documents played into the motivations behind this very serious conversation.

In 1940 on the tracks of the train station of La Charité-sur-Loire German troops had captured a trainload of French army headquarters' documents. Among these highly confidential papers German officers discovered a convention regulating the entry of French forces into Switzerland in case of a

---

146. Gautschi, *General Henri Guisan*, 538. Braunschweig, *Secret Channel to Berlin*, 380.

German attack. Clearly these records implied certain specific qualities of Swiss neutrality not necessarily acceptable to the Germans. In addition, it was evident from the records that General Guisan was fully informed and indeed had participated in these apparently somewhat unneutral Swiss dealings with the French. The enemies of the Swiss Chief of Staff naturally had their day, and Guisan could do little but try to minimize the harm done to Switzerland and, of course, to himself. The Germans, incidentally, did not overreact to the Charité documents in 1940 or later, and the Swiss must have been pleased with the low-key resonance from Berlin. Schellenberg, of course, knew of the vulnerability of Guisan and evidently drew this card to pressure the Swiss Chief of Staff.[147]

Schellenberg did come to the point. He very unceremoniously requested a written document from the Swiss Chief of Staff, clearly stating that Switzerland would without any reservations defend itself against any attack regardless of the intruder. Guisan understood and delivered such a statement in person just a couple of days later. While the Swiss worked out the text of the document, Meyer-Schwertenbach, his wife Patricia, Eggen and Schellenberg drove out to Arosa, the well-known resort in Graubünden, where Guisan had to attend to an official function and was to meet up with them. On March 6, 1942, Guisan arrived at the Hotel Excelsior where Schellenberg had checked in as Dr. Bergh. The handwritten statement was presented to Schellenberg in the course of a brief meeting of the two men. The contents of the extremely short paper were absolutely to the point and left no room for misunderstandings: "The balance [of power] in Europe requires Switzerland to be neutral toward all sides and in every respect ... We are aware that our country's sovereignty depends on whether this conviction is abandoned or slackens. Therefore all Swiss ... are perfectly willing to sacrifice everything in order to defend their independence and honor. Whoever invades our country is our enemy ... This statement will remain unshakeable and unchangeable ... There is no room for any doubt about that, neither today nor tomorrow." That was exactly what Schellenberg had wanted to take with him, and he had reasons to be pleased with the results of the entire risky operation. Whether the text of the document was of great political significance is quite another question, but one that may not have been of primary concern to Schellenberg at the time.[148]

---

147. Regarding the Charité documents see undated MS and article excerpt from Major General Ulrich Liss in Bonjour, *Geschichte der schweizerischen Neutralität*, vol. 7: *1939-1945*, 63-67.
148. German text, dated March 3, 1943, in Gautschi, *General Henri Guisan*, 545, naming as source a copy in Swiss Federal Archives with handwritten addition by Guisan: "La défense de notre neutralité est un engagement d'honneurs auquel nous ne faillirons pas ..." English translation in Braunschweig, *Secret Channel to Berlin*, 195. On the dinner at the Hotel Bären Gautschi, *General Henri Guisan*, 540-541 (also detailed dinner bill).

More meaningful in some ways may have been the lengthy discussions between the two men after the party had left Arosa, met up with Masson in Zurich and returned to less hectic environs of Wolfsberg Castle. Meyer-Schwertenbach took notes on what Masson told him about the meeting, and there seem to be no important reasons to doubt what he wrote down. Both Guisan and Schellenberg considered their talks at Biglen and Arosa to have been successful steps in the right direction, but Guisan also clearly registered that the Germans still grossly underestimated the extensive military reserves of Soviet Russia and, possibly of greater interest for the Guisan/Masson-Schellenberg line, that Schellenberg was no "optimist" or, one might add, that Schellenberg did not believe in German victory.[149]

When it was time to leave, the Chief of Swiss Military Intelligence very personally accompanied the Germans to the border, making certain that they could depart from Swiss territory without being checked. Schellenberg rushed back to Berlin and attempted to compose the appropriate reports and to obtain the needed support in important quarters. He later remembered that it was the statement from Guisan that helped him persuade the wily Himmler "of the genuine intentions of Switzerland to remain neutral." In fact, Schellenberg who by 1943 had come to know Himmler much better and to some degree had gained the latter's confidence—as much as that was ever possible—reports that he was able to turn Himmler into "an outspoken partisan of his standpoint" and to win his support against those who had little concern for Swiss neutrality and worked against his personal lines to Switzerland. He felt that Himmler would go a long way to support him but that Ribbentrop would be on the lookout for any opportunity to interfere in his Swiss dealings.[150] A "Memorandum for the Führer" signed by Ribbentrop in Fuschl, his Austrian estate, on June 22, 1943, clearly shows that Schellenberg had informed the Foreign Minister about the Swiss undertaking and the specific results of his meeting with General Guisan. Documents of the German Foreign Office also establish that Otto Karl Köcher, Nazi Germany's Minister at the Legation in Bern, felt excluded from Schellenberg's operations in Switzerland and, as the official German representative to that nation, requested to be informed to an extent hardly helpful in the difficult business of a strictly confidential intelligence line.[151] Köcher who was playing his own not always transparent games in Switzerland actually went so far as to demand to be informed about

---

149. Diary of Meyer-Schwertenbach, March 6, 1943, Swiss Federal Archives, quoted in Braunschweig, *Secret Channel to Berlin*, 196.
150. "Final Report," Appendix XII, 271. "Translation of Schellenberg's Report–96a," NAK, KV 2/98. Cf. Bob [Blum] to Dear Allan [sic] [Dulles], October 9, 1945, NA, RG 226, E 106, Box 13.
151. Ribbentrop to Hitler, June 22, 1943. Köcher to Foreign Office, October 1, 1943, and October 7, 1943, both Confidential, PA, AA, R 100692.

Schellenberg's meeting with the Swiss Chief of Staff. When he found out that there was someone called Senner having to do with the travel contacts between Bern and Berlin, he wanted to be told who that was. Since Schellenberg had his own informants in Ribbentrop's Foreign Office, he heard about Köcher's interferences and must not have felt inclined to share his Swiss operations with this quarrelsome Minister.[152]

To increase the tension of those concerned, the Wiking (Viking) line, a Swiss intelligence source apparently very well placed in Berlin, transmitted the worrisome news to Bern that Germany could be on the brink of acting militarily against Switzerland in order to put an end to the undesirable or unhelpful neutrality of that country. What later found its way into history books as the "Märzalarm" (March alarm) had rung. Bernard Barbey, chief of Masson's personal staff, noted on March 20, 1943, that "Fall Schweiz" (Case Switzerland), according to Wiking, was again being given serious consideration by the *Oberkommando der Wehrmacht* (OKW, Supreme Command of the Armed Forces). Barbey, of course, was aware that Erwin Rommel's much propagandized *Afrikakorps* (Africa Corps) was defeated, that the Germans had occupied what had been unoccupied France, and that German advances in Soviet Russia had been stopped. Would the German troops still massed in Austria and Bavaria invade a weakening Italy to save the day? Or would they grab another piece of Europe like Switzerland to reinforce their *Festung Europa* (fortress Europe)? Whether the Germans suddenly had actually decided on an attack on neutral Switzerland or whether such action was as before just a matter of discussion among those in power in Berlin, but now was used as a menacing threat by someone such as Schellenberg, remains an uncertain and complex speculative topic. Whatever the case, Schellenberg did not miss the opportunity to polish his standing with the Swiss contacts by assuring them shortly thereafter that the danger had been removed and a German invasion was no longer imminent.[153]

That the Germans continued to be very much interested in the Swiss line can be seen in the somewhat bumptious attempt to bring Roger Masson to Berlin in mid-1943. The invitation does not appear to have originated with Schellenberg, for no other reason than his understandable disinclination to

---

152. Dr. Otto Karl Köcher, born 1884 in the Alsace, suicide 1945 in American internment camp. Studied Law, joined Foreign Office 1912, NSDAP 1934, since 1937 Minister in Berne, expelled from Switzerland 1945, arrested by American C.I.C. at Chiasso when leaving Switzerland. Cf. Keipert, Grupp, eds., *Biographisches Handbuch des deutschen Auswärtigen Dienstes 1871-1945*, vol. 2, 573-574. See "Report on Dr. Otto Koecher," August 30, 1945, NA, RG 59, E 1082, Box 2.
153. Regarding the "Märzalarm," cf. Gautschi, *General Henri Guisan*, 563. Fuhrer, *Spionage gegen die Schweiz*, 82-86.

share his lines to Masson and Guisan. Meetings of Masson with Himmler and other political Nazi leaders, Schellenberg certainly knew, would have destroyed the very personal character of his Swiss line. Moreover, Schellenberg was fully aware that his encounters with Guisan had brought forth rather critical reactions in some top echelons in Switzerland, and he could have no desire to further damage his contacts.[154]

The final act of Schellenberg's very personal participation in this productive *Sonderlinie* (special intelligence line) was his last journey to Switzerland in October 1943 when he spent three days at Paul Meyer-Schwertenbach's Wolfsberg Castle. In some ways it was a typical Schellenberg reaction to a crisis, in this case one others had caused, namely the rejection of a German invitation to Masson, first to come to the Nazi capital and, when that was turned down, to just about any place in Germany. He does not seem to have been someone who would just accept defeat. Instead, as often in the course of his short life, he did what he had decided should be done and in the process at times took defeat and punishment, often without visible regard for his staff and even his family. In this particular situation, working under great stress in Berlin as well as in various risky international operations, he does not really seem to have comprehended that Roger Masson had already stepped over the generally accepted limits of his position as Chief of Swiss Military Intelligence and had paid a professional and personal price for allowing himself to participate in this covert connection.[155] What Schellenberg did not know was the fact that the Office of Strategic Services (OSS) somewhere along the line had closed in on Schellenberg's *Sonderlinie* to Masson. In early 1944 the Americans were observing "a perilously close association between Masson, the head of Swiss G-2, and Schellenberg of the Gestapo [*sic*]." While the records indicate that Masson always kept General Guisan posted on his contacts with the Germans, Allen Dulles and his OSS apparently even in the spring of 1944 still thought that Guisan was uninformed about the supposedly clandestine line to Schellenberg.[156]

From Schellenberg's perspective the final encounter at Wolfsberg Castle apparently had a dual purpose. During his interrogations after the war Schellenberg emphasized that he thought it was necessary to again strongly assure the Swiss of the German intention to respect Swiss neutrality. Indeed, he was able to inform Masson that he had personally obtained the specific

---

154. On the German attempt to lure Masson to Berlin see "Attestation," May 10, 1948, for Masson's point of view. NA, RG 238, Microfilm 897, Roll 114.
155.. Cf. Gautschi, *General Henri Guisan*, 669-670.
156 OSS Bern to OSS for Director, March 15, 1944, NA, RG 226, E A1-170 (210), Box 469. Schellenberg, of course, since 1941 is not Gestapo (Secret State Police) but *Amt* VI Foreign Intelligence. A very common error in many documents and publications.

confirmation of this German policy from Himmler himself. The other purpose of his journey to see Masson personally was his and Himmler's absolute conviction of Germany's need to keep the Swiss in a friendly disposition, thereby reinforcing their desire to stay neutral. Following the defeat of Germany's Africa Corps in Tunisia, the successful landings of Allied forces in Italy, and—to crown it all—the collapse of Mussolini's fascist regime, Switzerland had gained a new strategic significance and the more sagacious political and military leaders in Berlin were aware of it. Some of those leaders in Berlin would have solved the problem simply by invading Switzerland and while they were at it gaining the use of the Swiss transport system, meaning the railroads and tunnels, for the forthcoming confrontation with the Allied forces heading north. However, there were also those in Berlin who thought they might need the neutral ground of Switzerland to meet with representatives of the Western Allies and in spite of the Casablanca decision discuss possible conditions of a German surrender. Schellenberg and Himmler were important voices in that group.[157]

If all previous incidents and developments had been handled in a more or less covert manner, there was one unforeseen event which by its very nature was somewhat public. It had all the markings of an explosive crisis and clearly required more than incidental encounters and confidential conversation. On April 29, 1944, a German jet of the type Messerschmitt ME 110 Cg + EN had made an emergency landing at the airfield at Dübendorf near Zurich. In contrast to numerous previous landings of other German planes in Switzerland this fighter was a late model with some of the newest equipment the Germans had available. Allied intelligence undoubtedly would have wanted to take a closer look at this German plane. By the same token the Germans could not really allow this Messerschmitt to fall into the hands of the enemy. Interestingly and maybe indicative of the quality and usefulness of the diplomatic representatives in this case, the precarious situation was not handled by diplomats, such as the German Minister Otto Köcher. Instead the negotiations were left to Schellenberg who, of course, commissioned his Swiss expert Eggen with the unpleasantly risky assignment. Eggen had excellent and, more important, actually working connections to both the Chief of Military Intelligence Masson and the Chief of Staff Guisan. It is of little relevance whether these two Swiss military leaders liked Schellenberg's man, but it is of immeasurable importance that they had worked with him and knew that he could be relied upon. There would be no slippery dealings. Apparently

---

157. There are few accounts of the final encounter at Wolfsberg Castle. "Final Report," 130-131. "First Detailed Interrogation Report on Sturmbannführer Hans Wilhelm Eggen," Secret, December 1, 1945, NA, RG 263, E A1-86, Box 9. "Translation of Schellenberg's Report–96a," NAK, KV 2/98.

Schellenberg sent a highly confidential message to Guisan, explaining the absolute necessity to keep this Messerschmitt ME 110 and all its contents out of the hands of the Allies, and he appealed to the principles of Swiss neutrality as discussed during the controversial meetings between them. Guisan who had not really recovered yet from the harsh criticism emanating from influential Swiss quarters concerning his previous encounters with Schellenberg, nevertheless decided to take on this new task. Not surprising though, he proceeded with the greatest possible care. As far as outside impressions were concerned, unwanted observers might even have concluded that the Swiss-German negotiations were led by the Swiss Military Attaché in Berlin, Major Peter Burckhardt. On the German side, Eggen could, of course, have no interest in damaging his good working lines to Switzerland, and he was extremely motivated therefore to ferret out some civil solution to this conflict.

The alternatives considered back in Berlin were ill foreboding indeed. There was the possibility of invading Swiss air space and bombing the Messerschmitt, risking considerable ground damage beyond the target and, of course, accepting a serious violation of Swiss neutrality. The other alternative which actually appears to have been seriously discussed in detail was the parachuting of a sabotage unit of Otto Skorzeny's men into Dübendorf where they would then proceed to blow up the German fighter.[158] The consequences of such an attack, including the likely confrontation with Swiss armed forces on the ground, are not difficult to imagine. Instead Hans Wilhelm Eggen with the assistance of a great number of persons on both sides managed to negotiate a package that served Switzerland and Germany and, most important, prevented a brutal German military intervention.

From the scant reports available, one is led to conclude that Eggen had been given full authority by Schellenberg, but that the situation was so thoroughly twisted that he was forced to leave safe grounds and consent to stipulations he was most likely not quite authorized to make. Eggen ended up agreeing that the Messerschmitt ME 110 would be destroyed at the airfield of Dübendorf and that Germany in return would deliver to Switzerland twelve Messerschmitt ME 109.[159] Fortunately for him—and it might be added, for Schellenberg—this deal found sufficient support in both Switzerland and Germany. Eggen was permitted to return to Switzerland with the explosives aboard his plane. In the presence of Eggen, the German flight captain Brandt, the Swiss Colonel Rihner, the Swiss Colonel Brigadier Karl von Wattenwyl, the

---

158. "Final Report," 146. The date given here, however, is incorrect.
159. Gautschi, *General Henri Guisan*, 564, speaks of 12 planes. "Final Report," 147, mentions 6 planes. Fuhrer, *Spionage gegen die Schweiz*, 354, writes of 12 planes at a total price of Swiss Francs 6,000,000. He adds that the sale had actually been agreed on prior to World War II.

Swiss Chief of Military Intelligence Masson and his assistant Meyer-Schwertenbach, the explosives were taken to the plane and lit with gasoline. Thus in view of these witnesses the Messerschmitt ME 110 with its equipment and ammunition was destroyed on May 18, 1944. It was a solution acceptable to all,[160] and the twelve Messerschmitt ME 109G were delivered to the Dübendorf airfield only two days later on May 20, 1944. Probably of little historical significance but nevertheless a curiosity in the context of the merciless war year 1944 and the continuing mass murder committed by Germans at home and in the occupied regions: The Swiss officers gave a festive dinner in honor of Schellenberg's emissary Hans Wilhelm Eggen.[161]

While there can be no doubt that Schellenberg's *Sonderlinie* to Masson and thereby to the Swiss Chief of Staff General Guisan was his most sophisticated operation in Switzerland, it must be remembered that the country, because of its neutrality and its very central location, served as an ideal arena for a great variety of international contacts. Such contacts, incidentally not always fully reflected in the records, at times could transcend apparent boundaries between different intelligence services and German interest groups. One of the German agents often mentioned but seldom clearly positioned was Hans Christian Daufeldt. He was neither liked nor much trusted by his chief Schellenberg, but he had been around the Berlin head office sufficiently long to have acquired some powerful protectors and even received assignments from Heydrich himself.[162] Often referred to as Schellenberg's permanent representative he was first installed in Geneva in the summer of 1942 and one week later moved to Lausanne under the cover of Vice Consul. His job list included building a network of agents to be used to spy on Allied representatives in Switzerland, collecting information on Swiss trade with the Allies, keeping an eye on the activities of Germany's allies Italy and Japan and, of course, observing very closely the many German exiles now living in Switzerland. An additional task was an attempt to set up a post-occupation net of agents in France and to connect it with the German network in Switzerland. Being attached to a German Consulate, he certainly enjoyed a broad spectrum of diplomatic and resident privileges largely unknown to traveling operatives, such as Eggen or Jahnke. Daufeldt and Eggen clearly did keep in touch, and one can easily

---

160. Eduard von Steiger, Federal Councillor and well-known Swiss politican, for instance, accused Masson of occupying himself with matters outside his responsibility as intelligence chief. Heinrich Rothmund, Chief of Police Section of Dept. of Justice and Police, tried repeatedly to prevent Eggen from obtaining entry visas for Switzerland.
161. Good treatment of Dübendorf incident in Gautschi, *General Henri Guisan*, 563-567.
162. Heydrich in October 1938 named Daufeldt as "SS-Adjutant" to Konrad Henlein, the leader of the Sudeten German Party. Heydrich to Jost, October 4, 1938, Fuhrer, *Spionage gegen die Schweiz*, 127. Regarding previous German landings in Switzerland, *Bericht des Kommandanten der Flieger- und Fliegerabwehrtruppen an den Oberbefehlshaber der Armee über den Aktivdienst 1939-1945*. (Swiss publ. without publ. data.)

imagine how the always transient Eggen may have needed some stabilizing assistance from the resident "diplomat" Daufeldt. Otherwise Daufeldt and his contacts, in spite of the recommendations in his personnel file, seem to have done little more than attend to the needs of some pro-German or pro-Nazi groups in Switzerland. This again would not be of special interest were it not that Schellenberg had reached the conclusion, known to his staff in *Amt* VI, that propaganda on behalf of Germany and all connections with pro-German underground groups in Switzerland were useless and of no help in his intelligence undertakings. As already pointed out, in line with this view he had actually instructed the *Amt* VI agents to refrain from any such activities.

Allied intelligence agents in a postwar report put it this way: "Daufeldt has been variously described as a playboy, a nincompoop, and a fool."[163] Schellenberg probably would have fully agreed with that appraisal, but one wonders why he let him go to Switzerland to begin with, and more, why he did not call him back to Berlin before Swiss authorities finally requested his removal in March 1945.[164] His apparent successor was SS-*Obersturmführer* Dr. Gustav Adolf Sonnenhol who according to some records took up his work in Switzerland already in December 1944. Prior to his departure to Switzerland, as a Vice Consul in Geneva, Sonnenhol made an agreement with SS-*Standartenführer* Eugen Steimle, Chief of Group VI B in Schellenberg's *Amt* VI to send him copies of reports he would be transmitting to the German Foreign Office. Indeed, some of the information would bypass the Foreign Office and go only to Steimle.[165] This arrangement was not surprising as "he was, in effect, looked upon as the chief liaison man between the Foreign Office and Amt VI" and "all requests of Amt VI for absorption of intelligence officers into the diplomatic service, etc., had to be submitted to him." Schellenberg learned from SS-*Sturmbannführer* Eberhard Reichel, a *Legationsrat* with the German Foreign Office, that the reports from Sonnenhol contained leads regarding possible contacts to French circles. As Sonnenhol had a personal connection to Germany's long-time Gestapo expert in Paris, Helmut Knochen, his information on possible French contacts could have been of some interest. But

---

163. SAINT London to SAINT Washington, October 26, 1945, Secret, NA, RG 263, E ZZ-16, Box 45.
164. Regarding Daufeldt, DB 5 to SAINT Rome, September 26, 1945, Secret, NA, RG 263, Entry ZZ-16, Box 45. OSS Mission for Germany to SAINT Washington, August 3, 1945, Secret, NA, RG 226, E 108A, Box 287. "Sixth Detailed Interrogation Report on SS Sturmbannführer Huegel, Dr. Klaus," June 21, 1945, Top Secret, NA, RG 226, E 174, Box 39. — Schellenberg and Daufeldt were on a first name basis which suggests a past or present close relationship.
165. Eugen Steimle (1909-1987), seventh child of a farmer, studied History to become a teacher, various SD assignments, in charge of *Sonderkommandos* (special commands) of *Einsatzgruppe B* (special task force in Eastern European occupied areas), since February 1943 chief of Group VI B of *Amt* VI, sentenced to death 1948, sentence commuted to life 1951, shortly thereafter released and employed as teacher. "Final Interrogation Report," December 12, 1945, Secret, NAK, KV 3/114. Kahn, *Hitler's Spies*, 265, refers to Steimle as "one of the most capable and gifted of [*Amt*] VI group leaders."

they were "pidgeon-holed" at the Foreign Office, and Schellenberg ordered Reichel to make Sonnenhol report to Berlin. The endgame, however, was already on, and Schellenberg later recalled that he saw no further signs of life from either Reichel or Sonnenhol. After the fall of Nazi Germany Sonnenhol tried to stay in Switzerland and left no stone unturned to prevent deportation. In July 1945 he even contacted Allen Dulles personally, explaining that he "had no direct connection with Schellenberg since I do not belong to the SD or to the Abwehr, but am an official in the Foreign Office." He emphasized his supposed anti-Nazi position and underlined his engagement for a quick end of the war. The Americans, however, who had already kept an eye on him when he was posted as Vice Consul at the German Consulate General in Casablanca had come to the conclusion that he was working for the SD both in Casablanca and Geneva and consequently felt little inclination to respond to his theatrics. As a result he was, like other Nazi officials, expelled from Switzerland and captured by American forces in Chiasso in late July 1945.[166]

The last emissary from Schellenberg's *Amt* VI to continue Daufeldt's work in Switzerland was Dr. Count Christoph von Dönhoff, brother of Countess Marion Dönhoff who during the war ran the family's estates in East Prussia and in postwar Germany as Chief Editor of the influential weekly *Die Zeit* became a powerful media personality. Count Dönhoff had gone to Kenya as a young man and from there joined the NSDAP before returning to Germany in 1939. Whatever his connections to the Foreign Office may have been, contrary to some records he did not obtain a position at the Wilhelmstrasse, but instead was assigned to the offices of the *Auslandsorganisation* (foreign organization of the NSDAP, AO) in Paris where he served as *Rechtsreferent* (legal expert) and eventually became involved in the interrogation of Allied POWs on behalf of Schellenberg's *Amt* VI. After being trained by SS-*Obersturmbannführer* Dr. Theodor Päffgen and SS-*Standartenführer* Eugen Steimle with Group VI D in Berlin and Waldburg, Schellenberg sent Dönhoff off to Zurich where he arrived on March 28, 1945. Thanks to the full support of the Foreign Office, particularly State Secretary Baron Adolf Steengracht von Moyland, Dönhoff was given a cover position as Vice Consul.

---

166. Gustav Adolf Sonnenhol (1912-1988), a farmer's son, studied Law, joined SA 1930, member of NSDAP 1930, Nazi activist as student in Berlin, joined SS as Obersturmführer 1939. A.F.H.Q., PF 602, 448 Sonnenhol, Adolf, Secret, NA, RG 226, E 119A, Box 39. "Final Report," Appendix XXIII, 330-331. "Final Interrogation Report" Eugen Steimle alias Dr. Hermann Bulach, 307th C.I.C. Detachment, December 12, 1945, Secret, NAK, KV 2/966. "Liquidation Report No. 7," Amt VI of the RSHA, Secret, NA, RG 226, E 109, Box 45. Cf. amazing "Oral History Interview with Dr. Gustav Adolf Sonnenhol," May 14, 1964, conducted in Bonn by Philip C. Brooks for Harry S. Truman Library, Independence, MO. In postwar Germany Sonnenhol held important government and Foreign Office positions. Hans-Jürgen Döscher, *Das Auswärtige Amt im Dritten Reich: Diplomatie im Schatten der "Endlösung"* (Berlin: Siedler, 1987), 287.

From the records, Count Dönhoff's only activity worth mentioning seems to have been his involvement in the so-called Seth Case. SS-*Obersturmführer* Ernst Schüddekopf later told Allied interrogators that Dönhoff had informed him that the Englishman "with a knowledge of Baltic languages" had parachuted into Estonia, but unable to recover his second parachute carrying a radio and supplies had surrendered to the Germans and apparently volunteered to work for them. As Count Dönhoff told the story, Seth was then posted in Paris with the *Abwehr*. As it happened, Ronald Seth, a British "intelligence analyst during [the] Russo-Finnish War" from 1939 to 1940 and a member of the Special Operations Executive (SOE) in 1941 survived all close calls and lived to write a number of books, some of them on intelligence. According to his own version of events, he joined SOE in January 1942 and was dropped over Estonia in October of that year. Following his capture by the Germans, he was interrogated, tortured and sent to public execution in Tallinn. Instead he was taken to Frankfurt for further maltreatment and from there shipped to Paris to be trained in the transmission of coded messages. If we can believe Seth, the Nazis had planned to send him to England "to transmit meteorological information" to occupied France. As it was, he found himself placed in a POW camp near Brunswick to spy on fellow British officers. When these officers suspected the nature of his activities, his life suddenly seemed to be in danger and someone from *Amt* VI came to rescue him. Again, according to his own version, he was taken to see Heinrich Himmler on April 1, 1945, and instructed to "carry to London a peace feeler from Himmler." Seth claims to have accepted the assignment and to have been freed into Liechtenstein on April 12 or 13. As he tells it, he was "refused access to Churchill." While available records do not contain any helpful substantiation, it is entirely possible that Count Dönhoff handled Seth at some stage, as his story told to Schüddekopf would suggest.[167]

Whether Dönhoff was able to take any steps in neutral Switzerland to contact French military representatives, an assignment he later claimed to have been given, would seem more than doubtful. His late arrival in Zurich would rather suggest that very little of any significance was accomplished during the brief span of time left until the final demise of the Third Reich. Later comments by Walter Schellenberg as well as Count Dönhoff's replies to his

---

167. Dr. Count Christoph von Dönhoff (1906-1992), to Kenya 1929, joined NSDAP from Africa, back to Germany 1939, interrogations of Allied POWs, with his sister Countess Marion Dönhoff in editorial office of *Die Zeit* 1945-1948. Dönhoff's own biographical information in *Wer ist wer: The German Who's Who*, vol. 25, 1986-1987 (Lübeck: Schmidt Römhild, 1986), 245. Liquidation Report No. 7, Amt VI of the RSHA, Gruppe VI B, Secret, NA, RG 263, E A1-87, Box 3. NAK, WO 204/12814. SAINT London to SAINT Washington, October 29, 1945, Secret, NA, RG 226, E 125, Box 28. Ronald Seth, *Encyclopedia of Espionage* (London: New English Library, 1972), 568-572. Dorril, *A Who's Who of the British Secret State*, 88.

interrogators and the Count's unguarded conversation while being recorded during internment do not suggest any remarkable activities. Schellenberg, incidentally, met with Count Dönhoff before the latter departed for Switzerland and apparently spoke to him with a frankness uncommon in Germany at the time. Dönhoff "was told to watch out for the tendency, as sometimes expressed in high Nazi circles, of leaving the future of Germany to Russia." Dönhoff recalled later that "Schellenberg regarded such thinking as dangerous and ordered … [him] to observe this trend in Switzerland and to counteract it." Following the collapse of Nazi Germany Count Dönhoff like many others insisted that he had no connections to the SD. The Swiss, however, were less gullible than he thought, expelled him from the country and as with other Nazi officials handed him over to American forces in Northern Italy in June 1945.[168]

Not all of Schellenberg's emissaries to Switzerland, however, were of the adventurous sort and in some cases the label agent does not really seem to fit. One such man with whom Schellenberg had lengthy risky conversations concerning his serious doubts about the outcome of the war was the psychiatrist Dr. Wilhelm Bitter. He had met him through Professor Maximinian de Crinis, his friend who held the Chair for Psychiatry at the University of Berlin and was a Director at the famous Charité Hospital. Schellenberg was much taken by the philosophical thoughts of Dr. Bitter who, he recalled later, was concerned with the "faults of the German character" and the search for remedies such as "the rebirth of the Christian soul." As Schellenberg, like many Germans, in conformity with Nazi ideology had left the Catholic Church in which he was raised, one is curious to know what he may have discussed with Dr. Bitter. He became aware that Dr. Bitter, who was almost twenty years his senior, had at least indirect connections to William Temple, the Archbishop of Canterbury, and to Carl Gustav Jung, the well-known Swiss psychologist. Apparently Schellenberg hoped that the psychiatrist could be used to establish totally fresh lines to Britain which eventually might lead to more real possibilities of negotiating an end to the war. As Dr. Bitter remembered it later, he had run into serious problems when trying to obtain the needed German exit permits in order to travel to Switzerland to join his family there during semester break. Professor de Crinis, with whom Dr. Bitter worked as an assistant at the university, had sent him to talk to Schellenberg who seems to have been able to get him the needed papers. Not being aware of who Schellenberg really was, Dr. Bitter in the course of their first meeting

---

168. Secretly recorded conversation, Report CSDIC/CMF/X 187, July 9, 1945, Top Secret, NAK, WO 204/11505. Fuhrer, *Spionage gegen die Schweiz*, 128.

apparently dropped all pretense and told Schellenberg about what he knew of the negative reactions to Nazi Germany in other countries. If Bitter can be trusted—and there seems to be no reason to doubt his word—he went to Switzerland and had conversations with a number of people who would pass on Schellenberg's views. Upon his return to Berlin, Bitter strongly emphasized to Schellenberg that the German evacuation of Western European countries, such as The Netherlands, Belgium, France, Denmark and Norway, was seen by his contacts as an absolute precondition to any talks about ending the war. As Bitter recalls, Schellenberg appeared to be somewhat holding back but generally prepared to broach the matter with Himmler and Hitler. While Schellenberg did not elaborate on this during interrogations after the war, Bitter remembers that he told him that Himmler had reacted positively, but that Hitler during a meeting with Himmler, which was attended by Schellenberg, had turned down any suggestions of this nature. When Bitter returned to Switzerland, he learned that the respective openings for negotiations had disappeared. In July 1943 Dr. Bitter again was able to travel to Switzerland and this time decided to stay. He later recalled that in 1944 he received a message from Schellenberg asking him to come to Germany. Bitter replied that chances for a negotiated peace were now nil and that at present he was ill and therefore regrettably in no condition to travel. Whether he actually sent a further message to Schellenberg, suggesting that an "overthrow of Hitler" might be a way out for Germany, cannot be ascertained. Schellenberg's suggestion that he received such a message through Daufeldt, however, does seem of some interest for it would clearly indicate that the psychiatrist was given a connection to the permanent representative of *Amt* VI in Switzerland. In view of the postwar academic status of Professor Bitter, this very personal short-term line into Switzerland is an indication of Schellenberg's own critical view of the system he served, not to mention of his willingness to take considerable risks in the pursuit of such ideas.[169]

Besides these somewhat unorthodox activities of the psychiatrist, Schellenberg early on also initiated what would appear to be quite traditional approaches to British diplomats stationed in neutral Switzerland. While the exact origins of the contacts between Nazi emissaries and British representatives still remain slightly blurred, some of the early encounters seem to go back to the operations of British Group Captain Malcolm Grahame

---

169. Wilhelm Bitter (1893-1974), in some records erroneously referred to as Hitter or Bueter, trained in Business and International Law, switched to Psychiatry. Professional stays in Switzerland, England and the U.S. In 1948 he headed a group of psychiatrists founding the Institute of Psychotherapy in Stuttgart, since 1971 called Academy for Psychoanalysis and Analytical Psychotherapy. Dr. med. et Dr. phil. Wilhelm Bitter, Statement under Oath, May 24, 1948, SAN, Rep. 501, LV, S-4. Internet data from Psychoanalytisches Institut Stuttgart e.V. (2007).

Christie and his already mentioned meeting with Prince Max Egon zu Hohenlohe-Langenburg in 1939. The wealthy Austrian aristocrat with a Liechtenstein passport had then communicated his opinion that it was not too late for Britain and Germany to seek a common ground from which to negotiate current differences and eventually arrive at results agreeable to both nations.[170] Group Captain Christie had studied engineering at Aachen, had served in the Royal Flying Corps in World War I, had been Britain's Air Attaché in Berlin from 1927 to 1930, and had created excellent personal ties to powerful names in German business and politics. Among Christie's acquaintances were such men as Hermann Göring, himself a fighter pilot in World War I, the industrialist Robert Bosch, the Mayor of Leipzig and major figure in the anti-Nazi underground Carl Goerdeler, the decidedly anti-Nazi diplomats Erich and Theodor Kordt, the former news correspondent in London Klop Ustinov,[171] the Secretary of the German Legation in The Hague Wolfgang Gans Edler Herr zu Putlitz,[172] and the diplomat and later Ambassador to the Court of St. James Hans Heinrich Herwarth von Bittenfeld.[173] Christie, while less affluent than Prince Hohenlohe and therefore not quite as personally connected to Europe's real or so-called social elite, certainly knew all the right people in Britain and even informed the British Foreign Office as well as Sir Robert Vansittart who ran what might be called his private intelligence agency in London.[174] In late 1939 Prince Hohenlohe let it be known that he was in touch with Hermann Göring personally and that

---

170. Prince Max Egon Maria zu Hohenlohe-Langenburg (1897-1968), married Maria de la Piedad Iturbide y Scholtz 1921, considerable property holdings in Southeastern Europe, Spain and Mexico, Skoda representative, in his intelligence activities relations with several services and personalities in different nations. Close connections with Germany's *Amt* VI and the OSS in Switzerland where he was referred to as Mr. Paul.
171. Klop Ustinov (1892-1962), of Russian/German parentage, served in German Army in World War I, joined London office of Wolffs Telegraphisches Büro (WTB, later Deutsches Nachrichtenbüro/DNB). When Germans insisted on proof of "Aryan" descent, he parted ways with them, worked for Vansittart, eventually joined MI5. Code name U 35. Much of his work was directed against Germany and the U.S.S.R. Assisted Wolfgang zu Putlitz escaping from The Hague to London. Stephen Dorril, *MI6: Fifty Years of Special Operations* (London: Fourth Estate, 2000), 407-408, 418-420. Nigel West, ed., *The Guy Liddell Diaries*, vol. I (London: Routledge, 2005), 21, 35-36.
172. Wolfgang Gans Edler Herr zu Putlitz (1899-1975), served in German Army in World War I, German Foreign Office since 1925, last positions with Embassy in London and Legation in The Hague, cooperated with Ustinov, fled to London 1939, moved to East Germany 1952. Keipert, Grupp, eds., *Biographisches Handbuch des deutschen Auswärtigen Dienstes 1871-1945*, vol. 2, 8-9. Cf. his memoirs *Unterwegs nach Deutschland: Erinnerungen eines ehemaligen Diplomaten* (Leipzig: Verlag der Nation, 1970).
173. Hans Heinrich Herwarth von Bittenfeld (1904-1999), German Foreign Office since 1927, positions in Berlin and abroad. Herwarth's English friends called him Johnnie. After the war cooperated with OSS. Keipert, Grupp, eds., *Biographisches Handbuch des deutschen Auswärtigen Dienstes 1871-1945*, vol. 2, 291-292. Andrew, *Secret Service*, 383, 426-427. David Cesarani, *Justice Delayed* (London: Mandarin, 1992), 155-156.
174. Sir Robert Vansittart, Permanent Undersecretary at the Foreign Office 1930-1937, early cultivated close contacts to important figures in British intelligence, close ties to Z organization, eventually developed his own intelligence gathering organization concerned largely with Germany. Through Group Captain Christie and others he had access to important Germans in industry and politics. His brother Guy Nicholas, an Oxford graduate and former officer in the Indian Army was with MI6.

even a removal of Adolf Hitler from the office of Imperial Chancellor was not at all unthinkable if conditions for an envisioned peace could be considered acceptable. Hohenlohe in the context of this scheme had told Göring that by "initiating World War II Germany has started from false premises and has miscalculated in every way" and that it might still be possible to persuade Franklin D. Roosevelt to mediate a way out of the conflict.[175]

The puppet master pulling the strings from London in this curious operation was Philip Conwell Evans, a former "admirer of Hitler" who had come around and was now connected to Vansittart's determined efforts directed against Germany.[176] They were in touch with Theodor Kordt, who from March to September 1939 served as *Botschaftsrat* (Secretary) at the German Embassy in London. Through Kordt they were rather well informed about underground rumors brewing in Germany, and they could well have surmised that replacement or removal of Hitler was a topic in certain circles in Berlin. To be closer to what somewhat optimistically may have been registered as significant German developments, Conwell Evans even journeyed to the Continent. That all this quickly lost its real or imagined meaning when after the Munich Bürgerbräu explosion the SS went out to kidnap the British operatives Best and Stevens at Venlo, should come as no surprise.

The covert connections between British intelligence and Prince Hohenlohe, however, were not completely broken off, and it should be remembered that Hohenlohe's extraordinary social contacts were, of course, quite independent of any particular mission or assignment he may have undertaken. By the same token, indications are that the very unclear maneuvers on both sides at the outset of World War II did not really suggest a common ground for negotiations. Göring, no more than the disorganized opposition groups among German military and political leaders, seems to have been able or willing to bring about meaningful changes in Germany. And if the German opposition wavered in uncertainty and disunity, the British could hardly sue for peace while the rest of the world was stunned in paralysis watching the German armies march from victory to victory. Hitler's public utterances that he wished no harm to Britain and the British Empire were neither reliable nor particularly conducive to seeking a rapprochement.[177] For Britain to have openly discussed peace at that time would certainly have meant a loss of face.

---

175. Quoted from Höhne, *The Order of the Death's Head*, 587, who cites a document in the "private papers" of Hohenlohe.
176. T. Philip Conwell Evans (b. 1891), had been a lecturer at the University of Königsberg. Cf. William L. Shirer, *The Rise and Fall of the Third Reich* (New York: Simon and Schuster, 1960), 649. Used his German connections to collect information for MI6. Dorril, *A Who's Who of the British Secret Service*. 22.
177. Cf. Saul Friedländer, *Pius XII and the Third Reich: A Documentation* (New York: Alfred A. Knopf, 1966), 60.

The mission in 1942, when Prince Hohenlohe acted on behalf of Schellenberg, appears to have had a rather obscure background. One of the early center pieces of the complex mélange of the diplomats, agents and freewheelers involved was Eric Grant Cable, since spring 1942 British Consul General in Zurich. Per chance or intentionally launched, intelligence gossip had it that he was interested in and authorized to engage in discussions with an important personality from the other side. It seemed no coincidence that Cable had earlier been stationed in Cologne and was therefore well known to men like Schellenberg. How exactly the message that Cable could be interested in meeting someone was transmitted remains unclear, but there can be no doubt that Schellenberg much welcomed the news.[178] Other than getting several more traditional German lines into gear, Schellenberg may have contributed to the matter by mobilizing SS-*Obersturmbannführer* Dr. Klaus Hügel whom he knew and probably respected for his Stuttgart activities into Switzerland. Apparently one of Hügel's *Vertrauensmänner* (agents), a businessman called Strobl, actually made the contact. Interrogated about this after the war, Hügel recalled that Schellenberg had had intensive exchanges with Himmler who "merely hinted to him that if things went wrong Schellenberg's head might be forfeit, whereas if they went well he would be considered a great man." Apparently even Himmler himself was most uncertain and very fearful that any of such peace feelers might find their way into the press with "consequent unpleasant reactions from Hitler." Schellenberg, however, quite in contrast to most Nazi leaders, did not shrink back and, in fact, directed his people in the field "that the lines of contact should not be dropped." He went so far as to authorize Klaus Hügel to take his "vacation" in Switzerland and get in touch with Allied representatives. Apparently Hügel was ready to go but was stopped in the last moment when Himmler withdrew even his tacit support of the undertaking. From the postwar interrogations of another *Amt* VI officer who enjoyed the trust of his chief Schellenberg, SS-*Obersturmführer* Otto Ernst Schüddekopf, we know that Himmler's insecurity in the operation may have been caused by interference from Ribbentrop. The Foreign Minister believed that Cable was a member of the British intelligence service, and anyway "he hated England far too much to want to come to an understanding with her." To the contrary, Ribbentrop "always gave the impression of having been an ally of the pro-Russian movement in Germany." All in all, the scanty evidence in the records leads one to conclude that in the absence of sufficient cover from Berlin and without the deployment of Hügel or Hohenlohe the potentially interesting

---

178. See especially Under State Secretary Martin Luther to the State Secretary for the Foreign Minister, September 26, 1942, Top Secret, PA, AA, R 100696, regarding content of a letter from Schellenberg (not in file) on contacts with Cable.

Cable operation fizzled away leaving no noteworthy traces. Later contacts such as towards the end of 1944 seem to have had no concrete results either[179]

In line with his view that negotiations were needed to bring the war to an end, Schellenberg threw his full support behind Prince Hohenlohe and, in fact, dispatched Reinhard Spitzy to join him in his efforts. The apparently internationally well versed and intelligent young man was the son of a well-to-do Austrian family who following a traditional Catholic education had spent some years studying in Germany, Austria and France. He had also rather early become an active member of the *Heimwehr* (home defense), an Austrian post-World War I movement with Christian-Socialist origins but soon clearly Fascist dominated. Joining the NSDAP, the SA and the SS for young Spitzy had seemed natural next steps. In his 1986 memoirs he refers to himself as an "alter Kämpfer" (old warrior). Drifting through Europe and getting an education on the way, Spitzy increasingly became actively involved in the German Nazi movement and eventually ended up as an adjutant or secretary to Joachim von Ribbentrop in his so-called *Dienststelle* (service office). There it did not take him long to learn to despise the insecure and somehow false Nazi Foreign Minister. Undoubtedly, the work for Ambassador Ribbentrop in London, however, not only had allowed him to look at diplomatic business from the inside, but also had helped him to better understand the English. Whether Spitzy's increasingly critical appraisal of Nazi foreign policy was also brought about by his low estimation of his rather incompetent chief, must remain a matter of speculation, but it is worth noting that his deprecatory view of Ribbentrop was clearly shared by Schellenberg and Prince Hohenlohe. In time Spitzy had come to share Schellenberg's regard for British ways and increasingly had found Ribbentrop's anti-English policy just plain foolish. As a result, he had left Ribbentrop's Foreign Ministry and managed to slip into Canaris' *Abwehr*, there mingling with and apparently sharing the views of a number of ranking Military Intelligence officers who were deeply involved in the military opposition to Hitler's regime. Looking at the political alignments in Germany, the SS officer serving in the *Abwehr* was certainly as strange as the *Abwehr* man then returning to the SS by working for Schellenberg's *Amt* VI Foreign Intelligence. Spitzy later recalled that he knew Prince Hohenlohe from encounters in London and social functions in Berlin and at Friedrichsruh, an estate of the Bismarcks' south of Hamburg. As Spitzy remembered, Prince Hohenlohe invited him to

---

179. "Sixth Detailed Interrogation Report on SS Sturmbannführer Huegel, Dr. Klaus," June 21, 1945, Top Secret, NA, RG 226, E 174, Box 39. "Report on Information Obtained from PW CS/2244 SS Ostuf Schüddekopf," October 1, 1945, NAK, KV2/2648. "Memorandum for the President," January 24, 1945, Top Secret, NA, RG 226, E A1-170 (210), Box 364. According to Bonjour, *Geschichte der schweizerischen Neutralität*, vol. VI, 109, Cable had extensive discussions with German-Swiss industrialist Emil G. Bührle.

join him in Spain in the so-called "Inspection West" of Skoda and related industrial and arms production interests now controlled by the Nazis. In the course of being accepted for the work with Prince Hohenlohe, Spitzy had to present himself to the Chief of *Amt* VI, Schellenberg, whom he had not known personally before. All went very smoothly and Schellenberg even arranged that Spitzy's mail from Spain would be sent unopened by diplomatic pouch via the Police Attaché in Madrid, Paul Winzer. While both Schellenberg and Spitzy were obviously gifted and personable negotiators, the pleasant ambiance of this encounter did have one other reason: Spitzy apparently was well acquainted with Walther Hewel, Ribbentrop's liaison official in Hitler's entourage, an important man to whom Schellenberg had no connections yet. Spitzy, apparently always quick to sense new openings, naturally was more than able and willing to introduce Schellenberg to Hewel, and the records indicate that Schellenberg indeed made use of this new access to the *Führer's* headquarters.[180]

Since Hohenlohe and Spitzy had known each other already for some years, there undoubtedly existed a comfortable feeling of trust between them, something almost essential when considering that while working for German interests they were also extremely critical of many aspects of Nazi Germany. Their purpose and Schellenberg's intent was a continued search for lines to the Western Allies. What it was that motivated these two obviously intelligent, internationally oriented, and rather well informed men to continue serving the criminal German state remains an enigma. One hesitates to make such judgment, but it does seem possible that both of them found the intelligence assignments challenging and welcomed the opportunity to live outside the thought-controlling German social structures. In this case, they operated in Switzerland, Spain and Portugal, and because of their social status and the apparent ease with which they moved in various national groups, they were in a position to obtain information of the kind Schellenberg knew he was not getting from regular *Amt* VI German representatives, such as Daufeldt, or from Gestapo-trained Police Attachés, such as Winzer.

Possibly due to Hohenlohe's excellent family and business connections, a good part of their activities was centered in Spain where they also benefited from the Skoda cover. As it happened, an old friend of Spitzy's and fellow

---

180. English edition of the memoirs of Reinhard Spitzy, *How We Squandered the Reich* (Norwich: Michael Russell, 1997; 1st German ed. 1986). "Final Report," 111, where Hohenlohe is referred to as "general agent for the Skoda works in West Europe." According to "Final Report," Appendix XXIII, Schellenberg's connections to Hewel did not last beyond spring 1944 "since he [Hewel] was completely under Hitler's spell." Hewel (1904-1945) studied Economics in Munich, sentenced for participation in Hitler's 1923 putsch, to Java 1926, NSDAP 1923, SS 1937, joined Foreign Office 1937, since 1940 representative of the Foreign Office attached to Hitler, suicide May 1945. Keipert, Grupp, eds., *Biographisches Handbuch des deutschen Auswärtigen Dienstes 1871-1945*. vol. 2, 300-301.

Austrian Hubert von Breisky, was attached to the German Legation in Lisbon since early 1940. We do not know whether Spitzy stretched matters many years later when he claimed that it was he who assisted Breisky to enter the German Foreign Office to begin with and later to be appointed to Lisbon, but we are certain that Spitzy fell in love with Breisky's sister-in-law, his later wife Maria, whom an Operational Information Report of the CIA some thirty years later described as "a gracious lady of regal bearing and manner."[181] As a well-connected diplomat, Breisky had made the personal acquaintance of two Americans also stationed in the Portuguese capital, namely the Naval Attaché Demarest and his assistant Theodore Rousseau. Inviting them for dinner at his home was a natural gesture of hospitality and so to speak incidentally gave Hohenlohe and Spitzy a new line into the U.S. Embassy in Portugal. Breisky thought the encounter sufficiently rewarding to inform his chief at the German Legation, Minister Baron von Hoyningen-Huene. The Minister apparently listened with great interest and actually agreed not to broach the subject in his mail to the Berlin Foreign Office. Good working conditions for this operation therefore seemed to have been established.[182]

Spitzy apparently introduced Breisky to Schellenberg's *Amt* VI and the conversations with Demarest and Rousseau were considered an informative link to the Americans. Breisky later under oath stated on behalf of Schellenberg, that he had met him through Spitzy "in the winter of 1942" and three to four times in later years, meaning that this German diplomat had an ongoing contact with SS Foreign Intelligence in Berlin. About Theodore Rousseau Breisky later recalled that the American was looking for contacts to members of the German resistance movement and was hoping for his assistance in this matter. If Schellenberg's memory was correct in 1945, and there seems no particular reason to doubt his word in this case, the connection to Demarest and Rousseau "was maintained from early 1943 till the end of the war," the results eventually showed a "decreasing importance," and "it was purely for political purposes, not for intelligence." The contact was attended to by Spitzy and Breisky who in their reports to Berlin referred to the Americans as Hero and Leander. As none of the reports on Hero and Leander seem to have survived the end of the war, it is impossible to come to an estimation concerning their intelligence value at the time. As in Switzerland, Schellenberg

---

181. Dr. Hubert von Breisky-Breisky (1908 Vienna-1967 Lisbon), studied Law in Vienna and Paris, legal practice in Austria, NSDAP 1938, since 1939 with German Foreign Office. Keipert, Grupp, eds., *Biographisches Handbuch des deutschen Auswärtigen Dienstes 1871-1945*, vol. 1, (Paderborn: Ferdinand Schöningh, 2000), 274-275. Spitzy, *How We Squandered the Reich*, 335. IFZ, ZS 3066. Operational Information Report, Central Intelligence Agency, August 30, 1974, NA, RG 226, RC Box 50, "Spitzy" (no other NA information). From this: "He [Spitzy] boasts of being the only admitted Nazi in all of Europe."
182. Spitzy, *How We Squandered the Reich*, 335.

and his representatives of *Amt* VI of the RSHA in Portugal and Spain were confronted by the mostly silent ill will of their Gestapo colleagues, the so-called Police Attachés and their staff. In Lisbon this was SS-*Obersturmbannführer* Kriminaldirektor Dr. Erich Schroeder who reportedly enjoyed a good relationship with the German Minister. Later Breisky recalled that some SD men in Lisbon had even surmised that Schellenberg was actually working for British intelligence.[183]

Meanwhile an American emissary had arrived in Bern who seemed more challenging than the operations around the British Consul General in Zurich or the American Attaché in Lisbon. Obviously with the strong approval of Schellenberg Prince Hohenlohe began to activate the needed contacts in order to prepare an encounter with Allen Dulles, later to become Director of Central Intelligence and since November 1942 busily engaged in setting up an Office of Strategic Services (OSS) station in neutral Switzerland. Prince Hohenlohe did not have to exert himself to meet the American, maybe because, as some sources suggest, Allen Dulles himself was not at all averse to such an encounter. Agent *110* or, in German code, Mr. Bull, while officially a kind of assistant to the American Legation, in fact was on his way to become the mysterious chief of U.S. intelligence in war-torn Europe. Whatever the claims and reports on both sides may suggest, it seems firmly established that Prince Hohenlohe stopped by to see Allen Dulles in January or February of 1943.[184] They weren't really strangers. They had come across each other on the international circuit, certainly in Vienna in World War I and in Berlin in the 1920s. The decision of Dulles to talk and exchange views with Schellenberg's emissary Hohenlohe was therefore less difficult than might be assumed under other conditions. The preparatory moves of the Germans in Portugal, explained in some detail by Heinz Höhne, may have contributed to arranging the encounter, and it should be added that the man undertaking these preparatory steps in Lisbon was none other than "Alfonso" or rather Reinhard Spitzy. Most likely the Americans in Lisbon who had been told by Spitzy what Schellenberg had in mind were Hero and Leander. Whether Schellenberg in his discussions with Spitzy ever used the term *Separatfrieden* (separate peace), as Spitzy wrote in 1978, we shall never know.[185] That Schellenberg did seriously

---

183. "Special Interrogations of Schellenberg" (1945), NAK, KV 2/98. Dr. Hubert von Breisky, Statement under Oath, January 27, 1948, in Lisbon, SAN, Rep. 501, LV, S-3. Schellenberg Document 7, Defense, May 11, 1948, NA, RG 238, Microfilm M 897, Roll 114. C.S.D.I.C. (U.K.) Report, August 26, 1944, Secret, NA, RG 165, E 179, Box 661.
184. Cf. Peter Grose, *Gentleman Spy: The Life of Allen Dulles* (Amherst: The University of Massachusetts Press, 1996; 1st 1994), 157. Burton Hersh, *The Old Boys: The American Elite and the Origins of the CIA* (2nd ed. with new "Preface," St. Petersburg: Tree Farm Books, 2002; 1st 1992), 95. Clipping (*Der Spiegel?*), NA, CREST.
185. Reinhard Spitzy to Lew Besymenski, February 14, 1978, IFZ, ZS 3066. Here Spitzy writes that he had three cover names: Bauer, Alfonso, and Gerber. Hohenlohe was Pauls (Paul), Schellenberg was der Baron

consider the necessity of seeking negotiations, most likely already since some time in 1941, is clearly evident from the records, and it might be added that the year 1942, from his perspective, had only worsened the outlook for Germany. At the time of the Hohenlohe-Dulles operation in the winter of 1942/1943 German forces were headed for disaster in the vast spaces of the Soviet Union, Allied forces had landed in Africa making the defeat of Rommel and the sparing of the Jews in Palestine from the brutalities of the German Africa Corps almost predictable, and the eventual attack of the German occupied European continent by American forces massing in Britain indeed seemed not too far off.[186] Yes, Schellenberg felt that he needed open lines to Germany's enemies in order to explore chances for a negotiated end to the war in the West. More than twenty years later and long after Schellenberg's death, Prince Hohenlohe wrote to the German expert Heinz Höhne: "Schellenberg went so far as to tell me that he knew that the West would never make peace with Hitler and therefore some internal changes in Germany were necessary ... he told me that he hoped Hitler would be patriotic enough to subordinate his own interests to those of the German people. If he did not, he must be removed by force."[187]

The meeting between Dulles and Prince Hohenlohe in Bern was a long shot and required preparations beyond Spitzy's busy contacts in Lisbon. Others who seem to have worked as go-betweens in helping make this top level event feasible were William Walton Butterworth, an American economic warfare expert stationed in Spain, and Royall Tyler whom Dulles knew from the peace conference after World War I and who now pursued various business interests out of Geneva. Presumably also Leland Harrison, the American Minister to Switzerland, who had run across Prince Hohenlohe repeatedly, most likely would have been inclined to support and sufficiently prepare any initiative coming from the attractive, smooth talking social figure.

The first encounter between Allen Dulles and Prince Hohenlohe must have gone well enough for there were several follow-up meetings. How serious the conversations between the two experienced men of the world actually were is still somewhat uncertain. The fact that they met more than once would suggest not only that Prince Hohenlohe may have been a persistent emissary,

---

(the Baron), Breisky was Rodrigo and Allen Dulles was Mr. Bull. Höhne, *The Order of the Death's Head*, 588, does not identify Alfonso as Spitzy.
186. The Jews in Palestine were very much aware that Rommel's Africa Corps would continue the German program of mass murder begun by other German armies in Poland and the Soviet Union. Unlike the European Jews, many of them not accepting extermination were preparing to fight the Germans. Cf. Dina Porat, *Israeli Society, the Holocaust and its Survivors* (London: Vallentine Mitchell, 2008), 58, 242, 339, 357.
187. Prince Hohenlohe to Heinz Höhne, February 1967, here quoted from Höhne, *The Order of the Death's Head*, 588.

but also that Dulles found the matters discussed not entirely boring. What was supposedly said, especially by Franklin D. Roosevelt's OSS representative, has been reported numerous times, and there can be no doubt that the opinions said to have been voiced by Dulles are somewhat astonishing to say the least—if indeed he said what various sources claim he said. The sundry explanations of these reports, that is above all the assumed unreliability of Schellenberg's agent Prince Hohenlohe and beyond that the peculiar circumstance that the reports fell into the hands of the U.S.S.R. and were released only years later, may be of interest, but they cannot serve as persuasive arguments concerning the genuineness of the texts. It should be remembered that Allen Dulles had become acquainted with pre-war Germany and that there are no indications that he was taken up in any way by either the Kaiser's Empire or Adolf Hitler's Third Reich. That his appraisal of German political acumen may have been quite different from his personal and professional interest in dealing with the Germans legally and in business need not necessarily be seen as a contradiction.

As most reports on intelligence operations, those concerned with what was said during the meetings of Dulles and Hohenlohe should be read with a cautious eye. Hohenlohe was an internationally well connected personality who would have had little interest to sell out to either the Germans or Allied intelligence. Whatever he reported to anyone would therefore have been directed by a natural desire to appear professionally successful without ever allowing himself to be used as a tool by one side or the other. It is therefore not to be excluded that Prince Hohenlohe may also have told the Germans what he thought they wanted to hear. If he did this, it would not have lessened his chances of obtaining a line for the Germans to the obviously important American representative. There is also, of course, maybe even more significant, the position of Allen Dulles somewhere between his government in Washington being at war with Hitler's Germany and the enemy who continued to deliver a stream of agents, opponents, collaborators and freewheelers to his front door at Herrengasse in Bern. Looking at Allen Dulles' background in international business and politics, not forgetting his earlier professional ties to major German enterprises, it is quite conceivable that what he said to Hohenlohe may not in all aspects have reflected official opinion on the Potomac. Also, it would not be surprising if Dulles had employed these unusual conversations with the German representative Prince Hohenlohe to create certain impressions which he supposed might induce positive reactions from the German side and thus help him open access routes to German centers of power. As disturbing as Dulles' purported views of the Nazi regime, on the need to control Soviet expansion and of nations and their borders may appear, they may well have been part of a well-planned political scheme to get closer to the Germans. One may or may not share the view of Fred J. Cook in his controversial article in 1961 claiming that some people "would say, too, that he [Allen Dulles] retained the strong prejudices, or the stout convictions (depending on how you look at it), that led him at the age of eight to refuse to dignify the British with a capital letter." Did Mr. Bull or Allen Dulles indeed say to Prince Hohenlohe in early 1943 that he was "fed up with listening to outdated politicians, émigrés and prejudiced Jews"? Future historians may discover additional records and be better able to continue the difficult task of ascertaining what was actually said and the specific qualities of the context of the respective conversations.[188]

While Hohenlohe was undoubtedly also pursuing his own contacts and interests—he was not a member of *Amt* VI or any related organization—he did approach Allen Dulles on behalf of Schellenberg who for his part had to be on constant guard to keep Himmler on his side. A particularly controversial operation in Berlin, closely related to the attempts to create useful lines to London and Washington, was Schellenberg's involvement in the still somewhat mysterious activities intended to rid the German Foreign Office of its chief Joachim von Ribbentrop. One of the center pieces of the operation, often referred to by historians and journalists, is said to have been a document or a series of documents composed by Under State Secretary of the Foreign Office Martin Luther, listing the deficiencies and failures of Ribbentrop and going as far as to suggest that he was mentally unbalanced and thus hardly fit to preside over Germany's foreign affairs. While such a document has not surfaced, specialists tend to agree that it existed. It is generally concluded that the document was written by Luther and possibly other Foreign Office officials also opposed to Ribbentrop, and small attention has been given to a 1967 letter from Walter Büttner, a man at the time close to Luther in the Foreign Office, to the German magazine *Der Spiegel*. In it Büttner clearly states that the document in question was dictated to a secretary in Schellenberg's office in the presence of the latter and Martin Luther. Prior to this Schellenberg had told Luther that Himmler would be supporting the dismissal of Ribbentrop and that all that was needed was a written statement listing the problems of the

---

188. Fred J. Cook, "The CIA," *Nation, Special Issue*, June 24, 1968, CIA Release, NA, CREST. On p. 534, he is referring to *The Boer War*, a brochure Allen Dulles published at the age of eight. At the time Dulles wrote: "It was not right for the british to come in and get the land because the Boers came first ..." Cf. Grose, *Gentleman Spy*, 13-14. Grose, 157-158, offers a slightly different quotation: "... sick of listening to bankrupt politicians, émigrés and prejudiced Jews." According to Grose, the Russians published and commented these texts in 1960 to slander Allen Dulles and the American government. That these texts would later be used by the Communist press, regardless of their reliability, is not surprising. Cf. "Deutschland Über Alles," from *Prague Mlada Fronta*, September 16, 1961, NA, CREST.

Foreign Minister. According to Büttner, this conversation and the creation of the document took place on February 8, 1943. Schellenberg's account regarding this background reads rather differently, but there seems little doubt that shortly thereafter he and Himmler discussed the possible dismissal of Ribbentrop. If we can believe the general report by Schellenberg, Himmler was in full agreement with him but changed his mind when SS-*Obergruppenführer* Karl Wolff, an ambitious SS leader who was anything but a friend of Schellenberg, entered the scene. Wolff easily persuaded Himmler that Ribbentrop, "one of the highest ranking members of our order," could not possibly be kicked out of office "by this scoundrel Luther." As often Himmler sought to avoid a conflict and submitted to Wolff. As a result, the Foreign Minister stayed in office and no one less than the Gestapo Chief Müller was given the assignment to investigate the case.[189] All of this would be but an almost common occurrence among ranking Nazi leaders. In this case, however, the problem and Schellenberg's doubtful performance were connected to his engagement for lines to the enemy with the ultimate purpose of negotiating an end to the war. He was fully aware that Ribbentrop was unwilling to consider such negotiations in the West and therefore would block his efforts. Schellenberg was somewhat certain of Himmler's qualified support which he needed to survive the risky game. As it was, Ribbentrop's removal did not take place. The odds were not in Schellenberg's favor.[190]

Whatever useful information may have been collected by either side in the course of the Hohenlohe-Dulles encounters, at the time quite independent from any obstruction originating with Ribbentrop's Foreign Office, no progress was registered on the stony path to German-American negotiations. The main reason was simple and there was not much that Schellenberg could do to alter the conditions: Apparently for the Allies the person of Adolf Hitler

---

189. Walter Büttner (1908-1972), studied Mining Engineering, joined NSDAP 1929, SA 1929-1938, SS 1938, joined Foreign Office 1939. On Büttner and Luther cf. "Fourth Detailed Interrogation Report on SS Sturmbannfuehrer Huegel Dr. Klaus," NA, RG 226, E 174, Box 39. Keipert, Grupp, eds., *Biographisches Handbuch des deutschen Auswärtigen Dienstes 1871-1945*, vol. 1, 344-345. *Der Spiegel*, April 3, 1967, 7-10. Cf. Schellenberg, *The Schellenberg Memoirs*, 364-369. Lutz Hachmeister, *Der Gegnerforscher: Die Karriere des SS-Führers Franz Alfred Six* (München: C. H. Beck, 1998), 244. Hans-Jürgen Döscher, "Martin Luther—Aufstieg und Fall eines Unterstaatssekretärs", in R. Smelser, E. Syring and R. Zitelmann, eds., *Die Braune Elite II* (Darmstadt: Wissenschaftliche Buchgesellschaft, 1993), 179-192. Hiller v. Gaertringen, ed., *Die Hassell-Tagebücher 1938-1944*, 582-583. Christopher R. Browning, "Unterstaatssekretaer Martin Luther and the Ribbentrop Foreign Office," *Journal of Contemporary History*, vol. 12, no. 2, (April, 1977), 313-344.

190. Martin Luther (1895-1945), served in German Army World War I, later in export business, NSDAP 1932, SA 1938, Foreign Office 1938, dismissed and to Concentration Camp Sachsenhausen February, 1943, later imprisoned by Russians. Joachim von (since 1925) Ribbentrop (1893-1946), various jobs, wine import Canada, married Annelies Henkell of sparkling wine family 1920, NSDAP 1932, SS 1933, Ambassador in London 1936, Foreign Minister 1938-1945, sentenced and executed Nuremberg 1946. Maria Keipert, Peter Grupp, eds., *Biographisches Handbuch des Deutschen Auswärtigen Dienstes 1871-1945*, vol. 3 (Paderborn: Ferdinand Schöningh, 2008), 146-147, 644-645.

was the major barrier that would have to be removed before any substantial exchanges could take place.[191]

This confusing picture of early intelligence lines from *Amt* VI to the Western Allies becomes even more disorderly if the curious journey of Gerhard Alois Westrick, an international business lawyer in Berlin and a partner of Allen Dulles and his New York law firm Sullivan and Cromwell is looked upon in this context. Until 1938 Westrick had been a partner in the law firm of Heinrich F. Albert at Bellevuestrasse in Berlin. These lawyers knew Allen and John Foster Dulles well and for years had acted as legal advisors and representatives to powerful financial and industrial interests in both Germany and the U.S. They appear to have moved on the fringe of an American elite, entertainingly described in Burton Hersh's *The Old Boys*.[192] Heinrich Albert, the senior partner of the firm, it should be said, in the course of World War I had become all too well acquainted with the U.S. and its early intelligence organizations. The Kaiser's Germany had dispatched the young man, falsely declared as Commercial Attaché, to Washington to act as accountant and general manager for German propaganda and sabotage agents in still neutral America. When the less than efficient manager of German intelligence one day dozed off on a New York subway train, an FBI agent attended to his briefcase, the contents of which offered Americans a pretty overview of illegal German operations in their country.

After World War I and other more harmless governmental assignments Albert had built up his law firm, and one of his important clients was the mighty International Telephone & Telegraph Corporation (IT&T) which among numerous other business interests controlled a number of companies operating in Germany, such as Standard Electric and Lorenz AG.[193] When Gerhard Westrick founded his own law firm in Berlin in 1938, he apparently took some of his clients in the Albert partnership with him, IT&T being one of them. When the German Government decided to dissolve the IT&T companies and confiscate the German holdings of Sosthenes Behn, Schellenberg did his best to prevent this. He had early on scrutinized several large international enterprises and found their commercial networks a most suitable cover for intelligence work. The colorful and dynamic entrepreneur

---

191. Cf. Bernd Martin, "Deutsche Oppositions- und Widerstandskreise und die Frage eines separaten Friedensschlusses im Zweiten Weltkrieg," in Klaus-Jürgen Müller, ed., *Der deutsche Widerstand 1933-1945* (Paderborn: Ferdinand Schöningh, 1986), 88.
192. Burton Hersh, *The Old Boys*.
193. Heinrich F. Albert (1874-1960) during the Hitler years played an important role as director of the large Ford Motor Company production facilities in Germany and was able to prevent a German confiscation. Regarding Albert's illegal activities in the U.S. before 1917 see Reinhard R. Doerries, *Imperial Challenge* (Chapel Hill: University of North Carolina Press, 1989). For the later period see Johannes Reiling, *Deutschland: Safe for Democracy?* (Stuttgart: Franz Steiner, 1997).

Behn was known to him, and Schellenberg saw him and his far-flung corporation as ideal lines to the United States. It turned out to be an uphill fight against the powerful *Reich* Postal Minister Wilhelm Ohnesorge who perceived IT&T as an undesirable foreign competitor. Schellenberg's ally in the ugly conflict was Army General Fritz Walter Thiele, the Deputy Chief of Signal Communications in the OKW, who for obvious professional reasons was highly interested in a continued access to IT&T know-how and products. Schellenberg and Thiele had learned to cooperate for good reasons. In his postwar interrogations, both the Americans and the British were particularly interested in the decoding work of the Germans, and Schellenberg frankly told them that he had worked with Thiele since 1942. Schellenberg's interest was two-fold, for he not only wished to see as much as possible of the decoded or deciphered material, but he also wanted to learn from Thiele's coding practice. As a result, "Schellenberg's relations with Thiele were very good." With the evident cover from Himmler both Schellenberg and Thiele managed to become members of the board of the European IT&T structure, thereby strengthening their own cooperation even more. The infuriated Ohnesorge even stooped to public comments about IT&T and its German companies being enemy enterprises and about the "fraudulent" roles played by Schellenberg and the OKW General. This was dangerous slander in Nazi Germany. Schellenberg later recalled that his interest in the matter was the "preservation of the American controlled combine as a bargaining lever to establish contact with the U.S. Government through a certain Westrick and Colonel Behne [*sic*]."[194] After the war Schellenberg quite frankly also conceded to Allied interrogators that aside from gaining a potential line to the U.S., there was the matter of professional prestige within the Nazi hierarchy. If he had not fought it out but given in to Ohnesorge and his clique, his enemies would have assumed that their accusations were justified and, besides, without him Thiele and the others would not have been able to hold the fort.[195]

We cannot be certain just when Schellenberg and Sosthenes Behn began to cooperate. Gerhard Westrick's still somewhat mysterious journey to the U.S. took place already in 1940 when Schellenberg officially was not yet in

---

194. Sosthenes Behn (1882 St. Thomas, Virgin Islands-1957), educated in Corsica and France, became a U.S. citizen prior to World War I, served in the American Expeditionary Forces in France, U.S. Medal of Merit, French Legion d'Honneur. In the postwar years he built up the IT&T enterprise in the U.S. and abroad. Later involved in the management of a great number of companies in many countries. Buried Arlington National Cemetery. *Who's Who in American History*, vol. 3: *1951-1960* (Chicago: A. N. Marquis, 1963), 63.
195. Statement by Schellenberg, October 16, 1945, Secret, NA, RG 226, E 109, Box 45. Testimony of Walter Schellenberg taken at Nuremberg, February 12, 1946, Confidential, NA, RG 319, IRR, PS, Box 195, and RG 263, E A1-86, Boxes 37-38. Testimony, Schellenberg, February 13, 1946, SAN, S-45b. "Final Report," 91-92. Concerning the fight over IT&T cf. Interrogations of Gerhard Alois Westrick, April 1947, SAN, Rep. 502, W 79, and Schellenberg Interrogation, October 26, 1946, SAN, S-45b.

command of *Amt* VI Foreign Intelligence. Of course, even when he was still running the counterintelligence Group IV E under Heinrich Müller, he might well have occupied himself with the German operations of IT&T. Westrick was later to claim that he had gone to the U.S. entirely on his own initiative and that, in fact, he had planned to stay. Taking his wife and two sons with him would appear on first sight to lend some support to that version. The records, however, and, most of all, the gentleman's activities in America, do seem to more than suggest that he had significant business motivations, not only per chance very closely linked to Nazi interests. When he left Berlin in January 1940, he traveled as an official representative of Hitler's government, taking the route through the Soviet Union, still allied with Nazi Germany and Japan.[196] If Charles Higham has it right, Westrick's journey had been planned and organized largely by Sosthenes Behn who also arranged for Torkild Rieber, the affluent Norwegian-born American oil business executive, to attend to Westrick's mundane needs. Behn's own suite at the Plaza Hotel in Manhattan and a respectable leased property in Scarsdale, Westchester County, became his pied-à-terre on the East Coast. There were press meetings, receptions, festive gatherings and indeed—it must have gone over well in New York City—on June 26, 1940, a grand party at the Waldorf-Astoria to celebrate the defeat of France. In his appearances before the press the German emissary, just like his law firm partner Heinrich Albert in World War I falsely declared as Commercial Attaché, had no hesitation to advise Americans of economic progress to be expected after the German victory. Following peace negotiations, Germany, Japan and America would become a powerful economic threesome, regulating trade for the better of business and mankind. It is, of course, conceivable that Westrick was not as simplistic as he may have sounded. Possibly the real purpose of this colorful one-man stage show was to persuade U.S. business leaders to take a stronger stand against Roosevelt's apparently increasing readiness to go to war against Adolf Hitler. This clearly would not have been too far removed from the business oriented international perspectives of a whole range of big-time entrepreneurs, such as Sosthenes Behn or Henry Ford.

Whatever may have been the real mission of this German international business lawyer, the undertaking had obviously been shoddily prepared and very little attention had been paid to the political climate in the U.S. which by 1940 had become somewhat jittery. Westrick with his overdone and over-self-confident appearances apparently wished to be noticed and he must have expected or been told by his dispatchers that Americans were waiting to listen

---

196. Westrick's family chose the shorter route across the Atlantic in April.

to him. Apparently quite unaware of the evidently increasing anti-German feelings in New York, a city that had welcomed a great number of Jews and other victims who had been fortunate enough to escape the murderous Germans, Westrick acted or was shocked and helpless.[197] The apparent need to shield the German guest and his family from unpleasant events had necessitated FBI guards around the property, he and his family had been exposed to what he felt was open hatred, and possibly worst of all, the metropolitan press had latched on to his every word and move. In the end there remained only the unceremonious departure of this untimely, unqualified and generally unwelcomed representative of the new Germany. From all appearances, the evident failure of the undertaking does not seem to have harmed Gerhard Alois Westrick who would share the IT&T board of directors in Europe with the *Amt* VI Chief Schellenberg and simultaneously maintain good relations with Sosthenes Behn and Allen Dulles which survived the dreadful depths of the German Nazi period.[198]

Schellenberg's perception of large international companies as ideal networks for the collection and transmission of intelligence actually was not a new development. Not only did and do international combines often maintain economic intelligence departments, but the governments of industrialized nations have been well aware of this possibility of infiltrating their agents under a convenient international business cover. One of Schellenberg's more colorful undertakings in this direction was his scheme to join forces with the far-flung company network of the almighty I. G. Farben. Indications are that some inroads were actually made, but in contrast to Sosthenes Behn, the foreigner running some German operations from outside the country, Dr. Hermann Schmitz was one of Germany's most powerful executives controlling a good number of enterprises, some of which by themselves played significant roles in the German business world. Schmitz had no need to go out of his way to please the Chief of SS Foreign Intelligence. Actually Schellenberg must have thought that matters could be worked out. Although business leaders originally had taken no notice of the almost juvenile Schellenberg, after Heydrich's death

---

197. Westrick in his position knew that numerous well-known Jewish families had left Germany, but like other Germans does not seem to have understood the consequences for the nation, not to mention the moral implications. Cf. Max M. Warburg (who had left Hamburg in August 1938), *Aus meinen Aufzeichnungen* (New York: private publication, 1952), 158: "My German life was brought to an end." (Transl.)
198. Regarding Westrick, his connections with the Nazi hierarchy, his journey to the U.S., and some information about his role as an executive see Reiling, *Deutschland: Safe for Democracy?*, 344, 395-401. Grose, *Gentleman Spy*, 134. Charles Higham, *Trading with the Enemy: An Exposé of the Nazi-American Money Plot 1933-1949* (New York: Dell, 1984; 1st 1983), 115-118. Schellenberg Testimony, February 12, 1946, NA, RG 319, IRR, PS, Box 195. Interrogation Gerhard Alois Westrick, April 1947, SAN, Rep. 502, W 79.

in 1942 Fritz Kranefuss and his *Freundeskreis Himmler*[199] (Friends of Himmler) made all sorts of friendly gestures and were obviously interested in a congenial cooperation. Schellenberg already had become well acquainted with Karl Lindemann[200] of the North German Lloyd and would soon use the internationally well-connected shipping magnate in his operations with Prince Hohenlohe and in connection with his attempts to find access to the Western Allies through Sir Victor Mallet, the British Minister in Stockholm. Through Kranefuss Schellenberg was able to meet other top managers of I. G. Farben, such as Dr. Max Ilgner of the I. G. VOWI (*Volkswirtschaftliche Abteilung*/Economic Dept.) and Dr. Max Bütefisch, a member of the *Freundeskreis* and the I. G. Farben board and Chief of the I. G. Farben offices in Berlin. Schellenberg worked very hard to gain access to Schmitz himself for he knew that large-scale cooperation with I. G. Farben could only be approved at the top. The result was a cold shoulder from Schmitz who, as it happened, never had the time to receive the intelligence man in his office. Schellenberg typically did not give up and made successful efforts to reinforce his contacts just below the top, such as to Wilhelm Rudolf Mann, Director of Bayer, who controlled a huge sales organization of I. G. Farben abroad, and some officials in the Economic Department. In fact, Canaris' Military Intelligence had gained some ground inside the huge I. G. Farben combine, and it may be assumed that this less formalized cooperation was continued without much fanfare when Schellenberg's *Amt* VI took over the *Abwehr* in 1944. When after the war, Bütefisch was interrogated by U.S. Military Intelligence, he explained that Schellenberg had planned to place his own agents inside I. G. Farben in addition to making use of good company men. This was to be done in Germany and abroad and completion of the difficult process was not envisioned until the postwar period. The G-2 officers handling Bütefisch noted that Schellenberg "intended thus to create an organization similar to the British Secret Service."[201]

International intelligence work, whether carried out through company networks, such as Sosthenes Behn's IT&T, or other covert intelligence organizations, as a rule takes place in various locations or countries simultaneously, and it is not at all unusual that several operations are part of a

---

199. The *Freundeskreis Himmler* grew out of the *Keppler Kreis*, a group of German businessmen who strongly supported the National Socialists. Fritz Kranefuss, a nephew of Wilhelm Keppler, was a banker and well connected to the SS leader Karl Wolff. Cf. Henry A. Turner, Jr., *German Big Business and the Rise of Hitler* (New York: Oxford University Press, 1985), 244-246, 256, 433.
200. Karl Lindemann (1881-1965) influential businessman, member of the *Freundeskreis Himmler*, executive of Norddeutscher Lloyd (North German Lloyd).
201. Interrogation Report of G-2, Special Section S.H.A.E.F., NAK, KV 2/2708. Declaration under Oath, Schellenberg, January 8, 1947, SAN, Rep. 502, NI-2784.

larger concept and pursue the same ends. This was certainly true with a good part of German intelligence activities in Northern Europe, particularly in Sweden. Even working conditions in Sweden were not unlike those in Switzerland. Both nations were strongly determined to guard their vulnerable neutrality and offer no excuses to any of the warring powers to meddle in their internal affairs or foreign policy. For Sweden, occupied Norway to the north and occupied Denmark to the south meant being surrounded by aggressive German military forces and Gestapo units. The German desire to turn the country into a highway for the transport of troops and material into occupied Norway was also somewhat comparable to German considerations of Switzerland as a thruway between Central and Southern Europe, particularly following the defeat of the Germans' overrated Africa Corps and the Allied landings in Southern Italy. Notable differences, of course, were Sweden's proximity to the Soviet Union and its traditional connections to Finland. Because of this and a strongly perceived uncertainty in the general Baltic area, diplomatic and intelligence representatives of the nations concerned seem to have been even more numerous here than in Switzerland. Moreover, Stockholm evidently had become a particularly busy place or intersection where the intelligence lines and networks of very different interests met, crossed each other and at times overlapped. In addition and also rather comparable to the much valued German business connections in Switzerland, there were important business relations with Sweden, and some of them, such as the ball bearing industry, were of such industrial and financial significance that no one was willing to sacrifice them just to please one or the other belligerent. One is all the more surprised to find that the lines from *Amt* VI to Sweden and the far-flung German intelligence activities in the country have not been examined as thoroughly as the Nazi operations in Switzerland.[202]

Not unlike the Swiss situation Schellenberg while conscious of his lack of international experience, was also much aware of the pressing need to check the lines inherited from his predecessor Jost and to gain a more thorough understanding of activities in Sweden. What he found was not unlike the conditions in Switzerland. Germany's enemies, especially Great Britain, the Soviet Union and the United States, maintained generously staffed diplomatic representations in Stockholm, and all of them controlled a number of operatives either clearly in the field of intelligence or somewhere in the foggy landscape where diplomatic, intelligence and business interests cannot always be clearly distinguished from each other. In addition, not unlike Switzerland,

---

[202]. A real exception is the well researched and most informative study by McKay, *From Information to Intrigue: Studies in Secret Service Based On the Swedish Experience 1939-45*.

Sweden had attracted a great number of refugees who had escaped persecution and murder in Nazi Germany and the regions overrun by German forces. Due to geographic proximity many of them had come from Denmark and Norway. Finally, much like in neutral Switzerland, there were those Swedes who sympathized with German political and racist ideologies. They, of course, had found allies and supporters inside Germany, persons who were neither desirable nor trustworthy individuals and of no interest to Schellenberg. In other words, conflicts here too were programmed well before he took on his responsibilities as Chief of *Amt* VI Foreign Intelligence.

In November 1941 he made his first journey to Stockholm. However one may be inclined to evaluate his various contacts, there can be little doubt that his meeting with Martin Lundqvist in a café in Stockholm was probably quite a coup. Though Schellenberg's relationship with Lundqvist, the chief of the important Stockholm bureau of Sweden's civilian Security Service, appears to have been no more than a sober working relationship which never approached anything like cooperation of services, it was precisely this kind of connection that could be essential to assure smooth movement throughout the country. We are now aware that Lundqvist in 1943 also seems to have been quite willing to "exchange information on German activities" with British intelligence representatives in Sweden,[203] but even knowing that would not in any way have lessened his considerable usefulness to Schellenberg, who later recalled: "I had with him a fairly close personal contact. During my various stays in Sweden I met him regularly. Our conversations were always of a general political nature, and I never received any political or military information from him."[204] To all appearances this was a mutually profitable connection, and both partners intelligently seem to have left it at that.

From a personal and professional perspective another early contact in Stockholm may have been even more important, but during interrogations after the war Schellenberg hardly ever mentioned the man's name. It was SS-*Hauptsturmführer* Hans-Hendrik Neumann, a trusted close personal friend from the Berlin head office and a former *Begleitoffizier* (a type of adjutant) of Heydrich. He had been sent to Stockholm as a Police Attaché to be attached to the German Legation. As in some other cases, the Swedes evidently did not sense a necessity to be overly accommodating to the Germans and just told them that they saw no reason to accept this new type of so-called diplomatic representative. When Schellenberg met his friend in Stockholm, he was officially working as an Assistant to the Press Attaché at the Legation.

---

203. Regarding Lundqvist's arrangement with the British Secret Service and the go-ahead given by the Swedish Minister of Justice, see McKay, *From Information to Intrigue*, 101.
204. "Translation of Statement handed in by Schellenberg on 20.8.45," NA, RG 226, E 125A, Box 2.

Apparently Neumann had already established himself so well that he was able to introduce Schellenberg to the Swedish intelligence chief.[205]

The early official representative of German Military Intelligence in Sweden was Lieutenant Colonel Dr. Hans Wagner whom Canaris had withdrawn from the *Abwehr* station in Bucharest. Wagner, also occasionally referred to as "the Doctor," used the cover name Dr. Neumann and was attached to the Military Attaché Lieutenant General Bruno von Uthmann. Wagner and his staff arrived in the fall of 1940 and officially he was occupied with problems of an economic nature. Wagner's deputy was Captain Albert Utermark, and in 1943 the *Abwehr* had dispatched a third man by the name of Eberhard Schrott who was stationed at the German Consulate in Gothenburg.[206] The other prominent German operative in the Swedish capital, also an *Abwehr* officer, was Dr. Karl Heinz Krämer who seems to have been introduced to Schellenberg by Daufeldt who in turn had become acquainted with Krämer during his earlier brief tour of duty in Hamburg. Prior to fully committing himself to intelligence, Krämer had practiced law in the port city and occasionally worked with Colonel Nikolaus Ritter of the *Abwehrstelle* Hamburg (AST, Office of Military Intelligence). Aside from these two Military Intelligence men, who at this time would not really have been *Amt* VI operatives but nevertheless were both more than inclined to work with the SD, Schellenberg had his own SD representative August Finke in Stockholm who took the place of Hans-Hendrik Neumann when the Swedes could see no urgent reason to allow the latter to stay at the German Legation after they had turned him down as a Police Attaché. Finke cultivated a busy social life and became acquainted with a great number of public and not so public persons. For those who did not know him personally he preferred to be known as Herr von Schilling.[207]

From February 1943 on Minister Hans Thomsen took over the German Legation. Succeeding Victor Prince zu Wied, who was regarded as a not very effective but devout Nazi, Thomsen was an experienced diplomat who as Chargé d'Affaires had run the German Embassy in Washington in a very

---

205. Neumann and Schellenberg were on first name base, and Schellenberg called him Hans. Various items in BA Berlin, R 58/Anhang 51. Statement under Oath, Hans-Hendrik Neumann, NA, RG 238, Microfilm 897, Roll 114.
206. Hans Wagner is said to have been recommended for the Stockholm post by Hans Piekenbrock, Chief of Department I of the *Abwehr*. Cf. "Camp 020 Report on the Case of Karl Heinz Kraemer," NAK, KV 2/151. Ladislas Farago, *The Game of the Foxes*, 527 ff. For information from the Swedish perspective McKay, *From Information to Intrigue*, 160-163.
207. Karl Heinz Krämer (b. 1914), studied Law in Göttingen and Hamburg, to Stockholm 1940, arrested in Germany May 1945, taken to Camp 020. On his sources "Josephine" and "Hektor" cf. Horst Boog, "'Josephine' and the Northern Flank," *Intelligence and National Security*, vol. 4, no. 1 (January 1989). Oliver Hoare, ed., *Camp 020: MI5 and the Nazi Spies* (Richmond: Public Record Office, 2000), 354. "Final Report," 88, 319, 360.

difficult political climate from November 1938 until the Germans declared war on the United States on December 11, 1941. The Norwegian-born Thomsen came to that position when Franklin D. Roosevelt recalled his Ambassador, the historian William E. Dodd, following the so-called *Reichskristallnacht* (Reich Crystal Night) of November 9–10, 1938, when Jewish businesses and synagogues were ravaged and burnt down all across Germany. Hitler in turn had called back his Ambassador in Washington, Hans Heinrich Dieckhoff, and it had become Thomsen's unrewarding task to hold the fort on the Potomac. While there are some indications that Thomsen was considered to be someone who might be approached with thoughts about an eventual removal of Hitler, indecision and hesitation in the end seem to have gotten the better of him. Quite to the contrary, before departing from the U.S., Thomsen, in fact, enthusiastically announced that he was returning to Berlin to serve as "personal assistant to the Führer." If those were his expectations, the posting to Stockholm must have been something of a disappointment. Whatever he may have felt, there are no indications that he undertook any efforts to make use of the unique qualities of the neutral Swedish capital to spin off even the most covert lines to Britain or the United States.[208]

Schellenberg, however, in sharp contrast to this lethargic German diplomat, set out to do just that. Unlike his secretive personal lines into the more subdued and guarded atmosphere of Switzerland, he almost naturally established a rather broad variety of important contacts on different levels of Swedish society. In several aspects working conditions in Stockholm were quite different from those in Switzerland. Two nations which had been less visible in Bern, were strongly represented in Stockholm and offered many new challenges to Schellenberg. To the outside world, Soviet interests were attended to by the illustrious feminist and Bolshevik revolutionary, the Minister Alexandra M. Kollontai[209] and her counsellor Vladimir Semyonovitch Semyonov,[210] and Schellenberg, though in his international and geopolitical views clearly Western oriented, made certain that German connections to Stalin's Russia were not lost.

The key Japanese figure in Stockholm certainly was General Makato Onodera, the Military Attaché who lived and worked with his wife from the fifth floor at Linne Gatan 38. A secretive and highly respected member of the

---

208. Ingeborg Fleischhauer, *Die Chance des Sonderfriedens: Deutsch-sowjetische Geheimgespräche 1941-1945* (Berlin: Siedler, 1986), 54-56.
209. Alexandra Michailovna Kollontai (1872-1952), early participant in revolutionary activities, since 1915 member of Bolsheviks, various positions, stationed in Stockholm since 1930.
210. Vladimir Semyonov (1911-1992), diplomat and intelligence functionary, 1940 with Soviet Embassy in Berlin as 1st Secretary, since 1941 Secretary at the Legation and NKVD Resident in Stockholm, numerous appointments after the war, finally Soviet Ambassador to West Germany.

international military and intelligence community, he was by some observers thought to be more effective and influential than the Japanese diplomatic representatives in Stockholm.[211] Considering that Onodera was said to have a direct line to the Emperor and that his important position in Stockholm was matched by the impressive standing of Lieutenant General Hiroshi Oshima, the Japanese Ambassador in Berlin, it would appear natural that German intelligence had little choice but to closely observe Japanese activities and cultivate friendly relations.[212] That the alliance between Hirohito's Japan and Hitler's Germany would be disturbed from time to time by such unpleasantnesses as mutual distrust and even recurrent moments of disloyalty should come as no surprise. Schellenberg from his counterintelligence activities in *Amt* IV, of course, was all too well acquainted with the intricate Japanese network in Europe which would have no hesitations of operating against its German ally if conditions appeared to require it. What Schellenberg could not know was that the Japanese Ambassador in Berlin reported in great detail to Tokyo what he thought he had learned from conversations with Hitler, Ribbentrop and other Nazi brass, and naturally neither Schellenberg nor Oshima had an inkling that with their Magic system the Americans were reading what Oshima thought he only told Tokyo. When Oshima went inspecting installations at the German front, it was as if Americans were right there with him.[213]

For his part Schellenberg not only intently observed the international lines crossing in Stockholm, but also allowed himself to become personally involved in the hazardous business of assisting various Swedes in their attempts to free Swedish or, in some instances, non-Swedish friends captured by the Nazis for any number of reasons and now being held in some German jail or concentration camp. Amazingly, as in Switzerland, Schellenberg was able to contact the right people with influence and get things done that needed to be done. The question whether Schellenberg's engagement for others was in all cases motivated by his plans to survive what since late 1941 he saw as the likely

---

211. Makato Onodera (b. 1897), upper-class background, educated and later instructor at Japanese war college, wife highest class background, appointed Military Attaché in Stockholm 1939, knew Russian and some German, probably sent some of his reports to the Emperor via German transmitters in Berlin, well connected internationally, left Europe from Naples 1945, interrogated and briefly imprisoned in Japan 1946, back in Sweden 1953 "to recover bank account and other properties." CIA Name Files, NA, RG 263, E ZZ-18, Box 97.
212. Hiroshi Oshima (1886-1975), many years in Berlin first as Military Attaché later as Ambassador. He was a strong supporter of the Nazi government and William Shirer, *The Rise and Fall of the Third Reich*, 90, refers to him as "the fiery and hot-tempered Japanese ambassador, General Hiroshi Oshima, who had often impressed this observer as more Nazi than the Nazis." On Oshima especially Carl Boyd, *The Extraordinary Envoy: General Hiroshi Oshima and Diplomacy in the Third Reich, 1934-1939* (Washington, D.C.: University Press of America, 1980).
213. Cf. Ronald Lewin, *The American Magic: Codes, Cyphers and the Defeat of Japan* (New York: Farrar Straus Giroux, 1982), passim.

outcome of the war, has been asked before and appears justified. By the same token it should not be overlooked that the stakes were very high. If in the course of any of these rescue operations he had stumbled or if his enemies inside the SS structure had more successfully denounced him in the highest places, he most likely would not have survived to see the end of the Nazi regime. That too he certainly knew.

His *Amt* VI representative in Stockholm, August Finke, was involved in a broad spectrum of different operations. While there was an understanding that none of the work would be directed against the host country Sweden, the use of Swedes in some of the activities or the occasional need to achieve certain targets at any price would make it appear more than doubtful that tactfulness toward the Swedish Government could be maintained in all operations. Both, paying people for their services or ignoring law and national interest, could easily become part of covert operations or even be taken for granted in certain complicated undertakings. The people Finke used in Sweden came from different walks of life and probably did not know about one another in most cases. Schellenberg later recalled that reports from Finke contained very little of real intelligence value. In fact, they were of such inferior quality that Finke's *Gruppenleiter* (Chief of Group VI D inside *Amt* VI Foreign Intelligence) SS-*Obersturmbannführer* Theodor Päffgen, one of Schellenberg's own appointments in 1942, several times requested that Finke be recalled. Even bringing him back to Berlin to give him a good straightening out does not seem to have improved his reports on military topics. There was, however, another sector of information where Schellenberg in his otherwise very critical appraisal of Finke's work did see some good results. Finke apparently had successfully built himself a social network of contacts who knew much about internal conditions in Sweden, Swedish relations with Finland and Western nations, business aspects of Swedish-German relations and Swedish trade unions and Communist organizations. Schellenberg believed such data to be of considerable interest, and he tried to use this as a point of departure to put Finke on the right track for information about the Soviet Union. In this Russian work Finke apparently cooperated with Hermann Rasch, a businessman operating in Sweden who may also have been part of the larger more nebulous group of German nationals connected to the Gestapo and the foreign intelligence activities of the German Legation. More significant in this connection may have been Finke's acquaintance, if not to say cooperation with SS-*Obersturmbannführer* Dr. Bruno Peter Kleist, one of Ribbentrop's trouble shooters in Northeastern Europe who actually was able to establish what appeared to be a line to Moscow. Finke's business and society contacts in Sweden included a number of journalists, such as Herman Johansson of *Folkets*

Dagblad. This newspaper, originally run by Nils Flyg who had come from the Swedish Communist Party via the Swedish Socialist Party, had pursued a Socialist anti-Stalinist line and soon experienced severe financial difficulties. The paper had actually ceased publication in 1940 and when it surfaced again in July 1942 had become National Socialist. The Germans paid monthly subsidies to the paper and when Flyg died in 1943 Johansson continued to receive the money from Finke. McKay points out an interesting aspect of this operation, namely the proximity of *Folkets Dagblad* to the Socialist Party. Johansson apparently was able to dispatch two party members to Germany, have them trained there, and to return them to Stockholm where he put them on hold as future illegal radio stations in case of a break of diplomatic relations between Sweden and Germany.[214]

Another journalist often mentioned in connection with August Finke was Heinz Pentzlin who in Stockholm represented the *Frankfurter Zeitung*, the official Nazi paper *Das Reich* and the *Deutscher Verlag*. Pentzlin had close connections to the German Foreign Office and therefore to the Legation in Stockholm. His ties to a number of Nazi organizations in Germany would suggest that his appointment to the Swedish capital was more than a purely journalistic assignment. His contacts with Bruno Peter Kleist and Piotr Ivanov would even suggest an involvement in the intermittent German-Russian contacts in Sweden. What it was that Pentzlin accomplished for Finke remains unclear, but his status within the large group of German journalists in Sweden may have been helpful in opening doors.[215]

A particularly colorful agent of August Finke's was Countess Armgard Innhausen zu Knyphausen who is said to have cultivated good social contacts in Sweden about whom she freely reported to German intelligence. Schellenberg in his interrogations after the war called her a "paid agent" in late 1943 and 1944. According to available records, the Countess had separated from her husband Count Anton von Knyphausen who had gone to Sofia for the *Deutsche Allgemeine Zeitung* at the outset of World War II but was soon in trouble with Gestapo representatives there. With assistance from the *Abwehr* his employers were able to bring him back to Berlin. A short time later he had left his well-meaning protectors and switched to the *Hamburger Fremdenblatt* from where he was dispatched as a correspondent to Helsinki. In 1944 he must have had enough of pro-German Finland and luckily found asylum in Sweden. When Allied interrogators after the war quizzed Finke about the Countess, he

---

214. McKay, *From Information to Intrigue*, 225-226.
215. Heinz Pentzlin (in some records Penzlin) was well connected in journalistic and social circles in Stockholm and does not seem to have proclaimed his political preferences in public. Fleischhauer, *Die Chance des Sonderfriedens*, 323. "Situation Report No. 9," Confidential, NA, RG 319, IRR, IS, Box 1.

said that until 1944 her reports were mailed sealed to Schellenberg. When in 1944 Finke obtained permission to see her reports before they were dispatched, he found them to contain mostly society information and nothing of interest for his own work. In addition, from that time on, the Countess often sent letters marked "personal" to SS-*Obersturmführer* Otto-Ernst Schüddekopf in *Amt* VI. When Schüddekopf was questioned in 1945, he recalled that the Countess had had important contacts in the SD hierarchy in Berlin and in fact had served in Switzerland as an agent for SS-*Sturmbannführer* Klaus Hügel prior to being admitted to Sweden purportedly to see her son who was staying with her parents in Stockholm. Schüddekopf also claimed that Finke had pressured her to undertake more important assignments in Sweden but that she had refused. In February 1945 Countess Knyphausen wrote a letter to Schüddekopf, announcing that she and her parents were moving to a small estate on the Mälaren. "... I can consider myself lucky to be able to lead such a pleasant life whilst the whole of Europe is being reduced to ruins ... The best wish I can think of for you is that you should survive."[216]

While the activities of these representatives of *Amt* VI Foreign Intelligence and of Canaris' *Abwehr* (Military Intelligence) were an important part of the ongoing cat and mouse game in Stockholm and produced information as well as disinformation of more than occasional impact, Schellenberg rather than merely running an office in Berlin, quickly began constructing his own personal lines into neutral Sweden. Very much like his early initiatives in the Swiss context, his first operations in Stockholm were closely connected to the misfortune of a group of men who had been apprehended by the Nazis and were now in real danger of losing their lives. Schellenberg certainly was fully aware of what he got himself into and the consequences he might have to face if these issues could not be fixed smoothly and without negative publicity. Five of those imprisoned were high-ranking managers of "Spolka Akcynja Do Eksploaticji Panstwowego Monopolu Zapalczanege N Polsce [*sic*, MONZAP]," the Polish subsidiary of the famous Jönköping enterprise Svenska Taendsticks Aktiebolaget (STAB) and two were managers of AB L.M. Ericsson. Swedish companies had been permitted to continue operations in German-occupied Poland, and the imprisoned Swedes had all been stationed in Warsaw. The Germans were accusing them of espionage and claimed that they had been in contact with the much hated and, one could add, feared Polish

---

216. SAINT London to SAINT Washington, "SS Ostuf Schueddekopf," November 13, 1945, Secret, NA, RG 226, E 119A, Box 28, containing several OSS reports and letter from Countess Knyphausen. Otto-Ernst Schüddekopf (1912-1984), Ph.D. in History in Berlin, connected with the Hielscher Circle, claimed to have been anti-Nazi. On Count Knyphausen Helmut Müssener, *Exil in Schweden: Politische und kulturelle Emigration nach 1933* (München: Carl Hanser, 1974), 318-319, 478. Karl Silex, *Mit Kommentar: Lebensbericht eines Journalisten* (Frankfurt: S. Fischer, 1968), 144-145.

underground. At least some of the Swedes obviously were more than just businessmen. Carl Herslow had served as Military Attaché in Moscow and Berlin and while running MONZAP, the STAB operation in Warsaw, had been named Swedish Consul General, thus officially gaining diplomatic privilege.[217] The others were Tore Widén, a company executive, the Chief of Accounting Stig Lagerberg and two engineers Reinhold Grönberg and Einar Gerge. The directors from Ericsson were Sigfrid Häggberg and Nils Berglind. All of them had not exactly been in sympathy with the German occupation forces and their excessive brutality. The Swedes had soon become acquainted with members of the Polish underground, and it took very little persuasion to assist the Poles in the transport of much needed funds from Stockholm to Warsaw and the smuggling out of Warsaw of valuable reports on the situation in the country. Some of these reports are said to have contained information on German massacres. The Poles in exile had strong bases in Stockholm and in London, and McKay may not be far off with his suggestion that the Germans had gotten on to the Poles by cracking the Polish code used between Stockholm and London. The Swedes themselves indeed had broken into that signal traffic in 1942.[218]

When the Swedes realized that urgent steps had to be taken to spare the imprisoned executives, Alvar Möller, the successor of Axel Brandin as chief executive officer of the German STAB affiliate in Berlin, by rather roundabout ways was able to get in touch with Felix Kersten, a masseur who was treating Heinrich Himmler and other influential Germans with apparent success and therefore correctly was thought to be in a position to carefully assist his important patient in reaching certain desirable decisions. When no tangible results were achieved, Brandin and Möller decided to approach Kersten directly and press for action. However one may be inclined to evaluate the somewhat controversial role of Felix Kersten in Nazi Germany, there can be no doubt that he knew his way around the dangerous venues of power in Berlin.[219] He surely had access to a great number of people. The Swedish executives learned from Kersten that Schellenberg was "helpful and completely trustworthy." Either because he sensed the possibility of big name Swedish contacts or because he was indeed willing to allow himself to be used to help

---

217. Statement under Oath, Carl Herslow, April 20, 1948, SAN, Rep. 501, LV, 54.
218. McKay, *From Information to Intrigue*, 89-90.
219. (Eduard Alexander) Felix Kersten (Dorpat, Estonia 1898-1960), acquired Finnish citizenship, courses in Medicine in Finland and Germany, studied Physiotherapy with a Chinese masseur in Berlin, moved to The Netherlands where he treated members of Royal Family, acquired estate Hartzwalde a ways north of Berlin near Gransee. Left memoirs entitled *Totenkopf und Treue: Heinrich Himmler ohne Uniform* (Hamburg: Robert Mölich, [1952]). A slightly altered version is *The Kersten Memoirs 1940-1945*. Cf. John H. Waller, *The Devil's Doctor: Felix Kersten and the Secret Plot to Turn Himmler Against Hitler* (New York: John Wiley, 2002). Joseph Kessel, *The Man with the Miraculous Hands*, (Short Hills: Burford Books, 2004; 1st Paris, 1960).

the troubled Swedes, Schellenberg agreed to meet with Brandin and Möller. The encounters actually took place at the private home of Alvar Möller in the fashionable Berlin-Wannsee sector and on Kersten's estate Hartzwalde out in the country. What the Swedish executives asked for was nothing less than the release of the suspected spies. Schellenberg used what influence he had and talked to Dr. Rudolf Dix, Finnish Consul General in Berlin and a successful lawyer, who succeeded in getting the prisoners' diet improved. While this was an important change for those held in the inhuman Nazi prison system, it was not enough. Schellenberg now decided to take the more drastic but also more dangerous step and spoke to Himmler himself. Emphasizing the well-known significance of excellent Swedish-German relations, he underlined the far-reaching negative consequences if these men of some social and professional standing in Sweden were to be sentenced in a German court. If Schellenberg remembers correctly, Himmler actually agreed to see to it that any sentencing that might occur would be diffused or wiped off the records altogether. Intent on getting results while they seemed obtainable Schellenberg then used his connections to have the trial moved ahead. He and Kersten even attempted to win the support of Foreign Minister Ribbentrop who was out to punish the Swedes. Ribbentrop refused to change his mind. As things turned out, however, even Schellenberg's considerable clout could only achieve a very partial success. When on June 30 and July 1, 1943, the trial finally took place in the much feared People's Court in Berlin, two of the Swedes were acquitted, one received a life sentence, and the remaining four were sentenced to death. Their defense lawyer was *Justizrat* Dix. Alvar Möller attended the trial. In the corrupt German legal system the next urgent intervention obviously would have to achieve the change of the death sentences into life imprisonment.

Needless to say, Schellenberg knew that even this was not enough and that he would have to do much better if he wished to keep his new very highly placed lines into Sweden. In August 1943 he went so far as to take Brandin and Möller to Himmler's headquarters in East Prussia. It took considerable effort first to extract the Swedes from the ill reputed Alexanderplatz prison, from where they were moved to Bautzen, and then, once again with Himmler's assistance, to have them freed and returned to their families in Sweden in late 1944.

Upon their release the Swedes found themselves in the Hotel Bristol in Berlin where they were attended to by Schellenberg's "adjutant" (probably Franz Göring). The SS officer told them that they were now guests of the German *Reich* and shared dinner with them. After dinner Director Möller joined them and informed them that their liberation had only been possible thanks to the cooperation of Schellenberg and Kersten. The next evening all gathered at Möller's house in Berlin-Wannsee where they celebrated until the early morning hours. Schellenberg himself was present and both Möller and Herslow spoke to express their gratitude to him. Then Schellenberg and Göring personally took them to the airport to be certain there would be no last minute snags.[220]

In retrospect, the engagement on behalf of the seven Swedes could be seen as an isolated case of mercy or even as the humanitarian instinct of an SS official. In the case of Schellenberg such a view would certainly be an oversimplified understatement of what he was trying to do in Scandinavia. Perhaps through his very personal and much of the time open relationship with the mysterious masseur Felix Kersten, he seems to have understood rather early in the game that not only was Sweden an important arena but that such men as Brandin and Möller were extraordinarily well connected in Swedish society and had access to a vast network of business, political and often influential personal relationships. Following his initial journey to Stockholm in 1941, there were therefore numerous other trips and opportunities for encounters with some of Sweden's most powerful and influential individuals at the time.

Neutral Sweden was not only an important economic partner for Germany, but following the German occupation of Denmark and Norway, it had become the one nation which could openly represent Scandinavian interests and simultaneously function as a communication channel to Great Britain and even the United States, not to forget its role as a somewhat uncertain path to Eastern Europe and the Soviet Union. Schellenberg recognized very early on that the stakes in Sweden were high, and looking back it is evident that he was absolutely correct. Depending on the accuracy of the records, he first met Jacob Wallenberg, the influential Swedish banker, either in October 1943 at the home of Count Gottfried von Bismarck in Potsdam or in December 1943 in the course of a visit to Stockholm. A third possible date for a first encounter would appear to be November 1943, when Schellenberg, as he remembers, undertook a journey to Stockholm in an attempt to patch up the brittle relations between Germany and neutral Sweden. Germany urgently needed Swedish ball bearings, and the Swedes were more than disgruntled because of the miserable treatment of Norwegian students and Danish policemen held in German camps. Jacob Wallenberg later recalled: "Brandin, Möller and I at that time and at later occasions spent considerable time with him ... We told him that as long as such things were happening in our

---

220. Regarding the Swedish executives, "Final Report," 28-29, 109-110, 363. Statement under Oath, Alvar Möller, April 22, 1948, SAN, Rep. 501, LV, S-4. (Transl.) Statement under Oath, Carl Herslow, April 20, 1948, *Ibid*. McKay, *From Information to Intrigue*, 88-90, 229-231. Kersten, *Totenkopf und Treue*, 280-284.

neighboring countries, Germany should not be surprised if it was disliked in Sweden. Schellenberg understood our points of view and expressed his disapproval of such brutal measures. He declared his willingness to use his entire influence with Himmler to achieve an end or at least a moderation of such measures." Considering the power and position of Jacob Wallenberg, one may be fairly certain that he could hardly be pressured into voicing positive comments on Schellenberg or for that matter on anyone else. In retrospect, there can be no doubt that Schellenberg's positive reception by Wallenberg and his friends and business partners was of considerable significance. By the same token, of course, Schellenberg must have been aware that suggestions or requests from Wallenberg, perhaps in that way comparable to requests from Masson or Guisan, could hardly be ignored or rejected if he had the slightest interest in securing somewhat congenial working conditions in Sweden.[221]

One of the important persons Schellenberg encountered in Stockholm in 1943 was a personal friend of the American President, and some documents suggest that Roosevelt may have sent him to Sweden in order to determine any possibilities of ending the war in Europe. How the OSS agent and Roosevelt emissary, Abram Stevens Hewitt,[222] happened to meet up with Walter Schellenberg, the Chief of SS Foreign Intelligence, remains somewhat uncertain. Indications are that the connection was first made through J. Holger Graffman in whose home in Stockholm Himmler's masseur, Felix Kersten,[223] so-to-speak accidentally met the OSS man Abram Hewitt over coffee. Whether further initiatives came from Hewitt or Kersten is still rather unclear. The coffee chat it would appear did lead, however, to a treatment of Hewitt's back problem by the masseur. The daily massages that followed obviously helped the two men become better acquainted and learn more about each other's political views. As is often the case, the real background of this acquaintance was probably a bit more complicated. Richard Breitman's suggestion that Jacob Wallenberg, whose connections with important members of the German resistance against Hitler are well known, might have inspired Hewitt to seek the

---

221. "Final Report," 130, 134. Statement under Oath, Jacob Wallenberg, NA, RG 238, Microfilm M897, Roll 114. (Transl.)
222. *Foreign Relations of the United States* (FRUS). *Diplomatic Papers 1944*, vol. I, *General* (Washington: USGPO, 1966), 489, refers to Hewitt as "an official of the United States Commercial Company in Sweden." R. Harris Smith, *OSS: The Secret History of America's First Central Intelligence Agency* (Berkeley: University of California Press, 1972), 215-216, identifies Hewitt as "a wealthy New York attorney," the grandson of a New York Mayor in the 1880s and "a large contributor to the Democratic Party." Joining the OSS in 1942, he was probably more a representative of that organization than of Franklin D. Roosevelt.
223. Felix Kersten still owned his estate Hartzwalde outside Berlin, but in fact had obtained permission from Himmler to move himself and his family to Sweden. The agreement was that he would periodically return to Germany and, of course, at all times be available for treating Himmler. At the time of the Hewitt/Schellenberg meeting, Kersten had his first extended stay in Stockholm. Cf. Kersten, *Totenkopf und Treue*, 237-238. — Waller, *The Devil's Doctor*, 146, identifies Graffman as a Swede "who held a key position in Wallenberg's business organization."

German contact, is rather plausible and would make the resulting encounter of Hewitt and Schellenberg even more significant. It would fit in with Wallenberg's interest to support those who were considering a removal of Hitler, and it certainly would fit in with Schellenberg's interest to link up with persons who might be in a position to assist him in communicating with London and Washington about acceptable ways to end the war. In the absence of reliable information about the manner in which the two men were brought together, suffice it to say that Kersten, Hewitt and Schellenberg met in early November 1943 in a hotel suite in Stockholm.[224] Schellenberg later recalled: "Kersten did no more than introduce us, and then left us alone. Hewitt came to meet me in a very friendly manner; he was a quiet, pleasant man with whom I soon felt on good terms. We very soon agreed not to waste time in diplomatic fencing, but to come to the point clearly and directly. From the beginning Hewitt was at pains to make it clear that he had no official function and was not a diplomat, and that on that account our conversation was valuable only from the point of view of information. This attitude agreed entirely with my own ... With complete frankness, therefore, I explained to Hewitt my view of the general situation in Germany." He explained to the American that he wished to persuade Himmler to propose some sort of compromise to the Western powers at the earliest possible moment. According to Schellenberg, Hewitt expressed concern that "Europe would be saved from bolshevization" but left no doubt that Germany would have to make considerable concessions such as "the cession of the occupied territories in the West"—and "regarding the acquisition of territory in the East ... Germany must have no illusions."[225]

Neither of them could offer any kind of assurance to the other, but both agreed to report to their superiors. If reactions in Washington were interested or positive, Hewitt could return for another meeting with Schellenberg, for instance in Lisbon or Germany. They agreed to give some thought to the entire matter and, in a couple of days, see each other again. That second encounter took place at the home of the German agent August Finke. The main point of discussion seems to have been the manner in which Hewitt would inform Schellenberg about the outcome of his planned discussions in Washington. If prospects on the Potomac appeared somewhat promising, a Stockholm daily paper would on eight consecutive days in February 1944 carry the ad "For sale. Valuable goldfish aquarium at 1524 Kr." In that case further arrangements

---

224. "Translation of Statement by Schellenberg," August 6, 1945, NA, RG 226, E 125A, Box 2. Richard Breitman, "A Deal with the Nazi Dictatorship?: Himmler's Alleged Peace Emissaries in Autumn 1943," *Journal of Contemporary History*, vol. 30 (1995), 414-415.
225. "Translation of Statement by Schellenberg," August 6, 1945, NA, RG 226, E 125A, Box 2.

were to be made secretly through Hubert von Breisky at the German Legation in Lisbon or another German representative in the Portuguese capital. If messages were to become necessary, Hewitt would send such under the cover name Siegel. If there was no ad, Schellenberg would know that Hewitt had not been able to achieve any results.[226]

Whether Schellenberg actually told Hewitt "that Himmler was ready to oust Hitler from power" we cannot ascertain. Hewitt, however, evidently informed the American Minister in Stockholm, Herschel V. Johnson, that during his meetings with Kersten and Schellenberg such matters were discussed and that Kersten had emphasized that "Himmler has become the most important man in the country." Himmler, Kersten told Hewitt, "knows that the war is lost, and is anxious to arrive at an arrangement with the Americans and the British which would leave something of Germany." Probably largely for the record the American Minister in Stockholm "informed the American citizen [Hewitt] ... that proposals such as Dr. Kersten's were completely unacceptable ..." To make certain that no American diplomats in Stockholm could be said to have participated in the half-covert talks with Walter Schellenberg, the State Department then unmistakably "confirmed ... the Minister's understanding that the only terms which the Government of the United States is prepared to give are those of unconditional surrender, and that under no circumstances would peace proposals from Himmler be considered."[227]

By 1943 Schellenberg, of course, might have had more than an inkling that an end to this period of German history would not be negotiated, most certainly not by the Western Allies treating with Heinrich Himmler. Schellenberg was obviously fully informed on the extent of the crimes committed by Germans inside Germany as well as in the countries under occupation. He knew that the British were planning a White Book about German atrocities against Jews and Catholics in occupied Poland.[228] And last but not least, he had had very personal conversations with Masson and Guisan and was therefore more than familiar with the views of informed and educated persons outside Germany. Still, Schellenberg upon his return from Sweden reported his agreements with Abram Hewitt, apparently expecting some how-

---

226. "Final Report," 132-133.
227. Interrogation of August Finke by Peter Beauvais, January 1948, SAN, Rep. 502, F 30. Aide Memoire from State Department, January 24, 1944, to Foreign Office, NAK, FO 371/39085. According to this text, the same information was given to the Soviet Embassy in Washington.
228. Cf. "Geheime Reichssache," Wagner for Foreign Minister, May 14, 1943, PA, AA, Inland IIg 173, "Judenfrage: Allgemein." Cf. USTRAVIC London to OSS, October 19, 1943: "... mass executions of Poles in concentration camps by the use of gas have taken place since the middle of June." NA, RG 226, E A1-170 (210), Box 458.

ever moderate consent. Himmler, however, had had other problems, was unwilling to become part of Schellenberg's dangerous undertaking, feared Hitler's reaction and therefore rejected Schellenberg's proposals across the board. Of course, Schellenberg had not been authorized to seek the American contact, and through his discussions with Hewitt, he had put in question Himmler's loyalty towards Hitler. Looking back, it is difficult to avoid the conclusion that Schellenberg was probably very fortunate that Himmler's emotionally excited refusal and Kaltenbrunner's ice-cold repulse did not have more serious consequences for him and his family.[229]

Though not exposed to ominous threats and possible personal harm, Hewitt too had not been particularly successful with his undertaking. While it may not be inconceivable that his OSS superiors in Stockholm, Bern or Washington had not really considered negotiating with the much despised Himmler but instead had speculated on the welcome unrest in Nazi Germany in the event of a Himmler putsch against Hitler, indications are that Hewitt indeed may have thought it possible to develop through Kersten and Schellenberg a line to Himmler which somehow might lead to negotiations about compromises and an end to the war. The records show that American diplomats in Stockholm and certainly official Washington did not share such expectations—if indeed they existed—and had no intention to deal with Heinrich Himmler. While some questions about the background of Hewitt's operation remain rather unanswered, there can be no doubt that unconditional surrender continued to be the mantra worn in public and that Hewitt therefore had nothing better to show for his efforts than did Schellenberg.[230]

Looking at the military situation, Schellenberg's recognition that negotiations were necessary was certainly correct. The Germans had lost North Africa and Allied forces had landed in Calabria and begun pushing north. Erwin Rommel, the once much venerated commander of the German Africa Corps, had been dispatched to France to supervise the reinforcement of the German defense installations along the Channel Coast where Allied forces were expected to land. The last German offensives against the vastly superior forces of the Soviet Union had failed, and after the debacle of *Unternehmen Zitadelle* (Operation Citadel) in the summer of 1943, all that could be done in the East was a continuous defensive withdrawal accompanied by immense losses of men and material. The *Schlacht im Atlantik* (battle of the Atlantic), after initial much propagandized successes such as *Operation Paukenschlag* (Operation Drumbeat) on America's very shore in early 1942 and the fierce battle against

---

229. "Translation of Statement by Schellenberg," August 6, 1945, NA, RG 226, E 125A, Box 2.
230. Hewitt's report "summarized" by the American Minister in Stockholm Herschel V. Johnson and other relevant documents in FRUS, *Diplomatic Papers 1944*, vol. I, 489-496.

Allied convoys, had collapsed and Hitler's replacement of Grand Admiral Erich Raeder with the faithful Nazi Grand Admiral Karl Dönitz was symbolic of the obvious defeat of Germany's navy. Schellenberg's very high level of information concerning the atrocities committed and the military campaigns being lost would suggest that he might have considered taking his family and himself out of Germany, as in fact had been recommended to him by some of his well placed foreign contacts. Alvar Möller later recalled that in the course of his meetings with Schellenberg regarding the seven Swedish managers held by the Germans, he suggested that it might be wise to consider leaving the sinking ship. Though certainly aware of the situation, Schellenberg only responded that such a move was out of the question for he would not only risk his own life, but also the lives of his entire family. As a dead man, he added, he would not be able to achieve anything good which in fact "was now his endeavor."[231]

All this, of course, does give us an indication as to how much Schellenberg was taken up by the idea of still achieving a negotiated compromise with the Western Allies and simultaneously blocking the Soviet onslaught in the East. How he could possibly think that the Western Allies might find a way to hold such negotiations with Heinrich Himmler, continues to be an unanswerable question. Although there are some indications that he and other German leaders may have seriously entertained the idea of gaining Western support against their former ally the Soviet Union, this does not make sense for men who like Schellenberg because of their international contacts were well informed about the realities outside National Socialist Germany. Moreover, it remains an enigma how such men could not have been concerned with an aftermath to their mass murder in Eastern Europe and the destruction of the Jews. It would seem evident that they would hardly be able to block the question of guilt from their minds entirely.

---

231. Möller's German text: "... worauf doch jetzt sein Bestreben gerichtet sei." Statement under Oath, Alvar Möller, April 22, 1948, SAN, Rep. 501, LV, S-4.

Chapter III

Twilight of the Gods

The persistent efforts of Schellenberg in 1943 to construct some meaningful lines to the Western Allies were undoubtedly serious, and they reflected his conviction, already held for some time, that Germany would not be able to win the war. That most Germans continued to be loyal to their government may in part explain why Schellenberg had to be on constant guard in his undertakings and could rely on only a very small number of men in the political and military Nazi structures. Even while Allied bombing raids nearly wiped out their cities from Stuttgart in the south to the Hanseatic port city of Hamburg in the north, a great majority of Germans, in marked contrast to Schellenberg, apparently wanted to believe in the promised *Endsieg* (final victory) and enthusiastically supported their *Führer*, denouncing and punishing those who dared to think otherwise.

Schellenberg's operations in 1944 were to become even more hectic and dangerous, particularly following the belated bungled attempt in July by parts of the military to take over the government and finally change Germany's course. It was also the year that would see the merger of the two German foreign intelligence organizations, something he had wanted ever since leaving Müller's *Amt* IV in 1941. Developments, not only those related to the failed putsch of July, but many of them connected to persons outside of Germany, would increasingly create situations where victims of the Nazi system he served needed to be rescued or assisted in one way or the other. His personal involvement in such humane activities seems to have been caused by a variety of circumstances and motivations, and it is rather difficult in many of these operations to arrive at persuasive explanations. Evidently it would not suffice to merely assume that the intelligent and still very young SS leader merely realized that the Nazi system was scheduled for certain defeat and that it was therefore essential to assure one's own survival. Interpretations of this nature have been offered but often tend to overlook the complexity of Schellenberg as a functionary at that level and they do not take into consideration the multifaceted moral and political conflict he had gotten himself into and which he does not appear to have mastered. Self-preservation as a strong personal motive must be considered, but very likely it was only one of several forces driving him. In Germany it was blind perseverance until the final almost complete destruction in 1945 that appears to have been the dominating force. Schellenberg was aware that he was part of the system, and it is indeed more than conceivable that he considered extracting himself and his family in time. However, whatever his motives may have been, he stayed.

As would be expected, foreign intelligence and related operations continued to occupy the visible part of Schellenberg's life in early 1944. While, in contrast to numerous Army and SS officers looking East, it is undeniable that his own interests and therefore the great majority of his personal contacts and intelligence lines were clearly in the West, it would be a mistake to overlook his activities related to Eastern Europe, especially the Soviet Union, and to the Middle East. One very significant and highly controversial but not overly successful organizational effort against the U.S.S.R. was *Unternehmen* Zeppelin (Operation Zeppelin). It was an intelligence operation that had its beginnings some time in late 1941.[232] Its main purpose was the infiltration of Russian territory behind the front lines and farther inland. Russian POWs were passed through the front or, in somewhat safer manner, dropped from planes far behind the lines. Operation Zeppelin had become necessary because other attempts to collect information from inside the vast Soviet Union had been less than rewarding. The whole operation was directed from a central office not in *Amt* VI but on the Potsdamer Strasse. From the records, as well as from his memoirs, one gains the impression that Schellenberg invested less effort in Soviet affairs than in Western matters and that he showed much less personal involvement in the Eastern European operations thereby allowing for more independent action on the part of those running that section of *Amt* VI.

---

232. Cf. XX5315, February 6, 1945, NA, RG 263, E A1-86, Box 37. The beginnings of Operation Zeppelin, contrary to what some historians have concluded, were in the autumn of 1941. Directives from *Amt* IV Chief Müller "for the commandos of the Chief of the Sipo and the SD which are to be assigned to the permanent prisoner of war camps and the transit camps," October 13, 1941, *Trials of War Criminals before the Nuernberg Military Tribunals under Control Council Law No. 10*, vol. 13, *Nuernberg October 1946-April 1949* (Washington, D.C.: USGPO, 1952), 557-558. Cf. also Müller to same, October 25, 1941, *Ibid.*, 558-559.

Consequently, Schellenberg most likely also was not always correctly informed. The interrogation, selection and subsequent training of the Russian soldiers, POWs as well as deserters, could be delegated to qualified officers of the responsible *Amt* VI section.[233] One of the fundamental problems of the entire operation appears to have been a lack of suitable POWs. For the difficult missions the Germans wanted educated and anti-Communist Russians, but instead discovered that such men had been weeded out rather thoroughly by the Russian authorities "leaving only anti-Communists who were illiterate."[234] The responsible Group VI C was led by SS-*Obersturmbannführer* Dr. Heinz Gräfe with the subdivision VI C1-3 being run by SS-*Sturmbannführer* Dr. Erich Hengelhaupt and the Operation Zeppelin itself, internally referred to as VI C(Z), being supervised by SS-*Obersturmbannführer* Dr. Rudolf Oebsger-Röder. For obvious reasons Operation Zeppelin would also seek close cooperation with Reinhard Gehlen's *Abteilung Fremde Heere Ost* (FHO, Foreign Armies East), which was the German Army's military intelligence section in the East, and with the Vlasov Army. Gehlen was informed about Zeppelin operations and his FHO frequently provided the information needed for the undertakings behind the Soviet lines.[235] When Gräfe was killed in a car accident in January 1944, Hengelhaupt filled in until summer when the position was given to SS-*Sturmbannführer* Karl Tschierschky who in 1941/1942 had been with *Einsatzgruppe* A (special task force). According to the records he was "dismissed for inefficiency" at the end of the year and replaced with SS-*Standartenführer* Albert Rapp.[236] Organized largely along lines developed by Gräfe, Zeppelin main-

---

233. In the above-mentioned directive of October 25, 1941, Müller clearly states that he (Amt IV) will control at least the early stages of the Zeppelin work: "... the representatives of Amt VI [Schellenberg] will be subordinated to the leaders of the Einsatzkommandos of the Sipo and the SD during their activity in the prisoner-of-war camps." (p. 559)
234. Counterintelligence Special Report 61, March 6, 1948, NA, RG 319, IRR, IS, Operation Zeppelin, Box 6.
235. Reinhard Gehlen (1902-1979), since 1920 service in German Army, 1935 General Staff, 1942-1945 Chief of FHO, 1946 Chief of *Organisation* Gehlen, later Chief *Bundesnachrichtendienst* (BND, Federal Intelligence Service). Gehlen's memoirs *The Service: The Memoirs of General Reinhard Gehlen* (New York: World Publishing, 1972; German Copyright 1971). Heinz Höhne & Hermann Zölling, *The General Was a Spy: The Truth about General Gehlen and His Spy Ring* (New York: Coward, McCann & Geoghegan, 1972; 1st German ed., 1971), 39. Cf. James H. Critchfield, *Partners at the Creation: The Men Behind Postwar Germany's Defense and Intelligence Establishments* (Annapolis: Naval Institute Press, 2003).
236. Situation Report No. 8, Records of the Federal Bureau of Investigation, NA, RG 65, E A1-136P, Box 56. Heinz Gräfe (1908-1944), studied Law in Leipzig, joined NS-*Juristenbund* and *Stahlhelm* June 1933, later in the year following an encounter with Heydrich member of SS and SD. Wildt, *Generation des Unbedingten*, passim. Erich Hengelhaupt (b. 1911), according to some sources a Soviet agent, joined NSDAP 1930, studied Journalism and Sociology, after the war connected to C.I.C. and *Organisation* Gehlen. Klaus-Michael Mallmann, "Der Krieg im Dunkeln. Das Unternehmen 'Zeppelin' 1942-1945," 332, and Lutz Hachmeister, "Die Rolle des SD-Personals in der Nachkriegszeit. Zur nationalsozialistischen Durchdringung der Bundesrepublik," 364, both in Wildt, ed. *Nachrichtendienst, politische Elite und Mordeinheit*. Rudolf Oebsger-Röder (1914-1992), SS, SD, after the war correspondent of German newspapers and connected with BND. Helmut Roewer, Stefan Schäfer, Matthias Uhl, *Lexikon der Geheimdienste im 20. Jahrhundert* (Munich: Herbig, 2003), 325-326. Cf. on Röder's activities in 1951 CC2 Report, May 30, 1951, NA, RG 263, E A1-86, CIA

tained relatively small administrative staffs in Berlin and instead shifted most of the decision making and the training of the POWs to various outlying camps. Among such locations were Sandberge Training School for advanced training in all aspects of espionage work, wireless transmission and sabotage, the much smaller Sachsenhausen Camp for men who had already absolved Sandberge, the Pleskau Camp training men for operations in the Baltic nations and in Northern Russia, various camps of *Hauptkommando Mitte* (Command Center Area) located in 1944 near Prague, Tepl Camp in 1945 located near Marienbad but due to the advance of Russian forces not completed, Jablon Camp destroyed by enemy bombing raids already in late 1942, Auschwitz Camp training "Caucasians" only and shut down in 1944, and Special Camps T and L engaged in technical projects and map research on the Soviet Union.[237]

As is often the case with this particular type of covert operation, a correct and fair appraisal of results achieved can be problematic. Naturally, supervising officers involved in unpleasant and undesirable assignments would not be overly talkative later. A possible exception could be still classified information given by surviving *Amt* VI and German Army officers to Allied intelligence services or to the *Organisation* Gehlen/BND which took on some of these men during the early years of the Cold War. As in the case of the Police Attachés coming from *Amt* IV but stationed in German diplomatic posts, the strong rivalry between *Amt* IV Gestapo and *Amt* VI Foreign Intelligence also took its toll in the Operation Zeppelin. In this case, the records suggest that Gräfe was much closer to the Gestapo Chief Heinrich Müller than to his official chief Walter Schellenberg and that some of the activities of Zeppelin inside the Soviet Union may indeed have originated outside of *Amt* VI. In fact, it would appear that Gräfe and Müller decided on certain measures behind the Russian lines without Schellenberg being sufficiently informed. As in numerous other operations, matters were not helped by Schellenberg's antipathy towards the Gestapo Chief.[238] In addition to management deficiencies of this nature, it needs to be pointed out that, as in many German operations, there was a continuous lack of planes and pilots to take the agents behind Russian lines. Moreover, following their crushing defeat at Stalingrad in early 1943, the Germans found it increasingly difficult to recruit Russian POWs for dangerous missions inside their home country. Also, the Germans had begun to have doubts about the wisdom of dropping off large numbers of men who were expected to operate mostly uncontrolled and on their own, but in fact often simply had

---

Name Files, Box 18. Jeffrey Burds, "The Soviet War against 'Fifth Columnists': The Case of Chechnya, 1942-4," *Journal of Contemporary History*, vol. 42 (2007), 287.
237. Situation Report No. 8, Secret, NA, RG 65, E A1-136P, Box 56.
238. Statement under Oath, Otto Skorzeny, June 4, 1948, SAN, Rep. 501, LV, S-5.

vanished after hitting the ground. Instead *Amt* VI in cooperation with *Abwehr*, FHO and the Vlasov people in 1944 made an effort to be more selective in the camps and to dispatch only small units or even individual men who seemed to be sufficiently qualified and, more important, personally motivated to go on these suicide missions.[239]

What to this day German authors call the Vlasov Army was neither an army nor an effective instrument of war in any other way. Instead there was for a long time no more than a rather large number of men in a general state of disorganization. Some authors speak of 1,000,000 men, but most likely are referring to planning figures or uncommitted POWs in German camps. Lieutenant General Andrei Andreyevich Vlasov had been the commanding officer of the 2nd Soviet Shock Army on what was known as the Volkhov Front and his assignment seems to have been to remove some of the German pressure on Leningrad.[240] When that Army was defeated by the Germans and Vlasov had stayed with his troops rather than having himself flown out of the kettle, he was captured and taken to Vinnitsa, a special German POW camp for more important prisoners.[241] Here Vlasov and Colonel Vladimir Boyarsky, it is thought because they felt let down by the Soviet Government, offered the Germans to organize a National Russian Army. It has later been argued that the Russian officers were too naïve to know what they were getting involved in and that their German captors were too ignorant to develop a vital interest in Russia and its future. One of the exceptions on the German side was Captain Wilfried Strik-Strikfeldt, a *Fremde Heere Ost* (FHO) officer and attached to the OKW. A Baltic German, educated in St. Petersburg and having served in the Russian Army, he was, in marked contrast to most Germans who were dealing with the Soviet Union, intensely interested in Russian matters and in some ways his lively concern with Russia may have contributed to the rather optimistic expectations Vlasov appears to have developed in his contacts with the Germans.[242] Whether it was a very intelligent move by the Germans to use Vlasov's name in their propaganda campaign directed toward the U.S.S.R. is

---

239. Schellenberg Statement about Zeppelin, November 13, 1945, Prosecution Document Book 71-C, United States Holocaust Memorial Museum Archives (USHMMA), Kempner Collection, Box 197, F 2.
240. Andrei Andreyevich Vlasov (1901-1946), youngest of thirteen children of a poor family, educated in religious schools prior to revolution, after revolution studied Agriculture, served in Red Army during Civil War, became a successful professional soldier, Chief of the Soviet military mission in China 1938, back in U.S.S.R. under General Semyon Konstantinovich Timoshenko at Kiev 1939, Lieutenant General January 1942, by June 1942 2nd Shock Army defeated, taken prisoner by Germans, captured by Soviet troops May 1945, tried and executed 1946. Cf. Catherine Andreyev, "Andrei Andreyevich Vlasov," in Harold Shukman, ed., *Stalin's Generals* (New York: Grove Press, 1993; 1st ed. London 1993).
241. Alan Clark, *Barbarossa: The Russian-German Conflict, 1941-1945* (London: Phoenix/Orion, 1996; 1st 1965), 199-200.
242. Wilfried Strik-Strikfeldt (b. 1897), close to later BND Chief Reinhard Gehlen. He published his memoirs of the war years *Gegen Stalin und Hitler: General Wlassow und die russische Freiheitsbewegung* (Mainz: v. Hase & Koehler, 1970).

quite another matter. On the other hand, men offering their services to the enemy traditionally have not been able to count on a great amount of respect and often have been used and abused without any concern for their own future. Hitler, driven by a loathing for the supposedly inferior Slavs, certainly did not want an independent Russia, and his views of Russia and the Russians certainly must have contributed to his unwillingness to even consider a Russian liberation army fighting alongside his supposedly superior Aryan forces. Instead of a National Russian Army under the command of someone such as Vlasov, the Germans organized different Russian combat units attached to various German divisions and only ineffectively and very loosely united under the overall command of General Ernst Köstring. The General came from a proud Hanoverian family that had moved to Russia when Hanover fell to Prussia. He had gone to school in Moscow and spoke Russian like a native. He cared for Tsarist and revolutionary Russia and as a young officer had been on the staff of Hans von Seeckt, the main promoter of German-Russian cooperation after World War I. He was a rather typical officer in the traditional sense and lacked all interest in loud public appearances. Köstring's standing with Hitler was not good for he had warned the *Führer* that the Soviet Union was vast and, like a bear, after the initial surprise would mount a most powerful counterattack. From a military perspective much valuable time was lost until November 1944 when with the specific agreement of Himmler a Committee for the Liberation of the Peoples of Russia was finally founded. But even then the decision to let Vlasov organize two divisions for combat in the East caused little serious interest among German military leaders now intensely preoccupied with the Battle of the Bulge and its consequences on the Western Front, as well as the expected onslaught of large Soviet forces on Poland and East Germany. In addition, the German High Command lacked the energy and the material needed to outfit a new Russian army most ranking Nazis did not want anyway.[243]

All this meant that Vlasov was given very limited freedom of movement, not to mention an opportunity to serve as an intelligent advisor to the German General Staff. Instead he found himself surrounded by Russian nationals, united only by their common hatred of Joseph Stalin, and a number of enthusiastic Nazis who despised all Russians as inferior human beings. When Schellenberg met Vlasov through SS-*Standartenführer* Rapp and SS-*Oberführer* Dr. Erhard Kröger, he had actually hoped to employ the Russian General as a kind of central figure in his rather vague plans to bring some order to the masses of

---

243. Re: Vlasov and Himmler cf. Weinberg, *A World at Arms*, 295, 756. Clark, *Barbarossa*, 199-200, 408. On Köstring cf. Hans von Herwarth, *Zwischen Hitler und Stalin: Erlebte Zeitgeschichte 1931 bis 1945* (Frankfurt: Ullstein Propyläen, 1982), 253 ff.

different ethnic Eastern Europeans and Russians working in Germany mostly as slave labor. Apparently unaware of the antagonism most of these imprisoned and maltreated people must have felt for their captors who kept them in prison camps, concentration camps or industrial forced labor situations, Schellenberg seems to have had curious ideas regarding a Union of European Peoples in which "foreign workers consisting of the racial minorities" could be brought together in a politically feasible way.[244] Rapp had actually come to some agreement with the Russian General concerning cooperation in intelligence work on the Soviet Union, and to all appearances Vlasov indeed was happy to collaborate with the German officers of the former *Abwehr*, which since 1944 was part of Schellenberg's Foreign Intelligence organization. That a man like Vlasov would also have his own personal network of intelligence lines to exiled Russians in Europe, as well as to men still loyal to him inside the Soviet military structures, may be assumed, and it was here that Vlasov was likely to come in conflict with the watchful counter-intelligence of *Amt* IV Gestapo. As in the related Operation Zeppelin, Schellenberg's *Amt* VI would therefore be forced to tolerate interferences from Müller's Amt IV. While the various Russian units out in the field were still under the well-meaning but by necessity inefficient command of General Ernst Köstring, Vlasov was largely tied down in Berlin and subject to all the shenanigans and political intrigues of the Nazi system.

One of the most colorful and, as some authors would have it, dangerous figures in these German-Russian operations was Prince Turkul, in actuality Anton Turkul, a White Russian leader with a considerable network of personal contacts all over Europe. Much of the time Georg Sergei Romanov appears to have been or acted as his personal secretary or advisor. From the records it would appear that Turkul, originally an officer in the Tsarist army, served in the White Russian Wrangel Army, and after the victory of the Red Army fled to Sofia, moved on to Paris, and for fear of being kidnapped by Russian intelligence or expelled by the French, he went on to Berlin. Here he stayed until the Hitler-Stalin Pact of 1939 when he thought it wise to depart for Rome where he felt safer. In 1938, while still in the Nazi capital, he was contacted by *Generalmajor* Hans Piekenbrock of the *Abwehr*. Chapman Pincher describes him as "a prewar agent of the British Secret Service in Paris" and "a friend of Himmler before the war," suggesting the latter to have been the reason for the former. Whatever Turkul's experience was as an intelligence agent, the initial, apparently fruitful period of cooperation with the *Abwehr*, the Nazi Military

---

244. "Final Report," Appendix XIII, 272-273. Kröger was a trained lawyer from Latvia, SS member 1938, very active for Nazi programs in Latvia and Estonia. George C. Browder, *Hitler's Enforcers: The Gestapo and SS Security Service in the Nazi Revolution* (New York: Oxford University Press, 1996), 206.

Intelligence Service, was interrupted by a falling-out. The cooling-off period cannot have been very long for the records clearly indicate that, following an undisclosed time of apparently no contacts, in the course of World War II the *Abwehr* was again working very closely with the Russian.[245] Around Turkul was a group of men whose loyalty was not undisputed and who for that reason proved to be extremely difficult to handle. Probably the most significant person in this network was Richard Klatt who was "run" by Colonel Wiese of *Abwehr* Vienna.[246]

While Vienna seemed more than pleased with what Klatt delivered, the Chief of the *Abwehr* station in Sofia, Colonel Otto Wagner, alias Dr. Delius, took a decidedly different view. After the war U.S. intelligence came to the decision that Wagner was a personal enemy of Klatt, suggesting that information from Wagner concerning Klatt should be taken with a grain of salt. Wagner, in fact, thought that Klatt was working for the Russians or for the British and had informed the *Abwehr* Chief Admiral Wilhelm Canaris of his suspicions. Canaris, however, had responded by pointing out that *Abwehr Luft* (Military Intelligence Air) was always very pleased with the quality of Klatt's material. Wagner understood the message from above, but, of course, as a watchful intelligence officer continued to keep a close eye on the Klatt situation. Another attempt to obtain Canaris' permission for an official investigation received the same reaction. Wagner realized that he would get nowhere with his Chief in Berlin and apparently did not repeat his grave suspicion of Klatt's apparatus until Schellenberg's *Amt* VI had absorbed the *Abwehr* in 1944. Schellenberg, although not well informed on Soviet matters, decided to listen and arranged for Klatt's operation to be thoroughly checked, ostensibly because there were strong reasons to suspect Black Market deals and other irregularities. When the investigation made no real headway, Schellenberg actually summoned Colonel Wiese from Vienna and gave him unmistakable instructions. After the war Schellenberg told Allied interrogators that he had

---

245. Anton Turkul (Odessa 1892-1959), often called Prince Turkul, alias Tourkout, alias Papa, stayed in several countries after leaving Russia following the defeat of the White Army, most likely expelled from France 1938, to Berlin with German papers, contact with Hans Pieckenbrock, moved to Rome after Hitler-Stalin Pact, survived end of war. Georg Sergei Romanov (also referred to as George Leonidovitch Romanoff), b. Tiflis 1901, left Russia 1920, in Paris 1923-1939, was a White Russian, very close to Turkul until there were differences between them, causing Romanov to change from Turkul to the German Embassy in Budapest. There are suggstions that he lived as a priest called "Father George" in Geneva after World War II. Top Secret "Report on the Interrogation of George Leonidovitch Romanoff" in Geneva, November 19 and 20, 1946, NAK, KV 2/1630. Chapman Pincher, *Their Trade Is Treachery* (London: Sidgwick & Jackson, 1987; 1st 1981), 126. On Turkul cf. Burds, "The Soviet War against 'Fifth Columnists',". passim.
246. Richard Klatt, b. Richard Kauder (Kauders) Vienna 1900, alias Karmany, parents Jewish, parents and children baptized Catholic Church 1904, mechanical engineer, married and divorced, arrested in Hungary 1939, handed over to Gestapo 1940, freed by Count Rudolf von Marogna-Redwitz, Chief of *Abwehrstelle* (Military Intelligence Post) Vienna, since then with *Abwehr* responsible to Colonel Count von Marogna-Redwitz.

become aware that Klatt was moving closer to Wilhelm Höttl and Wilhelm Waneck, which if one wished to avoid additional trouble could actually have prevented a serious inquiry at a later time.[247] For this reason Schellenberg's decision to act sounds entirely plausible. Schellenberg knew what he was talking about, with Höttl and Waneck being Austrian protégés of his Austrian Chief Kaltenbrunner and considering the frosty relations if not to say evident antagonism between him and Kaltenbrunner. Wiese did what he was told and getting down to serious work he came up with a most significant detail: The informants of Klatt were Prince Turkul and "a Slovac Lawyer (Ira Lang)."[248] Presumably Schellenberg did have some previous information on these two names that caused him to react. In any case, he moved instantaneously and ordered Turkul to Berlin, ostensibly needing his assistance to keep an eye on the frustrated and at times difficult Vlasov. Curiously, though speculations regarding Turkul's work for the Soviets run high, there is almost nothing to be found on his real activities following this quasi forced transplantation to Berlin. There are indications that he may have been the real or pretending leader of a large number of anti-Soviet Russians scattered over much of Europe. If Schellenberg asked Turkul to follow the activities of the hapless Vlasov, this would suggest that he had no more confidence in the Russian General than Hitler himself. Considering that Schellenberg was not well informed about the Soviet Union and Eastern Europe, he may have taken a sceptical view of the Russian operations even without sharing the unintelligent racial prejudices of his fellow Nazi leaders and a great number of Germans. If that was his frame of mind, however, one is inclined to ask why he would have put Turkul onto Vlasov. There are a number of claims that, once in Berlin, Turkul aspired to push Vlasov aside and to form a Russian National Army under his own leadership. If that could not be achieved, he tried to persuade Schellenberg to agree "to infiltrate his men into the Vlassow army as political commissars." Chapman Pincher also reports that Turkul convinced Himmler and the German High

---

247. When Schellenberg restructured *Amt* VI Foreign Intelligence in 1942, he reorganized Group VI E with group leader Helmut Knochen going to Paris and new names gaining influence. Höttl and Waneck, regardless of their somewhat unclear status in Amt VI, were among the winners in the reorganization. In late 1943 they and a good part of that group had moved their base to Vienna. Group VI E included intelligence work in Italy, Hungary, Serbia, Slovakia, Croatia, Rumania, Bulgaria and Greece. Cf. Wildt, *Generation des Unbedingten*, 404-405.

248. Ira Lang, also referred to as Ira Longin, Ira Longhin Patronymic Fedorovitch (Fedorovich), alias Ilya Lang, Dr. Lang, Vasya, 02. Probably born 1896, Russian, to Constantinople 1920, later studied in Prague, school teacher, several languages, arrested 1939 by Hungarian police, met Klatt/Kauder in prison, 1940 with Klatt in Budapest, possibly joined *Abwehrstelle* in Vienna, late 1941 said to have brought Romanov into intelligence group. — Cf. Dick White's clear placement of Turkul and Lang: "Klatt's interrogation ... throws a sinister light on his two main sources — General Turkul and Ira Lang. The theory is now held that these two White Russians are members of the NKVD ..." Note, August 23, 1946, NAK, KV 2/1629. Concerning Klatt and postwar interrogation cf. Nigel West, Oleg Tsarev, *The Crown Jewels: The British Secrets at the Heart of the KGB Archives* (New Haven: Yale University Press, 1999; 1st 1998), chptr. 8.

Command that Vlasov's army, if deployed on the Russian front, would switch sides. Supposedly Turkul told the Germans that Vlasov "had been secretly in touch with the Kremlin." Much of this makes sense and one could feel inclined to follow Pincher's apparent view that Turkul was a Soviet agent. Final evaluation of Turkul and his role in Soviet Russia and Nazi Germany will have to be postponed until declassification of the respective documents.[249]

With Turkul out of the picture—first in Berlin and during the final weeks of World War II in the area of Salzburg—Colonel Wiese and his men wasted no time in arresting Klatt and his team of operatives, some sources speak of 28 men, charging them with illegal Black Market and currency activities. Fitting in well with the curious and contradictory appearance of this entire operation, the Klatt people were let go a few days after Turkul's departure, and it is said that after a brief period of stalling, results quickly picked up and the Klatt apparatus, in the view of the recipients, became as excellent a source as it had ever been. Klatt's other productive information found that Ira Lang had been connected with Turkul for a great number of years, but Turkul, for reasons unknown, in World War II had allowed him to also work directly for Klatt. Quite independently from any assessment of Vlasov's ties to Russia and his personal plans for a Russian future, there are certainly sufficient indications that both Klatt and Lang served more than one side and that both in some way directly or indirectly were linked to Soviet intelligence. In the case of Klatt, Wagner was fairly certain that Klatt's claimed network inside the Soviet Union did not even exist and that the information supplied by Klatt came from the NKVD. Indeed, it turned out, Klatt had a relationship with a Colonel Otto Hatz, Budapest's Military Attaché in Sofia and later in Istanbul. Apparently Klatt and Hatz exchanged intelligence and the latter had a brother who was known to work for the Russians.[250]

In the absence of reliable documents of the time and being limited to a few interrogations of the postwar period, an appraisal of how the Germans handled this, still presents some difficulty. Apparently they arrested Hatz and then hired him to work for their side against the Soviet Union. When both Klatt and Hatz, as Wagner saw it, delivered the same disinformation of apparent Russian origin, Wagner felt he had sufficient proof. The entire case was apparently openly discussed at a conference in Berlin in the autumn of 1944, and it is in

---

249. "Final Report," Appendix XXIII, 322-323, 331-332. NAK, KV 2/1495-1497. "Interrogation Report of Richard Kauder @ Klatt @ Karmany," NA, RG 319, IRR, PS, Boxes 234b-234c. "Translation of Statement by Schellenberg," July 21, 1945, NA, RG 226, E 125A, Box 2. Pincher, *Their Trade Is Treachery*, 126.
250. On Otto Hatz (also Hatszeghy) "Translation of Statement by Schellenberg," August 7, 1945, NA, RG 226, E 125A (?), Box 2. "List of Alphabetical Names and Cover Names of LMK Organisation," NAK, KV 2/1497. "Interrogation of Oberstleutnant Wagner ... by Mr. Arnold Silver," February 3, 1947, NA, RG 319, IRR, PS, unmarked box (234b-234c?).

retrospect difficult to say whether Schellenberg actually agreed with Wagner's findings as presented or whether he, in fact, sided with Military Intelligence Air who praised Klatt's information as genuine and valuable. Wagner later said that Schellenberg had told him during a telephone conversation after the conference that he shared his view of Klatt. As in other intelligence operations of this nature, it is tempting to surmise that men like Schellenberg, to assure the continuity of their services and to maintain a minimum of personal security, may be almost forced to keep the lid on certain embarrassing developments. If that was the case here, the Klatt operation could have continued, even if scrutinized somewhat more closely than before. The outcome of this particular affair seems to have been that Klatt was kept on and indeed very much survived the end of the war. His presumed friend, the Hungarian Colonel Hatz , who continued to be seen as working for more than one side, chose in late 1944 to cross the lines and turn himself over to the Soviet Union, reportedly only to end up in a camp for war criminals near Moscow.[251]

The fact that the engineer Richard Klatt or Richard Kauder was Jewish seems to have had little effect on his intelligence activities, other than that occasionally someone would wonder why as a Jew he would wish to be such an engaged and successful agent on behalf of Nazi Germany. That Klatt's problems with Wagner were also or even to a considerable extent caused by the latter's stubbornly anti-Semitic Nazi persuasions, as Herbert Rittlinger, another *Abwehr* officer, would have it, appears very likely. Yet, if that was what moved Wagner, it seems not to have been sufficiently important for *Abwehr* and *Fremde Heere Ost* to sacrifice the highly valued services of Klatt and his people.[252] Besides, Colonel Wagner had repeatedly presented in Berlin what he considered the unreliability of Klatt. In contrast to the case of Andor (Bandi) Grosz, another Jewish agent, who was "blackmailed into working" for the Nazis because his smuggling activities had gotten him into legal difficulties, Richard Klatt seems to have operated on a more sophisticated level and to have been just too well connected to be simply blackmailed.[253] Possibly surprising when considering what Wagner thought he knew, but indeed Klatt's standing with other *Abwehr* men was of such extraordinary quality that they dis-

---

251. NAK, KV 2/1497. "Translation of Statement by Schellenberg," August 7, 1945, NA, RG 226, E 125A(?), Box 2.
252. Interestingly one of Klatt's men, a Hungarian Jew by the name of Mirko Rot (in some documents Roth) fled Sofia to avoid problems with the Germans and by way of Portugal made it to England. Apparently he was interned in Camp 020 and willingly talked about his work in the Klatt group. Various documents, NAK, KV 2/1712-1714. Herbert Rittlinger, *Geheimdienst mit beschränkter Haftung. Bericht vom Bosporus* (Stuttgart: Deutsche Verlags-Anstalt, 1973), 224-225.
253. Cf. Bela Vago, "The Intelligence Aspects of the Joel Brand Mission," *Yad Vashem Studies on the European Jewish Catastrophe and Resistance*, vol. X (Jerusalem, 1974), 114-115. Otto Hatz, the Hungarian Military Attaché in Sofia, was one of the many recipients of information from Grosz. In 1942 Grosz is said to have smuggled for Richard Klatt.

obeyed Hitler's orders. When their *Führer* in 1943 personally decreed that "non-Aryan" representatives were to be dismissed from the *Abwehr* and that no exception was to be made in Sofia, these *Abwehr* officers with the full knowledge of Reinhard Gehlen (*Fremde Heere Ost*) clandestinely moved Richard Klatt and a good part of his group from Sofia to Budapest where they would be less exposed to harassment and worse from the Gestapo. When the Mussolini regime tumbled in the summer of 1943, the same officers together with Klatt hurriedly flew to Rome and in an adventurous operation evacuated Prince Turkul, his family and his secretary Muchanov to Budapest. Incidentally, Turkul's assistant Georg Romanov also moved to Budapest in 1943.[254] Altogether, aside from normal personal rivalries and the sensible suspicions voiced by Wagner, it seems evident that the Klatt apparatus continued to serve German Military Intelligence, undisrupted by their absorption into *Amt* VI in 1944 and, for whatever reasons, covered by the Chief of *Amt* VI Walter Schellenberg. One might question whether Schellenberg was actually sufficiently informed on Soviet policy and intelligence methods to enable him to arrive at a competent appraisal of men such as Klatt, Turkul or Lang. Instead Schellenberg seems to have been almost completely Western oriented and therefore thought that it was possible for the Germans to join an anti-Soviet alliance that he anticipated for awhile.

The intelligence reports coming from Klatt were divided according to their source into two main groups, namely *Max* and *Moritz*. *Max* was used to describe the Turkul apparatus, also referred to by the White Russians as "Union," as well as to name the intelligence reports emanating from that group and containing data largely on the Soviet Union and Soviet policies. *Moritz* was the name given to the intelligence reports treating Mediterranean topics and apparently including at times Southeastern Europe, Turkey and the Mideast, reaching as far as North Africa. While Turkul and Lang as sources for *Max* finally became known to the Germans—certainly through the investigations of Wagner and Wiese—information on the source or sources for *Moritz* still appears to be largely unsatisfactory. One of the suppliers of *Moritz*, from the records at least, would seem to have been Enomoto Momotaro, a Japanese journalist working in Europe. Another may have been Ira Lang whose non-Russian reports are said to have been labeled *Moritz*.[255] Apart from those authors who have cast a special light on Turkul and the related Soviet disin-

---

254. Director CIA to CIA Germany. February 18/19, 1953, Secret, NA, RG 263, E A1-86, "Gehlen File," Box 13. Joan Paine to British Army Headquarters, Intelligence Division. December 3, 1946, Top Secret, NAK, KV 2/1496. "Interrogation Report No. 1 of Richard Kauder @ Klatt @ Karmany," date missing on ripped page, NA, RG 319, IRR, PS, Boxes 234b-234c.
255. NAK, KV 2/1497. CI Special Interrogation Report No. 39, Otto Wagner, March 4, 1947, Top Secret, NAK, KV 2/1631.

formation game, most intelligence experts and authors, including some otherwise often critical voices from the Allied side, tend to agree that the Klatt apparatus ran one of the successful operations of the German services. Curiously, even if it was a Soviet game that was played and even if some intelligence reports grossly mislead the Germans, for instance prior to Stalingrad, it is very likely that the game also gave the Germans data which could be and were used to their advantage.[256]

Doubtful as the reliability of the work of Klatt and Turkul may have been much of the time, it appears justified to ask why the Western Allies decided to hang on to these agents in the postwar years. One of the reasons may have been that the Americans, not unlike some *Abwehr* officers a few years before, confirmed or discovered during interrogation of the Russian what they called Turkul's "MVD affiliations." If their knowledge were to become public, the Americans felt, their sources were very likely to freeze up. This way men like Turkul simply became part of the early Cold War maneuvers which incidentally for the individual agent in the field were no less perilous than many a conflict in World War II. A British intelligence memorandum by J. Chenhalls of October, 1946, weighs the possibilities of handing Turkul and Ira Lang over to the Russians or holding them in the United Kingdom or in the United States and comes to the conclusion that it would be best to recommend to Washington that the two men be taken back to the American Zone of occupied Germany and be held there in some prison without contact with each other and "available for reference."[257]

Richard Klatt, though until the end of 1944 Schellenberg had held his hand over him, finally did fall victim to anti-Semitic Nazis and *Abwehr* officers who saw him as a Soviet agent. He found himself arrested and transported to the Gestapo-*Leitstelle* (Regional Head Office) in Vienna, but Klatt, of course, would not have been Klatt if he had accepted the Germans' hospitality and waited around for the approaching Soviet forces. Exact details of his escape are unknown, but he somehow managed to get on the road going West, joining the masses of civilian refugees and military heading in the same direction and always aware that the slightest mistake could land him again in the hands of German military police or the SS. Being hung from a tree or a lantern pole was the ongoing procedure then in areas still under German control. Rumors that

---

256. Cf. David Kahn's interesting speculations on the value of Klatt in *Hitler's Spies*, 312-317 and especially 369. Kahn also cites a few Klatt messages which with the Sofia-Berlin traffic were read by the British. See also Kahn's point that the Russians when told by the British "did not appear interested." "The German Intelligence Service and the War," December 1, 1945, NA, RG 319, IRR, IS, Box 5. (This report is very similar to one by Hugh Trevor-Roper of the same time.) Pincher, *Their Trade is Treachery*, 126-127.
257. U.S. Forces Heidelberg to War Dept., October 16, 1946, Top Secret Control, NA, RG 226, E 216, Box 1. Memorandum by J. Chenhalls, October 4, 1946, NAK, KV 2/1629.

he had been shot were without foundation, for Klatt or Kauder was lucky enough to run into American troops who passed him on to the C.I.C. Declassified records in the National Archives so far do not contain any enlightening hints on this top agent for the immediate post-war years. One exception is a curious letter from U.S. intelligence to MI5, informing the British that Kauder and his family were taken from Frankfurt to Salzburg by military train and were now checked in at the Old Fox Hotel. Kauder had been instructed by the C.I.C. to stay away from any intelligence activities and that his telephone and mail would be censored.[258] A much later and surprising German document of May 1949 in the OSS records is actually a report on the intelligence activities of Dr. Hugo Kittel, Police Commissioner in Vienna in the 1930s and since 1945 supposedly in the import-export business and located in Salzburg. Kittel's chief agent is said to be the engineer Richard Kauder. According to this document, Soviet intelligence agents disguised as American MPs turned up one day and tried to abduct Kauder. Fortunately for him, the Russian operation had been betrayed and Austrian police was on hand to prevent any harm. Also the document suggests that Kittel and Kauder had confidentially let on that they were in touch with a British intelligence service, needless to say a splendid cover if they were Soviet agents. Kittel, it is reported, in fact traveled regularly to London, Paris and Norway. The former *Abwehr* officer Herbert Rittlinger, who in 1973 or earlier is rather unlikely to have seen the Kittel document which was released only in 2001 by the CIA, remembers that the abduction attempt by the Russians was but a cleverly laid trap by the OSS who were fully aware that the Soviets wanted to get their hands on Klatt. According to this undocumented tale, the Soviet Military Mission in Salzburg took the bait. The entire episode, if it happened that way, would certainly indicate that the Americans were still interested in Klatt and for whatever reasons certainly inclined to protect him.[259] Following the attempted kidnapping by the Russians, Klatt was taken to the 7707th European Command Intelligence Center, also known as Camp King, at Oberursel just outside Frankfurt. There he was protected to prevent a repeat performance by the Russians and incidentally interrogated by Arnold M. Silver. The Americans suspected Klatt to have been used by the Soviets or to have been their agent. When the British discovered him to be at Oberursel, MI6 sent—who else—U 35 or rather Klop Ustinov. When Klatt would not open up, he was placed in a cell rather than in

---

258. Winston M. Scott, Attaché, U.S. Embassy London, to Lt. Colonel T. A. Robertson, MI5, March 27, 1947, NAK, KV 2/1497.
259. [Name whitened out] to "Sehr verehrter Herr [name whitened out], May 4, 1949, enclosure "Nachrichtengruppe Kittel," NA, RG 263, E A1-86, Box 22, Folder: Krallert. Rittlinger, *Geheimdienst mit beschränkter Haftung*, 230. CIA report, March 17, 1952, Secret Control U.S. Officials Only, NA, RG 263, E A1-86, Box 18, states that "Klatt ... allegedly worked for the Russians in the area around Salzburg."

the separate safe house he and his mistress had been given. That must have done the trick for after trying to hang himself, Klatt/Kauder finally decided to talk.[260]

We cannot be certain that Schellenberg was fully informed about Klatt's connections to a Japanese citizen who, it would appear, years earlier had already worked with Turkul. Certainly Turkul could easily have assisted Klatt in contacting this Japanese national. We may assume that the Japanese in question was Enomoto Momotaro, presenting himself as a journalist, among other things a correspondent of *Nichi-Nichi Shimbun*. The fact that Klatt changed Momotaro's Japanese currency into European money would suggest that they knew each other well. In retrospect, indications are that Momotaro was a Japanese agent in Sofia and one of the recipients of his information was either Klatt or someone like Turkul feeding Klatt. What Momotaro actually produced still remains rather unclear. British intelligence reading the German cable traffic observed that his reports covered an area roughly from Syria to Libya, but there were "no clues to the sources of the *Moritz* reports." Still somewhat surprising, the British shared what they thought they knew with their Russian ally. More surprising, however, was Moscow's reaction to London's friendly gesture: "There was no reaction from the Russians and the Max reports continued until February 1945."[261]

Some time in January 1945 Momotaro packed his wife and belongings into a car and drove all the way to Stockholm. That on the way he spent a few days in bombed-out Berlin and was even seen visiting the RSHA, not to mention traveling through the disorderly and dangerous police state of Germany, would suggest that the Germans had outfitted him with the right papers. His visit to the Foreign Intelligence Offices in the RSHA would imply that someone in *Amt* VI knew about his work for the Germans. Upon arrival in the Swedish capital he linked up with the very active but secretive Japanese Military Attaché Makato Onodera who controlled a sizeable Japanese intelligence organization in Scandinavia. Over the years the Japanese apparently had established valuable and reliable contacts with the Poles who were known for their good lines into the Soviet Union. When interrogated in 1946, Onodera claimed that "the origin of the collaboration between the Polish and Japanese General Staffs dates back to the Russo-Japanese war [1904–1905] and is based on a common hatred of

---

260 See Arnold M. Silver, "Questions, Questions, Questions: Memoirs of Oberursel," *Intelligence and National Security*, vol. 8, no. 2 (April 1993), 202-206.
261. F. H. Hinsley, C. A. G. Simkins, *British Intelligence in the Second World War*, vol. 4 (London: HMSO, 1990), 198-199. McKay, *From Information to Intrigue*, 288. The Germans, Pandur (Wenzlau) to Ludwig Otto, January 24, 1945, NAK, KV 2/157, called him a correspondent of *Jomiuzi*. The Americans, SAINT Copenhagen to SAINT Washington, May 10, 1946, NA, RG 226, E 214, Box 1, called him a *Mainichi* correspondent. Cf. Makato Onodera file, NAK, KV2/243.

Russia." While he may have been right in this, the "hatred of Russia" had neither been a traditional mark of German Eastern European policy nor had most of Germany's military leaders during the Weimar Republic and under their *Führer* exhibited a particular dislike for Russia. Quite to the contrary, a good part of German military preparations for the Second World War, maneuvers as well as the testing of new weapons, had taken place in the Soviet Union and the relationship between the Soviet and the German General Staff had been friendly to say the least. But war and the destruction of Poland had altered all this and between the Soviet Union and Hitler's Germany operated a Polish underground with exiled representatives in various nations and in its efforts certainly also directed against Germany. Which was what had led the Germans to arrest such agents as Kuncewicz and Lapinska. Because "K," as he is often called in the records, was linked directly to Peter Ivanov and thereby to Onodera, Schellenberg's men had in fact destroyed an important line of their allies, the Japanese, into Poland and thereby into Russia. However one may be inclined to rate the significance of the Kuncewicz-Ivanov line, the case demonstrates that, at least concerning Eastern Europe, Germans and Japanese at the top certainly were not seeing eye to eye. On a lower level things clearly looked different. Schellenberg's *Abwehr* man in Stockholm Karl Heinz Krämer at least since 1943 had become personally acquainted with Onodera and indeed was receiving reports from the Japanese which he passed on to Berlin. Schellenberg had never thought very highly of the intelligence reports or the efficiency of Krämer but considered Krämer's information on Swedish society very useful. While watching Krämer and his "private secretary" Nina Siemsen, his go-between to Onodera and other operatives in Stockholm, Schellenberg certainly must have become well informed about the cooperation of the intelligence services.[262]

Although Schellenberg's overwhelming interest was clearly directed to the West where he hoped to find an opening for contacts that might lead to a negotiated end of hostilities, he obviously could hardly ignore the very strong presence of the Japanese in Berlin. Around the key figure of the former Military Attaché, now Ambassador Hiroshi Oshima, an array of apparently well trained and very engaged Japanese representatives played their game. The most important players among the Japanese, besides Oshima, were the Military Attaché Major General Mitsuhiko Komatsu, the Naval Attaché Rear Admiral Katsuo Abe, and the First Counsellor of the Japanese Embassy Kawahara. The surviving records, not very plentiful regarding Schellenberg, do not suggest a

---

262. CIA Name Files, NA, RG 263, E ZZ-18, Box 97 (2nd release). Someone writing for Major P. J. Mason to Major A. F. Blunt, MI5, May 6, 1945, NAK, KV 2/243. "Army Intelligence Activities in Sweden. May 1945," NAK, KV 2/148.

quick patent answer to the question about Schellenberg's view of the Japanese and their tactics. There are some indications that he considered closer connections to Asian nations, especially Japan and China, but most of the evidence instead points to Western inclinations. He could therefore hardly be enticed to give serious thought to occasional Japanese visions of a Japanese-Russian-German alliance, nor would he have been much inclined to share the often freely expressed blunt hatred of the Japanese for the Americans. There were exceptional situations, such as in 1943 after the defeat of the Germans at Stalingrad, when rumors spread that something like secret Russian-German negotiations were planned or underway, but as an OSS cable of October 1943 puts it, "the rumors had no basis in truth."[263]

Even if Schellenberg had not thought very highly of the Japanese alliance schemes bantered about, there was no way to avoid the social obligations in the German capital including those with Japanese guests. After the war Schellenberg recalled one of these occasions, a dinner party at the residence of Ambassador Oshima. Some of the Japanese present had been taking to the alcohol, and it had bothered them that Schellenberg had not consumed more drinks. One of the Japanese, the Embassy expert on Soviet Russia, sat down next to the German Chief of Foreign Intelligence loudly encouraging him to drink like the others. Pushing matters, he continued by asking if he had heard correctly that "his policy always had rather a pro-British orientation" and "why he had no weak spot for Russia instead." When Schellenberg replied that he "had not asked the Japanese about his own attitude towards Russia," the Japanese threw a glass of whisky into Schellenberg's face. In a helpful but rather brutish manner other Japanese gentlemen dragged their misbehaving colleague out of the room "by his ears and hair."[264]

In certain respects this dinner might not be considered atypical for Japanese-German relations at the time. What the Germans saw as Aryan or Aryan culture had strong racial aspects which would not have escaped the Japanese. One could safely assume that some of the well-educated Japanese officers stationed in Germany would have taken a look at Germany's most important publication at the time that is Adolf Hitler's *Mein Kampf*. Here they could read that all creative and cultural impulses or progress had come from

---

263. USTRAVIC, London, to OSS, October 7, 1943, Secret, NA, RG 226, E A1-170/210, Box 458. Contradicting the often cited and still widely accepted B. H. Liddell Hart, *History of the Second World War* (New York: G. P. Putnam's Sons, 1971), 488: "In June, Molotov met Ribbentrop at Kirovograd ... for a discussion about the possibilities of ending the war." Cf. Vojtech Mastny, "Stalin and the Prospects of a Separate Peace in World War II," *The American Historical Review*, vol. 77, no. 5 (1972), 1378.
264. "Final Report," 239. Cf. Colonel Chas. E. Rayens to Major General Clayton Bissell, May 30, 1945, reporting this incident and identifying the Japanese as "Admiral Koshima." Rayens could be referring to Admiral Hideo Kojima, the Japanese Naval Attaché. NA, RG 226, E 119A, Box 26.

one race, the Aryan "Kulturbegründer" (creators of culture). Moreover, while considering Germans and so-called Germanic culture superior to the *Untermenschen* (inferior human beings), many Germans in fact were lacking international experience and tolerance. The Japanese came from a different cultural sphere and, though often more international than the Germans and certainly more open towards Russia in World War II, had insufficient knowledge of European mannerisms. Schellenberg, much aware of the ignorance of the Germans, had tried to clear the way to send a group of well selected and generally prepared German Army officers to Japan, not to work in intelligence but to become acquainted with the people and their culture, as well as to learn the language. When his proposal was turned down, he became involved in getting a group of naval officers ready for the same assignment only to be blocked by the Navy which rejected the idea of political indoctrination, what Schellenberg called "a short political training." From appearances, one gains the impression that personal contacts between Japanese and Germans at the time were rather limited and, more serious, their intelligence efforts and political approaches to problems often followed rather diverging paths. To amend things Schellenberg in 1943 even planned to travel to Japan himself.[265]

However, while considering such occasional differences in mentality and culture and remembering that Washington, though of course unbeknown to the Germans, was reading the detailed and wordy cables of Hiroshi Oshima, it should not be overlooked that both *Abwehr* and *Amt* VI had constructed with the Japanese an intricate net of connections, relationships and exchanges, many of them undiscovered by Allied intelligence. As would be expected, the Japanese representatives in neutral Switzerland, not unlike Onodera's apparatus in neutral Sweden, played a major part in this network. Schellenberg's personal representative for the Swiss contacts, Hans Wilhelm Eggen, maintained an excellent working relationship with Naoe Sakai, one of Hideo Kojima's intelligence officers. Sakai, who is said to have had a line to the Russians, apparently was used by the Germans to make contact with Lieutenant General Kiyotomi Okamoto, the Japanese Military Attaché in Bern, who in turn worked closely with Onodera. It was through Onodera, incidentally, that Karl Heinz Krämer, the *Abwehr* man in Stockholm, received information originating in Okamoto's Swiss office. On the surface, which is what Schellenberg told his Allied interrogators after the war, the Sakai connection served mostly economic purposes which indeed would have fit nicely with Eggen's diverse personal business operations in Switzerland. In fact, however, the goals pursued were rather

---

265. Adolf Hitler, *Mein Kampf* (München: Zentralverlag der N.S.D.A.P, 1934), 317-318. "Final Report," 239. "Eighth Detailed Interrogation Report on SS-Sturmbannfuehrer Huegel, Dr. Klaus," June 26, 1945, Secret, NA, RG 226, E 119A, Box 71.

more serious. Sakai in 1951 clearly stated that Schellenberg's emissary approached him in late 1944 through a mutual acquaintance in the financial world "to explore the possibilities of establishing direct confidential contact with the staffs of President Roosevelt and Premier Stalin." If we can believe Sakai's version, the Germans at that stage of the war wanted to prevent their country from becoming a battlefield and were therefore willing to withdraw their armies to the German borders on whichever side was prepared to accept their proposal of an armistice. Sakai recalled that the Germans counted on an "inevitable clash between the West and the Soviets," presumably seeing themselves on the side of the West following an acceptance of their armistice offer by the Western Allies. The unrealistic assumption that Germany in spite of the mass murder committed all over Europe could somehow slip into the camp of the Western Allies, of course, is known to have been a part of Schellenberg's increasingly erroneous view of Allied perceptions, and the records demonstrate that the idea of replacing Hitler with Himmler certainly by late 1944 had become a part of this larger illusionary Western-oriented context. Related to these contacts in Sweden, Germany and Switzerland are the even less known activities of Dr. Friedrich-Wilhelm Hack, a colorful individual who in World War I had fought on the German side at Tsingtao, consequently had been a prisoner-of-war of the Japanese, had learned Japanese and after returning to Germany had been involved in the arms trade with Japan. In that connection he had come close to Hiroshi Oshima and indeed introduced the latter to Ribbentrop. Hack, who is said to have been affiliated with Ribbentrop's *Dienststelle* but for reasons unknown was arrested by the Gestapo, used the first opportunity to depart for neutral Switzerland. He resided in style at the Grand Hotel Dolder in Zürich and cultivated his numerous international contacts from there.[266] Among these were Naoe Sakai, Oshima's right-hand man in Berlin, and Katsuo Abe, Tokyo's extremely well connected chief military representative and among other things heading the Tripartite Commission in the German capital. Recent research has revealed that what might be called vague "peace feelers" between the U.S. and Japan continued here all the way until May/June 1945. Apparently the Japanese involved in these contacts hoped to avoid a repetition in Japan of the near total destruction they were witnessing in Nazi Germany. Sakai later recalled that he visited Hack in October 1944 "with the approval of Admiral Kojima" and in personal consultations attempted to persuade him "to use his open channel to the American authorities." The

---

266. Friedrich Wilhelm Hack (1885?-1949) studied Business, worked for railroad in China, military service in Asia World War I, 1920s and 1930s involved in German-Japanese business connections, active in German foreign policy in Asia, connections to Japanese. On Hack see also John W. M. Chapman, "A Dance on Eggs: Intelligence and the 'Anti-Comintern'," *Journal of Contemporary History,* vol. 22, no. 2 (April, 1987), passim.

frustrating reply from the Americans was that they did not trust the Germans, presumably meaning Hack. In January 1945 there were further encounters between Sakai and Hack, and they came to the conclusion that Kojima or Abe should come to Switzerland and meet with U.S. officials, referring most likely to OSS representatives. When Abe hesitated and Kojima failed to obtain a Swiss visa, Commander Yoshikatsu Fujimura was dispatched to tackle the difficult task, to all appearances without any visible results. A far-fetched scheme to employ Sakai's line to Moscow by bringing Eggen and Sakai together with a Russian representative in Switzerland, only identified as Orlowski, at the residence of Lieutenant General Okamoto could not be realized due to the latter's illness.[267] Times indeed had changed from the glowing reports of early German victories in Russia in 1941 that Oshima had rushed to Tokyo and, without knowing, to the MAGIC-reading Allies: "... the Soviet air forces ... were completely annihilated and the German air force has gained ... the mastery of the air." General Okamoto having observed the collapse of the German Nazi regime put an end to his life to preserve what in Japanese tradition he considered his personal honor in the afternoon of August 15, 1945, when he received the news of Japan's final surrender.[268]

One might be inclined to ask what it may have been that the Japanese Ambassador General Hiroshi Oshima and Admiral Wilhelm Canaris, Chief of the German *Abwehr* until February 1944, shared. They had known each other well since the mid-thirties, and, yes, they had become personal friends. Canaris, of course, came from the undoubtedly conservative background of the quasi-illegal and nationalist *Schwarze Reichswehr* and the anti-republican Kapp Putsch, and it seems apparent that the strong emphasis given by historians to his connections to men in the resistance against the Hitler regime has created a slightly stilted picture of this traditionally trained German naval officer. Like many of his military and political contemporaries, Canaris had not accepted Germany's defeat in World War I, and after 1918 was personally engaged in the remilitarization effort. His international experience consisted of military duty on land and at sea in the First World War, military assignments between the wars, and extended activities in Spain that had led to close connections in that country, including even a very positive relationship with General Francisco Franco. He had come to despise Communism and fought Communists on all

---

267. "Final Report," Appendix IV, 237-242. Statement by Naoe Sakai, March 9, 1951, NA, RG 263, E A1-86, Box 9. SHAEF FWD to ALP/SHAEF, July 5, 1945, NA, RG 226, E 119A, Box 26. Gerhard Krebs, "Operation Super Sunrise? Japanese-United States Peace Feelers in Switzerland 1945," *The Journal of Military History*, vol. 69 (October, 2005), 1081-1120.
268. Carl Boyd, "Significance of MAGIC and the Japanese Ambassador to Berlin," *Intelligence and National Security*, vol. 2 (January, 1987), 154. DB 001 to SAINT London, August 22, 1945, NA, RG 226, E 108, Box 434.

fronts, including Spain. When he met Oshima, they discovered that they had much in common and their alliance against the Soviet Union seemed but a natural step. Canaris had helped to build the Nazi state that Oshima admired, and, as in the case of Schellenberg, there remains the open question how he continued to serve in view of his full knowledge of events.[269]

In many ways both Canaris and Schellenberg represented a German class of rather rigidly trained professionals, one in the military, the other in German law. Both had grown up in a system that had taught them to accept a given structure. Though several authors have made that point, the records do not offer any evidence that Schellenberg pursued the destruction of his professional competitor Canaris. Quite to the contrary, in expressing their political views to each other the two men were surprisingly frank, their intelligence services in many instances worked together more intensively than required, and Schellenberg had never hesitated to express his admiration for the older professional. In fact, their relation was such that, as has already been pointed out, the restless young Reinhard Spitzy could even switch from Canaris to Schellenberg and suffer no problems of adjustment. What brought about the demise of Canaris' *Abwehr* was instead a series of intelligence failures which may not have been avoidable in all cases, but which caused him to lose his once considerable standing with Hitler and other leaders in the Nazi hierarchy. Even German military commanders increasingly lost faith in their military intelligence chief.[270] Finally in early February 1944, much later than expected by many, came the humiliating discharge.

When Hitler, reacting to a train of embarrassing developments and strongly encouraged by underhanded slander from the enemies of Canaris, removed the *Abwehr* Chief from his post and empowered Heinrich Himmler to take over his responsibilities, this was the beginning of the end for the *Abwehr*. It implied the upcoming merger of the two intelligence services into one service, something that fully corresponded with the plans of both Himmler and Schellenberg, though often forgotten for quite different reasons. Himmler from his power perspective had long had a vision of bringing all police, security and intelligence functions in Germany under his control, and Military Intelligence or the *Abwehr* so far had continued to be a notable exception. In contrast to Himmler's schemes of concentration of power, Schellenberg wanted an efficient, all-encompassing security service situated independently outside such

---

269. There is no reliable, more recent biography of Canaris taking into account declassified records in London and Washington. Still rewarding the thoughtful earlier Heinz Höhne, *Canaris: Patriot im Zwielicht* (München: Bertelsmann, 1976).
270. Most often mentioned is the failure of German Military Intelligence to predict the landing of Allied forces in North Africa in 1942, but there was a consistent string of slipups, not to mention the inability of Canaris to operate with any success in Great Britain or the U.S.

power structures as the RSHA or the military. A further difference would have been the time span considered by the two SS leaders. Himmler knew that he needed the concentration of power to stay in power and, as we know now, to reinforce his position for the time when he would become Hitler's successor. Schellenberg's plans were long-term, and he was certain that a unified intelligence service, modeled as he saw it on the British secret service, could only be perfected in the post-war period.[271] Schellenberg would have been pleased to know what his American counterparts thought of his new intelligence structure in Germany: "The greatest practical effect, as far as we are concerned, will probably be an increased efficiency on the part of German Intelligence ... It can be expected ... that more trustworthy individuals from the German standpoint will be employed ... efforts toward gathering information will likely be better coordinated ... Key positions will be held by trusted officers and there will be less desertions to the Allies."[272]

Indications are that neither Himmler nor Schellenberg were personally, directly or indirectly, involved in the final debacle that led to the destruction of Canaris and his *Abwehr*. That decisive event took place in Turkey, was at least in part brought about by arrests made in Berlin and, it should be said, might not have had quite the same effect had it not been for timely and expert assistance from British intelligence. The Gestapo arrests in Berlin came after months of close observation and what would appear to be rather careless habits of the victims, a resistance group around Hanna Solf, the widow of the politician and diplomat Wilhelm Heinrich Solf.[273] One of those arrested was Otto Kiep, the former German Consul General in New York and now also associated with another resistance group, the Kreisau Circle. That was the final ring of the alarm bell for Erich Maria Vermehren, the second man in charge under Paul Leverkuehn at the AST (*Abwehrstelle/Abwehr* office) in Istanbul. He and his wife Elisabeth (née Countess von Plettenberg) had already made contact with the British and now wasted no time accepting generous assistance from the British Embassy. They were spirited out of Turkey into Syria and

---

271. For Himmler, a man extremely loyal to Hitler, the thought of wanting to or having to take over from Hitler developed only very slowly over time, but by late 1943 had become part of the larger context of seeking an end to the war.
272. L. L. Tyler to D. W. Ladd, August 23, 1944, NA, RG 65, E A1-136P, Box 45.
273. The Solf Circle carelessly tolerated the presence of an unknown guest who reported them to the Gestapo. He is said to have been a medical doctor by the name of Paul Reckzeh. If he was a Gestapo agent or reported to the Gestapo, he was not Schellenberg's "agent," as stated by Brissaud. He would have been a member of Müller's Gestapo *Amt* IV, not of Schellenberg's *Amt* VI Foreign Intelligence. Peter Hoffmann, *The History of the German Resistance 1933-1945* (Cambridge: The MIT Press, 1977; 1st German ed. 1969), 32-33, 541. Brissaud, *Canaris*, 314.

then flown to Cairo.[274] Much to the chagrin of the Germans, two more Nazi operatives, Willy Hamburger and Karl Alois Kleczkowski, both working under cover in the Turkish capital, decided to leave while they still could and to turn themselves in to the Americans. Altogether it was quite a haul for Allied intelligence. London, extremely correct in this case and intent on avoiding any possible misinterpretation of British covert operations in the Mideast, notified Moscow: "The first of the fugitives, whose name is Erich Vermehren ... had been in touch with the British authorities shortly before he made his escape ..." In fact, Kleczkowski had worked for Germany against the United Nations in the Near and Far East and therefore was also rather well informed about Japanese intelligence activities in Turkey, including their native Turkish network. The records suggest that these German agents were properly shielded against all harm from their furious fellow citizens and in return were quite willing to tell their interrogators whatever they wanted to know. Although evidence remains sketchy on this, it would appear that the escapees also took with them German material of considerable interest to the Allies.[275]

Turkey, however, did not just serve as a point of departure for German agents or receiving station for information or disinformation from inside the Soviet Union, but the Germans used or tried to use to their advantage the strong nationalist sentiments in Turkey and the Balkans. While Schellenberg had no special personal inclinations to become involved in the troublesome regions South of Russia, both *Abwehr* and *Amt* VI could hardly afford to overlook the potential problems one might be able to create for the Soviet Union if the right nationalist movements were supported at the right time. Not surprising, Allied intelligence was most interested in what the German defectors of the *Abwehr* knew about Berlin's lines to the various nationalities in that large region. From the declassified records one could gain the impression that neither Vermehren nor Kleczkowski or Hamburger had much to offer during the debriefings. It should be recalled though that these records are often reports on interrogations in 1944 and it would be justified to assume that what the German agents said regarding cooperation with such nationalist movements was filed separately and probably never passed on to Moscow.[276] The

---

274. Erich Maria Vermehren (1919-2005) studied Law, specialty shipping law, selected as Rhodes Scholar. Paul Leverkuehn helped him to be posted with the *Abwehr* station in Turkey in 1942. For a detailed, critical appraisal Höhne, *Canaris*, 521-525.
275. British Ambassador Archibald Clark Kerr to People's Commissar for Foreign Affairs V. M. Molotov, March 5, 1944, NAK, FO 371/39193. Lt. Col. Carroll Gray to James R. Murphy, March 27, 1944, Secret, NA, RG 226, E 210, Box 503. Regarding a lengthy list of questions from Moscow to be given to the Germans, OSS felt that the Germans may not know all the answers and "it is not our intention to furnish the Russians with answers from other sources." SAINT to Links, March 25, 1944, NA, RG 226, E 171A, Box 72. Extract for File P.F. 66208, March 27, 1944, NAK, KV 2/956.
276. Diverse records, NAK, KV 2/956.

Western Allies, especially Great Britain, had a long tradition of political involvement in the Mideast and certainly were observing every move by the Germans very closely. The general impression is that the British, mostly due to their larger presence in the region, had a better understanding of developments there and a much greater number of their own experts as well as local contacts in the region than the few area specialists the Germans were able to activate. Men such as the excellent Near East expert and adventurous diplomat Werner Otto von Hentig, the specialist for Russia and the Mideast Oskar Ritter von Niedermayer, or Fritz Grobba, the Arab expert, were exceptions on the German side.[277] Possibly as a consequence of this shortage of experts, the Germans often too hastily became tied up with regional nationalist leaders whose reliability they were unable to ascertain. Schellenberg later recalled that the gamut of ventures from Turkey against the Soviet Union was closely related to Operation Zeppelin. He remembered that these activities were planned in "close cooperation with the Turkish Secret Service" and that "specially trained Georgians, Caucasians, Azerbaijans and Turks" were deployed in Russian territories as far away as the Ural Mountains.[278] One of the well-known leaders in these covert operations was Nuri Pasha Killigil, a brother of the equally well-known Young Turk leader Enver Pasha. Both he and his brother, of course, had an allegiance to the Germans dating back to World War I and both were deeply implicated in the Turkish mass murder of Armenians. Nuri Pasha had come to Berlin already in late 1941 to sell the Germans his ideas of a Greater Turkey. The fiercely anti-Semitic Germans fell for Nuri's strong nationalism and took the bait. Hitler personally agreed to the organization of Muslim divisions for volunteers from Central Asia and the Caucasus. As a result the Germans began to mobilize so-called *Orientlegionen* or, less specifically, *Ostlegionen* (Oriental Legions, Eastern Legions). Like his brother, Nuri Pasha, who actually functioned as a well-connected businessman and manufacturer of explosives, longed for a greater Turkish state based on Muslim ethnic minorities several of them located in the Soviet sphere of power. In this he was merely one of many often radical leaders who represented different nationalist goals, Muslim groups, ethnic cultures and local patriotic bodies who all seem to have operated under that old adage that the

---

277. Werner Otto von Hentig (1886-1984), except for military service in both wars in German Foreign Service 1911-1954. Fritz Grobba (1886-1973), studied Law and Turkish, with interruptions in German Foreign Service 1913-1944. Oskar Ritter von Niedermayer (1885-1948), studied Geology, Geography and Farsi, in World War I expeditions to Mideast and military service, later active in German-Russian relations, military service in World War II, died in Soviet prison. Memoirs and other publications by all three.
278. Schellenberg, *The Schellenberg Memoirs*, 378.

enemy of my enemy is my friend.[279] Following the German defeat at Stalingrad, however, and the gains of Soviet Russia versus an apparently weakening Germany, the far-reaching plans for a greater Turkish state or for free Muslim nations in the Caucasus region in most cases were shelved and instead local and regional leaders began to seek a modus vivendi with the superior Soviet power.

That Nuri Pasha's connections included a good number of persons whose background had not been sufficiently checked and who, in fact, are now thought to have been Soviet agents should not come as a surprise. A dangerous mixture of ignorance in Middle East and Near East affairs, blinding anti-Semitism and the lack of experienced personnel made up the background of German failure in that region. To this must be added the excessive brutality of German troops entering Southern Russia. Members of ethnic minorities must have had serious doubts whether life under German occupation would always be an improvement. One of Nuri Pasha's connections was Prince Turkul who first helped deliver what were said to be reports from Soviet Russia and who later stayed in Berlin, apparently covered by Schellenberg's *Amt* VI and supposedly advising Vlasov. If Turkul was also a Soviet agent, he fit in well with another man who cultivated close contact with Nuri Pasha, namely Michael Kedia, actively working with *Amt* VI in Berlin and directly involved in the decision making processes for covert operations into the Caucasus. He too, it has been argued convincingly, is more than likely to have been a Soviet agent, namely the mysterious 59. These and other German intelligence failures would indeed suggest that Moscow was fully informed on most ventures of Abwehr and *Amt* VI against the Soviet Union.[280]

In view of the importance of Istanbul for intelligence work against the Soviet Union and against British interests across much of the Near East, *Amt* VI, of course, maintained its own representatives in the region, and in 1943 Schellenberg himself, traveling as "*Oberregierungsrat* Schenkendorf," flew to Istanbul to strengthen his base in Turkey and reinforce cooperation with Turkish intelligence. The journey was not only an initiative on Schellenberg's part but in many ways responded to strong interests expressed by visiting Turkish officials in Berlin earlier that year. High point of Schellenberg's sensitive activities in Istanbul was his encounter with Naci Perkel, the Chief of the Turkish Intelligence Service. Not surprisingly, one of their main topics was Turkish cooperation in the just mentioned difficult smuggling of German

---

279. Nuri Pasha Killigil (1889-1949) visited Germany more than once. "German Intelligence Activities in the Near East and Related Areas," p. 174, NA, RG 319, IRR, IS, Box 40. Burds, "The Soviet War against 'Fifth Columnists'," 286.
280. See especially Burds, "The Soviet War against 'Fifth Columnists'," 279, 282, 286-287.

agents across the Caucasus into Soviet Russia. Schellenberg later recalled that as a consequence of their very congenial discussions Perkel not only looked the other way when such activities of the Germans became necessary, but also, more astonishingly, assisted in "providing suitable candidates." In fact, Schellenberg's direct contacts with Perkel and Pepily, the Police Chief of Istanbul, were so successful that covert connections between German and Turkish intelligence services continued even after Turkey broke diplomatic relations with Germany in 1944. Schellenberg interpreted this Turkish policy as an indication that Ankara wished to be prepared for a resumption of fruitful intelligence cooperation "in the event of a change in the German regime." Franz von Papen, the German Ambassador in Turkey whom Schellenberg had seen during his visit, shortly afterwards reported on the impressive success of Schellenberg's talks in Istanbul. "Mr. Schellenberg has, as I hear from others, made an excellent impression on the Turkish gentlemen with his balanced and quiet personality. In Istanbul the Chief of the Secret Police here has given a larger evening reception in his honor …"[281] Papen's very positive appraisal of the SS leader's activities in Turkey could be considered as politics, but it might be of some interest to recall that Schellenberg in his memoirs claims to have had rather frank exchanges with the Ambassador even on the need to discover ways "to reach a compromise peace with the western Allies." Schellenberg's dangerous talk with Papen would suggest that through his own sources he had become aware that Papen had changed somewhat politically and though certainly not a man of the resistance was now open to consider ways to get out of the war. It is true that Schellenberg in 1938 had left the Roman Catholic Church, but it would be very surprising if he had neglected to keep himself well informed on German Catholic leaders and their political views. If his memoirs are correct, and there is no apparent reason why he should have presented matters incorrectly in this case, he specifically addressed the Catholic personality von Papen and apparently got through to him. Needless to say, Ambassador von Papen in his report to the Foreign Office did not mention this particular segment of their conversation. Schellenberg, for his part, was so pleased with the results of his exchange with Franz von Papen that he instructed his chief agent in Istanbul, Ludwig C. Moyzisch who had been most helpful during his stay and whose family he had taken a liking to, to stay close to Papen and keep him informed, "for I felt that a relationship of confidence between them was emphatically necessary." That Schellenberg's visit in Turkey

---

281. A. J. Kellar to Major G. P. West, S.I.N.E., August 23, 1945, Top Secret, NAK, KV 2/97. SHAEF Forward to War Room, July 6, 1945, Secret, NA, RG 226, E 119A, Box 26. Von Papen to Foreign Office, July 16, 1943, USHMMA, Kempner Collection, Box 40, F8. (Transl.) Staff Intelligence Analysis, March 5, 1947, SAN, Rep. 502, SEA, NO 2449. — Naci Perkel's first name is often spelled Nacy.

was generally considered a success and therefore led to much improved cooperation of the Turkish Intelligence Service with Moyzisch, interestingly was reported to British intelligence by Erich Vermehren following his defection in February 1944.[282]

Brief mention should be made in this context of Elyeza Bazna who had become a valet for the British Ambassador in Ankara, Sir Hughe Montgomery Knatchbull-Hugessen. Though much has been written about Cicero, the cover name given to him by the Germans, documents permitting a final appraisal of the case have not been declassified in London or Washington.[283] Bazna or Cicero apparently brought photographs of sensitive British documents to Ludwig Moyzisch, Schellenberg's man in Ankara, who for cover functioned as an Attaché at the German Embassy. Some of the photographed British documents undoubtedly contained rather sensitive information, and one can easily imagine the German Ambassador Franz von Papen smirking about some of the news not meant for him concerning Allied political perspectives and military operations. In retrospect one of the more conspicuous words in a particular group of papers he read was Overlord, the code word for the planned cross-Channel operation against the Germans in Northern France. When Fritz Kolbe, alias George Wood, alias *674* or *803* skimmed through this particular document in the German Foreign Office, he had the presence of mind to include it in his next batch of German papers delivered to Allen Dulles. The British must have been absolutely delighted to learn that the Germans had access to the confidential papers at their Embassy in Ankara. When London took the necessary steps to stop the intolerable leak, Bazna most likely got a whiff of all the covert commotion in the Turkish capital and having no desire to encounter any British agents, wisely decided to close shop.[284] Schellenberg's extensive treatment of the case in his memoirs[285] could suggest to the informed reader that he had some doubts concerning Bazna's interesting and important

---

282. Statement under Oath, Franz von Papen, June 6, 1948, SAN, Rep. 501, LV, 55. Schellenberg, *The Schellenberg Memoirs*, 380-382. "Final Report," 122-123. — Franz von Papen (1879-1969), officer's career, Military Attaché in Washington World War I, declared persona non grata and expelled 1915, contributed significantly to Hitler's rise to power, Ambassador in Turkey 1939-1944. On October 17, 1944, OSS Chief William J. Donovan notified the Secretary of State that von Papen was in Madrid "urging Franco" to influence the Vatican to obtain acceptable peace conditions for Germany. Secret, NA, RG 226, E 190 C, Box 13.
283. Elyeza (various spellings) Bazna (1904-1971), cover name Cicero, uncertain background, briefly valet for Albert Jenke, German Minister in Ankara, late 1943 to early 1944 valet for British Ambassador. Germans said to have paid him considerable sums — particularly in forged bills. Elyeza Bazna, *I Was Cicero* (New York: Dell, 1964; Copyright 1962). L. C. Moyzisch, *Operation Cicero* (London: Wingate, n.d.). Cf. Christopher Baxter, "The Cicero Papers," London, "Foreign & Commonwealth Office," March 2005.
284. Cf. Joseph E. Persico, *Roosevelt's Secret War: FDR and World War II Espionage* (New York: Random House, 2002; 1st 2001), 286-287.
285 Schellenberg, *The Schellenberg Memoirs*, 388-397. His German *Memoiren*, 315-322, offers no additional information.

deliveries, but there are no indications that he earnestly considered the possibility that the messenger might have been controlled by British intelligence, that Cornelia (Nele) Kapp, Moyzisch's secretary,[286] might have connections to another intelligence service or that even Moyzisch himself might not be what he appeared to be.[287] Unquestioning accounts of the Cicero Case have continued to treat it as one of the more remarkable successes of German intelligence—which it might have been if all was what it seemed to be. A sound evaluation of the colorful episode, however, will be possible only when more records are released.[288] The news that Cornelia Kapp absconded shortly after the Vermehren Affair, though apparently pretty much covered up in Berlin, could only contribute to the German impatience with the avoidable intelligence calamities in Turkey.

While all this transpired, an enraged Hitler, urged on by General Field Marshall Wilhelm Keitel, had personally and to begin with apparently orally ordered the formation of a unified intelligence service under the direction of Heinrich Himmler. He and Keitel, Chief of the High Command of the German Armed Forces, were assigned to prepare the merger of the old *Abwehr* with the SD into a completely new intelligence service.[289] A conference presided over by Himmler decided that such a unified service would be set up, that Himmler would be in charge of the organization, and that Himmler for the SD and Keitel for the Armed Forces would work out the merger of *Amt* VI and the *Abwehr*. On February 12, 1944, Hitler signed the written top secret order, of which only two originals exist.[290] That Ribbentrop and his Foreign Office had

---

286. Scattered unreliable information on Cornelia Kapp (b. 1919), father Karl Kapp (1889-1947) German diplomat serving as Consul and Consul General in Cleveland 1936-1941, she finished high school in Cleveland, attended Case Western Reserve University, said to have been recruited by OSS and to have informed Americans about Bazna when she worked as secretary for Moyzisch. Cf. Anthony Cave Brown, *Bodyguard of Lies* (New York: Quill/Morrow, 1975), 401. Rittlinger, *Geheimdienst mit beschränkter Haftung*, 246. Richard Wires, *The Cicero Spy Affair: German Access to British Secrets in World War II* (Westport: Praeger, 1999), ch. 12.
287. Some sources report that Moyzisch was partially Jewish, by German Nazi racial laws a *Mischling* (person of mixed racial background) and may have joined the SS and asked for a position abroad to protect himself and his family. Adam LeBor, Roger Boyes, *Surviving Hitler: Choices, Corruption and Compromise in the Third Reich* (London: Simon & Schuster, 2000), 229: "Perhaps Moyzisch had been a double agent all along ..."
288. Cf. meagre information divulged by British intelligence in Hinsley and Simkins, *British Intelligence in the Second World War*, vol. 4: *Security and Counter-Intelligence*, 214 ff. Kahn, *Hitler's Spies*, 340-346, also on Moyzisch. Anthony Cave Brown, ed., *The Secret War Report of the OSS* (New York: Berkley Medallion, 1976), 295-296. Oscar Reile, *Treff Lutetia Paris: Der Kampf der Geheimdienste im westlichen Operationsgebiet, in England und Nordafrika 1939-1945* (Wels: Welsermühl, 1973), 328-329. For a more recent analysis see Robin Denniston, *Churchill's Secret War: Diplomatic Decrypts, the Foreign Office and Turkey 1942-44* (Stroud: Sutton, 1997), chptr. 8.
289. Contrary to James Srodes, *Allen Dulles: Master of* Spies (Washington, D.C.: Regnery/Eagle, 1999), 298, Schellenberg was not given "direction of the RSHA." Wilhelm Keitel (1882-1946), military service since 1901, General Staff officer in World War I, rose quickly in Nazi military structure, dedicated Nazi leader, sentenced to death in Nuremberg as a war criminal.
290. Original No. 2 of this order in PA, AA, Pol. IM, acc. to George O. Kent, ed., *A Catalog of Files and Microfilms of the German Foreign Ministry Archives 1920-1945* (Stanford: The Hoover Institution, 1966), 47,

long wanted to have their own foreign intelligence service or, in fact, even control German foreign intelligence altogether, was of little concern to their *Führer* or to Himmler. The ensuing deliberations about the future of German intelligence turned out to be somewhat complicated because Schellenberg— Chief of *Amt* VI Foreign Intelligence, not Chief of *Amt* IV Gestapo as stated by the French intelligence officer Paul Paillole—who would absorb the *Abwehr* into *Amt* VI faced a difficult task. On one hand he intended to create one unified intelligence service but on the other he wished to minimize his own responsibility for purely military information that had been or should have been handled by Canaris' *Abwehr*. He remembered all too well what the failure to predict the Allied landings in North Africa had done to the *Abwehr*. Whether his proposed and indeed accepted structural solution, a political intelligence service and a military intelligence service separated but under one roof, was an intelligent move to achieve both goals, in retrospect is difficult to assess. Schellenberg's idea of creating the new *Amt Mil* (*Amt Militär*, Military Intelligence Dept.) did, however, protect the *Abwehr* against falling fully into the power sphere of Heinrich Müller, the Gestapo Chief, who surely would have relished nothing more than a chance to clean out what to him had been a nest of traitors.[291] While not wishing to prevent the rather questionable separation of Military Intelligence from the German Armed Forces, the formation of *Amt Mil* and its placement under Colonel Georg Hansen allowed Schellenberg to preserve intact almost the entire *Abwehr* of Canaris and yet move the complete organization into the larger realm of his *Amt* VI. Undoubtedly, Heinz Höhne has it right when he emphasizes that indeed *Abwehr* and *Amt* VI "were working on parallel lines." Many members of both intelligence services by spring 1944 "had ceased to believe in an ultimate German victory" and both services were therefore scanning the horizon for any possibility of negotiating an end to this war. Höhne at the time of his writing in the 1960s, however, assumed that very few of the leaders of one service were informed about the views held by members of the other service.[292] Decades later, following the voluminous declassification of intelligence records in Washington and London and the appearance of memoirs of participants in the events, it can be said that a good number of *Abwehr* officers in personal and official contacts had become acquainted with the views of officers in *Amt* VI, and Schellenberg himself with his access to Canaris and ranking members of the *Abwehr* was certainly aware that similar

---

"Handakten Schellenberg, Abwehr, 1942-1944." Cf. Chief of High Command of Armed Forces, Top Secret, May 22, 1944, and related documents, Bundesarchiv-Militärarchiv Freiburg (BAMA), RH 2, 1537.
291. Special Interrogation of Schellenberg, September 15 and 21, 1945, NA, RG 226, E 125A, Box 2. Paul Paillole, *Fighting the Nazis: French Military Intelligence and Counterintelligence 1935-1945* (New York: Enigma Books, 2003; 1st French ed. 2002), 402.
292. Höhne, *The Order of the Death's Head*, 552.

views were rather more common than an outsider might have expected. Whether the initially acceptable treatment of the deposed Canaris was a consequence of influences exerted by Schellenberg is open to question. It has also been suggested that Schellenberg may have protected Canaris to prevent Müller's Gestapo from investigating his new *Amt Mil*. Colonel Hansen, a traditional *Abwehr* officer, understood the situation completely and trying on his part to salvage as much as possible of the old *Abwehr*, agreed to all the salient points of the new intelligence structure.[293] The views of Hansen and Schellenberg were so similar that they had no difficulty coming together on most issues, going as far as to become deputy for each other. From the perspective of the *Amt* VI Chief this was a momentous decision because, since taking over Foreign Intelligence, Schellenberg for reasons of circumspection and personal security had chosen not to appoint a deputy. Or, in the words of British intelligence officers in the "Counter Intelligence War Room" in London: "… he [Schellenberg] had not sufficient faith in any one single person."[294] Colonel Hansen was the exception.

However one might be inclined to appraise the structural separation of Military Intelligence from the OKW, it seems to have been a successful merger. With the Thousand Year Empire of the Germans unmistakably heading for an early termination, conditions inside the power echelons and on all fronts were such that the new intelligence organization really had no opportunity to test its strengths and weaknesses. Time was literally running out even before the new service took its first blow from the fundamental shake-up following the abortive putsch attempt on July 20, 1944. When the poorly organized and ill prepared military leaders failed, a veritable killing spree was unleashed across the nation by the Nazi government. Not surprising, the traditional conservative German military class, including a good number of *Abwehr* officers, was made to pay an exorbitant price for its failure.

In the brief period prior to these events Schellenberg maintained very close relations with Colonel Hansen, and the two men basically achieved a new intelligence structure, including the realistic beginnings of a fruitful cooperation and even attempts at some organized socializing to improve relations between the officers of the two services who in some cases had clearly worked against each other in the past.[295] Possibly even more significant was the formidable struggle to keep the espionage function of the old *Abwehr* out of the Gestapo's

---

293. Srodes, *Allen Dulles: Master of Spies*, 298.
294. Liquidation Report No. 6, Amt VI of the RSHA, Secret, NA, RG 226, E 119A, Box 24. "Final Report," 137. Hoettl's postwar claims that Schellenberg "never trusted Hansen" but "saw in him an awkward competitor" have no base. Interrogation Report No. 15, Wilhelm Hoettl, NA, RG 319, Box 617, File XE 00 08 82.
295. "Final Report," 143.

reach. Heinrich Müller had seen a grandiose opportunity when he thought that he had discovered a gross deficiency of German intelligence in the so-called Jebsen Case. As he saw it, this was the opportunity to salvage the espionage function for his Secret State Police. Johannes Jebsen or Johnny was a rather affluent and socially very well connected *Abwehr* officer who had invited Dusko Popov, an equally affluent and socially well connected Yugoslav or rather Serb whom he had known during his student years in Germany, to come and work for German Military Intelligence.[296] As Jebsen did not survive 1945, we cannot be certain whether he asked Popov to work as a German agent in Britain or whether Popov accepted Jebsen's invitation to join the *Abwehr* and then on his own initiative contacted the British who were more than pleased to run him as a double agent called Tricycle and offered that he move to Britain. In any case, upon his arrival in London Popov was taken to meet no lesser person than C, that is Sir Stewart Graham Menzies, Director of MI6 since 1939. By the time he turned up in Lisbon in early 1941, prior to going to the U.S., it is more than likely that Jebsen was his handler. When he arrived in New York in mid-1941, his assignment from the Germans was to set up a new functioning network of agents, it is thought to make up for the loss of the extensive *Abwehr* network steered by the old fox Frederick Joubert Duquesne but totally blown by William G. Sebold or Tramp.[297] Incidentally, it has been reported that the U.S. might have been warned of the Japanese attack on Pearl Harbor—if they had taken the time to listen to Popov. The German-American Sebold had been pressed into *Abwehr* service by Nikolaus Ritter of the AST Hamburg. Sebold, however, had kept his head clear and prior to leaving for the U.S. had contacted American representatives in Germany who had promptly put him in touch with the FBI, who in turn set him up against Duquesne and his network in New York.[298] German Military Intelligence obviously had failed to observe Popov and what he was doing with whom. Moreover, the Germans had not discovered that Johannes Jebsen was double-crossing them with British intelligence under the cover name Artist. Jebsen was a well-educated *Abwehr* agent who had no sympathies for the Nazi regime but apparently much enjoyed playing the hazardous game. In the course of his work he was able to assist many who had gotten into trouble with the Nazis and among other things

---

296. Dusko Popov (1910–1981) has written an informative volume about his activities and especially about his friendship with Johannes Jebsen. For an appraisal see "Foreword" by Ewen Montague. *Spy/Counterspy* (London: Weidenfeld and Nicolson, 1974). Anthony Cave Brown, *"C": The Secret Life of Sir Stewart Graham Menzies* (New York: Macmillan, 1987), 307 ff., quotes Popov extensively.
297. Frederick Joubert Duquesne of Boer background had already worked for German intelligence in World War I, not because he cared for Germany, but because of his great antipathy towards Great Britain.
298. On William G. Sebold see Kahn, *Hitler's Spies*, 331–333. Cf. Ritter's somewhat colored memoirs Nikolaus Ritter, *Deckname Dr. Rantzau: Die Aufzeichnungen des Nikolaus Ritter, Offizier im Geheimen Nachrichtendienst* (Hamburg: Hoffmann und Campe, 1972).

became involved in financial work that is the exchange business of *Abwehr* agents moving about. His base seems to have been in Lisbon. Whether other *Abwehr* or SD officers in Lisbon or Madrid denounced him in Berlin or whether the Gestapo belatedly discovered that he was also working for the British, still seems somewhat uncertain. The skimpy data available suggest that in May 1944 he was lured to the German Embassy in Madrid, made unconscious by something added to food or drink he consumed and, following an injection, packed into a trunk and shipped out of Spain, presumably as diplomatic luggage.[299]

Military Intelligence in Berlin, not entirely incorrectly, insisted on handling the prisoner, one of their agents, under military jurisdiction. Müller, putting his own powerful connections to work, in contrast demanded that Jebsen be handed over to the Gestapo. Remarkably, Hansen actually won this contest and was able to keep his prisoner, most likely, it should be said, with the support of Schellenberg's *Amt* VI. In post-war interrogations Schellenberg did not specifically recount that he used his personal clout in the Jebsen Case, but the records show that Dr. Eduard Waetjen, a German lawyer and *Abwehr* agent under cover at the German Consulate in Zurich, also a major link between the resistance group around General Ludwig Beck and Dr. Carl Friedrich Goerdeler and the intelligence office of Allen W. Dulles in Bern, made a chancy approach to C. L. Sebastian whom he knew to be connected to *Amt* VI. Waetjen had previously met the SS officer through Jebsen, and Sebastian had repeatedly passed on confidential warnings that someone was in danger. Waetjen thought that his intervention may have helped. In fact, Jebsen appears to have been moved from the inhuman Gestapo prison at Prinz Albrecht Strasse to the somewhat less dangerous Concentration Camp Oranienburg. If Dusko Popov has it right, the *Abwehr* or rather *Mil Amt* worked hard on getting Jebsen out and things did look very promising. But: "He was about to be released. Schellenberg's office had given the order. An Abwehr officer was detailed to pick him up at Oranienburg. When he got there, he was informed that Johnny was shot while trying to escape." Either Müller or Kaltenbrunner had his way in wasting another life, but the Gestapo was not able to use the Jebsen Case in their obsessive battle against Schellenberg's *Amt* VI. The foreign espionage function stayed, at least pro forma, with *Amt Mil* by now part of *Amt* VI. In the course of his interrogations after the war Schellenberg reservedly commented: "Jebsen ... had been forcibly abducted...to Berlin at a

---

299. BB092 to SAINT London, May 8, 1945, Secret, NA, RG 226, E 108, Box 433. Statement under Oath, Eduard Waetjen, May 3, 1947, SAN, Rep. 501, LV, S-4. It seems uncertain whether he was taken captive in Madrid or Lisbon. In the records he is also referred to as Jepsen. British intelligence which produced "Final Report," 144, does not care to fully identify him.

certain Kuebarth's [*sic*] instigation, possibly working under Hansen's orders, for purposes directly connected with the prestige of the old Abwehr." Whether Karl Friedrich Kuebart, Lieutenant Colonel with the *Abwehr*, himself handled the kidnapping of Jebsen or whether he ordered some underling to do the dirty work, he was in any case not exactly rewarded for the kidnapping of a comrade. That same summer the Gestapo arrested him for treason. Luckily he was only discharged from the Armed Forces and in the spring of 1945 managed to be picked up by the advancing U.S. troops.[300]

The real hiatus of the German Nazi system—or was it merely a bell ringing in the last act?—on July 20, 1944, found Schellenberg sitting in his office. Before casting some light on his role during the days of the attempted assassination of Adolf Hitler and the bloody aftermath, it should be underlined that there cannot be the slightest doubt that Schellenberg was informed about all significant military and civilian resistance groups and that he could have easily and without any harm to himself arranged for the destruction of any of those groups or individuals had he wished to do so. To be sure, this in no way moves him even into the proximity of any of the resistance groups, but it fits into the picture of the high-ranking internationally oriented SS intelligence officer who probably since 1941 had ceased to share the unrealistic expectations of the vast majority of Germans who even at this late stage still counted on their *Endsieg* (final victory) and fully supported the Nazi regime.

In this connection Schellenberg later recalled that he had been expecting something of significance, because shortly before the attempted putsch, Hansen on one of their frequent walks together had intimated that "in the near future" there would be an opportunity to bring about a better intelligence network for Germany and that in connection with such developments it might be possible to appoint Schellenberg as ambassador to London. If Schellenberg remembers correctly, he certainly did expect that something like a military coup was being planned, and he decided "to maintain a diplomatic silence." Another earlier incident seems to have been a rather frank conversation with General Fritz Walter Thiele with whom he had worked together most fruitfully and established a feeling of mutual trust. Thiele, second in command of Signal Communications, had alluded to a planned coup by the military and anticipations of negotiating an end to combat in the West in order to better hold the lines against the Soviet Union. Following this exchange, Schellenberg, as he later remembered, in order to protect himself in case the apparently upcoming event should fail, wrote a memorandum for Kaltenbrunner that some of the

---

300. "Final Report," 144-145. Popov, *Spy/Counterspy*, 247-249, 263. Secret Personalia and other documents, NA, RG 226, E 119A, Box 28. SHAEF to War Room, June 30, 1945, Secret, NA, RG 226, E 119A, Box 26.

higher military "were discontented" with the High Command. To have something in hand, he had Kaltenbrunner initial this memo. We shall not know whether he was informed about the specific date or whether, as he claimed later, he happened to be in his office at Berkaer Strasse when he suddenly became aware of certain unrest in the streets outside. He remembered that he had a frantic telephone call from Thiele late that afternoon that all had gone wrong. Presumably aware that the call most likely was being wiretapped, he had to put himself in the clear quickly and therefore called Müller at the Gestapo to tell him that he had just received a call from Thiele about a "tremendous uproar" and gun shots in the Bendlerstrasse area. The political and military events in the German capital on that day are well known, and we may assume that Schellenberg indeed was, as he recalls, very upset by the near emotional collapse he experienced with Thiele. The latter had a brief reprieve when he found himself appointed successor of General Fritz Erich Fellgiebel, his Chief of Signal Communications. The apparent reprieve, however, lasted all but a couple of days when Thiele himself would fall victim to the murderous dragnet. Colonel Hansen too was caught when Müller confronted him with the accusation that evidence had turned up in the papers of another conspirator linking him unmistakably to the attempted coup. By now reduced to a psychological wreck, Hansen apparently gave up and was promptly arrested. Schellenberg then was ordered by the sly Müller to have Hansen's offices searched for incriminating papers, the result of the search being a note book suggesting Hansen's involvement. Not at all surprising, with Hansen out of the way, Müller's hopes to finally get ahold of Foreign Intelligence were rekindled. While Hansen and Schellenberg had fully agreed to keep this intelligence work away from the Gestapo, Schellenberg now, in order to squelch Müller's ambitions, was forced to approach Kaltenbrunner directly. There were some changes Schellenberg did not care for, but on the whole Foreign Intelligence was left with *Amt Mil* which with Kaltenbrunner's blessings Schellenberg himself took over on July 28.[301]

Schellenberg may have painfully understood just how close he came to being sucked up into the general turmoil when only three days after the failed coup[302] and following the somewhat astonishing and still unclear damning confession of Colonel Hansen, Müller by telephone ordered him to personally

---

301. Regarding the Schellenberg-Hansen relationship see "Did Himmler know of the 20th of July?," USAMHI, William J. Donovan Papers, Box 87B. Special Interrogations of Schellenberg, September 15 and 21, 1945, NA, RG 226, E 125A, Box 2. "Final Report," 145-150.
302. Although *The Schellenberg Memoirs* (p. 409) and the German *Memoiren* (p. 333) both give the date as early August, other sources agree that Schellenberg was sent to arrest Canaris on July 23. Cf. Karl Heinz Abshagen, *Canaris: Patriot und Weltbürger* (Stuttgart: Union Deutsche Verlagsgesellschaft, 1955), 375. Karl Bartz, *Die Tragödie der deutschen Abwehr* (Salzburg: Pilgram, 1955), 206. Höhne, *Canaris*, 543.

arrest Wilhelm Canaris. Schellenberg undoubtedly knew that this was a surprising order from one head of department (Müller, *Amt* IV) to another head of department (Schellenberg, *Amt* VI) and possibly a threatening indication of his still relatively weak standing within the RSHA. We have no way to determine what was said over the telephone or whether Schellenberg later correctly reported his own reactions to Müller's order. Roger Manvell and Heinrich Fraenkel have labeled Schellenberg's recollections of this event "an almost sentimental account." In some ways it certainly was, but the question of whether Schellenberg reported truthfully in this context would seem more relevant.[303] As in several other instances, there are no comments of witnesses and we are faced with the alternative of accepting or rejecting Schellenberg's own description of events. Quite aside from this question, there is, of course, no doubt that both Müller and Kaltenbrunner, who were heading the investigation into the coup, seriously disliked Schellenberg and would have welcomed the opportunity to silence him or better yet to eliminate him. Whether Schellenberg would actually, as he remembers, respond to Müller that he would first speak to Himmler and whether in such an encounter Müller would just disregard the person of Himmler and threaten Schellenberg in case he were not to comply is quite another question. There is no reason not to believe Schellenberg that he would rather not have arrested the Admiral whom he considered something of a friend but that he felt he had no choice but to do what Müller and Kaltenbrunner demanded of him. To accompany him on this loathsome assignment, he chose SS-*Hauptsturmführer* Adrian Baron von Foelkesam, a respected officer and paratrooper of the well-known German special forces unit called *Die Brandenburger* and a man whom he trusted. At Canaris' house Foelkesam stayed by the car and Schellenberg went to the door. Canaris himself opened, and after sending his guests away, Schellenberg and the Admiral had a brief exchange of words pertaining to the turn of events and the fact that of all the officers available Müller and Kaltenbrunner had chosen Schellenberg to arrest his older friend. In this particular situation the brief exchange between the two men—Schellenberg's suddenly impersonal and formal offer and Canaris' response—deserves to be noted. Schellenberg later recalled that he said: "If the Herr Admiral wishes to make other arrangements, then I beg him to consider me at his disposal. I shall wait in this room for an hour, and during that time you may do whatever you wish. My report will say that you went to your bedroom in order to change." Schellenberg's offer needs no explanation, and Canaris's words are equally clear: "No, dear Schellenberg,

---

303. Roger Manvell, Heinrich Fraenkel, *The Canaris Conspiracy: The Secret Resistance to Hitler in the German Army* (New York: David McKay, 1969), 194.

flight is out of the question for me. And I won't kill myself either. I am sure of my case, and I have faith in the promise you have given me." In the course of their brief prior conversation, Canaris had asked Schellenberg to arrange in the course of the next three days a meeting for him with Himmler. Canaris also warned the younger Schellenberg that he had better be on guard, stating that the scoundrels Müller and Kaltenbrunner were after him as well. No doubt Schellenberg knew that any wrong move on his part could mean the end of his career and for that matter of his life. However, in view of his very recent promotion to the rank of SS-*Brigadeführer*, Schellenberg, not unlike the older Canaris, may have thought that he would survive all adversities.[304]

Following his removal from office as Chief of the *Abwehr*, back in early February 1944, Canaris had been ordered to stay at the secluded Castle Lauenstein near the Franconian woods until further notice, in fact a sort of house arrest. Why a man with his clandestine international connections did not leave the country, in retrospect is very difficult to say. He may actually against all odds have speculated on a comeback or, if he saw his situation realistically, he may have realized that anywhere, at least within continental Europe, the Germans would arrange for his murder. There are some suggestions that Schellenberg may have visited Canaris at Lauenstein for an extended discussion of the new structures of German intelligence,[305] but nothing is known of those results—if such meeting actually took place. The curious decision in Berlin at the end of June 1944 to bring the Admiral back, even if only in a powerless function as so-called Chief of the High Command Special Staff for Commercial Warfare, may have caused Canaris to briefly believe in a return, but there is no tangible evidence of any plans to reintroduce him to the center of power. Rumors that had originated in Sweden, suggesting that the Admiral's total removal would lessen Germany's chances to reach any kind of understanding with the Western Allies, may have had some slight influence, but it is difficult to believe that such vague hints could have freed him. Quite to the contrary, it is often forgotten that Canaris after the defeat in World War I had joined the ranks of those who did not accept that defeat and instead decided to rebuild Germany's military might. He had been close to many who later played their roles in the Nazi system. In other words, Canaris had had a widespread network of military and political leaders who respected him, including such

---

304. "Beförderung des SS-Oberführers Walter Schellenberg, SS-Nr. 124 817, zum SS-Brigadeführer," Personnel File Schellenberg, NA, BDC Microfilm, Roll No. A 3343 SSO-074B. — It is not entirely clear from the records whether Foelkesam waited outside by the car or in a hallway inside the house. — Suggestions that "Canaris had no knowledge of the preparations for the assassination" would appear removed from reality. Cf. Horst Mühleisen, "Die Canaris-Tagebücher — Legenden und Wirklichkeit," *Militärgeschichtliche Zeitschrift*, vol. 65 (2006), 180. (Transl.)
305. Cf. Gert Buchheit, *Der deutsche Geheimdienst: Geschichte der militärischen Abwehr* (München: List, 1966), 433.

men as Himmler and Heydrich and even Hitler, or who actually had struck up good relations with him on the personal level, such as Schellenberg. Taking that into consideration, it is not inconceivable that it was this larger frame of goodwill which in the short term prevented the worst. Now, on July 23, Schellenberg had been ordered to take him to Fürstenberg in Mecklenburg where a police academy had been turned into a kind of reception facility for the overflow of arrested high ranking military officers who had survived the ruthless purges of the first two days after the coup attempt. As they parted, the Admiral, whom Schellenberg respected enormously but to whose downfall he and his *Amt* VI had certainly contributed, looked at him and said that as he saw it Schellenberg had no part in his dismissal. Canaris may or may not have known better. It was the last time the two men saw each other.

Schellenberg did immediately contact Himmler who assured him that he had not known that Kaltenbrunner had involved Schellenberg and he promised he would speak with the Admiral. In his memoirs Schellenberg points out that later Himmler never mentioned such a meeting with Canaris but that he assumes it took place, for it would be the only plausible explanation why Canaris, in spite of all the evidence collected against him, was allowed to live for another nine months. It was indeed only during the desperate last-minute German murder campaign that on April 8, 1945, Canaris was sentenced by an SS court and hanged in the early hours of the next day in the Concentration Camp Flossenbürg. Very likely Schellenberg did not even know what happened to Canaris and those who were hanged with him in April 1945, but it is difficult to come to any appraisal on just how he could have continued to live and work with the knowledge of the ongoing murders all around him and the specific accounts of the fate of so many to whom he had been close. Looking at the frantic activity of Schellenberg in the course of the final nine months of the Thousand Year German Reich, it appears possible that he may have tried to make good in some small way for having been part of that Reich. It is conceivable that to him suicide would have been the equivalent of surrendering to the evil he had personally helped to bring about and therefore was not an alternative.[306]

Other than being responsible for a vast network of agents in many parts of the world, Schellenberg's significant activities from Berlin in the course of those final months can be divided into two major areas, namely a series of less than promising undertakings directed toward almost any kind of negotiations with the Western Allies and very risky attempts to rescue all sorts of people

---

306. For Schellenberg's view of the events of summer 1944 see Schellenberg, *The Schellenberg Memoirs*, chptr. 36. Schellenberg, *Memoiren*, 325-337. "Final Report," 136 ff.

from the worst excesses of the system he was part of. All this it must be pointed was rather atypical activity for a high ranking Nazi official and taking place very close to Himmler who was often informed. Himmler usually cared not to know officially, protected the loyal protégé and even permitted him to act in his name. Without that protection Schellenberg would not have been able to practically ignore such men as Kaltenbrunner, Müller and several others. Why Himmler protected Schellenberg has been and will continue to be a difficult question. Among the possible explanations there appears to be only one constant and visible factor: Himmler seems to have trusted Schellenberg and, to all appearances, the latter while not respecting Himmler to a great extent certainly remained loyal to him to the end.

In some cases Schellenberg had had close contact with those who needed help, so close that he might indeed have been concerned that under torture those interrogated by the Gestapo might inadvertently incriminate him. Also, however, it should be recalled that Schellenberg had built up a large network of contacts, a number of whom had spoken and acted against the Nazi regime but had not been apprehended. Some of those who strongly disliked him, such as his official ultimate superior Ernst Kaltenbrunner or Otto Skorzeny, the man of action who cared little for the low profile executive type, or Wilhelm Höttl who actually owed Schellenberg his professional reinstatement but was not inclined to show gratitude, for various reasons would not or could not easily attack him. All this meant that Schellenberg was able to continue to play the curious double role of an SS department head and a benefactor for those who in the lawless German system had ended up outside the then normal legal procedures. One of the more significant rescue operations was the already described freeing of the seven Swedes which had required his very personal attention and cooperation with Felix Kersten for many months and had a satisfactory ending at Christmas 1944 when the last of these Swedes returned home. Evidently Schellenberg in this case had not only rescued a number of Swedish executives, but in the course of events had made the personal acquaintance of such powerful figures as Jacob Wallenberg, Alvar Möller and Axel Brandin. These men had dealt with him in dangerous situations and discovered that he was reliable and, most importantly, there was no price tag on his assistance. It was right after July 20, 1944, that these Swedish contacts turned to him once more in a case that seemed very urgent to them. Gottfried Count von Bismarck, a nephew of the earlier illustrious German chancellor, had been picked up by the Gestapo in the aftermath of the attempted coup and, as Sir Victor Mallet learned from Jacob Wallenberg, it was "a very near thing for his life." In retrospect, one might be inclined to comment cynically that in this case Schellenberg had to intervene for his own good. A simple explanation along those lines, however, would not do justice to the rather complicated context. Schellenberg had been in contact repeatedly with Count Bismarck. There had been visits by the Count to Schellenberg's office in Berlin, and Schellenberg had paid personal visits to the Bismarcks. In other words, the two men, the SS leader and the apparent member of the resistance, who was planning the overthrow of the German government, had spoken to each other rather openly and addressed the need to terminate the present German regime. Bismarck, if Schellenberg recalls correctly, thought it a wise step to eliminate Hermann Göring, and he had hoped for Schellenberg's advice regarding persons who could be trusted with the execution of such an operation. Schellenberg, however, had expressed his view that Göring was no more than a glittering showman. Instead he felt that it was Hitler who would have to be removed and had told Bismarck that he had hoped to move in that direction with Himmler's support. We have no way of knowing why a man like Bismarck trusted someone like Schellenberg whose uniform alone normally meant the threat of death to the hunted members of Germany's small resistance.[307] Schellenberg, in fact, almost never wore that uniform and according to those who met him, had a pleasant open personality. We are also uncertain whether Schellenberg was fully aware that Bismarck was actually tied in with the group that would attempt to overthrow the regime. From the somewhat incomplete records it would appear that Schellenberg must have been contacted by Alvar Möller of Svenska Taendsticks on behalf of Bismarck almost immediately following the failed coup, because Schellenberg remembers that he spoke with Himmler about the Bismarck Case at the same time he approached him for urgent assistance in the Canaris Case which we know came only days after July 23. Schellenberg and Himmler, much aware of the weight of the Bismarck name even for Hitler, discussed the possibility of having Bismarck's mother or grandmother write a personal letter to Hitler. According to Schellenberg's memoirs, Himmler also offered to personally take the matter up with Hitler. Moreover, Himmler apparently ordered the much feared President of the ill-famed People's Court, Roland Freisler, to his office and told him in no uncertain terms that Bismarck must be acquitted. Undoubtedly, a good part of the exchanges relating to the Bismarck Case were concerned with the international renown of the name and the sheer impossibility of having a member of that family sentenced in a German court. The entire operation, as in most

---

307. "Notes on a conversation with Mr. Jacob Wallenberg," Sir Victor Mallet, March 25, 1945, NAK, FO 188/487, File 65. Gottfried Count von Bismarck (1901-1949), *Regierungspräsident* (President) in Potsdam, closely connected to Jacob Wallenberg, a member of the inner circle of the German resistance. Count Bismarck had also been one of the founding members of the Keppler *Kreis*, later called *Freundeskreis*, a group of industrialists and other influential Germans who in 1932 organized themselves in support of the Nazis.

cases of this nature, certainly took longer than Bismarck would have wished, but considering the state of German law at the time and the political climate in Germany, it was a fortunate event for Count Bismarck when he was released to return to his estate. Surely, Schellenberg alone would not have been able to protect the Count from Freisler's vengeful blood justice if it had not been for the meaningful assistance of his extremely well connected Swedish friends and his own direct lines to Himmler and the Nazi Minister of Justice Otto Georg Thierack with whom he may not have had much in common otherwise but who was, most importantly, his corps brother. We are fortunate in this case to have the later statements of Bismarck, Wallenberg and Moeller. As a historical document, Jacob Wallenberg's testimony before the Military Tribunal at Nuremberg is of great interest not only for the rescue of Count Bismarck, but also as reliable evidence that Wallenberg, Brandin and Möller from December 1943 on met with Schellenberg on numerous occasions. Incidentally, this document proves in addition that Schellenberg personally rescued a number of individuals who were of particular concern to Jacob Wallenberg. He specifically credits Schellenberg with having saved his brother-in-law the Austrian Ferdinand Count Arco auf Valley and the two Norwegian shipping line operators Wilhelm Klavenes and Arne Bjoern-Hansen. Without touching on his own personal contacts to the British Minister in Stockholm, Sir Victor A. L. Mallet, Wallenberg adds that he learned that Schellenberg had made repeated attempts to arrange an end of hostilities with the Western Allies.[308] Alvar Möller fully confirmed Schellenberg's report on the Bismarck Case. In August 1944 Jacob Wallenberg asked Möller to come and see him. He introduced him to the *Fürstin* (Princess) Anne Marie von Bismarck. After this visit to the Wallenbergs Möller immediately traveled to Berlin and saw Schellenberg on the day of his arrival. The latter promised help and influenced Himmler to call on Freisler to make sure that Bismarck would not be found guilty by the People's Court. Bismarck indeed was then transferred to a concentration camp from where he was later released. Möller also underlined that Schellenberg arranged for the freeing of Egon Freiherr (Baron) von Ritter, his friend whose wife was a Swede. Finally, Möller confirmed Schellenberg's important role in the release of Count Arco auf Valley, a brother-in-law of Jacob Wallenberg who had been imprisoned in Austria. Of considerable historical interest is Möller's clear statement that he invited Schellenberg to his home, presumably in Berlin, where he arranged a meeting with Arvid Richert, the Swedish Minister. Richert was struck by Schellenberg's openness and, in Möller's words, "this encounter then

---

308. Notes on a conversation with Mr. Jacob Wallenberg, May 25, 1945, NAK, FO 188/487, File 65. Statement by Jacob Wallenberg, NA, RG 238, Microfilm M897, Roll 114. Statement under Oath, Count Gottfried von Bismarck, February 19, 1948, SAN, Rep. 501, LV, S-3.

led to the meeting of Count Bernadotte and Schellenberg in February 1945 and the following Swedish Red Cross operation whereby more than 20,000 persons were rescued from the concentration camps and brought to Sweden."[309]

The Swedish executive certainly was correct in his appraisal of the significance of Schellenberg's contacts with men such as Richert who had the ways and means to open doors in Swedish Government circles and thus get the extensive and costly rescue operations under way that were to bring a large number of concentration camp inmates out of Germany, thereby saving thousands from the excessive brutality practiced by the Germans until the final collapse of their system. Not wishing to detract from the significant roles played by men like Richert or Count Bernadotte, it must be understood, however, that the rescue operations directed by Schellenberg and Bernadotte are part of a much wider context which includes Schellenberg's continued efforts to contact the Western Allies for talks leading to an end of hostilities in the West. Moreover, and this has often been overlooked, it is very clear that Schellenberg and others would not have been able to pursue lines to the Allied camp if Heinrich Himmler had not silently tolerated such activities and, even more so, in several instances actively taken part in the deliberations leading to such contacts. Whether Himmler's motives had their origin in anything resembling an even faintly realistic appraisal of the situation cannot be analyzed here, but the very fact that Himmler was providing cover is a key aspect and in part an explanation for Schellenberg's ability to organize the rescue operations. This in no way is to imply that Schellenberg could continuously rely on Himmler's support. Quite to the contrary, Himmler's boundless loyalty to Hitler was a supremely important factor to contend with almost to the end of the German Reich, and Schellenberg had to proceed with the greatest circumspection to be sure that he himself would not be caught in the cauldron of reckless murder and destructiveness characteristic of life in Germany at that time.

This is not only relevant in the large rescue operations which Schellenberg undertook together with former Swiss President Jean-Marie Musy or Count Bernadotte, but more than likely the personal risk taken by Schellenberg was even greater in the much smaller operations involving individual persons or small groups. One of these cases was the complicated maneuver to free a captured American general and to use this release in order to establish a line of contact to the United States. Brigadier General Arthur W. Vanaman of the U.S. Army Air Force was a former U.S. Air Attaché to Berlin who had become a

---

309. Statement under Oath, Alvar Möller, April 22, 1948, SAN, Rep. 501, LV, S-4. Statement under Oath, Egon Freiherr von Ritter, February 21, 1948, SAN, Rep. 501, LV, S-3.

prisoner-of-war of the Germans.[310] In the autumn of 1944 when Schellenberg had given some serious thought to using high-ranking British POWs to open paths for negotiations with the Western Allies, he had also been aware of General Vanaman. Apparently no progress was achieved in that project, and it would appear that Vanaman was held in a POW camp in occupied Poland until January 1945. When Soviet troops threatened to overrun the area, the POWs were moved West, and General Vanaman and a small group of American officers were taken to Berlin. There is no doubt that Schellenberg wanted Vanaman released to Switzerland from where he would fly to the U.S. and contact President Roosevelt. Just what transpired in the bombed out Nazi capital is not entirely clear, but it seems certain that Schellenberg had a plan for which, for his personal security alone, he decidedly needed the approval of Himmler. The latter, however, much feared being drawn into an extremely risky undertaking and was not to be persuaded to give his consent. Whether a conference of American officer POWs and SS officials in Berlin was actually convened to find ways of obtaining food and supplies from Switzerland for American POWs in Germany or whether Schellenberg had organized the curious conference merely to create a plausible reason for dispatching Vanaman to Switzerland must remain an open question.[311] Whatever may have been the case, Schellenberg undoubtedly considered the matter sufficiently important to meet General Vanaman personally. Most likely Schellenberg had decided to send the American General to neutral Switzerland, if need be even without the agreement of Himmler, and SS-*Obergruppenführer* Berger had probably become involved too deeply to be able to withdraw and claim innocence. Eventually, it was now early April 1945, General Vanaman and Colonel Delmar T. Spivey on Schellenberg's order were outfitted with the necessary papers and taken to the German-Swiss border by a hand-picked SS officer. Apparently Vanaman until the actual crossing of the border was quite uncertain whether, for whatever reason, the Germans might decide to eliminate him on the way. On the Swiss side the case was being handled by the Chief of Military Intelligence Roger Masson and his right-hand man Paul E. Meyer, and it may be assumed that the Chief of Staff General Henri Guisan was also fully informed. Their German contact man was Hans Wilhelm Eggen, Schellenberg's personal representative in Swiss affairs. Somewhere in the background and much concerned about the outcome of the operation was Brigadier

---

310. Arthur W. Vanaman (1892-1987), studied Electrical and Aeronautical Engineering, Assistant Air Attaché in Berlin prior to World War II, May 1944 Assistant Chief of Staff for Intelligence with 8th Air Corps in Britain, probably shot down over Germany in June 1944.
311. On the events in Berlin Anthony Read, David Fisher, *The Fall of Berlin* (New York: Da Capo, 1995; 1st 1992), 246-249, 289-290.

General Barnwell R. Legge, the Military Attaché at the American Legation in Bern who is said to have been a friend of General Vanaman and handled the American side of the rather clandestine undertaking. To arrange for the illegal border crossing Legge worked with both Schellenberg and Swiss authorities. It is not clear from the records whether Himmler in the end gave his go-ahead or whether Schellenberg had to act entirely on his own. The mysterious delay at the border mentioned in some sources that caused the American officers some concern, may have been a consequence of Schellenberg's difficult attempts in Berlin to gain Himmler's approval.[312]

The ranking American officers were not the only military personalities of the Western Allies released to fulfill requests from abroad. About this time there also occurred the liberation of the British Major J. Bigelow Dodge who was apparently released in the same manner, that is being transported by one of Schellenberg's men to the Swiss border and there, handled by Hans Wilhelm Eggen, transferred to Masson's men, most likely Paul Meyer.[313]

A further rescue operation directed by Schellenberg and clearly of historical interest involved the freeing of the wife and fifteen family members of the well-known French General Henri Honoré Giraud.[314] Giraud had served many years in French Colonial North Africa, as well as in World War I. In early World War II he was in command of the 7th French Army. Following his capture by the Germans in 1940, he spent about two years in prison, but as in World War I he was able to escape, this time from the supposedly high-security prison at Königstein in April 1942. Possibly with some assistance from American intelligence, he actually made his way through Nazi Germany to the unoccupied part of France. On May 2, 1942, somewhere in France, the records give different locations, Giraud appears to have been met by the German Ambassador to France, SS-*Brigadeführer* Otto Abetz. The curious gathering was arranged and attended by Admiral François Darlan and the infamous collaborator Pierre Laval, and considerable pressure was exerted on Giraud to give himself up and return to Germany. Needless to say, this professional

---

312. Barnwell R. Legge to Brigadier General G. S. Smith, January 14, 1946, NAK, WO 204/12814. Statement under Oath, Paul E. Meyer, May 10, 1948, SAN, Rep. 501, LV, S-4. Schellenberg, *The Schellenberg Memoirs*, 447. Hans Rudolf Schmidt, "Klarheit über den 'Fall Masson'," newspaper clipping, NAK, WO 204/290, without naming a source states that the officer taking the Americans to the border, SS-*Sturmbannführer* Heinz Lange, at the border received order from Berlin "to liquidate" the American officers.
313. Schmidt, "Klarheit über den 'Fall Masson'"; Colonel Roger Masson to SCI/UNIT-Z/Milan, October 20, 1945; both NAK, WO 204/12814.
314. Giraud himself speaks of "ma femme et quinze personnes de ma famille." Most other sources speak of 13 persons. Henri Giraud "Attestation," June 4, 1948, SAN, Rep 501, LV, S-4. Henri Honoré Giraud (1879–1949), graduated from St. Cyr 1900, military experience in North Africa, wounded and captured by Germans August 1914, escaped October 1914, served again until 1918, after World War I service in North Africa, in World War II differences of opinion with de Gaulle, following second escape from Germans for awhile favored by Americans over de Gaulle. Cf. Mark M. Boatner III, *The Biographical Dictionary of World War II* (Novato: Presidio, 1999), 183–185.

soldier, who was soon to become a serious contender for the leading role in postwar France and thereby a controversial competitor for General Charles de Gaulle, had no intention of turning himself in to the enemy. Although the Gestapo was given the assignment to keep an eye on the General, he managed to successfully continue his escape and reach North Africa. As was then commonly practiced in Nazi Germany—*Sippenhaftung* the Germans called it[315]—the infuriated Germans arrested all the family members they were able to get hold of. Giraud's daughter and grandchildren were actually kidnapped in Tunis by men of Rommel's withdrawing Africa Corps.[316] The request for the rescue of the Giraud family was delivered to Schellenberg by Jean Marie Musy and his son Benoit when they arrived in Berlin in October 1944. Whether Schellenberg was told that the request now coming from Masson in fact originated with the French General is quite uncertain. The knowledge that it came from Masson certainly was sufficient reason for Schellenberg to do everything in his power. The Swiss emissaries actually had come to Berlin to persuade the Germans to shut down the concentration camps and release all prisoners. Among the individual cases they presented to Schellenberg, the Giraud family appears to have been especially important. It is of more than passing interest that Masson was especially concerned with the release of the Giraud family. The French General had been his instructor at the École superieure de guerre in Paris. It turned out to be an uphill fight, a particularly tough case because Kaltenbrunner had personally decided that the family members of the run-away French General were not to be released under any circumstances. The OSS whose members had dealt with General Giraud on various occasions after his escape from Königstein was unwilling at the time to see Schellenberg's rescue activities, particularly those on behalf of the Giraud family, as anything other than an attempt by the German to smooth conditions for himself in the postwar period. Allen Dulles put it this way: "Shellenberg [*sic*] is obviously attempting to buy immunity as he has just delivered Gen Giraud's family to Masson who repatriated them to France, and is apparently prepared to release further women and children." While selfish motives can never be excluded, these rescue operations more likely were caused simply by requests from highly placed persons abroad, such as Masson in the case of the Giraud family. Moreover, those who made the requests, be it Möller or Wallenberg in Sweden or Masson or Guisan in Switzerland, may well have

---

315. *Sippenhaftung* or *Sippenhaft* meant legal responsibility, i.e. arrest and punishment, for all members of the family clan of a person sought and sentenced by the German authorities.
316. Peter Witte et al, eds., *Der Dienstkalender Heinrich Himmlers 1941/42* (Hamburg: Christians, 1999), 404, 417, 435. Cf. somewhat unclear report on German reaction to Giraud's flight in Höhne, *Canaris*, 451-454. Jean-Paul Cointet, *Pierre Laval* (Paris: Fayard, 1993), 377-378. Michèle Cointet, *De Gaulle et Giraud: L'affrontement (1942-1944)* (Paris: Perrin, 2005), 26ff.

represented the only lines left if one wished to somehow still seek a negotiated end of hostilities in the West. This certainly was true for Schellenberg and, incidentally, it should be said, does not make the turn of events less fortunate for those who could be rescued. In this case, as in several others, Schellenberg used his own driver Hugo Buchwald to transport the French family to the Swiss-German border. Presumably they were then taken to the checkpoint by Schellenberg's man Hans Wilhelm Eggen to be handed over to Paul E. Meyer, Masson's personal assistant, who would accompany them into Switzerland and attend to the formalities of getting them on their way back to France.[317]

Several other such rescue operations are much less documented and information on the persons often remains less than reliable. Jean Marie Musy for instance brought the request from Janusz Prince Radziwil for the liberation of General Bor, the Polish resistance leader. General Bor was actually Tadeusz Komorowski, a courageous Pole who in the summer of 1944 had led the underground forces in Warsaw against the far superior German troops under the command of General of the *Waffen* SS Erich von dem Bach-Zelewski. Komorowski was captured, and Schellenberg and Müller had given permission to the officers of the Operation Zeppelin to contact him in the detention camp to see if he could be used for intelligence purposes. During postwar interrogations Schellenberg remembered that on April 24, 1945, just days before the end of the war, he actually managed to talk Himmler into allowing him to notify the Kaltnow Camp in Czechoslovakia that Komorowski should be escorted to the Swiss frontier and released to Swiss authorities. If Schellenberg's order still reached the camp, the Polish prisoner in any case appears to have gotten no farther than Innsbruck where he was fortunate to be liberated by American troops.[318] Musy had also pressed Schellenberg to create some goodwill in France by having the French political leaders Édouard Herriot and Paul Reynaud released from prison. Apparently Schellenberg made an attempt to gain Himmler's consent but no success could be achieved at this late stage. Himmler felt that he had more important problems to deal with than fighting Kaltenbrunner over the release of some Frenchmen.[319]

Prior to taking a closer look at the large rescue operations undertaken by Schellenberg, Musy and Bernadotte, it is necessary to examine several other

---

317. 110 (Dulles) to Director OSS, April 5, 1945, NA, RG 226, E 210, Box 364. Statement under Oath, Paul E. Meyer, May 10, 1948, SAN, Rep. 501, LV, S-4. Interrogations of Hugo Buchwald, May 24, 1948, SAN, Rep. 502, KV-Anklage, B 186. Questioning of Schellenberg by Dr. R. M. W. Kempner, December 18, 1947, SAN, S-45c.
318. "Final Report," 179-180. Boatner, *The Biographical Dictionary of World War II*, 288. Statement under Oath, Benoit Musy, May 8, 1948, SAN, Rep. 501, LV, S-4.
319. Statement under Oath, Colonel-Brigadier R. Masson, May 10, 1948, SAN, Rep. 501, S-4. Schellenberg, *The Schellenberg Memoirs*, 432. Both Herriot and Reynaud were held by the Germans until liberation by Russian and American troops respectively.

intelligence activities that need to be understood in order to obtain a more complete picture of the confusing final period of the Third Reich. One of the important sectors of German intelligence handled the Soviet Union. It has been pointed out that Schellenberg was not very much interested in exploring possibilities for negotiations with the Russians, and with that negative perspective he found himself in clear opposition to a number of Nazi leaders in politics and in the military who for various reasons disliked and even despised both Great Britain and the United States. Somewhere between those Germans who tended to be oriented towards the East and the Soviet Union and those who preferred to look towards Great Britain and in some cases to the United States were the Japanese, represented very strongly by Hiroshi Oshima in Berlin and Makato Onodera in Stockholm. It is difficult in this context to clearly define Japanese political positions in terms of East and West. We have already seen that the Japanese for instance used the Poles who were surely not pro-Russian to obtain much information about the Soviet Union, some of which ended up with their allies, the Germans. On the other side the Japanese repeatedly pressed the Germans in the direction of a more positive appraisal of the U.S.S.R. and even suggested the benefits of an understanding if not an alliance of Japan and Germany with the Soviet Union. One can easily guess who could turn out to be the enemy of such an alliance and how much it would strengthen the position of the Japanese versus the U.S. The German inclinations in this game were not altogether clear. While the German General Staff had worked with the Soviets during all those years when in the open spaces of the U.S.S.R. the Germans were testing their new weapons for the next war, there were also much older and traditional pro-Russian trends among other German leaders. To be sure, the Nazis with their perverted racial perceptions of humanity had classified the Slavs among the lesser and weaker tribes of mankind. Not without reason has it been said that Nazi Germany's military forces when entering the greater Russian regions might indeed have benefited to some degree from the anti-Russian sentiment of several ethnic populations which could have been and in some cases had turned already into pro-German sentiment. As is well known, however, the unfathomable brutality practiced by the supposedly superior Germanic Germans quickly destroyed any good will that might have existed prior to their arrival. The Zeppelin Operation, of course, had made a belated effort to use pro-German sympathies in Russia to the advantage of Germany. The Russian units fighting on the side of the Germans and the men signing up in large numbers for the so-called Vlasov Army also would appear to suggest that there was indeed an anti-Soviet sentiment in some regions of Russia that could have been used advantageously. Contrary to numerous SS leaders, Schellenberg who in 1941 had played an important role as a mediator in the preparatory deliberations of the SS and the regular Armed Forces, had never served in an *Einsatzkommando* (special detachment) of any kind, but in his position as Chief of *Amt* VI he was certainly aware of the reports of the bloody excesses and just plain mass murder among the civilian population of Eastern Europe that had passed through his office. Whether he read them or not, there can be no doubt that he was completely informed about the unprecedented crimes committed by German forces in the Soviet Union. We may assume that his knowledge of the primitive German behavior in Russia could well have been one factor reinforcing his apparently general view that Germany's future was in the West. There is nothing in the records to suggest that his views were influenced by a fear of an expected Russian revenge and, although it has been suggested by other authors, his desire to line up Germany with the Western nations does not seem to have included a long term idea of a united West moving against the U.S.S.R. When the now victorious Soviet armies were advancing towards Germany, he apparently hoped to negotiate a peace in the West and thereby stop the advancing Soviet forces in the East. An aggressive campaign of the West against the East does not seem to have been part of his belated attempts to stop the war. To prevent the creation of misconceptions about Schellenberg's orientation, it must be said that there is evidence of his interest in connections to China which he tried to create through contacts in Switzerland. One of the men who worked with Schellenberg in this sector was Kurt Jahnke, the already mentioned intelligence specialist in Rudolf Hess' office before the latter's journey to Britain. Most of the contacts with China, whether cultivated in Berlin or in Switzerland, appear to have been highly covert and the number of people involved was very small. The remaining records suggest that these activities produced nothing and that in any case they must have been in serious conflict with the German-Japanese alliance.

Schellenberg's aversion to closer political contacts in Eastern Europe and especially the Soviet Union may have kept his interest in lines into the U.S.S.R. at a relatively low level, but it could not mean that he would ignore these lines. There were two groups in Germany who were decidedly interested in Eastern Europe. Both, certain parts of the older military professionals and a strong section of the German Foreign Office, were oriented more to the East than to the West, and both of these groups had their own lines to the East. To avoid possible misunderstandings, it should be pointed out that these two groups obviously did not prevent the German attack on the Soviet Union and, more surprisingly, made no effort to prevent the inhumane treatment of Russian POWs in Germany. In other words, the pro-Russian sentiments in some sectors of German leadership were not stronger than the support of these same

Germans for an aggressive war in the East. Schellenberg certainly was aware of these seemingly contradictory sentiments and their relative strength among German political and military leaders. Ribbentrop, Hitler's Foreign Minister, with his fanatical dislike of Britain and a more than superficial inclination to deal with the Soviet Union was among those who from their positions of power were more than likely to hinder Schellenberg's predilections for Western Europe, Great Britain and the United States.

Following the total suppression of Poland and the destruction of much of its intellectual leadership, Stockholm had become the most important center for German political moves in the direction of Eastern Europe. The activities in the Swedish capital, however, were not expressions of a profound German interest in Russia nor were the Russian moves a reflection of a generally pro-German feeling. Quite the opposite, what transpired in Stockholm was heavily influenced by the turn of events registered on the battlefields inside the Soviet Union, and the representatives of both the Soviet Union and the Western Allies, while having their intelligence services watch the other side twenty-four hours a day, did their best to maintain the appearance of a reliable partnership. The successful landing of Allied forces in North Africa, the defeat of Germany's Africa Corps and particularly the visible weakness of the German armies in the Soviet Union after the defeat at Stalingrad made German maneuvers for negotiations on one side or the other increasingly difficult. Neither the Western Allies nor the Soviet Union could have a great interest in joining forces with what was left of the corrupt and brutalized Nazi dictatorship in Germany. The expected victory over Germany, however, did not automatically invalidate the many secondary interests relating to conditions following German surrender or faint German hopes for concessions from either side. While Schellenberg had been able to establish his own personal contacts to a number of influential personalities in Sweden, he appears to have avoided direct encounters with Russian agents or diplomats in Sweden and his regular agents in Stockholm apparently had neither the qualifications nor the international connections needed for risky undertakings of that nature. Of all the Germans involved in attempts to contact the Russians in Sweden, two agents seem to have been better qualified and less clumsy than the run of the mill SD and *Abwehr* men. One of them was Dr. Bruno Peter Kleist, a well educated man of diverse professional background who had a marked ability to react to changing conditions.[320] A member of the NSDAP since 1933 and the

---

320. Dr. Bruno Peter Kleist (1904-1971), also called himself von Kleist, occasionally referred to as Dr. Bruno, studies in Leipzig and Berlin, joined Ribbentro's staff 1936, Polish work and contacts 1937, worked for Ribbentrop in connection with Hitler-Stalin Pact 1939, came to Stockholm for Ribbentrop, Canaris, *Ostministerium* and probably Kaltenbrunner, since 1943 also worked for *Amt* VI, intelligence work in Sweden,

SS since 1938, he had come of age so to speak in the German Foreign Office working for Ribbentrop's inner circle in his *Dienststelle*. When the Germans occupied large areas in Eastern Europe, Kleist moved to Alfred Rosenberg's *Ostministerium* (Ministry for the East). Officially he came to Sweden on behalf of these two Ministries, and on the surface his work was connected with the settlement of ethnic Germans in occupied territories and most recently the resettlement of smaller ethnic Swedish groups from Estonia to Sweden. Kleist had also been used in some kind of advisory function for the Operation Zeppelin, clear evidence that he was more than superficially associated with parts of *Amt* VI. When he came to Sweden in 1942, he may in fact have been closer to Canaris than to Schellenberg. Kleist, who in 1939 had participated in Ribbentrop's negotiations leading to the Hitler-Stalin Pact, considered himself quite an Eastern expert and his generally somewhat conceited appearance had not helped him to establish close contacts with more traditional German diplomats. The fact that in his difficult work with the Russians he was trusted by both Schellenberg's *Amt* VI and the *Abwehr* may be seen as just one more example of the not infrequent cooperation of the two German intelligence services. When Kleist first made his appearance in Stockholm, the Germans had not yet been defeated at Stalingrad. Specialists in the field have later tended to emphasize that the Germans at the time pursued their contacts to Russia based on the assumption that German victory in the Soviet Union was still very likely. By the same token the point has often been made that the Russians came to feel more self-confident only after defeating the Germans at Stalingrad.

Whoever was actually responsible for sending Kleist to Stockholm may have known who his contact in Sweden would be. From appearances the dispatcher seems to have been Ribbentrop, but both Canaris and Schellenberg were certainly informed. Looking at the somewhat scanty evidence it would seem that in Stockholm Kleist was introduced to Edgar Klaus, a Jewish *Abwehr* agent of Russian-Latvian background and evidently multilingual who used the code name Schönemann. In the course of his adventurous life, much of it being on the run from Soviet Communism as well as from German anti-Semitism, he had found it necessary to change his official citizenship from Danish to German to Stateless. Available sources are rather uncertain regarding just when Klaus may have begun working for German intelligence as an informer on Russian matters. The initial work may well have occurred already

---

imprisoned in Special Detention Center "Ashcan" summer 1945, autumn 1945 offered his services to British in Germany, involved in organizing neofascist party in post-war Germany. Bruno Peter Kleist, Court Interrogation, SAN, Rep. 502, KV, K 82. Ministerial Dirigent Bruno Kleist, NA, RG 263, E A1-86, Box 22. "Eidesstattliche Erklärung," Dr. Dr. Kleist, May 4, 1948, NA, RG 226, CIA Name Files, RC Box 29. Detailed Interrogation Report, Joachim von Ribbentrop, NA, RG 319, IRR, IS, Box 8.

prior to World War II. Some time early in the war he was brought to the *Abwehr* by a man called Werner Boening who like Klaus was in the business of selling films. Whether in his intelligence business Klaus informed both Russians and Germans on each other, remains an open question. Being a stateless Jew in Europe in those years may well have caused him to consider buying insurance on both sides, regardless of the obvious high risks involved. Quite in contrast to Klemens von Klemperer who describes Klaus as "a thoroughly questionable character," Ingeborg Fleischhauer has come to the conclusion that whatever controversial information may be found in the documents related to the various intelligence operations, Klaus as a baptized Jew from Latvia had grown up to become a very loyal German who in reality was neither a Nazi nor a Communist. In the summer of 1945 the OSS found Klaus sufficiently interesting to consider approaching him as a potential agent, but the *Abwehr* man passed away in 1946, presumably inactive.[321]

Kleist and Klaus, in any case both German intelligence agents, had a number of meetings in Sweden in the course of which Klaus appears to have offered his assistance in arranging contacts to the Soviet Legation in Stockholm. "If Germany would accept the borders of 1939, you can have peace in eight days," he reportedly told the all too easily impressed Kleist.[322] When the latter informed Ribbentrop of what he thought was splendid news, the Foreign Minister hurried off to see the *Führer,* fully convinced that he had come up with a way to move in the direction of talks with Stalin. Needless to say when Hitler understood that the proposal of the Russians meant sacrificing the conquered territories in Eastern Europe he literally exploded.[323] This all led to a short break in the all too optimistic pursuits of Ribbentrop and Canaris, but already in the early summer of 1943 Kleist was back in Stockholm and not surprising once again met with Klaus. This time the apparently well connected Canaris man announced the upcoming arrival of one Andrey Mihailovich Alexandrov identified as the important chief of the Central European Department in the Foreign Commissariat but who instead may well have been just a

---

321. Edgar Klaus (1879-1946), also spelled Claus, Clauss or Clausson, Jewish father who became Protestant and raised Edgar as Protestant, in constant danger of persecution because of Jewish descent, studied Geology in Russia, early professional work in banking, interpreter in Russian prison camps, contacts with Communists possibly including Stalin, Danish identity papers when working for Danish Consulate in Riga, contacts to German Foreign Office, real estate business in Berlin, German identity papers 1931, to Yugoslavia 1933, back to Riga 1938, contact with *Abwehr*. Von Klemperer, *German Resistance Against Hitler*, 245. Fleischhauer, *Die Chance des Sonderfriedens*, passim. Alexander Slavinas, "'Treff' und 'Joker'," *Die Zeit*, June 2, 1989, 45-46. Several documents, NA, RG 226, Field Station Files, Stockholm, Box 28.
322. Fleischhauer, *Die Chance des Sonderfriedens*, 110. (Transl.)
323. *Ibid.*, 111. Bruno Peter Kleist, *Die europäische Tragödie* (Göttingen: K. W. Schütz, 1961), 212, recalled that he spoke to very few persons, among them Adam von Trott zu Solz, the German resistance member who attended to his own contacts in Sweden, and Friedrich Werner Count von der Schulenburg, Hitle's Ambassador in Moscow until 1941. Cf. H. W. Koch, "The Spectre of a Separate Peace in the East: Russo-German 'Peace Feelers', 1942-44," *Journal of Contemporary History*, vol. 10, no. 3, (July, 1975), 534.

member of the Soviet Legation in Stockholm.[324] Even the self-confident Kleist seems to have become hesitant. It might be too risky to attend to this matter without appropriate orders from above, the agent thought and delayed. It is not entirely clear just how his message to Berlin made its way to Ribbentrop and from there to Hitler. Some sources suggest that Klaus may have taken the matter into his own hands by forwarding the presumed Russian desire for a meeting by way of Hans Wagner, the *Abwehr* Chief in Stockholm, to Canaris. Even less certain seems to be the exact content of the message. When it reached Hitler it apparently identified the German agents and the Russian as Jews. Whoever composed this text in the *Abwehr* offices in Stockholm or Berlin knew or should have known how Hitler would react. Also it would seem unlikely that such a text would have found the approval of Admiral Canaris. The *Führer* indeed is said to have been enraged about this "audacious Jewish provocation" and to have threatened that all those involved would be held accountable.[325] At this stage of the war Hitler was strictly opposed to any contacts of this nature with Stalin. That some of his underlings, such as Ribbentrop and apparently Canaris, may have entertained certain ideas in that direction surely would have had little or no effect. There is also no evidence of any encounters of significance between Nazi and Soviet leaders, not to mention the often reported meeting of Ribbentrop and Molotov in the summer of 1943 that never took place. Contrary to all kinds of sensationalist reports published every so often, there is nothing to suggest a Soviet willingness to contemplate a new version of the Hitler-Stalin Pact.[326]

There can be no doubt that one of the more pressing concerns of intelligence men like Schellenberg in wartime was the ongoing search for lines to the neutral nations and the building of connections there to representatives of the enemy. Yet, it is often overlooked that he had just been appointed Chief of *Amt* VI and that this far-flung intelligence organization had to be revamped almost entirely when he took office in July 1942. It is clear from the records that following the inefficient years of his predecessor Heinz Jost the very existence of this foreign intelligence service was uncertain. Heinrich Himmler is said to have given Schellenberg a year to straighten out the malfunctioning apparatus. Schellenberg not only had the usual problems of reorganization following any takeover and abrupt change at the top, but he was also forced to justify the existence of the organization and therefore to present results much

---

324. Cf. Vojtech Mastny, "Stalin and the Prospects of a Separate Peace in World War II," *The American Historical Review*, vol. 77, no. 5 (December 1972), 1379. Fleischhauer, *Die Chance des Sonderfriedens*, 162-165.
325. Cf. Kleist, *Die europäische Tragödie*, 218-219. Fleischhauer, *Die Chance des Sonderfriedens*, 166.
326. For a still very useful analysis see Mastny, "Stalin and the Prospects of a Separate Peace in World War II."

faster than would normally have been expected in such a situation. To add a little spice to this undertaking he found himself faced with a group of ideological and professional enemies inside the Nazi structure who for many reasons would have been more than delighted to see him fail in the almost hopeless task. His management problems were considerable, and the personnel available was often ideologically programmed, if not to say politically blinded, and therefore quite incapable of rational analysis of international contexts and developments. Presumably circumstances were not helped by the fact that some of his more perceptive colleagues and employees realized or suspected that their Chief was not in fact a real *Nationalsozialist* (National Socialist, Nazi). In the words of Bruno Peter Kleist: "… he had a far more flexible mind than the majority of Nazis and was indeed not a convinced Nazi himself." During postwar interrogation SS-*Standartenführer* Martin Sandberger put it this way: "Schellenberg…[was] a politician rather than a dogmatic National Socialist and…favorably disposed toward the Allies."[327] It is moreover quite evident that repeated changes in personnel, the almost constant floundering of the overall RSHA organization, and the continuous moving of larger sections of *Amt* VI to new locations outside of the capital did not increase efficiency and in some cases worsened the already unsatisfactory working conditions he had to contend with.

The personnel changes originated with the already mentioned urgent need to clean out the less than optimal functional structures inherited from his predecessor, but they continued because qualified people were just not available in sufficient numbers and because some of his trained experts were increasingly called up to serve in the field. Schellenberg, quite in contrast to many of his German contemporaries, was painfully aware of the lack of international perspective in German education and professional training and had advocated a more international orientation. The British view following a few initial interrogations of Schellenberg in July 1945 was certainly somewhat exaggerated, but in some ways it was not so far removed from reality: "The consequence was that neither Schellenberg himself nor any of the officers under his command had the capacity to evaluate the political and other intelligence…"[328] In view of such dour conditions it is not surprising that some of his personnel choices were not ideal and that in several cases it became necessary to move people again. Also, as touched on earlier, Schellenberg quite naturally would try to take with him from *Amt* IV those men whom in the

---

327. Kleist to Ewan Butler, July 19, 1945, NAK, FO 371/46749. Interrogation of Martin Sandberger, July 8, 1945, NAK, KV 2/95.
328. Statement under Oath, Hans Hendrik Neumann, NA, RG 238, Microfilm M 897, Roll 114. "War Room Monthly Summary No. 4," July 23, 1945, NA, RG 226, E 119A, Box 24.

course of his brief tenure there he had found intellectually engaged and, possibly even more important, trustworthy. Gestapo Chief Müller may have been uncertain whether he would rather rid himself of this unliked Group Chief or keep the overly active and independently thinking upstart under his direct control in *Amt* IV. In any case, Müller understandably was very unwilling to assist Schellenberg in strengthening his *Amt* VI by allowing him to take some of the best people with him. In several instances Schellenberg actually had to fight before getting the men he thought he needed.[329] Needless to say, these confrontations would intensify the already highly unpleasant relationship between the two very different Nazi leaders. Whether the differences between the two men were linked to the fact that Schellenberg, who was clearly Western oriented early on, began to suspect Müller of being particularly Eastern oriented, if not more, may be a question of interpretation. Much has been made later in respective publications of Schellenberg's supposedly naïve and biased opinion that Müller may have had connections to Soviet Russia.[330]

Most likely it was this at times outright dangerous situation, added to a very distant and often disharmonious relation with Ernst Kaltenbrunner that led to Schellenberg's decision to seek a reliable and close working relationship with Heinrich Himmler, even more so after losing the always uncertain and threatening but undoubtedly powerful tutelage of Reinhard Heydrich. The consequences of the often very challenging and tense activities in *Amt* VI were easy to see. Those closer to him, including his opponents, all agreed that he was someone who never left matters unfinished nor ever learned to really delegate responsibility. Naturally, many of his plans could not be realized, and his protector Heinrich Himmler would not always budge. A very significant example was Schellenberg's decision that *Amt* VI Foreign Intelligence should operate outside the RSHA structure. He approached matters rather carefully and tried to persuade Himmler to lift the SS uniform requirement for *Amt* VI. Himmler, the *Reichsführer* SS, of course would have nothing of this and even rejected the more moderate request for discarding the SD insignia in *Amt* VI. Uniforms and insignia of every sort indeed were meaningful symbols for the men in the Nazi structure, but Schellenberg was aware that they also stood for a concert of outside ideological forces which almost prevented an independent evaluation of intelligence information.[331]

In contrast to various departments of his *Amt* VI, his own place of work saw very little change. Soon after moving from the Gestapo to *Amt* VI, his

---

329. "Eighth Detailed Interrogation Report," Klaus Hügel, June 26, 1945, NA, RG 263, E A1-86, Boxes 37-38.
330. Schellenberg, *The Schellenberg Memoirs*, 360-362, Cf. Schellenberg, *Memoiren*, 286-288.
331. Statement under Oath, Dr. Theodor Paeffgen, March 12, 1948, SAN, Rep.501, LV, S-3.

entire organization had been installed in the spacious quarters at Berkaer Strasse in downtown Berlin. The large modern building had been constructed only in 1930 by the architect Alexander Beer to serve as a retirement home for the Jewish community of the city. In 1941 the Nazis had confiscated the Jewish property and the last inhabitants, as well as the Jewish employees, had been taken away.[332] Actually Germans had disowned their Jewish fellow citizens for several years now, and countless Germans had happily moved their families into vacated Jewish homes. From that German perspective there would therefore have been no reason for Schellenberg to give any thought to the background of his daily surroundings. Yet, in his case this was a part of what went across his desk every day, of what he knew, and of what at least with his membership and career he had supported for years, and it is not impossible that occasionally he may have had more than passing thoughts about the society created. Because he was often working under enormous physical and psychological pressure, it had become a habit for him to stay overnight and to sleep a few hours in the office. On those days his secretaries would prepare light, digestible meals to avoid relapses of his almost constant liver and gall bladder problems. Under those circumstances, it can be safely assumed that what would be called his social life was practically nonexistent. In fact, it is easy to guess that many of the rumors going about were also created by colleagues and rivals who resented his social unavailability. Wilhelm Höttl, maybe somewhat unkindly, but not so far off, commented Schellenberg's work routine: "The dream in Schellenberg's life was the creation of one single espionage system omnipotent in the field of political decision and comparable to what he conceives the British Secret Service to be. To make this dream come true, he was willing to sacrifice everything, not excluding his health and the happiness of his family life. For years he had never, not even for a matter of hours, taken time off to relax and enjoy life. He knowingly drove himself to a physical collapse and his gall bladder ailment is primarily due to overstrain." Wilhelm Waneck later recalled that such false rumors as Schellenberg being a friend or student of Heydrich were actually spread quite intentionally. Klaus Hügel, whom Schellenberg had brought from Stuttgart to Berlin in early 1943, remembered that part of the problem may have been just plain jealousy inside the RSHA apparatus. Schellenberg was not only the youngest *Amt* Chief, but he had also served fewer years than any of the others.[333]

---

332. The building was not destroyed during the bombing raids and now serves as a retirement nursing home. (See illustration.) Alexander Beer was taken to the Concentration Camp Theresienstadt in 1943 and murdered there on May 8, 1944. (Memorial plaque at Berkaer Strasse.)
333. Statement under Oath, Wilhelm Waneck, April 21, 1948, SAN, Rep. 501, LV, S-3. "A Character Sketch of Schellenberg," by Wilhelm Höttl, July 12, 1945, NA, RG 319, IRR, PS, Box 195. "Eighth Detailed Interrogation Report," Klaus Hügel, June 26, 1945, NA, RG 263, E A1-86, Boxes 37-38.

Distasteful tattle passed around behind his back, such as that about the supposed close connections between Schellenberg and Heydrich's wife Lina, could be, as already shown, truly dangerous, and there are indications that he had to be constantly on guard. For later authors the SS officer's imagined affairs served to embellish their fictional accounts of historical events. Harry Patterson's (Jack Higgins) *To Catch a King*, a thrilling story of the Germans' attempt to kidnap the Duke of Windsor, goes so far as to present a dashing Schellenberg swept off his feet by a charming Jewish singer named Hannah Winter. A particularly insipid rumor that has survived in print is the unfounded tale of an affair between Schellenberg and Coco Chanel.[334] The actual encounter of the two was a rather sober presentation in Berlin of Chanel's unrealistic ideas for a direct line to Sir Winston Churchill. The unlikely enterprise was given the code name *Operation Modellhut* (Operation Model Hat). It was Coco Chanel's proposal to approach Churchill for negotiations to end the war. Presumably she had made the personal acquaintance of the British statesman at the time of her affair with the Duke of Westminster. During the war years Chanel resided at the always fashionable Ritz in Paris where she enjoyed the company of a German officer by the name of Hans von Dincklage.[335] He is said to have been connected with both *Abwehr* and SD and during the war was officially attached to the German Embassy in Paris. His role in this operation has remained rather hazy, but he was obviously somehow connected to Theodor Momm and SS-*Brigadeführer* Dr. Walter Schieber, one of Albert Speer's economic functionaries. These two turned up in Schellenberg's office in April 1944 and reported to him that the well-known French lady of some social standing had sufficiently direct personal connections to Winston Churchill to assist in reaching him for political negotiations. Later, after the war Schellenberg recalled that he had asked the two messengers to bring Coco Chanel to Berlin for more detailed information. Shortly thereafter she arrived in the German capital accompanied by Schieber, Momm and her German friend Hans von Dincklage whom she called *Spatz* (Sparrow).[336] Chanel's plan may have sounded quite feasible on first hearing. In fact, however, what Coco

---

334. For instance John Weitz, *Joachim von Ribbentrop: Hitler's Diplomat* (London: Phoenix/Orion, 1997; 1st 1992), 229: " … Coco Chanel was having an affair with a very senior Nazi (probably Walter Schellenberg, the Gestapo-SD espionage head)." Harry Patterson, *To Catch a King* (London: Book Club Associates, 1980, 1st 1979).
335. "Haute Coco," *Vanity Fair*, June 1994, 144. Judith Thurman, "Scenes from a Marriage," *New Yorker*, May 23, 2005, 86. Roewer, Schäfer, Uhl, *Lexikon der Geheimdienste im 20. Jahrhundert*, 112. Hans von Dincklage is sometimes referred to as Hans-Gunther or Hans-Günther von Dincklage. "Translation of Statement handed in by Schellenberg," July 23, 1945, NAK, KV 2/96.
336. Walter Schieber (b. 1896), an engineer and chemist, various economic positions in Nazi Germany, advanced to SS-*Brigadeführer*. Cf. Ulrich Schlie, ed., *Albert Speer: Die Kransberg Protokolle 1945* (München: F. A. Herbig, 2003), 468. Momm is often identified as *Hauptmann* (Captain) suggesting that he was an Army officer connected to the *Abwehr*.

Chanel presented was a complicated hackneyed undertaking that had little or no chance of success. Her scheme included Vera Bate, an English-born lady married to a presumably anti-Mussolini Italian officer by the name of Alberto Lombardi, who would travel to Madrid to contact the British Ambassador Sir Samuel Hoare who in turn would be willing and able to transmit a letter to Churchill. As it was, Mrs. Lombardi had been arrested by the Germans and at present was being held by them and their Italian allies in some Italian jail. Schellenberg's *Amt* VI, of course, had no problems getting her promptly released and without much ado transferred to Paris where she met her friend of years past Coco Chanel. Mrs. Lombardi must have been delighted about the sudden unexpected release, but it is difficult to understand why the Germans could have thought that after having been maltreated she would wish nothing more than to work for them as an agent. Mrs. Lombardi was obviously pleased to be sent to Madrid, and once out of the hands of her tormentors she indeed hurried off to the British asking for help. The final act in the Spanish capital not only had troublesome consequences for Coco Chanel, but also caused Reinhard Spitzy, Prince Hohenlohe's assistant and Schellenberg's representative in Spain, all sorts of problems because he had been in brief contact with Mrs. Lombardi prior to her departure from the scene. Based on the information available on Operation Model Hat one can only wonder what could have caused the wily Schellenberg to allow himself to become involved in this harebrained scheme. There was, it should be said, almost no limit to the inventive and unfounded rumors that involved the Chief of Foreign Intelligence. Aline Countess of Romanones in *The Spy Wore Red*, for instance, goes so far as to suggest that Gloria von Fürstenberg more than just worked for Schellenberg in Spain. [337]

More troublesome than the at least in retrospect rather naïve so-called Operation Model Hat was Schellenberg's ongoing confrontation with some of the other SD leaders who were almost on his level and just below him in the hierarchy. Contrary to some claims in the records, men such as Wilhelm Höttl, Helmut Knochen or Otto Skorzeny were not his friends. In most cases the contentious atmosphere was caused by different political orientations which in turn could lead to a loss of trust on the personal level. Some of Schellenberg's opponents belonged to what could almost be called a powerful Austrian group, particularly after Heydrich's assassination in 1942 and Ernst Kaltenbrunner's

---

337. For Coco Chanel see the more recent Isabelle Fiemeyer, *Coco Chanel: Un parfum mystère* (Paris: Payot & Rivages, 1999). Edmonde Charles-Roux, *Chanel: Her Life, Her World—and the Woman Behind the Legend She Herself Created* (New York: Alfred A. Knopf, 1975; 1st Paris 1974). Axel Madsen, *Chanel: A Woman of Her Own* (New York: Henry Holt, 1990). — Aline Countess of Romanones (Aline Griffith), *The Spy Wore Red* (New York: Charter, 1988; 1st 1987), 193, 291-292. Nigel West, *Counterfeit Spies* (London: St. Ermin's, 1999), 56.

effective rise to real power. Höttl, not unlike Schellenberg, had grown up in a Roman Catholic surrounding and like Schellenberg had completed very respectable university studies, in his case as a student of the well-known Austrian historian Heinrich von Srbik at the University of Vienna who supervised his Ph.D. dissertation on Friedrich Ludwig Jahn, the founder of the *Turnverein* movement. Höttl in later years liked to refer to his earlier academic work and to insinuate that he had almost become a professor of history.[338] Examining Höttl's colorful career, it is difficult to escape the impression that he was one to recognize opportunities as they presented themselves.[339] Arguably this might well be said with some justification about most of the well educated SS leaders, but in comparison Schellenberg leaves an impression of the more determined and sober executive type who would not necessarily be available at every turn. While not Chief of Group VI E, the section involved in intelligence work of every kind in Southeastern Europe or the Balkans, Höttl played a major role in a number of operations in that region. Whether there ever was, as some Allied interrogation reports of the postwar period seem to suggest, a "Höttl group," is quite another question, but there can be no doubt that he tried to be involved in all possible kinds of operations and deals. Somewhere in all this Höttl obviously lost touch with reality and his luck ran out. In late 1941 with Heydrich still running the show in Berlin as Chief of the RSHA—while he also was *Reichsprotektor* (Germany's Protector) in Prague— matters caught up with Höttl. As he recalled later, he was suspended from all positions and accused of being unreliable ideologically, having unacceptable church connections, and having had contacts with Jews. In the absence of any reliable documentation of such SS court-like procedure, it is quite impossible to test the validity of his claims.[340] The Austrian historian Oliver Rathkolb has suggested that Höttl in fact was suspended because of "highly dubious contacts" to other agents and a number of hazy operations.[341] Why Schellenberg would go out of his way to undertake efforts to retrieve Höttl from punishment, a low grade assignment as a military reporter with the *Waffen*-SS, remains rather unclear, but looking at the RSHA hierarchy, it would seem very likely

---

338. Höttl's most recent memoirs *Einsatz für das Reich* (Koblenz: Siegfried Bublies, 1997) are very colorful but continue to pass on untruths. His earlier memoirs *The Secret Front* (London: Phoenix/Orion, 1953) were originally published in Austria as *Die geheime Front* under the pseudonym Walter Hagen.
339. Cf. Höttl file, NA, RG 319, IRR, Box 617, File XE000882: "Former German SS Officer and former U.S. intelligence informant, who is allegedly currently employed in Austria as a Soviet intelligence operative."
340. Testimony of Wilhelm Hött before District Court Bad Aussee, Austria, June 19-21, 1961. Extensive document seen through Oliver Rathkolb.
341. Oliver Rathkolb, "Dritte Männer: Ex-Nazis als US-Agenten," *Das jüdische Echo*, vol. 39, no. 1 (October, 1990), 85. Cf. Thorsten J. Querg, "Spionage und Terror — Das Amt VI des Reichssicherheitshauptamtes 1939-1945," Doctoral Dissertation, Free University, Berlin, 1997, 309-311, commenting some of the problems of Höttl.

that Heydrich's successor Ernst Kaltenbrunner in late 1942 may even have pushed Schellenberg to reinstate Höttl. That would explain why Schellenberg would try to keep an eye on Höttl but also station him down in Austria far away from the daily *Amt* VI business in Berlin. Schellenberg's letter to SS-*Gruppenführer* Gottlob Berger would fit into such a constellation: "... Dr. Höttl was or rather is a full-time member of the SD. He is a specialist of Southeastern Europe and indispensable at this time. His earlier suspension took place to allow him to attend to an assignment [military service at the front] and there was a temporary disciplinary procedure which since has been decided in his favor ... Höttl is on leave until December 27, 1942, from his military reporting section and I would be grateful if ... Höttl would not need to return to Belgrade because he is needed in a current assignment directed from here." On February 10, 1943, Höttl signed a statement that he had just learned that the disciplinary procedure against him had been dropped. "I have, however, understood that I have been strongly reprimanded for my behavior and that my further work is to be understood as a time of probation."[342] Whether under pressure from Kaltenbrunner or otherwise, Schellenberg had undoubtedly extracted Höttl from a difficult situation and one wonders why in the course of postwar interrogations Höttl quite persistently gave negative information on Schellenberg and in some cases even invented matters.[343] In 1943 section VI E was completely restructured according to regions in Southeastern Europe and SS-*Sturmbannführer* Wilhelm Waneck, also an Austrian, became section chief. This reorganization and, not to forget, Kaltenbrunner's very personal interest in Austria may have contributed to the move in 1943 of much of section VI E, including Waneck and Höttl, to the Austrian capital. Schellenberg must have welcomed the relocation of the Austrians, but it seems evident that he would also have less control over their operations from the distance. In fact, what Schellenberg told Allied interrogators when asked what he thought of Höttl, was probably a rather correct estimate: "Hoettl is an intelligent, practical person ... I would think him useful in an intelligence service and use him again, if I could lead him. Otherwise I would not use him in an intelligence service because he is not sufficiently clear and sober." For many years after the war Wilhelm Höttl continued to cultivate relations with a number of intelli-

---

342. Schellenberg to Berger, December 12, 1942; Höttl statement, February 10, 1943; both NA, BDC Microfilm, SSO SS Officer Dossier, Roll A3343 SSO-105A. (Transl.)
343. Cf. "Notes by Dr. Wilhelm Höttl on Schellenberg Interrogation Report", Höttl claiming to quote Eduard Waetjen: " ... he [Waetjen] would ... reveal that Schellenberg's hands were not clean in financial matters." NA, RG 226, E 125A, Box 2. "A Character Sketch of Schellenberg," NA, RG 319, IRR, PS, Box 195.

gence services, and as late as May 1951 he served the Americans as a source of information on intelligence developments inside West Germany.[344]

Helmut Knochen was well known to Schellenberg, and they had been in close contact in connection with the Venlo Operation. Whether Knochen shared Schellenberg's ideas concerning rapprochement with Great Britain, as some sources suggest, seems at least doubtful. He was like Schellenberg well educated and had finished his studies with a Ph.D. in English Literature. He moved up quickly in the SS hierarchy and may have encountered Schellenberg more frequently in *Amt* IV Gestapo where he had come from the old *Amt* II. There under Franz Alfred Six Knochen was in charge of persecuting the Freemasons. When Schellenberg in 1942 reorganized *Amt* VI E, Knochen, who like Schellenberg had come from *Amt* IV, was sent off to command the SD in occupied France where he attended to SD business until driven out by Allied Forces in September 1944. Kaltenbrunner thought this an excellent excuse to place Knochen with Schellenberg in *Amt* VI. He "hoped that Knochen would be acceptable to Schellenberg and that through Knochen he would be able to obtain a better insight into Schellenberg's work." Schellenberg who in September 1944 was not part of that Germany described by Allen Dulles as "a cornered beast which will fight to the last drop of blood, knowing that it has no chance to escape or survive," was very much involved in dangerous contacts to the West and rescue operations thought intolerable by most Nazi leaders. Kaltenbrunner's watchman in his office at Berkaer Strasse was surely not what Schellenberg needed. He flatly turned down Kaltenbrunner's proposal of placing Knochen in *Amt* VI and got away with it.[345]

Otto Skorzeny, another Austrian SS officer and a contemporary of Schellenberg, like Höttl has often been erroneously described as a friend of the *Amt* VI Foreign Intelligence Chief.[346] Much as in the case of Höttl, Schellenberg and Skorzeny could not have been more different and both men were aware of it. Skorzeny was of middle class background and as a youth in Austria, much like Reinhard Spitzy, had been "engaged in the more militant sort of

---

344. Much of the Höttl material can be found in NA, RG 319, IRR, PS, Box 617. Interrogation of Schellenberg by Rudolph Pins, April 30, 1947, SAN, S-45c. CC 2 to CIA, May 30, 1951, NA, RG 263, E A1-86, Box 18.
345. Helmut Knochen (b. 1910), son of a school teacher, studied to become a teacher, brought into Berlin head office by Franz Alfred Six, responsible for much injustice and worse during German occupation of France, sentenced to death by British 1946 and by French 1954, changed to life imprisonment, pardoned by Charles de Gaulle, insurance business in West Germany. Cf. Wildt, *Generation des Unbedingten*, 515-517. Information from Kaltenbrunner file, June 28, 1945, NAK, KV 2/2745. Dulles in lecture at Council on Foreign Relations in New York, September 26, 1944, Records of Meetings, vol. XI, Council on Foreign Relations Archives, New York.
346. "Skorzeny's Biography," NAK, WO 204/11839: "Skorzeny is also a very close friend of Schellenberg." Skorzeny's claim, published after Schellenberg's death, that Schellenberg asked him to lie for him in 1946 in Nuremberg, tells much about the relation of the two men. Otto Skorzeny, *Meine Kommandounternehmen: Krieg ohne Fronten* (Wiesbaden: Limes, 1977; 3rd ed.), 277.

nationalist activities." From the *Steyrische Heimatschutz*, a regional reactionary organization, he found his way to the NSDAP and the SS. He was apparently very much involved in the planning for the so-called *Anschluss* and Austria's takeover by the Nazis. From a Nazi perspective he had an extremely successful military career and, in fact, a number of adventurous special operations soon endowed him with an international reputation for courage and manly action and a long list of high military decorations.[347] Fellow Austrian Ernst Kaltenbrunner brought him into the RSHA where he was made Group Chief of VI S, thereby placing him under Schellenberg's command. While this new sabotage section was first organized in the city at Berkaer Strasse, it soon moved to a place called Schloss Friedenthal near Oranienburg where Skorzeny could spread out and set up facilities for training purposes. As was the case with some other operations of *Amt* VI, for instance as pointed out for Zeppelin, here too it would be nothing out of the ordinary to have the man in charge of the sabotage section just bypass Schellenberg and report directly to Kaltenbrunner. When asked about this after the war, Schellenberg accurately responded: "The Group was in a perpetual state of reorganization, and my statements [about VI S] are therefore only guesswork as I was not responsible."[348]

Looking back at the rather circumspect handling by Schellenberg of such special operations as his assignment to persuade or kidnap the Duke of Windsor, it is plain to see that he and Skorzeny were inclined to handle crisis situations very differently. When Schellenberg called for Skorzeny to create some order at the time of the assassination attempt of July 20, 1944, it indicated that he thought him to be suitable for emergency occurrences requiring decisive action.[349] Skorzeny, however, was clearly not Schellenberg's man for long-term planning, sensitive diplomacy and the patient pursuit of lines to the enemy. Schellenberg thus had little or no connection to the various perilous undertakings or plans for such or the unrealistic German schemes for postwar underground resistance by such combat units as the *Jagdverbände* or the even more nebulous and imaginary guerilla forces named *Wehrwolf*.[350] As Schellen-

---

347. Otto Skorzeny (Vienna 1908-1975), courses of study in Engineering, strong supporter of Nazi party in Austria, impressed Kaltenbrunner early, SS-*Leibstandarte* Adolf Hitler, saw action in The Netherlands, Yugoslavia and the Soviet Union. Chief of VI S 1943, Mussolini rescue, unexecuted plans to kidnap Marshal Philippe Pétain and Josip Brozovitch Tito, successful operation against Miklós Horthy in Hungary 1944, active on Western front for instance with special forces in Battle of the Bulge, active on Eastern front 1945, surrendered to American troops in May, interrogated at Oberursel, many years in Franco's Spain after World War II.
348. "Translation of Statement," Schellenberg, July 23, 1945, NA, RG 226, E 119A, Box 26.
349. "Final Report," 148. Cf. Skorzeny's rather personal description of events in *Meine Kommandounternehmen*, 265-267.
350. The *Wehrwolf* (Werwolf, Werewolf) under the command of SS-*Obergruppenführer* Hans-Adolf Prützmann caused the Allied occupying troops some concern but after a brief period of sabotage and a few killings

berg was soon to find out, Skorzeny was not someone who followed protocol and hierarchy. He did pretty much what he thought he needed or wanted to do. As Schellenberg later told his interrogators: "I did not oppose Skorzeny anymore whatever he did. I can say, without exaggeration, that it was already a matter of indifference to me when high-up officers came to me and asked if I would rather resign, as the muddle was intolerable." And he added that in a way he was fortunate not to be responsible for Skorzeny. During postwar interrogations by Americans, Skorzeny, for his part, made no secret of his "personal dislike for Schellenberg." All this is of considerable interest because it describes the relationship of two SS officials who it was later claimed became friends again in postwar Spain where they are said to have had funds stashed away from the Nazi years and supposedly were closely working together in organizing some kind of neo-fascist movement.[351]

In view of the gruesome realities in Germany, more visible after the summer of 1944, and recalling Schellenberg's personal participation ordered by Kaltenbrunner and Heinrich Müller in the physical removal of Admiral Canaris, his fierce competitor and social friend, the pressing question of how he was able to continue to function seems even more unanswerable than prior to the events of July 20. It may well be that his decision to obey Kaltenbrunner's orders to arrest Canaris was indeed a hiatus in a life already torn by conflicting motives. If there had been a way to distance oneself from what one knew and to guard a small personal sector against the inhumane and incomprehensibly immoral system of which one was a part, that small sector after July 1944 must have become barely visible. One registers with even greater surprise the continuous frenzied activity of Schellenberg during the final months of the German Thousand Year Reich. With Allied armies closing in from west, south and east on a Germany increasingly showing the physical effects of the bombardment of its infrastructure, Schellenberg seems to have become even more involved in chancy moves in searching for a negotiated end to all this at least in the West and in almost incredible operations culminating with the rescue of a great number of unfortunate victims of the Germans. A plausible explanation of Schellenberg's engagement on behalf of the victims and one voiced by contemporaries, such as Allen Dulles, and by later authors

---

disappeared. The *Jagdverbände* or their small units were involved in sabotage operations in Denmark, France, Yugoslavia and elsewhere. Skorzeny's Operation Greif during the Battle of the Bulge, using German men in American uniforms, was not sabotage but "a para-military undertaking." Liquidation Report No. 13, Counter Intelligence War Room, Gruppe VI S, Secret, NA, RG 319, IRR, IS, Box 1.

351. "Consolidated Interrogation Report" No. 4, Headquarters USFET. Confidential, July 23, 1945, NA, RG 319, IRR, IS, Box 9. "German Nationalist and Neo-Nazi Activities in Argentina," CIA report, July 8, 1953, Secret, NA, CREST. Special Operations to Pullach, May 16, 1951, NA, RG 263, E A1-86, Box 38.

would have been his scheming to prepare for himself a way out of the raging sea of blood and guilt. How this fits together with his undoubtedly certain knowledge that, if he missed but one step in these rescue operations, he and his entire family would be extinguished remains just one of several imponderables. The odds for his destruction were overwhelming. We know that he had avoided service, if it can be called that, in the *Einsatzgruppen*. We also know that in contrast to other SS leaders Schellenberg had gone out of his way to avoid visiting the death camps. Now, again in contrast to most German leaders, he would deliberately occupy himself in his meetings with foreign emissaries—and with Heinrich Himmler—with the release of the victims. Much aware that the Allies for some years had known of the mass murder committed by the Germans, he now found himself negotiating the actually nonnegotiable. He did this, always in fear of the uncontrollable irrationality, but with the needed intermittent support of Himmler. These particular qualities of the rescue operations and the connected attempts to end the war have made a wholly reliable appraisal of Schellenberg's role well-nigh impossible.

That Schellenberg's partners in this context would come from Sweden and Switzerland is not astonishing. It had been in those two nations that he had found conversation partners who had come to trust him personally and to whose requests for human help he had been able to respond. These earlier rescue operations, however, had usually involved individual unfortunates whom he had been able to extract from German camps and prisons with the covert means available to him. When the elderly former President of the Swiss Confederation Jean-Marie Musy[352] and his son Benoit[353] arrived in the bomb-torn German capital in the autumn of 1944, they of course had been in touch with high ranking Swiss authorities as well as American representatives in Switzerland and, most important, with members of American Jewish groups. Musy, who in earlier years is said to have expressed pro-fascist views and who apparently had met Heinrich Himmler at anti-Communist conferences, certainly was a most experienced statesman and his bold, courageous son Benoit had decided to lend his father a hand in this hazardous operation. As an indicator of the great personal risk the two men took, it should be recalled that by this time many German cities had been turned into rubble by Allied

---

352. Dr. Jean-Marie Musy (1876-1952), studied Philosophy and Law finishing with a doctorate in *Strafrecht* (Criminal Law), career in banking and politics, traditional Roman Catholic, elected President 1925 and 1930, strongly anti-Communist politician, said to have sympathized with corporatism and fascism in the 1930s. Cf. Chantal Kaiser, *Bundesrat Jean-Marie Musy 1919-1934* (Fribourg: Universitätsverlag, 1999). Alain Dieckhoff, "Une Action de Sauvetage des Juifs Européens en 1944-1945: L'Affaire Musy," *Revue d'Histoire Moderne et Contemporaine*, vol. 2 (1989), 287-303.
353. Benoit Musy (1917-1956), studied Agricultural Engineering, served in Swiss Air Force, military sky diver, after the war motocycle racing, automobile racing, killed driving a Maserati.

bombing raids and German civilians had suffered great losses which only added to the grief of those whose fathers, husbands and sons would never return. The American and British bombing raids were seen by the Germans as an uncivilized and criminal war against civilians, quite forgetting the much applauded raids of Hermann Göring's *Luftwaffe* on English cities. Most Germans wanted to believe in their racial superiority, but now in 1944 the uncultured Americans and the despised British were beating the heroic German troops in the West and the Slavic hordes from the steppes of Soviet Russia were rapidly closing in on Germany's Eastern boundary. When the two dedicated Swiss emissaries drove into Germany, they must have had considerable doubts about the wisdom of their undertaking. Except for slave labor and camp inmates, Germany certainly did not seem to be a place for visiting foreigners to move about.[354]

There had, of course, been some preparations in Switzerland. In early 1944 Musy had been approached by a Bern family called Loeb for assistance in freeing some relatives who had been imprisoned by the Germans at Clermont-Ferrand in France. Musy had gone to Paris and actually succeeded in seeing the HSSPF France (*Höherer SS-und Polizeiführer*, Higher SS and Police Leader) Karl Oberg. Obviously Musy had the necessary know-how to reach this dangerous top German official in occupied France. Not unprepared he successfully argued that one of the two prisoners was a neutral Swiss citizen, and he was able to get them released. Although a second journey to Paris soon afterwards to pry loose a man by the name of Thorel seems to have had no success, word had gotten around in Swiss Jewish circles that Musy was willing and possibly able to talk to the Nazis on behalf of their victims. He was soon visited by Louise Bolomey of the Aid Society for Jewish Refugees (HIJEFS-*Hilfsverein für jüdische Flüchtlinge in Shanghai*/Aid Society for Jewish Refugees in Shanghai) and by Recha and Isaac Sternbuch who now begged him to go to Germany and arrange for a larger scale liberation of Jewish inmates from German concentration camps. Recha was a daughter of the Polish Rabbi Mordechai Rottenberg, a well-known member of Agudath Israel and Chief Rabbi in Antwerp when the Germans overran Belgium. The Germans had imprisoned the Rabbi and his wife, and Recha Sternbuch was hoping that Musy could get them freed. Rabbi Isaac Sternbuch had come from a Russian-Jewish family who by way of Rumania had reached Switzerland. His father Naftali Sternbuch was a very

---

354. A man expected them at the border at Constance and looked out for them until arrival in Berlin. Nevertheless, they experienced car damage by shrapnel, probably during an attack by low flying aircraft, not uncommon then. Monty N. Penkower, *The Jews Were Expendable: Free World Diplomacy and the Holocaust* (Urbana: University of Illinois Press, 1983), 278, reports that Recha Sternbuch on unnamed date went into Nazi Germany with the Musys to look for members of her family.

active member of the Orthodox Jewish community. The Sternbuchs were much involved in the efforts of HIJEFS and soon became connected with Vaad haHatzala, located with its head office in Manhattan and an affiliate of the Union of Orthodox Rabbis of the United States and Canada. With this background regarding his mission to Berlin, there can be no doubt that the elderly Swiss statesman represented one of the more important Jewish organizations of the time and that the internationally well-informed Musy was aware of that.[355] It would be correct to assume that Himmler and Schellenberg were not fully informed about the significance of the international Orthodox Jewish network, but they knew of Musy's former political standing in Switzerland, and Schellenberg, of course, always kept in mind the line to Guisan and Masson constructed with great effort during these difficult years. He certainly knew that Musy had written to Himmler and that the latter had agreed to receive him. Therefore, even if at this late point in the war Schellenberg more than welcomed the occasion to do something good on a greater scale, he was also much aware that if he wanted to continue his work in the direction of negotiations in the West, this could be an opportunity to polish up his image outside the Reich. A number of influences were therefore in place when Jean-Marie and Benoit Musy came to the German capital.

Upon arrival the two Swiss were not taken to Himmler's or to Schellenberg's office but instead to the Berlin International Red Cross offices where the *Amt* VI Chief was already expecting them. As Musy had written to Himmler referring to the desired release of only one specific prisoner—the full extent of his mission was not quite clear to him until shortly before his departure—he now informed Schellenberg about the larger purpose of his journey, and Schellenberg in that unconfidential, open encounter could do little more than respond that it was not his prerogative to decide on the release of prisoners from the camps. Things of that nature would have to be taken to Himmler himself. Two days later Schellenberg accompanied Musy to Himmler's temporary headquarters on his special train in the vicinity of Breslau and heading for Vienna. In the course of their conversation during the journey Schellenberg apparently felt drawn to Musy and developed a feeling that this Swiss emissary "might exercise a beneficial influence on Himmler." If Jean-Marie Musy recounted events correctly under oath in October 1945, Schellenberg did not join the two men in Himmler's private car on that special train. It was a confidential encounter which lasted for approximately two hours and no one else was present.

---

355. Cf. Livia Rothkirchen, "The 'Final Solution' in Its Last Stages," *Yad Vashem Studies*, vol. 8 (1970), 19.

Consequently there are no minutes by the participants or by a stenographer. From interrogations after the war, Schellenberg's memoirs relying on what he was told and a few other documents, it appears, however, that the powerful Nazi leader, who may have sensed that he was past his zenith, and the elderly Swiss gentleman covered two topics. The relatively modest request for the quick release of a handful of specifically named inmates may have been the more pressing from Musy's perspective for he must have felt that he owed it to those who trusted and sent him to Berlin to do the best he could. Astonishingly, published works often pay little attention to minor requests of this nature though it would seem obvious that for the authors of such publications the rescue of their own loved ones in any situation would have been of paramount importance. Here Jean-Marie Musy succeeded in freeing the already mentioned Alain Thorel, a member of a family close to Musy's wife, and in fact he had the great joy of meeting the lucky young man when he returned to Berlin. Others rescued at this time were two brothers of Recha Sternbuch, but in the words of Musy "they had not been able to find [Recha's] father and mother, who had been sent to Auschwitz, and were probably dead."[356] A further request was for the release of all women prisoners, most of them French, from the Concentration Camp Ravensbrück. His most far-reaching plea at that first meeting with Heinrich Himmler was the more general proposition of the Sternbuchs: "I asked Himmler to liberate...all the Jews who were confined in concentration camps for religious reasons." They would be transported to the Swiss-German border by the Germans, taken on by the Swiss and eventually sent to the United States. Unexpectedly for Musy, Himmler after about two hours of conversation in that railroad car generally seemed agreeable to allow all Jews to go free. His price was "material compensation such as trucks and tractors." From Musy's recollections under oath, we know that his response to that was that it would be difficult to obtain trucks "because of the Allies." Instead he proposed to organize a financial funding. It was agreed that Musy would go back to Switzerland and negotiate the financial transaction with interested international parties. Not because the often mentioned financial transaction was of significance but because some publications suggest that a sum of money was paid to Musy, it should be pointed out that 5,000,000 Swiss francs were indeed deposited with a Swiss bank by American aid organizations but that, according to a statement under oath by Jean-Marie Musy, the amount was "entirely paid back to the Americans." The impression given by Musy's description of the first meeting with Himmler is that the

---

356. Internal Memorandum, Capt. Oughton to Lt.-Col. Stimson, n.d., Piece 155a, NAK, KV 2/96. Musy under Oath to Major Robert Haythorne, October 26, 1945, in John Mendelsohn, ed., *The Holocaust*, vol. 16 (New York: Garland, 1982), 12-13. Alain Thorel's name is spelled in various ways in different records.

Reichsführer SS either was or acted as if he were tired "of the entire Jewish question ... they could have them all." Even more stunning was Himmler's agreement to start the releasing process immediately, not waiting for the result of Musy's deliberations upon his return to Switzerland. Hitler's most loyal soldier Heinrich Himmler may have appeared to Jean-Marie Musy more open than he actually was, and Schellenberg may have been correct when he wrote in his memoirs a few years later: "Himmler could not realize that the freeing of the thousands of Jews was important from the point of view of Germany's foreign policy." In retrospect, however, it does appear more than doubtful that after the senseless murder of millions a rescue of survivors of that German program could have created an international political landscape offering new vistas for whatever "foreign policy" the Germans might have come up with in late 1944.[357]

In contrast to Himmler's undefined and seemingly almost defeatist attitude exhibited during the encounter with Musy, Schellenberg must have continued to believe that an improvement of Germany's international reputation, possibly through a change of government, could be brought about and that some kind of political solution was still conceivable in the West. Whatever Schellenberg's motivations, the first visit of Jean-Marie Musy visibly prompted him to increase his rescue efforts begun a few years before and to press his search for lines to foreign, in particular neutral personalities. Somewhat astonishing for a political leader at his level and in view of the predictable inevitable defeat of Germany is the complete absence in the records of any indication that he sought to arrange for a safe escape for himself and his family. Respective accusations voiced after the war by surviving personal enemies have not been connected to any documentation.[358]

Following Musy's departure, Schellenberg's first task was to arrange the freeing of those individuals Himmler had agreed to let go. To extract these people from their keepers, Schellenberg had no choice but to contact Heinrich Müller, Chief of *Amt* IV Secret State Police who promptly objected by pointing out that the inmates were not part of Schellenberg's responsibility. Very much aware that Schellenberg was the man who in 1941 had left his Gestapo to take

---

357. Primary sources for the encounter of Musy with Himmler are Schellenberg, *The Schellenberg Memoirs*, 428-429. Schellenberg, *Memoiren*, 350. The lack of detail in both texts suggests that Schellenberg had little to do with the preparations in Switzerland. Interrogations under Oath of Jean-Marie Musy, reproduced in Mendelsohn, ed., *The Holocaust*, vol. 16. Statement under Oath, Jean-Marie Musy, May 8, 1948, SAN, Rep. 501, LV, S-4. "Internal Memorandum," Lt.-Col. Stimson to Capt. Oughton, August 8, 1945, NA, RG 226, E 119A, Box 26.
358. Statement in Court, Ernst Kaltenbrunner, Nuremberg, April 11, 1946, *Der Prozess gegen die Hauptkriegsverbrecher vor dem Internationalen Militärgerichtshof Nürnberg*, vol. 11 (Nuremberg: Internationaler Militärgerichtshof, 1947), 311.

over *Amt* VI Foreign Intelligence, a competitive *Amt* within the RSHA, it must have been with some satisfaction that he instructed Schellenberg that since he was not Gestapo he would have no access to the prisoners. As a result Schellenberg and his people had to spend much time and effort to first locate the unfortunates in the various camps and then try to alleviate their lot by slightly improving living conditions and allowing them to receive food parcels. How many of them were actually extricated is not clear from the records, and considering the uncontrolled brutality practiced by the Germans in their camps and the progressively evident disarray of the administrative apparatus, it is extraordinary that any of these individuals could be rescued.[359] Schellenberg, however, was as underlined earlier, fortunate to have brought together a number of people in his intelligence organization whom he could personally trust and who therefore could be given assignments such as these. Dealing with the Commanders of Nazi concentration camps and their dehumanized blindly obedient guards was not only repulsive but also often outright unpredictable and dangerous. Schellenberg's most reliable assistant in all these rescue activities was SS-*Hauptsturmführer* Franz Göring who previously had been with *Amt* IV and was now attached to Schellenberg's head office for direct, personal assignments. Other than Göring's "Annexe" written down in Stockholm in June 1945 as a sort of addition to or comment on Schellenberg's so-called "Autobiography" of the same date, we have very little documentary information on the activities of this significant eyewitness and events occurring during the rescue operations in the spring of 1945.[360] From the little we know Göring accompanied Musy and his son when they came to Germany, attended to their personal needs and rather fearlessly went to the concentration camps with Benoit Musy when people were to be released. Even with the authority given to him by his boss, the Foreign Intelligence Chief, and wearing his SS uniform for personal protection, facing the camp commanders could be a fearsome experience.

The Musy operation with its numerous attempts to free Jews and non-Jews from German captivity lasted into April 1945 and brought success, as well as bitter disappointment, for those engaged. Altogether Jean-Marie Musy traveled to the German capital eight times. On two occasions he met with Himmler

---

359. Archival holdings contain several long lists of names of what would appear to be French and Polish women which Musy is said to have given to Himmler. Penkower, *The Jews Were Expendable*, 259, also suggests that "a list of non-Jewish Swiss and French nationals and Recha Sternbuch's relatives" was presented at the later meeting in January 1945. Names found in various sources include the Rottenberg family, the Giraud family, a niece of Charles de Gaulle, members of the Donnebaum family, and a Mr. Torel.

360. Franz Göring (b. 1908), member of NSDAP and SS, with police in Weimar, *Kriminalkommissar* 1943, probably with *Amt* IV *Gestapo* until 1944, then to *Amt* VI. Highly sanitized U.S. documents suggest that after the war he was associated with CIA and BND. Diverse papers, NA, RG 263, E ZZ-16, Box 19; RG 263, E ZZ-18, Box 43. For cover he ran a bar in Hamburg.

himself; during his other six stays in Berlin he conferred with Schellenberg who was doing everything in his power to assist the two Swiss emissaries in their humanitarian efforts. During all these contacts the conservative Musy represented the Sternbuchs who in turn were unmistakably representing the Vaad haHatzala. We are uncertain when the parallel undertaking of Saly Meyer and the SS-*Obersturmbannführer* Kurt Becher began its work and to what extent the two operations competed and possibly hindered each other rather than efficiently doubling the rescue effort. Undoubtedly there were different Jewish interest groups at work, and it is entirely conceivable that their splendid efforts could have been more united and forceful if Washington had exhibited much earlier a more solid front on behalf of the Jews, first persecuted and outlawed and later slaughtered by the Germans. Because there was no mighty national American input to prevent the unimaginable even after the facts—in gruesome numbers and even photographs[361]—became known, the rescue attempts were carried out by amateur representatives of different Jewish groups in the U.S. who, not unlike other ethnic groups, were of course unaccustomed to always closely cooperate. Recha and Isaac Sternbuch, as representatives in Switzerland of the Vaad haHatzala, stood for the Orthodox Jewish community in America which clearly meant that they were not representing all or even most other American Jewish groups.[362] They helped numerous Jewish refugees enter Switzerland illegally, and in the course of their difficult work, which was understandably not always tolerated by Swiss police authorities, they increasingly had also been able to count on the benevolent assistance of Monsignor Philippe Bernardini, the Papal Nuncio in Switzerland. It may be assumed that this assistance may have contributed to Schellenberg's willingness to arrange for the release of Bernardini's nephew from a German camp.[363] Another group representing Jewish interests and very actively involved in rescue efforts and related controversial contacts with the Germans was headed by Saly Mayer, a Swiss-Jewish businessman in the textile industry who served as an agent of the American Jewish Joint Distribution Committee. His German opposite was the SS-*Obersturmbannführer* Kurt Becher, a man close to Kaltenbrunner and with direct access to Himmler, who had followed the German

---

361. In the spring of 1943 Schellenberg had notified his German officials of British intentions to produce a White Book "on the supposed German atrocities committed against Jews and Catholics in Poland." Wagner to Foreign Office, May 14, 1943, PA, AA, Inland II g 173, "Judenfrage." For what was known in Britain and the U.S. see the still revealing Richard Breitman, *Official Secrets: What the Nazis Planned, What the British and Americans Knew* (London: Penguin, 1999; 1st in U.S. 1998). Cf. Yehuda Bauer, *Jews for Sale: Nazi-Jewish Negotiations, 1933-1945* (New Haven: Yale University Press, 1994), 220-222.
362. While being Orthodox Jewish, Vaad haHatzala in January 1944 decided to save all Jews, regardless of their religious affinities. Efraim Zuroff, *The Response of Orthodox Jewry in the United States to the Holocaust: The Activities of the Va'ad ha-Hatzala Rescue Committee, 1939-1945* (Hoboken: KTAV, 2000), 273.
363. Friedensohn, Kranzler, *Heroine of Rescue: The Incredible Story of Recha Sternbuch*, 70-71. Internal Memorandum, Capt. Oughton to Lt.-Col. Stimson, Camp 020, August 8, 1945, NAK, KV 2/96.

occupation army into Hungary in 1944 and pursued what could be called Nazi economic interests. An OSS report of April 1945 called Becher "one of the chief fixers in the Nazi Party."[364] When questioned after the war, Becher, who had received his SS training at the *Junkerschule* in Bad Tölz, emphasized that he had allowed the Jewish Manfred Weiss family to escape from Hungary to Portugal, forgetting to mention that this was part of the German-arranged theft of that industrial family's property. His partner in the negotiations to permit Hungarian Jews to leave the country was Dr. Rezsö Kasztner, a Zionist leader in Budapest better known for his negotiations with the infamous Adolf Eichmann. On the positive side, if anything can be labeled such in this context, eventually two transports totaling 1673 Hungarian Jews were taken to the Concentration Camp Bergen-Belsen in June 1944 and moved on to Switzerland in August and December of that year.[365]

Although the efforts of Saly Meyer are quite a separate story from the rescue operations of Walter Schellenberg and Jean-Marie Musy, they are of considerable relevance because they are part of an unfriendly competitive situation which may not have been fully realized by all concerned at the time but which, in retrospect, certainly did not contribute to saving more Jews. In their earlier frantic efforts the Sternbuchs had worked on a trucks-for-Jews deal with the Germans, but Roswell D. McClelland for the World Refugee Board had declined any financial support. From other sources of their own Orthodox group and funds obtained from the American Jewish Joint Distribution Committee through Saly Mayer, they did what they felt they had to do anyway. Obviously McClelland was not fully informed. When the Sternbuchs began the promising operation with Musy, they for good reasons expected to have to pay ransom for the Jews they hoped Musy would pry loose from Himmler, meaning that again they did not keep the World Refugee Board or rather its Representative McClelland at the American Legation in Bern posted. When Musy returned from his first meeting with Himmler, it was his difficult task to scan the grey market for trucks, check the availability of other goods of interest to the Germans, such as medical drugs, and look for ransom money which had been mentioned to him by the Sternbuchs prior to his departure for Berlin and

---

364. Quoted from Adam LeBor, *Hitler's Secret Bankers: How Switzerland Profited from Nazi Genocide* (London: Pocket Books/Simon & Schuster, 1997), 262.
365. Kasztner (1906-1957) emigrated to Israel in 1948 and in 1954 was accused of collaboration with the Nazis. He was murdered but after his death acquitted by the Israeli Supreme Court. Dina Porat, *Israeli Society, the Holocaust and its* Survivors (London: Vallentine Mitchell, 2008), 426. Cf. David S. Wyman, *The Abandonment of the Jews: America and the Holocaust, 1941-1945* (New York: Pantheon, 1985; 1st 1984), 245. Theo Tschuy, *Dangerous Diplomacy: The Story of Carl Lutz, Rescuer of 62,000 Hungarian Jews* (Grand Rapids: William B. Eerdmans, 2000), 82. Statement, Kurt Becher to Norbert G. Barr, March 24, 1948, SAN, NG 5230. Declaration by Roswell D. McClelland, American Representative in Switzerland of the War Refugee Board, February 6, 1946, attached to Rezsö Kasztner, *Der Bericht des jüdischen Rettungskomitees aus Budapest 1942-1945* (Budapest: Vaadat Ezra Vö-Hazalah Bö-Budapest [1946]). (Machine typed, LC.)

which he had tried to push on Himmler as an alternative to trucks. Evidently Musy had no choice but to approach McClelland, and the records confirm that the two men did not much take to each other. Nevertheless, Jean-Marie Musy, an experienced politician, was not so easily turned away. The improbable outcome of the negotiations was an agreement to make available 5,000,000 Swiss francs to be deposited with Swiss banks until needed. We do not know whether McClelland's very positive comments regarding Saly Mayer and his activities were caused by his strong dislike for the formerly pro-fascist Musy or whether he had concluded that Mayer's operation into Hungary was more promising.[366] Unfortunately for the Schellenberg-Musy rescue efforts in the German capital there was an additional and most likely unforeseen problem, namely the already mentioned rapidly developing competitive struggle between Becher and Schellenberg. With Becher having direct access to Schellenberg's enemy and Chief of the RSHA Kaltenbrunner, this conflict was not only most unhelpful in the urgent campaign to save lives, but the internal SS conflict also bore the markings of danger for Schellenberg's very existence. It was just one more incentive for the Chief of Foreign Intelligence to assure himself of the protective arm of Himmler.

In mid-January 1945, following communications not by diplomatic pouch but apparently handled by the German police chief on the border in Constance, Musy and his son were back on the road. After a meeting with Schellenberg in Berlin he personally took them to Wildbad in the Black Forest where Himmler had another temporary headquarters. Benoit Musy recalled later that his father talked with Himmler "alone" for about two hours and that afterwards during dinner with Himmler he learned that the transport of the Jews in German camps to the U.S. by way of Switzerland had now "been approved by Himmler." In fact, during the conversation with Himmler and likely further discussions in the presence of Schellenberg, it was agreed that every two weeks a train with some 1,200 Jews would arrive at Constance at the Swiss-German border. The train would then continue to Kreuzlingen, the first Swiss town, where the Swiss would receive the released camp inmates and attend to first urgent needs, presumably eventually helping them to move on to the U.S. Absolutely reliable information on other points discussed during the confidential Musy-Himmler encounter or in the course of the surrounding meetings or at dinner is difficult to come by. Essentially we have memoirs, statements under oath, interrogation texts from the participants Walter Schellenberg, Jean-Marie Musy, Benoit Musy and second-hand reports, so to

---

366. Statement under Oath, Dr. Jean-Marie Musy, May 8, 1948, SAN, Rep. 501, LV, S-4. Wyman, *The Abandonment of the Jews*, 247 ff. Statement by Roswell D. McClelland, on U.S. Legation stationery, February 6, 1946, attached to Kasztner, *Der Bericht des jüdischen Rettungskomitees aus Budapest 1942-1945*.

speak, from Franz Göring, Schellenberg's adjutant, who was very close to the scene. Göring had the unenviable task of going to the concentration camps and making those in charge there somehow believe that Heinrich Himmler himself had ordered the releases now requested.

What can be said with some certainty is that at Wildbad they discussed financial arrangements, that is, payments to be made for the shipment of Jews. It was agreed that such payments would be made in form of deposits in Swiss banks. All indications are that Musy would no longer be obliged to try to turn these funds into trucks or other war material for the Germans. Instead this money would be held in trust—most likely in Musy's name—for later use by the International Red Cross which had its headquarters in Switzerland.

Another topic which Schellenberg and others have reported on concerned the representation of American Jews or rather their organizations in Switzerland. Supposedly "in January 1945 Himmler demanded from *Altbundespräsident* Musy that he should be the sole representative of all Jewish organizations dealing with him in Switzerland." This may have been worded slightly differently in the course of Schellenberg's postwar interrogations in London, but what British intelligence officers wrote down generally adds up to the same. Musy recalled in somewhat more detail that Himmler told him rather bluntly that the Union of Orthodox Rabbis was not a Jewish organization representing a majority of Jewish Americans. According to Musy, Himmler apparently also volunteered that "the organization which Saly Meyer [*sic*] represented...was more important." The embarrassed Musy quickly offered that he would be glad to withdraw if Himmler preferred to deal with Saly Mayer alone. As Schellenberg would hardly have minimized the significance of his own negotiation partners in Switzerland, we can be almost certain that it was Kurt Becher who had supplied the negative information on the Sternbuchs. The result of this unpleasant exchange, according to Musy, was that they concurred that he would obtain a declaration from the Americans regarding their prominence in the U.S. If Musy is correct in this, and there is really no reason why he should have invented it, he contacted the Union of Orthodox Rabbis upon his return to Switzerland and received the requested statement regarding their significance as a Jewish organization and confirming that the Sternbuchs were their representatives. Musy had this transmitted to Himmler but told his interrogators that he did not receive a reaction of any kind from Berlin.

Rather more important from a humane point of view was Musy's new list of individuals to be released and a request to permit the departure of some 60–70 so-called "illegal Jews," apparently Jews who were not yet known to the Germans as Jews. From the records it would appear that Himmler granted these specific requests and that the "illegal Jews" indeed soon made their way to Switzerland.[367]

In all this the elderly Jean-Marie Musy, though his primary concern may have been the rescue of Jews from those very Germans with whom he had sympathized a few years earlier, was, of course, very much aware of the linkage of these rescue operations to the hopes of a few Germans, such as the Foreign Intelligence Chief Schellenberg, to establish lines to the Western Allies. As a politician and being located in Switzerland, Jean-Marie Musy most likely had a more realistic view of the international scene towards the end of World War II and thus would have had fewer illusions than the Nazis in bombed out Berlin regarding the faintest chance of ending this conflict at the negotiation table. To negotiate with the Germans who had wanted the war and committed the murder of innocent millions was, of course, really not an option. By the nature of his job Allen Dulles, the OSS representative in Bern, was well informed on most developments. Staying on top of things and getting the needed information was his main function which at times could require even by-passing his own Legation or even Washington. As a result Musy's journeys to Germany were routinely covered by the Bern OSS. If Musy did not tattle about his contacts with American diplomats, Walter Schellenberg in this case may not always have been informed as well as Allen Dulles. To be sure, Schellenberg had several lines into Switzerland and indeed even to the Americans there. Although Dulles, the records indicate, made a point of turning down any approaches from him, we may assume that Schellenberg had a good idea of what the Americans knew about his hopes to come to some kind of talks with them.[368]

The first of the agreed transports of Jews from concentration camps in Germany took a lot of crisis management, primarily due to the progressive disintegration of Germany, but also because literally no one in Germany's administrative structure had the slightest interest to assist. Schellenberg had given Franz Göring far-reaching authority for all situations, but the requirements were considerable. There had to be a train with the needed personnel, food supplies for some 1,200 passengers had to be organized, and, most important, access to the prisoners had to be granted. In many of the camps the

---

367. Sources for the second Musy-Himmler encounter in Wildbad include Statement under Oath, Dr. Jean-Marie Musy, May 8, 1948, SAN, Rep. 501, LV, S-4. Schellenberg to Hillel Storch, Representative of the World Jewish Congress in Stockholm, June 17, 1945, NAK, KV 2/98. Testimony, Jean-Marie Musy to Major Robert Haythorne, October 26, 1945, in Mendelsohn, ed., *The Holocaust*, vol. 16, 5 ff. "Final Report," 161-162. Schellenberg, *The Schellenberg Memoirs*, 430.
368. 224 "to 110 [Allen Dulles] only," March 29, 1945, containing the curious sentence: "He [Musy] then went on to say that he believed that if Hitler were granted a Safe Haven, he would be willing to come to terms [letting more Jews go]." Musy had spoken to Sam Woods (U.S. Consul General in Zürich). NA, RG 226, E A1-170 (210), Box 276.

Commander and his staff made their decisions without interference from the outside, and they were not inclined to submit to any orders or suggestions delivered by some SS officer arriving from Berlin. For these men a release of the inmates of their camps was totally out of the question. The first camp where such a train was to be filled was Theresienstadt or Terezin, located in Czechoslovakia not far from Prague. To get the train on track and loaded with human beings, Franz Göring and Benoit Musy drove to Theresienstadt and took things in hand. Those inmates who were interested in boarding the train departing on February 5 to Switzerland had to report to a central office on February 4 to be scanned by supervisors and police before they would be allowed to go through the so-called *Schleuse* (normally a lock for the passage of ships). If Göring and Musy had worried about the onslaught of people who would want to leave this place of horrors, they had an unexpected surprise. Because Theresienstadt had been changed more and more from a camp for individuals and their Jewish husbands or wives and the respective children to a transit camp where victims were merely held until someone decided to ship them off to a death camp, to be shot, gassed or done away with in some other way, many of the present inmates had no wish to board a train that might take them to Auschwitz. The train to Switzerland looked like the latest hoax of their tormentors. Many of those who finally did get on board may simply not have cared any more, and when the train started moving, their faces were unhappy or apathetic. They had given up in every way, and it did not really matter where this train would take them. It would be more torture or death. Only when the names of the stations they passed seemed to suggest that they were indeed going West were there happy faces. Joy broke forth on February 7 when they reached the Swiss border and Franz Göring went through the cars announcing: "In the name of the Reichsleiter Himmler you are now free." Emil Kaim, one of the passengers on that train, recalled after arrival in Switzerland: "Good fortune has taken us here. On February 3, all of a sudden a transport to Switzerland of 1200 men and women was assembled in Theresienstadt. I can not express the emotions that filled us being freed after 20 months of imprisonment ... The transport consists of mostly older people of all classes, and we are grateful ..." [369]

Much to Schellenberg's and Musy's disappointment this operation, however, was not only the beginning but also already the end of their execution of

---

369. Regarding the train operation Franz Göring, "Annexe" (see edited text in this volume). Statement under Oath, Franz Göring, February 24, 1948, SAN, Rep. 501, LV, S-4. Penkower, *The Jews Were Expendable*, 260-261, who gives exact figure of 1,210 released Jews, including 58 children. Emil Kaim to Hans Schaeffer, Montreux-Chateau Belmont, February 19, 1945, Papers of Hans Schaeffer, Reel 9, Leo Baeck Institute, Center for Jewish History, New York.

an agreement they had made with Heinrich Himmler for bi-weekly trainloads of camp inmates to be taken out. In fact, Franz Göring and Benoit Musy were frantically preparing the second transport of about 1,800 inmates from the infamous Concentration Camp Bergen-Belsen, a gruesome place in the beautiful heather country just north of Hanover, when it all ended with an order from Hitler to stop all release operations immediately. Somebody had shown him some articles from foreign newspapers, reporting on the Musy operation. There are indications that Himmler had asked Musy, probably at the January encounter in the Black Forest, to arrange for some positive press coverage. His reason would have been to create a more congenial political climate in the West which would help to move closer to talks about an end to the war. This incidentally would fit with an idea Schellenberg and Musy discussed when the big operation was stopped. Under the enormous pressure, they came up with the scheme of asking the Western Allies for "a four days' truce on land and in the air" during which all Jews and foreigners held in German concentration camps could be released and transported through the front lines. Schellenberg later recalled that he had even brought the powerful SS-*Gruppenführer* Gottlob Berger into the deliberations.[370]

Whoever it was that arranged for Hitler to see such articles from the foreign press reporting the large scale release of Jews still remains uncertain. Evidently Himmler himself, who was backing Schellenberg's search for contact lines to the Western Allies, would have had absolutely no interest in exciting Hitler about the release operation. Nor would Schellenberg. However, there were others, such as Kaltenbrunner or Müller, who might have had precisely such interest. Schellenberg and others have left no doubt that the culprit was Kurt Becher, deeply involved with Saly Mayer in the Hungarian operations and feeling threatened by what he saw as competitive efforts of Schellenberg and Musy. Even more enraging for Hitler than the reports on the release of Jews must have been a specific news item revealing that the handover of the Jews was part of a larger deal guaranteeing the safe asylum in Switzerland for some 250 ranking Nazis. Though a source often mentioned was an outpost of Charles de Gaulle in Spain which dispatched a message with this content that was intercepted, the question of who placed this supposed news item has remained unclear and even serious historical experts, such as Yehuda Bauer, have not managed to fully solve the puzzle.[371]

---

370. Schellenberg, *The Schellenberg Memoirs*, 430-431.
371. Schellenberg to Hillel Storch, June 17, 1945, NAK, KV 2/98. Yehuda Bauer, "The Negotiations between Saly Mayer and the Representatives of the S.S. in 1944-1945," in *Rescue Attempts during the Holocaust* (Jerusalem: Yad Vashem, 1977), 41. Schellenberg, *The Schellenberg Memoirs*, 430. Interrogation of Kurt Becher, June 22, 1948, reproduced in John Mendelsohn, ed., *The Holocaust*, vol. 16: Rescue to Switzerland. The Musy and Saly Mayer Affairs (New York: Garland, 1982). Statement under Oath, Franz Göring, February 24, 1948,

As indicated earlier there was no love lost between Roswell D. McClelland of the War Refugee Board and Jean-Marie Musy. Observing the old Swiss gentleman's engagement for the Jews in German concentration camps, McClelland's appraisal of Musy in the summer of 1945 indeed seems slightly harsh: "Mr. Musy's motives in performing this service ... seemed to consist of a mixture of the desire for personal gain, the hope of playing a striking 'humanitarian' role and the belief that he might hereby obtain more favorable peace terms for the Nazis." The denigrating charge of "personal gain" needs no comment. The humanitarian efforts did help to rescue a very large number of Jews and others from German concentration camps. McClelland's "more favorable peace terms" may be just a slip in terminology, for there were no "terms" under the unconditional surrender agreed on by the Allies. Schellenberg's attempts to contact the Western Allies were instead motivated by the unrealistic idea of an armistice in the West.[372] However one may wish to evaluate the activities of Jean-Marie and Benoit Musy, fortunately for the victims these two men were not intimidated by Hitler's clamping down on their rescue operations. In spite of the harrowing conditions they continued to drive into Germany and managed to free many more people. Probably largely coming from Recha and Isaac Sternbuch, there were always more lists of names that Jean-Marie Musy thrust in front of Schellenberg, who continued to work with him and sent out Franz Göring to accompany and protect Benoit Musy on his risky errands to the camps.

What they saw on these errands acquainted them with a German system quite beyond any description. One of these journeys to free a group of people had to be made to the Concentration Camp Buchenwald just outside of the German cultural center of Weimar where the *Bauhaus* was born not so many years before. Göring and Musy were to meet at Weimar, but when driving up from the Constance border crossing, Musy had run into attacks from low flying aircraft, and their meeting could not be worked out as planned. In order to not lose time Benoit Musy drove on to the Buchenwald camp on his own, not really expecting what was ahead of him. Schellenberg and Jean-Marie Musy had discussed the desirability of surrendering the concentration camps intact to arriving Allied troops rather than evacuating the miserable inmates and thereby in many cases marching them to their certain death. Himmler had agreed and

---

SAN, Rep. 501, LV, S-4, who gives the figure as 200. Cf. Clark, *Barbarossa*, 487. Internal Memorandum, Lt.-Col. Stimson to Capt. Oughton, August 8, 1945, NA, RG 226, E 119A, Box 26.

372. Roswell D. McClelland, "Report on the Activities of the War Refugee Board through Its Representation at the American Legation in Bern, Switzerland, March 1944-July 1945," in Mendelsohn, ed., *The Holocaust*, vol. 16, 52. Cf. Dieckhoff, "Une Action de Sauvetage des Juifs Européens en 1944-1945: L'Affaire Musy," 291-292.

given an order to stop all evacuation procedures,[373] but Kaltenbrunner evidently saw things differently and planned to concentrate the surviving prisoners in some Southern German location to have something in hand for eventual bargaining with the enemy. Word therefore had gone out to continue the senseless and inhuman evacuations. When Musy arrived at the gates of Buchenwald on April 9, 1945, it was perfectly evident that the evacuation was in progress. There was great confusion everywhere, and Musy was unable to locate an SS officer who could help him find the inmates he had come to free. Everyone seemed fully occupied with beating the human wrecks into columns to be driven out onto the road to who knows where. Realizing that he would not be able to talk sense into anyone there, not to mention rescuing the people on his list, he gave up and headed for Berlin, never quite sure he would make it. In Berlin he learned, of course, that Kaltenbrunner had taken things in hand and with Hitler's support had countermanded Himmler's orders. In view of the hazardous travel conditions and the increasing risk of ending up between the battlefronts, Benoit Musy had no choice but to stay in the German capital for the time being.[374]

While the Musy rescue operations were taking their course, the Chief of *Amt* VI was more than fully taken up by another very extensive undertaking that was to save the lives of literally thousands of unfortunates held by the Germans in their concentration camps. To increase the pressure to almost a breaking point, constant devastating air raids and the threat of the Soviet Armies closing in on the Berlin area had created nearly impossible working conditions. As a consequence, Schellenberg had to move a number of sections of his *Amt* VI to safer locations. These moves were meant to increase security but by the same token removed those people and their work farther away from his close control. The first of a number of such difficult moves took several sections and their records to Burg Lauenstein, a castle far to the south of Berlin near the small town of Probstzella on the edge of the Franconian Forest. Schellenberg himself remained in Berlin to stay on top of two difficult tasks that were not always compatible. Since the summer of 1944 he was the only Chief of Intelligence in the true sense of the word and as such was involved with both military and SS commanders, not all of them to his liking. At the same time he had slowly become the key person on the German side for the

---

373. Jean-Marie Musy recalled later that Himmler was ready to counteract Hitler's order to evacuate the concentration camps, but in return he wanted the Allies to agree to treat "the personnel of concentration camps as prisoners of war, and not shoot them." Himmler, however, counteracted Hitler even without that assurance and ordered the evacuations to stop. Testimony, Jean-Marie Musy, October 26, 1945, in Mendelsohn, ed., *The Holocaust*, vol. 16, 24.

374 Regarding the visit at Buchenwald, Statement under Oath, Franz Göring, February 24, 1948, SAN, Rep. 501, LV, S-4.

extensive rescue operations of the Swedish Count Folke Bernadotte which had earlier origins in Sweden but in fact were begun at this point in time as a direct consequence of the good news concerning the successful Musy transport from Theresienstadt which Schellenberg had helped to make possible. What many Swedes and Jews in Sweden had envisioned suddenly appeared feasible.[375]

While the background of the first visit of Count Bernadotte in early February 1945 still is not entirely clear, it can be assumed that Schellenberg was more fully informed about the Swede and his activities than his memoirs would suggest. His first rather neutral reaction to the announcement of Bernadotte's upcoming visit to the German capital can probably be explained with his wish to avoid new complications for himself and with his already ongoing and sufficiently troublesome rescue operations. Himmler was fully informed about his contacts with Jean-Marie Musy and, though always avoiding real decisions, was completely aware that Schellenberg considered the Musy operations also as a political contact to the West. Schellenberg's later assertions that he was in no way involved in bringing Bernadotte to Germany may well have been caused by a desire to understate his own rather special role in Nazi Germany at the end of the war in order to avoid the appearance of a linkage between his contacts abroad in the rescue operations and his later stay in Sweden and the subsequent appearance as a rather consequential witness at the Nuremberg trials. Schellenberg, in fact, had known of Felix Kersten since about 1940 from his *Amt* IV Chief Heinrich Müller who had nothing good to say about the masseur attending to Himmler's health problems.[376] Later Schellenberg recalled that he actually first met Kersten at Himmler's temporary headquarters at Shitomir. When there, Schellenberg had one of his frequent and painful attacks of "liver and gall-bladder trouble," and Himmler ordered him to submit to the massaging treatment of Kersten, which indeed made him feel better almost immediately. Like all the others treated by Kersten, Schellenberg too became quite dependent on his treatments. Later it was often said that Felix Kersten could gain access to Himmler when others didn't and that he was able to make him do things he might not have done on his own intuition. Looking at the relationship that developed between Kersten and Schellenberg, the same might well be said, and one might add that in time the two men learned to trust each other, enabling them to have confidential discussions, something extremely rare and risky in the structurally corrupt system where everyone denounced

---

375 Telegram, Swedish Cabinet to Arvid Richert, February 10, 1945; second telegram, Swedish Cabinet to Richert, February 10, 1945; both in Steven Koblik, *The Stones Cry Out: Sweden's Response to the Persecution of the Jews, 1933-1945* (New York: Holocaust Library, 1988), 277-278.
376. Kersten is said to have known and treated Himmler since 1939. Kersten's application for Swedish visa, March 24, 1944, NA, RG 226, E 125A, Box 1. Kersten, *Totenkopf und Treue*. Kersten, *The Kersten Memoirs, 1940-1945*.

everyone else. That part of this relationship was shared with the much less dependable Himmler must have been evident to the observant Schellenberg.

Regarding the political network in Sweden, it should be recalled that Schellenberg made a number of trips to Stockholm to confer with leading entrepreneurs, such as Brandin, Möller and Jacob Wallenberg, usually related to his important and difficult endeavor to save the lives of their managers in Poland who had been arrested by the Germans.[377] On those visits Schellenberg had numerous political conversations and undoubtedly had gained important insights into the Swedish political arena though there are no indications that he met Count Bernadotte personally. Kersten certainly cultivated a net of contacts to Swedes and foreign diplomats, and it was he, it should be remembered, who through his connections had brought Schellenberg together with Roosevelt's emissary Abram Hewitt for their clandestine conferences. In fact, with Himmler's permission Kersten had been able to move to Sweden in late 1943. As Schellenberg played a significant role in obtaining that agreement, it seemed natural that on his visits to Stockholm he would always look up Kersten, not only to benefit from his much needed physiotherapeutic treatment but also to freely exchange views on a great number of highly political and confidential matters.

Not only had Schellenberg helped Kersten obtain the necessary permissions for taking much of his household from Hartzwalde to Stockholm, but he had also lent his support in arranging for Kersten to take along a number of concentration camp inmates who were employed at his country estate. Quite unbelievably, Kersten apparently succeeded in also getting permission to leave some concentration camp prisoners behind at Hartzwalde where in his absence they would attend to the necessary upkeep of the place. Even more unbelievable, they would be considered as released inmates and allowed to wear normal clothing. Who were these privileged prisoners? They were *Bibelforscher*, an earlier German name for the *Zeugen Jehovas* (Jehovah's Witnesses) who, like most other German *Sekten* (sectarian churches), were not tolerated by the Nazis. Second only to the Jews, the Jehovah's Witnesses seem to have been the most hounded people. Particularly disturbing to the Germans, Jehovah's Witnesses traditionally did not much care for what other people saw as the state, they would not carry arms or do military service, and they refused to renounce their Church—even when promised to be released from the concentration camps. While many Witnesses were murdered in the camps, others were put on farms and in households because they had a reputation of being

---

377. C. G. McKay, *From Information to Intrigue*, 231, reports ten visits of Schellenberg to Stockholm. This is a very plausible figure though journeys undetected or not noted by Swedish authorities certainly cannot be excluded.

honest and diligent, hard workers. Apparently Schellenberg himself had acquired at least one female Jehovah's Witness as a housekeeper for his wife. From the postwar interrogations of Schellenberg's driver Hugo Buchwald, who joined the NSDAP only in the late 1930s and was not a member of the SS, we know that in the spring of 1944 he drove Schellenberg to the Concentration Camp Ravensbrück where Schellenberg chose a girl to help in his household. "She was a Jehovah's Witness, a quiet nice girl." Of considerable interest is the driver's comment in connection with this trip to Ravensbrück: "Otherwise Schellenberg never went to the camps." How he would have been able to avoid visits to concentration camps and work for someone like Heinrich Himmler, who would go to a camp to observe the gassing of inmates, is a perplexing question. Jehovah's Witnesses who, not unlike many Poles and Russians, were given like slaves to private German farms and households were often less exposed to brutality than their brothers and sisters in the concentration camps. In the case of Kersten's helpers, they were practically freed. Kersten's liberal handling of the Jehovah's Witnesses naturally was strongly opposed by SS-*Obergruppenführer* Oswald Pohl and by Gestapo Chief Müller. It was possible only because Kersten quite visibly enjoyed the protection of both Himmler and Schellenberg. If Kersten remembered correctly, Schellenberg in 1944 even warned him that his life was in danger. Kaltenbrunner and Müller apparently had decided to attend to the bothersome masseur. Kersten and his Jehovah's Witnesses may indeed have been spared the worst.[378] On Kersten's estate Hartzwalde tolerance was considerable, and to Jehovah's Witnesses the place even became known for its supply of Biblical material so important to them. Schellenberg clearly also tolerated that situation and generally saw to it that nothing was undertaken against Kersten and his property.[379]

In view of Schellenberg's apparent closeness to Kersten and the importance of the Scandinavian network in his operations, it is somewhat astonishing that after the war Schellenberg clearly wished to set the record straight once and for all that he had nothing to do with arranging Count Bernadotte's first visit to Germany. With the overwhelming evidence from the

---

378. Germany in recent history has not been a haven for sectarian churches. The relatively small group of Jehovah's Witnesses was directed from the U.S. Statistical data on the number of victims vary considerably. — Interrogations of Hugo Buchwald, May 24, 1948, SAN, Rep. 502, KV-Anklage, B 186. Cf. Gellately, ed., *The Nuremberg Interviews*, 426, where Schellenberg tells the psychiatrist Goldensohn that he visited one camp, namely Oranienburg in 1943. On Himmler's inspection tour of Auschwitz Gerald Fleming, *Hitler and the Final Solution* (Berkeley: University of California Press, 1984), 126-127. Pohl was Chief of the SS Economic and Administrative Office, sentenced to death in Nuremberg and hanged on June 7, 1951. — Cf. [Felix Kersten], *The Memoirs of Felix Kersten* (Garden City: Doubleday, 1947) 239ff.
379. Michel Reynaud, Sylvie Graffard, *The Jehovah's Witnesses and the Nazis: Persecution Deportation, and Murder, 1933-1945* (New York: Cooper Square, 2001; 1st French ed. 1999), 172-174. Schellenberg comments on the Witnesses at Hartzwalde and his attempts to help Kersten in: Translation of Statement No. 6, July 16, 1945, NA, RG 226, E 119A, Box 26.

records that Schellenberg was clearly seen as one of the very few usable channels to Himmler, that he was evidently trusted by Swedish representatives in Germany, such as Arvid Richert, Stockholm's Minister in Berlin, and that he had been able to establish excellent personal contacts to a number of influential Swedish personalities, his insistence on not having been connected with the preparations for the Bernadotte mission seems all the more surprising. If we follow his account, Bernadotte's journey to Berlin was announced rather suddenly and through diplomatic channels, the latter procedure making it almost impossible to plan any confidential dealings with the Swede. Yet, unexpected as the visit may have been, Schellenberg would not have been Schellenberg if he had not come up with some ways to make the most of it. Because Bernadotte's arrival had to be handled as a diplomatic visit, Hitler had to be notified and, as might have been expected, he expressly forbade a meeting with this member of the Swedish Royal Family.[380] To bypass this problem Himmler and Schellenberg decided to have Count Bernadotte received first at the Foreign Office, of course without informing Ribbentrop of Hitler's uncompromising reaction, and then to have Kaltenbrunner meet the now quasi-official guest of the Foreign Office. As matters worked out, Kaltenbrunner ended up with receiving the Swedish emissary first, but all went surprisingly well, allowing Schellenberg to loudly sing praise of Kaltenbrunner's successful diplomatic finesse. This presumably so flattered Kaltenbrunner that he rushed to suggest that Himmler see the Swede too. Things were now on track and Schellenberg took Count Bernadotte out to Hohenlychen, a clinical sanatorium run by Himmler's favorite medical doctor, SS-*Gruppenführer* Professor Dr. Karl Gebhardt, where Himmler spent much time in care and relative seclusion towards the end of the war.[381] That encounter with Himmler seems to have taken place on February 17, 1945, and Himmler was so positively taken by his Swedish visitor that he asked Schellenberg "to remain in close contact with Bernadotte in order that he might keep his eye on the execution of the arrangements which had been agreed to."[382] Quite often in the course of international contacts atmospheric intangibles can be more influential for the outcome than apparently visible facts. In this case the uninhibited and

---

380. Cf. Swedish Cabinet to Arvid Richert, February 10, 1945, in Koblik, *The Stones Cry Out*, 277-278. — Count Folke Bernadotte af Wisborg (1895-assassinated in Jerusalem 1948), nephew of King Gustav V, married to an American Estelle Romaine née Manville, Vice-Chairman of Swedish Red Cross. In May 1948 sent to Mideast as United Nations Representative to mediate between Arabs and Jews. He and French officer Captain André Pierre Serot murdered by Israeli terrorist group, often identified as Stern Gang, well known Israeli leaders said to have been involved. Steven Koblik, "'No Truck with Himmler': The Politics of Rescue and the Swedish Red Cross Mission, March-May 1945," *Scandia*, vol. 51, nos. 1-2 (1985), 191.
381. Hohenlychen is located in Mecklenburg, north of Berlin, not far from Concentration Camp Ravensbrück. When Kersten was largely in Sweden, Gebhardt's medical advice may have become even more important for Himmler.
382. "Final Report," 167.

private conversation during the extended drive from Berlin to Hohenlychen apparently brought about a very comfortable ambiance of mutual understanding, if not, one may venture to say, of first indications of trust between the Swede, Count Bernadotte, and the German, SS-*Brigadeführer* Schellenberg.

What Count Bernadotte had come to achieve, and which obviously somehow had been agreed to by Himmler, was to transport all Scandinavian prisoners kept in German concentration camps to a single location, such as the Concentration Camp Neuengamme, just on the edge of Hamburg, thus facilitating the still to be permitted transfer of these prisoners across the nearby border to German-occupied Denmark and on to Sweden. As might have been expected neither Kaltenbrunner nor Müller were in any way inclined to lend their support to an undertaking of that nature, and they had no difficulty coming up with a string of supposedly insurmountable technical obstacles. For Schellenberg, whom both strongly disliked and who was still deeply involved in the frustrating but noble rescue efforts of Jean-Marie Musy, which had been all but throttled by Hitler after that memorable train from Theresienstadt, the potentially much larger operation of Count Bernadotte must have seemed to offer fresh possibilities. Doing everything in his power to get this challenging new venture on the road, Schellenberg was able to speedily deflate the first objection of not enough trucks and fuel being available by agreeing with Count Bernadotte that the Swedish Red Cross would try to deliver both, being aware of course that a fleet of foreign vehicles driving through the destroyed German towns would present him with considerable problems. Good luck would have it that the Swedes had planned on furnishing the transport vehicles even prior to Bernadotte's departure from Sweden. The second weightiest argument against this rescue operation was that the Concentration Camp Neuengamme was already so crowded that there was no chance to arrange for an even temporary reception of a large number of Scandinavian inmates from other concentration camps. Much aware of Germany's situation and the increasing number of victims being murdered in the camps or driven to their deaths on the senseless evacuation marches, Schellenberg knew that there was no time left and he simply told his opponents in the Nazi hierarchy that he was quite prepared to handle the situation at Neuengamme with his own men from *Amt* VI. While Schellenberg's prompt and plucky reactions to the evident problems of transporting Scandinavians from camps all over Germany and assuring a minimum of safety for them in the process are indeed impressive, there are, however, as suggested earlier, indications that to a certain degree he must have been prepared for this challenge. Not only did he maintain a group of agents in Stockholm, but his *Amt* or *Amt* IV had also penetrated the Swedish Legation in

Berlin,[383] and finally it would appear perfectly natural that the trusted Kersten would keep him posted on events in Stockholm. Supporting such a view of Kersten's activities would be our knowledge of the web of contacts Himmler's masseur had been able to establish in Stockholm and elsewhere. In other words, it would seem to have been almost normal for Kersten to be at least superficially informed on what for instance Sir Victor Mallet, the British Minister in Stockholm, wrote to his Foreign Office a day prior to Bernadotte's flight to Berlin: "Count F. Bernadotte of Swedish Red Cross is leaving for Germany today in charge of this convoy of cars and busses with the object of assisting the evacuation not only of the remaining Swedes in Germany but also of such Norwegians and Danes as he may be able to retrieve. He has instructions to visit Himmler if possible to impress upon him the explosive state of Swedish public opinion regarding recent executions in Norway ..."[384] Added to bits of knowledge regarding such developments in Sweden, Schellenberg would be driven by his undaunted wish to discover some kind of opening in the West, and for that, he knew well, he was in great need of positive reactions abroad.

All this in no way minimizes the significance of his attempts to rescue as many unfortunates as possible, but taking cognizance of the larger context could help us to better comprehend the reactions of the SS-*Brigadeführer*. Contrary to a number of authors stating that at this late stage in the war both Heinrich Himmler and Walter Schellenberg urgently sought an opportunity to negotiate in the West this is far from the truth. Probably as a consequence of his largely unbroken loyalty to Hitler, Himmler had always preferred to stand back when Schellenberg tried his best to construct some lines of contact to the Western Allies and that attitude of Himmler's—or was it a blend of loyalty to and fear of his *Führer*?—did not really undergo any change, maybe with the exception of the very last days of the Third Reich. Instead it was Schellenberg, the more internationally interested and informed intelligence chief, who continued to take great risks when attempting to draw Himmler to his side of the table. Risky indeed that was because the often unpredictable Himmler, though evidently trusting Schellenberg more than most other men in his surroundings, was at any given moment likely to change positions and even decisions already taken. It has also repeatedly been suggested that Schellenberg engaged in all these rescue activities and probably even in his search for a negotiated end to hostilities in the West merely in order to pave his own path

---

383. A Gestapo officer had "a close connection with a female secretary" in the Legation. Arrested in June 1946 she confessed having "passed secret information." "German Penetration of the former Swedish Legation in Berlin," undated copy, NAK, KV 3/109.
384. Sir Victor Mallet to Foreign Office, February 11, 1945, Secret, NAK, FO 371/48046.

out of the hell on earth the Germans had created. Others have argued that Schellenberg was compelled by his hunger for power and therefore wanted to build the base for a postwar Germany to be headed by Heinrich Himmler and with himself in some position of significance. Although some records seem to point in that direction, it is incomprehensible how a man with his knowledge of the unfathomable crimes committed by his people and particularly by the SS order he had joined when he was just twenty-three years old could have imagined that the Allies would accept a Germany governed by Heinrich Himmler. Whether it was a humane instinct and the moral base instilled in him by his mother years earlier when he was a young man at home or whether a boundless ambition was driving him even at this late moment, we shall never know. If it was indeed something like conscience that touched him in the final hours of the moral abyss of German society, he may have sensed that he was about to be drawn into the most far-reaching rescue efforts of the Nazi period. Stunning it is that the humane undertaking unfolding literally between fierce battles in the East and the West has been met with an almost complete disinterest by historians. For the many nameless human beings who were saved at the last moment this surely was the most important event in their lives.

From the very beginning the almost inconceivable operation appears to have been a mixture of a desperate rescue operation and, at least on the German side, of rather unrealistic conceptions about reaching the negotiating table in the West. Undoubtedly even if the German people did not want to know that their country had lost the war—the Allies, at the time of Count Bernadotte's first visit to Berlin, had convened at Yalta to deliberate upon the world after Hitler—Allied bombing raids on German cities underlined the country's defeat. Soviet Armies were speedily moving into eastern German regions, such as East Prussia and Silesia. The Battle of the Bulge had been a complete German failure, and Allied Forces in the west were pushing what was left of the German Armies and the SS forces back into an increasingly crumbling Nazi Germany. The confused and ill-planned mission to Stockholm of Fritz Hesse, a confidant of Ribbentrop who had been unsuccessful in Stockholm before, may serve as just one example of the opaque foreign policy produced at this critical point by the German Foreign Office. Hesse had worked in London in the 1930s, representing the *Deutsche Nachrichtenbüro* (German News Bureau, DNB) and in 1940 had come to the Foreign Office by way of the *Dienststelle* Ribbentrop. Because of his background, the German Foreign Office considered him a specialist in relations with Great Britain.[385]

---

385. Fritz Hesse (Baghdad 1889-Munich 1980), studied Law and Geography, journalistic work, until 1939 with DNB, 1939-1940 *Dienststelle* Ribbentrop, joined Foreign Office 1940, which sent him to Stockholm February 17, 1945. Joined NSDAP 1933. After the war interned and then employed by American Military

His previous journeys to Stockholm were connected to the undercover contact work of Bruno Peter Kleist and Edgar Klaus. During interrogation after the war, Hesse claimed that Ribbentrop had sent him to Stockholm because of his "pre-Nazi acquaintance with the Wallenberg family." His first assignment was therefore to revive contacts with Jacob Wallenberg. If we can believe Hesse, he saw Wallenberg at least twice and discussed various possibilities of seeking negotiations. Presumably he was to persuade Jacob Wallenberg to go to London and see Churchill. Hesse was to give Wallenberg a proposal for an armistice or peace. If the Western Allies should refuse to deal with the Germans, Hitler would "let the Russians conquer Germany." To that ingenious message Wallenberg supposedly replied that he would rather suggest contacting the Russians, because they were unlikely to inform their Western Allies and something might be achieved by such a contact. If, by contrast, the Western Allies were approached, they would inform the Russians who in that case would reject any German offer. Apparently there were no tangible results to the meetings with Jacob Wallenberg, and Ribbentrop's emissary went on to the next Swede, this time the well-known shipping line owner Gunnar Carlsson, who was said to be close to Churchill. According to Hesse, Carlsson "promised to take my message to London." Apparently, "nothing came of this," and Hesse next met with the Swede James Dickson, who had a connection to the British Minister Sir Victor Mallet and told Hesse that Mallet would be willing to receive him. Hesse claimed later that he was not sufficiently authorized and therefore was not able to meet with Mallet. With this out of the way, Hesse was able to meet Hillel Storch, a very active representative of the World Jewish Congress, who in the summer of 1944 had already conferred with Kleist, Klaus and Böning regarding transactions involving payments for the release of Jews. Hesse claimed he met Storch several times, discussing "the liberation of half a million Jews." Storch then put him in touch with Iver Olsen, the representative of the War Refugee Board posted to the American Legation in Stockholm. They met at Olsen's apartment outside the city and discussed the German offer to "humanize" the war. Apparently all of these encounters lacked serious substance, and there were no tangible results. When the Swedish press divulged the story of this German emissary negotiating in Stockholm, that was the end of a carelessly handled operation, and Hesse was on his way home. The German message he left with his conversation partners was neither surprising nor very new: If the Western Allies would not react positively to Nazi proposals of a negotiated armistice, Germany would simply open the gates for

---

Government in Germany, later with *Bundesnachrichtendienst* (BND). Keipert, Grupp, eds., *Biographisches Handbuch des deutschen Auswärtigen Dienstes*, vol. 2, 296-297.

Communism to engulf Central Europe. As Ribbentrop had nothing but contempt for the British, one is inclined to wonder what it may have been that he tried to achieve at this time, especially since his earlier attempts to reach the Soviets in Stockholm, for instance through Kleist and Klaus, had not really remained a secret. Moreover, it was well known that the Government which Ribbentrop and his emissaries represented had begun to expand its killing program to include almost anyone heard voicing a deviant opinion. Whatever it was that Ribbentrop was "humanizing" in Germany, people were being picked up and never heard of again, and during the final weeks of the war "traitors" could be seen hanging in the streets just to assure the continued loyalty of the people.[386]

The failure of the ill-conceived Hesse mission may serve to illustrate the political chaos reigning in Hitler's Reich in the spring of 1945. Though one might think that Schellenberg as Chief of *Amt* VI and *Amt Mil.* controlled a machine sufficiently strong to protect himself against treacherous attacks from other members of the top echelon of the Nazi government, it needs to be remembered that the Nazi hierarchy was not a traditional construct of top and bottom. Though Hitler's commands emanating from the secluded bunkers of the Chancellery still had an almighty quality, regional and local Gestapo, SS and even NSDAP functionaries often ruled in an uncontrollable manner over life and death in their respective realms. Such were the conditions inside Germany overshadowing Schellenberg's attempts to support the rather ambitious rescue operation of the Swedish Red Cross directed by Count Folke Bernadotte. In many ways Schellenberg became an intermediary between the international benevolent organization and the still very dangerous and completely unprincipled remnants of the German Government. Even in the case of Himmler Schellenberg could never be quite certain from day to day. If Himmler had suddenly decided that absolute loyalty to the *Führer* continued to be his utmost pressing obligation, Schellenberg could have found himself stripped of all positions or worse. This surely must have been in the back of his mind when following the visit of Bernadotte at Hohenlychen, he suggested to Himmler that the new line of contact should be used to now offer "capitulation" to the top Allied Commander General Dwight D. Eisenhower. "It was a stormy conversation but Himmler finally gave in and granted me the widest authority for negotiating with Count Bernadotte." If Schellenberg reports this correctly,

---

386. Re Hesse Mission: Hesse, "Top Secret. My Stockholm Mission," NAK, KV 2/915. Labouchere, Stockholm, to Foreign Office, April 21, 1945, NAK, FO 371/46784. Significant interpretation of related documents in Hans Jakob Stehle, "Deutsche Friedensfühler bei den Westmächten im Februar/März 1945," *Vierteljahrshefte für Zeitgeschichte*, vol. 30 (July 1982), 538-555. Cf. Fleischhauer, *Die Chance des Sonderfriedens*, 273-274. Cf. critical view of Hesse in Helmut Krausnick, "Legenden um Hitlers Aussenpolitik," *Vierteljahrshefte für Zeitgeschichte*, vol. 2, no. 3 (July, 1954).

Himmler reconsidered already the next day, and it took another patient struggle to move him to allow Schellenberg to "influence him [Bernadotte] to fly to Eisenhower on his own initiative." Whatever it may have been that Himmler still hoped to realize—and his horizon would change quickly during the few remaining weeks—the authorization to further pursue the talks about an armistice or capitulation in the West finally opened the gate for Schellenberg to instigate and accompany a great variety of rescue operations and political activities at the same time. Schellenberg, who actually at one point thought that he might fly to London with Count Bernadotte, now did have the green light and he used it to the fullest extent.[387]

The enormous venture now taken in hand by Count Bernadotte and Schellenberg would entail the transport of starved and ill people of all ages in large numbers through basically hostile territory.[388] These much abused human beings would be moved from various concentration camps to the outskirts of Hamburg where they would be held, temporarily it was hoped, at the Concentration Camp Neuengamme. In the early phase of the planning permission from Himmler for continuing the conveyance on to Denmark and even to Sweden was still missing, but that, of course, was the ultimate goal and both Schellenberg and Bernadotte were working on it. Also, initial talks with Himmler had always referred to Scandinavians, not really stating the fact that quite a few of the Scandinavian inmates were Jews. Aside from specific shorter lists of prisoners to be freed, presented by both Jean-Marie Musy and Count Bernadotte, the transport of Jewish camp inmates had not actually been discussed. The Swedes collecting these masses of helpless and very fearful people would have to extract them from often brutal commanders of the camps and then load them onto trucks and busses under the watchful eyes of the SS guards. On their way north, they would be exposed to a potentially dangerous German civilian population hardened by the loss of family members and the destruction of their cities, not to mention the endless wagon trains fleeing from the advancing Soviet troops in the East. Beyond that the long lines of trucks and busses would make ideal targets for low-flying aircraft. Even upon arrival in the Concentration Camp Neuengamme they would have to expect an unfriendly reception, to say the least, by commanding officers in charge. Anticipating these difficulties, the Swedish Government assembled a mighty force of volunteers from the Armed Forces, officers as well as enlisted

---

387. "Final Report," 168-169. Schellenberg, *The Schellenberg Memoirs*, 437-438.
388. For general treatment of the rescue operation see Koblik, *The Stones Cry Out*. Paul A. Levine, *From Indifference to Activism: Swedish Diplomacy and the Holocaust; 1938-1944* (Stockholm: Gotab/Almqvist & Wiksell, 1996). Wanda Heger, *Jeden Freitag vor dem Tor* (München: Franz Schneekluth, 1989; 1st Norwegian ed. 1984). Sune Persson, "Folke Bernadotte and the White Busses," *Journal of Holocaust Education*, vol. 9, nos. 2-3 (2000).

men. They would all be on leave from military service and would not wear military insignia but Red Cross emblems while in Germany. This way the Red Cross operation had the full approval and every possible assistance from the Swedish Government, including most importantly the diplomatic representatives of neutral Sweden in the war-torn Nazi capital.[389] The Germans had warned Count Bernadotte that there could be no assurance that military incidents would be avoided, and the British cautioned that there was no guarantee against aircraft attacks. The Americans were unable to respond in time before departure of the convoys from Sweden.[390] To make the many vehicles clearly identifiable on land and from the air, it was decided to paint all of them white and mark them clearly as Red Cross vehicles. In early March Bernadotte was back in Germany to clarify a number of uncertainties. Kaltenbrunner merely repeated his stance that no support whatsoever would come from his office. On the more positive side the Germans had begun to separate a section of the Concentration Camp Neuengamme to receive the Scandinavian inmates from the other camps. *Skandinavierlager* (camp for Scandinavians) they called it. To assist Count Bernadotte in his preparations, both Felix Kersten, who had flown in from Stockholm to treat an ill Himmler, and Schellenberg were active: Schellenberg trying to remove all kinds of obstacles and staying in close touch with Himmler, and Kersten influencing his patient who required treatment. A notable result of the combined endeavors was Himmler's go-ahead on March 7 for the rescue operation. On March 9 and 10 two endless convoys of trucks and busses started out for Malmö, there to be loaded onto ferry boats for Copenhagen. From there they headed for Korsör to take the ferry boats to Nyborg. Driving east, they would reach Kolding where they would turn south into Germany. After the ferry crossings the two convoys became one, consisting of approximately 95 busses, trucks and ambulances, as well as a group of vehicles carrying fuel, food and medical and other supplies. There were at least 250 drivers and a good number of doctors and nurses. The convoy had been organized with military precision, and there was not much that they could not attend to.[391] Overall responsibility and the command over the entire extensive operation rested with Colonel Gottfrid Björck and the destination was Friedrichsruh, a country estate of the Bismarck family southeast of Hamburg. When they arrived at Friedrichsruh in the middle of the night from March 12 to March 13, they were warmly welcomed by their

---

389. Ulrike Jensen-Lorenz, "Dänische Häftlinge im KZ Neuengamme 1944/45: Die Aktion Bernadotte und das Skandinavierlager," Master's Thesis, University of Hamburg, 1996, 131. Persson,"Folke Bernadotte and the White Buses," 241.
390. Koblik, *The Stones Cry Out*, 128-129.
391. Information on number of trucks and personnel varies slightly in different sources. Cf. Steven Koblik, "'No Truck with Himmler'," 173.

organizer Count Bernadotte. The Bismarcks had close family ties in Sweden and knew both Count Bernadotte and Schellenberg personally. To be of some assistance in the difficult undertaking, they had offered their country estate with its yards and buildings as headquarters. Count Bernadotte had just returned that night from Berlin where he had battled to clear away ever new obstacles thrown in his way by the almighty Chief of the SD and of the RSHA, Ernst Kaltenbrunner. Both he and Müller would have done anything to halt the Bernadotte/Schellenberg rescue operation. To be sure Count Bernadotte had the helpful and protective cover of the International Red Cross, and Schellenberg possessed the necessary experience in handling crises inside the small assortment of top Nazi leaders. Though just thirty-five, Schellenberg in the course of the tumultuous war years had learned all about the loyalties and fears, not to mention the psychological currents of men like Himmler, and his experience had helped him not only to survive in the daily struggle but to succeed occasionally in getting Himmler to do things he would not have done on his own. At times it had become necessary for Schellenberg to become involved in decisions and contacts which, if uncovered, could entail the gravest consequences for himself and his family. In the words of the British Minister, Sir Victor Mallet, reporting to the London Foreign Office: "Schellenberg, who is one of Himmler's principal assistants and believed by Bernadotte to be his intelligence officer, was described by Bernadotte to me as a decent and humane man who had been an immense help in the arrangement for the evacuation of Norwegian and Danish internees to Neuengamme Camp."[392] To minimize exposure Schellenberg in some cases even resorted to meeting foreign representatives at his private home.[393] One of his most important supporters in many chancy undertakings seems to have been Felix Kersten. It was a strange combination of efforts that persuaded Heinrich Himmler to permit the rescue operation even in the face of vicious opposition from Kaltenbrunner. The arrival of the Swedish volunteers at Friedrichsruh was the result of these efforts.

Already on March 15, 1945, the White Busses, as they came to be called, moved out from Friedrichsruh to begin the complicated enterprise of gathering inmates from the heavily guarded concentration camps and transporting them to Neuengamme. The first destination of the trucks appears to have been the Concentration Camp Sachsenhausen, north of Berlin, from where the Swedes

---

392. Telegram, Sir Victor Mallet to Foreign Office, April 12, 1945, NAK, FO 188/487.
393. Statement by Arvid Richert, reporting a meeting with Schellenberg in the latter's private home on April 9, 1945. NA, RG 238, Microfilm M897, Roll 114.

were able to liberate 2,176 Scandinavian prisoners in the course of the next two weeks. To avoid encounters with German refugees, who Schellenberg thought might have problematic reactions to Red Cross busses transporting prisoners, and to cut down daylight hours when they could be attacked by Allied planes, the convoys to Sachsenhausen usually started out in late afternoon to arrive at the gates of Sachsenhausen some time after midnight. Not being admitted to the concentration camp they would wait there and get some rest until around 4:00 a.m. when the guards would command bus load after bus load of the prisoners through the gates. Driving to the Concentration Camp Neuengamme would take about eight hours, worrying about mine fields, fearing exposure to low-flying aircraft and grudgingly submitting to directives from the Gestapo men accompanying every convoy. Also, at least at the outset of the rescue operation, the indescribable human misery witnessed was a rather shocking experience for Colonel Björck's military men, as well as for the doctors and nurses directed by Dr. Hans Arnoldsson. Distressing concerns about sufficient supplies were taken care of when their supply ship the *Lille Mathiesen* was able to dock at Lübeck on March 17.

With the Sachsenhausen operation well underway, more convoys were now sent to other concentration camps, such as Dachau, Mauthausen and Natzweiler. Other trucks and busses made their way to prison camps and jails all over what was still left of the German Reich to pick up more than 1,000 Danish policemen. Most of these policemen had worked under the German occupation forces and the Danish administration until September 1944 when the police and the border guards were disarmed and shipped off to camps and prisons in Germany. When the likely end of the war became more and more visible, destructive interferences in Denmark also increased. As Germany was rather dependent on food shipments from Denmark, sabotage activities against freighters in Danish harbors began to hurt. When needed shipments of pork were threatened, the Nazis even considered trading Danish policemen for Danish hogs. The deal would have assured normal hog shipments from Danish ports to Germany, and the Germans would have released 60 Danish policemen per week.[394]

If the collecting of Scandinavian prisoners at Neuengamme and their eventual transport to Denmark and Sweden seems to have been a relatively easy decision for the Germans, by comparison they reacted with extreme reticence when the liberation of Jewish inmates was even broached. As mentioned

---

394. Document referring to two ships loaded with pigs and sabotaged in the harbor. Reich Commissar for Oceangoing Ships to Foreign Ministry, with copy to Kaltenbrunner, February 9, 1945, NA, RG 226, E 123, Box 4, Folder 43. Therkel Straede, "Die 'Aktion Weisse Busse'," in G. Morsch, A. Reckendrees, eds., *Befreiung Sachsenhausen 1945* (Berlin: Hentrich, 1996), 46-47.

earlier, there had been lists with names, certainly including Jewish names, submitted by Jean-Marie and Benoit Musy, and Count Bernadotte had also taken lists of names with him to Germany. Some individuals inside or close to the Nazi hierarchy had been able to arrange for the release of all types of victims, certainly including Jews. To avoid possible unpleasant reactions from the by and large anti-Semitic surroundings, such releases took place quietly and certainly without any kind of public attention. In fact, such covert procedure continued to be practiced until the end of the war. When large numbers of Jews could finally be included among the inmates rescued from the camps by Schellenberg and Bernadotte, the organizers avoided any sort of public acknowledgment. The reasons for the subdued activities were obvious. A fierce hatred of Jews and everything Jewish over a long period of time had so much become part of public sentiment and was shared by many Nazi leaders that unnecessary publicity would have endangered not only Schellenberg and his assistants in this work but also men like Count Bernadotte and the Swedish volunteers.

Actually what has been said to have been the first inducement for the Swedish rescue attempts inside Nazi Germany was a suggestion made by Raoul Nordling, the Swedish Consul General in Paris. When Count Bernadotte spoke to Nordling in the autumn of 1944, the latter was well experienced in negotiating with the Germans in France and proposed that attempts should be made to rescue the large number of French women held in the Concentration Camp Ravensbrück. That some of the thousands of French women held by the Germans would be Jewish must have been obvious. A second impetus was undoubtedly Jean-Marie Musy who in his undertakings in Berlin and supported by Schellenberg had very pointedly declared that the French women at the Concentration Camp Ravensbrück should be released.

Thus it can be said that the release of Jews had for some time been an unpronounced part of the larger or more general rescue plans. As the war neared its inevitable end, fears grew in many international quarters that the Germans would opt for the total destruction of all concentration camp inmates. There could be various motivations for a decision to complete the genocide of diverse ethnic and cultural groups undertaken in their sphere of power. A desire to destroy all evidence of their abysmal crimes could indeed become a primary impulse at this stage of the war. Another impetus could come from the determination of the Germans to complete the Aryanization (*Arisierung*) at least in their own region. A group of Swedes in Germany tried to warn the Swedish Government: "A liquidation of the inmates in the concentration camps has been planned and will be executed if nothing unforeseen happens." These fears were not without base. Certain SS leaders were discussing ways and means to rid themselves of the KZ inmates before Allied troops would arrive, and their liquidation "through gas or other means" was seen as a possible answer to the problem. The HSSPF August Heissmeyer, responsible for the "combat region" Berlin, argued that he needed a "solution" for the Concentration Camp Sachsenhausen as he would be in no position to defend the German capital with 80,000 inmates threatening his rear. One might just wipe out the entire camp with heavy artillery fire or one could load the inmates on ships to be taken to the Baltic Sea to be sunk. In the Concentration Camp Mauthausen in Austria the SS commander thought about driving all his inmates into a tunnel which then would be blown up.[395] Ominous predictions these were indeed, and it seems to have been at the last moment that the very fruitful cooperation of the ever present Felix Kersten and the much engaged representative of the World Jewish Congress in Stockholm, Hillel Storch, delivered the necessary push to bring about an at least partial turn for the better in Himmler's mind. The Kersten-Storch connection combined with Himmler's dependence on Kersten and Schellenberg's protective and organizational assistance finally brought about the inclusion of the Jews in Count Bernadotte's unique rescue operation.

In early 1945 Hillel Storch, who was well informed and had closely followed the development from ugly anti-Semitism to mass murder in Germany, sought contact with Himmler's masseur to impress upon him the absolute necessity to move fast before the Germans would liquidate the Jews remaining in the concentration camps. Storch and Count Bernadotte knew each other well, and Storch therefore was fully informed about the rescue operation. Although Kersten had not met Storch before, their common interests quickly brought about a mutual understanding, and Kersten agreed to take a short list of Storch's suggestions to his patient in Berlin. What Storch wanted from Himmler at this point came down to a permission to send food and medicine to the inmates, the concentration of the Jewish inmates in a few camps to be run by the International Red Cross until the World Jewish Congress could take things in hand, the freeing of a number of specifically named Jewish prisoners, and the organization of first transports of Jews to Sweden and Switzerland. Prior to his departure for Berlin Kersten also had a meeting with Christian Günther, the Swedish Foreign Minister, who apparently assured him that Sweden was ready and willing to take in all inmates rescued from German concentration camps. If Kersten later remembered correctly, the Foreign Minister was clearly supportive and made a point of asking him to

---

395. Karin Orth, "Planungen und Befehle der SS-Führung zur Räumung des KZ-Systems," in Detlef Garbe, Carmen Lange, eds., *Häftlinge zwischen Vernichtung und Befreiung* (Bremen: Edition Temmen, 2005), 38. (Transl.) Heger, *Jeden Freitag vor dem Tor*, 177.

assist Count Bernadotte in his important undertaking. The fact that both Christian Günther and the Undersecretary of State in the Swedish Foreign Office, Erik Boheman, were completely in favor of the Swedish involvement was certainly important to increase the confidence of Kersten and Schellenberg. As must have been expected by all involved, including Schellenberg with his direct access to Himmler, the *Reichsführer* SS was not won over easily and no overall consent for the release of Jews could be worked out in the early hectic attempts. Nevertheless, taking all risks into consideration, there was some real intangible progress made, suggesting that more satisfying results might indeed be reached in the near future. Only in slow steps did Himmler allow himself to move toward his petitioners. He did agree that the concentration camps would not be evacuated when Allied Forces were approaching, and by the time Kersten flew back to Sweden, he had Himmler's assurance that on his next trip he could bring a representative of the World Jewish Congress with him and that such a visitor would have safe conduct. Kersten recalled that Himmler gave him his word of honor. When Schellenberg spoke to Himmler before Kersten and Storch were to return, it was very evident just how far Himmler had now moved away from his previous loyal closeness to Hitler. As Schellenberg was to recall later: "Himmler was well aware that to have a conversation with Herr Storch while Hitler was still alive would be an action of fundamental importance which would have the greatest consequences for his relations with his own associates in the Party and in connection with the Jews." Himmler's greatest fear was that Kaltenbrunner would learn of his meeting with a Jew and that he would report him to Hitler—with the evident consequences. When Kersten had first brought up the thought of a Jew coming to Germany and negotiating with him, Himmler had cried out: "I can never receive a Jew. If the Führer were to hear of it, he would have me shot dead on the spot."[396]

In most cases one might be inclined to ignore the man who may have played a role in the preparations for an event but then had little to do with it. This event, however, was not a routine happening nor were the preparations. The records show that Hillel Storch was a man engaged in all kinds of business, well connected to a good number of highly respectable and historically significant personalities and a Stockholm representative of the World Jewish Congress. As pointed out earlier, he had been approached by German agents, such as Fritz Hesse, who were serving different interests in Nazi Germany, fishing for lines to the Western Allies, as well as to the Soviet Union. In the spring of 1945 Storch and Felix Kersten had been introduced to each other by

---

[396]. "Final Report," 37. Schellenberg, *The Schellenberg Memoirs*, 439. The German *Memoiren*, 357, varies slightly in text but not in content. Felix Kersten, *The Kersten Memoirs 1940-1945*, 281.

Ottokar von Knieriem, identified by Kersten as a representative of the Dresdner Bank, and Storch had used the opportunity to persuade Hitler's masseur to speak to the Nazi leader to improve the lot of Jewish inmates in German concentration camps. Kersten had not been turned down by Himmler and had reported back to Storch that much had been achieved and that even the release of Jews to Switzerland and Sweden might be realized in the near future. Most significantly, Himmler by issuing a special order, Kersten reported, had taken the initiative to stop cruel treatment and the killing of Jews.[397] Kersten's message to Storch closes with: "Finally I must inform you that the Reichsführer SS Himmler, following my suggestion, would be prepared to negotiate with you personally about the questions on hand." In other words, Hillel Storch evidently had offered to Kersten to go to Germany, Kersten had presented Storch's viewpoints regarding the improvement of the treatment of Jews to his patient Himmler, and Himmler had declared that he was ready to discuss matters with Storch in person. One might indeed wonder why the dedicated Hillel Storch did not follow up that invitation of the Nazi leader. Only three days after Kersten's report to Storch, Sir Victor Mallet, the British Minister in Stockholm, wrote to "The Right Honourable Anthony Eden, M.C., M.P. etc., etc., etc." leaving no doubt that he and Iver Olsen, "the Refugee Attaché of the American Legation," were of the decided view that Storch "a stateless Latvian who lost his citizenship in 1940," a man of "considerable means" and "I am told by the American Legation, persona grata with the Soviet authorities for whom he has performed several services in the commercial field" was a troubled man who did not seem suitable for the mission to Himmler. "His present activities ... are leading him into very deep waters for his zeal on behalf of his Jewish compatriots and in his desire to play a prominent part in their cause he has certainly made himself out to possess more authority than of course he possesses ... it is not without significance that Dr. [Fritz] Hesse when he was in Stockholm made contact with him. For these reasons it would probably be extremely dangerous if Mr. Storch went to Berlin. The Refugees Attaché of the United States Legation holds this opinion very strongly and ... he also intends informing the Swedish Ministry for Foreign Affairs that they must in no circumstances grant him the necessary exit permit to visit Germany."[398] Taking a closer look at the available records relating to the Storch mission, it seems fair to conclude that neither the Americans, here particularly the Minister in Sweden Herschel Johnson and the War Refugee Board delegate at the American Legation Iver Olsen, nor the

---

397. "Medicinalrad" (medical doctor) Felix Kersten to Hillel Storch, Stockholm, March 24, 1945, Strictly Confidential, NAK, FO 371/51194. (Transl.)
398. Sir Victor Mallet to Anthony Eden, March 27, 1945, "Important: Top Secret," NAK, FO 371/51194.

British, particularly their Minister in Sweden Sir Victor Mallet, demonstrated the slightest interest in a visit of Storch to Germany. Not really plausible but in fact strongly suggested in the documents is the explanation that their firm aversion to Storch was caused by the latter's indirect association with the fudged Hesse negotiations in Sweden. "Humanizing" the war in the spring of 1945, following the unprecedented liquidation of millions and a war of aggression, did seem slightly ludicrous, and it is difficult to criticize British or American reactions to Hesse's offer. Incidentally, the German Chief of Foreign Intelligence Schellenberg was not drawn into this mission for the "humanization" of the war. Fritz Hesse, of course, was Ribbentrop's emissary and his rather infantile message to Germany's enemies, if anything, appears to have been an illustration of Joachim von Ribbentrop's lack of sophistication in diplomacy. Also, the Swedes were fully informed by their Minister in Berlin on how foreign policy was formulated there. Mallet's between-the-lines inferences regarding connections of Storch to the Soviet Union are less comprehensible, and there is no evidence that Hillel Storch was in any way connected with Soviet intelligence. The simple result of this unpleasant exchange of unsubstantiated opinions was that the Swedes refused to provide Storch with the needed travel documents.[399]

In retrospect it was fortunate for the Jews still languishing in German concentration camps that Norbert Masur, the quickly found replacement for Hillel Storch, was a highly qualified and dedicated Jew who like Storch represented the World Jewish Congress and thereby important Jewish interests in the U.S. When Masur and Kersten boarded a German plane in Stockholm on April 19, 1945, they were literally on their way into the lion's den not knowing what awaited them and solely relying on Kersten's experience with the Nazi leaders and the hopefully diligent preparations for their arrival in Berlin supervised by the apprehensive and exhausted Chief of *Amt* VI. Though a national of neutral Sweden and thus entitled to certain protection, Norbert Masur was also a Jew about to visit the country where Jews were put away and murdered, where the killing of Jews was official public policy. He was heading for a personal encounter with one of the organizers of the historically unprecedented crime. A few days later Masur wrote down: "For me as a Jew, it was a deeply moving thought that, in a few hours, I would be face to face with the man who

---

399. For the British side, also referring to the American reaction, see rather complete documentation in NAK, FO 371/51194. Cf. very considerate interpretation of the conflict over Hillel Storch in Penkower, *The Jews were Expendable*, 279. Additional data in Meredith Hindley, "Negotiating the Boundary of Unconditional Surrender: The War Refugee Board in Sweden and Nazi Proposals to Ransom Jews, 1944-1945," *Holocaust and Genocide Studies*, vol. 10 (Spring 1996). Elie Wiesel in the 1960s still was in contact with Hillel Storch and refers to him as "a Jewish leader." Elie Wiesel, *All Rivers Run to the Sea: Memoirs* (New York: Alfred A. Knopf, 1996), 312.

was primarily responsible for the destruction of several million Jewish people."[400] There were no other passengers on that German plane. When they put down at Tempelhof Airport in Berlin, it was evident that Schellenberg had ordered the guards to check only Felix Kersten's papers and admit unquestioned the person in his company. Indeed, the arrival of Himmler's masseur and the Jew from the World Jewish Congress had not been given any kind of publicity in the German capital. As it turned out, they could not even accept the car sent from the Swedish Legation but instead had to wait at the airport for a limousine that Schellenberg had dispatched. They were then taken to Hartzwalde, Kersten's estate in the country, arriving around midnight following a harrowing ride without headlights to avoid detection from the air. With the Allied bombers flying overhead and in the unnerving anticipation of the chancy encounter on the following day, Masur spent a restless night. After all he was staying overnight in Hitler's Germany. How could he ever have gotten himself into this!

Meanwhile Schellenberg, who had arranged everything, went through the usual frustrating exchanges with Heinrich Himmler. It was the day before Hitler's birthday on April 20, and Schellenberg worked hard to persuade his Chief, who was at Hohenlychen, not to drive into the bomb-torn city and expose himself to unpredictable terror in Hitler's bunker. Schellenberg had received a message that Masur and Kersten had arrived and he knew that Count Bernadotte, who like Kersten had helped Schellenberg in bringing the Jewish emissary from Stockholm to Berlin, was also on his way. Both Masur and Bernadotte were of great importance to Schellenberg's plans, and both had to be brought together with Himmler during their predictably very brief stays in Germany. For what he was doing, Schellenberg needed the consent and, as a life insurance, the cover of Heinrich Himmler. As might have been expected, Himmler insisted on driving into the city or what was left of it, because he still felt it necessary to be there when the *Führer* held a birthday reception for his inner circle in the bunker under the Chancellery. Consequently, it was agreed that Schellenberg would drive to Kersten's country place and already begin talks with the Jewish delegate on the morning of April 20. The encounter of Himmler and Masur would have to be postponed until that evening after

---

400. Norbert Masur, "My Meeting with Heinrich Himmler, April 20/21, 1945. Report to the Swedish Section of the World Jewish Congress, Stockholm, Sweden," "Translated from the Original German into English by Henry Karger on the occasion of Yom Hashoa, 1993." Original publication: Norbert Masur, *En Jude Talar Med Himmler* (Stockholm: Bonniers, 1945). Various similar texts available otherwise. A German translation of the original now in: N. Günther, S. Zankel, eds., *Abrahams Enkel: Juden, Christen, Muslime und die Schoa* (Stuttgart: Steiner, 2006). The German editors state that a German translation was not available before 2006, which would suggest that Karger did not translate from "the original German."

Himmler had attended the birthday celebration. It was midnight when Schellenberg finally departed from Hohenlychen just as Himmler was opening a bottle of champagne to toast Hitler's birthday. It was 2:30 a.m. when Schellenberg finally reached Hartzwalde and the entire place seemed sound asleep—except for his trusted friend Felix Kersten with whom he discussed the multitude of pressing problems until 4:00 a.m.

Therefore Schellenberg had but a few hours of rest before the surreal early morning event on Adolf Hitler's birthday April 20, 1945. Unimaginable as it was, that morning the SS-*Brigadeführer* Walter Schellenberg shared breakfast with the representative of the World Jewish Congress, Norbert Masur. Masur's reaction to the Nazi leader: "I was surprised to see a good-looking young man with soft features, in civilian clothing, not the hard Nazi type which I had expected. He was terribly depressed, considered the war as lost, and was very pessimistic about Germany's future." Judging from the surviving records of their conversation, it would appear that they had a very fruitful exchange and that Masur came away with the feeling that here was someone who was seriously interested in helping him with his rescue efforts. As they were sitting there, the skies over Hartzwalde were darkening with one formation of bombers after the other, most likely heading for Berlin. Suddenly the house was shaking from bombs dropped nearby. A little later a message from Himmler came, informing them that he would journey to Hartzwalde after Hitler's birthday reception, probably arriving about 2:30 a.m. on April 21. Soon after this breakfast meeting Schellenberg had to leave Masur to get back to Himmler and make certain that the two planned meetings with Masur and Count Bernadotte would actually take place.

Postwar interrogations suggest that Schellenberg did find Himmler and not only persuaded him of the absolute need to meet with Masur and Bernadotte, but also apparently arranged a kind of dress rehearsal for the Himmler/Masur encounter. For some time already they had in various ways touched on the probability that Hitler would be unable—or unwilling—to lead Germany out of this war, and they had considered different ways of handling the dilemma. When Himmler now told him that he wished to present to Masur the background and development of what the Germans had come to consider their Jewish problem, Schellenberg apparently took courage to suggest that "it was late in the day for vindicatory eloquence ... and [that] it would be much better not to speak of the past but instead to determine ... what had to be done to save those who could still be saved." When Himmler, following a brief attendance of the festivities in Hitler's bunker, finally got out on the road to Hartzwalde, it was way past midnight. Himmler was now accompanied by Schellenberg and his own adjutant, the SS-*Standartenführer* Rudolf Brandt. When the car rolled into the driveway of Kersten's country estate, it was indeed 2:30 a.m. Kersten went out to welcome the guests, and when they entered the room, Himmler, instead of calling out the common and practically required *Heil Hitler* (Hail Hitler) greeted the Swedish emissary with *Guten Tag* (Good Day). A couple of days later Masur noted that in spite of the early morning hour he had found Himmler "well groomed ... fresh and lively ... outwardly quiet, and in control." In the course of the ensuing exchange Himmler then proceeded to do exactly what Schellenberg had attempted to keep him from doing. He went into wordy descriptions of the past and explained what difficulties from his perspective the Jews had caused the German people. This indeed went so far that Himmler elaborated on the "just treatment" the Jews had received. Masur listened, interrupted the Nazi leader and listened again, his enduring patience strained but well realizing that he had to put up with this if he wished to achieve what he had come here for. Much in line with what Schellenberg had tried to tell Himmler the previous afternoon, Masur found an opening to bluntly state that the inmates of the concentration camps in the North and the Southwest should be evacuated to Sweden and to Switzerland, and he added that the other remaining camps should be surrendered without evacuation attempts and intact to the approaching Allied troops. Until such surrender of the camps the inmates were to be fed and receive medical care. In addition Masur pressed upon the Nazi leader that the prisoners listed individually on the lists the Swedish Foreign Office had prepared were to be released now. These demands, necessarily presented rather to the point may not have pleased Himmler, but he had changed in the course of the last weeks, and Schellenberg, trying against all odds, had almost constantly pleaded with him to create a better international climate for talks with the British and/or the Americans. Following this unusual exchange between the Jewish delegate and the Nazi leader, almost any reaction from Himmler seemed possible when he rose and asked for an intermission to talk with his adjutant Rudolf Brandt. While Schellenberg took Norbert Masur to another room, Himmler, meeting with Brandt and Kersten for some twenty minutes, agreed to the following concessions: There was no objection to the individual releases requested on the lists, including a number of Jewish prisoners in different camps. About a thousand Jewish women were to be released from the Concentration Camp Ravensbrück. An additional number of French women were also to be released. Indeed most of Masur's requests had been granted across the board, though under two slightly surprising conditions. Even at this late hour of the Third Reich, it was evident that Himmler, probably for fear of retribution from Hitler and his closer entourage, such as Martin Bormann and Joseph Goebbels, lacked the courage to release any "Jews" and therefore unmistakably stipulated that the Jewish women from Ravensbrück would be designated as Polish women. And very telling about his position and what was possible under existing conditions: "It is very necessary that not only your visit here must remain secret, but also the arrival of the Jews in Sweden must remain that way." As Masur was later to recall, it was a most depressing night with the German SS chief, but it was also the key for the liberation for uncounted unfortunates.[401]

The meeting, somewhat incomprehensibly labeled ten years later by British historian Hugh Trevor-Roper (Lord Dacre) "one of the most ironical incidents in the whole war," ended about 5:00 a.m.[402] Knowing how concerned Norbert Masur would be about getting back to Sweden, Schellenberg assured the visitor that all would be arranged and safe. Intent on making the second date, Schellenberg and Himmler then were off to the next encounter at Hohenlychen.[403] A 6:00 a.m. breakfast with Count Bernadotte was the result of the troubles Schellenberg had taken to make certain that Himmler would not have a relapse into a harsher policy regarding the remaining concentration camps. From the memoirs and reports of the participants it is not easy to determine what was actually discussed. A number of individual release requests appear to have been on the table, and Himmler confirmed that he had no objections to the transport of the women from the Concentration Camp Ravensbrück to Sweden. Bernadotte was pleased but pressed for a further permission to take the Scandinavians on to Sweden also. What he elicited from Himmler was continued hesitation, and he thought it well not to push matters. Schellenberg in his memoirs recalls that Himmler had reminded him to once again ask Count Bernadotte to travel to General Eisenhower's headquarters "to arrange for him [Himmler] to have a conference with the General." The Swede's reply to Schellenberg somewhere in the countryside of Mecklenburg before they parted was sufficiently clear: "The Reichsführer no longer understands the realities of his own situation. I cannot help him any more. He should have taken Germany's affairs into his own hands after my first visit. I can hold out little chance for him now. And you, my dear Schellenberg, would be wiser to think of yourself."[404] Schellenberg, of course, remembered that type of personal advice from friends in both Sweden and Switzerland and that his

---

401. List of people to be released, given by Swedish Foreign Ministry to Kersten, confirmed by Storch, given to Germans, NAK, FO 188/526. Re the Masur-Himmler encounter at Hartzwalde see Masur's report and Schellenberg, *The Schellenberg Memoirs*, 443-444. Schellenberg, *Memoiren*, 360. "Final Report," 177-179. Bauer, *Jews for Sale*, 246-248. Frank Fox, "A Jew Talks to Himmler," *Zwoje*, 1/38 (2004).
402. H. R. Trevor-Roper, "Introduction," to Kersten, *The Kersten Memoirs 1940-1945*, 15.
403. Hohenlychen was not "Kersten's sanatorium" as stated in Raymond Palmer, "Felix Kersten and Count Bernadotte: A Question of Rescue," *Journal of Contemporary History*, vol. 29 (1994), 45.
404. Schellenberg, *The Schellenberg Memoirs*, 445. Very similar in *Memoiren*, 360. "Final Report," 180.

reaction in the past had always been to stay in Germany and continue to run *Amt* VI. As indicated earlier, in spite of his view at least from 1941 on that the war could not be won, his reasons for staying are rather obscure, other than the fear for the lives of those in his family. Although at the end of April 1945 the Nazi police system was no longer as likely to catch up with his family, we may assume that he had already moved his children and pregnant wife to somewhere near Marquartstein in Bavaria. Had he decided to leave the sinking ship, other SS officers in the area could of course have destroyed his family there.[405]

On Schellenberg's return to Hohenlychen there were but two hours of sleep, followed by renewed frustrating exchanges with Himmler. Though fully aware of the irreversible fact that the war was lost, he apparently continued to push Himmler to take things in hand. The military situation was such that Schellenberg persuaded Himmler not to return to Berlin. Instead they headed for Himmler's temporary headquarters at Wustrow. On the road they ran into such unruly masses of refugees and soldiers that "a company of their escort"[406] was ordered to help clear the way. The sight of the total breakdown and the wagon trains of miserable Germans, Schellenberg reports, caused Himmler to exclaim: "Schellenberg, I dread what is to come." Surviving the attacks of low-flying enemy planes, they reached Wustrow to find a foreboding message from Hitler's bunker that Hitler and Joseph Goebbels[407] were raging because they wanted Gottlob Berger there to supervise the summary execution of Dr. Karl Brandt, Hitler's physician, who had moved his family to Thuringia where they were now under American occupation. While public order may have been nonexistent at this stage, the internal power network in a way still functioned and Himmler actually succeeded in getting Karl Brandt out of Berlin, protecting him against the bombing raids and holding him in Schwerin for a postponed execution to take place, Berlin was told, when Gottlob Berger had returned from an official journey to Southern Germany. In this case Himmler's manipulation merely extended a life that had been forfeited.[408]

Their hectic activities at Wustrow were abruptly ended by reports that Soviet detachments had been sighted in the region. Back at the clinic at Hohenlychen Himmler seems to have finally come to the realization that he,

---

405. To avoid falling into the hands of the Russians, several *Amt* VI Foreign Intelligence Sections were moved from Berlin, most of them south. Mrs. Schellenberg was sent south together with staff and documents.
406. Suggesting that Schellenberg was often accompanied by a truckload of SS men. "Final Report," 180. The information is missing in both the English (p. 446) and the German (p. 361) edition of the memoirs. Most likely this was no longer the case during the final days in Germany.
407. Dr. Joseph Goebbels (1897-1945), studied philosophy, art history and literature, joined NSDAP 1926, editor of Nazi journals, Minister for Propaganda 1933, fiercely anti-Semitic, suicide in Hitler's bunker.
408. Dr. Karl Brandt, personal physician to Hitler. Accused of medical experiments on humans in the so-called Doctors' Trial at Nuremberg, he was sentenced to death and hanged in June 1948.

Himmler, would now have to act. There was no time for Schellenberg to advise, other than counseling a possible last encounter with Count Bernadotte. Heinrich Himmler was evidently in a chaotic state. He said that he wanted to give Count Bernadotte a declaration of capitulation of the German Armed Forces to be passed on to the Western Allies. Expecting Bernadotte to be still in Lübeck, Schellenberg once more hit the road to arrive there late at night and learn that Count Bernadotte was spending the night in Apenrade across the Danish border. With some luck Schellenberg succeeded in reaching him by telephone and to meet on the following day at the Swedish Consulate in Flensburg. Coming together that afternoon, Bernadotte thought that it would be unnecessary to meet again with Himmler because all that was needed was a letter document from the German side offering capitulation. Quite correctly Schellenberg countered that this could be problematic if Hitler was still alive. When Schellenberg begged him instead to accompany him to Lübeck where he would see Himmler one more time, the Swede acquiesced, thereby putting Schellenberg once more on the telephone, this time to get Himmler to come to Lübeck. It worked. The conference was set for 10:00 p.m. After dinner Schellenberg and Count Bernadotte were back on the road heading for the Swedish Consulate in Lübeck. With the Swede being quasi on home ground there, Schellenberg was off to the Hotel Danziger Hof which had been turned into headquarters of General Alfred Wünnenberg and his *Ordnungspolizei* (special police force) and where Himmler intended to stay for the night. Schellenberg tried one more time to strengthen Himmler in his decision to announce the capitulation and then took him to the Swedish Consulate where Bernadotte was expecting them. They had hardly greeted each other when an air raid nearby forced them to seek shelter in the cellar. It was by candlelight that Himmler revealed his views about the state of the war and among otherwise wordy self-confirmation told the Swede: "We Germans must declare ourselves as beaten by the Western Allies ... To the Russians it is impossible for us Germans, and above all for me, to capitulate." And he emphasized that he had the authority to pronounce this proposal. Count Bernadotte replied that he was willing to deliver the proposal and added that the Swedish Government was particularly concerned that the entire "Northern Sector" should be spared any "senseless destruction." Finally Bernadotte agreed to take a letter from Himmler to the Swedish Foreign Minister Christian Günther in which the Germans would ask that Sweden lend its full support to the German capitulation offer. Himmler, it seems, then by candlelight wrote that note. It was past midnight, now April 24, when the two Germans took leave after agreeing that Schellenberg would accompany Count Bernadotte to the border. After taking Himmler back to the Danziger Hof, Schellenberg returned to the Consulate and drove the Swede to the border, having agreed that hopefully positive reports on first reactions to the proposal would come back through the Swedish Consulate in Lübeck.

Parallel to these difficult political negotiations which because of time and circumstances could not possibly be expected to deliver very surprising results, there was the equally demanding and risky but incomparably more rewarding sizeable rescue operation of the Chief of *Amt* VI Foreign Intelligence. We have seen that the hopes for negotiations in the West and the very late, but nevertheless immensely important rescue operations were linked, certainly in Schellenberg's mind, and there were calculations on his side that the rescue operations would lead to a more positive international climate in which a tolerable end of hostilities must still be reached. However one may be inclined to weigh the balance of the two operations in Schellenberg's frame of mind, even to the point of assigning a greater degree of importance to the envisioned negotiations—and a number of interpretations are conceivable—there surely cannot be the slightest doubt that for every single life saved, there was nothing more meaningful than those rescue operations. The two specific large-scale rescue undertakings, organized by Jean-Marie Musy and Count Folke Bernadotte and made possible because the SS-*Brigadeführer* Walter Schellenberg wanted them to happen, developed in an almost parallel fashion. In fact, when the larger Swedish rescue campaign could finally be activated, Benoit Musy was still in the country and attended to by Franz Göring, that somewhat enigmatic SS officer who may have been the product of the perverse ideological training of that imagined German elite, but who also was an absolutely loyal member of Schellenberg's personal staff and therefore appears to have enjoyed his Chief's unlimited trust. From available documents it is evident that Schellenberg's estimate of Göring was correct. Quite amazingly, this SS officer assigned to assist both Musy and the Swedish Red Cross managed to not only attend to the various needs and wishes of the many foreigners unaccustomed to Nazi Germany, but even more astonishing to also overcome most hindrances placed in his way by the Gestapo apparatus being fed with contradictory orders from Kaltenbrunner. To illustrate how these rescue operations actually transpired, it may be of some interest to take a closer look at the respective events at the Concentration Camp Ravensbrück. Here the Germans were keeping mostly women, Jewish and Gentile, and both Musy and Bernadotte had given this place of organized human misery the highest priority on their lists of rescue demands. It will be recalled that it was here that Himmler had granted the surrender of all women prisoners but had very specifically added the stipulation that the Jewish women would be released as Polish women.

By the end of March 1945 most of the Scandinavian inmates had already been hauled out from the different German concentration camps. The crews manning the White Busses had done very dedicated work under harassing conditions and in constant danger for their lives. There was death and human deprivation all around them. Their short reprieves at the country estate of the Bismarcks' were breaks from the daily horror. There had also been a number of transports of Scandinavian and other selected prisoners from Ravensbrück.[409] This meant that the arrival by car on April 22 of Schellenberg's representative Franz Göring and Benoit Musy should have been no surprise for the camp commander SS-*Hauptsturmführer* Fritz Suhren. Whether he and his men were still convinced Nazis looking ahead for the *Endsieg* (final victory) of from their perspective superior German men or whether they were merely putting up a front, there were no signs of any willingness to cooperate with the two visitors. Suhren had run this inhuman camp since 1942 and feelings or compassion do not appear to ever have entered into his decisions. Quite the opposite. What transpired under Suhren's command is revolting and quite beyond any description. Apparently the routine disposal of prisoners was shooting them in the neck and burning the remains in the crematory. Some time in late 1944 this procedure was seen as too slow and inefficient, and a special building for gassing people was constructed. Eyewitness accounts of the killings, of the breaking out of gold teeth and of the disposing of the bodies in the crematory can be found in the respective sources. How Benoit Musy and Franz Göring dealt with this German commander and his guards at Ravensbrück is hard to imagine. Indications are that Göring decided to act the SS official he was, applying the rude German tone he had learned during his own training, and that this assumed self-confidence had the desired effect. Aside from a specific request for the release of some individual French women whom Suhren first declared not to know and then claimed to be dead, the massive undertaking of moving thousands of women out of this camp under the given circumstances worked out tolerably well. To be sure there still were some hitches. To get the operation started Göring requested that the women inmates should be put on the road and start walking in the direction of Malchow, an affiliate camp of Ravensbrück to the north. The arriving Red Cross busses would then pick up those women first and fetch the rest later at Ravensbrück. Although Suhren seemed to agree, the busses coming down the road met no women at all. In the course of a new confrontation with the camp commander, Göring was told by Suhren that he was in receipt of new orders

---

409. Cf. Jack G. Morrison, *Ravensbrück: Every Day Life in a Women's Concentration Camp, 1939-45* (Princeton: Wiener, 2000), 296-298. Sigrid Jacobeit, Simone Erpel, eds., *"Ich grüsse Euch als freier Mensch": Quellenedition zur Befreiung des Frauen-Konzentrationslagers Ravensbrück im April 1945* (Berlin: Hentrich, 1995), 18-19.

from the Inspector of Concentration Camps SS-*Gruppenführer* Richard Glücks, specifying that all inmates were to be retained in the camp, presumably to proceed with their liquidation at any given moment. Göring had no choice but to call Himmler's adjutant Rudolf Brandt for new instructions. Fortunately for Göring and the imprisoned women, Brandt was able to get to Himmler and to report back shortly that the *Reichsführer* SS had personally ordered the release of all Ravensbrück women and that Suhren had better obey. With that having been taken care of, Suhren still seemed extremely hesitant to perform as told, and after some time and added pressure from Göring, the by now somewhat insecure commander hesitatingly revealed something shocking and ugly. Some 54 Polish and 17 French women prisoners had been subjected to medical experiments. The women had been infected with diseases which some Nazi doctors then treated by operating on their muscles and bones. To prove his point Suhren actually presented two of these "Kaninchen" (rabbits), as the Germans called them, to his visitors. Also, he confided that he was under strictest orders from Kaltenbrunner's office to liquidate these women. Again there was no way but to get back on the telephone to Himmler's temporary headquarters. Luckily again the often helpful Rudolf Brandt was there and clearly stated Himmler's explicit permission to include the women in the rescue transport. Göring arranged for the Swedish Dr. Arnoldsson to personally put these unfortunates on the convoy. As the undertaking progressed, it soon turned out that the White Busees did not have sufficient space to handle so many thousands at the given short notice and Göring had to become an organizer. To transport about 4,000 women, he calculated, only a sizeable freight train would do and that was what with the assistance of Colonel Björck's successor, Major Sven Frykman, and the dedicated Dr. Arnoldsson, he managed to press out of the chief of the *Deutsche Reichsbahn* (German Reich Railway) at Lübeck. Thanks to the immeasurable personal engagement of the Scandinavians the loading operation could be completed in a relatively short time, and Göring, pleased that all worked out in the end, noticed that the last vehicles leaving the forsaken place, were already coming under Soviet artillery fire.[410]

However the motivations of the negotiators and the organizers of the rescue operations may be interpreted, the remarkable outcome of all this was the freeing of a very large number of unfortunate human beings who, because

---

410. For the eyewitness account of the Ravensbrück rescue operation see "Annexe Written by Hauptsturmführer Göring," included in this volume. Statement Under Oath, Franz Göring, February 24, 1948, SAN, Rep. 501, LV, S-4. Regarding medical experiments Morrison, *Ravensbrück*, 245-249. Cf. concerning the killings Simone Erpel, *Zwischen Vernichtung und Befreiung: Das Frauen-Konzentrationslager Ravensbrück in der letzten Kriegsphase* (Berlin: Metropol, 2005), 69-73. Bernhard Strebel, *Das KZ Ravensbrück: Geschichte eines Lagerkomplexes* (Paderborn: Schöningh, 2003), 475 ff.

of the engagement and the selfless help of many foreigners and a few Germans, were given a chance to live. "Take all the Jews you want," the exhausted Heinrich Himmler had called out a few hours after his encounter with Norbert Masur, the representative of the World Jewish Congress. Count Bernadotte, Hillel Storch, Norbert Masur, Felix Kersten, Jean-Marie Musy and his son Benoit, and Walter Schellenberg, to name just a few, had taken personal risks and exposed themselves to false accusations in the course of the preparations for this act of humanitarianism. Bus drivers, doctors, nurses and, yes, men like Franz Göring had risked their lives in the humane enterprise undertaken in the twilight of the destruction of the German nation. For more than 20,000 imprisoned and tortured human beings they lit the light of hope for a new life.[411]

For Germans and their leaders who had created that darkness, the final act was still to come, the formal collapse of the system they had believed to be superior to other cultures. In the case of Himmler this meant that with Hitler still alive he continued to see himself as the inheritor of power and to all appearances still had a vision of becoming a mediator between the German people—his people—and the victorious Allies. Because of his need for Himmler's protection when constructing lines for negotiations in the West, Schellenberg of course had reinforced the unrealistic expectations of his chief. Not long before the nation's demise Schellenberg and Himmler had actually discussed ways of ridding the land of Adolf Hitler, and they had even consulted Maximinian de Crinis, Schellenberg's friend and Professor for Psychiatry at the Charité in Berlin, about the *Führer's* state of health. De Crinis thought he had detected symptoms of Parkinson's disease. Probably shortly thereafter, in April 1945, Schellenberg recalled later, he actually gathered his courage to advise Himmler that he should see Hitler and present him with the facts as they were. After "all that had happened during the last years," Himmler was to propose to Hitler that he should resign. When Himmler, probably correctly, countered that Hitler would simply turn mad and shoot him on the spot, Schellenberg replied that Himmler was certainly powerful enough to have some effective SS leaders in place to carry out the needed arrests. Finally Schellenberg remembers saying,

---

411. For obvious reasons there are some minor discrepancies regarding the exact number of people rescued. Count Bernadotte speaks of "about 20,000 inmates transported to Sweden" (Affidavit of April 19, 1948, SAN, Rep. 501, S-4). Franz Göring (Statement under Oath, February 24, 1948, SAN, Rep. 501, S-4) speaks of 9,000 Polish, 1,500 French, some 3,000 Jewish and other women and girls from Ravensbrück alone, 450 Jewish women from Malchow, and 1,500 women of different nationalities from Neubrandenburg, another affiliate camp. Ulrike Jensen, "'Es war schön, nicht zu frieren': Die 'Aktion Bernadotte' und das 'Skandinavierlager' des Konzentrationslagers Neuengamme" in KZ-Gedenkstätte Neuengamme, ed., *Kriegsende und Befreiung*, vol. 2 of *Beiträge zur Geschichte der nationalsozialistischen Verfolgung in Norddeutschland* (Bremen: Temmen, 1995), 32, 34 has exact figures for the various nationalities and speaks of a total of 20,937 or 20,936 inmates having been evacuated from German concentration camps by the Bernadotte/Schellenberg operation, i.e. not including other operations of Musy and Schellenberg.

"if there is no other way, the doctors must intervene." Still avoiding a personal commitment, Himmler's way out seems to have been a meeting of medical experts—with somewhat surprisingly Martin Bormann being present—who discussed questions of Hitler's health. Apparently there was disagreement over a diagnosis of Hitler's symptoms, but "an agreement on the use of certain medicines for Hitler."[412] Part of the general development in this context was also a curious conference of Himmler with the Minister of Finance Count Lutz Schwerin von Krosigk. Schellenberg appears to have been instrumental in arranging this encounter because he knew that Schwerin von Krosigk shared his views about the necessity of bringing the war to an end at the earliest possible moment.[413] Schellenberg himself stayed outside the room and later noted that Schwerin von Krosigk had indeed counseled Himmler to quickly end hostilities and take "control of the situation."[414]

Meanwhile what could be expected had occurred. The Allies bluntly refused to consider any negotiations with Himmler. Unconditional surrender across the board was the only way out. When Himmler and Schellenberg met shortly thereafter, it was evident that Himmler was very dismayed and extremely disappointed. He finally understood that he would not be accepted by the Allies and that he too, like his *Führer*, had reached the end of the road. For the moment, however, he seemed almost overwhelmed by fear that reports about his failed negotiation attempts might turn up in the international press. As one who had done more than anyone else to push Himmler into negotiations with the enemy, Schellenberg was keenly aware of the great danger to himself and his entire family. He "believed that he was now so discredited with Himmler that under certain circumstances he would even reckon with liquidation." Realizing that Himmler would be in a crisis and anticipating a grave personal conflict with his protector, Schellenberg had brought along the astrologer Wilhelm Wulff from Hamburg, who had been used before in difficult situations and was known to have the ability to calm Himmler, who apparently thought rather highly of him. Unbelievable as it may sound, Schellenberg's thinking was correct. Wulff was not only able to defuse the explosive mood Himmler seems to have been in, but he also succeeded in changing the emotional atmosphere of that nighttime encounter to such a degree that Schellen-

---

412. "Final Report," 173-175.
413. Johann Ludwig (Lutz) Count Schwerin von Krosigk (1887-1977), title "Count" by adoption 1925, studied Law, military service in World War I, 1920 to Ministry of Finance, made Finance Minister by Chancellor Franz von Papen 1932, stayed in office under Hitler until the end of Third Reich, Finance Minister and Foreign Minister under Dönitz, sentenced to ten years by Military Tribunal at Nuremberg, released 1951. Biographical Report, OSS, Confidential, Mission by Dewitt C. Poole, NA, General Records of the Department of State, RG 59, E 1082, Box 3.
414. For more detail "Final Report," 176.

berg was in a position to persuade him of the senselessness of continuing the war in the "Northern Sector," which would only achieve much useless destruction in Norway and Denmark, leaving a shameful mark on Germany's future reputation in the Scandinavian countries. Himmler withdrew to be alone and come to a decision. Apparently back on track and considering again his own role in Germany, he relented and at the crack of dawn on April 29 he agreed to authorize Schellenberg as *Sonderbevollmächtigter* (Special Envoy) to now negotiate the end of hostilities in Norway and to arrange for the German forces stationed there to be interned in Swedish camps until the end of the war. Himmler suddenly spoke again as if he expected to succeed Adolf Hitler.[415]

With large parts of the Third Reich already occupied by Allied troops, the final collapse of what remained seemed imminent. Unable to return to Berlin, with his *Amt* VI in various locations in Southern Germany or already dissolved and with his wife somewhere in Bavaria expecting another child, there was little left for Schellenberg but his ceaseless engagement, and it is difficult to escape the feeling that at this moment he knew no other way than a continued performance under high pressure. To complete this picture it might be well to recall that for some years he had been plagued by health problems which were constantly present but had not yet incapacitated him. Following the curious night sessions with Himmler and with the astrologer being around at least part of the time, Schellenberg did what he usually did. He drove off into the early morning to Apenrade just north of the Danish-German frontier and met with Count Bernadotte. The two men had come to trust each other, and we can therefore assume that Schellenberg well knew just how important a workable peaceful solution of the German occupation of Norway was to Bernadotte. Whether he was aware that solving that problem and preventing bloodshed in Norway, or Denmark for that matter, was a primary concern for the Swedish Government is quite another matter. Count Bernadotte certainly did know and because of his status and personality was in a position to act as a representative of the Swedish Government. As both of them knew, they were in complete agreement on most points and certainly felt that an end of hostilities had to be found immediately. Not surprisingly therefore Bernadotte, after conferring with Schellenberg, arranged a session for the next day at the Hotel d'Angleterre in Copenhagen. The Swedish request was clear: a German proposal for a solution to the strong military presence in Norway and Denmark. It was a friendly and congenial diplomatic event, held not in Nazi Germany but in German occupied Denmark and in fact organized by neutral Sweden.[416]

---

415. "Final Report," 188-189.
416. "Final Report," 189-190.

When the conference ended in the early afternoon, Schellenberg was once again back on the road, facing controls, delayed ferries and enormous time pressure. It was again in the early hours of the morning that he arrived in Plön. One of the first people he encountered in the small town, now crowded with officials and military, was SS-*Sturmbannführer* Dr. Giselher Wirsing, one of his men from *Amt* VI who in 1944 had produced the curious intelligence newsletters called the *Egmont Berichte* (Reports), carefully warning of possible defeat and available only to a very small number of top Nazis.[417] They had worked together on this and presumably trusted each other. Moreover, Schellenberg was quite certain that Wirsing shared his views about the urgency of ending the war. Wirsing at this point had just flown in from the now separated south of Germany, and he informed Schellenberg that the RSHA Chief Ernst Kaltenbrunner, who had never liked Schellenberg, had just stripped him of all positions and appointments. His two successors appointed by Kaltenbrunner were Wilhelm Waneck, like Kaltenbrunner an Austrian, for the political work, and Otto Skorzeny, another Austrian and like Waneck a man from Schellenberg's *Amt* VI, for Military Intelligence or *Amt Mil*. Skorzeny had handled mostly special forces assignments and sabotage, but his fame rested on the adventurous rescue of Benito Mussolini from the Abruzzi Mountains in 1943.[418] More upsetting must have been the news that Hitler had bypassed Himmler when he named a successor. The chief of Nazi Germany's last government was Grand Admiral Karl Dönitz, a passionate Nazi who greatly admired his *Führer*. Someone had informed Hitler of Himmler's capitulation offer passed on by the Swedes which meant that Himmler was now a criminal, guilty of high treason and to be punished accordingly. News from the bunker in Berlin, however, at this point in time had become more or less irrelevant. In fact, the *Führer* had ended his and Eva Braun's life on the afternoon of April 30. Rather more important for Schellenberg was a report from Rudolf Brandt that Dönitz had met with Himmler, without punishing the traitor as requested, and had appointed Schwerin von Krosigk as the new Foreign Minister. Himmler, he was told, was very insulted, because the rest of Germany's military leaders gathered around Dönitz had treated him like a traitor. When Schellenberg and Himmler then tried to confer with the Admiral, he indeed seemed to have no time for them. Following some more hurried jaunts between the Dönitz headquarters and the impatiently waiting Swedish representatives in Copenhagen, Schellenberg finally succeeded in seeing Germany's new Head of

---

417. The Egmont Reports had the support of Heinrich Himmler. Cf. SAINT London to SAINT Washington, "Amt VI of the RSHA, Gruppe VI A," October 29, 1945, NA, RG 226, E 109, Box 45.
418. The dramatic rescue of Benito Mussolini on Sunday, September 12, 1943, once and for all established Skorzeny's reputation as a flamboyant ruffian.

State, the Admiral, together with the Finance Minister and now also Foreign Minister Schwerin von Krosigk, and obtaining some instructions for his talks with the Swedes. It was a difficult and slow moving exchange but with the active support of Schwerin von Krosigk, it was decided to name Schellenberg an official emissary of the post-Hitler German Government and to give him the title of *Gesandter* (Minister). On May 4, 1945, Dönitz signed the respective document and Schellenberg was on his way to Denmark and Sweden—after taking leave from Heinrich Himmler.[419] Following a nerve-racking journey, repeatedly held up by aircraft attacks and other problems, Schellenberg arrived in Copenhagen. Driving in Count Bernadotte's Red Cross car, he first encountered bothersome German SS guards only to shortly thereafter be surrounded by masses of jubilating Danes celebrating the expected defeat and departure of the hated Germans. At the Swedish Legation where he drove for a meeting and dinner with Gustav von Dardel, the Swedish Minister to Denmark, crowds were singing the Danish and the Swedish national anthems. Schellenberg must have welcomed a few hours of quiet and rest planned at the Hotel d'Angleterre.[420]

On May 5, 1945, the SS-*Brigadeführer* Walter Schellenberg, now a Minister representing the curious Dönitz Government, climbed aboard the special flight to Stockholm arranged for him by Count Bernadotte.

---

419. The suicide of Heinrich Himmler, shortly after having been picked up by British Forces, has been questioned before. Most recently, the generally accepted British description of the suicide has been questioned again, this time based on documents held by the National Archives in Kew. This author was able to inspect the respective documents at NAK, and the National Archives have assured him officially in writing that these papers are considered to be forgeries. There has been a great amount of press coverage of this affair since 2005. On Karl Dönitz cf. Bodo Herzog, "Der Kriegsverbrecher Karl Dönitz: Legende und Wirklichkeit," *Jahrbuch des Instituts für Deutsche Geschichte*, vol. 15 (1986), 477-478, 483.
420. Sir Victor Mallet to Foreign Office, May 5, 1945, Top Secret, NAK, FO 371/47509. "Final Report," 197-198.

Walter Schellenberg, date uncertain.
(Courtesy of the National Archives, College Park, MD)

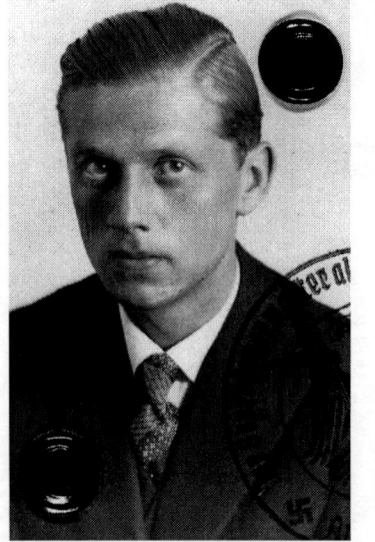

Walter Schellenberg 1933 Passport.
(National Archives, College Park, MD)

Walter Schellenberg 1934 Passport.
(National Archives, College Park, MD)

Walter Schellenberg 1937 Passport.
(National Archives, College Park, MD)

Walter Schellenberg 1938 Passport.
(National Archives, College Park, MD)

Schellenberg's office at Berkaer Strasse, Headquarters of RSHA SD *Amt* VI in Berlin.
(Private archive of Michael Foedrowitz)

Sigismund Payne Best.
(Courtesy of After the Battle, *London)*

Richard H. Stevens. *(Courtesy of* After the Battle, *London)*

Schellenberg is the second from the left. Probably in 1940.
(Private archive of Michael Foedrowitz)

Jean-Marie Musy.
(Private archive, Dr. Pierre Th. Braunschweig)

Benoît Musy.
(Private archive, Dr. Pierre Th. Braunschweig)

below
Brigadier Colonel Roger Masson, Chief of the Intelligence Service of the Swiss General Staff.
(Private archive, Dr. Pierre Th. Braunschweig)

Paul Meyer-Schwertenbach.
(Private archive, Dr. Pierre Th. Braunschweig)

Castel Wolfsberg meeting. *From the left:* Hans Wilhelm Eggen, Walter Schellenberg, Albert Wiesendanger, Patricia Meyer-Schwertenbach. *(Private archive, Dr. Pierre Th. Braunschweig)*

right
Walter Schellenberg probably during the war. *(United States Holocaust Memorial Museum Archives)*

Count Folke Bernadotte.
(Friedrich Reinhart AG, Basel)

Admiral Wilhelm Canaris,
Chief of the Abwehr.
(Enigma Archive)

Walter Schellenberg in either British or
American custody, after May 1945.
(National Archives, College Park, MD)

SS Chief Heinrich Himmler. *(Enigma Archive)*

Joachim von Ribbentrop, Nazi Germany's Foreign Minister. *(Enigma Archive)*

Reinhard Heydrich, Head of the RSHA and SD.
(Enigma Archive)

Walter Schellenberg at his wedding to Irene Grosse-Schönepauck, October 10, 1940. *(Enigma Archive)*

Allen W. Dulles code named Mr. Bull, OSS Representative in Bern, Switzerland in 1942-1945. *(Enigma Archive)*

Heinrich Müller, Head of the Gestapo. *(Enigma Archive)*

Ernst Kaltenbrunner, Head of the RSHA and SD, 1943-1945. *(Enigma Archive)*

Walter Schellenberg at the Nuremberg Trials.
(Courtesy of Der Spiegel, *Hamburg)*

Nazi SD and SS officers during the Nuremberg Trials *(from the left)*:
Alfred Naujocks, Viktor Zeichka, Wilhelm Höttl and Walter Schellenberg.
(Enigma Archive)

Chapter IV

Postlude to Hitler's Germany

When Walter Schellenberg, as usual in civilian attire but now a diplomat rather than a high-ranking SS officer, boarded a Swedish Red Cross flight at the Copenhagen airport on May 5, 1945, he could not really know just how long Nazi Germany might continue to exist. Because he passed away before some editors and publishers printed the first edition of what they called his memoirs, we are rather uncertain about what he did know and think in those very final days of the 12-year old German Thousand Year Reich. As most other educated Germans, he knew of the indescribable crimes committed and expecting some kind of punishment or retribution must have been part of his mental frame at the time. Also, even in the absence of completed memoirs, his activities during those final weeks allow us to come to certain conclusions. Schellenberg appears to have been fully aware of Germany's total military and political defeat. Moreover, he knew that his departure to neutral Sweden would take him away from further destruction and the uncertainties of final unconditional surrender and that such an exit from the stage would be available to only very few high-ranking Nazi officials. It is therefore unlikely that he thought he would actually fly back and report in person to Adolf Hitler's successor Admiral Karl Dönitz on the results of his negotiations for the surrender of the still considerable German forces stationed in the "Northern Sector," specifically in Norway.

On the more personal side, one might be inclined to wonder what Schellenberg knew of the whereabouts and fate of his wife and children whom he evidently had not seen for quite some time. From the few documents referring to his family, it seems possible that earlier in 1945 Schellenberg had succeeded in sending them south, probably in connection with the shipping out of some departments of *Amt* VI and of a good amount of the *Amt* VI records. That way the family's move would have been less noticed and therefore less quickly denounced as treason. If this is true, his family for a short while may have been at or near Castle Lauenstein near Probstzella. At least temporarily near Castle Lauenstein at a place called Wiburg, *Amt* VI Foreign Intelligence had set up camp under the cover designation of "Seedorf" (lake village), the *S* and the *d* referring to the SD (*Sicherheitsdienst*). With Allied Forces closing in rapidly from east and west, the *Amt* VI departments at Lauenstein apparently decided to move on to Marquartstein much farther south in Bavaria.[421] Some time in March 1945 SS-*Standartenführer* Dr. Martin Sandberger, at that stage responsible for much of the administration of *Amt* VI, checked on various of the strewn about staff groups and ran into Schellenberg who was visiting his family at Hechingen, south of Stuttgart, and attending to intelligence matters in Stuttgart. When interrogated in London and Camp 020, Schellenberg said that his family was at Marquartstein and that SS-*Sturmbannführer* Hans Wilhelm Eggen was there to keep an eye on them. When the Americans searched for Schellenberg's wife, they found her "in good health and expecting baby mid August," but "investigation at Marquartstein did not yield any traces Amt 6 Mil Amt Personnel."[422] On his flight to Sweden Schellenberg therefore assumed that Eggen was watching out for his family at Marquartstein.

Also on the personal side there remain many open questions regarding the state of health of this totally overworked functionary who for years had suffered from recurring gall bladder and liver problems and for some time now had spent even his nights sitting in tense meetings concerned with intelligence lines and the rescue of concentration camp inmates or driving from place to place under life threatening conditions. There are no indications that Schellenberg could or ever wanted to step out of the menacing daily routine to recuperate mentally or psychologically, for instance by reading something other than documents. His pleasant horseback riding with Canaris in the Grunewald

---

421. Some sections of *Amt* VI in April 1945 moved from Lauenstein to Rottach-Egern at the Tegernsee. Final Interrogation Report of Eugen Steimle alias Dr. Hermann Bulach, December 12, 1945, Secret, NAK, KV 2/966. SHAEF Report, June 29, 1945, Secret, NA, RG 226, E 119A, Box 26.
422. 12th Army Group to War Room London for Hampshire, July 20, 1945, Secret; J. J. Ferguson to Col. Stephens, Camp 020, July 23, 1945; both NAK, KV 2/96.

must have seemed years away.[423] His memoirs offer few hints about the *Mensch* Schellenberg away from desk and intelligence operations, and what we surmise about his personal characteristics is largely derived from official documents or hearsay passed on by those around him. All we really have on the personal side is a few private letters and some legal documents, as well as correspondence from his divorce proceedings that accidentally ended up in archival holdings. Otherwise, there is almost nothing to reveal the individual who at this moment was being welcomed in Sweden by the intelligent, well-educated and certainly internationally versed Count Bernadotte. Moreover, the number of rather cultured and influential personalities, who had made his closer acquaintance and relied on him for various types of assistance during the war years, would suggest the existence of another Schellenberg not evident on first glimpse in the voluminous official records.

One of the visible consequences of this dearth of personal information would appear to be the somewhat rash conclusions passed on by historians and other authors regarding Schellenberg's character and motivations. In the absence of sufficient evidence it has, for instance, been asserted that Schellenberg in his political and intelligence negotiations, as well as in his rescue operations, was driven by a desire to take out insurance, so to speak, for his personal well being in the time after the demise of Adolf Hitler and the end of the war. From what we know it seems justified to conclude that Schellenberg in no way shared the fatalistic outlook of many of his ideologically blinded colleagues, but that precisely for that reason at times he may well have thought about his life in an unclear future. In addition, it might be helpful to recall that this still very young man had already had a number of close brushes with death and, in fact, had known ever since taking over *Amt* VI that each new day might also turn out to be his last, if his enemies, such as Heinrich Müller or Ernst Kaltenbrunner, would have things their way. Keeping this in mind could be of some assistance when trying to understand Schellenberg.

Whatever mental or physical state Schellenberg may have been in when, following a change from the Red Cross flight to a Swedish military plane at Malmö, he landed at Stockholm's Bromma Airport, there was no break in the hectic schedule set out by the Swedish Government. Indeed, the Swedish Foreign Office at 3:50 a.m. had already notified the Allied ministers in Stockholm "that General Schellenberg is due Stockholm 10 hours today with

---

423. There are no references to writers or poets in his records, with the exception of a short list of book titles, then typically owned and possibly read by German middle class families, found in the divorce papers.

full power from Doenitz to arrange surrender to Swedes of troops in Norway."[424]

At Bromma Airport Schellenberg was met by the Swedish Foreign Office official Ostroem and taken straight to the private home of Count Bernadotte for a conference attended by Secretary of State Erik Boheman, the Head of the Political Division of the Foreign Office Eric von Post and Count Bernadotte.[425] To be diplomatically correct, Schellenberg formally presented his diplomatic credentials from the new Nazi government of Karl Dönitz. The authority given him by Dönitz in no uncertain terms concerned negotiations for the surrender of the German occupation troops stationed in Norway: "This is to authorize Walter Schellenberg to carry on negotiations with the Royal Swedish Government in the name of the German Reich Government on all questions that could result from the abandonment of the occupation of Norway by the German Armed Forces in the German-Swedish relations. At the same time, I authorize him to conclude agreements, subject to ratification where necessary on the basis of the present law. Headquarters, May 4, 1945."[426]

According to the memoirs of Count Bernadotte, at this meeting Schellenberg also "stated that the new German Minister for Foreign Affairs, Count Schwerin von Krosigk, had asked him to endeavour to arrange a meeting with General Eisenhower for the discussion of a general German surrender." Whether this additional mandate was something the new German Foreign Minister and Schellenberg had agreed on orally the day before at Dönitz's headquarters or whether this is one of the "special tasks" mentioned by Schwerin von Krosigk in his respective message to the German Minister in Stockholm, Dr. Hans Thomsen, cannot be resolved in retrospect, but under the circumstances such a request from Minister Schellenberg for an encounter with the Allied General was of little consequence. Not only had the Dönitz government by this time begun direct negotiations in the West, but also these contacts had developed so quickly that individual talks with a single emissary, such as Schellenberg, seemed quite unnecessary. Moreover, the Swedes, being correct, had notified Allied representatives in Stockholm about ongoing

---

424. Sir Victor Mallet to Foreign Office London, May 5, 1945, Top Secret, NAK, FO 371/47509. For background to the surrender of German troops in Norway cf. Peter Thorne, "Andrew Thorne and the Liberation of Norway," *Intelligence and National Security*, vol. 7, no. 3 (1992).
425. Count Folke Bernadotte in his memoirs *The Fall of the Curtain: Last Days of the Third Reich* (London: Cassell, 1945; 1st Swedish ed. 1945), 66, recalls that at this first meeting in his home only von Post, Schellenberg and he were present.
426. The document is signed by Dönitz. Department of the Army, U.S. Army Military History Institute, Carlisle Barracks, Carlisle, PA (USAMHI), William J. Donovan Papers, Box 87B.

developments, thereby practically defeating this attempt—if one can call it that—to surrender in the West only.[427]

As might have been expected, preparations for the surrender of German Armed Forces in Norway turned out to be more complicated. Like many Germans, the German commanders in that occupied nation were unwilling to accept defeat, and there remained the ominous threat that they would actually refuse an orderly surrender and, obeying their dead *Führer's* orders, continue to fight even Allied landing forces. Schellenberg, in line with his own concept of a quick surrender, however, continued to push the issue and asked the Swedes to have the German Minister, Hans Thomsen, sent to the Swedish-Norwegian border to motivate General Franz Böhme, Commanding Officer of German Forces in Norway, to consider laying down arms and allowing his troops to be interned in neutral Sweden. Already early the next morning, on May 6, 1945, Thomsen was taken in a Swedish military plane to the Norwegian border where, thus clearly indicating his disagreement, General Böhme was not to be seen. Instead Thomsen was met by a chief of staff who had been instructed by General Böhme to leave no doubt with this diplomatic peace emissary that German troops in Norway were in the best condition, "fresh, strongly entrenched and sufficient in number to hold out for nine months." General Böhme obviously had no intention to consider any kind of surrender other than ordered by Adolf Hitler or his successor. Incidentally, Hitler's successor, Admiral Dönitz, did not trust the Swedes and therefore was against such surrender of Böhme's army. Thomsen correctly saw no chances of getting anywhere and before flying back to Stockholm called his Legation to have Schellenberg informed about the obstinate soldier.[428] This led to another urgent conference attended by Schellenberg, the Swedish Minister to Berlin Arvid Richert, von Post and Count Bernadotte. Under the enormous time pressure caused by the evident collapse of Nazi Germany and with the Swedes wanting to have all German troops in Scandinavia surrender as quickly as possible to avoid military confrontation and unnecessary bloodshed, the deliberations were grave and tense. In the end it was agreed to seek a telephone connection to Dönitz himself and persuade the Admiral to inform the German Military Command in Norway that Schellenberg was fully authorized to negotiate their surrender. With some difficulty a telephone connection was finally made, but it was technically so deficient that a conversation with the

---

427. Bernadotte, *The Fall of the Curtain*, 66. Copy for Information for Minister Walter Schellenberg, Reich Minister of Foreign Affairs von Krosigk to German Minister in Stockholm Dr. Hans Thomsen, May 4, 1945, USAMHI, William J. Donovan Papers, Box 87B.
428. Interrogation of Hans Thomsen, DeWitt C. Poole Mission (State Department), October 10, 1945, NA, RG 59, E 1082, Box 4. Karl Doenitz, *Memoirs: Ten Years and Twenty Days* (New York: Da Capo, 1997; 1st 1990), 456.

Admiral proved to be impossible. From the records it would appear that a new attempt was made early the next morning on May 7, 1945, and Schellenberg was able to speak to the Foreign Minister who broke the very latest news to him, namely that total capitulation had been signed during the night. The German Reich was no more. The former SS-*Brigadeführer* and presently Minister had become a civilian guest of Count Bernadotte.[429]

Bernadotte's almost private guest was in the somewhat unusual situation of being to all appearances a free man, but at the same time being watched closely by an intrusive international press which registered his presence and not unreasonably wondered why this former ranking SS-officer was not a POW. Professionally, of course, Schellenberg had never sought unnecessary publicity and, unable to simply disappear in Stockholm, it is reported that he made a point of always changing his hats and sunglasses when it was unavoidable to go out.[430]

Moreover, it did not take the press very long to discover that the strange visitor had not come alone. Indeed Schellenberg's driver, Hugo Buchwald on May 1 or May 2 had received orders to drive to Sweden.[431] Literally at the last moment he had left the German capital, almost totally surrounded by Soviet forces, with Schellenberg's two secretaries Marie-Louise Schienke and Christl Erdmann, heading out northwest in the direction of Lübeck by way of Felix Kersten's estate Hartzwalde.[432] Hoping to avoid dangerous attacks from low flying aircraft, they had driven through the night. When they reached Lübeck, Buchwald was ordered to drive to Hamburg to find the astrologer Wilhelm Wulff and take him to meet with Himmler. Not surprising, under the totally chaotic conditions in the very small region still remaining of Nazi Germany, Himmler never turned up, and Wulff very impatiently demanded to be taken back to Hamburg which without destructive fighting would be surrendered to British forces in the afternoon of May 3, 1945. Buchwald later recalled that during the ride Wulff told him that already two years ago he had advised Himmler to stop the war for the simple reason that the Germans were unable to win. From Hamburg Buchwald drove to Flensburg, the seat of what called itself the Dönitz government. The small town was packed with military and Nazi brass. His next orders came already on May 4, instructing him to drive to

---

429. Bernadotte, *The Fall of the Curtain*, 67-68. "Final Report," 198-199.
430. Cf. "Schellenberg Reaches Sweden," *New York Times*, June 6, 1945: "It is expected that the Allies will, in due course, make demands for his extradition as a war criminal."
431. The following description of the journey to Copenhagen is largely based on his testimony. Interrogation of Hugo Buchwald, May 24, 1948, German text, SAN, Rep. 502, B 186.
432. We don't know whether Buchwald picked up papers or baggage there that had been taken out of bomb-torn Berlin earlier or whether they fetched Schienke's sister to safety who had been secretary to Felix Kersten at Hartzwalde.

Sweden. Buchwald, according to later testimony, spent the next hours packing suitcases and "the documents of Miss Schienke." From the number of passengers and the amount of luggage expected, one would conclude that they left in more than one automobile or indeed a larger vehicle. When they finally headed out of Flensburg, besides Buchwald and the two secretaries with their baggage, the group included Franz Göring and the SS-*Obersturmbannführer* Dr. Heinz Rennau with wife and daughter. Miss Schienke was Schellenberg's personal secretary who had worked for him since June 1, 1941, which would suggest that he may have brought her with him from *Amt* IV. She was "secretly engaged" to Franz Göring, who also came from *Amt* IV. Christl Erdmann functioned as a kind of assistant to Schienke.[433] Franz Göring was the man Schellenberg had completely relied on for the actual day-to-day dangerous efforts of extracting inmates from the concentration camps, including the most uncommon visits to such camps by a foreign rescuer like Benoit Musy. The records indicate that Göring was not one for theatrical performances but instead attended to the risky rescue assignments from Schellenberg with extraordinary loyalty and diligence. Schellenberg evidently had chosen a very good man for this type of work, and it appears that they trusted each other. Heinz Rennau had been a member of *Amt* IV Gestapo until the very end, and in fact seems to have been a personal adjutant to the Gestapo Chief Heinrich Müller. Indications are that Count Bernadotte had asked Schellenberg to get Müller to name a Gestapo officer to assist in the far-flung rescue operations they had planned. Conceivably Müller could have appointed this adjutant of his to report to him on the much resented Schellenberg and his, for the Gestapo, unacceptable rescue efforts. Whatever Rennau may have reported to the Gestapo Chief, his cooperation with the Swedish officers in the difficult Red Cross operations apparently had been so helpful that Count Bernadotte had arranged for the Rennau family to be allowed into Sweden.[434] Buchwald, of course, had driven Schellenberg almost daily, and they had come to know each other very well, to say the least. The daily closeness at work had brought about mutual trust and loyalty. Until their entry into Denmark all seems to have gone smoothly. At that point, however, the official German car was stopped and difficulties were created by uncontrolled "freedom fighters." Marie-Louise Schienke had to use all her skills in telephoning to what was left in Copenhagen

---

433. In various documents Schienke is called Schinke, and her first name is given as Marielouise or Maria Luise. Erdmann came to *Amt* VI in 1940 and worked for Schellenberg since 1942.
434. SS-*Obersturmbannführer* Dr. Heinrich F. (Heinz) Rennau (often called Renau), "Persönlicher Referent" (a personal adjutant) to SS-*Gruppenführer* Heinrich Müller, Chief of *Amt* IV. Situation Report No. 4, Amt VI of the RSHA, December 7, 1945, NA, RG 319, IRR, IS, Box 8. Interrogation of Christl Erdmann by Mr. Barr, April 1948, SAN, Rep. 502, E 41. Interrogations of Schellenberg also suggest that Kaltenbrunner appointed Rennau. Interrogation, September 3, 1945, NA, RG 226, E 119A, Box 26.

of a German administration after the Danes had already begun to set up their own provisional government. Much time was lost until they were finally allowed to pass and move on to Copenhagen, where they arrived past midnight, presumably now May 6, for they were told that Schellenberg had already flown on to Stockholm. Papers enabling them to continue their journey to Sweden were ready for all but the driver who was left with no choice but to hand the car keys to Franz Göring and stay at the German Legation in Copenhagen—to become a POW for the next two years.

The rest of the group apparently made it to the Swedish capital, including Schienke and the papers she was carrying with her. As the departure from embattled Berlin had been predictable for some time, and Schellenberg, fully occupied with the hectic negotiations with Heinrich Himmler and Count Bernadotte, had not been there for a few days, Schienke not only had had sufficient time to select and pack certain Schellenberg documents, but she had also put aside for the journey considerable amounts in cash. In both cases it may be assumed that she acted on instructions from Schellenberg. Documents released in Washington more recently show that Allied intelligence took considerable interest in both the papers and the money and, as is common in such cases, there has been much sensationalist speculation on the nature of these papers and the amount of money brought to Stockholm. From the records it is unclear to what extent American and British intelligence may have acquired papers of Schellenberg in Stockholm.[435]

Nazi Germany having capitulated, Count Bernadotte and Schellenberg were now able to slow down and turn to other matters. They could freely exchange views on the ethical, as well as the military and political demise of the German Reich, and because there are no minutes or other records, we are obliged to check the evidence left to us by the two participants in this rather personal encounter very closely. The Swedish aristocrat of very high social standing and with excellent connections in numerous countries was facing the former German SS officer from a middle class background who was respected by a number of influential foreigners but to a greater number of people was a defeated and not very respectable enemy. To all indications they knew each other well enough to acknowledge each other's viewpoint. In fact, Count Bernadotte thought Schellenberg's story, as he heard it in the course of their

---

435. Paehler's conclusion ("Espionage, Ideology and Personal Politics," 465) that Schellenberg and his staff came to Stockholm together at the same time in view of the documentary situation is therefore incorrect. For details of journey to Stockholm, Interrogations of Hugo Buchwald, May 24, 1945, SAN, Rep. 502, B 186. According to Preliminary Interrogation Report, Heinrich F. Rennau, November 27, 1945, Secret, NAK, KV 3/109, Rennau was "in Stockholm and environs" from May 7 to August 18, 1945, suggesting that the group arrived in Stockholm on May 7. For documents and currency see comments below.

conversations, should be told. The result was an inclusion of what Schellenberg told him in Bernadotte's memoirs *The Fall of the Curtain*, published immediately after their exchanges. In Bernadotte's view "his [Schellenberg's] account, for the accuracy of which he himself must be responsible, appeared to me, from the point of view of history, and as supplementing my own impressions, to be of so great an interest that the main points should be given publicity."[436] This clearly refers to that part of Bernadotte's publication which is entitled "Schellenberg's Story" and was written as a report of what Walter Schellenberg told him in the course of their conversations about the events and developments in which they had participated during recent weeks. Though Bernadotte could not have been clearer in form and content—here Schellenberg tells his view of events and Bernadotte passes this on to the reader—this has not deterred some authors from charging that Schellenberg in fact wrote Bernadotte's book. Usually such claims are embedded in allegations that Bernadotte had not given deserved credit for the rescue operations to Felix Kersten. Regrettably this battle over who is to be credited with how much of the great rescue operations has led to curious excesses of occasionally less than scholarly argumentation. Thus, while the respected British historian and former member of British intelligence Hugh Trevor-Roper right after Schellenberg's death in Italy and following the murder of Bernadotte in Jerusalem informed a broad international audience that "of Count Bernadotte's activities in these negotiations little need be said, for he was an agent—'a transport officer, no more'—," Raymond Palmer bluntly tells us that Bernadotte's memoirs were "ghost-written by Schellenberg."[437] Expressing himself more reservedly, Louis de Jong from The Netherlands discusses a manuscript published under the name of Count Bernadotte which in fact "came about in large part from the pen of Walter Schellenberg, the former Chief of Amt VI (Foreign Intelligence) of the RSHA, who had found refuge in the home of Bernadotte in Stockholm."[438] In view of such heated accusations, all of them without naming any sources of information, it might be of some

---

436 Bernadotte, *The Fall of the Curtain*, 72.
437. H. R. Trevor-Roper, "Kersten, Himmler, and Count Bernadotte," *The Atlantic Monthly*, vol. 191, no. 2 (February, 1953), 44. Cf. H. R. Trevor-Roper, "Introduction," to Felix Kersten, *The Kersten Memoirs 1940–1945* (New York: Macmillan, 1957), 14-15: "... the facts, amply documented, are clear. They show that he [Count Bernadotte] first sought to fill a larger *rôle* than had been assigned to him, and that afterwards, in a foolish attempt to monopolize the glory of the achievement, he allowed himself to claim a position which could only be defended by unfortunate exhibitionism and unfair persecution ... But for the self-glorifying myth which he manufactured, it is unlikely that he would ever have been chosen as U.N. mediator in the Arab-Jewish war of 1948, or fallen in Palestine a premature victim of the assassin's bullet." Palmer, "Felix Kersten and Count Bernadotte: A Question of Rescue," 46.
438. Louis de Jong, "Hat Felix Kersten das niederländische Volk gerettet?," in Hans Rothfels and Theodor Eschenburg, eds., *Zwei Legenden aus dem Dritten Reich* (Stuttgart: Deutsche Verlags-Anstalt, 1974; 1st Dutch ed. 1972), 138.

interest to take a closer look at the time Walter Schellenberg actually spent in Stockholm. We know that he arrived there by military plane on May 5 and that the following days, until the official capitulation of Germany pronounced by the Nazi government of Grand Admiral Karl Dönitz on May 7, were spent in difficult meetings in Stockholm with Swedish and German officials. Their purpose was to get the German military forces in the "Northern Sector" to agree to surrender and to the internment in neutral Sweden of the German troops stationed in Norway. In addition, Schellenberg continued to push for a total surrender of all German forces in the West including his own readiness to meet with General Eisenhower. For the neutral Swedes, who were feeling closer to the Western Allies than to the Germans, it was mostly about a quick end of all hostilities in Scandinavia and the avoidance of any military incursions into Sweden. From the records we know that Schellenberg had his final telephone conversation with the German Foreign Minister Count Schwerin von Krosigk on May 9. From the scattered bits of information it is evident that Schellenberg was a guest at the Bernadotte home during the first days of his stay in Stockholm. After that Schellenberg, while continuing to meet with Swedes and Americans at the Bernadottes, apparently was moved to a small private hotel in the village of Trosa, a short ways south of the capital in the country. Also at Trosa were the secretaries Schienke and Erdmann, Franz Göring and the Rennau family who had not stayed with him at the Bernadottes. Though we have no exact arrival date for Schellenberg in Trosa, it would seem reasonable to assume to have been some time around May 15. Since he was taken from Stockholm to Frankfurt, Germany, on June 17, he would have stayed at Trosa for about four weeks during which, however, a good number of days were spent traveling to Stockholm for meetings and conferences with men like Brandin and Möller, Swedish diplomats and politicians, undoubtedly a few Americans, and possibly a few British, though the records contain no hints concerning the latter. Besides these other activities it was during those four weeks that Schellenberg, most likely with the assistance of Marie-Louise Schienke, produced what later became known as his "Autobiography." Looking at that text, it would appear rather unlikely that Schellenberg could have written Count Bernadotte's book alongside or somehow in between. That Bernadotte had encouraged Schellenberg to write down his experiences, among other things as a kind of counterpart to his own memoirs, and that the two men, who knew each other well by now, may have frequently discussed events and appraisals of people, would be a very natural procedure and in no way suggests that one of them would have written all or parts of the other's text.

Quite in contrast to the later published memoirs, no one has doubted that Schellenberg wrote the short "Autobiography" himself.[439] Specialists have known for some time that this document existed, but, as has been the case with most other records relating to Walter Schellenberg, authors have generally overlooked it.[440] A notable exception to this apparent lack of interest has been the publication of a Russian translation of the document with comments by Sergei A. Kondrashev, a Russian intelligence officer who reports that Russian intelligence in Stockholm was able to procure a copy soon after Schellenberg finished writing and that both Joseph Stalin and Vyacheslav Molotov were given a translation in October 1945. As recently as 2000, the well-known historian of the SS, George C. Browder, refers to this Russian publication as a source "for peace feelers," apparently unaware of the nature and background of the so-called "Trosa Memorandum." The disinterest of historians seems all the more perplexing since we know that copies of this "Autobiography" were much sought after in 1945 and consequently a considerable number of photographic reproductions were made. Indeed Soviet interest, according to Kondrashev, was so strong that they tried to get Schellenberg for interrogations. That they did not succeed was a consequence of the refusal of their Western Allies to cooperate.[441] Schellenberg himself, in the course of his interrogations by British intelligence officers in the summer of 1945, recalled that he "dictated" the text of the "short biographical summary," presumably to Marie-Louise Schienke, and that copies were given to Count Bernadotte, the Swedish Foreign Minister Christian Günther and Hillel Storch of the World Jewish Congress. Two copies he packed and carried with him to Frankfurt, though they may have been taken from him there or elsewhere in Germany following his imprisonment in Frankfurt.[442] When questioned later in London, Schellenberg certainly was not aware how many copies of his document were floating around, and British intelligence, of course, had no interest in commenting the

---

439. See commented English version of complete "Autobiography" in this volume.
440. The existence of the "Autobiography" has been known for decades because already in "Final Report," 201, Schellenberg responded in some detail to respective questions of his British intelligence interrogators. "Final Report" has been available at NA since the 1980s.
441. Russian translation of so-called "Trosa Memorandum" with comments by Sergei A. Kondrashev in *Otecestvennye Archivy* (*National Archives* or *Patriotic Archives*), nos. 2 (pp. 58–78) and 3 (pp. 79–96) (1997). Sergei Kondrashev to Swedish National Archives, October 6, 1998, private holding. George C. Browder, "Walter Schellenberg: Eine Geheimdienst-Phantasie," in R. Smelser/E. Syring, eds., *Die SS: Die Elite unter dem Totenkopf* (Paderborn: Schöningh, 2000), 430.
442. R. D. Scott Fox to R. A. Clyde, B.W.C.E., August 16, 1945, NAK, FO 371/46749. Clutton to G. W. Harrison, June 22, 1945, Top Secret, NAK, FO 188/487. J. J. Ferguson to Section V.F., October 8, 1945, NAK, KV 2/98. SAINT London to SAINT Washington, October 20, 1945, NA, RG 263, E ZZ-16, Box 45. British Legation Stockholm to Anthony Eden, June 22, 1945, Top Secret, NAK, FO 371/46749. Schellenberg to "Prison-Command," n.d., in Charles Hamilton, *Leaders & Personalities of the Third Reich*, vol. 2 (San Jose: R. James Bender, 1996), 65, asking for manuscript that was in his luggage but had disappeared. Origin of letter could not be established, because, according to publisher's letter to me, author has passed away.

matter. From the records declassified in recent years, we know that the British Foreign Office was mailed a copy only days after Schellenberg left Stockholm in June 1945. That fall OSS representatives in Germany, Sweden, the U.S., Switzerland and Austria also had copies. Again from the records, it is evident that the British Legation in Stockholm obtained a copy from the World Jewish Congress even before it was translated. That copy and copies of it could later easily be identified because Hillel Storch had asked Schellenberg to initial each page of his copy, which Schellenberg had done at the bottom right of the pages.[443]

Of considerable historical interest is the report Schellenberg asked Franz Göring to write about his part in the rescue operations of early 1945. Here too one encounters curious reactions from the apparently few readers who have taken a closer look at this document. It has, for instance, simply been assumed that Göring did not write his own memoirs but instead merely penned down what his chief told him. We have no way of knowing what, if anything, Schellenberg may have suggested to write, but it might be useful to recall that Schellenberg was not himself present during the rescue operations at the concentration camps Theresienstadt and Buchenwald. In both cases Göring acted under orders from Schellenberg, but he was accompanied, as described earlier, by the young Swiss emissary Benoit Musy, who acted in the name of his father Jean-Marie Musy. Therefore, it does not make too much sense to infer that Schellenberg instructed Göring what to write about his experiences. Technically, of course, it would have been possible for Schellenberg to even write large parts of Göring's report, but, as pointed out, it would not have made very much sense.[444] Considering the kind of human misery and brutality Franz Göring must have observed during these last weeks of the Third Reich, his report is written in descriptive terms largely bare of any emotional comment. The names and figures presented would suggest that Göring and Schellenberg were able to discuss the various rescue activities and people involved. Names, dates and other details may have been corrected. Otherwise this document appears to be what it is declared to be, namely a rather exacting report by a police officer schooled and trained as such and normally not called upon to offer his personal views. His training and general demeanor were common qualifications for intelligence service functionaries which incidentally is what

---

443. One of these German texts with Schellenberg's initial on each page can be seen in NAK, FO 371/46749. In the finding aids of the German IFZ, ED 90/7, the user is still informed that this document is an "addition to the chronological diary notes (memoirs)." This has to be an error because there is no evidence so far that Schellenberg wrote biographical notes or memoirs before the end of World War II. Aside from other reasons, writing a diary of this nature would have cost him his life had he been denounced.
444. A copy of Göring's German text, entitled "Anlage," with his intial at bottom right of each page is located in NAK, FO 371/46749.

Franz Göring became again following World War II, apparently staying in touch with American intelligence and becoming an employee of the West German *Bundesnachrichtendienst* (BND).[445] Of the many important personalities Schellenberg encountered in Stockholm, Norbert Masur and Hillel Storch of the World Jewish Congress may have had a particular influence on the still young German SS leader who in his function and through his position had supported the programmed mass murder of Jews and others in Germany. While Schellenberg had personally met Masur shortly before during the tense deliberations with Himmler, he had only heard of Storch and the activities of the World Jewish Congress which he represented. As Kersten and Storch were well acquainted, one might assume that it was Felix Kersten who now introduced them when Schellenberg was in Stockholm and in need of treatment by the masseur. Storch was a most inquisitive man, and the records suggest that extensive discussions must have taken place, even leading to an exchange in writing of questions and replies, reaching a high point on June 9, 1945, when Schellenberg sent him a copy of his "Autobiography."[446]

In the historical context and certainly when considering the consequences of their encounters, except for Count Bernadotte, decidedly the most important conversation partner of Schellenberg in Stockholm was the Assistant Military Attaché at the U.S. Legation, Colonel Charles E. Rayens, who back in 1943 had made the acquaintance of Alvar Möller who had told him of his struggle to free the seven Swedish managers, some of whom had been sentenced to death by the Germans. Möller in turn had established a very pleasant relationship with Schellenberg and several times had offered that he leave Germany and come to Sweden or at least try to somehow move his family there. Not surprising, Möller had passed on to Rayens his own very positive impression of Schellenberg as "a young SS General ... having the courage to speak his mind." When Count Bernadotte became actively involved in the rescue operations in Germany, he too was in touch with Colonel Rayens who closely followed the difficult dealings with the Germans. After Schellenberg's arrival in Stockholm on May 5, 1945, Rayens quickly found out that this curious visitor, looking like a diplomat, was in fact the German who had made both rescue operations possible. Rayens, the Military Attaché, of course realized the advantages of the situation and decided that it might be of considerable interest to question Schellenberg on the Japanese, still very much at

---

445. Sanitized document, "Upswing Security," May 2, 1959, Classified Message, Secret, NA, RG 263, E ZZ-18 (CIA Name Files, 2nd Release), Box 43.
446. Storch-Schellenberg correspondence in June 1945, USAMHI, William J. Donovan Papers, Box 87B. NAK, KV 2/98.

war with the United States. Alvar Möller was able to arrange a meeting and, it turned out, that Schellenberg was ready to answer any questions "but that he asked for no special considerations, that he was answerable for himself, and that anything he might do to help the Allies would be done by him not for favour but for the good of Germany and its people." Their first meeting was at the home of Count Bernadotte on May 27, 1945, and the exchange was so rewarding that the American Military Attaché had Schellenberg over to his own house the next day for another session. Col. Rayens just two days later reported to Assistant Chief of Staff, Major General Clayton Bissell, in considerable detail. What was said corresponded largely with what we know since then from other sources. A notable exception would be Schellenberg's view that "Himmler disposed of Hitler" with an injection. Such a version of Hitler's death is found in other records but has not been substantiated. The background of Schellenberg's knowledge would be the discussions in Berlin, for instance with the Charité professor de Crinis and other doctors, on the subject of eliminating Hitler before Germany's total defeat. Of greater interest is Schellenberg's report about attempts to strive for a reconciliation agreement between Japan, the Soviet Union and Hitler's Germany. As pointed out earlier, there were indeed Japanese moves in that direction, and certain Nazi leaders may have strongly considered them. Schellenberg, in sharp contrast to this influential group, always sought lines to the West and never seriously supported any eastward ventures.[447]

Significantly, Rayens concluded from this that if what Schellenberg said was true, and it should be possible to verify that easily enough, then he should voluntarily offer to go to Supreme Headquarters, Allied Expeditionary Forces (SHAEF). Apparently Schellenberg was more than willing to do that, and it was suggested that Count Bernadotte would accompany him to SHAEF. An interesting aside to this would be Rayens' notification to his superiors in the General Staff that "no other legation in Stockholm has been informed on these arrangements." In view of later developments in this matter one might indeed wonder whether it was quite intentional that the British Legation was not informed. Nevertheless and not entirely surprising, the records do show that British intelligence must have heard the news rather quickly, even before the Americans had Schellenberg flown out of Stockholm. Possibly quite inadvertently Count Bernadotte stirred British interest when he contacted the British Military Attaché in Stockholm in connection with flight arrangements. All in all, the scanty records contain some strong hints that some Americans

---

447. Colonel Chas. E. Rayens to Major General Clayton Bissell (G-2), May 30, 1945, NA, RG 226, E 119A, Box 26. The English spelling in this American document catches the eye, but it could be caused by a Swedish secretary in the U.S. Legation.

were more than interested in getting hold of Schellenberg, but there are also indications that the British, almost by coincidence or because American intelligence in the end was not that interested, obtained the German Foreign Intelligence Chief instead. Even before he was taken to Oberursel, a largely American interrogation center near Frankfurt, there was correspondence regarding the further handling of this case, containing the surprising comment: "Propose dispatching him to the UK, if agreement of appropriate authorities is obtained, in order that he may be dealt with as special case, not 020. Probably by U 35 if latter is available." Of course, 020 was the well-known British interrogation camp for Nazi prisoners, and U 35, it should be added, was Klop Ustinov, a British intelligence officer considered by his superiors to be a particularly successful interrogator.[448]

On June 17, 1945, Schellenberg was taken to Frankfurt on a U.S. military flight accompanied by Colonel Rayens and Count Bernadotte After being registered at SHAEF Forward Headquarters[449] he was not, as would have been routine procedure, transported to Camp Ashcan in Luxembourg or Camp Dustbin near Frankfurt. Ashcan was the designation given to a large hotel at Mondorf Les Bains, then used as a "detention center ... surrounded by two rows of barbed wire with machine gun posts at each corner." Had Schellenberg been deposited at Ashcan, the colorful crowd of fellow inmates would have included such leading Nazis as Hermann Göring, Wilhelm Keitel, Karl Dönitz, Alfred Jodl, Count Johann Ludwig Schwerin von Krosigk, Albert Speer, and Franz von Papen.[450] Dustbin, located at Kransberg Castle in the Taunus region, was quite different. Here Germany's financial, industrial and technical elite was collected and had Schellenberg, as found desirable by some Allied representatives, been sent there he would have encountered such leading figures of the Third Reich economic system as Ferdinand Porsche, Wernher von Braun, Hjalmar Schacht and other brass from such enterprises as Krupp, Thyssen or I. G. Farben. Ironically Albert Speer, who eventually also ended up here, had personally supervised the renovation of the castle in 1939 for Hermann Göring.[451]

---

448. "HP" from D.S.O. Hut 3 to Section V, June 9, 1945, Secret, NAK, KV 2/94. Air Attaché to Air Ministry, secret message from Sir Victor Mallet to Air Marshal Tedder, June 5, 1945, NAK, FO 188/487.
449. Walter Schellenberg, 3408, XE 001752, I6A044, released to me by Freedom of Information/Privacy Office, Department of the Army, Fort George G. Meade, MD.
450. Memorandum by J. D. Beam, June (?) 1945, following visit to Ashcan with Cavendish Bentinck and Major Keith of G-2 SHAEF; SHAEF Forward to AGWAR, May 28, 1945, containing list of inmates; both NAK FO 371/46778. Some prisoners continued to be moved, like Speer who was taken to Dustbin. Richard Overy, *Interrogations: The Nazi Elite in Allied Hands* (New York: Penguin Putnam, 2001), 60, reports that Ashcan was run by Americans, while Dustbin was under British control.
451. E. Tilley, Major GS G-2 F.I.A.T., to Major P. M. Wilson, June 23, 1945: "An attempt should be made to have both Schellenberg and Kersten extradited as two of the most obvious war criminals and to have them brought to Dustbin for an examination of their connections with industrial leaders and their plans for espionage through German industry. After a thorough examination they should be passed on to Ashcan for

Just who it was that decided not to place Schellenberg with the Nazi elite at Ashcan or Dustbin still remains uncertain. One of the few hints in the records suggests that Colonel Dick White about June 9, 1945, had already told someone, probably Helenus Patrick Milmo of MI5, "that he [White] was now able to arrange for Schellenberg to be held for a short period, say a week or ten days, at a private house in Frankfurt, where U 35 could operate on him."[452] Assuming that U 35 gave the correct date of the first interrogation that would suggest that Schellenberg was kept inactive as long as fourteen days at the safe house in Frankfurt. When Allied intelligence finally got to him, early reactions were rather positive: "The first interrogation of Walter Schellenberg left nothing to be desired and justified reasonable hope that complete answers will be received to all queries which Schellenberg is competent to answer."[453] Not surprisingly, most Allied interrogation reports prior to the Nuremberg Military Tribunals do not reveal names of interrogators. From the documentary evidence, however, we can be rather certain that Schellenberg, while being held in the U.S. occupied part of Germany, was questioned at least by U 35, Sir Stuart (Newton) Hampshire and Sir Helenus Patrick Milmo.[454] From discussions with Lord Dacre (Hugh Trevor-Roper) and Sir Stuart Hampshire this author learned that while in Frankfurt, London and Camp 020, Schellenberg was also interrogated by an American called Rory Cameron, Hugh Astor of the famous Astor family and Herbert Hart. Regarding his own part in the Schellenberg interrogations, Lord Dacre preferred to skip over the Frankfurt period and stated that he did "not see" him in London. With due respect, the records and Trevor-Roper's own frequent personal appraisals seem to indicate otherwise.[455] Regarding locations of interrogation centers, safe houses and the like, information is scarce. Safe houses in the city of Frankfurt and its surroundings or the large facilities at Camp King or Military Intelligence Service Center (MISC) were the most likely venues for holding and interrogating important prisoners in the American Zone, but a number of SHAEF offices were located in the I. G. Farben building where, for instance, Hampshire recalled questioning Schellenberg. Another location mentioned in this context is the Combined Services Detailed Interrogation Center (CSDIC) in Bad Nenndorf west of

---

further treatment." NAK, KV 2/94. For Dustbin see Ulrich Schlie, ed., *Albert Speer: Die Kransberg-Protokolle 1945* (Munich: F. A. Herbig, 2003), 62ff.
452. H. P. Milmo to Major (name removed), Secret, June 9, 1945, NAK, KV 2/94. Sir Helenus Patrick Milmo, born 1908, was a well-known barrister of the Middle Temple and judge of the High Court of Justice, Queen's Bench Division.
453. First interrogation of Walter Schellenberg at SHAEF, June 27, 1945, NAK, KV 2/94.
454. Sir Stuart Newton Hampshire (1914–2004), studied History at Oxford, Professor of Philosophy at Princeton and Stanford. While with intelligence he used initials SH and SNH.
455. Lord Dacre to this author, November 7, 1999. Herbert L. A. Hart (b. 1907), Radio Security Service. Dorril, *A Who's Who of the British Secret State*, 43.

Hanover in Northern Germany. Camp King was probably the best prepared for these activities, for it was here that the Germans previously had interrogated American and British Air Force officers.[456] From a lively article by an old hand at interrogations of prisoners, the American Arnold M. Silver, we learn that the inherited German facilities were a rather complete installation, and Silver recalls some of the more colorful prison inmates they questioned, among them "Axis Sally," or rather Mildred Gillars, an American teacher in Berlin, who broadcast for the Nazis to U.S. troops, and Hannah Reitsch, Hitler's famous female pilot whom the Americans almost appointed to a significant position to rebuild the school system in the American Zone until they discovered that "she was as convinced and unreconstructed a Nazi as we have ever come across." More importantly, Arnold Silver also interrogated such German agents—or double agents?—as Anton Turkul, Richard Klatt and Ira Longin. Trying to determine just who this trio might have been working for, the British sent U 35 who joined Silver in handling these three gentlemen. Even if not sharing all of Silver's appraisals of his inmates at Camp King, there can be no doubt that Silver had it right when he concluded that Klatt "was a maneuverer *par excellence*."[457] The most visible result of Schellenberg's interrogations in the Frankfurt area at this time is the "Report on Interrogation of Walter Schellenberg, 27th June–12th July 1945," dated July 12, 1945, not overly impressive in analysis and conclusions but densely packed with information and data gathered in the obviously rewarding sessions with Schellenberg.[458]

While this first report is dated July 12, Schellenberg was clearly taken to London already on July 7. The records contain numerous documents showing that the British unquestionably wanted to get hold of him and that somewhat inexplicably they managed to succeed without any real opposition from their American Allies. Evidently this lack of American resistance was caused at least in part by the wide ranging cooperation of Allied intelligence services. That these services, however, did not in all cases work together without friction is well known, and the Schellenberg case is no exception. The occasional competitiveness of the services can be easily illustrated with the following example.

At issue in this case are papers or documents in Schellenberg's possession in Stockholm and to all indications missing shortly thereafter without leaving

---

456. Camp King originally was the 7707th European Command Intelligence Center. In the records it is often simply referred to as Oberursel. For Bad Nenndorf cf. Ben MacIntyre, *Agent Zigzag: A True Story of Nazi Espionage, Love and Betrayal* (New York: Harmony/Random House, 2007), 293.
457. Silver, "Questions, Questions, Questions: Memoires of Oberursel," 199–213. Kevin Ruffner, ed., "Forging an Intelligence Partnership: CIA and the Origins of the BND, 1945–49. A Documentary History," vol. 1, SVI, NA, RG 263, E A1-87, Box 2.
458. NA, RG 226, E 125A, Box 2. While spelling suggests British author, report is probably product of both English and American officers.

much of a trace. It has already been pointed out that Marie-Louise Schienke, who did not travel to Sweden together with Schellenberg, carried in her baggage papers and cash belonging to her boss. There have been no suggestions that these papers were confiscated from Schienke at the border or upon arrival in Stockholm. The fact that Schellenberg then worked together with Schienke getting his "Autobiography" typed, would suggest that the papers were still in his possession. In July 1945 someone in the War Room in London urgently wanted Schellenberg's papers and turned to the Americans in Frankfurt where Schellenberg had just been. Real or fabricated confusion was the only reaction, the sole response being that Schellenberg's papers had not been in his possession during the flight on June 17 from Stockholm to Frankfurt, but adding "that it is a well-known fact that the material was captured separately." Somehow at least one part of his papers ended up with "X-2 OSS Mission to Germany," clearly not British but American intelligence. American officers later recalled that Schellenberg papers were held for a time by the American Major Saxe and that Sir Stuart Hampshire was supposed to pick them up. An OSS investigation suggested that Schellenberg's papers came with him from Stockholm to Frankfurt, were there taken from him by U.S. officials who sent them on to another U.S. office in Wiesbaden where they ended up with Major Saxe. A U.S. intelligence officer wrote a large "NO" into the margin of the respective document. There are also hints that these papers were not taken from Schellenberg but "captured separately." Somehow the trail was lost. Whether the papers the British did get, were these, remains uncertain, but British intelligence in late July notified Colonel Stephens, the Chief at Camp 020 in London that "documents, the personal property of Schellenberg, have become available to us."[459] As is well known, the British, still rather disgruntled about the Venlo incident, were much interested in German documents relating to it. Apparently they had reason to be pleased. These Schellenberg papers included a number of "files on the Venlo case." They were now looking forward to quizzing the German Chief of Foreign Intelligence to learn what the Germans knew about British intelligence. As they were most eager to determine just how sincere Schellenberg was during the interrogations, they could now easily compare what he said with what his personal Venlo papers "show that he must know." It had to work because Schellenberg was "of course unaware of the fact that we hold these personal documents of his. They did not come from Sweden with him."[460] Examining U.S. records more

---

459. Diverse documents, NA, RG 226, E 119A, Box 26. "Memorandum for Schellenberg File," August 8, 1945; SAINT London, August 15, 1945, Secret; Schellenberg File, August 15, 1945, Secret; all NA, RG 319, IRR, PS, Box 195.
460. Ferguson to Colonel Stephens, July 31, 1945, NAK, KV 2/96.

closely, one discovers that the Americans in Frankfurt also obtained some "personal files of Schellenberg." In a letter of June 8, 1945, from the FBI representative Frederick Ayer, Jr., to the FBI Director J. Edgar Hoover, there is mention of "letters taken from the personal files of Schellenberg, which disclose that a considerable amount of money had been sent to Switzerland for Schellenberg's account." Of particular interest are three enclosures to this message for Hoover, namely a blank U.S. passport, another U.S. passport belonging to a Maurice S. Gagnon and issued by the U.S. Consulate General in German-occupied Paris, and finally a U.S. passport with the same number as the Gagnon passport but purportedly belonging to a William G. Bellmount, whose passport picture clearly shows Walter Schellenberg. We do not know whether the translation of the German words Schelle and Berg into bell and mount produced a smile from the FBI agents, but they did conclude that "the forging of the United States passport for Schellenberg might lead one to believe that he intended to seek refuge in America." Incidentally, when questioned about it, Schellenberg told the Americans the forgery had been but "a joke!" The letters mentioned referring to money sent to Switzerland "for Schellenberg's account" could have suggested, however, that the Chief of Amt VI Foreign Intelligence opted for Switzerland instead. Although it would be interesting to know how such papers fell into the hands of the U.S. agents, it is surprising that the FBI did not recognize the names in these financial documents. One of the "letters," dated April 10, 1942, is clearly a receipt from the Swiss Dr. Paul E. Meyer, adjutant of the Swiss intelligence chief Roger Masson, confirming acceptance of "$25,000" as a first down payment in a commercial deal involving the sale of wooden huts to Germany. As already mentioned, Meyer, in his time off, was actively engaged in various business transactions. The other "letter" is also a receipt signed by the same Dr. Meyer and confirming acceptance of "25 000 S. Franken in bar [Swiss Francs in cash] 5795 $ in Noten [in bills]" from "H. W. Eggen Berlin," Schellenberg's man in Switzerland. In this case the money is to be held in trust for Hans Wilhelm Eggen and most likely involves another business transaction of Eggen's firm in Switzerland. Recently declassified documents indeed inform us that certain Schellenberg papers were confiscated by FBI representatives in occupied Germany and forwarded to Washington. In the words of Frederick Ayer, writing to J. Edgar Hoover: "This material was secured in a highly confidential manner, and it is suggested that the source remain confidential."[461] All of this

---

461. JED: VA, Frankfurt, to Director, FBI, June 18, 1945, Confidential, NA, Records of the Bureau of Investigation, RG 65, IWG Classification 100 Name Indices, Box 2. The U.S. concluded that Gagnon had given his passport to the Germans for the forging operation. — Frederick Ayer to Director, FBI, June 8, 1945, Secret, NA, RG 65, E A1-136P, Box 5. Papers in NA, RG 65, E A1-136P, Box 59.

would suggest that both, Americans and British, had managed to obtain some Schellenberg papers which they were not sharing with each other. Cooperation between the intelligence services, while efficient and fruitful in general, obviously was turned off in certain cases of particular interest.

Speaking of Schellenberg's papers, it should be noted that the Allies, of course, were specifically interested in learning more about Schellenberg's finances and whether he had stashed away funds or transferred money to accounts abroad. What Schienke brought with her to Stockholm in cash, at the time certainly was not a small amount but still within reasonable expectation under the circumstances. When Schellenberg came to Stockholm he had US$ 29,000 and Swiss Fr 30,000, of which he immediately transferred US$ 1,000 to Jean-Marie Musy in Switzerland with the request that it be used to assist needy Germans and especially his wife and children who, as far as he was informed, were still in Southern Germany. Schellenberg told his interrogators that he gave the remaining US$ 28,000 to Count Bernadotte, but that this money had been confiscated by the Swedish government. The Swiss money was also given to Count Bernadotte with instructions to use it to help Germans in need and Schellenberg's family. According to the interrogation reports, Count Bernadotte and Schellenberg then decided to advance a three months' salary to his staff in Stockholm, leaving Swiss Fr 14,000 and Swedish Kr 3,000. Although there have over the years been a number of publications and press reports concerning a money forging project called Operation Bernhard and forged currency being available, they are not based on reliable sources and therefore, in most cases, are of little interest to the informed reader. There certainly is no documentary evidence that any such money may have been available to Schellenberg..[462] Finally, there have been repeated suggestions that he may have been involved in shipping funds to Spain and possibly elsewhere, but reality was that the former intelligence chief would in fact spend the next years as a prisoner and that the brief period of freedom, following his release, was marked by permanent suffering from terminal illness without indications of a lifestyle suggesting access to any substantial funds hidden away somewhere.[463]

---

462. Progress Report in the Case of Schellenberg, July 17, 1945, Secret, Camp 020, NA, RG 226, E 119A, Box 26. Comments, Christl Erdmann, April 1948, interrogated by Mr. Barr, SAN, Rep. 502, E 41.
463. Cf. Lt. Col. Ellington D. Golden of C.I.C. Region IV to Commanding Officer, 970th C.I.C. Detachment, December 30, 1947, NA, RG 319, IRR, PS, Box 195. German text by M., July 1, 1951, from the correspondence of Hans Heinrich Dieckhoff. I am grateful to Sylvia Taschka for informing me about this document. —"Final Report," Appendix VII: "Financial Affairs of the RSHA and *Amt* VI." "Re: Walter Schellenberg," n.d., NA, RG 65, IWG Classification 100 Names Indices, Box 2. For a lively and biased introduction to the Operation Bernhard, which used concentration camp inmates to forge especially British Pounds but also other bank notes and documents, see Walter Hagen [Wilhelm Höttl], *Unternehmen Bernhard: Ein historischer Tatsachenbericht über die grösste Geldfälschungsaktion aller Zeiten* (Wels: Welsermühl, 1955).

The differences in handling interrogations or personal papers would seem to suggest that the Americans and the British, while avoiding clashes, certainly at times worked from different perspectives and did not share views on how to go about things. If the Americans meant what they said in the Schellenberg case, they should have applied a little more pressure on their Allies. Though they had notified the London War Room in the name of General Eisenhower that the "War Department Washington advises Schellenberg greatly needed in USA," the political mood in London was such that a real U.S. countermove or protest was not expected, and it needs to be said that the basic premise in London, on paper as well as in reality, was cooperation between British and American representatives.[464]

Schellenberg therefore was not taken to some camp in the U.S., but on July 7, 1945, his British interrogators flew him to Croydon Airport and he was probably driven to Camp 020 soon after his arrival. The officers accompanying him had quite a time watching the German look down at London from the plane, wondering why the British capital had survived Göring's air raids and the ruthless V-bomb attacks.[465] Latchmere House, or later Camp 020, to where his hosts transported him, was a high security camp located in the Richmond section of greater London. Organized to imprison various types of enemy agents or persons suspected of being such, the camp also housed Nazi political and military prisoners of every shade. Among those who spent time there with Schellenberg were prominent fellow Nazis like Naujocks, Kuebart, Jost and Schellenberg's bitter enemy Kaltenbrunner.[466]

Following his arrival, Schellenberg was given a physical checkup, and the camp physician on duty, most surprisingly, "found [him] ... apparently fit and free from infection." From his voluminous medical records we are fully aware that Schellenberg was anything but "fit" and surely not in the right condition for what the British had in store for him. Life at Camp 020 was not well suited for this very ill prisoner.[467] When Robert M. W. Kempner, a German born lawyer who had left in time and become a U.S. citizen to return to Germany as an important member of the prosecution team at Nuremberg, interrogated Schellenberg much later that year, Schellenberg spoke of the harsh interrogation treatment in London. When Kempner asked him "With light?," Schellenberg told him "With light, being hollered at, cold water baths." When Kempner

---

464. USFET Main, Sands/Sibert, signed Eisenhower to UK Base/CI War Room, August 4, 1945, Secret, NAK, KV 2/96.
465. Report on Interrogation of Walter Schellenberg, 27th June-12th July 1945, NA, RG 226, E 125A, Box 2.
466. Hinsley, Simkins, *British Intelligence in the Second World War*, vol. 4, 70 ff.
467. Certificate of Health, July 9, 1945, NAK, KV 2/95.

added "Was it useful?" the former Chief of Foreign Intelligence, normally not one to dramatize matters, replied despondently "I was finished. Eight weeks in a lightless cell. I wanted to kill myself. It was not possible."[468] What British intelligence officers managed to force out of Schellenberg was based on and a continuation of the early interrogations in the Frankfurt area, and the end product was the "Final Report on the Case of Walter Friedrich Schellenberg," a most informative document for Nazi military and intelligence history of which it has been said that in some ways it is more rewarding than the memoirs written later and edited and published after his death. Clinton Gallagher, a CIA officer, in 1957 considered "a reading of the Schellenberg report...a rewarding professional experience." Even so there are indications that the "Final Report" does not reflect the full extent of information collected in the course of the interrogations in London and at Camp 020. "Schellenberg ... supplied ... information ... omitted from the general report at the request of the Special Agencies."[469] Regrettably, the original texts or notes from the London interrogators do not seem to have survived—or have not been declassified—thus depriving researchers and historians of many personal nuances in the exchanges. From the scanty data available it is quite impossible to determine all the locations where interrogations were held in and around London. Besides the sessions at Camp 020 Schellenberg was certainly often interrogated at the War Room inside the city. At this Counter Intelligence facility in London, initially referred to as the Counter Intelligence War Room, MI5, MI6 and OSS/X-2 worked together, and when Schellenberg was taken there for interrogation, the place was run by the British Lieutenant Colonel T. A. Robertson and an American, Mr. R. Blum.[470]

One of the most curious aspects of Schellenberg's stay in the British prison camp and the strenuous interrogations during that time is the highly contradictory appraisal traceable in the British records. On one hand there were highly qualified men like Hugh Trevor-Roper who said of the German SS leader that he was "among the universally parochial minds of the SS... enjoyed an undeserved reputation...[and] was in fact a very trivial character," but there was also the equally qualified Helenus Patrick Milmo who advised "that as Schellenberg was quite the most important character with whom we had to

---

468. Interrogation of Schellenberg by Dr. R. M. W. Kempner, November 13, 1945, (Transl.), SAN, S-45c.
469. See edited version published by this author. — For an appraisal of the "Final Report" cf. for instance Steven Koblik, "Sweden's Attempts to Aid Jews, 1939-1945," *Scandinavian Studies*, vol. 56 (1984), 113. Richard Breitman, Shlomo Aronson, "The End of the 'Final Solution'?: Nazi Plans to Ransom Jews in 1944," *Central European History*, vol. 25, no. 2 (1993), 203. — Clinton Gallagher, "Review of *The Labyrinth*, *Studies in Intelligence*, vol. 1, no. 4 (Fall 1957), 121. "Secret Appendix. Report on Interrogation of Walter Schellenberg 27th June–12th July, 1945," Top Secret, NA, RG 226, E 119A, Box 26.
470. Hinsley, Simkins, *British Intelligence in the Second World War*, vol. 4, 70-71, 184. Rather an informative document than a historical study is Hoare, intr. and ed., *Camp 020: MI5 and the Nazi Spies*.

deal it was essential that we should complete our interrogation before he was handed over [as a witness to the Nuremberg prosecutors]."[471] While a group of gifted intelligence men, among them certainly Klop Ustinov, Sir Stuart Hampshire, Rory Cameron and Hugh Trevor-Roper, worked on Schellenberg in a number of Greater London locations, some of them and their superiors not only decided to produce a major report on this German Foreign Intelligence Chief and his operations, but they also came to the conclusion that for a maximum exploitation of Schellenberg, they would need much more time than was apparently allotted to them. They had good reasons to be nervous, for soon after Schellenberg's arrival in London powerful attempts to get him back to Germany were being made and were considered a real threat to the long-term stay of the German intelligence leader which they had anticipated. Naturally British intelligence realized that using Schellenberg, so to speak, publicly as a witness at the Nuremberg Military Tribunals might open up the German intelligence chief to a degree that would destroy "his usefulness to Counter Intelligence." Evidently the British therefore left no stone unturned to keep Schellenberg in London, and indeed Colonel H. G. Sheen, Chief of the Counter Intelligence Branch, the officer who had collaborated with Colonel Charles E. Rayens to extract Schellenberg from neutral Sweden, went so far as to attempt to influence matters in such a way that Schellenberg "not be called as a witness." His reasoning was simple. In marked contrast to Trevor-Roper who saw Schellenberg as a "parochial mind," Sheen wanted "to save for Counter Intelligence the great value of Schellenberg's knowledge."[472] To complete the picture, it was not only the prosecutors in Nuremberg who were after their prisoner, but American intelligence continued to propose that in time Schellenberg should be brought to Washington. Even after he had been moved from London to Nuremberg, the Americans continued to press for an eventual transfer to the U.S.: "When his interrogation [at Nuremberg] is completed, he is to be transferred to the United States War Department ..." Naturally, MI5 lost no time to put their own interest on record: "Since Schellenberg is now being used in connection with the Nuremberg proceedings it seems unlikely that he would be shipped to the U.S.A. in the very near future. If, however, any consideration is given to his being transferred to Washington before the end of February, we should like ... to hold the option of keeping him available for

---

471. H. R. Trevor-Roper, *The Last Days of Hitler* (London: Macmillan, 1947), 27-28. H. P. Milmo, B.I.W., to D. B., August 3, 1945, Secret, NAK, KV 2/97.
472. Colonel H. G. Sheen, GSC, Chief, Counter Intelligence Branch to Deputy Judge Advocate, USFET, August 29, 1945, Confidential Secret, NA, RG 319, IRR, PS, Box 195.

interrogation until that time."⁴⁷³ Being aware that it could be more difficult to get their man back from Washington than from the international court proceedings in Germany, British intelligence obviously had seen Nuremberg as the lesser problem of the two. Other than their still incomplete far-reaching report on Walter Schellenberg and German intelligence operations, British motivations for holding on to their German prisoner are not really clear. As pointed out, Trevor-Roper's rather deprecatory estimate of Schellenberg's mental faculties was definitely not shared by all his colleagues. Nevertheless, the final product written by largely MI5 officers in the War Room in its "Conclusion" informs the readers: "His demeanour at this camp [Camp 020] has not produced any evidence of outstanding genius as appears to have been generally attributed to him. On the contrary his incoherency and incapability of producing lucid verbal or written statements have rendered him a more difficult subject to interrogate than other subjects of inferior education and of humbler status."⁴⁷⁴ Reading that verdict, one is indeed inclined to ask why British intelligence felt such a pressing need to continue interrogating him. In retrospect, even completion of the report was a flimsy excuse, for MI5 by September knew that the special Group 20, occupied with the Schellenberg report, would be "demobilized" in late October. Therefore, whatever it may have been that motivated British intelligence to keep their prisoner, Schellenberg's stay in London was definitely coming to an end. While exact dates of the transfer back to Germany are somewhat scarce, the records show that on October 22, 1945, U.S. Headquarters USFET inquired when Schellenberg "will be available for interrogation ... at Oberursel" and that the London War Room replied that he could be collected at Frankfurt Airport on "Sunday 28th October at 1600 hours." Another War Room message of October 29, 1945, confirms that Schellenberg was "escorted to Croydon Airport and returned to American Zone" the previous day. To all indications, possibly after further interrogations in the Frankfurt area, Schellenberg was taken to Nuremberg in early November and, in contrast to various published claims, did not stay in London or work for the British during the years before his own trial.⁴⁷⁵

We can be certain that Schellenberg was somewhat relieved to be leaving Camp 020. The move meant that he would trade the hospitality of British

---

473. USFET MAIN to UK Base/CIWAR, August 4, 1945, Confidential Secret, NA, RG 319, IRR, PS, Box 195. HQ, USFET, G-2 to C.I. War Room, December 4, 1945, Secret; response, no sender given, December 11, 1945, Secret; both NAK, KV 2/99.
474. "Final Report," 203-204.
475. Major J. C. Scott Harston to Lt. Col. Stimson, September n.d., 1945; HQ BAOR to CI War Room, October 24, 1945; War Room to USFET, October 26, 1945; D. B. Stimson to B.L.W. Major Forrest, October 29, 1945; all NAK, KV 2/98. Sándor Radó, *Deckname Dora* (Stuttgart: Deutsche Verlags-Anstalt, 1971), 274.

intelligence services for what is named euphemistically the Palace of Justice in Nuremberg, located in the American Zone of Occupation and under the command of U.S. Forces for its day-to-day management. The entire nature of the place was completely different from the covert procedures at Camp 020 and the Counter Intelligence War Room. Being put up in the so-called witness wing and for all matter of speaking still a prisoner with few rights and privileges, the Nuremberg Military Tribunals constituted a legal venue with all the usual attendant formalities, but, in contrast to the interrogations in London, with distinct regulations for those guarding and interrogating the prisoners and witnesses. A homecoming it certainly was not. Although one might assume that he did not see very much of the inner city, almost totally destroyed by air raids, the records indicate that members of the U.S. Forces drove him to various locations for what appear to have been more interrogations. For reasons quite unknown Schellenberg was taken out into rural Franconia, even as far as Hersbruck, for questioning sessions. There are no helpful explanations in the records for these trips, but they clearly show that American intelligence services, especially C.I.C. continued to interrogate Schellenberg on German intelligence operations during World War II and that these sessions had little to do with the ongoing cases at the Military Tribunal in Nuremberg. Moreover, these trips to other towns in the American Zone would suggest that Schellenberg, while still a witness and not yet a defendant, may have spent some nights in quarters other than his cell in the Palace of Justice.

Schellenberg's actual "Testimony" at the court began on November 12, 1945, when he faced Lt. Col. Smith W. Brookhart, Jr., with Leo Katz functioning as an interpreter. In this context, it should be noted that while Schellenberg had a more than superficial knowledge of English, a back and forth exchange as commonly develops in the course of an interrogation was difficult and in most cases, therefore, seems to have taken place through an interpreter. This would also mean that the minutes of the hearings would be minutes of what was said by the translator. Because of that and because most court notes and original German texts were destroyed, we are forced in most instances to use translated minutes. Questions concerning the loss of individual nuances or incorrect translations would obviously be one aspect of any attempt to evaluate the form and content of these interrogations and the court procedures. In the case of Schellenberg we are fortunate that some of the German material almost by coincidence has survived in the holdings of the State

Archives in Nuremberg.[476] A careful comparison of a great number of original German texts with the generally available English versions allows the conclusion that the translations in most instances are of a very high quality and do not in any way alter what was written down originally in German. In the case of Schellenberg it is rather evident that here and there nuances of what he may have tried to say between the lines or what would appear to be German colloquialisms have been flattened or lost their specific color, but such leveling of spoken German expressions to a sober and understandable English text does not appear to have altered the content or the specific meaning of what was said. Finally, it should be added that in most cases the testimony was given under oath. The SS leader who in 1937 at the age of twenty-seven had left the Catholic Church now swore "to tell the truth, the whole truth, and nothing but the truth, so help you [me] God."[477]

Already during his first court session in Nuremberg on November 12, 1945, it became clear that as a witness for the prosecution he would be used especially in the case against Ernst Kaltenbrunner. He had been Schellenberg's most dangerous enemy and his actual chief in Berlin. While being on guard against Kaltenbrunner every moment, he had by necessity learned to cooperate with this successor of Reinhard Heydrich since 1943, but had attempted to avoid personal contact and threatening proximity. When Kaltenbrunner on one of the final days of the Third Reich dismissed Schellenberg from all SS ranks and offices, it was undoubtedly a moment of great pleasure and belated satisfaction for him.[478] Little did either one of them expect that very soon they would encounter each other again, both as prisoners of the Allies and housed in the cells of the Palace of Justice at Nuremberg, one as defendant, the other a witness for the prosecution. When questioned by Colonel Brookhart on his relationship with Kaltenbrunner, Schellenberg was under oath but obliged to be courteous in his comments on his brutal RSHA chief: "He was from the beginning against me personally. As far as my office [*Amt* VI] was concerned, he made no difficulties for me the first two or three months, but then so many adversary powers were working against me that he started to treat me unjustly and insultingly, evidently with the aim to throw me out of my position." And: "…he insulted me… in front of the leaders…he…branded me a liar."[479] When

---

476. According to information from SAN, many of these papers were left behind in the Palace of Justice when it was returned to German authorities.
477. District Court Berlin, April 30, 1937, BA Berlin, R 58, Anhang I/48. See chptr. I above.
478. Contrary to some published versions, Schellenberg was dismissed by Ernst Kaltenbrunner, not Heinrich Himmler. Contrary to numerous publications, his function was Chief of *Amt* VI Foreign Intelligence, not Gestapo.
479. Testimony of Walter Schellenberg, taken at Nuremberg, November 12, 1945, NA, RG 238, E 7A, Box 18. "Adversary powers" here refers to general problems with operations rather than to persons.

Ernst Kaltenbrunner was later asked about his relationship with Schellenberg, he in turn made no secret of his strong dislike for "the most intimate friend of Himmler" who had let out a few Jews just to get positive reports in the American press. In retrospect, Schellenberg's testimony certainly did not contribute to a better image of the inhuman Kaltenbrunner, but it seems to have had no measurable influence on the court's decision to pronounce the sentence of death by hanging in October 1946.

Of greater interest and more significant than the nonexistent relationship of the two men was the information collected regarding the complex question of the connections between the military and the planned German genocide. From Schellenberg's vantage point, and he was probably aware of it by this time, the negotiations between the German Army and the SS prior to the German attack on the Soviet Union were an important topic. The matter came up in the case against Kaltenbrunner, because following the assassination of Reinhard Heydrich, Kaltenbrunner had become Chief of the so-called *Sicherheitspolizei* (security police) and the SD, thus being responsible for the murderous operations of the SS behind the front lines. In the spring of 1941 Schellenberg became involved in the negotiations between Army High Command and SS when Heydrich ordered him to take over from Heinrich Müller who made no progress in his conferences with Quartermaster General Eduard Wagner. As Schellenberg then was still with *Amt* IV and therefore a subordinate to Heinrich Müller, the assignment did spell trouble. As usual, however, Heydrich left him no choice, and Schellenberg contacted General Wagner. Preparations were not possible since the documents relating to the negotiations were still with Müller, and Heydrich had demanded immediate action. Schellenberg knew that Müller's meetings with Wagner had not gone well because, as Heydrich informed him, the Gestapo Chief had been "clumsy." It concerned the operations of *Einsatzgruppen* (special task forces) behind the front lines of the German Army and the practical cooperation between military and SS, in other words a sort of interdependence of combat forces and police units.[480] Heydrich wanted "full support" from the Army including "material equipment, fuel and other supplies," and "transport vehicles." In retrospect it would seem that Heydrich's target was to set up

---

480. On the Wagner/Schellenberg meetings see especially Schellenberg's recollections in IFZ, ED 90/6, 78-82. — Continuing German claims regarding the innocence of German combat forces cannot be treated in this context. Available records suggest that the German Armed Forces were informed about and participated in the crimes committed. For the views of the German military historian Manfred Messerschmidt critical of the German Army see "Hitlers ehrenhafte Komplizen" in *Die Zeit*, January 29, 1993, 40. For a recent treatment of this German controversy see Günther Gillesen, "Unsere letzten Zweifel und Hemmungen waren 1941 beseitigt," *Frankfurter Allgemeine Zeitung*, July 18, 2008, 37. For reactions to Schellenberg's views see below.

completely independent operations of the SS in the rear of the Army and secure the full support from the Army at the same time in all matters of logistics and material supplies. When Schellenberg met the Quartermaster General on the following day, by pure coincidence the chemistry seems to have been right. The young SS officer and the ranking military general were able to conduct a civil and sober conversation on all disputed issues, and Schellenberg recalled later that he made a point of not fighting over relatively unimportant questions of detail. "My purpose was to conclude the negotiations as quickly and as objectively as possible." To finalize their generally cordial deliberations, Schellenberg proposed to draw up a document containing all the points he thought they had agreed upon and to present that paper to the general for possible alterations. Wagner accepted and Schellenberg had his work cut out. After two days of tedious effort he was able to complete a draft agreement for General Wagner that was considered to be generally acceptable. When it came to the final meeting of Wagner and Heydrich, the latter asked him to come along, just in case. If Schellenberg's memoirs are correct, both Wagner and Heydrich came up with a growing number of suggestions for changes, but he wisely decided to keep quiet, knowing that the entire agreement would have to be rewritten once textual changes from one or the other side were agreed to. It worked. Both signed the document with Wagner passing comment on how much pleasure it had been to negotiate with Schellenberg.

Seconds later, however, the always unpredictable Heydrich rather coldly made the point that there was something he wanted to discuss with Wagner alone. Obviously, Schellenberg was invited to leave the room. What was said by the two men behind closed doors in the course of the next half hour remains unknown, but undoubtedly it concerned Hitler's orders for secret police forces to operate in concerted action with the Armed Forces in the coming war against the Soviet Union. Schellenberg in his memoirs does not speak about the planned murder of partisans, Communist leaders, political functionaries, Jews, gypsies, in other words from the German point of view the cleansing of all these elements of the population considered undesirable for any number of reasons. Whether Schellenberg knew then what the agreement he had just negotiated would be used for, we cannot be certain. What does seem certain is that soon afterwards he was fully informed about the extent of the crimes committed by the German Armed Forces and the SS in the occupied regions of the Soviet Union.[481]

---

481. The deployment of *Einsatzgruppen* also was not new, and Schellenberg must have been acquainted with many of the earlier decisions. On the earlier deployment see Wildt, *Generation des Unbedingten*, 421ff.

What he could not know at the time of his assigned deliberations with General Wagner was that his authorship of the agreement between Army and SS would be held against him in the future and that he would be charged with having played a role in the planning and preparation of mass murder.[482] For the time being, in Nuremberg in 1946 the crimes committed behind the German front lines were part of the charges brought against his RSHA chief Ernst Kaltenbrunner, and Schellenberg found himself interrogated under oath about what he remembered. What he told the court does not differ greatly from his memoirs written later, and it would therefore appear justified to accept his description of his role in the creation of the Heydrich-Wagner agreement. Some may prefer to doubt Schellenberg's claim about the special encounter of Heydrich and Wagner behind closed doors, but much of the evidence surrounding the origin of the agreement would suggest that Schellenberg's version is more than plausible.[483] Questioned in a different context right after his arrival in Nuremberg in the late fall of 1945, Schellenberg under oath made this statement: "Therefore today I must express my certain persuasion that during the secret and oral deliberation between Wagner and Heydrich the extensive future activities of the Einsatzgruppen and the Einsatzkommandos within the frame of the fighting unit of the Army [des Kampfverbandes des Feldheeres] including the planned mass killings [geplante Massenvernichtungen] were probably discussed and agreed upon. The above mentioned and already during the first weeks of the Russian campaign practiced cooperation between Army and Einsatzgruppen leads me to express today my decided persuasion, that the Supreme Command of the Army Groups and Armies who were to participate in the Russian campaign were exactly informed through the normal channels of communication of the OKH [Supreme Command Army] already prior to that campaign about the future broad assignment of the Einsatzgruppen and Einsatzkommandos of the SIPO and the SD including mass killings of Jews, Communists and all other elements of resistance."[484] Statements of this nature, of course, reflect Schellenberg's state of mind, particularly in view of his personal connection to the abysmal crimes referred to, and they may help us to understand in some way how the young and extremely ambitious SS officer later came to be actively involved in the rescue of thousands of helpless victims of the Nazi system. In contrast, German historians have found it difficult to accept that both the Army and the

---

482. For the trial of Schellenberg in Nuremberg see below.
483. For court session on January 4, 1946: *Der Prozess gegen die Hauptkriegsverbrecher vor dem Internationalen Militärgerichtshof. Nürnberg 14. November 1945-1. Oktober 1946*, vol. 4, (Nuremberg: Internationaler Militärgerichtshof, 1947), 415-418. Schellenberg, *The Schellenberg Memoirs*, 209-214.
484. Statement under Oath, Walter Schellenberg, signed November 26, 1945, SAN, Rep. 502, PS-3710. (Transl.)

SS were guilty of mass murder in Eastern Europe. The sharp dividing line, however, once drawn by Germans between the extermination squads of the SS and what they saw as the traditional German military forces has disappeared. A few authors' claims that Schellenberg's recollections are unreliable will also not diminish the historical evidence of the participation of the German Armed Forces in the willful destruction of Jews, gypsies or indeed any other persons perceived as enemies during the campaign in the east.[485]

The very complex question of the murderous special task forces (*Einsatzgruppen*) in the case of Schellenberg has an important aside. Though we know from the records that Schellenberg did not believe in a German military victory as far back as 1941, the fact that, in contrast to other young aspiring SS leaders, he did not lead an *Einsatzgruppe* has continued to confuse some and caused others to proffer curious explanations. There are some indications that his superiors, first Heydrich and later in fact Himmler, felt that they needed him in Berlin to attend to assignments more meaningful than the pursuit of undesirables in some occupied territory. Höttl, after 1945 often critical of Schellenberg, in a testimony before the District Court Bad Aussee in 1961 claimed to remember that Schellenberg had been selected to command the "Einsatzgruppe of the Security Police of the SD in Hungary" but had persuaded Himmler that following the takeover of the Abwehr he could not be spared in Berlin.[486] Whatever may have been the case, Schellenberg could have easily volunteered to command one of the infamous *Einsatzgruppen* and contribute to the cleansing of the racially polluted eastern regions. More likely would be the explanation that Schellenberg knew rather early—how early we do not know—of the bloody massacres committed by various special detachments and that in consequence he left no stone unturned to avoid his own participation. The fact that even so he continued to be a responsible and guilty participant in the system may have troubled him considerably, but as suggested earlier in another context he may not have seen a way out for himself without risking his entire family's and his personal extermination. Consequently he remained a guilty participant who assisted the victims when he was approached. When responding in such cases, he did take enormous risks, but he survived to stand in court at Nuremberg.

---

485. Cf. Eugene Davidson, *The Trial of the Germans* (Columbia: University of Missouri Press, 1997; 1st 1966), 316. Helmut Krausnick, Hans-Heinrich Wilhelm, *Die Truppe des Weltanschauungskrieges* (Stuttgart: Deutsche Verlagsanstalt, 1981), 127-128, 136.
486. Testimony of Dr. Wilhelm Höttl before the Bezirksgericht Bad Aussee (Austria), June 19-21, 1961, IFZ 2904/62. I am grateful to Oliver Rathkolb for this document. Schellenberg in Nuremberg also quite frankly stated: "I had a good relationship with Mrs. Heydrich and I confess that I used her also to keep away from all these matters." Hearing, December 4, 1945, SAN, S-45b. (Transl.)

Because there are almost no papers or letters of a personal nature, anything offering some insights on the individual is of great interest. One rather personal source on Schellenberg—at the time of his appearances as a witness for the prosecution—are the recently discovered notes taken at the Palace of Justice by Leon Goldensohn, an American psychiatrist who arrived in Nuremberg in January 1946. Actually his duties were at the same time those of a prison doctor and a psychiatrist. The young American was thirty-four years old, nearly Schellenberg's age. Apparently Goldensohn had only a scanty knowledge of German and his conversations with the prisoners, defendants as well as witnesses, were either held in English, not allowing a very relaxed exchange with some of the Germans, or they took place with the help of a translator. The meetings with Schellenberg recorded by Goldensohn were on March 12 and 13, 1946, but it is more than likely that Goldensohn had other informal discussions with Schellenberg which were not recorded.[487] The interview text now available shows that the two men did not know each other and would suggest that Schellenberg did not relate well to Goldensohn. We know that Schellenberg was well acquainted with psychiatrists, such as Dr. Bitter and Professor de Crinis, and had discussed conceptual approaches with them. We may therefore assume that he had no objections to a psychiatrist's somewhat inquisitive way of talking to him. The questions regarding Schellenberg's professional life do not reveal any surprises. However, his implausible claims of ignorance as voiced here about the millions of murdered Jews would appear to reflect his unreceptive reaction to this interviewer: "I always thought the Jews were for the main part still alive." And when Goldensohn more pointedly mentioned the 5,000,000 dead Jews: "I thought the Jews were alive in concentration camps." When pressed what as a young lawyer in the 1930s he had thought of the Nazi health laws which attempted to control certain diseases by means of sterilization or castration, he bluntly responded: "I had no opinion. I had little interest in it." Now, in 1946, he saw it as "too deep a violation of human rights" but "at that time I had no opinion." The observant Goldensohn may have come close to a correct appraisal of Walter Schellenberg's state in the spring of 1946 when he noted that he had the feeling that Schellenberg spoke "without much concern or affective reaction."[488] The conversation, if recorded

---

487. Gellately, ed., *The Nuremberg Interviews: An American Psychiatrist's Conversations with the Defendants and Witnesses. Conducted by Leon Goldensohn*, XXII, reports that Goldensohn only recorded "formal interviews" done with the assistance of a translator, thereby giving the interviewee time to consider the questions.
488. Gellately, ed., *The Nuremberg Interviews*, 417-418, 422. I was able to compare the edited text with the older version, Eli Goldensohn to Ashbel Green, September 15, 2006, author's collection. From this source it is evident that an interpreter was present during the conversation, that it was therefore not a personal or private encounter of the two men.

correctly, was brief and unrewarding. There appears to have been almost no rapport, and Schellenberg remained largely unresponsive.

We have no indications that Schellenberg received any private visitors. His mother whom he respected and maybe idolized had passed away years ago. His father seems not to have been very close, and the connections to his brothers and sisters appear to have been distant. But there were two pictures in his cell, one of his wife taken in some studio long ago and the other a snapshot of his wife with the children, the last born in late summer 1945. Had he not seen her since March 1945?

The so-called "Wilhelmstrasse Case," officially Case No. 11 United States of America vs. Weizsaecker et al., was obviously not of primary concern to the Allies, and two full years went by in Nuremberg before Schellenberg had his turn. During that time he found himself carted around to safe houses and offices in various locations for interrogations, mostly by military intelligence, counter intelligence and even representatives of the Federal Bureau of Investigation. In addition, he underwent seemingly endless interrogations, mostly under oath, for the prosecution at the Military Tribunal. Moreover, of course, he personally experienced the trial and the sentencing of once powerful Nazi leaders. Some of those tried were well known to him, and he had worked with some. Others, like Kaltenbrunner, he had feared and despised and had it not been for his own uncertain situation at Nuremberg, he might have welcomed their fate. Schellenberg's physical condition was as problematic as ever. His confinement to a cell, the lack of normal human contact and the constant personal psychological stress of being in or near the court certainly did not improve his physical condition or for that matter his mental composure. In fact, one is tempted to wonder whether continued and repeated questioning about the same however criminal context could not over time produce a degree of intellectual fatigue. The prisoner's complaints, still voiced clearly when his living conditions became worse following a change of cells, would indicate that he indeed succeeded in retaining a minimum of strength and will power to resist undesirable occurrences in daily life.[489] Because of his experience and fight for survival in the internecine atmosphere near the top of Nazi leadership, we may assume that he would not have considered writing a diary or making notes about his changing physical and mental conditions. Looking at the very disorderly state and the almost unstructured collection of notes for his later memoirs, it is however quite conceivable that he produced some of the text pieces already in his cell at Nuremberg. His own trial of which somewhat un-

---

489. Interrogation of Schellenberg by S. Hartmann, March 8, 1947, SAN, S-45c.

realistically he had hoped to be spared was part of Case No. 11 and the last Chief of Foreign Intelligence was just one among twenty-one defendants coming from a great variety of Nazi government offices and organizations. Indictments were filed only on November 4, 1947, and the large number of defendants can be seen as the main cause for the very extensive legal procedures generated by prosecution and defense during the coming months. The bare statistics of the "Ministries Case," as it also became known, may serve as an indication of what was in store for the participants in this historic legal event. Of the 21 defendants 19 decided to testify on their own behalf; altogether 339 witnesses were heard; the prosecution presented 382 affidavits versus 2,298 affidavits from the defense; the English text of the trial transcript has a length of 28,813 pages.[490] A most impressive array of judges and experienced lawyers ventured to determine the innocence or guilt of those accused. There were no precedence cases other than those tried in this very court since the autumn of 1945. In spite of all the however justified positions regarding the legitimacy of military tribunals, the accused in Nuremberg were afforded a legal procedure that bore no resemblance to the legal injustice meted out to those charged in German courts during the Third Reich. In Nuremberg, the city of Adolf Hitler's party rallies and race laws, the accused were treated in accordance with the legal principles imported from the United States of America. In the words of the "dissenting opinion of Judge Powers": "All the elements necessary to establish the personal guilt of the individual charged must be proven beyond a reasonable doubt." Regrettably we have no reactions by the highly trained German lawyer Walter Schellenberg to the legal proceedings of the Military Tribunal held at Nuremberg.[491]

One of the more colorful and inquisitive personalities on the prosecution side was Robert Kempner, an American lawyer of German background, just ten years older than Schellenberg and with a very similar education. Kempner played an important role at several of the trials in Nuremberg, and because of the time he spent in Germany when the Germans decided to trade what little democracy they had after the *Kaiser* for a dictatorship, Kempner understood their mentality well.[492] The fact that he was able to communicate with the accused in their own language probably helped him get closer to them than

---

490. *Trials of War Criminals before the Nuernberg Military Tribunals under Control Council Law No. 10*, vol. 15 (Washington, D.C.: USGPO, n.d.), 105.
491. "Statement from the Dissenting Opinion of Judge Powers," *Ibid.*, 108. The variety of legal views on individual and collective guilt cannot be considered here.
492. Robert Max Wasilii Kempner (1899-1993), born in Germany, studied Law and Political Science at Berlin, Breslau and Freiburg, worked in the Prussian Ministry of the Interior, opposed Hitler before he came to power and wrote legal brief proposing Hitler's trial or expulsion to Austria, persecuted in Germany, to Italy 1935, to the U.S. 1939, U.S. citizen 1945, returned to Germany as member of prosecution team, after Nuremberg other cases related to Nazi Crimes. Obituary, *New York Times*, August 17, 1993, p. B6.

other American lawyers could have. Very telling therefore are the minutes of an extended conversation between Kempner and Schellenberg on November 4, 1947, only days after the official beginning of Case No. 11.[493] After a discussion of Schellenberg's past in the Nazi hierarchy, his futile attempts to find a path to some kind of compromise peace, and his personal hopes for a future, Kempner inquired why the German Foreign Office had been so opposed to his rescue activities in cooperation with Jean-Marie Musy in Switzerland. Schellenberg's reply was to the point: "It was that sort of disaster policy which had gotten the upper hand everywhere. They did not have the courage to pursue an open policy [zum Bekennen]." Looking back at their conversation, Kempner responded by summarizing what one German lawyer thought he had just heard another German lawyer say: "Correct. Your own overall standpoint is, if I summarize it correctly, 'I was in that position and have recognized after 1940, how terrible it is, I have done my best and I have proof'." When Schellenberg consented that that was what he felt, Kempner inquired "Can you swear to that?" and when Schellenberg responded "Yes," Kempner asked him to rise and repeat after him the oath formula and swear. Schellenberg did just that. Studying these somewhat awkward but very exact minutes, it would appear that a misunderstanding can be excluded and that Schellenberg with his seemingly unrealistic hope that he might be spared a trial after all was not that far off the mark. Since we can be certain that as a member of the prosecution team Kempner was fully informed about the filing of the indictments for Case No. 11 a week earlier, we must conclude that Kempner too, at the time of his conversation with Schellenberg, still thought it possible that Schellenberg might not be charged in the upcoming trial after all.[494]

Matters, however, turned out differently. He was indeed included among the defendants in the "Ministries Case." Those charged in the case, though apparently thrown together somewhat haphazardly, were quite an elite group of Nazi functionaries, including such names as the State Secretary of the Foreign Office Ernst von Weizsäcker; Gustav Adolf Steengracht von Moyland, Weizsäcker's successor in office when the latter became Hitler's Ambassador to the Vatican in 1943; Johann Ludwig Count Schwerin von Krosigk, Minister of Finance until the end of the Hitler regime and then, in addition to that position, Foreign Minister of the very brief Nazi government of Admiral Karl

---

493. Interrogation by Dr. R. M. W. Kempner, in the presence of Research Analyst Jane Lester and stenographer, November 13, 1947, (German text), SAN, Rep. 502, S-45c.
494. Conversation quoted from Interrogation by Dr. R. M. W. Kempner, see above. (Transl.) Cf. Werner Otto von Hentig's appraisal of the way State Secretary von Weizsäcker handled his problems: "What disturbed me was how with an incomprehensible fear he avoided everything that could have created problems for him in the Foreign Office." Questioning of Werner Otto von Hentig by R. M. W. Kempner, August 7, 1947, SAN, KV-Anklage, Interrogations, H 101.

Dönitz; the former SS-*Obergruppenführer* Gottlob Berger, Chief of the SS Main Office and a man close to Himmler with whom Schellenberg had built a working relationship; SS-*Brigadeführer* Edmund Veesenmayer, closely connected to the Foreign Office and Hitler's Minister to Hungary towards the end of the war; SS-*Obergruppenführer* Richard Walther Darré, Minister for Food and Agriculture and in the 1930s directing Himmler's infamous Race and Settlement Office; and SS-*Obergruppenführer* Wilhelm Keppler, attached to the Foreign Office and economic consultant to Hitler in the 1930s, and, of course, the organizer of the "Freundeskreis Himmler." With the exception of Gottlob Berger, Schellenberg knew none of them well, but for diverse reasons he had collaborated with them over short periods.[495] To complete the picture it should be noted that the defendants could be charged under eight counts of the indictment.

"Count One" concerned "Planning, Preparation, Initiation, and Waging of Wars of Aggression and Invasions of other Countries," and Schellenberg was one of those charged. "Count Two" referred to "Common Plan and Conspiracy" ("to commit ... crimes against peace") and Schellenberg was included among those charged. "Count Three" cited "War Crimes: Murder and Ill-Treatment of Belligerents and Prisoners of War" and did not list Schellenberg among those charged. "Count Four" concerned "Crimes Against Humanity: Atrocities and Offenses Committed against German Nationals on Political, Racial and Religious Grounds from 1933 to 1939" and did not name Schellenberg among the accused. "Count Five" concerned "War Crimes and Crimes against Humanity: Atrocities and Offenses Committed against Civilian Population" and it mentioned Schellenberg, specifically pointing to his draft for the *Einsatzgruppen* in 1941. "Count Six" concerned "War Crimes and Crimes against Humanity: Plunder and Spoliation" and Schellenberg was not listed among the sixteen (of twenty-one) charged under this Count. "Count Seven" referred to "War Crimes and Crimes against Humanity: Slave Labor" and Schellenberg again was not named among those charged. "Count Eight" concerned "Membership in Criminal Organizations" and Schellenberg, of course, was listed among those charged.[496] In summary, his case looked somewhat less threatening than several others, but having said that, some of the charges pressed against Schellenberg were potentially very dangerous, and he would certainly be in need of excellent defense lawyers. Unfortunately the documents released so far do not seem to contain any information on the respective decisions or regarding influential friends and supporters who might

---

495. Complete list of defendants and their functions in *Trials of War Criminals before the Nuernberg Military Tribunals under Control Council Law No. 10*, vol. 12,1 (Washington, D.C.: USGPO, n.d.), 14-20.
496. *Ibid.*, 20ff.

have become active on his behalf. From appearances Schellenberg was represented in court by Attorneys Dr. Fritz Riediger and Kurt Mintzel who at the time shared a law office in Nuremberg.[497] Even if Schellenberg's case from the indictment appeared slightly more positive than some of the other cases in the "Ministries Case," the two lawyers had their work cut out. From the perspective of the defendants, court procedures did not really get under way until January 7, 1948, when the presentation of evidence began.

That Schellenberg would have a hard time defending himself under Count One, particularly against British charges in connection with the Venlo affair, was predictable, and from the extended interrogations in London Schellenberg certainly knew that the British had not forgotten the case and that, as seen through British eyes, he was the main instigator of the treachery at Venlo. The view that Venlo was among the excuses for the German invasion of The Netherlands was also no surprise for Schellenberg. His personal testimony regarding Venlo was presented on May 11, 12, and 13, 1948, and complete texts are available in the records of the Military Tribunal. Schellenberg delivered a rather clear description of the development of Venlo, particularly the when and how he was instructed by Heydrich to take over a *Nachrichtenspiel* (intelligence game) that British and German intelligence agents had played in The Netherlands. At the time, in October 1939, Schellenberg was still in charge of the counterintelligence section of *Amt* IV Gestapo, and in Nuremberg he expressed the opinion that Heydrich may have addressed him in that position; he had been busy pursuing foreign espionage networks in the Rhein-Ruhr area. Heydrich's view at that meeting had been that Schellenberg should shut down the game, but he also advised him to see Jost of *Amt* VI and discuss the matter. When asked in court why Jost of *Amt* VI, since he, Schellenberg, was in *Amt* IV, he responded correctly that the work of the counterintelligence section of *Amt* IV in many ways was closely related to the efforts of *Amt* VI Foreign Intelligence. The result of the meeting with Jost was a decision to continue the game in the same fashion. Schellenberg then presented a report to the court which even in retrospect by and large corresponded with the facts suggested in the records presently available. The complete alteration of the undertaking, namely from an intelligence game to a kidnapping, was ordered by Himmler on the day following the assassination attempt on Hitler in Munich. In court Schellenberg put it this way: "I remember ... that Himmler's order contained the sentence that ... the sense of taking these British officials into custody was to transfer these Britishers alive into German hands and thus to furnish

---

497. List of defendants, Counsel, and Co-Counsel, File Case No. 11, NA, United States High Commissioner for Germany (HICOG), RG 466, E 55, Box 8. Various correspondence from the two lawyers in respective files.

evidence for their participation in the attack in Munich." His statement that, when looking back from 1948, he was certain that "the German intention of attacking the West by violating the neutrality of Belgium and the Netherlands, was an accepted fact at the time" appears reasonable. Venlo was not needed to facilitate a German attack on The Netherlands.[498] In any case, quite aside from questions one may have regarding the kidnapping of the two British intelligence officers Best and Stevens, the death of Dirk Klop, and the interrogations of the kidnapped men, there are no indications that in connection with the Venlo operation Schellenberg had anything to do with "pretexts for aggression" or "preparations for aggressive war."

More threatening for Schellenberg than Venlo, at least as worded in the indictment under Count One, was the charge that "Schellenberg participated in the creation of special task forces of the SS, called 'Einsatzgruppen', for the extermination of all opposition in the territories of the Soviet Union." While the disturbing question of what and when Schellenberg knew about the mass murder committed by these special detachments remains open, the charge spelled out under Count One refers to the conference of Schellenberg with General Eduard Wagner and the text for a proposed agreement written by Schellenberg afterwards. There are no indications that Schellenberg at this meeting in the spring of 1941 knowingly created or helped to create any forces "for the extermination of all opposition" in the Soviet Union. Not surprisingly, the *Einsatzgruppen* therefore appear to have played a much smaller role in the court deliberations on the charges under Count One than the Venlo operation. Consequently, while not employing the term innocent, the verdict under Count One clearly states: "There is no evidence tending to prove that he took any part in planning, preparing, or initiating any of the wars described in Count One ... We therefore ACQUIT the defendant SCHELLENBERG under Count One."[499]

Count Two, the charge of "a common plan and conspiracy" was dealt with by the court, one might say, through administrative procedures. After three of the defendants, on a motion from the prosecution, were taken off the list of defendants under this Count, the court came to "the opinion that no evidence has been offered to substantiate a conviction of the defendants in a common plan and conspiracy." As a consequence all defendants charged, including Schellenberg, were acquitted.[500]

---

498. *Trials of War Criminals before the Nuernberg Military Tribunals under Control Council Law No. 10*, vol. 12 (Washington, D.C.: USGPO, 1951), 1233ff.
499. *Ibid.*, 20-30. *Ibid.*, vol. 14, 418. Count One Acquittal, NA, RG 466, E 55, Box 6.
500. *Trials of War Criminals before the Nuernberg Military Tribunals under Control Council Law No. 10*, vol. 14 (Washington, D.C.: USGPO, 1952), 435-436.

Count Three related to diverse acts of maltreatment, torture and murder. The cases treated here opened but a small window on the indescribable brutality that had begun to dominate German life and culture in those years. "An official policy" of lynching downed pilots and murdering unarmed prisoners was part of this gruesome German picture. Schellenberg was not indicted under this Count.[501]

Count Four concerning "Crimes against Humanity" opened another window on the crimes committed by Germans, in this case "against German nationals." Germans ruthlessly persecuted anyone who did not fit into their *Volk* (people), such as Jews, Free Masons, Jehovah's Witnesses, gypsies, individuals of mixed racial background and many others. Schellenberg was not indicted under this Count.

Count Five, concerned with "War Crimes and Crimes against Humanity," included an indictment of Schellenberg, and he seemed hard pressed to demonstrate that he had neither been a "principal in," an "accessory to" nor taken "a consenting part" in war crimes and crimes against humanity. Under Point 45 of Count Five the prosecution specifically spelled out its opinion that "in May 1941, the defendant Schellenberg drafted the final agreement which established special task forces called 'Einsatzgruppen' for the purpose of exterminating hundreds of thousands of men, women and children populations regarded as racially 'inferior' or 'politically undesirable'. Through the execution of this program, the eastern territories regarded by the defendants as 'Lebensraum' (living space) for a greater Germany, were to be vacated of all people viewed as dangerous to plans for German hegemony in the East."[502] Under oath Schellenberg had already described in some detail how he was ordered by Heydrich to mediate between the RSHA and the Army when Quartermaster General Wagner could or would not deal any longer with the ill-mannered Heinrich Müller. Schellenberg correctly pointed out that at that time he was in fact still working under Müller. The agreement between Army and SS had become necessary, he pointed out, because Hitler had ordered that a cooperation of Police and Army was to break all forms of resistance behind the German lines. Finally, Schellenberg underlined that though he was present when Heydrich and Wagner signed the agreement he was asked to leave the room afterwards and therefore did not hear the discussion of the *Führer*'s order by the two men. We do not really know when Schellenberg first saw actual reports containing figures relating to the mass executions by various means carried out by German forces in the Eastern regions, but Schellenberg, while

---

501. *Ibid.*, vol. 12, 35-38.
502. *Military Tribunals. Case No. 11.* (Nürnberg: Office of Military Government for Germany/US, 1948), 41.

still a witness for the prosecution, as pointed out earlier, under oath had been quite lucid about his reactions when he did see reports from the special detachments.[503] After careful consideration of the evidence or rather lack of it on this part of Count Five the Court arrived at the following verdict: "While we doubt that Schellenberg was as ignorant of the mission of the Einsatzgruppen as he now asserts, the proof that he had knowledge does not convince us to a moral certainty. We therefore give him the benefit of the doubt and as to this incident we ACQUIT him."

As can be seen from the "Final Brief on the Criminal Responsibility of Walter Schellenberg" of August 10, 1948, there were, however, other serious charges against Schellenberg under the same Count Five. Actually not from his own work area but sent out over his name was a document of May 1941, informing Police and SD offices in Belgium and France that due to the flow of Jewish emigration through Spain and Portugal and the insufficient "emigration possibilities" in those countries and in view of the "undoubtedly coming final solution of the Jewish question," Jewish emigration from France and Belgium was to be "prevented." The final sentence of that document reads: "An immigration of Jews into the areas occupied by us is to be prevented in view of the undoubtedly coming final solution of the Jewish question."[504] The specific reference here to the "final solution" at the Military Tribunal in Nuremberg could be and apparently was seen as an indication of Schellenberg's participation or collaboration in the infamous "Final Solution" program developed by the Nazis. Obviously Schellenberg was obliged to take a stand on this implied charge. His detailed response, of course, could not wipe away the suspicion that Walter Schellenberg had known more in May 1941 than he wished to admit already in 1941 and certainly in January 1948. Within the legal context of the Military Tribunal his "Vermerk" (Comment) did make some rather essential points: His own department in *Amt* IV Gestapo was IV E Counterintelligence, not IV B, and if the document in question had been issued by him, it would indeed have named his department in the letterhead, which it did not. Moreover, he pointed out, not incorrectly, that the meaning of the term final solution would have varied in different situations and that the Wannsee Conference about the final solution of the Jewish question would only convene

---

503. Statement under Oath by Walter Schellenberg, signed November 26, 1945, SAN, Rep. 502, PS-3710. See above for extensive quotation. — Apparently *Amt* VI had "its own agents" with the special detachments, and their reports would have been seen by Schellenberg. Cf. Affidavit by SS-*Sturmbannführer* Kurt Lindow, January 22, 1948, USHMMA, Kempner Papers, Box "Buffalo" 3, Folder F4.
504. Early photographed copy of the document on RSHA stationery with *Gestapo* stamp at bottom ("Geheime Staatspolizei. Geheimes Staatspolizeiamt"), "In Vertretung gez. Schellenberg" to all State Police Offices, Representatives of the Chief of the Security Police and the SD in Belgium and France, May 20, 1941, Secret, SAN, Rep. 502, NG 3104.

in January 1942.[505] Indeed, the document in question, signed by Schellenberg in May 1941 was signed "in Vertretung" (on behalf of) and according to the letterhead, originated with "Reichssicherheitshauptamt IV B 4b," not Schellenberg's department IV E. While not exculpating him from a connection to the holocaust reality or the Final Solution, be it by knowledge or by holding an important position in the RSHA, it would appear that the implied accusation of a role in the Final Solution program was not sustainable in court, and there indeed is no evidence in the records that it was further pursued. The records of the Military Tribunal also do not appear to contain a separate pronunciation of a partial verdict, such as in the case of the *Einsatzgruppen*.[506]

However, Schellenberg's involvement with, if not to say responsibility for, what was called Operation Zeppelin was quite another matter. This project had been directed by *Amt* VI C which had been in charge of intelligence and related covert military activities in the Soviet Union, other Eastern European states, the Far East including India and, following a reorganization in the *Amt*, also Turkey and the Near and Middle East, including the Arab countries and Palestine, but also extending as far as Iran and Afghanistan. One of the more influential regional leaders Schellenberg was forced to deal with was Amin El Husseini, Grand Mufti of Jerusalem and a descendant of an important Palestinian family. The Mufti, following earlier cooperation with the British, had now parted ways with them and after seeking refuge in various locations had arrived in Berlin in late 1941. He had been known to the Germans for some time and upon arrival was received by Adolf Hitler personally. From the records one gains the impression that while hating Jews and very much agreeing with their persecution and destruction by the Germans, Husseini in the final analysis was a rather costly, ineffective and unsuccessful operative.[507]

---

505. "Vermerk (14.1.48) zum Thema der Anklage in ihrem 'Opening Statement'," IFZ, ED 90/5. — The so-called Wannsee Conference, presided over by Reinhard Heydrich, took place on January 20, 1942, and was attended by representatives of ministries and Nazi organizations. Their decisions concerned methods of represssion and extermination of Jews, the "Endlösung" or Final Solution. Walter Schellenberg, who had moved from *Amt* IV Gestapo to *Amt* VI Foreign Intelligence, was not among the participants.
506. On the structure and history of *Amt* IV Gestapo Situation Report No. 4, *Amt* IV of the RSHA, Counter Intelligence War Room London, December 7, 1945, Secret, NA, RG 319, IRR, IS, Box 8. *Amt* IV B4 was concerned with "Judentum" (Jewry) while other sections of IV B were concerned with Catholicism, Protestantism and Freemasonry. Revision Notes No. 2, RSHA Amt IV, December 25, 1944, Secret, Security Information, *Ibid.*, Box 5. Cf. Translation of Statement by Schellenberg, July 18, 1945, NA, RG 226, E 119A, Box 26.
507. Re Husseini (1893-1974): "Final Report," 128-129, Appendix V, 243-244. SIME Report No. 9, March 6, 1944, NAK, KV 2/2085. Sönke Zankel, "Der Jude als Anti-Muslim: Amin Al-Husseini und die Judenfrage," in Günther/Zankel, eds., *Abrahams Enkel*, 41-52. R. D. McClelland to Paul Blum, June 29, 1945, with comments by Rabbi Michael Weissmandl on the Mufti's views regarding "the extermination of the Jewish population in Europe," NA, RG 226, E 211, Box 12. Dina Porat, *The Blue and the Yellow Stars of David: The Zionist Leadership in Palestine and the Holocaust, 1939-1945* (Cambridge: Harvard University Press, 1990), 20. Statement under Oath by Werner Otto von Hentig, August 7, 1947, SAN, KV-Anklage, Interrogations, H 101.

The other highly influential and colorful Arab personality in Berlin was Rashid Ali El Ghailani, the Iraqi politician who had left his courtry after the upheavals of 1941. Prior to Schellenberg's takeover of *Amt* VI Foreign Intelligence there had been an ill-planned and, thanks to massive British intervention, miscarried attempt to unseat the government in Baghdad. Most unwisely and poorly informed about local conditions, the Germans had intervened with covert anti-English activities, had sent a small detachment of the *Luftwaffe* (air force) and wasted financial assistance in the wrong places. As in World War I, when the Germans had attempted to unleash a Jihad against the British, and advised by some of the same Near East specialists as thirty years earlier, such as Max von Oppenheim, they tried to fulfill their dreams to cut back British domination in the region and construct a German sphere of influence, stretching from the Caucasus to the Arab Middle East. Victorious German forces would come down from the defeated Soviet Union to meet up with Erwin Rommel's victorious Africa Corps somewhere in Palestine. Husseini would return and rule over a large Palestinian state. Saudi Arabia's King Saud was to become Caliph and territorial concessions were to enhance his influence in the region. Anti-British and therefore occasionally pro-German sentiment in Egypt, Iran, Afghanistan and even Northern India was to be instrumentalized. All looked very promising to the Germans as long as their armies were advancing into the endless spaces of Soviet Russia and across the desert of North Africa toward the Suez Canal. But then came Stalingrad and the Russian winter and Rommel's men and tanks succumbed to the sand and superior British forces. Husseini was not to return to Palestine until after Germany's defeat, and King Saud was not attracted by flimsy offers from Berlin. The grandiose German scheme for the conquest of the Muslim world had obviously underestimated the enormous military requirements for an intercontinental campaign, and their knowledge of Arab and Muslim culture had been insufficient. In sharp contrast to Britain Germany lacked experts of the Middle East, and men such as Werner Otto von Hentig were rare exceptions and not always appreciated in official Berlin. To make matters more difficult, Husseini and Ghailani did not work together well and increasingly competed with each other. Related to such German plans, but lacking any military support were the underground activities of Roman Gamotha, another Austrian National Socialist who had risen in the SS and found himself dispatched to Iran by the then *Amt* VI Chief Heinz Jost, Schellenberg's predecessor in office. If Schellenberg's later recollections are correct, Gamotha's partner became involved in some private affair with a local family, and when matters became too dangerous, they were forced to leave Iran. Schellenberg had not sent him and thus in a way was not responsible for his activities. After some initial support on his return to Berlin, not surprisingly Schellenberg broke off contact with him.[508]

Schellenberg was not charged with anything in connection with these and other operations by *Amt* VI C in the Near and Middle East, but Operation Zeppelin, extending in some of its aspects all the way to Turkey and involving some of the same people as in the Caucasus, was a different matter. The other operations beyond the eventual consequences, for instance for Jewish settlements in Palestine, appear to have been rather haphazard or in fact irresponsible. Operation Zeppelin, as shown earlier, was not really run by Schellenberg either, but there could be no doubt about his personal responsibility extending in fact to crimes committed that he may not have ordered but which he somehow allowed to take place within the frame of an operation for which he was accountable as Chief of *Amt* VI Foreign Intelligence. The main object of Operation Zeppelin was the deployment of Russian POWs for espionage and sabotage assignments behind the lines of the Soviet Army. Considering the variety of ethnic backgrounds and nationalities in the Soviet Union, it was not surprising that the prisoners would volunteer for such risky undertakings. Following a brief period of instruction and training often by other Russians in special camps under better than normal prison camp conditions, they were either dropped off inside the Russian hinterland or infiltrated through the lines. Evidently most of them were apprehended and killed, and many others just seem to have disappeared. The indictment under Count Five charged that in certain cases men who had gone on these missions and against all odds had managed to come back, for whatever reasons were executed upon their return "without trial or notice of any offense of which they were alleged to be guilty." In this case, there were witnesses or survivors of concentration camps who testified at Nuremberg. Kasimierz Smolen, a prisoner at Auschwitz from 1940 to 1945, who worked in the "reception office of the Political Department of the concentration camp," remembered "executions carried out in Block 11" and that the men killed were Russians brought to the camp "by SD men." Smolen remembered that the prisoners were not recorded at entry and not given a number as was done otherwise. "The code word 'Zeppelin' I

---

508. "German Intelligence Activities in the Near East and Related Areas," NA, RG 319, IRR, IS, Box 40. C. L. Sulzberger, "German Preparations in Middle East," *Foreign* Affairs, vol. 20, no. 4 (July 1942). Both *Amt* VI and the *Abwehr* were active in the Middle East. A recent study by Klaus-Michael Mallmann, Martin Cüppers, *Halbmond und Hakenkreuz: Das Dritte Reich, die Araber und Palästina* (Darmstadt: Wiss. Buchgesellschaft, 2006) refers to a few documents from *Amt* VI C 13, the department in charge of Middle Eastern activities, but has no information on Schellenberg's policy in the region. Archival records suggest that this was clearly not an area of prime interest to Schellenberg. — Gamotha (also called Ramon Gamotta) broke a basic rule of intelligence by going to the press after his return. On Gamotha especially "Final Report," 246-248. Postwar documents suggest that Gamotha worked for Soviet intelligence in Alexandria, Egypt. Allied Commission for Austria, MI3, Secret, n.d.; S.I.M.E. Report, March 22, 1947; both NAK, KV 2/1492.

know from these documents concerning the arrest" and in "some of these documents 'person in possession of secret information' was mentioned as the reason for the arrest." Smolen also recalled that the executions took place between 1942 and 1944 and "as a conservative estimate, the number of people who were taken in during this period ... was approximately 200 altogether ... they were murdered by a shot into the neck within 4 or 5 days." Under questioning Smolen remembered that "the commitment papers which had originated with Gestapo agents mostly in Spago, Oppelen, and Breslau always had been filled in by the Gestapo ... the committing agency was never the 'Zeppelin Kommando' but it was the Gestapo agencies." Asked whether he had ever seen "a decree from defendant Schellenberg about a commitment into the concentration camp," Smolen responded: "No." When asked whether he knew "that this Political Department in the concentration camp was exclusively subordinated to Amt IV [Gestapo] of the Reich Security Main Office [RSHA]," Smolen said: "I don't know that, but, for example, I know the marking IV C2."[509] Reinforcing the impression that these executions were arranged by *Amt* IV Gestapo (Müller) rather than *Amt* VI Foreign Intelligence (Schellenberg) are directives presented in court, for instance from October 1941 and signed by Müller as Gestapo Chief and stating that a "transport leader" taking such Soviet prisoners to a concentration camp for execution "is to be furnished with a certificate stating" that the "execution has been ordered by the Chief of the Sipo and the SD" which would have referred to Heydrich and later Kaltenbrunner. However, the bottom of the document indicates that this directive from Müller is also being sent to all *Amt* chiefs for information, which would have included Schellenberg, meaning he was or could have been fully informed about the murder of these Russian prisoners.[510]

Schellenberg's defense statements are elaborately descriptive, but on the whole evasive and demonstrating an uncertainty very atypical of this, one could say, extremely engaged and ambitious young *Amt* Chief. He appeared uninformed to a degree that was hardly believable. There was a brief moment when the prosecution was very certain that it had proof of Schellenberg's personal guilt. They were excitedly producing a document that supposedly came from him and ordered the execution of two Russian prisoners suffering from tuberculosis. Seconds later it was clear that the document sending the two

---

509. *Amt* IV C2 stood for "Protective custody (Schutzhaftangelegenheiten). Commitments to and releases from concentration camps on political grounds." Revision Notes No. 2, RSHA Amt IV Gestapo, Secret, NA, RG 319, IRR, IS, Box 5.
510. *Trials of War Criminals before the Nuernberg Military Tribunals under Control Council Law No. 10*, vol. 13 (Washington, D.C.: USGPO, 1952), 551-569.

Russians to their death was not from him at all but from an SS officer of Operation Zeppelin, named Weissgerber.[511] But then came the question attempting to conceal the slip of the prosecution: "the Sonderkommando Zeppelin was within your jurisdiction in Amt VI, wasn't it?" and Schellenberg replied very straight forward: "Zeppelin was subordinated to me." With that sentence Schellenberg—the man who had served a criminal system in which since 1941 he probably no longer believed in and who had done everything in his power to avoid commanding a bloody special detachment (*Einsatzkommando*)—had reached the end of the rope. The court recognized that Walter Schellenberg had not individually committed murder but was responsible for the "official practice" of "criminal acts" committed under his leadership. "We hold that Schellenberg in fact knew of these practices and is GUILTY of the crimes as set forth."[512]

Under Count Six concerning "War Crimes and Crimes against Humanity: Plunder and Spoliation" Schellenberg was not indicted. The decision of the court seems reasonable enough, since Count Six, when one takes a closer look at the more detailed charges, refers to inexcusable injustice done to those under German occupation. The Count does not seem to be concerned with crimes committed in Germany, or the knowledge thereof, regarding for instance the use of real estate taken unlawfully from its legal owners.[513] Schellenberg's position under Count Seven "War Crimes and Crimes against Humanity: Slave Labor" was very similar. He was not indicted because he did not participate in any form or at any time in "enslavement and deportation to slave labor on a gigantic scale of members of the civilian populations of countries and territories under the belligerent occupation of the Third Reich." Count Eight concerned "Membership in Criminal Organizations ... subsequent to 1 September 1939" and Schellenberg was charged with having been a member of the SS and the SD, both of which had been declared to be criminal by the International Military Tribunal. That his membership in the two Nazi organizations might turn out to be problematic was certainly known to Schellenberg at least since his rather conversational interrogation by Robert Kempner on November 13, 1947, prior to the start of actual court proceedings. When Schellenberg had very carefully voiced a hope that he might soon be done with the trial, Kempner had reminded him tactfully: "There is

---

511. *Ibid.*, 571-572, Weissgerber to SS Special Detachment, Auschwitz, December 1, 1942, concerning prisoners Jakow Semjenow and Wassili Gatschkow.
512. *Ibid.*, 593-594. "Schellenberg," NA, RG 466, E 55, Box 6.
513. *Military Tribunals, Case No. 11*, 44-50. — The main office of Schellenberg's *Amt* VI was located in a building confiscated from its Jewish owners.

your membership in the organizations."[514] The prosecution indeed argued that he voluntarily joined "the SS, SD and Gestapo" and that he continued his membership even after he had "full knowledge of the criminal activities" of these organizations. There was no doubt that he did join the SS in 1933 and that he became a ranking officer. Although both Gestapo and SD were not really separate organizations but instead connected to the SS through the RSHA, membership was considered separately. From the prosecution's perspective membership in the Gestapo was evident due to his brief work with the Gestapo office in Dortmund in the late fall of 1939 and, not surprisingly, due to his period as Chief of Section IV E in *Amt* IV Gestapo. The fact that IV E did not deal with secret state police work against Germans in Germany, the regular function of the Gestapo as generally known, but was engaged in counterintelligence in the sense of work against foreign agents active in Germany, was not taken into consideration in this context. In contrast, the Final Brief of the prosecution emphasized Schellenberg's nominal designation as deputy of Gestapo Chief Heinrich Müller. Undoubtedly Schellenberg knew of or had seen reports of the *Einsatzgruppen* on their murderous activities. When he changed to *Amt* VI Foreign Intelligence, first as a deputy to Heinz Jost and from 1942 as Chief of the *Amt*, he became, as the Final Brief argued, automatically a member of the SD because *Amt* VI "is included in the SD." The Final Brief made a special point of regretting not to have pressed specific charges against Schellenberg regarding his membership in the Gestapo and added that "the defendant's activities in the Gestapo should be considered in weighing his guilt in the SS and assessing his punishment, inasmuch as the Gestapo was a component part of the SS."[515] The verdict was Guilty.

As might be expected, Schellenberg's trial also had to consider a great number of affidavits and witness testimonies, presenting in most cases positive appraisals of Schellenberg and often what might be referred to as mitigating circumstances. That such documentation would be argued over heatedly by prosecution and defense is a routine ingredient of any court procedure. Many of the affidavits, it would appear, quite correctly emphasized that Schellenberg had neither personally committed such crimes, as for instance charged under the headings *Einsatzgruppen* and Operation Zeppelin, nor ordered the execution

---

514. *Ibid.*, 51-58. Vernehmung durch Dr. R. M. W. Kempner, November 13, 1947, SAN, Rep. 502, S-45c. (Transl.) Regarding the legal aspect of "membership in organizations declared to be criminal" by the Military Tribunal see Final Brief on the Criminal Responsibility of Walter Schellenberg, August 10, 1948, 63-68, NA, RG 65, IWG Classification, 100 Name Indices, Box 4.

515. *Ibid.*, 67-68. For the two specific charges in the indictment regarding SS and SD membership see *Trials of War Criminals before the Nuernberg Military Tribunals under Control Council Law No. 10*, vol. 12.1, 62. Cf. The United Nations War Crimes Commission, comp., *History of the United Nations War Crimes Commission and Development of the Laws of War* (London: His Majesty's Stationery Office for the United Nations, 1948), 314-315.

of such criminal acts. Obviously those writing and speaking on his behalf would not be able to assist the Court in the difficult search for answers to the question just when Schellenberg knew what about the crimes committed. The assumption of the prosecution that he must have known a lot seems correct, but, of course, from a legal viewpoint, it remains an assumption. However one may be inclined to value or disregard the affidavits and oral statements made in connection with the Schellenberg trial, it has generally been accepted, probably correctly, that those documents contributed in some measure to what several critics have called a rather mild sentence.

Of those speaking up for Schellenberg, the former Vice President and later President of the Swedish Red Cross Count Folke Bernadotte[516] certainly had the highest international standing and, with the exception of Hugh Trevor-Roper, he had few detractors. Already in June 1945 Count Bernadotte had visited the Acting Supreme Commander of the Allied Expeditionary Force and requested to state "that he had had considerable dealings with Schellenberg and that Schellenberg had been of great assistance to him in evacuating from German occupied territory both Swedes and Danes who were in danger of persecution by the Gestapo. This work had been done on purely humanitarian basis ... He concluded by saying that while he did not know what charges, if any, the Allies would make against Schellenberg, he felt it was his duty to make a record of these instances of humane and enlightened conduct on the part of Schellenberg." This document was filed with the Schellenberg papers of the Military Tribunal.[517] Count Bernadotte planned to come to Nuremberg and attend the trial to be available if need be. Instead he found himself dispatched by the United Nations to the Near East to mediate between warring Jews and Arabs. Because of this important and unavoidable mission, Count Bernadotte wrote an affidavit for Schellenberg in Stockholm to be presented to the Military Tribunal in Nuremberg. In connection with the long planned rescue operation of concentration camp inmates he had, on the advice of Arvid Richert, the Swedish Minister in Berlin, made contact with Schellenberg who arranged for him a meeting with Himmler, during which Schellenberg tried to carefully push for greater concessions. Bernadotte remembered a high point of the cumbersome bartering when they succeeded in getting Himmler to agree to let them take all women from the Concentration Camp Ravensbrück. "Schellenberg never stopped supporting me wholeheartedly and I can say with certainty that without the very positive and valuable engagement of Schellenberg the entire undertaking would not have been brought about and success

---

516. In 1946 Count Bernadotte became President of the Swedish Red Cross.
517. Brigadier General, GSC, T. J. Betts to Chief, C.I.C. Subdivision, G-2, June 19, 1945, NA, RG 319, IRR, PS, Box 195.

would not have been there either. Through the action of the Swedish Red Cross about 20,000 inmates were brought to Sweden ..." Count Bernadotte and Walter Schellenberg were able "to speak very openly about the political situation." And of some relevance because several authors have claimed that Schellenberg had ulterior motives: "Any advantages of a material or any other sort for his support in the large Swedish aid operation he neither requested nor received from me." The dedicated Swedish aristocrat incidentally was unable to come to Nuremberg a little later because on his peace mission he was shot in cold blood by Jewish terrorists.[518]

Also from neutral Sweden came a noteworthy affidavit from Jacob Wallenberg, the powerful mover in the international business world. He told the Military Tribunal that he had met with Schellenberg several times and that Schellenberg had well understood that Germany's behavior in its neighboring countries was unacceptable. Wallenberg, aware of the need to be specific and clear, listed the cases in which he had approached Schellenberg for assistance in getting a number of prisoners freed, such as Danish policemen, Norwegian students, his cousin Count Ferdinand Arco auf Valley, and two Norwegian shipping entrepreneurs. "I also learned from third parties that Schellenberg tried several times to bring about an end of hostilities between Germany and the Western Powers."[519] Other Swedish affidavits were presented by Baron Egon von Ritter who was arrested after the assassination attempt of July 20, 1944, and freed by Schellenberg after Alvar Möller, top manager of Svenska Taendsticks Aktiebolaget, asked him for his assistance. Arvid Richert, the Swedish Minister in Berlin during the difficult war years, wrote that it had been Schellenberg who had kindly assisted him in the troublesome negotiations for the freeing of Danish and Norwegian inmates of concentration camps. He recalled the strenuous deliberations, in one case even in Schellenberg's private home in Berlin, some of them connected to the huge rescue undertaking by Count Bernadotte. Richert remembered that he was able to approach Schellenberg on behalf of individuals such as Raoul Wallenberg who in his daring efforts to save Hungarian Jews was getting into deep trouble with the Gestapo in Budapest. A Statement under Oath from Alvar Möller covered the very problematic rescue of seven Swedish managers, particularly difficult as

---

518. Affidavit, Count Folke Bernadotte af Wisborg, signed Stockholm, April 19, 1948, SAN, Rep. 501, LV, S-4. (Transl.) The murder of Count Bernadotte in Jerusalem on September 17, 1948, has been ascribed to the so-called Stern Gang. The terrorists shot Count Bernadotte and the French Colonel André Serot in spite of the fact that they represented the United Nations. For details see Kati Morton, *A Death in Jerusalem* (New York: Arcade, 1996; 1st 1994). Persson, "Folke Bernadotte and the White Buses," 248. Solomon Grayzel, *The History of the Jews* (New York: Meridian/Penguin, 1968; 1st 1947), 686. Cf. Wiesel, ... *und das Meer wird nicht voll*, 93. Regarding Serot see comments in Paul Paillole, *Fighting the Nazis: French Military Intelligence and Counterintelligence 1935-1945* (New York: Enigma Books, 2003).
519. Affidavit, Jacob Wallenberg, this copy n.d., NA, RG 238, Microfilm M 897, Roll 114.

Ribbentrop had decided to prevent the release of the Swedes. In this connection Möller had many meetings with Schellenberg, and he emphasized in his Statement under Oath how he had offered several times that Schellenberg leave Germany and come to Sweden and how Schellenberg had declined his offer each time. Like Minister Richert, Möller noted how Schellenberg did seriously take personal action on behalf of Raoul Wallenberg and was successful in stopping "the measures that were to be taken against Wallenberg." The liberation of Count Gottfried von Bismarck from the claws of Roland Freisler and his bloodthirsty People's Court is specifically mentioned by Möller. These and other similar testimonies from Sweden, even keeping in mind the somewhat pro-German sentiments existing in Sweden during the early Nazi years, clearly conveyed the message to the Military Tribunal that Schellenberg had not only performed a handful of humanitarian favors for some rather influential Swedes but that he also was respected and accepted by these cultured and internationally known personalities from the world of business and diplomacy.[520]

Further meaningful affidavits on behalf of Walter Schellenberg came from personalities in neutral Switzerland who had maintained connections with him or whom he had been able to assist in important matters. Among the Swiss testimonies certainly that of Roger Masson, the Swiss intelligence chief, was one of the most significant and influential. Quite aside from the varied interpretations by contemporaries and later authors of Masson's contacts with Schellenberg, his depositions on behalf of Schellenberg, even in retrospect, are sensitive personal statements of recognition. The background of the affidavit, dated Mont Pelerin a/Vevey, May 10, 1948, has not received much attention outside of Switzerland. In fact, largely as a consequence of his contacts with Schellenberg and the more or less justified criticism by Swiss contemporaries arising from the risky dealings with Nazi Germany, at the end of World War II Masson had left the intelligence service "under regrettable circumstances," and the subsequent public debate about what soon came to be called the Masson Affair overshadowed his visible achievements for Swiss intelligence. In the words of Pierre Braunschweig, the by and large exaggerated critique "caused the fall of Switzerland's Chief of Intelligence." By 1947 Masson retired altogether from federal service. His quiet life off-stage was briskly interrupted when Schellenberg's defense lawyers decided that testimony by the former Swiss Chief of Intelligence would be helpful in court. All indications are that

---

520. See for instance Statement, Arvid Richert, President of Royal Swedish Trade Office, n.d.; Statement, Jacob Wallenberg, n.d.; Statement under Oath, Egon Freiherr von Ritter, n.d.; all three NA, RG 238, Microfilm M 897, Roll 114. Statement, Arvid Richert, former Swedish Minister in Berlin, n.d., SAN, Rep. 501, LV, S-3.

Masson was actually invited to appear at the Military Tribunal in Nuremberg and followed routine procedures by requesting permission from the authorities in Switzerland. Not entirely surprising the Swiss Government did not allow him to appear in court or write an affidavit connected in any way to his previous responsibilities in military intelligence. However, Masson's written "Attestation" on behalf of Walter Schellenberg had apparently already made its way to the German law office in Nuremberg when he requested official permission to appear in court. To Masson's further embarrassment, the authorities not only sharply disapproved of the affidavit but demanded to receive a copy of what he had written. This affidavit is available in the respective records as a 10-page typed document signed "R. Masson" at bottom right of each page and, after brief descriptions of his own and Schellenberg's functions during World War II, introduces a sober and factual list of developments and events with the words "My connection and my personal contacts with Walter Schellenberg (1941–1945) can be explained and justified by the summary that follows." Among the significant points listed are the need to reduce friction between Switzerland and Germany, especially freeing Lieutenant Mörgeli, silencing the hate campaign against General Guisan, particularly the work of the IPA, neutralizing German propaganda against Switzerland and tuning down German press propaganda against the Swiss people. It was he, Masson, who had asked for the first unpublicized encounter with Schellenberg, not the other way around. When they met, it was his feeling that Schellenberg admired Switzerland for its "social, economic and patriotic synthesis of our four races." Masson was touched by the way Schellenberg talked about his family, and he had come to form the opinion that Schellenberg was a sensible man, open to other people's needs. Masson's listing of "services rendered" by Schellenberg "to Switzerland and to the Allies" includes the silencing of IPA and therefore the end of the attacks on General Guisan, the availability of visas for traveling athletes, the liberation of Lieutenant Mörgeli, the release of the Swiss citizen Cramer from the prison in Fresnes (Paris), the freeing of several American and British officers from the prison camp at Oranienburg, the relocation to Spain of Ernst Sigismund Baron von Bibra "considered by us an enemy of Switzerland," the smooth handling of the immense problem of the German plane at Dübendorf, the liberation of thirteen members of the family including the wife of General Giraud, and a great number of liberating activities such as on behalf of President Herriot, Paul Reynaud, Léon Blum and 6,000 French women from the Concentration Camp Ravensbrück. Masson further points to the humanitarian work pursued by Schellenberg in the north of Germany with Count Bernadotte after Germany had been cut in half by the advancing Allied forces. The final point on this list was Schellenberg's engagement in Berlin against any preventive German military action against Switzerland. General Guisan, it should be noted, personally confirmed the contents of this affidavit with a brief but very significant statement added by hand to Masson's text: "Je confirme l'exactitude de la présente déclaration, notamment en ce qui concerne les services rendus à la Suisse par W. Schellenberg.—Gen. Guisan.—10 mai 1948.—Cdt. en Chef de l'armée 1939-1945—"[521]

In some aspects, because it is less related to military and intelligence questions, the affidavit of the former Swiss President (*Altbundespräsident*) Dr. Jean-Marie Musy carried even greater weight as a document for the procedures in this particular court. The Musy affidavit concerned a daring and in some ways outright dangerous attempt to free large numbers of inmates from German concentration camps. Beginning with the fruitful link between Rabbi Isaac Sternbuch of the Vaad haHatzala Emergency Committee of the Union of Orthodox Rabbis of the United States of America and Canada and Musy, a retired Swiss politician extracting Jewish prisoners from the Nazis for instance in France, this document casts a light on the journeys to Germany undertaken by Musy and his son Benoit and the complicated encounters with Heinrich Himmler arranged and assisted by Schellenberg. The rescue operation from the Concentration Camp Theresienstadt and the unfortunate blocking of further such transports to Switzerland through Kaltenbrunner's personal intervention with Hitler are briefly mentioned. Furthermore, the affidavit clearly corrects two supposedly very negative aspects of the Musy rescue operation that are often alleged. First of all, the full amount of Swiss Fr 5,000,000 promised to Himmler in return for the continuation of the rescue transports and deposited for that purpose with a Swiss bank was entirely transferred back to the U.S. Neither the Musys, Schellenberg, nor anyone else involved in the Musy operation received any payments. Second, contradicting another accusation voiced repeatedly, Musy states for the records "It is not true that Himmler made the release of Jews from concentration camps dependent on obtaining a right of asylum in Switzerland for some Nazis ..."

Jean-Marie Musy's very complimentary personal appraisal of Schellenberg may sound slightly excessive, but he added that he would be willing to come to Nuremberg and take the witness stand if necessary. "I see it as my obligation to

---

521. Complete French text, NA, RG 238, Microfilm M 897, Roll 114. (Transl.) Gautschi, *General Hènri Guisan*, 672-673. General Guisan (Transl.): "I confirm the correctness of the present declaration, notably as the services rendered to Switzerland by Walter Schellenberg are concerned. General Guisan. May 10, 1948. Commander in Chief of the Army 1939-1945." — Bibra (1894-1973) was stationed at the German Legation in Bern. Apparently the British and the French shared the negative appraisal of von Bibra. He was a fierce National Socialist and an engaged propagandist. X-2 Branch, memorandum for the U.S. State Dept., November 14, 1944, NA, RG 226, E 171A, Box 57.

declare that Schellenberg on all occasions tried to fully support me in order to help human beings to recover their freedom. I hold the persuasion that Schellenberg supported my goals because he himself disapproved of all violent and brutal actions, and I think that the rescue [of the people] as it was done would not have been possible without the cooperation of General Schellenberg. I am fully certain that all this was done by General Schellenberg only for humanitarian reasons."[522] An additional affidavit from Musy's son, Benoit Musy, treats the same context but adds a considerable number of rescue efforts on behalf of various individuals, such as the members of the family of General Giraud, General Charles de Gaulle's niece Geneviève de Gaulle, the Polish General Tadeusz Komorowsky[523] and 161 so-called "illegal Jews" from Theresienstadt. Benoit Musy, who with his father had negotiated with Himmler and Schellenberg, had also spent some time in Germany without his father, had been in several concentration camps, such as Buchenwald and Theresienstadt, with and without Schellenberg's right-hand man Franz Göring and had become even better acquainted with Schellenberg than his father. In his affidavit Benoit Musy told the Military Tribunal that he was under the impression that Schellenberg had realized the crimes that had been committed and felt a need to make up for what had been done. He too was convinced that the rescue activities would not have been successful without Schellenberg's support.[524]

In this context, one of the most informative documents related to the Musy rescue operation and addressed to the Military Tribunal "in matters concerning Schellenberg" in November 1948 must be briefly considered. Signed in Montreux by Isaac Sternbuch of the "European Executive Council" of the Vaad haHatzala Emergency Committee of the Union of Orthodox Rabbis of the United States of America, it clearly states that they "put Dr. Musy in charge of the Himmler Mission" and that from the beginning they directed it "under supervision of the American Legation"; that they did not know Schellenberg before and that they know him since from the reports made by Musy following his journey to Germany; that Schellenberg "supported the Musy operation" and that it "was not limited to the 1,200 Jews from Theresienstadt," but that their target was "the liberation of Jews to a greater extent" with an estimate brought from Berlin by Musy of 700,000 to 800,000; that the operation was "constructed on a political base" and constituted "a purely charitable mission"; and that "this petition intends no defense of any

---

522. Statement under Oath, Dr. Jean-Marie Musy, Fribourg, May 8, 1948, NA, RG 238, Microfilm M 897, Roll 114.
523. Komorowsky's release came late and respective information is still incomplete.
524. Statement under Oath, Benoit Musy (on stationery of Jean-Marie Musy), Fribourg, May 8, 1948, NA, RG 238, Microfilm M 897, Roll 114. Also SAN, Rep. 501, LV, S-4.

persons." The document, which like the entire Musy rescue operation has not been sufficiently considered by the experts, is of such significance in the context of the Schellenberg trial before the Military Tribunal at Nuremberg, because, following the attempted extermination of Jews by the Germans, an affidavit of the Union of Orthodox Rabbis of the United States in favor of a ranking SS leader constitutes a most unusual legal step. The petition to the court gains additional importance when it is taken into consideration that the positive comments on Schellenberg are part of a text accusing Kurt Becher of preventing the continuation of the Musy operation after the Theresienstadt liberation of 1,200 Jews. All in all this kind of positive testimony for someone like Schellenberg was certainly not expected, and one can only guess the influence it may have had on the decision-making process in court before a sentence was pronounced.[525]

For the sake of completing the picture, it should be said that there were, of course, numerous other affidavits, such as Emil Berndorff of Müller's *Amt* IV who had been in charge of the "protective custody" section and witnessed under oath that Schellenberg had never asked to have anyone taken "into protective custody." Hugo Buchwald, Schellenberg's driver from 1941 to 1945, knew of several rescue involvements by Schellenberg and the related comments made by Schellenberg while being driven. Franz Göring, who had worked very closely with Schellenberg in the rescue operations, witnessed about these undertakings and specific problems relating to the Concentration Camps Theresienstadt, Ravensbrück, Malchow and Neuengamme. In contrast, the interrogations of Kurt Becher in March and June 1948 not only revealed important data regarding Becher's activities in Hungary and the dealings with Rezsö Kasztner and Saly Mayer, but they also to a surprising extent exposed just how much Becher detested Schellenberg, whom he referred to as Heinrich Himmler's staff officer for foreign visitors.[526] More astonishing, if not to say outright shabby, however, was the untrue information about Schellenberg offered during interrogation by SS-*Obergruppenführer* Karl Wolff who for a number of reasons had become Schellenberg's fierce competitor in the top echelon of the ever-threatening SS hierarchical structure. Wolff was fully aware of Schellenberg's position in the direct surrounding of Himmler, and

---

525. Notarized copy of notarized copy, signed German text from Isaac Sternbuch to "President of Allied Nuremberg Court," Montreux, November 17, 1948, NA, RG 466, E 53, Box 30. (Transl.) Cf. photocopy of clipping from *La Suisse*, December 15, 1948, NA, Foreign Service Posts of the Department of State, RG 84, E 3223, Box 83.
526. Statement, Kurt Becher, March 24, 1948, to Norbert Barr, SAN, NG-5230. Interrogation of Kurt Becher by Norbert Barr, June 22, 1948, reproduced in Mendelsohn, ed., *The Holocaust*, vol. 16, 4 pp. text. In the Becher operation considerable sums are said to have changed hands, while clearly neither Schellenberg nor Musy accepted any funds in their operation.

Schellenberg was equally aware that Wolff had gained access to Allen Dulles and his OSS apparatus in Bern and that his success with Dulles may well have contributed to the clear lack of interest by Dulles in any of the approaches launched by Schellenberg's people in Switzerland in the final period of World War II. Without going into the somewhat unpleasant detail of the relationship between the two SS leaders, it may be said without reservation that there was no love lost between them. For Wolff, however, to attempt to damage Schellenberg in the course of the interrogations in front of the Military Tribunal at Nuremberg, accusing him of things he must have known were untrue, would seem to cast a shadow on the wily SS leader. Besides telling the Americans that Schellenberg "in contrast to me" was "heavily incriminated" by, for instance, the arrest of the British intelligence officers at Venlo, he informed the court that Schellenberg had commanded an "Einsatzgruppe." When pressed to reveal his source for that obviously false information, he had nothing more convincing to say than that he must have heard it in a POW camp or in the hospital. While Karl Wolff "again succeeded in wriggling off the hook," largely thanks to his role in Sunrise, the surrender of German Armed Forces in Northern Italy at the very close of World War II, Schellenberg was sentenced at Nuremberg.[527]

With the Honorable William C. Christianson presiding, sentences were pronounced in the Palace of Justice in Nuremberg on April 14, 1949. Walter Schellenberg was sentenced *in absentia* because in connection with his long-term illness he had undergone an operation very recently and was still quite incapacitated, unable to sit or stand up in court. The records indicate that Schellenberg must have also missed considerable parts of the trial due to severe illness. On the day of sentencing he was one of four of the accused in the Weizsäcker Case who for reasons of illness had been excused from attendance. Considering the strongly worded charges under the indictment, Walter Schellenberg's sentence was relatively generous: "… the Tribunal now sentences him to a term of imprisonment of six years. The period already spent by him in confinement before and during the trial is to be credited on the term stated, and to this end the term of his imprisonment as now adjudged shall be deemed to begin on 17 June 1945."[528]

---

527. Interrogation of Karl Wolff by Norbert Barr, July 29, 1947, SAN, Rep. 502, W 136. Christopher Simpson, *The Splendid Blond Beast: Money, Law and Genocide in the Twentieth Century* (New York: Grove Press, 1993), 236-242. Cf. Jochen von Lang, *Top Nazi: SS General Karl Wolff. The Man Between Hitler and Himmler* (New York: Enigma Books, 2005; 1st German ed. Munich, 1985).
528. "14 April 1949-M-EM-1-1," Court IV, Case XI, NA, RG 466, E 55, Box 8. Extract from press cutting, *The Times*, May 21, 1949, NAK, KV 2/99.

Schellenberg has not received much attention by scholars until now, and when he was discussed, it was usually within the general frame of the SS.[529] In his case, however, this could mean overlooking some possibly significant aspects of his life which may lead to a better understanding of the role played by the SS elite. Not only did Schellenberg develop personal relations with men like Wilhelm Canaris, Roger Masson, Jean-Marie Musy or Count Folke Bernadotte, but the extent to which some of these personalities tried to assist the accused and physically debilitated SS leader and war criminal during the Nuremberg trials would suggest a side of this man not fully covered in the available routine documents of the time. The depositions and testimonies from these and other personalities do not in any way propose that the SS-*Brigadeführer* was not guilty, but the intonation chosen by those who spoke and wrote for him would indeed suggest that our understanding of the events might be helped if we looked closer.

As one might expect, the flood of misunderstandings and plainly false information in the case of Schellenberg did not stop with the verdict. Though certainly not unknown earlier, following the release of his personal health documents, it can now be stated with certainty that Schellenberg had been ill for a number of years and that his forced absence on the day of sentencing was by no means an exception. He had missed many days in court and a good part of his time had been spent in a hospital rather than in the cell assigned to him at the Palace of Justice. But even after the verdict nobody seems to have bothered to attempt to find out where he was. More recent publications still insist on repeating what has been said in print incorrectly for half a century. "Schellenberg was taken to jail in Landsberg."[530] The truth of the matter is that Schellenberg was never considered fit to be sent to Landsberg, a German prison compound where a large number of Nazi leaders spent years of their sentences. As none of the Landsberg prison records contain his name as a prisoner held there in custody, it would have been a relatively easy task to discover that Schellenberg had never been at that prison. Nobody seems to have made the effort to find out.

Though Schellenberg's personal health records were not available until recently, the fact that the former SS leader was at the General City Hospital (*Allgemeines Städtisches Krankenhaus*) in Nuremberg was no secret. From a medical affidavit written by Professor D. Jahn, Chief of the 1st Medical Clinic

---

529. Other than this author's "SS-Brigadeführer Walter Schellenberg" in Doerries, *Hitler's Last Chief of Foreign Intelligence*, the only study dealing with Schellenberg and his career remains George C. Browder, "Walter Schellenberg: Eine Geheimdienst Phantasie," in R. Smelser, E. Syring, eds., *Die SS: Die Elite unter dem Totenkopf* (Paderborn: Schöningh, 2000).
530. Blandford, *SS Intelligence*, 252. K. Bosl, G. Franz, H. R. Hofmann, eds. *Biographisches Wörterbuch zur deutschen Geschichte*, vol. 3 (Munich: Franke, 1975), 2474.

of that hospital, we now know that Schellenberg was permanently moved from his cell at the Palace of Justice to a police hospital already on July 22, 1948, and that his very serious condition forced the authorities to move him to the 1st Medical Clinic on December 3, 1948. The medical diagnosis at the time was a grave case of "cholangitis and cholecystitis" causing serious problems for liver and gall bladder. When none of the treatments led to any improvement, it was decided to operate. On April 7, 1949, his gall bladder was removed and artificial drains were positioned.[531] Although the difficult medical operation saved his life for the time being, his general condition only improved slightly. The tubing was removed in late summer and he apparently had begun to walk again. Some time in September of the same year, however, there was a relapse accompanied by "severe liver cell damage resulting in jaundice...a poor nutritional state, and mental depression over his condition." The diagnosis in October 1949 corresponds with such findings: "… this man is suffering from a wasting disease, to all appearances slowly increasing in intensity. A prognosis of recovery and/or life expectancy cannot be made at this time, but it must be considered 'guarded'."[532]

Under these conditions for longer periods of time there was obviously no social contact, although indications are that his wife Irene visited him at times. His location during these months is described in an Office Memorandum by the Chief of the Prisons Division: "Because of his critical illness, Schellenberg was never transferred to Landsberg, and is not now carried on their prison roster. Schellenberg occupies a private room on the ground floor of building II of the Nurnberg City Hospital. The room is reported as being large, sunny and airy. A 24-hour guard is furnished by the 42221st Labor Service Company. The guard's post of duty is in the corridor and the large window in the prisoner's room, which overlooks the hospital yard, is open and unguarded."[533]

Except for the increasing seriousness of his illness, living with health problems was nothing very new for Walter Schellenberg. Though different sources give different locations, even a journey to Africa is occasionally mentioned, where he may have first infected himself, we have it from the records that he experienced rather serious bouts of illness at least since about 1940, and indications are that even prior to that curious interruptions of his hectic schedule were caused by illness.[534] Keeping in mind that by 1940 he was all of

---

531. Medical Affidavit, Prof. Dr. med. D. Jahn, May 16, 1949, NA, RG 466, E 53, Box 30.
532. "Physical Condition of Prisoner Schellenberg," Prison Physician, Captain MC, Frank V. Sander to Prison Officer, Nurnberg Post Stockade, U.S. Army, October 17, 1949, NA, RG 466, E 53, Box 30.
533. Office Memorandum, S. H. Souter, Jr., Chief, Prisons Division, December 13, 1949, NA, RG 466, E 53, Box 30.
534. Indications are that Schellenberg already as a child suffered from digestive problems which later receded.

30 years old, he was certainly not a very healthy man. Also, his almost constant health problems may in part explain why he developed such a close personal relationship with Felix Kersten, the "Medizinalrat" who may not have been a trained physician but who obviously knew ways to alleviate discomfort and pains of numerous well-known and often affluent personalities. Moreover, Schellenberg's almost ascetic life as a non-smoking and non-drinking workaholic,[535] who apparently could not leave a task unfinished and tended to make night into day, may well have been part of his generally fragile physical condition. That this rigidity in his professional life was forced, can be seen quite easily from the extent to which he appears to have enjoyed the social company of interesting professionals, as well as rides in the Grunewald and the rather common hunts of the upper middle and upper classes at the time in Germany.

Imagining this gravely ill person in his hospital room and knowing of his strong will power and self-control, it is not at all difficult to see him, in spite of his physical debilitation, using every moment of respite to write down memories of events and persons as they came to his mind in his solitude. In some way this could explain the mass of often unmatching sheets of paper filled with very quickly dashed out notes. If all or many of these sheets, which were evidently the base for a large part of the memoirs published after his death, were indeed scribbled full in 1949 and early 1950 when Schellenberg was alone in his hospital room and much of the time physically very sick and weak that might explain the somewhat unstructured and disorganized quality of their content. Just how much his strength was failing him can be seen in the explanation offered by Fritz Riediger for the absence, except for a signature, of any comments from Schellenberg on a formal petition for parole. Instead Riediger passed on Schellenberg's request that he may be permitted to submit his personal comments at a future date when he would be in better health.[536] The brief time period between Schellenberg's parole in late March 1950, or rather his departure from the hospital in May 1950, and his death in March 1952, filled with recurring attacks of his illness and various journeys, all consuming his limited strength, could not have sufficed to write those memoirs, irrespective of their textual condition.[537] The legitimate question whether his American supervisors from the Prison Division would not have confiscated

---

535. His active Corps membership would suggest that as a student he was not aware of serious liver or other health problems. In his student years he may also have smoked. During professional life in the German capital social drinking was difficult to avoid. Various people from his professional surroundings have stated that he was not a smoker. Photographs showing him with a cigarette in hand appear to be posed.
536. "Petition" to the "Military Governor of the American Zone of Occupation in Germany," filed April 29, 1949, with Secretary General for Military Tribunals, Defense Center. NA, RG 466, E 53, Box 30.
537. Schellenberg Papers, IFZ, ED-90, vols. 1-7. According to official finding aid of IFZ, text is incomplete and IFZ has unsuccessfully attempted to obtain missing texts from the family. IFZ is of the opinion that the texts they hold were written from 1951 to 1952.

such scraps of paper from the prisoner's hospital room, can be answered with some assurance. From the records all indications are that once the trial ended and the prisoners had been taken to their designations, supervision seems to have been reduced to routine daily guard duty. Because Schellenberg had become a serious medical case, he received treatment by German hospital doctors, and U.S. authorities were merely informed periodically on his physical state. It can be assumed that the personal notes of this prisoner were of no interest to those who guarded him.

Other than medical care, the only outside activity that occupied the sick prisoner and that periodically challenged his mental awareness was the almost continuous work of his lawyers to obtain a ruling of parole. The visits of the lawyers and the discussions with them about new petitions and their contents may have been highpoints of mental challenge in the otherwise extremely regulated hospital life of the former SS leader and Foreign Intelligence Chief. Hints of clandestine intelligence connections during the time spent in the General City Hospital in Nuremberg, found occasionally in the literature, must be considered pure nonsense under the prevailing conditions.[538]

With the active assistance of a number of personalities, such as the well-known German diplomat Werner Otto von Hentig,[539] and the presentation of detailed medical reports from medical experts of the General City Hospital in Nuremberg, Schellenberg's lawyers in the spring of 1950 succeeded in obtaining a Medical Pardon. It was signed on March 27, 1950, in Frankfurt by the United States High Commissioner for Germany John J. McCloy.[540] In the final documents from General Counsel Robert E. Bowie of March 24, 1950, leading up to that parole, reference is made to medical affidavits from American and German medical experts, confirming that Schellenberg is suffering from "lingering cholangitis associated with jaundice and liver

---

538. Ian Sayer, Douglas Botting, *America's Secret Army: The Untold Story of the Counter Intelligence Corps* (London: Fontana, 1990; 1st 1989), 329, without naming source: "He [Klaus Barbie] had been recommended to British intelligence and employed by them to recruit agents for a new, British-initiated intelligence organization in Germany run by his former wartime chief in the SD, Walter Schellenberg." It should also be noted that Barbie was Gestapo chief in Lyons, not an intelligence agent. Müller, not Schellenberg, was therefore Barbie's "wartime chief."— Referring to the time period between the end of the war and Schellenberg being prosecuted as a war criminal, Alexander Hardy, Counsel for the prosecution in Nuremberg, who should have known better, reports that "Schellenberg had been successful in remaining free after the war and, in fact, had established himself as a confidential advisor to the American Occupation Forces." Alexander G. Hardy, *Hitler's Secret Weapon: The "Managed" Press and Propaganda Machine of Nazi Germany* (New York: Vantage Press, 1967), 142.
539. Correspondence of Dr. Werner Otto von Hentig for the Kirchliches Aussenamt der Evangelischen Kirche in Deutschland (Leitung: Dr. Martin Niemöller), NA, RG 466, E 53, Box 30. From 1946 to December 1949 Hentig was responsible for international matters in that Church office.
540. Order, Office of the United States High Commissioner for Germany, dated Frankfurt-am-Main, March 27, 1950, signed by John J. McCloy, United States High Commissioner for Germany, *Ibid.*

disease." Moreover, "the possibility of recovery is most remote," and the doctors were of the opinion "that Schellenberg's death within a period of six months to two years is probable."[541] The Order for Medical Parole prepared by U.S. officials and issued by John J. McCloy states that "during the period of his parole the Petitioner shall not engage, directly or indirectly, in any business or profession or in any writing for publication, whether alone or in collaboration with others." Presumably the period of Medical Parole would end with the regular termination of Schellenberg's sentence, or as Bowie informed McCloy, "in accordance with the established system for earning good [conduct] time, Schellenberg will be eligible for release on June 21, 1950."[542] In other words, the restrictions listed in the text of the parole order would be lifted automatically as of June 21, 1950.

From the records it would appear that Walter Schellenberg left the General City Hospital in Nuremberg on May 14, 1950. He told Dr. Gerhard Wendel that he would go for one day to Frankfurt and then travel to "his home town." On May 15, 1950, he was indeed taken in at the Saint Francis Hospital in Iburg. Doctors there reported his physical condition as bad and generally corresponding to the very negative medical reports from Nuremberg in the months prior to his discharge.[543] A little more than a month later Schellenberg received notice from S. H. Souter, Chief of Prisons Division, that "in accordance with the system of good conduct time established for War Criminals" he had "become eligible for this type of release." His status officially changed from that of "medical parole" to "conditional discharge." Walter Schellenberg, five years after turning himself in to the U.S. Military Attaché in Stockholm was now a free man.[544]

In view of Schellenberg's physical condition in mid-1950 there can be little doubt that he was forced to spend a good part of the next months under rather close medical observation. A few personal letters to Wilhelm Höttl clearly indicate that his health was very problematic that summer and that he suffered at least one relapse which seems to have destroyed unrealistic plans for publications in his own name or in some form of cooperation with Höttl. He knew

---

541. R. R. Bowie, General Counsel, to John J. McCloy, March 24, 1950, Petition of Walter Schellenberg for Medical Parole, *Ibid*.
542. *Ibid*.
543. Dr. Bremer to S. H. Souter, Jr., June 3, 1950, *Ibid*.
544. S. H. Souter, Jr., Chief, Prisons Division, to Walter Schellenberg, June 23, 1950. The "conditions" referred to in connection with the "discharge" are that laws of Germany or of the occupation authorities may not be violated. If such violations should occur prior to the date of expiration of the sentence, he would be imprisoned "to serve the remaining amount of his full term." Document for "Conditional Releases" from the Office of General Counsel. F. Walter Schellenberg to S. H. Souter, Jr., and enclosure, handwritten, June 20, 1950.

from the doctors in Nuremberg that another operation would be necessary and that he needed to recover considerably before submitting his weakened body to such an ordeal. There are also indications that he had learned that few surgeons in Germany were able to perform the needed operation and that better professional treatment might be available elsewhere.[545] Very little is actually known about Schellenberg's contacts and activities during the later months of 1950. Evidently, both American and British intelligence services were likely to keep an eye on the former Chief of *Amt* VI Foreign Intelligence. Clearly, we have what appears to be sufficient evidence to state that American intelligence was very interested to gain reliable information on Schellenberg and his possible activities. Moreover, their covert inquiries were channeled through an organization referred to as Zipper and closely linked to their involvement with an individual referred to as Utility. Thanks to a rather liberal declassification policy pursued by Washington on the basis of the Nazi War Crimes Disclosure Act of 1998 and related legislation, we have known for some time that Utility was a code name for Reinhard Gehlen, former chief of *Fremde Heere Ost*, Nazi Germany's military intelligence in the war against the Soviet Union, and that Zipper was the code name given to Gehlen's organization rebuilt under the tutelage of the U.S. Army and, merging similar groups called Bolero and Keystone, originally code-named Rusty. Regrettably, the *Bundesnachrichtendienst* (BND), the follow-up organization of Zipper and today the intelligence service of the Federal Republic of Germany, has not released any records relating to its founding years, and the German Government, in marked contrast to the Americans and more recently also the British, has seen no need to pass legislation leading to a declassification of such records. Under these conditions we are, for documentation, still largely confined to American sources.[546]

Though by 1950 this was no news for Washington insiders, it should be noted that in view of the Cold War and a generally much changed international situation, Americans had begun to look differently at the employment of useful Nazis. A rather clear statement from the CIA files might be helpful: "In the meanwhile, the developments in Germany and probably also in Austria have

---

545. Hagen [Höttl], *Unternehmen* Bernhard, 273-275. — There is no information regarding possible attempts by Schellenberg to be treated or operated by any of the supposedly three German surgeons coming into question. After the murder of Count Bernadotte in 1948, Schellenberg may not have considered Stockholm. In Switzerland he could have thought of Masson and Musy as persons possibly willing to help him.
546. For a recent review of Gehlen's relationship with the Americans see Timothy Naftali, "Reinhard Gehlen and the United States," in Richard Breitman, Norman J. Goda, Timothy Naftali, Robert Wolfe, *U.S. Intelligence and the Nazis* (Washington, D.C.: National Archives Trust Fund Board, 2004). Kevin C. Ruffner, "Forging an Intelligence Partnership: CIA and the Origins of the BND, 1945-49," vol. I, NA, RG 263, E A1-87, Box 2.

been such that membership in the SS, or in the SD, or in the Abwehr no longer is regarded as a strike against any personality."[547] Whether the vivid interest expressed by the Karlsruhe intelligence people was related to this more general statement of policy cannot be determined with any certainty, but their concern with "Brigadeführer u. Oberregierungsrat Dr. Walter Friedrich Schellenberg" fits well with their new way of looking at intelligence problems in Europe. Apparently the American intelligence officers corresponding here had just come upon a copy of the "Final Report" on Schellenberg produced by British intelligence officers in the summer and autumn of 1945.[548] What they wanted was "a check of the British allegation [text blocked out] that Utility [Gehlen] had offered his services to Himmler in setting up post defeat resistance." Gehlen apparently not only had not told his new American friends and supervisors that he and Schellenberg "were well acquainted," but in one situation Gehlen had actually claimed that he did not know Schellenberg. According to the documents, the Americans were "mildly dismayed." Evidently not completely trusting Gehlen or Utility, who was supposed to be in their service, they were now interested in speaking with Schellenberg— possibly to become better informed, one might think, about the possible availability of Schellenberg.[549] Quite contrary to their British colleagues who in their "Conclusions" to the "Final Report" had emphasized that Schellenberg had "not produced any evidence of outstanding genius" but instead had demonstrated "his incoherency and incapability of producing lucid ... statements," the Americans found that Schellenberg's "account of Utility's offer [concerning a resistance network in the defeated Germany] is both lucid and credible."[550] As to the origins of the negative appraisal of Schellenberg's mental abilities, one keeps stumbling over the name of Hugh Trevor Roper. A secret message from "Special Operations" to "Pullach/Karlsruhe" of June 16, 1950, and released to Pullach with the information copy to Karlsruhe over the names of William K. Harvey[551] and R. Helms[552] on June 17, 1950, informs Pullach: "1. No current info here. 2. Emphatically avowed low [text blocked

---

547. Chief Pullach (name blocked out) to Chief Karlsruhe (name blocked out), April 19(?), 1950, Secret, NA, E ZZ-16, CIA Name Files, Box 8.
548. See "Final Report."
549. Chief Foreign Relations (blocked out) to Chief Karlsruhe (blocked out), April 18, 1950, Secret, released by CIA 2001, NA, RG 263, E A1-86, CIA Name Files, Box 13.
550. *Ibid.*
551. William King Harvey (1915-1976), FBI agent, then CIA, professional contact with Kim Philby and Guy Burgess, later stationed for CIA in Germany. He would certainly have kept contact with British intelligence. Brief summary in Norman Polmar, Thomas B. Allen, *Spy Book: The Encyclopedia of Espionage* (London: Greenhill/Random House, 1997; 1st 1996), 255.
552. Richard Helms (1913-2002), later Director of Central Intelligence, joined OSS 1943, later to CIA, for a time head of Office of Special Operations (OSO) internally just called Special Operations, served in Britain, Germany and other locations.

out] estimate Schellenberg, view his wartime megalomania and incoherent behavior under interrogation, probably genuine. Seriously doubt [text blocked out] use for intended use. 3. Above opinion may be passed [text blocked out] recommend Trevor-Roper's 'Last Days of Hitler', published with blessings [text blocked out], for reading. 4. We interested any further info."[553] In retrospect the British derogation of their wartime opponent, of course, causes one to question why, if they saw him as incoherent and generally unrewarding, they would have insisted on getting him to London, intensely interrogating him for several months, and struggling to keep him in London rather than handing him over as a witness to the Military Tribunal in Nuremberg.

Even taking into consideration that Schellenberg in the autumn of 1950 would have been in such a state of general physical weakness that he would hardly be able to work in earnest for any intelligence organization, a lot of uncertainty remains about his changing whereabouts and his activities from fall 1950 to summer 1951. Being careful not to read too much into any statement by Reinhard Gehlen on Walter Schellenberg, one still registers with some surprise that shortly after Schellenberg's death Gehlen asked a Frankfurt CIA officer to "confirm" that Schellenberg had passed away recently. Apparently at the time Gehlen thought it possible that the report of Schellenberg's death might be some sort of trick, "referring to Schellenberg's travels during the past year between Switzerland, Italy and Spain 'presumably on behalf of either the British or the Americans'." The CIA officer replied that he was "not aware of any of Schellenberg's recent activities," but he would "inquire." Though one can read from this that Gehlen had tried to follow Schellenberg around, but that his sleuths had not done very good work, it cannot be excluded that Gehlen merely wanted to find out how much the CIA would tell him. An internal CIA message clearly shows that they kept a very loose tab on Schellenberg ever since May 1950 and that, in fact, they had "no detailed reports on Schellenberg's activities." In view of Schellenberg's constant affliction with serious illness, this is not at all surprising, and it is borne out by the total absence of any hints of substance pointing to any intelligence activity.[554]

---

553. Washington (blocked out) to Pull F, Secret, June 16/17, 1950, NA, RG 263, E A1-86, Box 38. The book referred to is Trevor-Roper, *The Last Days of Hitler*. In the preface Trevor-Roper states that the book was written after his intelligence chief Dick White "invited" him to do so in 1945. Trevor-Roper's book contains a number of erroneous informations on Schellenberg, some of which are repeated in his *The Philby Affair: Espionage, Treason, and Secret Services* (London: William Kimber, 1968). For a strongly worded response to Trevor-Roper's Philby book see Robert Cecil, "Five of Six at War: Section V of MI6," *Intelligence and National Security*, vol. 9, no. 2 (April 1994).

554. Chief (blocked out) to Chief EE, May 6, 1952, Secret, NA, RG 263, E A1-86, CIA Name Files, Box 38.

Whether Schellenberg, after his release from the hospital in Nuremberg, traveled to Spain more than once, must remain an open question. His reasons for going there, however, according to a few less than fully reliable sources, were at least two. According to one report from Madrid in July 1951, he was there some time prior to that date and like most other former Nazi officials, he was received "with open arms." According to this report, he pursued two goals. Supposedly he attempted to collect support for his idea of forming a militarily organized protection force not unlike the German SS, disbanding at the same time all political parties. He is said to even have presented some organizational proposals, but the Spanish supposedly were not greatly interested because at the time they had already what seemed to be more important political problems to deal with. His second purpose, according to this source, was an urgent search for funds, stemming, he is said to have argued, from some holdings of Heinrich Himmler and allegedly hidden somewhere in Spain. Unfortunately for him, this source claimed the ranking Nazis who had found refuge in Spain had known for some time that he would be coming to look for funds and consequently were well prepared to be unable to help. There is talk of some Spanish Pts 12,000,000 which, it is claimed, he declared to be "his private money." Presumably this particular visit lasted about two weeks. An approximate date of his stay in Spain can also be inferred from a later CIA report, informing that earlier CIA reports of May 16 and June 30, 1951, have Schellenberg "undoubtedly residing in Spain." The earlier report also tells us that Schellenberg was "in contact [with] Skorzeny" and adds "You may pass Zipper. No apparent ... interest Schellenberg at present but would appreciate details [text blocked out] activities coming Zipper's attention."[555] Contrary to later claims, Schellenberg and Skorzeny were not at all good friends. These two men were very different in every respect and therefore in professional situations often came to rather different conclusions. The case of the German plane grounded at the Swiss airport Dübendorf may serve as an illustration of their differences. Skorzeny was ready to attack Dübendorf with a special commando and destroy the plane. Schellenberg instead proposed negotiating and blowing up the plane under the supervision of Swiss and German officials. Fortunately his side won the heated debate in Berlin, thereby almost certainly preventing a state of war between Switzerland and Germany.

Somehow connected with Skorzeny's underground network of Nazis was a man called Otto Horcher, apparently an alumnus of Nazi intelligence in Berlin.

---

555. Correspondence between Hans Heinrich Dieckhoff and Richard Kempe. Dated Madrid, July 1, 1951. Could be someone's report or a collection of news from the Spanish press. Special Operations to Pullach/Karlsruhe, May 16/17, 1951, Secret, NA, RG 263, E A1-86, CIA Name Files, Boxes 37-38.

His role in Madrid remains unclear but there are unconfirmed hints in the records that Schellenberg saw Horcher in Madrid either on his own or in the company of Skorzeny.[556] Very possibly indeed Schellenberg was searching for funds to alleviate his probably extremely uncomfortable financial situation. Whether his contact with Skorzeny in Madrid was also related to any political plans, in the absence of documentation must remain an open question. Less likely are the doubtful reports claiming that "the former Gestapo [sic] leader Schellenberg conducts an information service under the name 'Anbeter der absoluten Macht'" or Worshippers of Absolute Power. A report dated February 7, 1952, shortly before Schellenberg's death, asserts that this organization was already well connected in Spain and North Africa and that it was in the process of establishing itself in Austria. This buzz would match other unconfirmed rumors of an "expanding international neo-Fascist movement" supposedly represented by the well-known Fascist Jean Bauverd, who was said to be linked to the Grand Mufti of Jerusalem and a number of Arab personalities and organizations. He was, it was claimed, in touch with Otto Skorzeny and Walter Schellenberg. On the basis of presently available records and research results published, it is safe to say that nothing reliable on this organization has surfaced and there is no confirmation anywhere which would suggest any political activities by Schellenberg in such a direction.[557] Additionally, it should be recalled that Schellenberg was a very sick person, handicapped by bodily deficiencies of a grave nature. Moreover, we are made to believe that in spite of this physical debilitation he was continually at work on his voluminous memoirs. We know that he may have been able to move about carefully by late 1950, and as already mentioned, he did travel at least once to Spain. Though lacking reliable information it would also appear plausible that his Swiss contacts helped him cross into Switzerland occasionally.

What does appear rather reliable, however, beyond such tales and rumors, is the very personal account of a "médecin de campagne," a Swiss country doctor, who in May 1951 was suddenly contacted by Roger Masson. They had not met before, but Masson had been given the doctor's name by Georges Ducry, a lawyer and police official, a long time friend of the doctor. Masson came with "a very particular request," namely for the doctor to take charge of the medical care of the former Nazi officer Walter Schellenberg. Obviously

---

556. 30 to 25 (BND report?), May 13, 1952, NA, RG 263, E ZZ-16, CIA Name Files, Box 45. Other documents suggest a connection of Otto Horcher to the BND.
557. "German Nationalist and Neo-Nazi Activities in Argentina," prepared by WH Division, Case K-10046, July 8, 1953, Secret, CREST, NA. B-2/GW 121, February 7, 1952, Secret, NA, RG 263, E A1-86, Box 38. According to Pierre Péan, L'Extremiste: François Genoud, de Hitler à Carlos (Paris: Fayard, 1996), 173, 209, Bauverd used his Spanish connections to obtain permission for Skorzeny to stay.

unprepared for such assignment, the doctor begged for time to give it some thought. He must have agreed later, for some time in the autumn of 1951 Walter Schellenberg arrived at the home of Dr. Francis Lang in Romont, a town situated between Fribourg and Lausanne. The car in which Schellenberg had traveled was driven by Sven Hinnen. As apparently agreed with Masson, the mysterious patient was put in Room 30A of the Hospital of Billens, and to the hospital employees he soon became known as le Monsieur du 30A (the gentleman from 30A). Dr. Lang visited him every two to three days, usually in the evening, and in the course of their apparently congenial conversations they became well acquainted. In fact, Dr. Lang must have begun to enjoy the company of the German patient, whom he barely knew. This went so far that he and his wife took Schellenberg along to a movie theater in Fribourg. What might have been a pleasant social occasion, however, became a potentially unpleasant event. As it turned out, in one of the seats in front of them sat the chief of the cantonal police who felt inclined to inquire about the stranger unknown to him. Dr. Lang does not tell how the police chief went about it, but as Lang later remembered the chief decided to keep to himself what he found out at the movie theatre. More risky was an unexpected encounter on a shopping street in Romont shortly thereafter. Apparently Schellenberg needed a winter coat—suggesting that it was now late fall 1951—and Dr. Lang as usual had taken him to shop. Quite unbelievably, while walking down the street, they ran into a couple of policemen who happened to be the men who had served as body guards for General Guisan when the latter met with Schellenberg a few years earlier at Biglen and Arosa. "Ils ont bien sûr reconnu W. Schellenberg."[558]

Dr. Lang knew, of course, that Switzerland was overrun by all kinds of people, seeking refuge and in many cases running away from their past related to the Nazi period, but he was also aware of the high degree of tolerance often exercised by Swiss authorities in such cases. Moreover, the doctor felt that someone staying at a hospital would be less exposed to bureaucratic chicanery than other more visible personalities. As a medical doctor he thought the hospital at Billens was not the optimal place for getting the treatment he would have prescribed for Schellenberg. From the very personal and direct expressions in his memoirs, one gains the impression that Dr. Lang was a little confused about what might be best for the rather helpless patient at Billens. Apparently Schellenberg told him about his work with Masson and Guisan, for some time in the fall of 1951, following the unexpected encounters with the police officials, the doctor decided to seek advice from Masson and Guisan, as well as from his old friend Ducry. From the memoirs it is evident that Dr.

---

558. "They certainly recognized W. Schellenberg."

Lang began his search for advice with General Guisan. He was received very kindly, but when the doctor explained his plans of getting Schellenberg transferred from the hospital at Billens to a better clinic in Lausanne, the general froze up and much regretted that he could be of no assistance, as he was very concerned that certain members of the federal government of Switzerland were just waiting for an opportunity to attack him in public. Being able to connect him again with the Nazi intelligence chief would be just what his adversaries needed. The country doctor left knowing that he could not expect much help from the general.

Dr. Lang next visited his old friend Georges Ducry, who had given Lang's name to Masson to begin with. To all indications Ducry had no helpful advice either, other than to suggest going and seeing Jean-Marie Musy. The former Swiss president, already advanced in age at the time of the rescue operations in Germany, had become in the meantime confined to a wheelchair and was suffering from multiple sclerosis and other ailments. In spite of being handicapped, however, Musy as always tried to come up with some solution for Schellenberg and proposed to approach the Papal Nuncio Philippe Bernardini whom Musy's wife knew well. More important, the Nuncio had supported the dedicated rescue work of Recha and Isaac Sternbuch and Schellenberg, in that connection, had seen to arrangements to free a nephew of Bernardini from a concentration camp. Musy now called the Monsignor in Dr. Lang's presence and obtained an appointment for him. Full of hope for assistance Dr. Lang was off to Bern. To his great disappointment, however, the Papal Nuncio was not very enthused about doing something for Schellenberg, indeed letting the doctor know that it was not Schellenberg who had saved his nephew from certain death in a German camp but Jean-Marie Musy. In fact, he said he did not know Schellenberg. Somehow the doctor succeeded in making the impatient Monsignor at least listen to his proposal to move Walter Schellenberg, who was living in Switzerland secretly and by now certainly under surveillance by the police, to a refuge in the Vatican. Dr. Lang seriously suggested that Bernardini send a telegram to Pope Pius XII to arrange for the reception of Schellenberg in the safe grounds of the Vatican. Apparently the Papal Nuncio did feel obliged to do something, and a telegram was sent. It has survived as an insufficiently identified handwritten text and reads: "From Bern: — Bernardini To Vatican General Schellenberg, former head of the German Information Service, who is now in Rome, will ask to be received by Your Excellency for personal reasons."[559]

---

559. To all appearances the document which contains this handwritten text is an FBI report. The handwritten text does not mention an author, is classified as Secret Security Information X58/52, and is

The doctor later recalled that a telegram was indeed sent, and we have no reason to doubt that. In the Vatican it was received by Cardinal Luigi Maglione who for whatever reason came to the decision that Walter Schellenberg was not to be given shelter.[560] Although he does not explicitly say so, the general impression from the memoirs is that the combination of the threatening situation for Schellenberg, caused by his illegal status and the refusal from the Vatican, persuaded Dr. Lang to look for another way for Schellenberg to leave Switzerland and stay within reach of urgently needed medical treatment. He learned about a special dietetic clinic known for treatment of liver diseases and located in Pallanza on Lago Maggiore just across the border in Italy. His good friend Georges Ducry with his police connections was even able to locate someone who could produce a false Swiss passport in the name of Louis Kowalki. As Dr. Lang remembered, Schellenberg had stayed at Billens for about six months until the "période de Pâques" (Easter Season) of 1952. Again Roger Masson's man Sven Hinnen handled the border formalities and transported Schellenberg past frontier controls without any difficulty. We also learn from Dr. Lang that Schellenberg's wife Irene was able to join him in Italy, implying that during the months in Switzerland at Billens she probably was not with him. Dr. Lang and his wife visited Schellenberg in Pallanza where, among other things, they must have talked about financial matters. Understandably, the memoirs do not offer much detail, but "in the course of one of their conversations" the doctor for whatever reason must have intimated that he was in considerable financial straights. He apparently explained that since Schellenberg's arrival at Romont he had covered medical and other expenses of around Swiss Fr 20,000. With few words Dr. Lang then reports that Schellenberg contacted Coco Chanel and explained his dire financial problems. If the doctor remembered correctly, the lady of haute couture indeed arrived in a black Mercedes, curtains drawn, and gave Schellenberg about Swiss Fr 30,000.[561] There are no other explanations from the doctor, other than the fact that during the war Schellenberg had been helpful to her and to others in the fashion world.[562]

As the country doctor recalls, Schellenberg stayed at Pallanza for some five weeks. André Brissaud, a French journalist and author of a number of important books, happened to be driving near the Lago Maggiore on a very frosty night "at the end of February 1952" when his rented car broke down,

---

dated October 29, 1951. It was declassified 1999/2000. NA, RG 65, IWG Classification 100 Name Indices, Box 2.
560. Reports that Schellenberg was granted an audience with the Pope appear to be baseless.
561. The currency may have been French francs.
562. Information regarding Schellenberg's stay in Switzerland is derived from Francis Lang, *Mémoirs d'un Médecin de Campagne 1940-1990* (Fribourg: Fragnières, 1991).

forcing him to walk and look for help. When he saw some light and discovered "a large villa," he decided to ask whether he might use the telephone to call a mechanic. The friendly servant opening the door spoke to the master of the house and Brissaud found himself invited to stay overnight. Later it turned out that the gentleman was a Milanese lawyer who at dinner introduced Brissaud to a "Swiss friend" of his. This Swiss friend was a relatively short, very well dressed man, who looked very slight, had yellow facial skin and in many ways appeared to be "very ill." Brissaud, always much interested in political and military history, had the distinct feeling that he knew this man, but it was only after dinner in the course of their conversation in French that he learned that the Swiss friend in actuality was Walter Schellenberg, an SS leader and the former Chief of *Amt* VI Foreign Intelligence. On the personal side Schellenberg mentioned his health problems and explained that he had come to Pallanza because "some old friends" were there. He also talked about regular trips to Milan for "treatment." Shortly, he said, he would be going to Turin "to consult an eminent cancer specialist." Fortunately for Brissaud, his generous host, off to Milan the next day, invited the Frenchman to stay on and continue his conversations with Schellenberg. Brissaud stayed a week. On closer reading, the information concerning Schellenberg, as remembered by Brissaud some twenty years later, contains a number of inaccuracies and cannot be considered completely reliable. On the other hand, Brissaud was a very observant visitor of Schellenberg, and his impressions of the SS leader, for different reasons than those of the country doctor, are of considerable value.[563] Very important also, the Frenchman's account confirms that Schellenberg indeed was staying in Pallanza in Italy in late February 1952 and that he did not live at the hospital or some guest house in town but instead with an unidentified Italian who some seven years after the war was willing to offer hospitality to the SS officer.

Of some significance is Brissaud's remark about Schellenberg working on his memoirs every afternoon, presumably at the Italian lawyer's villa. Apparently one day, in the course of the lively discussions with Brissaud, he went to his room and fetched a folder containing a part of the text. From what Brissaud remembers, Schellenberg actually then proceeded to read from his memoirs.[564] The question of when exactly Brissaud stayed with Schellenberg at the villa in Pallanza takes on some significance if one attempts to establish even in most general terms just where Schellenberg spent the final months of his life. In the course of his assignment to put some order into and even edit the disorganized texts Schellenberg had already written, the young German

---

563. One needs to remember that Schellenberg's memoirs had been published and that Brissaud had probably seen them when he wrote *The Nazi Secret Service* (*Histoire du Service Secret Nazi*) in 1972.
564. Brissaud, *The Nazi Secret Service*, 28.

journalist Klaus Harpprecht may have seen even more of Schellenberg than Brissaud. From the memoirs of Dr. Francis Lang we learn that Schellenberg only came to Italy in early 1952, meaning that he would still have been in Billens in Switzerland at the time when Harpprecht remembers working with him in Pallanza. The German journalist wrote the "Foreword" to the German edition of the memoirs which was published seven years after Schellenberg's death and three years after the first English edition of 1956. In Harpprecht's own words: "I saw him [Schellenberg] last in October 1951 as a very ill man, who was unable to complete the work he had begun … When I met him for the first time on a pleasant late summer evening in Pallanza on Lago Maggiore, I almost overlooked him among the guests of the large hotel." Shortly thereafter Harpprecht refers to a "plush resort hotel." If Harpprecht, who in 1951 was a very young man, remembers correctly, this would mean that he worked with Schellenberg on the latter's memoirs from "late summer" until "October 1951" which would not appear to be a long time for this type of assignment and, more baffling, a time when, according to Dr. Francis Lang, Schellenberg was still in Billens staying in Room 30A.[565] The British historian Alan Bullock in his "Introduction" to the first English edition of the memoirs reports that Alfred Scherz of the Swiss publisher Scherz sent Harpprecht to Pallanza where he arrived "at the end of August." According to Bullock, who may have met Harpprecht later in connection with the British publication, the latter's "task was to put the draft into order and help fill the gaps in Schellenberg's memory."[566]

While these reports demonstrate remarkable discrepancies regarding dates and locations, there is no doubt that some time in March 1952, Walter Schellenberg, accompanied by his wife Irene, boarded a train in Pallanza, most likely heading for further medical checkups in Turin. In his memoirs Dr. Lang adds to the mystery by reporting that Schellenberg actually had planned to leave Pallanza in order to return to Billens or even to go back to Germany. Based on archival sources, the Swiss historian Hans Rudolf Fuhrer states that Schellenberg was heading for Rome and had to be taken off the train at Alessandria. It does seem certain that while traveling Schellenberg suffered severe attacks of pain in his lower abdomen and had to be removed from the train and given medical attention, according to Dr. Lang, at Domodossola. After calling Schellenberg's doctor at Verbania (near Pallanza) and in view of

---

565. Klaus Harpprecht, "Vorwort," in Schellenberg, *Memoiren*, 7-9. Harpprecht has informed me that the hotel may have been a sanatorium. Harpprecht and Gita (Margarete) Petersen, who worked together on the memoirs, did not live in the hotel/sanatorium.
566. Alan Bullock, "Introduction," in Schellenberg, *The Schellenberg Memoirs*, 15-17. When, according to Alan Bullock, André Deutsch acquired the Schellenberg memoirs for publication, Harpprecht was asked to come to England and "inspect the manuscript."

his threatening condition, his wife had him transported to Turin where, according to Dr. Lang, he was operated several days later by a well-known surgeon by the name of Dr. Dogliotti. While Schellenberg was at the hospital in Turin the surgeon apparently telephoned Dr. Lang, reporting on his patient's condition. When the grim news suggested that Schellenberg would not have much longer to live, Dr. Lang rushed to call Father Franz Emmeneger of the Salvatorians in Rome and asked him to administer the final sacraments to Schellenberg in Turin.[567] This would fit with information offered by Pierre Braunschweig who writes that a priest approached Roger Masson in Chatel-St. Denis on March 29, 1952, to tell him: "[Schellenberg] died yesterday. I was his confessor. Based on what he confided to me under the seal of secrecy, I know all the things he did for Switzerland." Schellenberg apparently died not long after the operation in Turin on March 31, 1952, and was buried on April 2, 1952.[568]

Instead of obituaries and other public comments on the life of Hitler's last Chief of Foreign Intelligence, intelligence services of other nations in an almost ironic underground contest pursued his memoirs, incomplete and as some authors would later have it, "fictitious," "suspect and self-serving," or "ghost-written." Charles Whiting even proposes: "The SIS probably wrote his memoirs for him and paid him afterwards to keep his mouth shut about operations concerning the UK, especially Operation Willi (1940), dealing with the Duke and Duchess of Windsor."[569] Some sections of these memoirs were certainly seen and worked on in some manner by Klaus Harpprecht who according to Alan Bullock had been asked to do so by Alfred Scherz. Bullock, certainly not uninformed about these memoirs, also writes that Schellenberg when in Switzerland had "contracted to write for ... Scherz Verlag" which would appear to contradict a former member of the Scherz Verlag who recently wrote that Alfred Scherz had not asked Harpprecht to work for him. This former member of the management of Scherz publishers also reports that contacts with Schellenberg were handled by a very tall man living in Lausanne. Apparently Alfred Scherz had planned to pay Schellenberg a visit in late 1951, but the records contain no information that any such encounter between author and publisher took place. Most likely the tall man was Sven Hinnen,

---

567. A priest at the Palace of Justice in Nuremberg is said to have assisted Schellenberg in returning to the Catholic faith. While in Switzerland and Italy he wore a cross and took communion regularly.
568 Braunschweig, *Secret Channel to Berlin*, 272-273. Fuhrer, *Spionage gegen die Schweiz*, 134-135. The slight confusion of the last dates could not be cleared up. — He did not die "in his bed in Rome" as reported by Edward Crankshaw, *GESTAPO: Instrument of Tyranny* (London: Greenhill Books, 2002; Copyright 1956), 224.
569. Cf. Breitman, "Hitler's Alleged Peace Emissaries," 426. Neale H. Petersen, ed., *From Hitler's Doorstep: The Wartime Intelligence Reports of Allen Dulles, 1942-1945* (University Park: The Pennsylvania State University Press, 1996), 985. Charles Whiting, *Hitler's Secret War: The Nazi Espionage Campaign against the Allies* (London: Leo Cooper/Pen & Sword, 2000), 151.

named by Dr. Francis Lang as someone working for Roger Masson, who sent Hinnen to deal with various chores for Schellenberg, such as the border crossings.[570]

According to recently declassified CIA documents, the Americans first took notice of Sven Hinnen in 1951 when he turned up in the U.S. with a copy of Schellenberg's memoirs. There is no way of telling whether he was traveling in his own interest or whether he was indeed representing Walter Schellenberg who was still alive. Whatever it may have been, American intelligence caught up with Hinnen and discovered how unsuccessful he was in his efforts to locate a publisher for Schellenberg's memoirs. After Schellenberg passed away, his wife apparently took matters into her own hands, and the Schellenberg manuscript ended up with the German illustrated magazine *Quick*. An author of popular German war literature, Jürgen Thorwald, saw the manuscript at *Quick* where the managers supposedly encouraged him to edit the texts.[571] Reading the rather vague intelligence reports on the affair one gains the impression that perhaps Scherz already had picked an editor who indeed may have been Harpprecht. The Americans, at the time of these reports in the spring of 1953, a year after Schellenberg's death, had obviously not yet seen the memoirs and certainly were more than interested. To all indications they obtained their information from Zipper, Gehlen's intelligence organization, which in turn was in contact with Jürgen Thorwald. Also, while Thorwald was unable to get himself appointed editor, presumably for *Quick* rather than for Scherz, additional difficulties cropped up in Switzerland suggesting that Scherz was trying to avoid rumored problems with Swiss authorities concerned for whatever reason with the Schellenberg memoirs or rather potential legal aspects of their publication. Considering the controversies over the wartime connections of Schellenberg to Masson and Guisan, carried out rather publicly in Switzerland after World War II, Swiss authorities may have had good reasons for not lending support to the publication in Switzerland of Schellenberg's memoirs.

Intensely interesting is an intelligence report regarding "the team of Best and Schmitz" who according to this American—or BND?—source "made some arrangement with Frau Schellenberg according to which nothing can be published without their concurrence." Werner Best, of course, had been Nazi governor of occupied Denmark, sentenced after the war, but released in 1951. His partner in this affair, Schmitz, was, according to the CIA documentation,

---

570. Scherz letter, private archive. Bullock, "Introduction," 15.
571. Chief Pullach to Chief EW, April 2, 1953, Security Information Secret, NA, RG 263, CIA Name Files, E ZZ-16, Box 45. Chief (blocked out) to Chief EE, March 17, 1953, Secret, RG 263, CIA Name Files, E A1-86, Box 38.

"the Zipper man in the picture," probably the mysterious agent U-13910 who played a covert role in numerous U.S. activities in postwar Germany. Schmitz or Zipper or U-13910 evidently had a CIA assignment to procure the Schellenberg memoirs and the delivery man was supposed to be Jürgen Thorwald. Altogether it is difficult to comprehend how it could have been that the CIA had difficulties to get their hands on a copy of the Schellenberg manuscript. The sole reason for the American interest—and there may well have been others—spelled out in the documents was to discover what Schellenberg had written about their man Reinhard Gehlen. Surely they were aware that Schellenberg didn't regard Gehlen very positively and they now wanted "to learn the details of the anti-Utility[Gehlen] remarks contained in the manuscript." When Alan Bullock wrote the "Introduction" to the first edition of Schellenberg's memoirs, he knew of the contacts between Irene Schellenberg and Werner Best and that the former high-ranking SS officer had persuaded her to drop publication plans with the Swiss and to find a German publisher instead. Best, according to Bullock, at the time had joined a law firm in Düsseldorf. Somehow, the controversial manuscript in spite of the efforts of Werner Best was "bought by ...André Deutsch, from *Quick* Verlag in Munich."[572]

Once the book was published, the Americans who apparently had observed Schellenberg during his time in Switzerland and Italy and who had tried so hard to obtain a copy through Zipper, very quickly lost interest. In the summer of 1957, one reaction from the FBI would go as far as to suggest that there was nothing new for them in these memoirs. Quite to the contrary, the CIA and its contacts in Germany, some of them certainly related to Zipper or the BND, decided that there was "considerable information value" and that they wanted to acquire all "documents" (the complete memoirs), including all those texts kept out of the published memoirs and still in the possession of the widow and that these papers would be "of considerable value and worth reasonable expenditure... Would appreciate advice soonest."[573]

In the following years the Americans gathered up an extensive amount of papers related to Walter Schellenberg, Hitler's last Chief of Foreign Intelligence, so much material in fact that in 1960, eight years after his death and four years after the British publication of the memoirs, there was an official recommendation to destroy the Schellenberg papers. Ten years later, by 1970,

---

572. Chief (blocked out), Pullach, to Chief EE, April 2, 1953, Security Information Secret, NA, RG 263, CIA Name Files, E A1-86, Boxes 37-38, declassified by CIA 2001. Alan Bullock, "Introduction," in Schellenberg, *The Schellenberg Memoirs*, 17.
573 Berlin to Director, July 2, 1957, Secret; Chief Pullach to Chief EW, April 2, 1953, Security Information, Secret; both NA, RG 263, CIA Name Files, E 22-16, Box 45. Berlin to Director, July 2, 1957, Secret, NA, RG 263, E A1-86, CIA Name Files, Boxes 37-38.

when a further request for a decision "as to the retention or disposition of the material" was presented, the intelligent response was: "Although subject reportedly died in 1952, this detailed report of the life and activities of 'Heinrich Himmler's right-hand man' is of historical and research value. It also contains some details of German State Security operations during World War II" and the decision was "Retain."[574]

---

[574] S.B. Donahoe to A. H. Belmont, January 28, 1960, NA, RG 65, E A1-136P, Box 57. J. W. Marshall to Mr. Tavel, April 6, 1970, NA, RG 65, IWG Classification 100 Name Files, Box 2.

Appendices

Editor's Comment

Appendix I
Brigadefuehrer Schellenberg
Autobiography, Compiled During
His Stay in Stockholm, June 1945

Appendix II
Franz Göring

Annexe Written by Hauptsturmfuehrer Goering to
Schellenberg's Report on His Transactions with
Count Bernadotte and Events in the Last
Weeks of the German Reich

Franz Göring

Annexe Written by Hauptsturmfuehrer Goering to
Schellenberg's Report on His Transactions with
Count Bernadotte and Events in the Last
Weeks of the German Reich
Part II

Editor's Comment

Reinhard R. Doerries

Walter Schellenberg, Chief of *Amt* VI Foreign Intelligence until dismissed shortly before the end of the Third Reich, wrote this brief "Autobiography" in the few weeks after May 5, 1945, in Stockholm and Trosa.[575] While in Stockholm he was for several days a guest in the home of Count Folke Bernadotte, a member of the Swedish Royal Family and Vice-President of the Swedish Red Cross. Presumably the text was originally written in German. It was certainly begun while Schellenberg stayed with Count Bernadotte. It was finished after Schellenberg had moved to Trosa and most likely somewhat prior to his departure from Sweden. We can safely assume that Count Bernadotte read and discussed with Schellenberg at least those text parts written at the Bernadotte residence. As they saw each other frequently even when Schellenberg was staying out in Trosa, Count Bernadotte probably saw the entire text and exchanged views about it with Schellenberg. We don't know whether Count Bernadotte in any way influenced Schellenberg while writing his text.

The German text, as available in various archives, does not appear to have had a formal title, which may have been the reason why some people have referred to it as "Trosa Memorandum" or "Schellenberg's Dagbok." The title "Autobiography" would appear to be a creation of the translators. Every page

---

[575]. The English translation of the "Autobiography" used for this edition is part of the records in the custody of the National Archives and Records Administration, Washington, D.C., and College Park, MD, and is published with their generous permission.

of the German typescript bears Schellenberg's handwritten initials or rather his paraph at bottom right. The German text is rather clearly written and often quite to the point.[576] Moreover, it is neither an apologia nor an indictment. Both the original German text and the English translation convey the impression that the author felt a personal need to write down what he experienced during the final months of Nazi Germany.

There is no reliable information as to who the translators may have been, but indications are that parts of the text or all of it was already translated in Stockholm very soon after Schellenberg completed it. One of the British translations may also have been done by staff members in the War Room in London.[577] Both the evidently British translation and the possibly American translation have left out words and parts of sentences, apparently without political motivation. The editor has used the original German text to include any items missing in the "Autobiography" offered here.

A personal need or desire of Schellenberg to write down his very recent experiences, of course, does not exclude the possibility that Count Bernadotte may have prompted him to jot down his perspective of the events they had shared.[578] We know that Count Bernadotte wrote his own recollections during these same few weeks, and it would have been very natural for the two men, who had come to know each other rather personally, to exchange views on events and persons. Claims by a few authors that it was Schellenberg who wrote the recollections of Count Bernadotte apparently have no base.[579]

The English text of the "Autobiography" has been reproduced faithfully here.[580] Occasionally an inadequately translated word or term has been replaced with a correct English word, always using the original German typed version as a guideline. In no case has the editor tried to read a certain interpretation into the given text. In cases where the English text reproduced here may be considered somewhat bumpy, the editor has made no attempt to change sentences or words. Missing first names or names of organizations are supplied for the reader in parenthesis. Outright spelling errors have been corrected. In a few

---

576. The German text used for comparison by the editor may be found in a number of archives, such as The National Archives, Kew.
577. Cf. J. C. Scott-Harsten, October 12, 1945, Summary of Interrogation of Schellenberg, NA, RG 226, E 125 A, Box 2.
578. Cf. Schellenberg Office Memorandum, H. Plummer to Col. Knox Pruden, December 29, 1947, SAN, S-45a.
579. Cf.Louis de Jong, "Hat Felix Kersten das niederländische Volk gerettet?" in Hans Rothfels and Theodor Eschenburg, eds., *Zwei Legenden aus dem Dritten Reich* (Stuttgart: Deutsche Verlags-Anstalt, 1974), 138, without naming source.
580. The editor has seen another English translation of the "Autobiography" in Walter Schellenberg, *Report and Documents, The William J. Donovan Papers*, Box 87B, USAMHI. While it appears to be a somewhat better translation than the above mentioned in other archives, considerable parts of the German text have not been translated. The editor has used it for comparison.

cases where the translation appears unclear or could be argued, the original German words are supplied in parenthesis. Because the various unknown translators have altered Schellenberg's paragraphs, the editor in all cases has accepted the paragraphs as used by Schellenberg in his original text. Round parentheses are a part of the text; square parentheses have been added by the editor. The so-called "Autobiography" was not an exercise in good historical writing, but instead was meant to be and still constitutes an informative document.

The two appendices to Schellenberg's text by Franz Göring were almost certainly written upon special request from Schellenberg, or for that matter Count Bernadotte.[581] Indications from the records are that Göring, who had come to Schellenberg's *Amt* VI in 1944, was very loyal to his chief. While this should not imply Göring being obliged to write in a certain way, it could suggest that he would not wish to contradict Schellenberg. Being aware of this, however, does not mean overlooking the fact that in the course of the rescue operations, Göring obviously did as he was told by Schellenberg and that, therefore, there would be no plausible reason to assume that the events took place differently than described by Göring. In the editorial work the same general procedure was followed as outlined above for the Schellenberg text. Here too, for comparison and the checking of errors, the presumably original German text as well as another translation have been used. Every page of the German text has a handwritten G, for Göring, at bottom right. In the case of Franz Göring almost the same German text, without his paraph, was presented at the Nuremberg trials.[582]

Because we know that Franz Göring in the postwar years worked for the Americans and Zipper (BND), or more directly for the Americans but connected to Zipper, we may assume that the Americans read his texts in support of Schellenberg and did not find them troublesome. If Göring's texts had been found to be largely untruthful, U.S. intelligence presumably would have hesitated to have any connections with him or comments to that effect would be found in the American intelligence records dealing with Franz Göring.[583]

---

581. The English translations of the Franz Göring texts used for this edition are parts of the records in the custody of the National Archives and Records Administration, Washington, D.C. and College Park, MD, and they are published with their generous permission.
582. The German text used for comparison by the editor may be found in a number of archives, such as The National Archives, Kew.
583. Respective intelligence files on Franz Göring can be found in NA, RG 263, E ZZ-18, CIA Name Files, Second Release, Box 43.

Appendix I

BRIGADEFUEHRER SCHELLENBERG
Amtschef VI

Autobiography
Compiled During His Stay in
Stockholm, June 1945.

The sudden change from the high tension of my last weeks in Germany to the calm and peace of my present stay compels me to write an account of the events of these last weeks. A full comprehension of what I had to live through will not be possible without taking into account:—
1) That this statement can only be compared with sketches in a diary—that is, it is mainly a collection of chronological jottings from memory—and
2) That these last weeks were but the manifestation of long-felt presentiments and forebodings.

Since these are just diary sketches, I have done my best to avoid a completely false picture of my own situation by presenting my professional development and the resulting basis for my political convictions:

The last year of my studies was decisively influenced by financial difficulties at home and my own need of money. To prove my entitlement to a state grant I had to pass diligence examinations. Then after I had passed the "Referendar" examination on March 3, 1933, the question of a further state grant depended on my belonging to the Party and organizations. That was the first reason why I joined the Party and the SS in June 1933. That I joined the SS then was not the result of any political consideration. It was because the majority of my fellow students did not join the S.A., but also went to the SS. The uniform pleased us more. We were looked on unfavorably as undergraduates and as late-comers (people joining in May and June). Duties consisted of stupid exercises three times a week in the evening or late afternoon and mostly the whole of Sunday. I was soon employed at the office desk, and there had to produce plans for the training in "Weltanschauliche Schulung" [ideological training] which, because I was a lawyer, I based mainly on old Germanic law and similar subjects. Through legal colleagues I succeeded in being transferred to the Government presidency [Regierungspräsidium] at

Frankfurt/Main as "Referendar" for training in the administration.[584] In addition to the administrative police training, I was temporarily also given State Police training. Here I made the acquaintance in 1935 of an inspecting higher SS leader from Berlin, who requested that I should be sent to Berlin to the Reich Minister for Justice for a time, to write a state legal [staatsrechtliche] work on Reich reform.[585] This offer pleased me, because the work interested me and I was relieved of all the material difficulties of a legal "Referendar." Otherwise my family intended for me to enter the legal practice of a friend of my father's. For this purpose I left Berlin in 1936 and put in 6 months of intensive work at the [State] Supreme Court [Oberlandesgericht] at Düsseldorf, then 2 months in the legal practice of my father's friend—I represented him there—and on December 8, 1936, passed my Assistant-judge examination [Assessor-Examen] with distinction. After long consultations with my father's friend I decided to go for another year to Berlin. He was prepared to keep a partnership in his lawyer's practice open for me for the time being.[586] At that time everything pointed to the lawyer [Rechtsanwalt] profession disappearing altogether, for legal reform was tending so acutely towards nationalization, that this profession in the eyes of the people became almost completely discredited as being "liberal."

In Berlin during 1937, I worked again on questions of Reich reform and on legal questions of the remuneration and the career of the SS in relation to the Civil Service laws, to the Armed Forces, etc. In 1938 I worked on questions of international law—legal questions concerning Sudetenland, Danzig, Austria—and at the same time I was made to participate in the mobilizing of the entire Reich Administration.

At the beginning of 1939 I was appointed Chief of Counter-Espionage [Spionageabwehr]. This department of the State Police, formed from the old Landespolizei, could only be headed by an experienced professional jurist, as crime cases most often were complicated and legally standardized, and a continuous collaboration with the Reich Court—Supreme Reich attorney [Oberreichsanwalt]—was necessary. I was occupied with this until 1941.[587]

As I had been taken on in 1937 as "Regierungsassessor" in the Ministry of the Interior, I was promoted in the Civil Service to the rank of "Oberregierungsrat." It is interesting to note that I was paid as a Civil Servant and

---

584. Referendar is a title used in several professions in Germany to designate the first position, so to speak in training after a university exam, for instance in law or teaching.
585. This appears to have been Wilhelm Albert, then head of administrative section of the SD head office in Berlin. — Reich or Empire usually refers to the nation or national government.
586. The Düsseldorf lawyer was Justizrat Bartholomäus. SAN, Rep. 501, S-3; S-45c.
587. Schellenberg from 1939 to 1941 was Chief of Section IV E Counter-Intelligence of *Amt* IV, the Secret State Police (Gestapo), headed by the infamous Heinrich Müller.

held the SS-rank as a purely honorary title. On my promotion to "Ministerialdirigent" at the end of 1944, Himmler, against my express wish, on the suggestion of Kaltenbrunner appointed me Major General of the Police. I had occasion to inform Himmler during several consultations that I was not in agreement with a police career, as I had not been trained for it, and I requested my transfer back to the Ministry of the Interior [Innenministerium] as "Oberregierungsrat" or "Ministerialdirigent." Himmler was unsympathetic to my continuous pressure in this regard, but one day he explained to me that he wished to compensate me and had arranged to appoint me Major General of the Waffen-SS, thus making available a definite Armed Forces career. Therefore on January 30, 1945, I was appointed Major General of the Waffen-SS and paid accordingly.[588]

In 1939 I had attempted to obtain leave from the Ministry of the Interior and the SS-Service and to obtain an officer's commission at the front, as I wished to practice law after the war. I could not carry out this plan, as Himmler forbade it. He believed that he could compensate me by doing me the favor of sending me as a liaison officer to the Supreme Command of the Army [Oberkommando der Wehrmacht] for two months.

During this entire time I keenly observed the results of our foreign policy and all questions connected with it. My specialized knowledge gave me new ideas on the European economic situation, and this led to contacts with leading German economic experts [Wirtschaftlern]. From the cooperation with them I realized that there were problems totally unsolved of economic espionage in Germany and of its prevention, and I saw above all the great meaning of the economy for the existence of the state. This persuaded me more and more to occupy myself with the question of the basic principles on which German foreign policy, and particularly German foreign trade policy, was being conducted. Among these questions especially one aspect became increasingly clear to me: Germany and many influential Germans were forming a completely false impression of the entire outside world, that is, they had neither an instinctive nor an acquired understanding of foreign countries. There was experience with political space. Maybe the latter was just sufficient for areas which the German people had penetrated, but not elsewhere, not even in the nearer European areas.

These thoughts drove me, as if by an inner force, to go whole-heartedly into the question of creating an information center about foreign countries.

---

588. Schellenberg was promoted to the rank of SS-Brigadeführer on June 21, 1944. He was appointed Major General of the Waffen-SS and the Police on December 1, 1944. Other documents suggest that respective papers were not signed until much later, such as some time in January 1945. NA, BDC Microfilm, A 3343, SSO-074B.

There was no such center in Germany for the political and political-economic sectors. The military information service was narrowly confined to military matters. In 1941 I finally succeeded to devote my whole attention to this question.[589] I worked on this until the end of the war, though in 1944 the military sector was given to me as well.[590]

The results of this work confirmed me in my convictions, and I recognized more and more clearly the abuses and mistakes of the regime, which I had seen earlier on. Apart from many local defects of incompetent bigwigs ["unzureichender Bonzen"], the crux of the matter was the absence of the principle of selection, the fact that performance was no criterion and that important positions thus were given to stupid or unworthy men. If there was anything approaching selection of the individual in Germany, it was, I still believed, to be found among the good parts of the SS. In Himmler I saw a man about whom much was said, but about whose alleged brutality I was never able to ascertain exact information. I never got to the bottom of that matter during those years. Perhaps my work was too difficult, for it held me prisoner and diverted me from other problems. He was the only man I could see in the whole corrupt leadership, who with any success stood up as a factor of order against the many large and small popes of the regime. My conviction was that if I could convey to this organization and its leading head a knowledge of the formative political forces of the world, i.e. a knowledge of foreign countries in the larger context, there was a chance to protect Germany from the yawning abyss, which I saw coming since the end of 1940.

The task itself had two main objectives: First to solve the task as such, and secondly to use the results to provide Germany with an antidote to the obstructive Fuehrer-Ribbentrop policy. The Reichsfuehrer [Himmler] was the only genuine counterpart that one could use at all for this purpose. If I succeeded in working my way up to him and to inform him as completely as possible of the true power situation of the world, I considered him to be sensible and clever enough to still in time reach a compromise with the outside world.

It was a long and tiring road that I had to travel, a road presumably predestined, and in the end without success. It was not lack of will and industry, but stupidity, vanity and brutality on the one hand—my internal enemies

---

589. Schellenberg was Deputy Chief of *Amt* VI Foreign Intelligence since July 2, 1941 Cf. Schellenberg, *The Schellenberg Memoirs*, 227, giving the date as June 22, 1941. Following the dismissal of his predecessor Heinz M. K. Jost, Schellenberg became Chief of *Amt* VI. The official confirmation of this is Himmler to Schellenberg, February 25, 1943. Documents named here in NA, BDC Microfilm, A 3343. SSO-074B.
590. This refers to the absorption of the military intelligence service (*Abwehr*) by *Amt* VI in 1944.

[inside Nazi leadership circles?]—and the indecision of the Reichsfuehrer [Himmler] himself on the other, which ruined all these plans. This refers to that part of the task which had to do with the utilization, i.e. the implementation of a sensible and thereby conciliatory foreign policy. The other part of the task, namely the task itself with its manifold difficulties, was obstructed by the very nature of the German national character. Either, because it was not understood, or worse still, because it was believed unnecessary—thus Ribbentrop among others.

The Fuehrer [Hitler] rejected me and my work entirely. The only person who more or less understood me was indeed Himmler, although he too, caught up in his prejudices of the National-Socialist persuasion and his policeman's way of looking at political events, made things difficult for me. Slowly in the course of time, things, however, took a turn for the better and gradually I gained a greater understanding on his part. Unfortunately the results were never such as needed, since his hesitancy always spoilt everything. For me personally, the whole thing was often a struggle in which I had to play Don Quixote. My "Rosinante" was the relatively weak human material [Menschenmaterial][591] and the "windmills" were the above mentioned prejudices of the regime and the German character as such. One must understand that I did not give up this struggle, because I love my fatherland and I was always determined to turn things to the good. I believed that the easiest way to achieve this was, as pointed out above, through the only man who was capable of offsetting Hitler.

Already in 1940 I counseled peace with France; in 1941 I warned against a war on two fronts and saw the danger threatening from Russia. At the end of 1942 and the beginning of 1943 my reports on Russia led to Hitler, and later Himmler—at the instigation of Obergruppenfuehrer Dr. Kaltenbrunner—wanting to imprison me and my associates in a concentration camp for defeatism. In 1943 I managed to save Switzerland from being invaded by Germany, thanks to my adept negotiating with General [Henri] Guisan. In the same year I attempted through [Franz] von Papen in Turkey and some Turkish contacts, to solve the Ukrainian and Crimean-Tatar questions; via Spain, Portugal and Sweden I had contact with individual personalities in England and America and tried especially at this time to persuade Himmler to compromise. The situation in Rumania and Bulgaria and the turn of events there appeared so devastating to me that, in view of the incomprehensible stubbornness of Ribbentrop, Hitler and all the others who had to do with these questions, I thought seriously of giving up my efforts.

---

591. An unfortunate, not uncommon German expression, i.e., not a specifically intended choice of words of Schellenberg.

I continued work, however, for as I said at the beginning of 1944 in a conversation with Gottfried von Bismarck and thought to be correct: "One must do everything to try, using the strongest man of the internal opposition, to prevent in time the coming chaos."

Gottfried von Bismarck, whose life I had an opportunity of saving at the beginning of 1945 by interceding with Himmler, allegedly had taken part in the events of July 20. The accusation called for the death penalty. Himmler first refused to intervene effectively. However, I managed to persuade him by using as a warning the argument of my Swedish friends, with whom von Bismarck had good connections: "The death of the living descendant of the great Bismarck will have as bad an effect in England against Germany as the V-weapons." Himmler was very impressed with the importance that was placed abroad on von Bismarck, and obviously discussed the matter thoroughly with Hitler. Von Bismarck was, as I know from Kaltenbrunner, unexpectedly acquitted. My talks with Himmler at the time resulted not only in his being not transferred to another prison, but in his being merely confined to his estate. I also gave advice on this matter to the Bismarck family via a Swedish acquaintance.[592]

I do not wish to mention my role in the July 20 assassination attempt in these diary sketches.[593]

One thing I did achieve in the course of the years, and that was to attain such a position with Himmler, that I could always be sure that I myself and my work would always be judged broadmindedly or, as I would like to say, by "non-party political" standards. In addition Himmler somehow had a human weakness for me. This was first evident in 1940 when in spite of greatest scruples, he allowed my marriage to my wife, who was of pure Polish descent on her mother's side.[594] In all, the "broadmindedness" cost daily battles, each day brought new difficulties, but for that I had the advantage of being able to work in Germany itself on a broader "national" basis. The result was that I came increasingly into conflict with the State Police and the Security Service [Sicherheitsdienst], because under the cloak of my foreign activities I became the silent protector of many "Untrustworthies" [Unzuverlaessiger] and so-

---

592. Gottfried Count von Bismarck had been arrested following the events of the assassination attempt of July 20, 1944. SAN, Rep. 501. Cf. NAK, FO 188/487, "Notes on a conversation [of Minister Victor Mallet] with Mr. Jacob Wallenberg on May 25th, 1945": "Gottfried von Bismarck ... was imprisoned after the July coup ... and it was a very near thing for his life, but eventually some of his friends succeeded. I think through Schellenberg and Himmler, in getting him released ..."
593. No evidence of an active role of Schellenberg has turned up so far.
594. Schellenberg's first marriage to Käthe Kortekamp ended in divorce. He married his second wife Irene Grosse-Schönepauck in October 1940. See family tree (SS-Ahnentafel) and respective documents of the SS-Race and Settlement Head Office (Rasse- und Siedlungs-Hauptamt-SS), NA, BDC Microfilm, A 3343-RS-FO 270.

called "shady individuals" [schraeger Voegel]—actually all good Germans who recognized my honest intentions and helped me in spite of all political difficulties.

The more critical the whole military and political picture, the more difficult also became my own personal situation. Slanders, serious insinuations and the resulting control and surveillance made this life of uncertainty often unbearable. My sole protection, of my person as well as of my position, was the systematic extension of my trusty relationship with Himmler, which proved so powerful as to prevail against the strong attacks of [Martin] Bormann or [Ernst] Kaltenbrunner. The latter expressed his opinion about 1½ years ago that he had sufficient proof in his possession to prove that I worked for the [British] Secret Service.[595] Or, as in March 1945, that immediate measures must be taken against me, as I had taken my wife and children to Lake Constance and that they were on the point of fleeing to Switzerland.

This gives a small idea of the atmosphere when at the beginning of February [1945] we received the report from Minister [Gesandte Hans] Thomsen in Stockholm, that Count Bernadotte was intending to come to Berlin to talk to Himmler.[596] The personal counsel of Ribbentrop, Geheimrat Wagner, came to me twice on orders from his Minister on the day the report arrived to ask me, if I, with my personal connections in Sweden was behind this plan.[597] Ribbentrop and Kaltenbrunner, of course, saw in me the motivating, and therefore responsible force behind the pardoning and freeing of the so-called seven Warsaw Swedes, and both attempted to prove, mostly by referring to the Swedish Press that my active intercession for Sweden was a great political stupidity. The Fuehrer in this way was encouraged in his antipathy towards Sweden, above all by showing him reports on the training of Norwegian policemen in Sweden.

The freeing of the seven Warsaw Swedes was an activity stretching over a period of almost three years. I worked on this case with great effort and in closest contact with Mr. [Felix] Kersten, Director General [Alvar] Moeller, and [Axel] Brandin. After lengthy efforts and internal conflicts it was possible to

---

595. Neither the voluminous holdings of the National Archives, Washington, D.C./College Park, MD nor the respective more recently released records at the National Archives at Kew (particularly the KV series) contain reliable documentation suggesting that Schellenberg worked for British intelligence.
596. The German Minister in Stockholm, Hans Thomsen, had been stationed in Washington, D.C. until Germany's declaration of war against the United States, which he personally delivered to the State Dept. on December 11, 1941. He was born a Norwegian in 1891 and acquired German citizenship in 1913. Cf. NA, RG 226, Entry 125A, Box 3.
597. In Schellenberg, *The Schellenberg Memoirs*, pp. 388, 433-434, Wagner is referred to as "Ribbentrop's right-hand man, Legationsrat H. Wagner" and Ribbentrop's "personal adviser, Geheimrat Wagner." This is probably Horst Wagner of the German Foreign Office who, according to John Weitz, *Hitler's Diplomat* (London: Phoenix/Orion, 1997), p. 289, after the war "fled to South America ... [and] returned to Germany in 1952."

have them first pardoned, then in time evacuated from Berlin and given better accommodation and food, and finally even to have them freed. How much effort and trouble, and I must add personal danger, this meant to me must be left for a more detailed account.

It should not remain unmentioned that here too chance gave me decisive assistance. Reichsjustizminister [Reich Minister of Justice] Dr. [Otto] Thierack was in the same Corps—Student Corps—of which I was an active member. Unlike me, he had withdrawn from the Corps for party political reasons. In spite of, or perhaps because of this, he felt slightly awkward with me, for I think that privately he still clung to the student corps tradition. This fact was of inestimable value in my personal discussions with him on the question of the evacuation, accommodation and treatment of the Swedes and the presentation of my case to Ribbentrop and Hitler.[598] Had he taken a strong position against me, it would have been almost impossible for Himmler, with the existing difficulties vis-à-vis Ribbentrop and Kaltenbrunner, and also the negative attitude of Hitler, to bring this matter to a successful conclusion in the course of time. It is important, however, to mention here the motive for Himmler's decisive, final intervention with Hitler. Because all my attempts to exert influence in the matter so far had only prepared the ground, I now submitted a report to the effect that besides suspending trade relations between Germany and Sweden, I felt convinced, on the basis of my intelligence reports that Sweden was playing with the idea of entering the war against Germany at the end. A positive action in this case would have a favorable effect on Swedish circles interested in Germany and bring about a turn for the better, that is, assure the non-entry of Sweden into the war. That was Himmler's true motive, without which the humanitarian step would hardly have been possible.

At the same time I would like to mention that I do not wish here to offer details of the individual actions, which I have carried out, either in connection with the freeing and pardoning of the seven Warsaw Swedes, or the Norwegian students,[599] or the individual cases which were transmitted to me on Swedish recommendation—[Jacob] Wallenberg, [Axel] Brandin, [Felix] Kersten, etc.

At the time I explained truthfully to Geheimrat Wagner that I knew nothing of the travel plans of Count Bernadotte. I informed Kaltenbrunner and Himmler of this conversation. Himmler found the event very interesting,

---

598. The Minister of Justice, Otto Georg Thierack, and Schellenberg were members of the same fraternity, Corps Guestphalia, and Schellenberg was able to use the influence of Thierack in various difficult legal cases. On Thierack see Höhne, *The Order of the Death's Head*, pp. 455-457. Imprisoned after the war, he committed suicide in 1946.

599. A greater number of Norwegian students and Danish policemen were released from German prisons and concentration camps following personal contacts between Schellenberg and the Swedish Minister in Berlin, Arvid Richert.

but was all the same somewhat angry that it had occurred via the Legation and therefore through the Foreign Office, as he was thereby forced to treat the visit as an official matter and to report it to Hitler. He therefore ordered Kaltenbrunner—at the time Himmler himself was commanding Heeresgruppe [Army Group] Weichsel[600] and was with his staff in Prenzlau—to talk to Hitler at an opportune moment and to cleverly find out his position. I admit that I presented the visit of Count Bernadotte politically somewhat more interesting than I felt it was, in order to keep awake Himmler's interests in these political events while his attention was diverted by military matters. Kaltenbrunner, who at this time was present every noon at a long discussion of the military situation at the Chancellery and often following this was closeted alone with the Fuehrer, asked Gruppenfuehrer [Hermann] Fegelein to speak to Hitler, probably to avoid a personal turndown. Already the next day Fegelein reported Hitler's refusal and explained it with Hitler's own words: "With such nonsense nothing can be gained in this war."

In the meantime, however, Count Bernadotte had already arrived in Berlin. I thereupon spoke personally with Himmler on the telephone and begged him earnestly not to disregard this gesture of Sweden. He must [sic] receive the Count, I told him. I emphasized again that I could well imagine that apart from all technical questions, certainly one or the other aspect could prove politically interesting. After much humming and hawing he agreed to the following alternative proposal: Kaltenbrunner should speak to [Joachim von] Ribbentrop, while at the same time I should talk to Ribbentrop's personal counsellor, Geheimrat Wagner, both with the object that Ribbentrop should receive Count Bernadotte without Hitler knowing of this meeting in advance and without mentioning the refusal that Hitler had already given to the visit. If Ribbentrop agreed to receive him, then Kaltenbrunner and I could receive the Count afterwards. Himmler thus would have gained time and one could see how the matter would work itself out further.

What actually took place during the first visit was that Count Bernadotte, who got in touch with me from the Swedish Legation, was first invited to Kaltenbrunner and to me, and then on the same morning went straight from us to Ribbentrop.

In the course of this first conversation, during which I kept myself very much in the background, I immediately had the feeling of a good contact with the Count and was able on two decisive points to guide the discussion along the lines which the Count wanted it to take. By referring to various in-

---

600. On Himmler as commander of Army Group Vistula see Manvell and Fraenkel, *Heinrich Himmler*, pp. 210-211. Cf. Padfield, *Himmler*, pp. 562-563.

conspicuous cases of assistance, I gave the Count to understand my honest opinion regarding Sweden, and it was decisive for myself and my plan, namely under all circumstances to bring Count Bernadotte to Himmler, that the Count intimated to Kaltenbrunner at the end of the meeting that he had the wish to speak to Himmler himself, as he had something very personal to say only to him. I personally saw in Count Bernadotte's visit the possibility of realizing in this way my original basic idea of getting Germany out of the war, and regarded the connection with Sweden as always as particularly favorable, since from the perspective of power politics Sweden had to be especially interested in a pacification of the Nordic [nordisch] area. The Count this way brought his line of interest into harmony with my original endeavour to intervene in favor of Denmark and Norway. This interest, if rightly used by Germany, would prove a profitable partnership for both Sweden and Germany, in order to win Sweden over to act as mediator for a compromise peace. There was also the humanitarian side which had always moved me deeply, and the solution of which I also felt to be absolutely necessary. In order to circumvent Hitler's negative attitude, I had to take a great chance and try to get the slow-thinking Kaltenbrunner over to my side despite all his personal antagonism towards me and to counter Himmler's aloofness caused by military matters. When Count Bernadotte had left the house, I took the following steps: I praised Kaltenbrunner for the splendid way in which he had conducted the discussion with Count Bernadotte, for the subtlety with which he had cleverly adapted himself to all the Count's questions, and how he had really demonstrated a good example of Austrian Ballhaus-diplomacy.[601] I took this opportunity to explain to him that I had for some time wished to say something to him, and that I definitely intended to say to Himmler, when I next talked to him, that in this critical situation Ribbentrop would have to be relieved and Kaltenbrunner made Foreign Minister. Kaltenbrunner swallowed the bait so thoroughly that I thought he would take line and rod as well. In the telephone conversation which followed he was the most ardent of champions of the necessity of a meeting between Count Bernadotte and Himmler despite the fact that the Fuehrer had forbidden it. Himmler declared himself ready to meet Bernadotte, but Kaltenbrunner was excluded from the meeting itself, which so embittered and so to speak sobered him, that in a short time he returned to his old enmity against me. The meeting between the Count and Himmler took place two days later at Hohenlychen.

On the journey there I spoke openly to the Count of how I personally viewed the political situation, and in particular of my attitude towards Sweden.

---

601. Ballhausplatz in Vienna was the location of the Austrian Foreign Ministry.

We were soon on such good terms that I was even able to give Count Bernadotte some tips about the coming interview, in regard to the idiosyncrasies and peculiarities of Himmler. I knew that the Count's original plan to take the Danish and Norwegian prisoners for the duration of the war to Sweden and to intern them there, could not succeed and advised him to start with the compromise suggestion of a central camp for the prisoners in northwest Germany. Himmler, with whom I had an opportunity of speaking immediately after his discussion with the Count, was very favorably impressed by their conversation. He requested me to keep in close contact with the Count, and to keep an eye on the actual execution of the scheme which, as he himself knew, would meet with difficulties from Kaltenbrunner and [Heinrich] Mueller and, in some circumstances, also from Ribbentrop, and to assist everywhere. I was to inform the Reich Foreign Minister immediately of the essential content of the discussion and to acquaint him with the decisions reached, so that Ribbentrop—from Himmler's perspective—could give the official wording on the matter to the Count and so cover Himmler with Hitler.

I next informed Kaltenbrunner of the positive results of the conversation, and he immediately began to reproach me for having influenced Himmler far too strongly in favor of Count Bernadotte and the fulfillment of his wishes. He immediately drew Gruppenfuehrer Mueller into the discussion, who on several points brought up the supposedly insuperable difficulties entailed in the practical carrying-out of the matter, and finally announced his opinion: "This entire matter is utopian, because I am not in a position to provide trucks and fuel for the transportation of these widely scattered Danish and Norwegian prisoners. Nothing can be done regarding camp Neuengamme as the camp is completely overcrowded. It is always the same when so-called politicians spin their tales to Himmler." I repudiated the objection regarding the trucks and fuel by explaining that the Swedes could provide these. Owing to the swiftness of my suggestion, Mueller agreed without fully considering the implications. I stated further that I would inform the Reich Foreign Minister, who also wished to receive Count Bernadotte, of this point, so that Ribbentrop could, so to speak, put it to the Count as a German suggestion to help in putting the overall plan through. I also telephoned immediately to Standartenfuehrer Dr. [Rudolf] Brandt, so that Himmler should know of the extension of the plan.

On the next day Mueller again began to remonstrate with Kaltenbrunner against this plan, saying that the Germans, and above all the countless columns of refugees could not be expected to have to watch Swedish Red Cross buses driving past them with prisoners. The situation once again grew critical and the whole plan was endangered, particularly since Himmler considered this objection very important. I removed it by suggesting that all the transports would only be allowed to travel by night and declared myself ready to provide the personnel to ensure the observance of this agreement from my own department [*Amt* VI].

This utilization of personnel loyal to me incidentally influenced the fate of many. Their activity in the many camps, into which the Swedish Red Cross transportation of Danish, Norwegian, Polish and Jewish prisoners had brought them, introduced so much uncertainty into the issuing of orders by the camp commanders that these when pressed by them [my personnel], were prevented from carrying out the "orders of the Reichsfuehrer" [Reichsfuehrerbefehle]. Many instructions which, as explained below, were issued by Kaltenbrunner and other offices and which in fact were not orders of the Reichsfuehrer, were therefore never acted upon. The problem of overcrowding in the camp Neuengamme, the organization of the transports, the visiting rights of the Swedish Red Cross in the camps, the issuing of permits to individuals to whose departure from Germany Himmler had agreed as well as to collective transports, all that required a considerable amount of tact and engagement to overcome the extensive refractoriness and offensiveness of reluctant state police offices [Gestapo]. These things will be reported separately in the appendix. (By my assistant [Mitarbeiter] Goering!) [Text in parenthesis handwritten by Schellenberg.][602]

Incidentally, it may suffice at this point, if I may refer to my, so to speak, best witness in this whole matter and during this time, Count Bernadotte himself. He knows how much resistance, indeed almost chicanery, had to be overcome to solve the humanitarian questions involved and beyond that to free [disengage?] Germany and perhaps thereby Europe from this war. At that time, too—as so often before—I had a serious conversation with Himmler. It was after a military conference of his generals at Army Group Vistula [Heeresgruppe Weichsel] that I put to him the approaching collapse of the Reich as an almost inevitable event and implored him at least to use the hand of Sweden in order to steer the German wreck into the harbor of peace on his own initiative before it capsized. I suggested to him that he might ask Count Bernadotte to fly to General [Dwight D.] Eisenhower to convey the offer of capitulation from Himmler. After a very excited discussion, in which I also made it clear to Himmler, that I considered his place to be in Berlin and not here as the commander of an Army Group, to which Hitler's entourage had appointed him already for the second time in order to keep him away from Hitler, I made the concrete proposal, that he should return as quickly as possible to Berlin,

---

602. SS-*Hauptsturmführer* Franz Göring, in some sources mistakenly called Fritz Göring, came from *Amt* IV and had served on Schellenberg's staff since 1944 as a personal adjutant.

and there take the preparations for a peace into his own hand, with or without the use of force. Himmler gave in to my insistence and gave me that night the most far-reaching powers to talk to the Count. The next day he rang me up, began to take back everything, apparently under the influence of the "Hesse" action in Stockholm,[603] and merely permitted me to keep good contact with the Count and to get him, if possible, to fly to General Eisenhower on his own initiative. From this day on, it was the beginning of March, there began a daily struggle between Himmler and myself. Neither Kaltenbrunner nor Himmler's entourage took much notice of this. It was a struggle in which I fought like a devil for a soul.

I had given Count Bernadotte a comparatively wide insight into this quiet conflict. After long discussions we agreed, that as soon as Himmler finally brought himself to act, I should get into touch with him immediately. Even then it was already my intention to fly with him to General Eisenhower. Unfortunately I was unable to bring Himmler to make a decisive move. My arrangements with Count Bernadotte went so far, that were the Reich area to be split, as was possible, and Himmler, circumstances permitting, would fly to the South with me, I should still be able to find a way to contact the Count via the Swedish Minister in Switzerland.

Count Bernadotte after that went twice with me to see Himmler. Once it was exclusively on Swedish Red Cross business. The last visit will be dealt with later. In connection with the second visit, it is of interest to remember that there was a long discussion about the King of Belgium and his family as well as his place of residence, and that at the urgent request of the Count on May 4 [or April 5?] I again brought up the matter, and that Kaltenbrunner in the Southern area was ordered to have King Leopold taken without delay to the Swiss frontier and hand him over to the Swiss authorities. Kaltenbrunner does not appear to have complied with this order, that is, I was unable to check the matter because of my constantly changing whereabouts.[604]

Concerning the conversation between Count Bernadotte and the Reich Foreign Minister Ribbentrop, the Count among other things told me, that he had seldom been able to get a word in. Ribbentrop, he said, had stated his opinion of the political situation and pointed out that, if the Western Powers

---

603. The so-called England specialist Fritz Hesse had been in Stockholm representing Ribbentrop. He had unsuccessfully attempted to arrange peace contacts. For the professional career of Hesse see Maria Keipert, Peter Grupp, eds., *Biographisches Handbuch des deutschen Auswärtigen Dienstes*, vol. 2, pp. 296-297. According to this reliable source, he worked for the Bundesnachrichtendienst (BND) from the 1950s onward.
604. Leopold III, King of Belgium, had capitulated to the Germans in May 1940 and thereafter resided under German supervision at Castle Laeken in Brussels. Following the Allied invasion of France in 1944, he was taken to Germany. He was not able to return to the throne and in 1951 stepped down in favor of his son Baudoin I.

were to show no understanding, Germany would just become Bolshevist. Ribbentrop among other things, had made the interesting statement that he, Ribbentrop, had started to try to get into conversation with the Western Powers through one of his private channels in Stockholm. That he should say this to him seemed strange to the Count. It must have sounded, also in my opinion, like an insult, especially as it appeared later, that what was meant was the "Hesse" action.

It will give a particularly good insight into my battle of the last years and weeks, if I describe the attempt to bring about, in spite of all earlier fruitless efforts, some tolerable solution of the Jewish question[605] in Germany — that is to save, so to speak, at the last minute those Jews still alive in Germany:

1. Already in 1943 I had both used and helped Medizinalrat [Felix] Kersten, Himmler's personal doctor, in many humanitarian questions. Already early we discussed the possibilities of achieving a fundamentally good solution of the Jewish question in Germany. He had a very personal relationship with Himmler, which could be used in an extraordinary manner to influence the pursuit of humanitarian questions. After his move to Sweden and his only temporary availability in Germany, I did not allow my personal connection with him to be broken off, so as not to lose the means of influencing Himmler via this channel.

2. At the end of October 1944 I arranged a meeting between the former President of the Swiss Federation [Altbundespräsident Jean-Marie] Musy and his son and Himmler. I took Altbundespräsident Musy to see Himmler at Vienna, where he was conducting business in the Southeast. During the journey from Berlin to Vienna via Breslau, as on the previous evening, I had an opportunity to discuss in great detail with Altbundespräsident Musy the principle aspects of the Jewish question in Germany. I was able to tell him that I had no part in the events of the last few years and had no direct influence. He could not, I said, therefore expect any concrete help from me, such as release from imprisonment and similar matter.

Altbundespräsident Musy was apparently informed about my attitude to the Jewish question. He showed full understanding for my position and appreciated my silent efforts to work for good results in individual cases. — In many individual cases, I was the protector of many a Jewish family, especially

---

605. Schellenberg, in the German text, uses the term "Judenfrage."

of many half Jews ["Mischlinge"] and of numerous mixed couples.[606] The Cassel family, Major ret. Schmidt and others may be considered examples. He knew my every carelessness on my side endangered not only my own life, but what was more important to me, my wife and children. He was astounded to learn that he was better informed about many things than I, and the insight I was then able to give him into the structure of State and Administration showed him how cleverly the "System" separated the individual and his work. Such realizations only came to one slowly, since the Regime—the System—constantly played off State and Party against each other. Thus he also realized that though I had obviously remained "Trustworthy" [Zuverlaessiger] as far as the state apparatus was concerned, I had lately become "Untrustworthy" [Unzuverlaessiger] in the eyes of the party hierarchy. That was, as shown above, my strength, as well as my weakness, because I never possessed enough power against Kaltenbrunner and his associates.

In his first conversation with Himmler, Altbundespräsident Musy touched upon the question of a final settlement of the Jewish problem in Germany and urged Himmler at great length to free at last the Jews still imprisoned in Germany. The possibility was also discussed, that if such a solution was carried out, Germany for its part should receive tractors, trucks and in certain circumstances foreign exchange, for a definite number of Jews. Himmler had evidently determined to handle matters this way on the basis of previous undertakings, of which I had no idea—the Manfred Weiss-Enterprise, the activities of Standartenführer [Kurt] Becher with Sali Meyer [Saly Mayer] etc. Already then I made no secret of my opinion that this was a completely impossible attitude of Himmler. Altbundespräsident Musy, however, did not oppose it, so as not to destroy in advance his basis for further discussion. Regarding this question I too tried to study Himmler. In his tactics he was as changeable as a chameleon and one had to watch him carefully in order to be able to continue negotiations at all. As I had only discussed questions of foreign policy with him for years, I had no clear idea on this point. I noticed that even in 1944 he obviously did not consider the solution of the Jewish question as a matter of foreign policy to be considered carefully, but more as a question of internal politics in relation to the party clique on one side and to the Fuehrer on the other. There was no doubt, or so I felt, that he wished to free himself from the chains of the past, but he did not have the courage to take a fundamental decision. I think that from the outset he considered the solution I proposed to be the moral one, but that considerations of internal politics made him bring up the question of a quid pro quo to Altbundes-

---

606. Germans used the designations Halbjude (Half Jew) and Vierteljude (Quarter Jew).

präsident Musy in a hateful way. As much as I could comprehend the situation, I explained the internal problems involved to Altbundespräsident Musy.

Also the question of an agreement between the American and the Swiss governments was discussed, whereby Switzerland was to be declared a transit land. On the whole this was a general preparatory discussion, though one already with fundamental content. Nothing was definitely fixed, as Altbundespräsident Musy for his part wished first to settle further matters with the Jewish organization. On parting, I left Altbundespräsident Musy in no doubt, that I, personally, would do everything to see that the solution of the problem was under no circumstances to be linked to material gains. The only thing I thought possible in this connection would be certain political agreements. Altbundespräsident Musy agreed with my standpoint.

Himmler requested me to maintain contact with Altbundespräsident Musy and to assist him at the appropriate state police offices [Gestapo] in the freeing of individual Jews and Frenchmen which had been granted to him. I first contacted Gruppenfuehrer [Heinrich] Mueller, Chief of the Secret State Police [Gestapo], and requested permission to be allowed to take care personally of these prisoners. Mueller refused this, on the grounds that I was not a member of the Secret State Police and therefore could not be allowed insight into internal administrative procedure. He referred me to the respective officials in the individual state police offices and merely allowed me to get in touch with these. In this way I managed to trace the prisoners and in some cases arrange for them better accommodation and food, the delivery of parcels [Liebespakete]from abroad, and in some cases the supply of civilian clothes, accommodation in hotels and their despatch abroad—Alain Thorel, brothers Rottenberg, family Donnebaum, family Rosenberg, Dr. Stiassny, Helene Stein—. This entailed endless finicky dealings with the offices of the State Police because of questions concerned with food, clothing and transportation...

During the second conversation on January 12, 1945, at Wildbad/Schwarzwald between Himmler and Altbundespräsident Musy through my active intervention the following decisions were arrived at:

1. Every fortnight one train with about 1200 Jews would leave for Switzerland, travel conditions, food, etc., to be as good as possible.

2. The influences of the Jewish organisations with whom Altbundespräsident Musy cooperated, should positively support the solution of the Jewish problem as permitted by Himmler, and thereby even bring about the beginning of a fundamental change in the world propaganda against Germany.

3. According to my proposal, there would be no more payment of money but proof of the fact that a certain amount of money per train would be made

available to be held in trust by Altbundespräsident Musy for free disposal [by Germany?] later. Himmler originally spoke of later using this money for tractors, cars, medical supplies or similar things, but then let me persuade him that this money must be transferred to the International Red Cross.

The first train transport was carried out at the beginning of February [1945] and worked splendidly. Altbundespräsident Musy was able to present the respective press publicity, for example the statement by President von Steiger of Berne, and the New York Times article of February 8 etc., furthermore the proof that five million Swiss Francs had been deposited with him as trustee—end of February 1945—.[607]

On this last point I informed Altbundespräsident Musy both at the end of February and again in the middle of March that it had been decided on Himmler's authority that this amount and additional sums at the end of the undertaking should be transferred without delay to the International Red Cross.

Of this decision I also informed Mr. [Felix] Kersten, whose help I had enlisted in influencing Himmler towards a solution of the Jewish problem, when he was there in March. Unfortunately Kaltenbrunner got Hitler to stop any further transport of trains to Switzerland. Hitler forbade any German, under threat of death, to help one more additional Jew, but interestingly enough also any American or English P.O.W.—to cross the frontier. Each attempt was to be reported to him personally. Someone had shown Hitler a decyphered report from a de Gaulle office in Spain in which it was asserted that Himmler, through his deputy Schellenberg, had carried on negotiations with Altbundespräsident Musy in order to obtain the right of asylum in Switzerland for 250 "Nazi-leaders" [Nazi-Fuehrer]. This obvious nonsense all the same made Hitler issue the above order, and it had disagreeable consequences for me personally. Altbundespräsident Musy was very unhappy that his undertaking had been stopped and in my presence he shed tears of anger and of bitter disappointment. During his last stay in Berlin we decided to make one final effort together. I proposed to Himmler to ask the Western Powers for a four-day cease fire on land and in the air, in order to use this time to conduct all Jews and also other foreign prisoners in an orderly manner through the front lines, and thus show Germany's "good will." On my own I brought the head of the prisoner of war administration, *Obergruppenfuehrer* [Gottlob] Berger, into this project—who incidentally much listened to me in these matters and as a result of my advice and his not passing on many of Hitler's orders, has saved

---

607. The English translation mentions "5,000 Swiss francs," the German text speaks of "fünf Millionen Schweizer Franken." (Swiss Fr 5,000,000). Eduard von Steiger was Bundesrat from 1940 to 1951.

the lives of thousands. Altbundespräsident Musy and I thought that if such a four-day truce was accepted, as was to be expected, we would approach the Allies with the offer not propagandistically, but seriously through official channels, which, under certain circumstances, might lead beyond the rescue of these people to a discussion about a compromise, which would be to everybody's benefit. Himmler did not have the courage to discuss this matter with Hitler. Personally apparently agreeing with the plan, he turned to the leader of the Camarilla surrounding Hitler, Kaltenbrunner, who then conveyed to me the following negative decision: "Have you also joined the idiots [?]". That was on April 3, 1945.

The Altbundespräsident and I were agreed that there was only one thing left to be done, namely to persuade Himmler to give strict orders in view of the rapidly deteriorating military situation that the concentration camps, when it was expected that they would be overrun, were not to be evacuated any more. Himmler finally gave in after a long discussion. In this I had the support of Mr. Kersten, who urged Himmler from Stockholm that the camps should not be evacuated and thereby did much to convince him to give his agreement. On April 7, 1945, I was able to inform Altbundespräsident Musy of the positive decision and that it was Himmler's express request that it should be transmitted as quickly as possible to General Eisenhower. Altbundespräsident Musy, in spite of being over 70, started off by car the same night, and was able to report to me three days later that Washington had received the communication and was reacting positively.

Altbundespräsident Musy immediately had sent his son [Benoit] back from Switzerland with the car to pick up some Jews, promised to him by Himmler himself—Bernard Bemberg, Bernheim de Villiers—in Buchenwald. Musy junior saw the camp commander, was treated rather badly, and when he saw that the evacuation of the camp had begun, came to me in Berlin on April 10, 1945, being shocked by what he had experienced [mit allen Zeichen des Entsetzens].

I firmly believed that Himmler's original order would be carried out in any case. After [Benoit] Musy's disclosure I concerned myself with the entire procedure. — I myself in fact actually had absolutely nothing to do with these State Police matters. — I now found out that Himmler, as a result of countless intrigues, once again was completely discredited with Hitler, and that now orders had been given through Kaltenbrunner to evacuate all camps. So far the facts were totally clear to me, though I was still uncertain, how matters stood in regard to the prisoner of war camps. I cleared this up with [SS-*Obergruppenfuehrer* Gottlob] Berger, who, however, in contrast to Kaltenbrunner, had not passed on the order for the fresh evacuation of prisoner of war camps. In an urgent telephone call I complained about the entire situation to Himmler, who was obviously very embarrassed by the extent to which orders were by-passing him, and he promised me to intervene. An hour later I spoke to Dr. [Rudolf] Brandt about this matter, and he assured me that Himmler has [had?] done everything possible, to ensure that his promise that the camps should not be evacuated, was kept under all circumstances. Through the constant pressure on Himmler in this entire period, this I may well rightly claim at this point, it was accomplished at least to bring a positive direction [Linie] into the whole line of command [Kommandogebung] and to prevent the worst consequences of contrary orders from Kaltenbrunner and others, thereby effectively saving the lives of countless people. Himmler was particularly grateful to me for this, when Mr. Kersten came to visit him with Mr. [Norbert] Masur, a representative of Mr. [Hillel] Storch from Stockholm, who had the authorization of the World Jewish Congress to converse with Himmler, because otherwise he, Himmler, would not even have been able to have this conversation.

Through our frequent meetings Altbundespräsident Musy and I were on intimate terms [engen menschlichen Kontakt]. We understood each other very well. He told me much out of his rich political experience, while I took the opportunity in return, of explaining to him the pressing worries I had in my position. Particularly his great understanding made it easier for me to confide in him the great difficulties of the situation, in the hope that, together, we might avoid as many of them as possible.

He once made the proposal to me to release [Edouard] Herriot[608] under all circumstances, a gesture which would do a real service to France, while it would show that I had the political situation at my fingertips. Altbundespräsident Musy was even prepared to intervene in London in this question, which he considered highly important. I discussed this matter with Himmler, who, apparently after consultation with Kaltenbrunner, brusquely declined my proposal.

During this entire time there were also constant requests from various other Swiss friends to release the former Minister [Paul] Reynaud.[609] This failed because of Kaltenbrunner's resistance. I then tried at least something, namely to have the relatives of General [Henri] Giraud sent to one of my Swiss friends for further dispatch. My various attempts to achieve this failed. It required altogether six weeks of systematic pressure on Himmler to finally be given per-

---

608 Edouard Herriot, former président du conseil, had denounced Marshal Philippe Pétain and his Vichy government. Later he declared his support for Charles de Gaulle and eventually ended up a prisoner in Germany.

609. Cf. Schellenberg, *The Schellenberg Memoirs*, 432. Paul Reynaud was forced to resign as Premier in June 1940 and eventually was imprisoned by the Germans.

mission to free them, against the wishes of Kaltenbrunner and [Heinrich] Mueller. In order to carry out the release in a dignified manner I still had to overcome a number of difficulties—gasoline, a car, etc. My assistant [Mitarbeiter], [Hans Wilhelm] Eggen, helped me considerably in this matter, and he personally attended to their transportation into Switzerland. General Giraud thanked me in a personal letter that unfortunately is no longer in my possession.

To round off the complete picture, the following still remains to be mentioned: Through some Swiss friends I was in contact with the President of the International Red Cross, Professor Dr. [Carl Jakob] Burckhardt. He, too, apparently wished Germany to adopt a generous gesture [grosszuegigerweise] in the question of political prisoners, particularly those of French and Polish nationality, as well as in the Jewish question. He told a German friend of his in mid-March, that he considered it would be a good thing, if he could meet Himmler. I worked on Himmler for several days to get him to by all means write a letter to Professor Burckhardt and suggest a date for a meeting. Himmler several times put off a definite decision, then discussed it with Kaltenbrunner and got him to ask Hitler, if he—Himmler—might meet with Professor Burckhardt. Hitler refused this categorically. For tactical reasons I then suggested to Himmler that he should entrust Kaltenbrunner or me with the matter. Himmler decided on Kaltenbrunner, in order to cover himself with Hitler. Kaltenbrunner informed me of this decision and ordered me to draft a letter to President Burckhardt. I wrote this letter. Kaltenbrunner covered himself, on Himmler's orders, by informing Ribbentrop. Kaltenbrunner's and Himmler's plan was that, if the meeting should become known through a press notice, they could tell Hitler, that it was [the Foreign Minister] Ribbentrop who was responsible for the visit. President Burckhardt reacted favorably to the letter. A meeting took place between President Burckhardt and Kaltenbrunner, the procedure and content of which I prepared from the German side. President Burkhardt apparently was very pleased with the outcome of the conversation as it meant for him the beginning for the International Red Cross to finally take a decisive hand in the many pending questions concerning political prisoners, as well as prisoners of war [Haeftlings- wie Kriegsgefangenenwesens]. He confirmed the content of the conversation in a long letter and made concrete proposals, according to categories and urgencies on the procedure to be adopted in the exchange of prisoners of all nations. When shown this letter, Kaltenbrunner declared that it was far too concretely formulated. It was, he said, a particularly skillful, legally drawn up letter, whose individual proposals he could not fulfill at all. He merely declared himself prepared, in order to save appearances, to allow the International Red Cross, with Himmler's permission, to take a larger number of French women from Ravensbrueck. Kaltenbrunner essentially then kept me away from having anything to do with carrying this out in order to avoid my constant pressure for an answer to Burckhardt's letter. I again drew Himmler's attention to this matter and pointed out how Professor Burckhardt would necessarily lose confidence in him if his letter were not answered and delaying tactics, etc., were used. Himmler could not be moved to pursue the matter energetically. Only once more I was able to send consoling news to my friends in Switzerland, as from then on all further technical means of communication were closed to me. Thus this attempt to solve the humanitarian question on this basis was also destroyed.

In conclusion it is important to stress my cooperation with Count Bernadotte, especially on the Jewish question. Notwithstanding that the Count's mission was in connection with the Danish and Norwegian question, a very delicate one, the Count during his conversations intervened on behalf of the Jewish question, and drew attention to the importance of improving the situation of the Jewish inmates. Count Bernadotte skillfully managed to get the Danish Jews out. Relying on the authority of the Count, I was able to insist on an alleviation in the treatment of the Jews. During his conversations with Himmler, the Count always emphasized, and requested, that the Jews should receive better treatment. Here, too, we tried to achieve a total solution [eine totale Loesung]. Of very special importance was the conversation between the Count and Himmler at the end of March and the beginning of April 1945. Following a detailed conversation Himmler promised the Count that on the approach of the Allies the camps would not be evacuated, and would be handed over to the latter in complete order, especially Bergen Belsen, Buchenwald and Theresienstadt, as well as camps situated in Southern Germany. In view of the contrasts evident, this conversation was decisive and it enabled me thereafter to point out to Himmler that the promise made to the Count would have to be kept. Although it was not possible to save all the inmates, a large part of the camp inmates were saved, which I was able to achieve only because I could always base my activities on the promise given to the Count.

Thanks to the last discussions between the Count and Himmler I could finally on April 21, 1945, set in motion the liberation of the Jewish and other women from Ravensbrueck. Himmler gave me the authority to act as I saw fit under the circumstances, (that is, I arranged for the transportation of all women out of the camp as far as possible. This is based also on the intervention of the Count with Himmler.)[610]

I took all these examples to expound to Himmler again and again how completely the situation had gotten out of hand, and warned him that due to his hesitant attitude he would one day be held responsible before history for having endangered the whole biological substance [sic] of the German people [Volk] through his obvious blindness. In many discussions he always countered this by saying that he had built up the Order of the SS on the principle of loyalty [Treueprinzip], and that he was not in a position to break this principle, as otherwise he would destroy his own basis. I explained to him in long discourses that the Order of the SS, measured against the life of a nation [Volk] was only a small section, and that the whole German people [Deutsche Volk], after its superhuman sufferings expected at last a rational and liberating act, and finally saw in him the man who, so far, had not enriched himself. The answer was always: "Then you demand from me that I remove the Fuehrer". He had days when the answer could not be "Yes", as otherwise I ran the risk of being removed myself, especially as the influence of Gruppenfuehrer [Hermann] Fegelein, [Ernst] Kaltenbrunner, Obersturmbannfuehrer [Otto] Skorzeny and their clique [und Genossen] was often still too overpowering, particularly in view of their right of direct communication with Hitler. — Mrs. [Gretl] Fegelein is the sister of Eva Braun, Hitler's girlfriend. Kaltenbrunner and Skorzeny were befriended with both women.

During these conversations with me Himmler often spoke of Hitler's deteriorating health. To my objection, how was it then that he still had so much influence, Himmler answered that his energy was undiminished; the completely unnatural way of life, turning night into day and sleeping at most two to three hours,[611] his continuous activity and constant outbursts of fury had completely exhausted those around him and created an unbearable atmosphere. I often suggested that perhaps through the [attempted] assassination of July 20 Hitler had suffered health injuries, particularly of his head as an aftereffect. Himmler thought this possible. He mentioned, above all, the increasing stoop, the pale complexion and the severe trembling of his left arm and the operation on Hitler's ear which took place in November [1944], apparently as the result of the concussion of the brain suffered in July [damals]. He spent eight days in bed in November.

Because of this information, I then spoke at the beginning of April [1945] to my friend the Director of the Psychological Department of the Charité,

---

610. The text in parenthesis is part of the German text but missing in the English translation. The respective page of the German text bears Schellenberg's initials at bottom right.
611. The German text reads "two to three hours," not "3-4 hours" as some British translations have it.

Professor [Max] de Crinis. I brought up the matter of Hitler's state of health, whereupon he spontaneously answered: "I have the impression on the basis of Hitler's completely lame movements, which I observed in the pictures in the news [Wochenschau], that these could be the visible signs of Parkinson's disease." I arranged a meeting between Himmler and de Crinis. Himmler brought along Reich Health Leader [*Reichsgesundheitsfuehrer*] Conti[612] to the meeting. Himmler listened to their statements, as de Crinis later informed me, with much interest and the greatest understanding.

April 13, 1945

A few days later, it was April 13, Himmler had me come to see him at Wustrow, where he took a walk with me in the woods and said: "Schellenberg, I think it cannot be done with Hitler anymore. Do you think de Crinis is right [?]" I answered: "Yes, I haven't seen Hitler since two or more years, but from all I recognize from his actions recently, I am inclined to assume that the very last moment for you to act has now come."

I took this opportunity of pointing out to him once more the necessity of a fundamental solution of the Jewish question, as he had promised Alt-bundespräsident Musy already in September. The conversation turned to Mr. Kersten and the possibility that Mr. Kersten wanted to come to Germany with Mr. [Hillel] Storch in the next few days to discuss the Jewish problem with Himmler personally. As the visit had already been suggested, but Himmler still could not bring himself to give a binding answer, I let him know that both out of regard for Mr. Kersten and for reasons of principle the date of the visit could hardly be put off any longer. Himmler sensed how fundamental a step such an encounter with Mr. Storch, later [Norbert] Masur, would be, because he felt that such a meeting would constitute an act, that must have tremendous consequences for him, as long as Hitler was alive, in his relationships toward his Party colleagues, as well as toward the Jews [Judenschaft]. This was one of the reasons for his constant vacillation. I encouraged him in every way, to avail himself of the discussion, perhaps only because I had a premonition that this discussion might one day be of symbolic importance. Himmler said: yes, he was indeed ready to do this, but if Kaltenbrunner should then discover it, it could hardly be carried out, because he would then be completely dependant on Kaltenbrunner, who could report it to the Fuehrer at any time. I then

---

612. Dr. Leonardo Conti, born in Lugano, Switzerland, was appointed Reich Health Leader by Hitler in 1938. He committed suicide in his cell in Nuremberg in 1945.

suggested to Himmler, that as Kaltenbrunner had already had himself sent to the Ostmark by Hitler, this should be repeated on some pretext or other and the meeting with Storch could then take place on the estate of Mr. Kersten.

Himmler was in great mental distress. Apparently even outwardly having an almost total fall-out with the Fuehrer—Hitler had ordered, on the advice of Fegelein, the Leibstandarte "Adolf Hitler" to take off their armbands as a dishonoring punishment[613]—he said to me that I was the only one besides, perhaps, Standartenfuehrer Dr. [Rudolf] Brandt, in whom he could completely confide. What should he do, he asked. He could not kill Hitler, he said, he could not poison him, and he could not arrest him in the Reich Chancellory, because the whole military machine would then come to a standstill. I explained that all this was of no importance, he had only two possibilities, either to go to Hitler and openly inform him of all that had happened during the last years and force him to resign [sentence *sic*]. Himmler replied that would be totally impossible, Hitler would get into one of his rages, and shoot him out of hand. I replied: "Against such one must protect oneself. You have enough high SS-leaders who are in a position to prepare and carry out such surprise arrests, and if there is absolutely no other way, the doctors must intervene." Our walk lasted an hour and a half. Himmler was unable to reach any decision, but wanted to bring together Professor de Crinis, Professor [Theodor] Morell, Hitler's personal physician,[614] Dr. [Ludwig] Stumpfegger,[615] the second physician, an SS-leader and [Martin] Bormann [*sic*].

I asked Professor de Crinis about the result two days later. He told me quite disappointedly that he had discussed particularly with Dr. Stumpfegger the symptoms of Parkinson's disease which he had suspected. Dr. Stumpfegger had not been of the same opinion, but had to admit many of his arguments. They had agreed on certain medicines. He had them prepared in his clinic. Dr. Stumpfegger had, however, not sent for them. Dr. Stumpfegger had also wanted to get medicines, so it was quite possible that Dr. Stumpfegger would not send someone to pick up the medicines from his clinic. I informed Himmler of this, who urgently asked me to maintain the strictest silence about these matters.

---

613. The Leibstandarte Adolf Hitler originally was a bodyguard unit of the SS for Hitler, commanded by Sepp Dietrich.
614. Theodor Morell, a medical doctor of somewhat unclear training, was Hitler's personal physician. Some members of Hitler's immediate surrounding did not share his trust in the doctor's professional skills.
615. Ludwig Stumpfegger worked at Karl Gebhardt's hospital at Hohenlychen as an orthopedic surgeon. In late 1944 he became one of Hitler's personal physicians and stayed in Hitler's bunker until the latter's suicide.

Another thing I pointed out to Himmler was the senselessness of the Wehrwolf organization,[616] which would only bring more suffering to the German people [Deutsches Volk]. This organization would open the floodgates of crime, because everyone in the absence of control could claim to act in the interest of national law. Added to this was the frivolity with which these things were emphasized by Germany, it was even announced over the Deutschlandsender [a government radio station] and the Hague-Convention was voluntarily renounced. I closed my speech with the words: "Criminal and stupid." Himmler was obviously so wearied by this battle of souls with me that after a passionate outburst he drew no consequences from my accusations but instead said: "I must consider, whether I can even dissolve the thing [the Wehrwolf organization] again."

During the days following April 13—the date of our walk in the woods—all the things I had been observing for months and over which I had so often struggled with Himmler, began to move with breathless speed. Through a trustworthy colleague [Mitarbeiter] from my office—Oberstleutnant von Dewitz[617]—I got in touch with Reich Finance Minister [Johann Ludwig] Graf Schwerin von Krosigk during the first week of April. In lengthy conversations with von Krosigk we were in full agreement that the war ought to be brought to a speedy end, in order to save as much as possible of the biological substance [sic] of Germany. Because I was able at this time to speak openly with Himmler about things, while Himmler had quarreled with von Krosigk in the course of the years, I brought the two together for a discussion in the afternoon of April 19.

April 19, 1945

Before the meeting I had lunch with Himmler, in the presence of [Gottlob] Berger, Obersturmbannfuehrer [Werner] Grothmann,[618] and Dr. [Rudolf] Brandt. Himmler was very nervous. Berger attempted to lead the conversation to Fegelein's failure,[619] the bad situation on the whole and Hitler's reaction to it. Himmler prevented this attempt and took the wind out of Berger's sails by

---

616. Werwolf was a kind of underground German army or rather a network of largely autonomous quasi-military units conceived to operate in the areas occupied by the Allies. The commander of this planned force was SS-*Obergruppenfuehrer* Hans Pruetzmann. He was captured and committed suicide. "Final Report," Appendix XIX, 292-294.
617. Probably Eckhardt von Dewitz, an officer whom Schellenberg found trustworthy. "Final Report," 176, 187.
618. SS-*Obersturmbannführer* Werner Grothmann was on Himmler's personal staff and stayed with him until the very end. Cf. Padfield, *Himmler*, 608-609.
619. At this time Hermann Fegelein, an SS officer, had married Gretl Braun, the sister of Hitler's companion Eva Braun, and was one of the persons surrounding Hitler in the Berlin bunker at the end of the war. After he left the bunker in late April 1945, he was arrested and executed.

saying, that such and such a situation existed, he knew well enough, decisive was only how [*sic*] this could be altered, and apparently he, Berger, had nothing new to report about that. Berger then became quite unsure of himself and only managed to make disconnected general conversation. Grothmann also got into a little argument with Himmler, because he pointed out, as was his duty, that the Wallonian Division under [Léon] Degrelle[620] was no longer very reliable. Obergruppenfuehrer Steiner[621] had brought this to his notice, Grothmann said. Himmler worked himself up over Steiner and gave various instructions, which Grothmann, rightly defending Steiner in this case, misunderstood, and the whole thing resolved itself into a lengthy discussion between the two. Himmler by then was so nervous that he asked me at the end, what it was that he wanted to meet von Krosigk for. The meeting almost did not take place.

At the meeting with Reich Finance Minister Count Schwerin von Krosigk Reich Labor Minister [Franz] Seldte also was present.[622] Von Krosigk and Himmler talked together alone, while I withdrew with Seldte for a conversation. Seldte was of the opinion, that Himmler had to take over and force Hitler on his birthday to broadcast an appeal to the German people stating that a general election would be held, a second Party formed and the People's Court [Volksgerichtshof] abolished. Seldte talked for almost two hours on this subject and then turned to the topic what chances I thought a defense of the Alpine area would have. Concerning the latter I explained to him that I saw absolutely no chance from the military point of view, but that it was only by some last, quick political action that anything could be achieved under the circumstances. In the meantime the meeting between von Krosigk and Himmler had ended.

I then spoke to von Krosigk, who was very pleased with his discussion with Himmler, although we both knew that it was very late and that there was no longer any prospect of success. All the same we kept to our original plan.

We then talked of Reich President von Hindenburg[623] and some of von Krosigk's experiences with him, of Hitler, Ribbentrop's failure, etc. Von Krosigk then still asked me to continue influencing Himmler to dare the decisive step with Hitler or without him [German text unclear]. — Von Krosigk apparently wrote a letter to Himmler the next day, in which he reminded him

---

620. Léon Degrelle, a Walloon Belgian Nazi, after the war survived by fleeing to Argentina. Cf. Snyder, *Encyclopedia of the Third Reich*, 62.
621. Probably SS-*Obergruppenführer* Felix Steiner whose units Hitler at the end of the war had ordered to attack the Russian forces that were taking the outskirts of Berlin.
622. Franz Seldte, Hitler's Reich Minister of Labor, in December 1918 had been one of the founders of the Stahlhelm, a nationalist veterans' organization.
623. Paul Ludwig Hans von Beneckendorff und von Hindenburg (1847-1934). Supreme Commander of Germany's Eastern Armies in World War I, elected Reich President 1925.

again of their discussion and urged him to take decisive action, as he was answerable to the entire German people. I asked von Krosigk whether he had communicated to the Reichsfuehrer [Himmler] all the plans we had discussed. He answered in the affirmative and said that he had been particularly emphatic about it.

As we drove from Krosigk's home to Hohenlychen, Himmler thanked me for arranging the discussion with von Krosigk. I told Himmler, that in my opinion, von Krosigk, as I had known for a long time, was the only personality in Germany he could make Foreign Minister.

After arriving at Hohenlychen, the military reports gave a very depressing picture. I urgently counseled Himmler not to travel to Berlin the next day for Hitler's birthday. He did not, however, wish to miss the occasion. Meanwhile Himmler, in my presence, repeatedly telephoned about military questions with Fegelein at the Reich Chancellory. At the same time the report came in that Mr. [Felix] Kersten had arrived at the airport Tempelhof with Mr. [Norbert] Masur and had driven off to [his estate] Hartzwalde. As Count Bernadotte was also expected in Berlin at the same time, and there was danger that the two meeting dates would overlap because of the difficult military situation, Himmler asked me to drive to Mr. Kersten that night in order to begin the first preliminary talks with Mr. Masur and arrange a meeting for him and Himmler in Hartzwalde at a time I considered suitable.

After supper, which we had together at Hohenlychen and which was also attended by Professor [Karl] Gebhardt, whom I completely reject as a person, but whom I am unable to judge as a physician, I intentionally brought up the question of sending Berger to southern Germany, in order to emphasize once again the importance of this action. I had thought of Berger as a counter weight to Kaltenbrunner in the southern region, as I mistrusted Kaltenbrunner in every respect and did not even know if my family would be safe from him. Thus I thought of Berger only as a personal safety factor.

Interestingly enough, Himmler did not react to this, but immediately started talking about Kaltenbrunner, whom in the course of the conversation he now tried to present as a politically clever, circumspect and very wise man. From the coldness of my reaction he was able, as always, to recognize my attitude, but apparently my obvious disagreement only caused him to hold forth the more about Kaltenbrunner's alleged achievements in earlier days. Gebhardt knew nothing of my forthcoming journey to Hartzwalde. I used his lack of knowledge, which had to be maintained for reasons of secrecy, to put an end to this discussion of "Kaltenbrunner," by hinting that my further work during this night would hardly be in agreement with Kaltenbrunner's political cleverness. Himmler finally paid attention and the subject was changed.

Shortly before midnight I took my leave, as Himmler—contrary to his usual practice—ordered still another bottle of champagne in order to toast to Hitler's birthday at midnight. I did not have to wait for this, however, and was able to leave for Hartzwalde. It was a moonlit night. Because to make time we tried different field roads, we were somewhat off our path and finally just before Hartzwalde we were held up by flares set by aircraft obviously coming back from Berlin. I arrived at Gut Hartzwalde about 02:30 hours. Everyone was already fast asleep.

April 20, 1945

As I had to share a room with Mr. Kersten, there was an opportunity to exchange a few thoughts with him at 04:00 hours in the morning. He was very annoyed over Himmler and his hesitant attitude and thought that a successful discussion between Himmler and Mr. Masur was hardly possible any more, but all the same this would be a way for Himmler once again to show his "good will" [sic in the German text]. Kersten then again brought up the subject of my negotiations with Herr [Jean-Marie] Musy and said that it was fortunate that the solution of the Jewish problem had been lifted out from monetary considerations and that, as he had heard from me, the money deposited was to be transferred to the International Red Cross. I explained to Mr. Kersten how difficult the whole situation had been for me, especially in recent times, but that I had tried everything and as it was finally had achieved the coming off of this conference. I then spoke at some length to him about Kaltenbrunner's recent behavior, which Mr. Kersten noted with great interest and from his knowledge of the facts was able to confirm again and again.

On April 20 at 09:00 hours in the morning—Mr. Kersten had risen a little earlier—I was woken up by the noise of aircraft flying overhead. While I was still shaving a heavy bomber had evidently dropped a bomb on Hartzwalde, which had fallen about one kilometer away, near a narrow-gauge railway. For Mr. Masur this was not a pleasant surprise. I breakfasted with Mr. Masur and afterwards we had our first conference. Mr. Masur was at first somewhat nervous, but then I was able to establish contact with him and we discussed freely all the problems that interested us. At fairly great length I also explained to Mr. Masur why the operation Musy in Switzerland could no longer be continued. He regretted this very much and said that all the same he would be interested to know how such things took place in Germany. In the early hours of the afternoon I went again for a walk in the woods with Mr. Masur and he used the opportunity to enquire about many things in Germany about which, as far as it was possible, I willingly gave him information and explanations. He laid great stress on being able to leave Berlin again under all circumstances by plane on Monday at the latest. He could not agree to any postponement of his meeting with Himmler, as he would then regretfully have to depart, without having had the talk. I knew that Himmler intended postponing the talk once again, and I now had the task to see that the agreed date was adhered to under all circumstances.

On return from the walk I was rung up from the Swedish Legation where Count Bernadotte was staying. He told me that he would like to talk to Himmler once again, but that under all circumstances he would have to leave on the 21st, i.e. the next day at 06:00 hours in the morning. A postponement of his departure would not be possible under any circumstances. The task now was to bring Himmler and Mr. Masur together and to ask Count Bernadotte to a place, where he too could talk undisturbed with Himmler that night. I had indeed hoped that everything I had discussed with the Count would now, at the very last minute, be decided upon [zum Spruch kam]. In order to adhere to the last deadline I had the Count taken to Hohenlychen, where on my instructions he was to be looked after.

I myself at about 17:00 hours drove to the Ziethen Castle at Wustrow in order to wait there for Himmler. Dr. Brandt in view of the deadlines tried several times to hasten Himmler's departure from the Reich chancellory, but this was apparently impossible because of air raids. Himmler did not reach Wustrow till about 22:30 hours. Even before supper I explained the situation regarding Masur and Count Bernadotte to him and asked him above all to finally use the channel of Count Bernadotte to put an end to the war. The discussion lasted comparatively long, because he again had doubts about the meeting with Masur. He did finally decide, however, to drive with me to Hartzwalde and, from there, in the same night to Hohenlychen to have breakfast with Count Bernadotte at 06:00 hours.

Himmler then still outlined to me what he wished to say to Masur. It was essentially a chronological summary of events with an attempt at a skillful justification. I asked him not to speak of the "Karma" [sic] between the two peoples, nor of Weltanschauung, etc., which Mr. Masur would not be able to understand properly. It would be much better not to speak of the past, but instead to lay down shortly and precisely what had to be done to save those, who still could be saved, and what he, as the man responsible for these things, had undertaken in this direction. This would be what Mr. Masur would want to hear too and it would be a good thing, if he showed that, by the measures he was taking, he was putting himself in open contradiction and disobedience to Hitler and his camarilla, this being, however, what he must now finally take upon himself to make amends for his personal conduct. Himmler wished to think over my advice.

<u>April 21, 1945</u>

We left Wustrow for Hartzwalde about 01:15 hours, accompanied only by a driver and Dr. Brandt. On the way we had to stop in a wooded area, as low flying enemy aircraft [Tiefflieger] were very active in the area. After a quarter of an hour we were able, however, to proceed without further incident. We arrived at Hartzwalde about 02:30 hours. After a short greeting the conference between Mr. Masur and Himmler, and Mr. Kersten and myself began. Himmler really led the conversation which turned about proving that he had wanted to solve the Jewish question by forced emigration, but that this could not be successfully implemented, on the one hand because of opposition from the world, but on the other hand also because of opposition from our own ranks. I had the feeling that the conversation in its various points was correctly appreciated by Mr. Masur. Viewed as a whole, however, it was only an attempt to justify what I usually call "the cosmic sequence of events" [*sic*]. Mr. Masur did not reply to the individual points with lengthy argumentations, but merely said after about three quarters of an hour that these explanations to him had been very interesting, but that they were not suited to alter the actual situation. Therefore, he said he was in the main there in order to obtain the following assurances:

1) That there must be no more killings of Jews, which as he had heard had already been ordered earlier by Himmler.
2) That the existing number of Jews, a number very uncertain and disputable, should under all circumstances be kept in the camps and no longer be evacuated.
3) That all camps in which there were still Jews should have lists compiled which would be made public.

These points were agreed upon, Himmler always saying that he had already ordered this earlier and that everything would be done to now bring these problems to a conclusion in this smooth way. He hinted at the difficulties he had with Hitler in this question. The above-listed points were to be confirmed once more in writing. This was discussed between Mr. Kersten, Dr. Brandt and Himmler. I knew that Himmler was also ready to release Jewish women from Ravensbrueck to Mr. Masur, as he had permission from Hitler to remove all Polish women from Ravensbrueck. He had said to me before that then one could very well also let the Jewish women go from there, as he would be in a position to say, in case of an inquiry, that the women in question had been Poles.

I had gone into another room with Mr. Masur in order to discuss with him there all the points he wished to ask Himmler at the end of the conversation. After starting [again?] the joint conference, I tried very much to bring the meeting to an end because it was becoming increasingly unclear and gliding into totally unimportant incidentals, in order to still reach Hohenlychen with Himmler punctually at 06:00 hours. After a short leave taking we drove away from Hartzwalde at about 04:30 hours. On taking leave I promised Mr. Masur again that I would do everything in my power to make his departure on the next day possible.

We arrived at Hohenlychen punctually at 06:00 hours that is on April 21, and were able to have breakfast with Count Bernadotte straight away. I had hoped that the frank talk between Himmler and the Count that I had so long desired, would at last take place. Again Himmler dodged the issue. It remained a general conversation, in which, as a new offer, Himmler gave the Count permission to transport all Polish women from Ravensbrueck to Sweden. Regarding this point, Himmler had told me before that Hitler had only agreed to this proposal, because he had made it clear to him that the reception of these Polish women by Sweden would not only represent a humanitarian act, but, under certain circumstances, a political point versus Russia. The reason for Himmler's action was as follows: Through Mr. Musy Junior I had connections with the Polish Prince Radziwil in Geneva.[624] The Prince already in January had sent me a list of Polish women in the Ravensbrueck camp whom I had decided to free under all circumstances, because by age they were children and young girls. I had urgently presented Himmler with the indignity of this state of things and in the process could go as far as trying to move him to allow a release pointing out the racial qualities of the Polish people, in which connection I carefully referred [Andeutung machte] to my own wife. He was deeply impressed and I had the feeling that, as he repeatedly brought up the question of his own accord, he occupied himself with it a great deal. More I could not achieve at the time. Apparently in order to gain his point with Hitler without giving away his real motives, he tried to solve the question by using the above-mentioned political background.

---

624. Janusz Prince Radziwil (1880-1967), Polish aristocrat, various underground connections, said to have had access to Göring and to Russians, also to actress Olga Chekhova. Cf. Pavel Sudaplatov and Anatoli Sudaplatov, *Special Tasks: The Memoirs of an Unwanted Witness—A Soviet Spymaster* (Boston: Little, Brown, 1995), 112-115, 364. "Final Report," 179.

In addition Prince Radziwil urgently requested the release of General Bor.[625] This too I discussed with Himmler, who did not want to make a decision on the question without Hitler. I succeeded in saving General Bor at, so to speak, the last moment in that I was able to give the effective order in the name of Himmler to the prison camp in Klattnow in Czechoslovakia. He was then taken in the general direction of Munich and Himmler likewise gave me the authorization to send General Bor over into Switzerland. This was on April 24, 1945. I gave the order but was not able to verify its execution anymore.

Count Bernadotte expressed thanks for this offer and for his part asked whether it would not be possible to transport the Danish and Norwegian prisoners to Sweden. Himmler declared that he was not in a position to give such a permission, but agreed that if Neuengamme were overrun as a result of military operations, an evacuation of the Danish and Norwegian prisoners would not ensue [*sic*].

The Count expressed thanks for this willingness to oblige and for the confidence he had been shown in the earlier conversations. The conversation ended by turning to general matters and in an official leave taking.

Himmler knew that I would accompany the Count for part of the way and secretly hoped that during that time I would ask the Count again to fly to General Eisenhower on his own initiative, in order to make possible a mediation operation or a meeting between Himmler and General Eisenhower. The resulting conversation we had on the road near Waren in Mecklenburg, where we parted, revealed the situation to be approximately as follows: "The Reichsfuehrer does not see his real situation any more. I cannot help him any more, for, for that, he would have had to have taken things in the Reich entirely into his own hands after my first visit. I think he hardly has any more chances and you, my dear Schellenberg, would do better to think of yourself." There was nothing I could say to him in reply and we took leave as though we were not to see each other again within a reasonable period of time. I was extremely sad.

I drove back to Hohenlychen, slept two hours and was then at about 12:30 hours called to Himmler, who was still in bed. He told me that he was not feeling well, and he was such a picture of a torn soul and of unrest and dissatisfaction that I could only say to him that I too could do nothing any more for him, that it was up to him to act, act in any way he liked, as I simply did not see a way out for Germany any more. We then had lunch together. Our conversation produced no new points of view. The ever-worsening military situation of Berlin was discussed.

---

625. General Bor, or rather General Tadeusz Komorowski, led the uprising on August 1, 1944, in Warsaw. His troops held out against the superior forces of Erich von dem Bach-Zelewski for 63 days. Cf. John Toland, *The Last 100 Days* (London: Phoenix, 1996; 1st ed. 1965), 45–46.

Towards 16:00 hours we left for Wustrow after I had convinced Himmler that it would not be good for him to drive into Berlin. We came into great traffic difficulties in Loewenberg, because numerous troop contingents had become entangled with endless columns of refugees, closing all the highways from and to Berlin and Mecklenburg. I asked Himmler to detach a company from his escort to help these people and also to get the troops to move on. It was then that, for the first time, Himmler said, as we drove on: "Schellenberg, I dread all that is still to come." I replied that this ought at last to give him the courage to act. He did not reply. Shortly before Wustrow we met an attack of low flying enemy aircraft, but these apparently intended rather to attack the sector behind us with refugee columns and troop movements.

Obergruppenfuehrer [Gottlob] Berger and [Maximilian] von Herff had been ordered to report to Himmler in Wustrow, Berger so as to learn the latest intentions of Himmler before he flew off to the South in Himmler's aircraft. I sat alone with Himmler. The subject of conversation was my impression of the discussion with Masur. I again pointed to the great guilt of Kaltenbrunner who constantly obstructed the orders issued since the operation Musy and on this evening Himmler at last was strongly impressed. "Yes, yes, Schellenberg, if only I had listened to you earlier." After the meal we were alone and talked about general problems, the food supply, the danger of epidemics, clearance operations, the prisoner of war camps administration, etc., and then again and again about the senseless attitude of Hitler which was so greatly influenced by Kaltenbrunner, and about the complete evacuation of the camps. When I called the operation a crime Himmler became very restless, almost angry and said "Schellenberg, now don't you start too. Hitler has been furious for days that Buchenwald and Bergen-Belsen were not evacuated a hundred per cent." To that I said for the first time to Himmler: "But in that case Parkinson's disease must have advanced very far." Himmler accepted this answer without further reaction, but our conversation became more official and he immediately asked Berger to join in. At the same moment Fegelein telephoned with the information that Hitler and Goebbels were furious that Berger had not stayed in Berlin. The latter was required on account of the sentence against Gruppenfuehrer Professor Dr. [Karl] Brandt, Hitler's previous personal physician, who had been sentenced to death during the last few days because he had knowingly let his wife fall into American hands in Thuringia. From the conversation between Berger and Himmler, I was able to gather that this had to be a great game of intrigue among those closest to Hitler, in which Hitler's girlfriend, Eva Braun and Fegelein's wife were playing their parts. Himmler did everything to delay and prevent the execution of the sentence. I saw that from his attitude and from the instructions which he gave over the telephone to

Gruppenfuehrer Müller, Chief of the Secret State Police, in my presence. Professor Dr. Brandt was taken to Schwerin to protect him from air raids and Fegelein was told that Berger was already on the way south with the aircraft. In view of this, he was told, the execution could not take place at the moment unless Reichsleiter Bormann and Goebbels would make available trusted Party members for the action. As all these things about Berger and the current conversation were uninteresting to me, I took my leave.

After an hour, however, I was called for again. Himmler sat down again with me at a table and told me how he would do things once he had the power in Germany in his hands. He asked me to consider this very night a possible name to give to a new party, which I had suggested to him. I gave him the name "Nationale Sammlungspartei" [National Coalition Party]. He then began to speak again of removing Hitler. But there were only vague hints. Towards 04:30 hours he dismissed me and went to bed.

April 22, 1945

At 10:00 hours, it was Sunday morning, Himmler had breakfast with me and Dr. [Rudolf] Brandt. The military situation had deteriorated over night to such a degree, as Himmler said, that four Waffen-SS divisions of Obergruppenfuehrer [Felix] Steiner had to be deployed on Hitler's orders in a last deathly attack. I cannot say accurately anymore what the strategic situation was. It was to be a flank attack against the Russians somewhere. Himmler was still completely convinced of the necessity for this order of the Fuehrer, while I was in agreement with my military Adjutant [Werner] Grothmann that this too would become an unnecessary spilling of blood. My respective objections were rejected, because I allegedly understood nothing of military matters.

After breakfast Berger and Lorenz[626] arrived who were to drive with us to Hohenlychen because Ziethen Castle at Wustrow had to be given up because it was threatened by the enemy.

I then still discussed the Vanaman case with Berger. [Arthur W.] Vanaman, an American Air Force general, now German prisoner of war and previously American military attaché in Berlin, at the suggestion from Berger and myself was supposed to leave Germany illegally together with another American Air Force colonel. Vanaman was to fly to Roosevelt via Switzerland, first of all to obtain better aid for the American prisoners of war and secondly to explain to him that Himmler wanted peace with the Western powers.

---

626. If Schellenberg remembered correctly, this would be SS-*Obergruppenfuehrer* Werner Lorenz, chief of the Volksdeutsche Mittelstelle or Reference Office for Racial Germans. Höhne, *The Order of the Death's Head*, 312-313. "Final Report," 183.

I had conceived this plan already months earlier, when I had wanted to release English prisoners of war, who had a name in England, for example Mr. Dodge and many others, with the object of them propagating an understanding. Hitler and Himmler, however, firmly refused permission in both cases.

I spoke at length with Vanaman, and we were in complete agreement. His dispatch could not, however, be carried out, as, in spite of all my requests, Himmler would not give me permission. On my own responsibility together with Swiss friends and the American Military Attaché General Legg[627] in Bern, Switzerland, I prepared the illegal border crossing and sent Vanaman and the American Air Force Colonel, who accompanied him in a car—despite the great gasoline shortage—to Constance for the frontier crossing. As I had no news of the two men, I asked Berger in Himmler's presence to take a special interest in this case. Himmler now agreed with the plan.

There was a very hasty departure from Wustrow at about 12:00 hours, because Russian tank spearheads were reported near Oranienburg in the general direction of Löwenberg—Kremen. We drove from Wustrow in a northerly direction to Mecklenburg and then turned east in order to reach Hohenlychen. Army columns, guns and tanks that were being brought up and constant activity by low flying aircraft delayed the drive by more than an hour and a half.

In Hohenlychen we had a very late lunch together. The table conversation largely concerned affairs of the two Obergruppenfuehrer Berger and Lorenz. I took absolutely no part in the conversation.

After the meal Himmler begged me to stay behind alone and asked me: "I almost think Schellenberg that you are right, I must act now in some way or other. What do you suggest?" I explained to him that it was naturally too late for everything. The operation Vanaman unfortunately could not be counted on anymore. There would, however, perhaps still be a possibility to discuss the situation absolutely openly with Count Bernadotte, whom I had on my own responsibility put into the picture to a much greater and more comprehensive extent than he, Himmler, knew. I explained, however, that I was not accurately informed as to whether I could still reach Count Bernadotte in Germany or Denmark. I supposed that, as far as I could remember, I said, he had wanted to possibly remain in Lübeck till Monday. Himmler thereupon decided straight away that I should drive to Lübeck immediately in order to talk openly with the Count. He, Himmler, was now prepared, he said, to request the Count

---

627. This is Brigadier General Barnwell R. Legge, the U.S. Military Attaché in Bern. In OSS documents Legge is referred to as 520. "Final Report," 182-183.

officially in his own name to carry the declaration of capitulation to the Western Powers.

I immediately prepared my departure and drove off to Lübeck at about 16:30 hours. Owing to great activity of low flying enemy aircraft, clogged highways, etc., I did not arrive in Lübeck till night and ascertained after a short time that the Count was neither in Friedrichsruh, nor Lübeck, nor Flensburg but in Apenrade in Denmark. After a relatively short time I succeeded, despite all difficulties, in speaking to the Count on the telephone and asking him to receive me the next day in Flensburg. We arranged to meet on April 23, 1945, at 15:00 hours in Flensburg at the Swedish Consulate.

April 23, 1945

In the meantime it was morning again and after 3 hours rest and telephoning Himmler to inform him of my telephone conversation with Count Bernadotte, I drove on to Flensburg. At the Swedish Consulate in Flensburg towards 13:00 hours I met Attaché Chiron, who conducted me to the Swedish Consul—Honorary Consul—Petersen where I had lunch with the gentlemen.

At 15:00 hours Count Bernadotte arrived. I discussed with him the entire situation and Himmler's intentions.. The Count during the conversation thought that it was probably no longer necessary to go to Lübeck, as Himmler could put his intentions down in a letter to General Eisenhower, i.e. he could in this letter declare the unconditional surrender to the Western Powers. That would certainly be the best solution. I replied that such a course did not seem possible especially since Hitler was still alive, and asked him to drive with me to Lübeck for a short meeting with Himmler. After one hour of conversation the Count declared himself ready to do that. I telephoned from Flensburg with the Sonderzug Steiermark [special train called Steiermark and used by Heinrich Himmler and his staff] to ask Himmler to come to a meeting in Lübeck. Dr. [Rudolf] Brandt answered, but as he was unable to reach Himmler for the moment, he promised to call me back in Flensburg. — That the telephone connections were functioning in this way was particularly lucky, because generally telephone connections were not possible due to the overloading of the network with military communications. Towards 18:00 hours Dr. Brandt called back. He said that Himmler would be glad to see the Count in my presence at about 22:00 hours in Lübeck.

After a quick snack we drove at about 19:00 hours from Flensburg to Lübeck. We arrived there at the Swedish Consulate at 21:00 hours. I went to the office rooms which in the meantime had been fixed up in the hotel "Danziger Hof" [*sic*] and contacted the office of General Wünnenberg—

Ordnungspolizei—where Himmler intended to stay.[628] Towards 22:00 hours I was called to Himmler, reported briefly the main points of my conversation with the Count, and strengthened him in his intention to forward the declaration of capitulation through the Count to the Western Powers. Himmler still vacillated for a short time, but then agreed to my arguments which I had summarized again and said, "good, we will drive to the Count at 23:00 hours—prepare the meeting."

I drove then with Himmler at 23:00 hours to the Swedish Consulate, where we arrived at 23:10 hours. As the electricity was cut in Lübeck at that time, the discussion took place by candlelight, that is the alarm went off after the formal greetings, and since apparently there was a heavy attack on an airport nearby, we had to go into the cellar. After one hour, i.e. at about 24:00 hours, the conversation was continued. Himmler described at length the military and political situation of the Reich to the Count and explained to him in an almost honest account the whole situation: "We Germans have to declare ourselves as defeated by the Western Allies. That is what I request you to convey through the Swedish Government to General Eisenhower, so that further senseless fighting and unnecessary bloodshed be avoided. To capitulate to the Russians is impossible for us Germans, especially for me. We will then continue to fight there until the front of the Western Powers has, so to speak, relieved the fighting German front." Himmler also pointed out that he had the authority to communicate these things to the Count for transmission, as in the normal course of events it could certainly now be only a question of one or two, or at the most three days before Hitler gave up his strong life in this dramatic struggle. It was a consolation, he said, that he should fall fighting against Bolshevism, the idea [Idee] against the triumph of which he had dedicated his life [sein Leben verschrieben].

Count Bernadotte declared that in principle he was prepared to pass on Himmler's proposal [Vermittlungsvorschlag], indicating that for him, and probably also for the Swedish Government, it was a matter of first importance to save the entire Northern Sector from a senseless destruction through the continuation of this war. This consideration for him as a Swede was, he said, the deciding justification for carrying out such a request of Himmler at all. Himmler explicitly affirmed this point and, in answer to a question from the Count, now declared himself prepared to agree to the transfer of Danish and Norwegian internees to Sweden for internment.

Much time was needed for the discussion of the question how the transmittal of the declarations of capitulation to the Western Powers should take

---

628. SS-*Obergruppenfuehrer* Alfred Wünnenberg was Chief of the Ordnungspolizei (Opo) or Order Police.

place. The original plan that Count Bernadotte should, without using official diplomatic channels fly to General Eisenhower to submit to him Himmler's declarations was dropped. Instead, it was agreed that Himmler should write a letter to his Excellency Guenther, in which he would ask him to give his sympathetic support to the points of which Himmler had informed Count Bernadotte, and which Count Bernadotte would report to him. Himmler discussed briefly with me the form this letter should take, which then was written by himself in handwriting by candlelight on notepaper which had been hurriedly obtained. The Count said he was prepared to fly to Stockholm with this letter on the following day, i.e. on April 24, to initiate the necessary steps. We agreed that I should travel with the Count as far as Flensburg or Apenrade, in order to remain there as a connecting link in case of possible further questions or adjustments and also to be ready to serve as a fast communication channel to Himmler. Himmler and I left the Swedish Consulate after a cordial farewell, at about 01:30 hours.

April 24, 1945.

I once more accompanied Himmler to the office of General [Alfred] Wünnenberg where I sat with him for another half hour. This half hour served to lighten his anxiety over the steps which he had taken now and to imbue him with strength to feel that what he had done was in no way disloyal to the German people [Deutsche Volk]. At about 02:30 hours he then drove off to his official quarters [Kommandostelle]. I went back to the "Danziger Hof" [*sic*] where I still had meetings with some of my men in order to then punctually at 05:00 hours fetch the Count from the Swedish Consulate in order to drive with him to Flensburg.

It is perhaps of interest to note here that on the way to the Swedish Consulate Himmler drove his large car himself. As a guide I had taken one of my men with me, who was bathed in perspiration because of Himmler's appallingly bad driving—sidewalks, trucks coming towards us. He was normally not a good driver, but apparently his agitation was very great. When we left the Swedish Consulate he started too fast and with his left front wheel got off the paved drive and it took all of us together with the Count almost a quarter of an hour before we were able to drive on.

We left at 05:00 hours and arrived punctually at the German-Danish frontier. I took leave of the Count. He hoped soon to be able to send some in-between news to me by telephone through Count Lewenhaupt[629] or Attaché Chiron. I myself then went back to Flensburg with Attaché Chiron, where I stayed with Consul Petersen for the time being. There I lay down for a little rest at 10:00 hours in the morning and was awakened again at about 12:00 hours by an unpleasant raid of low flying aircraft with heavy strafing of the street and the nearby airfield. Only half-dressed, I went to the cellar only to meet there in this undignified get-up the lady of the house for the first time.

I then organized the necessary special telephone lines and went to Froeslev in the evening, where I lived. This place was convenient because on one hand I could be reached by telephone from Padborg-Apenrade, in other words for Count Lewenhaupt to send me a possible message from Count Bernadotte, and also through army lines from [to] Flensburg.

April 25, 1945.

On April 25 I had Standartenfuehrer [Otto] Bovensiepen[630] come to meet me in Flensburg in order to inform him of the authority and Special Powers which Himmler had given me in writing—in roughly the following words: "Acting on my express authority, has full powers to issue orders which are to be obeyed without objection"—that all Danish and Norwegian internees were to be transferred to Sweden without objection. I hinted to him that I would be in Copenhagen during the next days to discuss the political situation of Denmark with Dr. [Werner] Best,[631] and told him to already prepare this meeting by seeing to it that during the next few days no more death sentences would be pronounced or carried out. Bovensiepen was impressed by this conversation and promised to make contact with Dr. Best without delay. Of Dr. Best I had to assume that he was not a genuine follower of Hitler. This also came out in the course of my conversation with him in Copenhagen on April 30, when I was able to tell him that he had a bitter enemy in Kaltenbrunner, who had told me with pride that on receipt of a telegram from Best, Hitler had once said to him that it would be better if Best wrote his name with "ie", then he would be called "Biest" [*sic*, German for beast]—actually for Best a compliment.

---

629. Count Lewenhaupt was a Swedish diplomat (Counsellor at the Swedish Legation?) apparently at this point "attached" to Schellenberg in order to assist in the organizing of communications between Count Bernadotte and Himmler. Cf. "Final Report," 186-187.
630. SS-*Standartenführer* Otto Bovensiepen served as Chief of the SD in occupied Denmark. Wildt, *Generation des Unbedingten*, 332.
631. SS-*Obergruppenfuehrer* Werner Best, the Bevollmaechtigter des Reichs in Denmark (governor in occupied Denmark). For exact career data before and after 1945 see Keipert, Grupp, *Biographisches Handbuch des Deutschen Auswärtigen Dienstes 1871-1945*, vol. 1, 137-138.

April 26, 1945.

On April 26 I received an in-between message from Count Lewenhaupt indicating that the negotiations were not going well, mainly because Himmler was not acceptable as a person. This in-between message I did not pass on to Himmler.

In the late afternoon Oberstleutnant von Dewitz of my staff came to see me in the company of a radio expert and brought a wireless message received from the Chief of Front Reconnaissance [Frontaufklaerungschef], Colonel [Georg] Buntrock,[632] stating that a front reconnaissance unit [Frontaufklaerungkommando] had made contact with American reconnaissance men. Permission was requested to enter into an arrangement for us to cooperate. I discussed the matter in great detail with von Dewitz. We both agreed that the information was too vague and therefore needed to be checked. In my radio answer, however, I made it clear that the matter was certainly of greatest interest and that an exact report to me would be urgently desired. A reply did not reach me anymore. The radio message was exchanged between Hamburg and presumably Obing in Upper Bavaria.

April 27, 1945

In the night of April 26 to 27 I received a message to expect the Count on April 27 at the airport in Odense where he was to arrive from Copenhagen. On April 27 in the morning toward 11:00 hours I drove with Count Lewenhaupt to Odense. On account of bad weather the departure of the Count's plane from Copenhagen was delayed, and we spent the time with the air base commander [Fliegerhorstkommandant] Oberstleutnant von Maubeuge who treated us with exemplary hospitality and looked after us in every way. In view of the bad weather we were nevertheless anxious about the Count's plane and so all observation posts and antiaircraft zones [Flakzonen] were instructed to keep us constantly informed. We ourselves let off fire signals until the plane landed safely at about 16:00 hours. A delegation of magistrates had turned up from Odense.

I drove with the Count to Apenrade. Following a brief meal, we quietly discussed the negative result, above all the difficulty Himmler presented as a political figure vis-à-vis the Allies and the consequences arising out of this, and

---

632. Colonel Georg Buntrock became head of front reconnaissance in December 1944, having been transferred from army command to the SS in the course of the 1944 takeover of the *Abwehr* (military intelligence) by the *Sicherheitsdienst* (SD).

the advice which he, Count Bernadotte so to speak as private representative [Privatmann] of Norway and Denmark could give. Regarding the latter point, he expressed that he had good reason to believe the Swedish Government to be interested that the whole of the Northern Sector should be spared the complete destruction caused by continued fighting of the German army in Denmark as well as in Norway. The Count offered to drive with me to Himmler and discuss these things with him, as we had to accept the fact that my position with Himmler would not be easy, considering that not only the result was negative but that the press of the Allies had taken up these matters. I was therefore very happy that the Count wanted to drive with me to Lübeck for another discussion with Himmler. We arranged to meet on April 28 at 04:00 hours in the night to drive to Lübeck together.

I returned to Flensburg, tried to reach Himmler but was only able to speak to Dr. Brandt who very anxiously enquired about the result. I explained to him on the telephone that it was negative, but perhaps it was still possible to do something about the Northern Sector [Nordraum]. I said the Count wanted to come to Lübeck with me to discuss the entire matter with Himmler. This, however, was flatly refused. I was to report to Himmler alone, I was told.

April 28, 1945

As I did not wish to wake the Count—my telephone conversation had been at about 01:00 hours—I drove from Flensburg to Apenrade at 03:00 hours—where I asked the Count at 04:00 hours not to accompany me, as I had—and this Dr. Brandt had told me—to go further south than Lübeck to see Himmler. Mentioning the proximity of the front, I asked the Count not to come with me.

Shortly after 04:00 hours I then drove from Apenrade to Lübeck. As I knew that my position vis-à-vis Himmler would be very difficult, and that under certain circumstances I would have to reckon with my liquidation, I hit on the idea of sending for an astrologer from Hamburg, well known to Himmler, whom I took with me to Himmler, in order that an astrological advice might alleviate the gravity of his disappointment, for I knew that Himmler had a high regard for this particular gentleman.[633]

I waited till 20:00 hours in the evening at the "Danziger Hof" [sic] in Luebeck, until I was called again for a meeting to General Wünnenberg's office. I gave an account of my detailed discussion with the Count and the unofficial advice of the Swedish Government which he had transmitted with

---

633. This refers to the astrologer Wilhelm Wulff from Hamburg.

regard to the Northern Sector. The first part of my conversation with Himmler need not be mentioned here. The discussion was not easy for me and now that it is over I regard the result as quite unbelievably lucky for me as well as for the cause. I succeeded after some hours to point out the political significance of the Northern Sector, and to show the senselessness of a military battle to the end in Denmark and Norway and the great harm the meaningless destruction of these countries would do to what remained of Germany's reputation. After long deliberations about the form of the refusal of the Allies, his bitter disappointment, the publication in the world press, his fear that his letter to Foreign Minister [Christian] Guenther might also be put at the disposal of the world press, the consequences his step would have for him with Hitler, and the fact that my person was made responsible as the moving spirit in this, for him now seemingly so fatal step, made up a difficult base on which to carry through the plan I had in mind for saving the Northern Sector. All the same I had succeeded with the help of the above-mentioned gentleman to put forward the proposals for such a solution, in such a way, that he withdrew for an hour to think it over. Then at about 03:00 hours that night he gave me his permission to discuss with the Count first of all the suspension of the German military occupation of Norway and a consequent internment of the German troops in Sweden for the duration of the war. He declared himself prepared to accept a similar solution for Denmark, but wanted to reserve this for a later solution [*sic*]. But he already authorized me to prepare Reichsbevollmächtigter Dr. Best for such a plan. Finally he agreed to appoint me as Sonderbevollmächtigter [Special Deputy] for the execution of a peaceful solution of the North with the Swedish Government. At this point in time he still considered it self-understood that on the next day or a day later he would be in a position, as Hitler's successor, to decide these things at once.

Immediately afterwards I set off for Flensburg to speak with the Count within the frame of the authority given to me.

April 29, 1945

I arrived in Apenrade at about 11:00 or 12:00 hours on April 29 and lunched with the Count and Amtmann Thomsen—in the latter's quarters—in order to afterwards discuss with the Count the authorization I had received concerning the Northern Sector. The Count then prepared a meeting in his presence, between representatives of the Swedish Government and myself, for the next day, i.e. April 30.

We left Apenrade at about 17:00 hours—Amtmann Thomsen handed me a number of individual requests, suspension of sentences, release of Danish policemen, all of which I dealt with positively in Copenhagen on the next day. The Count drove himself. After an unproblematic trip we arrived in Copenhagen at about 23:30 hours where we took rooms at the Hotel d'Angleterre.

April 30, 1945

We met at 09:00 hours in the morning on April 30. I drove first to the Reichsbevollmächtigter [Governor] Dr. Best to inform him of my authorization, the decision to give up the military occupation of the Northern Sector without fighting and Himmler's succession to Hitler, etc. Dr. Best was, as I expected, voluntarily on my side. At 12:00 hours I met with Mr. [Erik] von Post of the Swedish government and Count Bernadotte.[634] Mr. Ostroem and Major von Horn, who belonged to the Swedish Commission, did not take part in the meeting. The conversation with Mr. von Post went positively, that is, the Swedish Government expected the German Government to make, through me, definite and clear proposals for the execution of the entire plan, in the first place for Norway and possibly also Denmark. After the meeting the Swedish Minister in Copenhagen, von Dardel gave a luncheon to which the Reichsbevollmächtigte [Dr. Werner Best] was also invited.

After the luncheon I immediately left for Korsoer in order to take the ferry to Nyborg, which had already been held up two hours for me. I arrived in Flensburg in the night, and after a short telephone conversation with Himmler, I drove on to Lübeck, where I arrived at 04:00 hours in the morning, i.e. on May 1, and where one of Himmler's adjutants met me to escort me to Himmler's new quarters—Kalkhorst near Travemünde.

May 1, 1945

In Flensburg I met a member of my Amt, Sturmbannfuehrer Dr. Wirsing, who had flown in a night fighter from Munich to Flensburg, to inform me as a representative of my closest associates that Kaltenbrunner had relieved me of all my official functions [Aemter] and had replaced me in the political section with Obersturmbannfuehrer [Wilhelm] Waneck, and in the military section with Obersturmbannfuehrer [Otto] Skorzeny. I took Dr. Wirsing with me immediately to introduce him to Himmler, so that he could return to the

---

634. Erik von Post was Chief of the Political Department of the Swedish Foreign Office. Regarding his contacts with Sir Victor Mallet cf. Koblik, "'No Truck with Himmler'," 181.

Southern Sector [Suedraum] armed with the respective orders from Himmler.[635]

From Lübeck to Kalkhorst we ran into the most difficult road conditions, as retreating troops from the entire Mecklenburg area, above all from Schwerin, were blocking the way, and it took us 3½ hours to do 40 km. During this time we were only once attacked by low flying enemy aircraft, otherwise it would have been nearly impossible to reach my destination. Long stretches of this journey I walked on foot as I could move ahead faster than our car.

I arrived in Kalkhorst at 08:00 hours in the morning. Himmler had only gone to bed at about 03:00 hours. I went to see Dr. Brandt who immediately informed me that Himmler had not become Hitler's successor but Grand Admiral [Grossadmiral] [Karl] Dönitz, that yesterday and until late at night the first meeting between Dönitz and Himmler had taken place at Plön, that Himmler on the strength of my earlier proposal had managed to get Dönitz, as his first order, to depose Ribbentrop and put in Count Schwerin von Krosigk as Foreign Minister. Himmler, I was told, was in the worst mood, for in the purely military surrounding of the Grand Admiral Himmler's political step in the direction of the Western Powers had not been understood. Himmler, Brandt said, was toying with the idea of having to resign. He was thinking of suicide. He wanted to speak once more with me about all these matters.

After half an hour of attempted rest Himmler asked me for breakfast at 09:00 hours to report about my meeting with Mr. von Post, Best and the Count [Bernadotte]. Himmler was very nervous and absentminded and told me that he was no longer up to dealing with these matters. He had only done one more thing, he said, and that was to suggest the Reich Minister Count Schwerin von Krosigk to Grossadmiral Dönitz as Foreign Minister, which after dismissing Ribbentrop Dönitz had done. Himmler wanted to take me along right away to Dönitz so that, so to speak as von Krosigk's first foreign policy assistant [Mitarbeiter], I should be actively engaged in all foreign policy questions. It would also be good if I expounded my ideas on the question of Norway and Denmark to the Government immediately. Himmler thought that it would be correct if I would remain permanently with von Krosigk and Dönitz in order to send someone else to Sweden, should I be successful in persuading the Reich Government to abandon the Northern Sector without fight.

After a longer discussion about the overall situation we left Kalkhorst at about 11:00 hours for Plön by way of Lübeck to meet Dönitz. After a difficult drive through refugee and military columns and attacks by low flying enemy

---

635. SS-*Sturmbannführer* Giselher Wirsing was a member of Schellenberg's *Amt* VI and would appear to have been a trusted colleague. "Final Report," 190-191. Wirsing became a well-known journalist in postwar Germany.

aircraft, we reached Plön at about 14:00 hours, where I contacted von Krosigk immediately. I also greeted Dönitz, Keitel and Jodl, but they were all taken up with the immediate military problems of the day. One could feel a great excitement among the entire staff.

In the afternoon alone with Himmler I succeeded again to convince him of the importance of the political solution that is of a solution without fighting for the Northern Sector. We agreed that von Krosigk was of the same opinion, whereas Dönitz, Keitel and Jodl in those days under no circumstances were prepared to surrender for instance Norway without fighting. On the other hand I had promised Mr. von Post to return to Copenhagen with a decision. A lengthy delay in Plön would have meant so much loss of time that the, so to speak, quietly granted option of the Swedish offer would have been forfeited. I was able to persuade Himmler to engage himself, together with von Krosigk, for the solution for the Northern Sector along the lines I had presented, and first of all to send me again to Copenhagen to explain the changed general situation to Mr. von Post and, despite this, to declare our readiness in principle to accept the discussed solution. Generaloberst [Franz] Böhme, Reichskommissar [Josef] Terboven, Generaloberst [Fritz] Lindemann and Reichsbevollmaechtigter Dr. Best in the meantime had been ordered to meet the Grand Admiral on May 2 in view of my proposal for the Northern Sector which Himmler had put before him. Himmler and I agreed that in any case I would not receive any definite decision from the Grossadmiral before this conference had taken place, and I therefore wanted to use this day, May 2, to explain the new situation to Mr. von Post in Copenhagen.

I left Plön at 15:00 hours and arrived in Flensburg at 19:00 hours, where I stayed three hours with Dr. Wirsing and worked out a draft I wanted to present to von Krosigk as my, so to speak, first task as his Mitarbeiter [assistant]. The primary intention was to show that any pretence at foreign policy was dependent on the internal political measures adopted by the new government. I suggested for this reason to von Krosigk, that Dönitz should first dissolve the Party, secondly the Secret State Police and the SD, and to announce this over the radio. Dr. Wirsing worked this out during the night and left it for me, because I wanted to rest for at least three or four hours before my drive to Copenhagen, as I was quite unable to fight against the need for sleep.

Dr. Wirsing wanted to fly back to the Southern Sector during the next night and, as Himmler did not consider Kaltenbrunner's dismissal order very important, perhaps under the pressure of the overall situation, to formally tell my closest colleagues to bow to higher authority, but inwardly to remain true and loyal to me in their work. I then drove during the night to Froeslev from where I telephoned Dr. Best, who wanted to meet me at the ferry on his way to the Grand Admiral at 07:00 hours on May 2, for me to tell him about the latest situation.

May 2, 1945

I left Froeslev at 04:30 hours for Nyborg. I may emphasize at this point that in Denmark, from Padborg on, I always had the personal Red Cross car of Count Bernadotte at my disposal, which was an enormous advantage and a very good camouflage for me at all army control posts, etc. I felt uneasy only when at times I was too much feted as a Swede and, without being able to speak word, even had to give autographs to school children and grown-ups.

The meeting date with Dr. Best could not be kept as we both had erred about the departure time of the ferry, that is I did not use the ferry coming from Korsoer on which Dr. Best was supposed to be, but took one which left Nyborg at the same time, so that we passed each other at sea. I arrived in Copenhagen at about 13:00 hours, telephoned with Minister von Dardel, and about 16:00 hours I could begin the meeting with Mr. von Post who brought Mr. Ostroem along. I once again described the overall situation, the change of Government and mentioned that at first the Grand Admiral had ordered the military and civil officials of Denmark and Norway to meet him, but that I had good reason to believe that the execution of my plan with the support of the Foreign Minister, Count Schwerin von Krosigk, and Himmler was still possible. Mr. von Post was still interested in the whole problem and stressed that Sweden, of course, had the greatest interest in a pacification of the Northern Sector without fighting, but he did not think that he could any longer make binding promises as the overall situation owing to both the change of Government and the passage of time, had changed so much that one had to reckon with a total capitulation within the next few days. In that case partial solutions in Denmark and Norway would no longer be of interest for Sweden. Nonetheless he suggested to further pursue the old plan and as soon as time and circumstances allowed, to present him a binding offer. We were agreed that everything was a question of time, that I should return as quickly as possible, or, if at all possible, should give an in-between report by telephone. We arranged the following code words [Stichworte] for the telephone conversation: "I should be glad to see the gentlemen again soon," meaning: binding offer of the Reich Government for Norway—the above sentence with the addition: "and to report to you," [meaning:] extension of the offer to Denmark. Mr. von Post and Mr. Ostroem emphasized that they could no longer remain in Copenhagen as also for reasons of secrecy this no longer seemed feasible. I must stress at this point that the entire conversation in Copenhagen was conducted in the strictest confidentiality.

May 3, 1945

During the night I experienced the first dive-bomber attack on Danish territory and only arrived at Padborg at about 04:00 hours in the morning. After a stay of two hours I drove on to Flensburg, picked up Dr. Wirsing's draft and in my car drove on to Plön to report to the Reich Government on the entire situation. The journey to Plön turned out to be one of the most difficult and dangerous I had experienced so far. On the comparatively short stretch of about 90 km, I experienced over a dozen dive-bomber attacks on totally jammed roads with retreating army columns stuck in part due to destruction and in part to lack of fuel. Through burnt-out truck columns, over streets strewn with corpses, past exploding tanks and ammunition trucks, we fought our way through with difficulty to Plön, having ourselves lain prone on the sides of roads, fields and meadows under heavy machine gun fire from low flying aircraft. In Plön we were told by the staff command [Stabswache] that the government had moved its seat to the Naval Academy at Mürwick [Marineschule Mürwick]. As the overall situation did not permit even an hour's delay, I had to take the same route back and fight the same difficulties. I may be permitted to state here, without exaggeration, that looking back on this particular trip, it seems like a miracle that I arrived with my car on the same day at Mürwick at about 17:00 hours to report to the Reich Foreign Minister and Himmler already at about 17:10 hours. The border police post at Kupfermühle near Flensburg had been informed of the relocation of the government, but I was not told of it at the border crossing and three search commandoes had been sent out to look for me on the road to Plön. One feared the worst.

In my report I once again pointed out the fundamental political importance of the entire Northern Sector, and I achieved in a comparatively short time that, in spite of the further deterioration of the overall situation, we came to the agreement that under all circumstances the military occupation of Denmark and Norway would have to be given up without combat, if at all possible, with the mediation [Einschaltung] of Sweden.

I then had a long discussion with von Krosigk alone. He was very glad to have someone with him to talk to and he told me that he would be glad if I could stay with him in order to make me his first assistant. On the other hand, he also considered it important that I should go to Sweden without delay to clear up the question of the Northern Sector, as discussed, with the Swedish

Government. We both agreed that this action was only a thing of the moment and could not delay the imminent total capitulation.

The declaration of a total capitulation at this point in time was still not feasible because of the problem of the Bohemian-Moravian area, where the army groups of Generalfeldmarschall Schoerner[636] and of Generaloberst [Lothar] Rendulic[637]—almost a million men, equipped with ammunition and provisions for another seven weeks—were still intact and defending the Eastern front [Ostfront]on the whole more than adequately.

Apart from my mission for the Northern Sector, which was primarily concerned with Norway, but also was meant to point out well founded expectations for Denmark, I had to try under all circumstances to arrange a meeting with General Eisenhower for myself or a suitable member of the Reich Government, be it via the Swedish Government or be it via the Swedish Red Cross. Von Krosigk and the so-called Reich Government were of the opinion anyway that I was permitted to do all I could to alleviate the upcoming emergencies in the present as well as in the coming difficult situation of the Reich through open talks with the Swedish Government, always keeping in mind the aim of opening a little the tightly closed doors of General Eisenhower. Then I discussed with von Krosigk and Staatsminister [Karl Hermann] Frank[638] from Prag the Czech problem. I myself could not hear Dönitz's decision on this anymore, so that I do not know how the matter was actually handled.

With regard to Denmark, von Krosigk thought that considering the ongoing military negotiations regarding the northwest German area between Admiral [Hans Georg von] Friedeburg[639] and Montgomery it would be wiser to include the Danish area immediately in this question. He asked me to include this problem in my discussion with Grand Admiral Dönitz, as the military

---

636. Probably General Field Marshal (since March 1945) Ferdinand Schörner. Cf. Trevor-Roper, *The Last Days of Hitler*, p. 121: "Kesselring and Schoerner were generally regarded as 'Hitler's field-marshals'." He left his troops at the end of the war and went to Austria, but the Americans turned him over to the Russians. Following extended imprisonment, he returned to Munich in 1955, only to be accused of crimes committed in the final months of the war.
637. *Generaloberst* (General) Lothar Rendulic was a well-educated Austrian officer who became part of the *Wehrmacht* (German Armed Forces) after the *Anschluss* of Austria.
638. SS-*Obergruppenfuehrer* Karl Hermann Frank following the assassination of Reinhard Heydrich in 1942 gave the order for the destruction of Lidice. As State Secretary and since 1943 as Reich Minister for the Protectorate (Bohemia and Moravia), he was responsible for war crimes. He was sentenced by a Czech court and publicly hanged on May 22, 1946. Gerhard Taddey, *Lexikon der deutschen Geschichte* (Stuttgart: Kroener, 1977), 356. Boatner, *The Biographical Dictionary of World War II*, 165.
639. *Generaladmiral* Hans Georg von Friedeburg was connected with the German submarine fleet during most of his professional life. During the final days of Nazi Germany, May 1-9, 1945, he served as *Oberbefehlshaber* (supreme commander) of the navy. Following the arrest of the last Nazi government on May 23, 1945, he committed suicide.

showed absolutely no understanding of the political problems of the Northern Sector within the general German situation.

At about 20:00 hours I began my report to Grand Admiral Dönitz, who at first would not hear of giving up the military occupation of Norway and interning the German troops in Sweden for the duration of the war. Apparently the military advisors not only of the navy but also of the army had pointed out the good strategic position especially of the army of Generaloberst Böhme. After I had succeeded in proving the political significance of a surrender without combat, that in fact bringing Sweden into the picture would be a political gain, I had to attend to the objection of the Grand Admiral just what sort of immediate gain this solution would mean for Germany. Reporting at length I had to explain to him that in the present situation of Germany I could naturally not prove any immediate gain, but that the gain, apart from the saving of the biological substance of the German people, would be in the long term political effects and the hardly still existent reputation of the Reich, particularly as Sweden was the only neutral country which even in the near future in the political play of the powers would not be without importance even for broken down Germany. Finally I said that after what I had witnessed of the collapse in the Reich, the continuation of the war in Denmark and Norway had no moral or ethical basis, since such a struggle had no political or other aims left.

The meeting was then interrupted. Count Schwerin von Krosigk, Generalfeldmarschall Keitel, Generaloberst Jodl and I went off for supper together at which these questions were, of course, further discussed. Keitel and Jodl both wanted that I did not go to Stockholm but that, as the best experienced in foreign affairs at the moment, I should always remain near von Krosigk and thereby near them. I again pointed out, however, the importance of the Northern problems and thought that I succeeded in getting Jodl to understand this.

I then discussed once more with von Krosigk the draft of Dr. Wirsing and advised him to carry out with the Grand Admiral as soon as possible the suggestion proposed there of dissolving the Party, the [secret] state police [Geheime Staatspolizei] and the SD. Further the question was discussed in what capacity I should best be sent to Stockholm. Von Krosigk left it up to me to advise him as to whether he should appoint me ambassador, special plenipotentiary, representative or whatever I wished to be called. I asked him to appoint me as Minister [Gesandter], a word which, in a true sense, would best reflect the tasks ahead of me. That night State Secretaries [Gustav Adolf

Baron] von [sic] Steengracht [von Moyland] and Henke[640] were called to the Foreign Minister to prepare the plenary powers and my appointment as Minister. Then we both again reported to the Grand Admiral. He again delayed a final decision until the next morning, saying he must sleep on it once more.

I then reported to Himmler once more who had a short but very meaningful conversation with me, the main point of which was in the words: "Had I only listened to you sooner" and "Perhaps you are the first German to be permitted to do something positive again for his poor fatherland."

May 4, 1945

The next morning at 10:00 hours I reported to von Krosigk. My appointment as Minister and the plenary powers to negotiate with the Swedish Government had been signed by Dönitz at 09:30 hours. I took leave of von Krosigk and left for Copenhagen at about 12:00 hours. On the stretch to Hadersleben in Denmark, I again ran into a heavy attack by low flying aircraft, suffered a delay of three hours in the Great Belt due to the low flying aircraft gathered there and arrived in Copenhagen at about 18:00 hours. I tried to inform Dr. Best about my mission and instructions as far as Denmark was concerned, and while I was still waiting for him in Dagmarhaus in order to go with him to the Swedish Minister von Dardel, a tremendous crowd gathered in the town hall square [Rathausplatz] in expectation of the imminent total capitulation of Germany. Shots were fired, emergency cars, ambulances, and the crowd grew to tens of thousands. Owing to this great upheaval in the entire city, Dr. Best was unable to make it in time, but I could not afford to lose any time either and under all circumstances had to reach the Swedish Legation, as the pre-arranged telephone communications had evidently not reached Stockholm via [the Minister] Mr. von Dardel although I had driven through the night specially from Mürwick to Padborg to ask Dr. Best to communicate the prearranged telephone message to Mr. von Dardel. After long negotiations with the SS-guard at the Dagmarhaus, I was taken away on the side of the house away from the square in Count Bernadotte's car through a clearing made in the wire fences. The driver had been ordered to bypass the crowded streets, but apparently he did not know his way too well, and in a short time we found ourselves in the middle of tens of thousands of people who recognized the car of Count Bernadotte and it was only a matter of minutes before the car, fully surrounded, was pushed and half carried by the enthusiastic crowd and in fact

---

640. Probably Andor Hencke (1895-1984), since 1943 *Unterstaatssekretaer* (Under Secretary of State) in the Foreign Office.

was stuck. I had enough presence of mind to close the doors from the inside and shut the windows, so that the people were unable to drag us out. I ordered the driver to step on it, and meter by meter we managed to push our way through the crowd. Those who were nearest shouted because of the pressure of the car and those a few meters away were pushing towards the car in wild excitement and gesticulating to each other. Finally the car was swamped by about 30 people on the running board, on the roof and on the hood, and it was only thanks to the driver's efficiency who again and again pushed ahead meter by meter that after one hour and a half we landed at the Swedish Legation, feeling as though we had come out of a Turkish bath. With much head nodding, saying 'Tak-Tak', waving our hats and all kinds of soothing friendly gestures, the driver and I succeeded again and again in detracting the wildest of the demonstrators.

I was immediately received by Mr. von Dardel, after I had met the lady of the house, and while we were still in the first minutes of our meeting the crowd had evidently come into the street of the Swedish Legation and there began to sing the Danish and Swedish national anthems. The tumultuous noise, the singing and shooting, was such that one could hardly hear one's own words. But in the quiet rooms of the Legation one felt in good safety. Mr. Berkholtz had immediately telephoned with Stockholm and preparations were made to enable me to fly the next morning at 07:00 hours to Malmoe on board a Danish ambulance plane in order to fly from there with another plane to Stockholm. After all questions of the moment had been attended to and Mr. Berkholtz had kindly undertaken to arrange the technical details for my further journey, I drove to the Hotel d'Angleterre to rest there for two hours.[641] The crowd had dispersed in the meantime and only now and then automatic gunfire could be heard. In front of the hotel I was held up by a wild military group of freedom fighters [Freiheitskaempfer] but on recognizing the Swedish car and reassuring words from the driver that I was a Swede, I was allowed to pass without trouble.

May 5, 1945

On the morning of May 5 at 07:00 hours after passing difficult controls by Danish freedom fighters [Freiheitskaempfer] as well as the last German airport control, I was able to leave Copenhagen in Count Bernadotte's Danish Red Cross plane [*sic*]. Already at 07:15 hours we landed safely in Malmoe, where I

---

641. This is an exact translation of the German text. In some English translations several sentences are missing.

was courteously received by the airport commander. Ten minutes later the commander informed me that a Swedish military plane was there to take me to Stockholm immediately. After a brief introduction to the pilot, I was strapped with oxygen apparatus and parachute and after two hours of flight with the Swedish bomber I landed safely in Bromma[642] at about 11:00 hours. Here I was picked up by Mr. Ostroem from the Foreign Office who escorted me to Count Bernadotte's home, where the meeting with Mr. von Post and state secretary [Staatssekretaer] [Erik] Boheman was begun immediately.

Presenting my credentials and the written authority I had been given for negotiations with the Swedish Government, I described to Mr. von Post and state secretary Boheman my special mission and the request of the Reich Government in this general situation. After a thorough discussion the two gentlemen decided to discuss the whole affair with the representatives of the Western Powers present in Stockholm as the course of events in Germany had advanced too far.

As an interim reply the Swedish Government received the statement that possibly a special commission, appointed by General Eisenhower, would be sent to Stockholm for a discussion of pending problems.

May 6, 1945

On Sunday, May 6, the Swedish state of affairs had not changed substantially. All those participating regarded the question of my plenipotentiary powers as important concerning the obligation of Generaloberst Böhme to obey agreements I might conclude with the Swedish Government. To lose no time, I decided to send Minister [Gesandter] [Hans] Thomsen, after I had explained my entire mission to him and General [Bruno von] Uthmann, the Military Attaché, to the Norwegian frontier, for preparatory discussions with Generaloberst [Franz] Böhme or [Hermann] Hölter about the question of ending the occupation in Norway and the internment of German troops in Sweden. Minister Thomsen flew in a Swedish bomber to .... [empty space in document] and met there at the border in the forenoon of May 6 the first General Staff officer of Generaloberst Böhme.

Around noon Thomsen telephoned an interim report to Stockholm and explained to me that only the First Officer of the General Staff had come, in himself an intelligent man, but whose attitude was different from what we had expected. Thomsen pointed out that he could not discuss the matter in detail over the telephone and said he intended to be back in Stockholm towards 17:00 or 18:00 hours, to talk to me personally.

---

642. Bromma Airport is the old Stockholm airport, located west of the city.

Minister [Arvid] Rieckert [Richert],[643] Mr. von Post, Count Bernadotte and I conferred on the further course of action. Minister Rieckert [Richert] recommended that under all circumstances we should get in touch with Grand Admiral Dönitz and inform him that Generaloberst Böhme apparently still had not been notified of my plenary powers. My suggestion of sending Dönitz a long telegraphic message was discarded after a general discussion. The procedure as suggested by Minister Rieckert [Richert] was: Through General [von] Uthmann's kind offices, a telephone conversation with the Grand Admiral via Oslo was actually made possible, but owing to technical difficulties it was hardly understandable. A second telephone contact was made available and I was able to talk to Reich Foreign Minister Count Schwerin von Krosigk myself. He told me that things had moved very rapidly over night and that Germany had declared total capitulation. Negotiations, however, were still under way. I should therefore take care to avoid bad feelings on the other—Anglo-American—side which now was included in the Norwegian question. He advised that the Swedish Government, if it had an interest in the matter, should contact the Western Allies directly.

The Swedish gentlemen then declared that at this stage of affairs they could no longer do anything, for evidently the Norwegian problem as well as the Danish problem had become part of the negotiations for the total capitulation. Therefore, one would have to wait and see if the Western Allies still had any intention to contact the Swedish Government, for instance concerning the question of the internment of the German forces stationed in Norway. All the same I did at the request of British Military Attaché, Suton Bratt, transmit through Mr. von Post and General [von] Uthmann to Generaloberst Böhme an announcement of the Western Allies about the possibility of Generaloberst Böhme contacting England directly on short-wave. The course of events then showed that the Western Powers, especially England, did not wish to include the Swedish Government in these questions, but that the negotiations for capitulation in Norway were concluded directly between the Reich Government and the Western Allies. With that the further plan of requesting the Swedish Government to officially intercede in behalf of a meeting for me or Schwerin von Krosigk with General Eisenhower fell through.

May 9, 1945

Another telephone conversation, my last one with Flensburg on May 9 [1945] revealed that the participation of the Swedish Red Cross in the process of possible internment of the German troops in Norway, was exclusively a

---

643. Arvid Richert, the Swedish Minister in Berlin.

question for the Swedish Red Cross and the British military authorities. In so far as I would be used in this connection the Reich Government would have no reservations [against my participation].

Walter Schellenberg
[handwritten]

Appendix II

Annexe
Written by
Hauptsturmfuehrer Göring
to Schellenberg's Report on His Transactions
with Count Bernadotte
and Events in the Last Weeks of the German Reich

Extract from my diary concerning the liberation of persons
from German Concentration Camps

On January 22, 1945, I received an order from General Schellenberg to free a number of Jews from various concentration camps in Germany and to hand them over to Altbundespräsident [Jean-Marie] Musy at the Swiss frontier at Constance. On this occasion General Schellenberg told me that he had been in contact with Mr. Musy since October 1944 and together with him he had already seen Himmler to obtain the permission for the release. Himmler at the time had already assured him of the release of some Jewish families. In spite of the permit by Himmler it had not been possible to locate the families and therefore he gave me the order to bring about under all circumstances the release of the respective persons on the basis of my personal contacts. First of all I got in touch with [SS-] Gruppenfuehrer [Heinrich] Müller, Chief of the Secret State Police [Gestapo] and asked him for permission to personally deal with the tracing of the Jewish families. Müller refused this request on the grounds that I was not a member of the Secret State Police and therefore could not be admitted into the inner workings of the administration. Finally he referred me to the respective officials and permitted me to contact these personally. Although the respective officials at an earlier point in time had failed to find the Jewish families concerned, I succeeded in tracing at least some of the persons via the Central Office for Protective Custody Matters

[Zentrale der Schutzhaftangelegenheiten] run by Dr. Berndorff,[644] thus among others the brothers Rottenberg; the Berger-Rottenberg family with the children; and some French people. Regarding the whereabouts of the remainder of these persons I was told I would hear within a few days, because some of the camps were in the process of evacuation as a result of being threatened by enemy forces. In spite of repeated enquiries and continuous search I was subsequently not able to learn anything about the whereabouts of these persons.

About the same time General Schellenberg explained to me that, in cooperation with [Jean-Marie] Musy, who in his turn was in contact with the Executive Committee of the Union of Rabbis of the United States of America, represented in Switzerland by Dr. Isaak Sternbuch [sic], he had drawn up a plan to release all Jews still in German concentration camps and transport them by rail to Switzerland. Dr. Sternbuch, Schellenberg said, had made an agreement with the Jewish organization in America that the Jews coming out of German concentration camps would be brought to America after a brief stay in Switzerland. This plan, he said, had been discussed with Mr. Musy and Himmler who already had given his consent. The object of this action was to bring about a more favorable reaction [Stimmung] in the international press in order to create for later times a better atmosphere for Germany. To ensure this operation on the one hand and to recognize the importance of the Jewish organization on the other hand, Himmler demanded that the organization of rabbis deposit the amount of five million Swiss Francs which should be held in trust by Mr. Musy until the operation was carried out. The intention was to later transfer this amount to the International Red Cross to create the prerequisites for possible relief measures for the suffering German civilian population.

The first transport [of the operation] now was supposed to take place as soon as possible. I therefore immediately contacted the Chief of the Secret State Police, [SS-] Gruppenfuehrer Müller, and the respective offices of the Security Police [Sicherheitspolizei], as well as the camp commander of Camp Theresienstadt, and I succeeded in spite of countless objections from these offices and last not least after overcoming difficult traffic conditions (daily bombardments) in getting the first special train rolling already on February 5, 1945, consisting of 17 express train cars with altogether 1,200 Jews from Theresienstadt. The train was scheduled to go to Konstanz and from there to

---

644. Dr. E. Berndorff headed Section IV A6 of *Amt* IV Gestapo. Subsection IV A6a handled *Schutzhaft* (protective custody), that is all arrest matters relating to people imprisoned by other Gestapo sections. Situation Report No. 4, Amt IV of the RSHA, NA, RG 319, IRR, IS, Box 8.

Kreuzlingen. It should be noted here that the availability of the special train for the transport as well as the inclusion of this train in the time table was achieved exclusively through my own negotiations as well as through the personal connections of General Schellenberg in the Reich Traffic Ministry. No support came from any Reich offices who with all possible means not only opposed the release but also the transportation of Jews.

To avoid a last minute failure of the transport due to the obstinacy of the camp authorities, I myself went to Theresienstadt. Here, in the course of the preparation of the transport, a situation appeared that seemed most curious to someone not acquainted with the internal conditions of a camp. When it was announced in the camp that a train with 1,200 [inmates] would leave for Switzerland and the inmates of the camp were called upon to volunteer for it, there was not the rush one might have expected but a hesitant trickle of only a few hundred people. As I could not understand this peculiar situation but on the other hand, was most intent to get 1,200 persons together, I enquired about the background of this more than questionable occurrence. In the end it turned out that they were all firmly convinced that this transport was one of the notorious death trips to Auschwitz. Even when the train was already on its way, there was still a large number of mainly older people who would not really believe in a trip to freedom. Only later, when the train was moving in the direction of Southern Germany, and I had succeeded by treating them humanly to gain the confidence of the passengers [der Teilnehmer], the mood became less tense, so that at the end the people, as though released from some frightful nightmare, were fully relaxed and showed cheerful faces.

This first transport, which had been very well organized, went so smoothly that even the Swiss authorities expressed their approval when taking over the 1,200 people in Kreuzlingen.[645] The participants of the transport were in the best of condition and with the exception of some persons weakened by age there were no casualties. The food I carried along on this transport was so plentiful that it would have been sufficient for all participants for two further days.

The second transport of about 1,800 Jews from the [Concentration] Camp Bergen-Belsen, prepared from lists made available by [Benoit Musy] the son of Altbundespräsident [Jean-Marie] Musy could not be carried through any more because [SS-] Obergruppenfuehrer [Ernst] Kaltenbrunner had given

---

645. Kreuzlingen is located on the Swiss side of the Swiss-German border at Constance. Jean-Claude Favez, *Das Internationale Rote Kreuz und das Dritte Reich* (Munich: C. Bertelsmann, 1989), 489, gives February 8 as the date of arrival of the transport. Cf. Leni Yahil, "Scandinavian Countries to the Rescue of Concentration Camp Prisoners," *Yad Vashem Studies on the European Jewish Catastrophe and Resistance*, vol. 6 (1967), 201.

instructions to Standartenfuehrer [Kurt] Becher[646] to do everything possible via his go-between in Switzerland, Saly Mayer, to arrange for a negative treatment [zu negieren] of the Musy operation in the foreign press. Therefore, immediately after the arrival of the transport press reports appeared in Switzerland which among other things said that with the release of the Jews a right of asylum in Switzerland was to be gained for 200 leading Nazis. These and similar reports were passed the quickest way by Saly Mayer via Becher to Kaltenbrunner who on the basis of his right to report personally presented them to Hitler, thereby in this way succeeding in stopping [inhibieren] the entire operation. Hitler abruptly ordered that the operation be stopped immediately and forbade the release of any Jew. Thus failed the operation that was founded on a decent and clean basis and free of any speculative intention, while on the other hand via Saly Mayer in connection with Becher small transports were still carried out whose background was nothing else but a dirty business. It has become known that Becher connected all kinds of compensation transactions with these transports. As one heard, he is said to have received 1,200 Swiss Francs per head for his transports of Jews. All these shady transactions were carried on with the permission of Kaltenbrunner.[647]

The efforts of General Schellenberg to get the Musy operation on the move again, failed because of the categorical refusal of Kaltenbrunner who simply referred to the fact that Hitler had forbidden the release of Jews.

Also refused was the request of Altbundespräsident Musy already at the end of 1944 and continually repeated after that date to release French and Polish women as well as women of other nationalities held at Ravensbrück. Altbundespräsident Musy particularly pointed out that especially the release of these women would create a very considerable impression which, in the course of time, could only have positive results for Germany. General Schellenberg who was of the same opinion as Altbundespräsident Musy left no stone unturned in the effort to bring about the release of these women. When this failed, he tried to bring about the release of at least a part of the women whose names were entered on a list. But here too, he came up against an absolute lack of understanding.

Later on, in spite of the strict prohibition of releases, General Schellenberg through clever manipulation was able to arrange for the release of still quite a number of Jews. Among others the families Donnebaum, Rosenberg, Stargarth and Cilzer, and also Dr. Stiassny and Helene Stein. It was no longer possible

---

646. Regarding Becher see Höhne, *The Order of the Death's Head*, 637-642. — Becher himself, interrogated by Norbert G. Barr on March 24, 1948, declared his final rank having been "Standartenfuehrer der Waffen-SS der Reserve." SAN, NG-5230.
647. For more detail on the Becher-Saly Mayer connection, see above.

for me to transfer these persons to Constance because of the development along the front in central Germany which had cut the connection between Berlin and Theresienstadt. Therefore the camp authorities at Theresienstadt were instructed by radio to get the persons in question on the move immediately to Constance on the Swiss border. In the course of searching for the families named, Mr. Musy, Jr., had an opportunity to thoroughly inspect the camp Theresienstadt together with me and to personally speak with individual detainees. It is interesting to note in this connection that prior to this inspection one of the officials from Theresienstadt, Hauptsturmfuehrer Moes, stated that the families we were looking for were all present. On the other hand, Sturmbannfuehrer Günther, the camp commander, answered to the repeated enquiries by Mr. Musy, Jr., that the Cilzer family had never been in the camp, that the Berger-Rottenberg family had been transferred to Auschwitz at the beginning of 1945, and that the men of the Donnebaum family had been handed over to a branch camp the name of which was not known. The contradiction between the official on the one hand and the camp commander on the other can be traced back to the fact that the families or rather persons who it was claimed were not present had come from Auschwitz in January 1945 and had witnessed events which were not to become public knowledge. Because Kaltenbrunner had given strictest order that such persons would not be allowed to be released, the camp commander simply used the excuse that the persons could not be found.

While the battle fronts in the East and the West increasingly closed in on German territory, the Germans began to evacuate concentration camps near the front lines and the inmates were marched on foot to the camps in the rear. This was an entirely senseless measure for, first of all, the traffic and rationing situation grew worse by the hour, with the result that the feeding of the human masses was no more guaranteed, and secondly because of the poor physical condition of the inmates hundreds of them perished daily.

A thorough discussion between Altbundespräsident Musy and General Schellenberg had the result that Himmler gave the order to hand the camps over intact to the Allied forces. Altbundespräsident Musy, who was in Berlin at the time, notified the American Legation in Switzerland which in turn informed Washington. Within a few days Washington replied that the Allies were in agreement with the proposal, that General Eisenhower had been informed [but that] for the moment no guarantee could be given [uebernommen] yet for the Russian side. Mr. Musy, Jr., who traveled from Constance to Buchenwald on April 9, 1945, in order to meet me at Weimar regarding the search for different inmates was instructed by his father to bring the reply of the Allies regarding the non-evacuation of the camps directly to

Berlin. Because of the nearness of the front and heavy attacks of low flying aircraft, the meeting with Mr. Musy, Jr., could not take place at the agreed time. In order not to lose any further time Mr. Musy drove alone to the Concentration Camp Buchenwald located in the proximity of Weimar. When he arrived at Buchenwald, he right away noticed a great nervousness and realized immediately that the evacuation had started. In spite of this he got in touch with the adjutant of the camp commander and asked for information regarding the inmates he was interested in. The adjutant explained he could give no information at that time, otherwise, he said, he was in the process of evacuating the camp on Himmler's order. According to the statement of Mr. Musy, Jr., the confusion was so total that it would have been useless to stay around longer. He was so shocked by the breaking of the agreement, which the Germans had made with the Allies, that since there was no other connection with Berlin, he went to Berlin immediately. At this point it should be noted that Mr. Musy was horrified by the treatment of the inmates who were put into marching columns in his presence. He described how the inmates were beaten with rods on their heads to form the marching column more quickly. It was a scene of horror to see how people who had death written over their face were driven onto the road.

After his arrival in Berlin Mr. Musy informed me of his experience in Buchenwald and thought a meeting with General Schellenberg urgently necessary. A few hours later Mr. Musy had occasion, in my presence, to inform General Schellenberg about the events in the Buchenwald concentration camp. General Schellenberg who at first could not grasp the things he was told, immediately asked for a connection with the personal assistant [Referent] of Himmler [Dr. Rudolf Brandt?] and informed him of what Mr. Musy had reported, adding the request to clarify the matter with Himmler and to give him a reply as soon as possible. As it turned out the next day, Himmler's order had been counteracted by Kaltenbrunner in disregard of the agreements with the Allies, insofar as he had gone to Hitler directly and persuaded him to evacuate by all means the camps threatened by the enemy in order to have at the end all inmates in the intact centrally located camps to serve as material for bartering with the Allies.

It must be emphasized here that at this time conditions in the parts of Germany not occupied yet had come to such a point where disorganization was more and more noticeable and orders and instructions could not be carried out any more partly on account of poorly functioning communications. Kaltenbrunner, of course, made use of this situation for the execution of his plans.

Convinced that he could do something even in the last minute for the inmates in the remaining concentration camps whose situation because of the overcrowding was becoming catastrophic, Mr. Musy, Jr., stayed in Berlin, especially since General Schellenberg also tried to transfer to Switzerland at least a part of the inmates drawn together in the camps in southern Germany. Unfortunately this was not possible any more for the quickly progressing Russian offensive already on April 16, 1945, had cut off the connection between Berlin and southern Germany with the result that it was not even possible any more for Mr. Musy to drive back to Switzerland in his car. Even the attempt to inform Dr. [Isaac] Sternbuch from Berlin was unsuccessful.

Appendix III

Annexe
Written by
Hauptsturmfuehrer Göring
to Schellenberg's Report on His Transactions
with Count Bernadotte
and Events in the Last Weeks of the German Reich

Extract from my diary concerning the liberation of persons
from German Concentration Camps
Part II

Count Bernadotte, Chief of the Swedish Red Cross, who since February 1945 together with General Schellenberg was fighting a battle for the release of the Scandinavian inmates in German concentration camps had, after overcoming endless difficulties, succeeded in being allowed to concentrate all Scandinavians in the Concentration Camp Neuengamme, located in Northwest Germany,[648] and to there care for them through the Red Cross. As he was not given any means of transportation from the German side, he had brought to Germany a convoy of vehicles, consisting of about 100 automobiles of the Swedish Red Cross, to carry out the transport of the inmates to Neuengamme. This operation was nearing completion by the middle of April, 1945. All Norwegians and Danes from the camps, except for a small number who in the meantime had come into Russian or Allied hands, were in Neuengamme. Only a group of about 450 Danish Jews were still in Theresienstadt against whose removal to Neuengamme Kaltenbrunner took a determined stand referring to Hitler's order. That it was possible to get these Jews out in the last minute in spite of the hopeless situation is the sole merit [in erster Linie] of General Schellenberg.

Medical Counsellor [Medizinalrat] [Felix] Kersten also exercised a decisive influence in the course of his personal conversations with Himmler and made it clear to him that the people still alive under all circumstances must be spared from destruction. Germany, he said, before history could not take the

---

648. The Concentration Camp Neuengamme was located just outside Hamburg.

responsibility. On this occasion Medical Counsellor Kersten also reminded Himmler again of the promise he had already given him, Kersten, earlier not to evacuate the camps, and demanded that this promise be kept.

When the last Swedish Red Cross column had left Theresienstadt on April 15, 1945, the Russian offensive had already advanced so far that on the following day a connection between North and South Germany did not exist any longer. Conditions in Germany grew more hopeless by the day and one could feel the approaching collapse. Berlin had been declared a fortress and the Russians had almost closed the ring around the city. On April 21, 1945, I heard from General Schellenberg, who kept me informed by telephone of his conversations with Himmler which he had had on one hand together with Count Bernadotte and on the other hand with Medical Counsellor Kersten and Mr. [Norbert] Masur, that from now on [nunmehr] I was explicitly authorized by him, General Schellenberg, to use the widest possible interpretation in the further removal [of inmates] from the concentration camps, even if there were other orders to the contrary. I also knew that in the course of the many meetings between Count Bernadotte and Himmler this question had often been raised by Count Bernadotte. Through Himmler it had been decided that all women from the Concentration Camp Ravensbrück could be evacuated provided they would be taken over by the Swedish Red Cross at the same time [bei gleichzeitiger Einschaltung]. This assurance Himmler had given Count Bernadotte at their last meeting. Because at this moment no means of transport were available for the transfer of the women, but a speeding up of the operation in view of the overall situation was imperative, I stopped the Swedish Red Cross convoy which was on the point of leaving Germany.

On April 22, 1945, I left Berlin by night at the last minute proceeding in a northerly direction in order to escape being taken prisoner by the Russians.[649] I stayed for several hours on an estate about 90 kilometers north of Berlin, when the news reached me from General Schellenberg that all women from the Concentration Camp Ravensbrück were to be set free. He gave me instructions to drive immediately to Ravensbrück in order to inform the camp commander of Himmler's decision and to prepare for the removal of the women. On April 22, 1945, at about 12:00 hours I arrived at the Ravensbrück camp. I immediately had a lengthy talk with the chief of the concentration camp, Sturmbannfuehrer [Fritz] Suhren.[650] Detailed enquiries showed that at present the camp contained about 9,000 Polish women, 1500 French, Belgian and Dutch women and women of other nationality, as well as some 3,000 Jewish

---

649. Felix Kersten took leave from Himmler on April 21 and departed from Tempelhof Airport in Berlin to Copenhagen on April 22, 1945.
650. On Fritz Suhren see above.

women. Several thousand inmates of German, Russian and Italian nationality, who were also imprisoned there, were not taken into consideration for this operation. Here too the negative attitude of the camp commander and his staff towards a release of the inmates once again became visible. Suhren always tried to evade precise questions and was vague in his answers. In all cases he excused himself by saying that he had already destroyed all documentary material, card indices and other papers, stating that this had been done on the orders of the Fuehrer. It was a characteristic situation when Mr. Musy, Jr., who was accompanying me, asked about the French women Madame Buteau and Madame del Marmoc. After about half an hour Suhren got the information from his adjutant that the persons named could not be found. When I then explained to Suhren that Himmler was particularly interested in these persons and had already ordered their release, he became very nervous and after another half hour told me that both had died in the camp a few weeks ago. I mention this example among many others to illustrate the situation in the camps at the time. Regarding the transportation of the women, I said to Suhren that the convoy of the Swedish Red Cross, which had already been on its way back to Sweden, had been stopped by me, so that, in order to speed up the release, it would be advisable to already march the women in question as far as Malchow.[651] I would then, I said, give instructions to the motor column to pick up the women in Malchow. Suhren promised me firmly that he would start the women off on the march towards Malchow still on the same day. I now drove by the fastest route to Lübeck to make contact there with the Swedish Red Cross. In the meantime, General Schellenberg had also spoken to Count Bernadotte about the possibility of the evacuation. Count Bernadotte had agreed and entrusted the execution of details to Captain [Rittmeister] Ancarcrona and Dr. Arnoldsson, both of whom I met at the Swedish Legation [Consulate?] in Lübeck.[652] The main difficulty now lay in the fact that the overall situation had changed in as much as the convoys of the Swedish Red Cross were engaged in transporting the Scandinavian inmates from Neuengamme to Denmark. In this context it should be noted that through the arrangement of General Schellenberg a new meeting between Count Bernadotte and Himmler had taken place with the happy result that the

---

651. Malchow was a kind of subsidiary concentration camp, located northwest of Ravensbrück. Cf. map in Sigrid Jacobeit, ed., "Ich grüsse Euch als freier Mensch" (Brandenburg/Ravensbrück/Sachsenhausen: Stiftung Brandenburgische Gedenkstätten, 1995), 44.
652. Hans Arnoldsson was a Swedish Red Cross physician who played an important role in the Swedish rescue operations. Ankarkrona during the rescue operations functioned as adjutant of Count Bernadotte. Schellenberg's secretary Christl Erdmann recalled later that they lived in a house of Ankarkrona when Schellenberg stayed with Count Bernadotte.

Scandinavian inmates from Neuengamme were to be taken to Sweden for internment.

Despite this state of affairs, the result of the discussion with Captain Ancarcrona was that on the following day a convoy of 17 buses of the Swedish, Danish and International Red Cross was made available for the transport of the women who according to the agreement with Suhren in the meantime should have arrived at Malchow. Together with Dr. Arnoldsson I drove ahead of the convoy the next morning, in order to get the loading of the inmates on the way in Malchow. When we arrived in Malchow, we learned from the camp commander that he knew nothing whatsoever about the arrival of the Ravensbrück inmates. He had spoken with the Ravensbrück commander, he said, only a few hours ago, and the latter had said nothing about a march. Thereupon we drove on to Ravensbrück and indeed found out that Suhren had not started the women on the march, as he had agreed to do. Upon my question why he had not kept the agreement, he stated that he had instructions from the Inspector of Concentration Camps, Gruppenfuehrer [Richard] Glücks,[653] that in accordance with the order from the Fuehrer the inmates were to remain in the camp. I thereupon telephoned Sonderzug Steiermark from the office of Suhren and in his presence, and had myself put through to Standartenfuehrer Dr. Brandt, Himmler's personal assistant. I described the situation to Dr. Brandt and asked for an immediate decision from Himmler. After a short time Dr. Brandt called back and gave Suhren the order to release the inmates for the evacuation, as agreed. After that Suhren told me between ourselves that he no longer knew where he stood, for he had received the express order of the Fuehrer, via Kaltenbrunner, to keep the inmates in the camp and to liquidate them at the approach of enemy troops. Suhren now became very uncertain and amongst other things confided to me that he had a group of women in the camp whom he was also to kill on express orders. They were 54 Polish women and 17 French women on whom experiments had been carried out. When I asked him what kinds of experiments he meant, he explained to me that the persons in question had been injected with bacilli, which had developed into a disease which then in turn had been healed through operations, partly muscle and partly bone operations. I thereupon had two women brought before me and saw the proof of this [überzeugte mich von diesem Vorgang]. I then pointed out to Suhren that under no circumstances was he to carry out Kaltenbrunner's order before

---

653. SS-*Gruppenfuehrer* Richard Glücks, Inspector of Concentration Camps since 1940. He is said to have disappeared at the end of the war (Snyder, *Encyclopedia of the Third Reich*, 117) or to have committed suicide. Institute of Jewish Affairs/World Jewish Congress, *Eichmann's Confederates and the Third Reich Hierarchy* (New York: Institute of Jewish Affairs, 1961), 29.

a decision of Himmler was at hand. From Lübeck I again called Dr. Brandt and reported this matter to him, with the request that he obtain a decision from Himmler as quickly as possible. I pointed out to him that under no circumstances could the women be liquidated, particularly as the women about to be released knew of the experiments. The experiments were partially known in the camp under the name "Rabbits" [Kaninchen]. After about two hours I received the answer through Dr. Brandt that Himmler had ordered the release of the so-called "guinea pigs" [Versuchskaninchen]. Dr. Arnoldsson, who was informed by me about the whole matter, personally supervised the evacuation of these women.

The vehicles at our disposal from the Swedish, Danish and International Red Cross were not sufficient for the removal of the mass of women from Ravensbrück before the advance of the Russian troops despite the fact that they drove day and night and did superhuman work in this. I therefore went with Dr. Arnoldsson, Major Frickmann [Sven Frykman?] and Captain Folke to the Reich Railway President [Reichsbahnpraesident] in Lübeck and asked him for a freight train for 4,000 persons. President Dr. Bauer first refused by pointing out the catastrophic traffic situation and expressed the view that troops and ammunition transports had priority. After long negotiations, however, I succeeded in getting the desired freight train. With the help of this freight train, which could be loaded with 4,000 persons from Ravensbrück at once, and the self-sacrificing efforts of the truck convoys, it was possible to evacuate the greater part of the women from Ravensbrück as well as 450 Jewish women from Malchow and about 1,500 Jewish, French, Belgian, Dutch and Polish women from Neubrandenburg.[654]

It should be noted here that the last transports of the Swedish, Danish and International Red Cross were already under Russian artillery fire when leaving Ravensbrück.[655]

When the last convoys had left German territory with the inmates in the direction of Denmark and the freight train with 4,000 persons had passed Lübeck in the direction of Copenhagen, I found out that in the area of Hamburg were still imprisoned 960 Jewish women, 250 French women and 790 Polish women who had been brought there from Neuengamme. On my own authority I made contact from Lübeck with the commander of the camp,

---

654. Neubrandenburg was a so-called work camp (*Arbeitslager*), located north of Berlin and somewhat east of Malchow.
655. For an inmate's perspective regarding the departure from Ravensbrück cf. Sigrid Jacobeit and Simone Erpel, eds., *"Ich grüsse Euch als freier Mensch"* (Oranienburg: Stiftung Brandenburgische Gedenkstätten, 1995), 61-62.

Obersturmbannfuehrer [Max] Pauli [sic][656] and gave him instructions to organize a freight train that very day, to load the inmates and with the cooperation of Reich Railway Direction (Reichsbahndirektion) in Lübeck get the train rolling in the direction of Copenhagen. From Lübeck I was unfortunately no longer able to notify the Swedish Red Cross about these measures and therefore I drove to the Danish border at Padborg, in order to there inform the Danish Red Cross (Baroness Wedel) of the arrival of the train.[657] I myself was at the station in Padborg when the train arrived, supervised by a Jewish woman who had been appointed leader of that transport. The 2,000 women who apparently had not received anything to eat for days were fed at the station in Padborg by the Danish Red Cross. The train later rolled on in the direction of Copenhagen. Thus ended an operation which saved thousands of human lives.

Franz Göring
[handwritten]

---

656. SS-*Obersturmbannführer* Max Pauli was camp commander (Lagerkommandant) of the Concentration Camp Neuengamme since 1942.
657. According to Therkel Straede, "Die 'Aktion Weisse Busse'" in Detlef Garbe and Carmen Lange, eds., *Häftlinge zwischen Vernichtung und Befreiung: Die Auflösung des KZ Neuengamme und seiner Aussenlager durch die SS im Frühjahr 1945* (Bremen: Edition Temme, 2005), 180, the quarantine receiving station at the border was directed by Baroness Fritse Wedel-Wedelsborg.

Abbreviations, Acronyms, Cover Names

AA	Auswärtiges Amt (German Foreign Office)
AAK	Alemannischer Arbeitskreis (Alemannic Study Group)
AB	Aktiebolaget (Inc.)
A.F.H.Q.	American Forces Headquarters
Alfonso	Reinhard Spitzy
AO	Auslandsorganisation (NSDAP abroad)
Artist	Johannes Jebsen
AST	Abwehrstelle (military intelligence office)
b.	born
BA Berlin	Bundesarchiv Berlin (Federal Archive)
BA Koblenz	Bundesarchiv Koblenz (Federal Archive)
Baron, der	Schellenberg
Bauer	Reinhard Spitzy
BDC	Berlin Document Center
Bergh, Dr.	Schellenberg
BND	Bundesnachrichtendienst (Federal Intelligence Service)
BSG	Bund der Schweizer in Grossdeutschland (Association of the Swiss in Greater Germany)
Mr. Bull	Allen Dulles
C	Sir Stewart Graham Menzies
CIA	Central Intelligence Agency
C.I.C.	Counter Intelligence Corps
CREST	CIA Records Search Tool (NA)
CSDIC	Combined Services Detailed Interrogation Center
Delius, Dr.	Colonel Otto Wagner
DNB	Deutsches Nachrichtenbüro
Doctor, the	Hans Wagner
Dressler	Hans-Christian Daufeldt
E	Entry (NA)
FBI	Federal Bureau of Investigation
FHO	Fremde Heere Ost (Foreign Armies East)
FHW	Fremde Heere West (Foreign Armies West)
F.I.A.T.	Field Intelligence Agency Technical
FO	Foreign Office (British)
FRUS	Foreign Relations of the United States
G-2	Military Intelligence, U.S. Army

G.B.	Grossbritannien (Great Britain)
GmbH	Gesellschaft mit beschränkter Haftung (limited company)
George Wood	Fritz Kolbe
Gerber	Reinhard Spitzy
Gestapo	Geheime Staatspolizei (Secret State Police)
HICOG	United States High Commissioner for Germany
HIJEFS	Hilfsverein für jüdische Flüchtlinge in Shanghai (Aid Society for Jewish Refugees in Shanghai)
HMSO	Her Majesty's Stationery Office
HQ	Headquarter(s)
HSSPF	Höherer SS- und Polizeiführer (Higher SS and Police Official)
HUB	Humboldt Universität zu Berlin, Universitätsarchiv
IFZ	Institut für Zeitgeschichte (Institute for Contemporary History)
IMT	International Military Tribunal
INSCOM	U.S. Army Intelligence and Security Command
IPA	Internationale Presse-Agentur (International Press Agency)
IRR	Records of the Investigative Records Repository (NA)
IS	Impersonal Series (NA)
IT&T	International Telephone & Telegraph Corporation
IWG	Interagency Working Group (NA)
K	Kuncewicz
Kowalki, Louis	Schellenberg
KSCV	Kösener Senioren-Convents-Verband (traditional student fraternity)
KZ	Konzentrationslager (concentration camp)
LC	Library of Congress
ME	Messerschmitt
MI5	British Counterespionage Service
MI6	British Foreign Intelligence Service
MISC	Military Intelligence Service Center
MP	Military Police
MS	manuscript
MVD	successor organization to NKVD (Soviet Russian secret state police)
NA	National Archives, Washington, D.C./College Park, MD
NAK	National Archives, Kew (formerly Public Record Office)
n.d.	no date
Neumann, Dr.	Hans Wagner
NKVD	People's Commissariat for Internal Affairs (Soviet Russian secret state police)
no.	number
NSDAP	Nationalsozialistische Deutsche Arbeiterpartei

	(Nazi party)
OKH	Oberkommando des Heeres (Supreme Command Army)
OKW	Oberkommando der *Wehrmacht* (Supreme Command Armed Forces)
Opo	Ordnungspolizei (Order Police)
OSAF	Oberster SA Führer (Highest SA Leader)
OSS	Office of Strategic Services
OVRA	Opera per la Vigilanza e la Repressione dell'Antifascismo (Italian Fascist secret state police. Abbreviation not undisputed.)
PA	Politisches Archiv (Political Archive of AA)
Pauls (Paul)	Prince Hohenlohe
POW	Prisoner of War
PRO	Public Record Office (now NAK)
PS	Personal Series (NA)
PG	Parteigenosse (party comrad or member of NSDAP)
RG	Record Group (NA)
Ritzburg, Dr.	Dr. Paul Meyer-Schwertenbach
Rodrigo	Breisky-Breisky, Hubert von
RSHA	Reichssicherheitshauptamt (SS security head office Berlin)
Rusty	Organization X, network of agents after end of World War II in Central Europe
S.A.	Societé Anonyme
SA	Sturmabteilung (storm troopers)
SAINT	X-2 counterespionage
Schenkendorf	Schellenberg
Schilling, von	August Finke
Schönemann	Edgar Klaus
SD	Sicherheitsdienst (security service)
Senner I	Roger Masson
Senner II	Paul Meyer-Schwertenbach
Senner III	Paul Holzach
SGAD	Schweizer Gesellschaft der Freunde einer autoritären Demokratie (Swiss Society of the Friends of an Authoritarian Democracy)
SHAEF (S.H.A.E.F.)	Supreme Headquarters(,) Allied Expeditionary Force(s)
Siegel	Abram Stevens Hewitt
SIS	Special (or) Secret Intelligence Service
SOE	Special Operations Executive
STAB	Svenska Taendsticks Aktiebolaget
Tramp	William G. Sebold
Transl.	Translation (by author)
U 35	Klop Ustinov
UK	United Kingdom

UNWCC	United Nations War Crimes Commission
USAMHI	United States Army Military History Institute
USFET	United States Forces European Theater
USGPO	United States Government Printing Office
USHMMA	United States Holocaust Memorial Museum Archives
USSR	Union of Soviet Socialist Republics
Utility	Reinhard Gehlen
VOWI	Volkswirtschaftliche Abteilung I. G. Farben (economics department of I. G. Farben)
vol.	Volume
WTB	Wolffs Telegraphisches Büro
WW II	World War II
Z	a British intelligence operation
Zipper	*Organisation Gehlen* (later BND)
59	Michael Kedia
110	Allen Dulles
520	Barnwell R. Legge
674	Fritz Kolbe
803	Fritz Kolbe

Glossary

German Intelligence Services

Abwehr

The *Abteilung Abwehr* (Department of Military Counterintelligence) had its origins in the *Abteilung* III b of the German General Staff in World War I. Though officially dissolved with the General Staff in 1918, *Abteilung* III b in fact continued its clandestine existence under Colonel Walter Nicolai until 1921 when it was succeeded by the *Abwehr* commanded by Major Friedrich Gempp. In 1928 this military intelligence service was united with the *Nachrichtenabteilung des Admiralstabs* (Intelligence Department of the Admiralty/Naval Intelligence), and in 1932 an officer of the Navy, Captain Conrad Patzig, became Chief of the *Abwehr*. Patzig was replaced by another navy man of considerable reputation in naval and German nationalist circles, Captain or shortly thereafter Admiral Wilhelm Canaris. He looked back on years of experience and by many was considered as someone able to handle difficult situations. Historians have been inclined to emphasize a spirit of dangerous competition between *Abwehr* and *Sicherheitsdienst* (SD, Security Service), especially the later *Amt* VI of the SD, Walter Schellenberg's Foreign Intelligence Service. A sober appraisal would instead indicate that both *Abwehr* and *Amt* VI were Nazi intelligence services and that most leading men in both services were convinced Nazis, certainly until the turn of events rung in by the defeat of Rommel's Africa Corps and the enormous losses suffered in connection with the German decision to hold out at Stalingrad. In addition, the records show that *Abwehr* and *Amt* VI not only competed for success but also cooperated in many operations. Moreover, while structurally tied into the OKW (*Oberkommando der Wehrmacht*, Supreme Command of the Armed Forces) and the RSHA (*Reichssicherheitshauptamt*, Reich Security Head Office), both German intelligence services were allowed a high degree of independence. In the final analysis the *Abwehr* was not a very efficient organization and failed to perform at critical points during World War II. Major campaigns of the enemy all too often came as surprises, and attempts to penetrate Britain and the United States were unsuccessful. The combination of generally unsatisfactory performance, a number of specific failures, and suspected connections of some *Abwehr* men to an anti-Nazi underground led to Hitler's dismissal of Admiral Canaris and placement of the *Abwehr* under the command of *Amt* VI where it continued to function as *Militärisches Amt* (*Mil. Amt* or *Amt Mil., Military Office*). Canaris was ousted from office in 1944, arrested following the unsuccessful assassination attempt of that year, and finally executed shortly before the defeat of Germany.

Amt VI (Foreign Intelligence)

Amt VI was one of originally six *Aemter* (departments) of the *Reichssicherheitshauptamt* (RSHA, Reich Security Head Office), the latter headed first by Reinhard Heydrich and after his death by Ernst Kaltenbrunner. The correct name of the Foreign Intelligence Department was *Amt* VI *Nachrichtendienst Ausland*, but it was often simply referred to as SD-Ausland (*Sicherheitsdienst*, Security Service Foreign). First Chief of *Amt* VI was Heinz Jost who was succeeded by Walter Schellenberg in 1942. In many ways *Amt* VI Foreign Intelligence became the main competitor of the older Military Intelligence, headed by Admiral Canaris and called *Abwehr*. Their interests were often quite similar, and the records indicate that the two intelligence services cooperated in a number of areas and operations. *Amt* VI Foreign Intelligence occasionally has been confused with *Amt* IV Gestapo (Secret State Police). The large head office of *Amt* VI was located on Berkaer Strasse in Berlin.

Amt Wehrmachtsnachrichtenverbindungen
(Office of Communications of the Armed Forces)

This intelligence service of the OKW (*Oberkommando der Wehrmacht*, Supreme Command of the Armed Forces) played a significant role in German attempts to intercept communications. The Signal Intelligence Section was headed by General Fritz Erich Fellgiebel who not only worked together with the *Abwehr* of Wilhelm Canaris, but since 1942 also had come to an understanding of cooperation with Walter Schellenberg, Chief of *Amt* VI Foreign Intelligence. Fellgiebel was involved in the preparations for the unsuccessful attempt in July 1944 to remove Adolf Hitler. In August 1944 he was therefore sentenced to death by the *Volksgericht* (People's Court). His successor was the former Deputy Chief of Signal Intelligence in the OKW General Fritz Walter Thiele who also knew Walter Schellenberg well and cooperated with him. As Thiele was involved in the attempted coup, he too was sentenced to death shortly thereafter.

Die Brandenburger (The Brandenburgers)

The *Brandenburger* was the common designation for the German special forces units organized in late 1939 and trained at Quenzgut, a military base and training camp near the town of Brandenburg just west of Berlin. These special forces units had their origin in a number of earlier nationalist paramilitary groups, and their first commander was Major Theodor von Hippel, who had served with the German forces in Africa in World War I. As a military unit, the *Brandenburger* was an arm of Department II of the *Abwehr* of Wilhelm Canaris. The cover name of the first *Brandenburger* unit was *Baulehrkompanie z.b.V. 800* (Construction Training Company, *z.b.V.* meaning zur besonderen Verwendung or for special assignments).

As Special Forces the *Brandenburger* were used in difficult military undertakings involving undercover campaigns, raids behind enemy lines, fighting in foreign uniforms, and other unusual operations not associated with traditional combat. As would be expected, a great number of foreign-born Germans, Germans living abroad, men from Eastern Europe, the Middle East and India and, of course, men looking for military adventure served in these special forces. In the course of World War II some of the *Brandenburger* detachments became attached to other units of the German Armed Forces. Following the failed assassination attempt of July 1944, the *Brandenburger* was dissolved altogether. In most cases the men joined the SS-*Jagdverbände* (Fighter Units) under the command of Otto Skorzeny or the *Panzerkorps Grossdeutschland* (Tank Forces Greater Germany). The *Jagdverbände*, like the *Brandenburger*, were special forces units deployed in difficult operations.

Bundesnachrichtendienst (BND, Federal Intelligence Service)

Officially founded in 1956, this intelligence service, first of West Germany and later of the reunited Federal Republic of Germany, had its beginning as a creation of the American Armed Forces in occupied Germany. Cover names of forerunner groups of agents included Bolero, Keystone, Rusty and Zipper. First Chief of the BND was Reinhard Gehlen, former Chief of *Abteilung Fremde Heere Ost* (FHO, Department Foreign Armies East). During the early phase of the Cold War Americans were interested above all in acquiring the expertise Nazi intelligence officers were thought to have in the affairs of the Soviet Union. In Germany this postwar intelligence organization was first called *Organisation Gehlen*, and Gehlen himself worked under American protection and, to a degree, difficult supervision. Former officers of the German Army and the SS, if not to say a number of war criminals and agents of the Soviet Union joined Gehlen's intelligence service during the early years, and their presence and the respective scandals have contributed to a critical appraisal in many quarters of the reliability of the BND. The Federal Republic of Germany up to the present has not passed legislation easing the access of researchers to the records of the BND, and publications regarding the history and earlier operations of the organization have had to rely heavily on documents declassified in the U.S. and in Britain. For this reason much of the literature about the BND remains incomplete and, not surprisingly, somewhat unreliable.

Since the postwar period headquarters of the *Bundesnachrichtendienst* have been located in Pullach, not far from Munich in Bavaria, the former American Zone of Occupation. There is an ongoing discussion about moving facilities from Pullach to Berlin, the new and old capital of Germany. While officially a foreign intelligence service, operating outside of Germany, there have been occasional complaints concerning presumably improper, politically motivated covert activities inside the country.

Forschungsamt (FA, Research Office)

The so-called Research Office was an intelligence service of a very special kind. Organized in 1933 when the Nazis came to power, the *Forschungsamt* was a part of Hermann Göring's personal sphere of influence as Prussian Minister President. Later when Göring expanded his power in the Third Reich, the *Forschungsamt* was moved to the *Reichsluftfahrtministerium* (Reich Air Ministry) where it continued to be very much his private service largely free of outside influences from other police or intelligence services. What began as a relatively small group of technicians tapping telephones, during World War II grew into a sizable and significant signal intelligence organization of several thousand employees. They tapped telephones of anyone anywhere, intercepted wireless traffic and tried to break codes. Diplomats and the military, foreigners and Germans, all were listened to, and it is thought that informed Germans feared Göring's Research Office more than the Gestapo (Secret State Police).

The records suggest that the *Forschungsamt* was able to do most of its work quite independent from other intelligence organizations, notably the *Abwehr* and *Amt* VI. Both the Gestapo and *Amt* VI would rather have taken over the *Forschungsamt* than have information developed there independently. In fact, the *Forschungsamt* or its protector Hermann Göring was so strong that it was possible to stay independent even after Hitler decreed the merger of SD (*Sicherheitsdienst*, SS-Security Service) and *Abwehr* in 1944. Ministries and other intelligence services, such as *Amt* VI Foreign Intelligence, were pleased to receive *Forschungsamt* information.

Headquarters of the *Forschungsamt* were at Schillerstrasse in Berlin for most of the war. Bombing raids finally forced a move to Breslau in Silesia, and when Soviet troops closed in, the offices were moved to Kaufbeuren, later to be occupied by U.S. Forces. In Germany most of the employees were civilians officially working for the Reich Air Ministry. Outside Germany, for instance in the offices in occupied France, military personnel filled most of the positions.

Forschungsanstalt (Research Institution)

The *Forschungsanstalt* was part of the *Deutsche Reichspost* (German Reich Postal Service). The *Reichspost* was responsible for the telephone system in Germany and therefore had access to all telephone lines. In fact, this postal intelligence service had the technical apparatus to tap telephones in Germany and other European countries. For obvious reasons telephone conversations between government officials in London and Washington were of special interest. Results of the interception work were passed on to intelligence services such as *Amt* VI Foreign Intelligence. Because of the importance of the interceptions, the Reich Postal Minister Wilhelm Ohnesorge found himself competing with Walter Schellenberg of *Amt* VI for up-to-date technical equipment and the respective information.

Fremde Heer Ost (FHO, Foreign Armies East)
Fremde Heere West (FHW, Foreign Armies West)

Both of these military intelligence services were successor organizations of *Abteilung* III b (Department III b) of the German General Staff. *Abteilung* III b was a "Section" of the General Staff since 1889 and became a "Department" only in the course of World War I. Its functions during World War I included military intelligence, counterespionage and sabotage. In time, *Abteilung* III b also became heavily involved in propaganda and press work in Germany and abroad. Though clearly a military service, it also had close connections with other arms of the Imperial German Government, one of the more significant links being to the German Foreign Office. Very early there developed a competitive situation involving the *Abteilung* III b and what was commonly referred to as the *Marinenachrichtendienst*, the Naval Intelligence Service, a "Department" of the *Admiralstab*, the Admiralty of the *Kasierliche Marine* (Imperial Navy). Germany's defeat in World War I (1918) and the Treaty of Versailles (1919) officially abolished the General Staff and the Admiralty. German military leaders, however, organized the so-called *Truppenamt* (troop office) which in fact served as the General Staff. Department "T 3" of this *Truppenamt*, also referred to as *Heeresstatistische Abteilung* (Army Statistical Department), was the continuation of the older or the beginning of a new military intelligence service. It was not until 1935 that T 3 was named *Abteilung Fremde Heere* (Department Foreign Armies). The final partition of this large intelligence department of the General Staff into two departments, namely *Fremde Heere Ost* and *Fremde Heere West* came in 1938. Major Ulrich Liss of the General Staff became Chief of *Fremde Heere West* and Major Eberhard Kinzel also of the General Staff took over *Fremde Heere Ost*. The offices of both intelligence organizations were at Tirpitzufer 66 in Berlin. Possibly due to the brief time span between this regional reorganization of the German Army's intelligence and the onset of World War II, *Fremde Heere West* did not reach the much more exposed but also more prestigious position of *Fremde Heere Ost*. With the quick defeat of France and the seemingly indefinite postponement of Operation Sea Lion, the planned invasion of Great Britain, the war against the Soviet Union clearly became the primary concern of German political and military leadership.

Fremde Heere Ost was responsible for military and, connected with that, political information from a number of countries in the east, reaching as far as Turkey and, on paper, covering even the Far East. Its main target was the Soviet Union. From 1942 on this intelligence service was under the command of Reinhard Gehlen, who lacked experience in that type of work but was thought to be an organizational talent. Although *Fremde Heere Ost* did not maintain its own agent networks abroad, there was frequent professional contact with men of the *Abwehr* and with Army and SS officers involved in such operations as *Operation Zeppelin*. Significantly, *Fremde Heere Ost* since 1942 reported directly to the General Staff, while *Fremde Heere West* operated under the *Oberkommando der Wehrmacht* (OKW, Supreme Command of the Armed Forces). During the final months of the war, Reinhard Gehlen and some trusted officers managed to hide a part of the records of *Fremde Heere Ost* in preparation for their plans to offer their services to the American Forces. The political climate of the early Cold War and Gehlen's experience with Soviet matters led to a cooperation of U.S. intelligence with former Nazi officers. It was the beginning of *Organisation Gehlen*, the later *Bundesnachrichtendienst* (BND).

Marinenachrichtendienst (Naval Intelligence Service)

The *Marinenachrichtendienst* has a long history going back to the time of Emperor Wilhelm II and his naval aspirations. During World War II Naval Intelligence was a section of the *Abwehr* and subordinate to the *Seekriegsleitung* (Skl, Naval War Staff).

Its most important work was Radio Reconnaissance (*Abteilung Funkaufklärung*), usually referred to as *B-Dienst* (*Beobachtungsdienst*, observation service). Some of this work was similar to the activities of Hermann Göring's *Forschungsamt* at the Reich Air Ministry. A particular weakness of Naval Intelligence or rather of the Naval War Staff was the refusal to assume that their code may have been compromised. It could be said that the Navy's negligence in this respect contributed to their defeat in the Atlantic. A very important part of German Naval Intelligence has always been its well-known *Etappendienst* (supply network or service). Its organization was undertaken some time prior to World War I, and it constituted a supply network consisting of bases normally functioning under civilian, often business cover. In these locations in coastal areas and port cities around the world persons well known to the Navy and considered reliable performed a great number of tasks for the benefit of Germany from providing supplies to German vessels to actual intelligence operations. In marked contrast to the Army and the SS, the German Navy had a great number of men with international experience and therefore a better functioning network of international contacts. In 1935 Canaris drew up a special agreement accepted by the German Foreign Office and the *Abwehr*. It concerned assistance by diplomatic representatives abroad to the *Etappen*, safekeeping of the *Etappen* agents and equipment and even the recruiting of new agents by the diplomats.

Seehaus (*Sonderdienst Seehaus*), (Special Service Lake House)

This news gathering service, located in a building on the Wannsee in Berlin, is seen by some authors as just that rather than an intelligence service. The Special Service began operations in 1940 and continued or expanded the news gathering activity begun much earlier in a number of ministries. *Seehaus*, an operation of the German Foreign Office and its *Meldedienst* RAM (Reporting Service Foreign Minister/RAM *Reichsaussenminister*), collected news from radio stations in other parts of the world for Joachim von Ribbentrop, Hitler's Foreign Minister. The news reports created at *Seehaus* and its growing number of branch offices in other countries were excerpted from foreign news broadcasts. Not surprising, Joseph Goebbels and his Ministry of Propaganda quickly became jealous and intervened in the operations of Ribbentrop's *Seehaus*. The result of this struggle was an agreement already in late 1941, dividing responsibilities at the Wannsee *Seehaus* between the two ministries. With increasing rumors and suspicions of what was called *Defätismus* (defeatism) among German officers, both Minister Goebbels and the *Abwehr* Chief Admiral Canaris decided to limit distribution of the *Seehaus* reports, i.e., of international news. It needs to be recalled that normal citizens were not permitted to listen to foreign radio stations and that foreign press was not available. The *Seehaus* reports, of course, were based on these inaccessible foreign news broadcasts. Under existing conditions German intelligence services and ministries undoubtedly profited from this foreign news service.

Bibliography

(This is a selective bibliography of published sources and Ph.D. dissertations. Preferably English language editions are listed here. All sources and related data are fully identified in the footnotes. Archival sources are cited in unabbreviated form in the footnotes when first mentioned. The Political Archive of the German Foreign Office has changed some holdings from descriptive titles to a numbers system. Some of the recently declassified records of the National Archives and Records Administration were kindly made available in unmarked boxes, and in a few cases documents have been reorganized.)

Andrew, Christopher. *Secret Service: The Making of the British Intelligence Community.* London: Heinemann, 1985.

Andreyev, Catherine. "Andrei Andreyevich Vlasov." In Shukman, Harold, ed. *Stalin's Generals.* New York: Grove, 1993.

Bauer, Yehuda. *Jews for Sale: Nazi-Jewish Negotiations, 1933-1945.* New Haven: Yale University Press, 1994.

Bazna, Elyeza. *I Was Cicero.* New York: Dell, 1964.

Bericht des Bundesrates an die Bundesversammlung über die antidemokratische Tätigkeit von Schweizern und Ausländern im Zusammenhang mit dem Kriegsgeschehen 1939-1945. Teil 1. n.d.

Bernadotte, Count Folke. *The Fall of the Curtain: Last Days of the Third Reich.* London: Cassell, 1945.

Best, S. Payne. *The Venlo Incident.* London: Hutchinson, 1950.

The Black Book (Sonderfahndungsliste G.B.). London: Imperial War Museum, 1989.

Blandford, Edmund L. *SS-Intelligence: The Nazi Secret Service.* Shrewsbury: Airlife, 2000.

Bloch, Michael. *Ribbentrop.* London: Transworld/Bantam, 1992.

Bonjour, Edgar. *Geschichte der schweizerischen Neutralität.* Vols. 5-7. Basel: Helbing & Lichtenhahn, 1970–1974.

Boyd, Carl. *The Extraordinary Envoy: General Hiroshi Oshima and Diplomacy in the Third Reich, 1934–1939.* Washington, D.C.: University Press of America, 1980.

———. "Significance of MAGIC and the Japanese Ambassador to Berlin." *Intelligence and National Security*, vol. 2 (January 1987).

Braunschweig, Pierre Th. *Secret Channel to Berlin: The Masson-Schellenberg Connection and Swiss Intelligence in World War II.* Philadelphia: Casemate, 2004.

Breitman, Richard. *The Architect of Genocide: Himmler and the Final Solution.* London: Bodley Head, 1991.

———. "A Deal with the Nazi Dictatorship?: Himmler's Alleged Peace Emissaries in Autumn 1943." *Journal of Contemporary History*, vol. 30 (1995).

———. *Official Secrets: What the Nazis Planned, What the British and Americans Knew*. London: Penguin, 1999.

——— and Shlomo Aronson. "The End of the 'Final Solution'?: Nazi Plans to Ransom Jews in 1944." *Central European History*, vol. 25, no. 2 (1993).

——— et al. *U.S. Intelligence and the Nazis*. Washington, D.C.: National Archives Trust Fund Board, 2004.

Brissaud, André. *The Nazi Secret Service*. New York: W. W. Norton, 1974.

Browder, George C. *Hitler's Enforcers: The Gestapo and SS Security Service in the Nazi Revolution*. New York: Oxford University Press, 1996.

———. "Walter Schellenberg: Eine Geheimdienst-Phantasie." *Die SS: Die Elite unter dem Totenkopf* edited by R. Smelser and E. Syring. Paderborn: Schöningh, 2000.

Buchheit, Gert. *Die anonyme Macht*. Frankfurt: Athenaion, 1969.

———. *Die deutsche Geheimdienst: Geschichte der militärischen Abwehr*. Munich: List, 1966.

Burdick, Charles B. *Germany's Military Strategy and Spain in World War II*. Syracuse: Syracuse University Press, 1968

Cave Brown, Anthony. *Bodyguard of Lies*. New York: Quill/Morrow, 1975

———. *"C": The Secret Life of Sir Stewart Graham Menzies: Spymaster to Winston Churchill*. New York: Macmillan, 1987.

———, ed. *The Secret War Report of the OSS*. New York: Berkley Medallion, 1976.

Chapman, John W. M. "A Dance on Eggs: Intelligence and the 'Anti-Comintern'." *Journal of Contemporary History*, vol. 22, no. 2 (April 1987).

Cesarani, David. *Justice Delayed*. London: Mandarin, 1992.

Clark, Alan. *Barbarossa: The Russian-German Conflict, 1941-1945*. London: Phoenix, 1996.

Clarke, Comer. *If the Nazis Had Come*. London: C. Nicholls, 1962.

Davidson, Eugene. *The Trial of the Germans*. Columbia: University of Missouri Press, 1997.

Delarue, Jacques. *The Gestapo*. New York: Paragon, 1987.

Denniston, Robin. *Churchill's Secret War: Diplomatic Decrypts, the Foreign Office and Turkey 1942-44*. Stroud: Sutton, 1997.

Dieckhoff, Alain. "Une Action de Sauvetage des Juifs Européens en 1944-1945: L'Affaire Musy." *Revue d'Histoire Moderne et Contemporaine*, vol. 2 (1989).

Doerries, Reinhard R. *Hitler's Last Chief of Foreign Intelligence: Allied Interrogations of Walter Schellenberg*. London: Frank Cass, 2003.

Dorrill, Stephen. *M.I.6: Fifty Years of Special Operations*. London: Routledge, 2005.

Döscher, Hans-Jürgen. *Das Auswärtige Amt im Dritten Reich: Diplomatie im Schatten der "Endlösung."* Berlin: Siedler, 1987.

Dulles, Allen. *The Secret Surrender*. New York: Harper & Row, 1966.

Farago, Ladislas. *The Game of the Foxes*. London: Hodder & Stoughton, 1972.

Favez, Jean-Claude. *Das Internationale Rote Kreuz und das Dritte Reich*. Munich: Bertelsmann, 1989.

Fisher, David. *Colonel Z: The Secret Life of a Master of Spies*. New York: Viking, 1985.

Fleischhauer, Ingeborg. *Die Chance des Sonderfriedens: Deutsch-sowjetische Geheimgespräche 1941-1945*. Berlin: Siedler, 1986.
Fleming, Gerald. *Hitler and the Final Solution*. Berkeley: University of California Press, 1994.
Fleming, Peter. *Operation Sea Lion*. New York: Simon and Schuster, 1957.
Foreign Relations of the United States. Diplomatic Papers 1944. Vol. 1. Washington, D.C.: USGPO, 1972.
Fuhrer, Hans Rudolf. *Spionage gegen die Schweiz*. Frauenfeld: Huber, 1982.
Garbe, Detlef, ed. *Kriegsende und Befreiung*. Vol. 2. Bremen: Temmen, 1995.
Gautschi, Willi. *General Henri Guisan*. Zurich: Verlag Neue Zürcher Zeitung, 1989.
Gellately, Robert, ed. *The Nuremberg Interviews: An American Psychiatrist's Conversations With the Defendants and Witnesses*. Conducted by Leon Goldensohn. London: Pimlico, 2006.
Hachmeister, Lutz. *Der Gegnerforscher: Die Karriere des SS-Führers Franz Alfred Six*. Munich: Beck, 1998.
———. "Die Rolle des SD-Personals in der Nachkriegszeit. Zur nationalsozialistischen Durchdringung der Bundesrepublik." In *Nachrichtendienst, politische Elite und Mord-Einheit*. Edited by Wildt.
Heger, Wanda. *Jeden Freitag vor dem Tor*. Munich: Schneekluth, 1989.
Herbert, Ulrich. *Best: Biographische Studien über Radikalismus, Weltanschauung und Vernunft, 1903-1989*. Bonn: Dietz, 1996.
Hersh, Burton. *The Old Boys: The American Elite and the Origins of the CIA*. St. Petersburg: Tree Farm Books, 2002.
Herwarth, Hans von. *Zwischen Hitler und Stalin: Erlebte Zeitgeschichte 1931-1945*. Frankfurt: Ullstein Propyläen, 1982.
Herzog, Bodo. "Der Kriegsverbrecher Karl Dönitz: Legende und Wirklichkeit." *Jahrbuch des Instituts für Deutsche Geschichte*, vol. 15 (1986).
Hewins, Ralph. *Count Folke Bernadotte: His Life and Work*. London: Hutchinson, n.d. (1950?).
Heydrich, Lina. *Leben mit einem Kriegsverbrecher*. Pfaffenhofen: Ludwig, 1976.
Higham, Charles. *Trading With the Enemy: An Exposé of the Nazi-American Money Plot 1933-1949*. New York: Dell, 1984.
Hindley, Meredith. "Negotiating the Boundary of Unconditional Surrender: The War Refugee Board in Sweden and Nazi Proposals to Ransom Jews, 1944-1945." *Holocaust and Genocide Studies*, vol. 10 (1996).
Hinsley, F. H. et al. *British Intelligence in the Second World War*. Vols. 1-4. London: HMSO, 1979-1990.
Hoare, Oliver, ed. *Camp 020: M.I.5 and the Nazi Spies*. Richmond: Public Record Office, 2000.
Hoare, Sir Samuel, Viscount Templewood. *Ambassador on Special Mission*. London: Collins, 1946.
Hoettl, Wilhelm. *The Secret Front: The Inside Story of Nazi Political Espionage*. London: Phoenix, 2000.

Hoffmann, Peter. *The History of the German Resistance, 1933-1945*. Cambridge: MIT Press, 1977.

Höhne, Heinz. *Canaris: Patriot im Zwielicht*. München: Wilhelm Goldmann, 1978.

———. *Mordsache Röhm: Hitlers Durchbruch zur Alleinherrschaft 1933-1934*. Reinbek: Rowohlt/Spiegel, 1984.

———. *The Order of the Death's Head: The Story of Hitler's SS*. New York: Ballantine, 1989.

——— and Hermann Zolling. *The General Was a Spy: The Truth about General Gehlen and His Spy Ring*. New York: Coward, McCann & Geoghegan, 1972.

Holt, Thaddeus. *The Deceivers: Allied Military Deception in the Second World War*. New York: Scribner/Simon & Schuster, 2004.

Jacobeit, Sigrid and Simone Erpel, eds. *"Ich grüsse Euch als freier Mensch": Quellenedition zur Befreiung des Frauen-Konzentrationslagers Ravensbrück im April 1945*. Berlin: Hentrich, 1995.

Jensen-Lorenz, Ulrike. "Dänische Häftlinge im KZ Neuengamme 1944/45: Die Aktion Bernadotte und das Skandinavierlager." Master's Thesis, University of Hamburg, 1996.

Joffroy, Pierre. *Der Spion Gottes*. Berlin: Aufbau, 1995.

Jong, Louis de. "Hat Felix Kersten das niederländische Volk gerettet?" In *Zwei Legenden Aus dem Dritten Reich* edited by Hans Rothfels and Theodor Eschenburg. Stuttgart: Deutsche Verlags-Anstalt, 1974.

Kahn, David. *Hitler's Spies: German Military Intelligence in World War II*. New York: Macmillan, 1978.

Kasztner, Rezsö. *Der Bericht des jüdischen Rettungskomitees aus Budapest 1942-1945*. Budapest: Vaadat Ezra Vö-Hazalah Bö-Budapest, [1946].

Kersten, Felix. *The Kersten Memoirs, 1940-1945*. London: Hutchinson, 1956.

———. *Totenkopf und Treue: Heinrich Himmler ohne Uniform*. Hamburg: Robert Mölich, [1952].

Kessel, Joseph. *The Man with the Miraculous Hands*. Short Hills: Burford, 2004.

Kessler, Leo. *Betrayal at Venlo: The Secret Story of Appeasement and Treachery, 1939-1945*. London: Leo Cooper, 1991.

Kieser, Egbert. *Hitler on the Doorstep*. London: Arms & Armour, 1997.

Kleist, Bruno Peter. *Die europäische Tragödie*. Göttingen: K. W. Schütz, 1961.

Klemperer, Klemens von. *German Resistance Against Hitler: The Search for Allies Abroad*. Oxford: Clarendon, 1994.

Koblik, Steven. "'No Truck with Himmler': The Politics of Rescue and the Swedish Red Cross Mission, March-May 1945." *Scandia*, vol. 51, nos. 1-2 (1985).

———. *The Stones Cry Out: Sweden's Response to the Persecution of the Jews, 1933-1945*. New York: Holocaust Library, 1988.

———. "Sweden's Attempts to Aid Jews, 1939-1945." *Scandinavian Studies*, vol. 56 (1984).

Koch, H. W. "The Spectre of a Separate Peace in the East: Russo-German 'Peace Feelers', 1942-44." *Journal of Contemporary History*, vol. 10, no. 3 (July, 1975).

Krausnick, Helmut. "Legenden um Hitlers Aussenpolitik." *Vierteljahrshefte für Zeitgeschichte*, vol. 2, no. 3 (July 1954).

―――― and H.-H. Wilhelm. *Die Truppe des Weltanschauungskrieges*. Stuttgart: Deutsche Verlagsanstalt, 1981.

―――― and H. C. Deutsch, eds. *Helmuth Grosscurth: Tagebücher eines Abwehroffiziers*. Stuttgart: Deutsche Verlags-Anstalt, 1970.

Krebs, Gerhard. "Operation Super Sunrise?: Japanese-United States Peace Feelers in Switzerland 1945." *The Journal of Military History*, vol. 69 (2005).

Lang, Francis. *Mémoires d'un Médecin de Campagne 1940-1990*. Fribourg: Fragnières, 1991.

LeBor, Adam and Roger Boyes, *Surviving Hitler: Choices, Corruption and Compromise in the Third Reich*. London: Simon & Schuster, 2000.

Levine, Paul A. *From Indifference to Activism: Swedish Diplomacy and the Holocaust; 1938-1944*. Stockholm: Gotab/Almqvist, 1996.

Lewin, Ronald. *The American Magic: Codes, Cyphers and the Defeat of Japan*. New York: Farrar Straus Giroux, 1982.

MacDonald, Callum A. "The Venlo Affair." *European Studies Review*, vol. 8, no. 4 (1978).

Mallmann, Klaus-Michael. "Der Krieg im Dunkeln: Das Unternehmen 'Zeppelin' 1942-1945." In *Nachrichtendienst, politische Elite und Mordeinheit*. Edited by Wildt.

Manvell, Roger and Heinrich Fraenkel. *The Canaris Conspiracy: The Secret Resistance to Hitler in the German Army*. New York: David McKay, 1969.

Mastny, Vojtech. "Stalin and the Prospects of a Separate Peace in World War II." *The American Historical Review*, vol. 77, no. 5 (December 1972).

Masur, Norbert. *En Jude Talar Med Himmler*. Stockholm: Bonniers, 1945.

Matlok, Siegfried, ed. *Dänemark in Hitlers Hand: Der Bericht des Reichsbevollmächtigten Werner Best*. Husum: Husum Verlag, 1988.

McKay, C. G. *From Information to Intrigue: Studies in Secret Service Based on the Swedish Experience, 1939-45*. London: Frank Cass, 1993.

――――. "The Krämer Case: A Study in Three Dimensions." *Intelligence and National Security*, vol. 4, no. 2 (April 1989).

Mendelsohn, John, ed. *The Holocaust*. Vol. 16. New York: Garland, 1982.

Military Tribunals, Case No. 11. Nürnberg: Office of Military Government for Germany/US, 1948.

Morrison, Jack G. *Ravensbrück: Every Day Life in a Women's Concentration Camp, 1939-45*. Princeton: Wiener, 2000.

Moyzisch, L. C. *Operation Cicero*. London: Wingate, n.d.

Orth, Karin. "Planungen und Befehle der SS-Führung zur Räumung des KZ-Systems." In *Häftlinge zwischen Vernichtung und Befreiung*, edited by Detlef Garbe and Carmen Lange. Bremen: Temmen, 2005.

Overy, Richard. *Interrogations: The Nazi Elite in Allied Hands*. New York: Penguin, 2001.

Paehler, Katrin. "Ein Spiegel seiner selbst. Der SD-Ausland in Italien." In *Nachrichtendienst, politische Elite und Mordeinheit*. Edited by Michael Wildt.

――――. "Espionage, Ideology, and Personal Politics: The Making and Unmaking of a Nazi Foreign Intelligence Service." Ph.D. diss., American University, 2004.

Paine, Lauran. *The Abwehr*. London: Robert Hale, 1984.

Palmer, Raymond. "Felix Kersten and Count Bernadotte: A Question of Rescue." *Journal of Contemporary History*, vol. 29 (1994).

Penkower, Monty N. *The Jews Were Expendable: Free World Diplomacy and the Holocaust.* Urbana: University of Illinois Press, 1983.

Persico, Joseph E. *Roosevelt's Secret War: FDR and World War II Espionage.* New York: Random House, 2002.

Persson, Sune. "Folke Bernadotte and the White Busses." *Journal of Holocaust Education*, vol. 9, nos. 2-3 (2000).

Petersen, Neale H., ed. *From Hitler's Doorstep: The Wartime Intelligence Reports of Allen Dulles, 1942-1945.* University Park: The Pennsylvania State University Press, 1996.

Pincher, Chapman. *Their Trade is Treachery.* London: Sidgwick & Jackson, 1987.

Popov, Dusko. *Spy/Counterspy.* London: Weidenfeld and Nicolson, 1974.

Porat, Dina. *The Blue and the Yellow Stars of David: The Zionist Leadership in Palestine and the Holocaust, 1939-1945.* Cambridge: Harvard University Press, 1990.

———. *Israeli Society, the Holocaust and the Survivors.* London: Vallentine Mitchell, 2008.

Der Prozess gegen die Hauptkriegsverbrecher vor dem Internationalen Militärgerichtshof Nürnberg. Vols. 4 and 11. Nuremberg: Internationaler Militärgerichtshof, 1947.

Querg, Thorsten J. "Spionage und Terror—Das Amt VI des Reichssicherheitshauptamtes 1939-1945." Ph.D. diss., Free University Berlin, 1997.

Read, Anthony and David Fisher. *The Fall of Berlin.* New York: Da Capo, 1995.

Reile, Oscar. *Treff Lutetia Paris: Der Kampf der Geheimdienste im westlichen Operationsgebiet, in England und Nordafrika 1939-1945.* Wels: Welsermühl, 1973.

Reiling, Johannes. *Deutschland: Safe for Democracy?* Stuttgart: Steiner, 1997.

Ritter, Gerhard. *Carl Goerdeler und die deutsche Widerstandsbewegung.* Stuttgart: Deutsche Verlags-Anstalt, 1955.

Rittlinger, Herbert. *Geheimdienst mit beschränkter Haftung: Bericht vom Bosporus.* Stuttgart: Deutsche Verlagsanstalt, 1973.

Schellenberg, Walter. *Invasion 1940: The Nazi Invasion Plan for Britain.* London: St. Ermin's, 2001. (Note: This book was not written or published by Walter Schellenberg.)

———. *Memoiren.* Cologne: Verlag für Politik und Wirtschaft, 1959. (First German edition.)

———. *The Schellenberg Memoirs.* London: André Deutsch, 1956. (First edition in any language.)

Schlie, Ulrich, ed. *Albert Speer: Die Kransberg Protokolle 1945.* Munich: Herbig, 2003.

———. *Kein Friede mit Deutschland: Die geheimen Gespräche im Zweiten Weltkrieg.* Munich: Langen Müller, 1994.

Silver, Arnold M. "Questions, Questions, Questions: Memoirs of Oberursel." *Intelligence and National Security*, vol. 8, no. 2 (April 1993).

Simpson, Christopher. *The Splendid Blond Beast: Money, Law and Genocide in the Twentieth Century.* New York: Grove, 1993.

Skorzeny, Otto. *Meine Kommandounternehmen: Krieg ohne Fronten.* Wiesbaden: Limes, 1977.

Smith, R. Harris. *OSS: The Secret History of America's First Central Intelligence Agency.* Berkeley: University of California Press, 1972.

Spitzy, Reinhard. *How We Squandered the Reich.* Norwich: Michael Russell, 1997.

Srodes, James. *Allen Dulles: Master of Spies.* Washington, D.C.: Regnery, 1999.

Stehle, Hans Jakob. "Deutsche Friedensfühler bei den Westmächten im Februar/März 1945." *Vierteljahrshefte für Zeitgeschichte*, vol. 30 (July 1982).
Steinert, Marlis G. *Capitulation 1945: The Story of the Dönitz Regime*. London: Constable, 1969.
———. *Hitler*. München: Beck, 1994.
Straede, Therkel. "Die 'Aktion Weisse Busse'?" In *Befreiung Sachsenhausen*, edited by G. Morsch and A. Reckendrees. Berlin: Hentrich, 1996.
Trevor-Roper, H. R. "Kersten, Himmler, and Count Bernadotte." *The Atlantic Monthly*, vol. 191, no. 2 (February 1953).
———. *The Last Days of Hitler*. London: Macmillan, 1947.
Trials of War Criminals before the Nuernberg Military Tribunals under Control Council Law No. 10. Vols. 12-15. Washington, D.C.: USGPO, 1951–1952.
Turner, Henry A. Jr. *German Big Business and the Rise of Hitler*. New York: Oxford University Press, 1985.
Vago, Bela. "The Intelligence Aspects of the Joel Brand Mission." *Yad Vashem Studies on the European Jewish Catastrophe and Resistance*. Vol. 10 (1974).
Waller, John H. *The Devil's Doctor: Felix Kersten and the Secret Plot to Turn Himmler Against Hitler*. New York: John Wiley, 2002.
Warburg, Max M. *Aus meinen Aufzeichnungen*. New York: private publication, 1952.
Weinberg, Gerhard L. *A World at Arms: A Global History of World War II*. Cambridge: Cambridge University Press, 1994.
———. *The Foreign Policy of Hitler's Germany*. Chicago: University of Chicago Press, 1970.
West, Nigel. *Counterfeit Spies*. London: St. Ermin's, 1999.
———, ed. *The Guy Liddell Diaries*. Vol. 1. London: Routledge, 2005.
Wheatley, Ronald. *Operation Sea Lion: German Plans for the Invasion of England 1939–1942*. Oxford: Clarendon, 1958.
Wiesel, Elie. *All Rivers Run to the Sea*. New York: Alfred A. Knopf, 1996.
Wildt, Michael. *Generation des Unbedingten: Das Führungskorps des Reichssicherheitshauptamtes*. Hamburg: Hamburger Edition, 2003.
———, ed. *Nachrichtendienst, politische Elite und Mordeinheit. Der Sicherheitsdienst des Reichsführers SS*. Hamburg: Hamburger Edition, 2003.
Witte, Peter et al., eds. *Der Dienstkalender Heinrich Himmlers 1941/42*. Hamburg: Christians, 1999.
Wyman, David S. *The Abandonment of the Jews: America and the Holocaust, 1941-1945*. New York: Pantheon, 1985.
Yahil, Leni. "Scandinavian Countries to the Rescue of Concentration Camp Prisoners." *Yad Vashem Studies on the European Jewish Catastrophe and Resistance*, vol. 6 (1967).
Zuroff, Efraim. *The Response of Orthodox Jewry in the United States to the Holocaust: The Activities of the Va'ad ha-Hatzala Rescue Committee, 1939-1945*. Hoboken: KTAV, 2000.

Index

Abe, Katsuo, 126, 129–30
Abetz, Otto, 153
Albert, Heinrich F., 90, 92
Albert, Wilhelm, 8–9, 12, 15, 43, 297
Alexandrov, Andrey Mihailovich, 160–61
Andrew, Christopher, 16, 21–22, 55, 79
Ankarkrona (Ancarcrona), Captain, 359–60
Antonescu, Ion, 49
Arco auf Valley, Ferdinand Count, 150, 265
Arnoldsson, Hans, 199, 213, 359–61
Artist. *See* Jebsen, Johannes
Astor, Hugh, 234
Axis Sally (Mildred Gillars), 235
Ayer, Frederick, 237

Bach-Zelewski, Erich von dem, 155, 327
Barbey, Bernard, 69
Barbie, Klaus, 275
Bartholomäus, Alfred, 9, 43, 297
Bate, Vera, 166
Baudoin I, King of Belgium, 308
Bauer (railway executive), 361
Bauer, Yehuda, 184
Bauverd, Jean, 281
Bazna, Elyeza, 137–38
Becher, Kurt, 178–81, 184, 270, 310, 353
Beck, Ludwig, 142
Beer, Alexander, 164
Behn, Sosthenes, 90–94
Behrends, Walter, 29
Bellmount, William G., 237
Bemberg, Bernard, 313
Bentinck, Cavendish, 233
Berger, Gottlob, 152, 168, 184, 209, 253, 312–13, 320–22, 328–30, 351, 354

Berger-Rottenberg (family), 351, 354
Berglind, Nils, 103
Berkholtz, 346
Bernadotte af Wisborg, Estelle Romaine Countess, 190
Bernadotte af Wisborg, Folke Count, x, xv, 3, 151, 155, 187–93, 195–202, 205–6, 208, 210–11, 214, 216, 218, 221–29, 231–33, 238, 264–65, 267, 272, 277, 293–95, 302–9, 316, 322, 324, 326–27, 330–39, 341, 345–48, 357–59
Bernardini, Philippe, 178, 283
Berndorff, Emil, 270, 351
Bernheim de Villiers, 313
Best, Sigismund Payne, 22–23, 25–26, 28, 80
Best, Werner, 19, 288–89, 334, 338, 340–41, 345
Bibra, Ernst Sigismund Baron von, 267–68
Bismarck, Anne Marie Princess von, 150
Bismarck, family, 82
Bismarck, Gottfried Count von, 105, 148–50, 198, 266, 301
Bissell, Clayton, 232
Bitter, Wilhelm, 77–78, 249
Bjoern-Hansen, Arne, 150
Björck, Gottfrid, 197, 199, 213
Blum, Léon, 267
Blum, R., 240
Bocchini, Arturo, 14–15
Boening (Böning), Werner, 160, 194
Boheman, Erik, 202, 222, 347
Böhme, Franz, 223, 340, 344, 347–48
Bolomey, Louise, 173
Bolschwing, Otto von, 49
Bonhoeffer, Dietrich, 24

Bonhoeffer, Karl, 24–25
Bonjour, Edgar, 60
Bor (General). *See* Komorowski
Bormann, Martin Ludwig, 48, 207, 215, 302, 319, 329
Bosch, Robert, 79
Bovensiepen, Otto, 334
Bowie, Robert E., 275–76
Boyarsky, Vladimir, 115
Brandin, Axel, 103–6, 148, 150, 188, 228, 302–3
Brandt (German pilot), 72
Brandt, Karl, 209, 328–29
Brandt, Rudolf, 206–7, 213, 217, 306, 314, 319–20, 324–25, 329, 331, 336, 339, 355, 360–61
Bratt, Suton, 348
Braun, Eva, 217, 317, 320, 328
Braun, Wernher von, 233
Braunschweig, Pierre Th., 57, 64, 266
Breisky-Breisky, Hubert von, 84–86, 108
Breitman, Richard, 106, 178
Brissaud, André, 12–14, 132, 284–86
Brookhart, Smith W., 243–44
Browder, George C., 229, 272
Brustmann, 40
Buchwald, Hugo, 155, 189, 224–26, 270
Bührle, Emil G., 82
Bullock, Alan, 5, 286–89
Bülow-Schwante, Vicco Karl Alexander, 15
Buntrock, Georg, 335
Burckhardt, Carl Jakob, 315–16
Burckhardt, Peter, 72
Burgess, Guy, 278
Burri, Franz, 59–60
Buteau, Madame, 359
Bütefisch, Max, 94
Butterworth, William Walton, 86
Büttner, Walter, 88–89

Cable, Eric Grant, 81–82
Cameron, Rory, 234, 241

Canaris, Wilhelm, xiii–xiv, 13–14, 51–52, 54, 82, 94, 97, 102, 118, 130–32, 139–40, 145–47, 149, 158–61, 171, 220, 272, 367–69, 372–73
Carlsson, Gunnar, 194
Cassel (family), 310
Chanel, Coco, 165–66, 284
Chekhova, Olga, 326
Chenhalls, J., 123
Chiron (Attaché), 331, 334
Christensen, Bernhard, 24, 28
Christian, Walter zu, 34
Christianson, William C., 271
Christie, Guy Nicholas, 79
Christie, Malcolm Grahame, 15–16, 23, 78–79
Churchill, Sir Winston, 33, 36, 76, 165–66, 194
Cicero. *See* Bazna, Elyeza
Cilzer (family), 353–54
Clemens, Wilhelm, 30
Conti, Leonardo, 318
Conwell Evans, T. Philip, 80
Cook, Fred J., 88
Copper. *See* Klop, Dirk
Cramer, 267
Crinis, Friedrich Alexander Maximinian de, 24–25, 30, 77, 214, 232, 249, 318–19

Dacre, Lord. *See* Trevor-Roper, Hugh
Dansey, Claude Edward Marjoribanks, 21–22, 33
Dardel, Gustaf von, 218, 338, 341, 345–46
Darlan, François, 153
Darré, Richard Walther, 253
Daufeldt, Hans-Christian, 54–56, 73–75, 78, 83, 97
de Gaulle, Charles, 153–54, 169, 184, 269, 312, 314
de Gaulle, Geneviève, 177, 269
Degrelle, Léon, 321
Delarue, Jacques, 13
Delius, Dr. *See* Wagner, Otto

Demarest (Naval Attaché), 84
Deutsch, André, 286, 289
Dewitz, Eckhardt von, 320, 335
Dickson, James, 194
Dieckhoff, Hans Heinrich, 98, 238
Dietrich, Sepp, 10, 319
Dincklage, Hans von, 165
Dix, Rudolf, 104
Dodd, William E., 98
Dodge, J. Bigelow, 153, 330
Dogliotti (surgeon), 287
Dollfuss, Engelbert, 14
Dönhoff, Christoph Count von, 75–77
Dönhoff, Marion Countess von, 75–76
Dönitz, Karl, 3, 110, 215, 217–19, 222–24, 228, 233, 252–53, 339–41, 343–45, 348
Donnebaum (family), 177, 311, 353–54
Donovan, William J., 137
Ducry, Georges, 281–84
Dulles, Allen, 45, 68, 70, 75, 85–90, 93, 137, 142, 154–55, 169, 171, 182, 271
Dulles, John Foster, 90
Duquesne, Frederick Joubert, 141

Eden, Anthony, 33, 203
Edward VIII. *See* Windsor, Duke of
Eggen, Hans Wilhelm, 56–57, 60–67, 71–74, 128, 130, 152–53, 155, 220, 237, 315
Eggi. *See* Eggen
Eichmann, Adolf, 18, 179
Eisenhower, Dwight D., 195–96, 208, 222, 228, 239, 307–8, 313, 327, 331–33, 343, 347–48, 354
Elser, Johann Georg, 29
Emmeneger, Franz, 287
Enomoto, Momotaro, 122, 125
Enver Pasha, 134
Epstein, Fritz, 33
Erdmann, Christl, 224–25, 228, 359
Ernst, Alfred, 60

Farago, Ladislas, xiii, 52, 97
Father George. *See* Romanov

Faupel, Wilhelm, 36–37
Fegelein, Gretl (née Braun), 317, 320, 328
Fegelein, Hermann, 304, 317, 319–20, 322, 328–29
Fehmer, 30
Fellgiebel, Fritz Erich, 144, 368
Feuchtwanger, Lion, 33
Finke, August, 97, 100–2, 107
Fischer, Franz, 22–24
Fleischhauer, Ingeborg, 160
Flyg, Nils, 101
Foelkesam, Adrian Baron von, 145–46
Folke, Captain 361
Ford, Henry, 92
Fraenkel, Heinrich, 145
Franco, Francisco, xiii, 36–38, 130, 137, 170
Frank, Karl Hermann, 15, 343
Freisler, Roland, 149–50, 266
Friedeburg, Hans Georg von, 343
Frykman, Sven, 213, 361
Fuhrer, Hans Rudolf, 286
Fujimura, Yoshikatsu, 130
Fürstenberg, Gloria von, 166

Gagnon, Maurice S., 237
Gallagher, Clinton, 29, 240
Gamotha, Roman, 259–60
Gans Edler Herr zu Putlitz, Wolfgang, 33, 79
Gebhardt, Karl, 190, 319, 322
Gehlen, Reinhard, 113–15, 122, 277–79, 288–89, 369, 371–72
Gempp, Friedrich, 367
Gerge, Einar, 103
Gerstein, Alfred, 9
Gerstein, Kurt, 9
Ghailani, Rashid Ali El, 259
Giraud (family), 153–54, 177, 267, 269, 314
Giraud, Henri Honoré, 153–54, 269, 314–15
Gisevius, Hans Bernd, 31
Glücks, Richard, 213, 360

Goebbels, Joseph, 10, 44, 207, 209, 328–29, 372–73
Goerdeler, Carl Friedrich, 79, 142
Goldensohn, Leon, 4, 189, 249
Göring, Franz, x, 50, 80, 104–5, 177, 181–85, 211–14, 225–26, 228, 230–31, 269–70, 295, 307, 350–62
Göring, Hermann, 10, 14–15, 23, 31, 38, 44, 48, 79–80, 149, 173, 233, 239, 326, 370, 372
Göttsch, Werner, 28, 30
Gräfe, Heinz, 113–14
Graffman, J. Holger, 106
Grobba, Fritz, 134
Gröbl, Willi (Wilhelm), 54
Grönberg, Reinhold, 103
Grosch, Lieutenant. See Christensen, Bernhard
Grosz, Andor (Bandi), 121
Grothe, Bruno, 30
Grothmann, Werner, 320–21, 329
Guisan, Henri, 57, 60–61, 65–68, 70–73, 106, 108, 152, 154, 174, 267–68, 282–83, 288, 300
Guisan, Henry, Jr., 57
Günther, Christian, 201–2, 210, 229, 333, 337
Günther, Sturmbannfuehrer (Theresienstadt), 354
Gustav V (King of Sweden), 190
Gut, Hedwig, 54, 323

Hacha, Emil, 16
Hack, Friedrich-Wilhelm, 129-30
Häggberg, Sigfrid, 103
Hamburger, Willy, 133
Hampshire, Sir Stuart Newton, 234, 236, 241
Hansen, Georg, 139–40, 142–45
Hardy, Alexander, 275
Harpprecht, Klaus, 285–88
Harrison, Leland, 86
Harster, Wilhelm, 45
Hart, Herbert L. A., 234

Harvey, William K., 278
Hassell, Ulrich von, 55
Hatszeghy. See Hatz, Otto
Hatz, Otto, 120–21
Hausamann, Hans, 56
Haushofer, Karl, 47
Heissmeyer, August, 201
Helms, Richard, 278
Hencke, Andor, 345
Hengelhaupt, Erich, 113
Henlein, Konrad, 15, 16, 73
Hentig, Werner Otto von, 134, 252, 259, 275
Herff, Maximilian von, 328
Herriot, Édouard, 155, 267, 314
Hersh, Burton, 90
Herslow, Carl, 103, 105
Herwarth von Bittenfeld, Hans Heinrich, 79
Hess, Rudolf, 47–49, 157
Hesse, Fritz, 193–95, 202–4, 308–9
Hewel, Walther, 83
Hewitt, Abram Stevens, 106–9, 188
Heydrich, Lina, 18, 165, 248
Heydrich, Reinhard, 7–10, 13–20, 22–23, 27, 30, 35, 38–43, 46–48, 51, 52, 55, 58, 73, 93–94, 96, 113, 147, 163–68, 244–48, 254, 256, 258, 261, 343, 368
Higgins, Jack, 3, 165
Higham, Charles, 92
Himmler, Heinrich, ix, xv, 3, 7, 13, 15, 19–20, 26–28, 31–32, 38–43, 47–48, 51, 56, 58, 63, 65, 68–71, 76–78, 81, 88–89, 91, 94, 103–10, 116–17, 119, 129, 131–32, 138–39, 145–53, 155, 161, 163, 172, 174–93, 195–98, 201–211, 213–18, 224–26, 231, 232, 244–45, 248, 253–54, 264, 268–70, 278, 280, 290, 298–342, 345, 350–51, 354–55, 357–61
Hindenburg, Paul L. H. von Beneckendorff und von, 321
Hinnen, Sven, 282, 284, 287–88
Hippel, Theodor von, 369
Hirohito, Japanese Emperor, 99

Hitler, Adolf, x–xi, xv, 3, 10–12, 14–16, 20, 23, 25–27, 30–31, 34–38, 40–41, 47–49, 51, 55, 58, 60, 62, 65, 68, 78, 80–83, 86–87, 89–90, 92, 98–99, 107–11, 117, 119, 122, 126–32, 134, 137–39, 143, 147, 149, 151, 158–61, 170, 176, 182, 184–86, 190–95, 202, 205–10, 214–19, 221, 223, 232, 235, 246, 251–54, 256, 258, 268, 279, 287, 289, 299–307, 312–13, 315, 317–32, 334, 337–39, 353, 355, 357, 359–60, 368, 370, 372
Hoare, Sir Samuel, 97, 166, 240
Hohenlohe-Langenburg, Max Egon Maria Prince zu, xiv, 23, 79–89, 94, 166, 365
Höhn, Reinhard H. A., 6
Höhne, Heinz, 10, 85–86, 139
Holt, Thaddeus, xiii, 166
Hölter, Hermann, 347
Holzach, Paul, 57
Hoover, J. Edgar, 237
Horcher, Otto, 280–81
Horn, Major von, 338
Horthy, Miklós, 170
Höttl (Hoettl), Wilhelm, 9–10, 17–18, 47, 49, 55, 119, 140, 148, 164, 166–69, 248, 276
Hoyningen-Huene, Oswald Baron von, 36–37, 84
Huerta, Victoriano, 51
Hügel, Klaus, 54, 81, 102, 163–64
Husseini, Mohammed Emir El, 258–59, 281
Huxley, Aldous, 33

Ilgner, Max, 94
Innhausen zu Knyphausen, Armgard Countess, 101–2
Iturbide y Scholtz, Maria de la Piedad (Princess Hohenlohe), 79
Ivanov, Piotr (Peter), 45, 101, 126
Iwanow. *See* Ivanov

Jacke, Fritz, 17
Jacubic. *See* Kuncewicz

Jahn, D., 39, 272
Jahn, Friedrich Ludwig, 167
Jahnke, Kurt, 48, 73, 157
Jakubaniec (or Jakubianiec). *See* Kuncewicz
Jebsen, Johannes (Johnny), 141–43
Jenke, Albert, 137
Jepsen. *See* Jebsen
Jodl, Alfred, 233, 340, 344
Johansson, Herman, 100–1
Johnson, Herschel V., 108, 203
Jong, Louis de, 227, 294
Jost, Heinz Maria Karl, 46–50, 53–54, 57, 73, 95, 161, 239, 254, 259, 263, 299, 368
Jung, Carl Gustav, 77
Jung, Edgar, 11

K. *See* Kuncewicz
Kahn, David, xiii, 123, 138, 141
Kahr, Gustav Ritter von, 11
Kaim, Emil, 183
Kaltenbrunner, Ernst, 49, 51, 109, 119, 142–48, 154–55, 158, 163, 166–71, 176, 178, 180, 184, 186, 189–91, 197–98, 199, 202, 211, 213, 217, 221, 225, 239, 244–45, 247, 250, 261, 268, 298, 300–6, 308, 310, 312–19, 322–23, 328, 334, 338, 340, 352–55, 357, 360, 368
Kapp, Cornelia (Nele), 138
Kapp, Karl, 138
Kapp, Wolfgang, 52, 130
Karger, Henry, 205
Karmany, Richard. *See* Klatt
Kasztner, Rezsö, 179, 270
Katz, Leo, 243
Kauder, Richard. *See* Klatt
Kauders, Richard. *See* Klatt
Kawahara, 126
Kedia, Michael, 135
Keim, 40
Keitel, Wilhelm, 138, 233, 340, 344
Keith, Major, 233

Kempner, Robert M. W., 44, 239–40, 251–52, 262
Keppler, Wilhelm, 94, 149, 253
Kerr, Philip, 4
Kersten, Felix Eduard Alexander, 19, 103–9, 148, 187–90, 192, 197–98, 201–8, 214, 224, 227, 231, 233, 274, 302–3, 309, 312–14, 318–19, 322–23, 325, 357–58
Kiep, Otto, 132
Killigil, Nuri Pasha, 134–35
Kinzel, Eberhard, 371
Kisskalt, Karl, 42
Kittel, Hugo, 124
Klatt, Richard, 118–25, 235
Klaus, Edgar, 74, 82, 89, 159–61, 194–95
Klavenes, Wilhelm, 150
Kleczkowski, Karl Alois, 133
Kleist, Bruno Peter, 100–1, 158–62, 194–95
Klemperer, Klemens von, xv, 160
Klop, Dirk, 24–26, 28, 255
Knatchbull-Hugessen, Sir Hughe Montgomery, 137
Knieriem, Ottokar von, 203
Knochen, Helmut, 22–23, 30, 45, 74, 119, 166, 169
Knyphausen, Anton Count von, 101
Köcher, Otto Karl, 54, 56, 68–69, 71
Koehl, Robert, ix
Kojima, Hideo, 127–30
Kolbe, Fritz, 137
Kollontai, Alexandra Michailovna, 98
Komatsu, Mitsuhiko, 126
Komorowski, Tadeusz (General Bor), 155, 269, 327
Kondrashev, Sergei A., 229
Kordt, Erich, 79
Kordt, Theodor, 79–80
Kortekamp, Käthe. *See* Schellenberg, Käthe
Köstring, Ernst, 116–17
Kowalki, Louis (Schellenberg)
Krämer, Karl Heinz, 97, 126, 128

Kranefuss, Fritz, 94
Kröger, Erhard, 116
Krosigk. *See* Schwerin von Krosigk
Kuebart, Karl Friedrich, 143, 239
Kuebarth. *See* Kuebart
Kuncewicz, Jerzy, 45, 126
Kybikowski. *See* Ivanov

Lagerberg, Stig, 103
Lahousen-Vivremont, Erwin Edler von, 13–14
Lang, Eugen, 54
Lang, Francis, 281–84, 286–88
Lang, Ilya. *See* Lang, Ira
Lang, Ira, 119–20, 122–23, 235
Lange, Heinz, 153
Lapinska, Janina (or Salomea), 45–46, 126
Laval, Pierre, 153
Ledochowski, Vladimir, 46
Legge, Barnwell R., 152–53, 330
Lemmens, Jan Frederick, 28–29
Leonhardt, Ernst, 59
Leopold III, King of Belgium, 308
Leverkuehn, Paul, 132–33
Lewenhaupt, Count, 334–35
Lienhardt, Otto Alfred, 59
Lindemann, Fritz, 340
Lindemann, Karl, 94
Liss, Ulrich, 67, 371
Loeb (family), 173
Lombardi, Alberto, 166
Longin, Ira. *See* Lang, Ira
Lorenz, Werner, 329
Lundqvist, Martin, 96
Luther, Martin, 88–89

MacDonald, Callum A., 23–24, 27
Maglione, Luigi, 284
Mallet, Sir Victor, 94, 148, 150, 192, 194, 198, 203–4, 338
Mann, Wilhelm Rudolf, 94
Manvell, Roger, 145, 304
Marmoc, Madame del, 359
Marogna-Redwitz, Rudolf Count von, 118

Masson, Roger, 56–58, 60–66, 68–71, 73, 106, 108, 152–55, 174, 237, 266–68, 272, 277, 281–82, 284, 287–88
Masur, Norbert, 204–8, 214, 231, 314, 318, 322–26, 328, 358
Maubeuge, Oberstleutnant von, 335
Mayer, Saly, 178–81, 184, 270, 310, 353
McClelland, Roswell D., 179–80, 185, 258
McCloy, John J., 275–76
McKay, C. G., 101, 103
Meade, Glenn, 3
Mehlhorn, Herbert, 8, 9, 19–20, 43
Menzies, Sir Stewart Graham, 21, 141, 363
Meyer-Schwertenbach, Patricia, 67
Meyer-Schwertenbach, Paul E., 57, 60, 62–68, 70, 73, 152–53, 155, 237
Miller, Hans Heinrich, 17
Milmo, Sir Helenus Patrick, 234, 240–41
Mintzel, Kurt, 254
Moes, Hauptsturmfuehrer (Theresienstadt), 354
Möller, Alvar, 103–5, 110, 148–50, 154, 188, 228, 231–32, 265–66, 302
Molotov, Vyacheslav, 127, 161, 229
Momm, Theodor, 165
Morell, Theodor, 319
Mörgeli, Ernst, 60–61, 64, 267
Morsey, Andreas, 25
Moyzisch, Ludwig C., 136–38
Muchanov (secretary of Anton Turkul), 122
Müller, Heinrich, 13–14, 18, 23, 39, 43–44, 46–47, 50–52, 60, 89, 92, 111–14, 117, 132, 139–42, 144–46, 148, 155, 163, 171, 176, 184, 187, 189, 191, 198, 221, 225, 245, 256, 261, 263, 270, 275, 297, 306, 311, 315, 328–29, 350–51
Mussolini, Benito, 71, 122, 166, 170, 217
Musy, Benoit, 154, 172, 174, 177, 180, 183–87, 200, 212, 214, 225, 230, 268–69, 309, 313, 326, 352, 354–56, 359
Musy, Jean-Marie, 151, 154–55, 172–82, 184–87, 191, 196, 200, 211, 214, 230, 238, 252, 268–70, 272, 277, 283, 309–14, 318, 323, 326, 328, 350–54

Naujocks, Alfred, 20, 27–28, 30, 239
Nelis, Heinrich-Josef, 7–8
Neubacher, Hermann, 49
Neumann, Hans-Hendrik, 17, 43, 96–97, 162, 364
Nicolai, Walter, 367
Nicolson, Harold, 33
Niedermayer, Oskar Ritter von, 134
Niemöller, Martin, 275
Nordling, Raoul, 200
Nostradamus, 32
Nuri Pasha. *See* Killigil, Nuri Pasha

Oberg, Karl, 173
Oebsger-Röder, Rudolf, 113
Ohnesorge, Wilhelm, 91, 370
Okamoto, Kiyotomi, 128, 130
Olsen, Iver, 194, 203
Onodera, Makato, 45, 98–99, 125–26, 128, 156
Orlowski (Russian representative), 130
Oshima, Hiroshi, 99, 126–31, 156
Ostroem, 222, 338, 341, 347

Paderewski, Ignacy, 33
Päffgen, Theodor, 11, 75, 100
Paillole, Paul, 139
Palmer, Raymond, 208, 227
Papen, Franz von, 11, 136–37, 215, 233, 300
Parilli, Baron Luigi, 44–45
Pasha, Enver. *See* Enver Pasha
Pasha, Nuri. *See* Killigil, Nuri Pasha
Patterson, Harry. *See* Higgins
Patzig, Conrad, 367
Pauli, Max, 361–62
Paulus, Friedrich, 64
Pentzlin, Heinz, 101
Pepily (Police Chief), 136
Perkel, Naci, 135–36
Pétain, Philippe, 170, 314

Peter, Ernst, 54
Petersen (Honorary Consul), 287, 331, 334
Petersen, Gita (Margarete), 286
Pfeffer von Salomon, Franz, 48
Philby, Kim, 278
Picot, Werner, 41
Piekenbrock, Hans, 97, 117
Pincher, Chapman, 117–20, 123
Pins, Rudolph, 169
Pius XII, Pope, 283–84
Planetta, Otto, 14
Pohl, Oswald, 189
Poole, DeWitt C., 56
Popov, Dusko, 141–42
Porsche, Ferdinand, 233
Post, Eric (Erik) von, 222–23, 338–41, 347–48
Powers, Judge, 251
Prützmann (Pruetzmann), Hans-Adolf, 170, 320
Putlitz (see Gans Edler Herr zu Putlitz), 79

Radziwil, Janusz Prince, 155, 326–27
Raeder, Erich, 110
Rapp, Albert, 113, 116–17
Rasch, Hermann, 100
Rathkolb, Oliver, 167, 248
Rayens, Charles E., 127, 231–33, 241
Reckzeh, Paul, 132
Reiche, Hans-Ulrich, 54
Reichel, Eberhard, 74–75
Reitsch, Hannah, 235
Rendulic, Lothar, 343
Rennau, Heinrich F. (Heinz), 225–26, 228
Reynaud, Paul, 155, 267, 314
Ribbentrop, Annelies von (née Henkell), 89
Ribbentrop, Joachim von, 34–38, 49, 63, 68–69, 81–83, 88–89, 99–100, 104, 127, 129, 138, 158–61, 190, 193–95, 204, 266, 299–300, 302–6, 308–9, 315, 321, 339, 372

Richert, Arvid, 150–51, 190, 198, 223, 264–66, 303, 348
Rieber, Thorkild, 92
Riediger, Fritz, 254, 274
Rihner (Swiss Colonel), 72
Rintelen, Franz, 33
Ritter, Egon Baron von, 150, 265
Ritter, Nikolaus, 97, 141
Rittlinger, Herbert, 121, 124
Robertson, T. A., 240
Robeson, Paul, 33
Röhm, Ernst, 42, 48
Romanoff, George Leonidovitch. *See* Romanov
Romanones, Aline Countess of, 166
Romanov, Georg Sergei, 117–19, 122
Rommel, Erwin, 69, 86, 109, 154, 259, 367
Ronge, Max, 13–14
Roosen, Count, 44
Roosevelt, Franklin D., 80, 87, 92, 98, 106, 129, 152, 188, 329
Rosenberg (family), 311, 353
Rosenberg, Alfred, 159
Rot, Mirko, 121
Roth, Mirko. *See* Rot
Rothmund, Heinrich, 64, 73
Rottenberg, Mordechai, 173, 177, 311
Rousseau, Theodore, 84
Russell, Bertrand, 33
Rybicki, Major. *See* Ivanov
Rybikowski, Michal. *See* Ivanov

Sakai, Naoe, 128–30
Salisch, Karl von, 24
Sandberger, Martin, 50, 162, 220
Saxe, Major, 236
Saud, King, 259
Schacht, Hjalmar, 233
Schaefer, Karl, 30
Schaemmel (Schellenberg)
Schambacher, Ernst, 30
Schämmel (Schellenberg)
Schellenberg, Guido Franz Bernhard, 4

Schellenberg, Irene (née Grosse-Schönepauck), 39–40, 209, 220, 273, 284, 286–89, 301
Schellenberg, Käthe (née Kortekamp), 16–17, 301
Schellenberg, Katherina Lydia (née Riedel), 4
Schemmel (Schellenberg)
Scherz, Alfred, 286–88
Schieber, Walter, 165
Schienke, Marie-Louise, 224–26, 228–29, 236, 238
Schilling, Herr von. *See* Finke
Schleicher, Kurt von, 11
Schmidt, Major (ret.), 310
Schmitz (works with Werner Best), 288–89
Schmitz, Hermann, 93–94
Schmitz, Wilhelm (Willi), 50
Schönemann. *See* Klaus
Schörner (Schoerner), Ferdinand, 343
Schroeder, Erich, 85
Schrott, Eberhard, 97
Schüddekopf, Otto-Ernst, 76, 81, 102
Schulenburg, Friedrich Werner Count von der, 160
Schulze-Bernett, Walter, 23, 30
Schumburg, Emil Johannes, 15
Schuschnigg, Kurt von, 12
Schwerin von Krosigk, Johann Ludwig (Lutz) Count, 3, 209, 215, 217–18, 222, 228, 233, 252, 320–22, 329, 339–45, 348
Sebastian, C. L., 142
Sebold, William G., 141
Seeckt, Hans von, 116
Seidlitz, Captain von. *See* Salisch
Seldte, Franz, 321
Semyonov, Vladimir Semyonovitch, 98
Serot, André Pierre, 190, 265
Serrano, Rosita, 44
Seth, Ronald, 76
Seydewitz, von. *See* Salisch
Sheen, H. G., 241

Shirer, William, 80, 99
Siegel (cover name). *See* Hewitt
Siemsen, Nina, 126
Silver, Arnold M., 124–25, 235
Sima, Horia, 49
Sinclair, Hugh "Quex", 22
Six, Franz Alfred, 6, 34, 169, 253, 262
Skorzeny, Otto, 72, 114, 148, 166, 169–71, 217, 280–81, 317, 338, 369
Smolen, Kasimierz, 260–61
Solf, Hanna, 132
Solf, Wilhelm Heinrich, 132
Solms, Major. *See* Travaglio
Sonnenhol, Gustav Adolf, 74–75
Souter, S. H., 276
Speer, Albert, ix, 165, 233
Spieker, Klaus, 22
Spitzy, Maria, 84
Spitzy, Reinhard, 82–86, 131, 166, 169
Spivey, Delmar T., 152
Srbik, Heinrich von, 167
Stalin, Joseph, 20, 41, 58, 98, 116–17, 129, 158–61, 229
Stargarth (family), 353
Steengracht von Moyland, Gustav Adolf Baron, 75, 252, 344–45
Steiger, Eduard von, 73, 312
Steimle, Eugen, 74–75
Stein, Helene, 311, 353
Steiner, Felix, 321, 329
Stephens, Colonel, 236
Sternbuch, Isaac (Isaak, Yitzchok), 173–74 177–79, 181, 185, 268, 269–70, 283, 351, 356
Sternbuch, Naftali, 173–74
Sternbuch, Recha, 173–75, 177–79, 181, 185, 283
Stevens, Richard H., 22–31, 80, 255, 365
Stiassny, Dr., 311, 353
Stohrer, Eberhard von, 36
Storch, Hillel, 194, 201–4, 208, 214, 229–31, 314, 318–19
Strassburger, Horst, 41–42
Strasser, Gregor, 11, 40–42

Strasser, Otto, 40–42, 46
Strik-Strikfeldt, Wilfried, 115
Strobl, 81
Stumpfegger, Ludwig, 319
Suhren, Fritz, 212–13, 358–60

Temple, William, 77
Terboven, Josef, 340
Thiele, Fritz Walter, 91, 143–44, 368
Thierack, Otto Georg, 150, 303
Thomsen, Amtmann, 337
Thomsen, Hans, 97–98, 222–23, 302, 347
Thorel, Alain, 173, 175, 311
Thorwald, Jürgen, 288–89
Timoshenko, Semyon Konstantinovich, 115
Tito, Josip Brozovitch, 170
Tourkout. *See* Turkul
Tramp. *See* Sebold
Travaglio, Johannes, 22
Trevor-Roper, Hugh R. (Lord Dacre), xv, 123, 208, 227, 234, 240–42, 264, 278–79
Tricycle. *See* Popov
Trott zu Solz, Adam von, 160
Tschierschky, Karl, 113
Turkul, Anton, 117–20, 122–23, 125, 135, 235
Tyler, Royall, 86

Urbannek, Erhard, 17
Ustinov, Klop, 33, 55, 79, 124, 233, 241
Utermark, Albert, 97
Uthmann, Bruno von, 97, 347–48

Valjavec, Fritz, 6
Vanaman, Arthur W., 61, 151–53, 329–30
Vansittart, Sir Robert, 15–16, 79–80
Veesenmayer, Edmund, 253
Verber, Otto, 5
Vermehren, Elisabeth, 132
Vermehren, Erich Maria, 132–33, 137–38
Vlasov, Andrei Andreyevich, 113, 115–17, 119–20, 135, 156

Waetjen, Eduard, 142, 168
Wagner, Eduard, 245–47, 255–56
Wagner, Hans, 97, 161
Wagner, Horst, 302–4
Wagner, Otto, 118, 120–22
Wallenberg, Jacob, 105–7, 148–50, 154, 188, 194, 265, 301, 303
Wallenberg, Raoul, 265–66
Waneck, Wilhelm, 119, 164, 168, 217, 338
Warburg, Max M., 93
Wattenwyl, Karl von, 72
Wedel-Wedelsborg, Fritse Baroness, 362
Weiss, Manfred, 179, 310
Weissgerber (SS officer), 262
Weizsäcker, Ernst Freiherr von, 250, 252, 271
Wendel, Gerhard, 276
West, Nigel (Rupert Allason), 34, 79, 119
Westminster, Duke of, 165
Westrick, Gerhard Alois, 90–93
White, Dick, 119, 234, 279
Widén, Tore, 103
Wied, Victor Prince zu, 97
Wiegand, Karl von, 55
Wiese, Colonel, 118–20, 122
Wiesel, Elie, 204
Wiesendanger, Albert, 65–66
Wilhelm II, German Emperor, 87, 90
Windsor, Duke of (Edward VIII), 33–35, 37, 46, 165, 170, 287
Winter, Hannah, 165
Winzer, Paul, 36, 40–41, 83
Wirsing, Giselher, 217, 338–40, 342, 344
Wolff, Karl, 20, 45, 89, 94, 270–71
Wood, George. *See* Kolbe
Wulff, Wilhelm, 215, 224, 336
Wünnenberg, Alfred, 210, 331–33, 336